Pancakes and Prangs

Twentieth-Century Military Aircraft Accidents in Shropshire

Thomas Thorne

Pancakes and Prangs
Twentieth-Century Military Aircraft Accidents in Shropshire
was first published in Wales in 2013
by
BRIDGE BOOKS
61 Park Avenue
WREXHAM
LL12 7AW

ISBN: 978-1-84494-087-5

A CIP entry for this book is available from the British Library

Printed and bound by
Gutenberg Press Ltd
Malta

Contents

Foreword *by* David Smith 4

Preface 5

Acknowledgements 6

Abbreviations and Terminology 7

Airfields 9

Military Aviation Accidents 19

Non-Flying Fatalities 298

Sources 300

Index to Crash Sites 301

Index to Airfields 303

Foreword

During the Second World War, Shropshire rivalled the eastern counties of England in the number of its airfields. Day and night, the skies were full of aircraft, the majority manned by raw trainees. As this book graphically describes, many succumbed to a variety of causes, ranging from collisions and bad weather to aircraft with tricky handling characteristics, even for an experienced pilot. For some, it was just sheer bad luck.

One very near disaster in Shropshire skies was recounted to me by the late Mike Edwards, flying instructor at Halfpenny Green in the 1970s. During a so-called rest period between operational flying with Fighter Command, he was instructing at Tern Hill. One dark night he was airborne in a Miles Master when, without warning, the pupil in the front seat put the aircraft into a violent dive. Mike opened his mouth to swear at him over the intercom when a huge black shape soared overhead. The bomber's crew probably never knew how close they had been to destruction. Many others were not so fortunate.

The Second World War casualties originated from all over the globe. Americans from the fighter training airfield at Atcham feature frequently. Unaccustomed English weather was the downfall of many, along with collisions, war-weary aircraft and the over-exuberance of youth. The same can be said of the RAF fighter pilots lost flying from Rednal. As with the so-called fighter boys, many would-be bomber crewmen perished before they got the chance to fly against the enemy. It is especially tragic to read of others who survived serious crashes, recovered from their injuries, only to die in action soon afterwards.

Tom Thorne has managed to trace more information on many First World War crashes, a difficult task as official records are often sparse. The toll of accidents between the wars and since 1945 is much reduced but no less tragic.

This remarkable book is a historical document and Tom is to be congratulated on his dedication and the depth of his research. In compiling it, he has ensured that these airmen and women and their misfortunes are recorded for posterity.

David Smith
Bagillt, Flintshire

Preface

This project was begun in 2000 whilst I was researching for a book on the history of Pulverbatch during the Second World War. One of the most vivid memories the local inhabitants was of an American pilot being killed whilst performing aerobatics over the village one sunny summer's evening as the congregation left the village church. While searching for information on the aircraft and its pilot, it soon became apparent that this was by no means an isolated incident and my initial thoughts of Shropshire being the quiet backwater of uneventful training flights were soon replaced with the realisation that the county's airfields had suffered a substantial number of casualties. Curiosity soon caused the research to broaden, covering all military crashes from the First World War to the end of the twentieth century.

Many of these young men and women were recently out of school, in their late teens or early twenties, and had joined up to do their bit for the war effort, or to pursue an exciting peacetime career. The sad truth is that the majority of the casualties in wartime never even had a chance to engage the enemy and were killed in training. For those airmen that were fortunate enough to survive accidents in wartime Shropshire, many would subsequently be killed flying operationally against the Axis powers, others were taken prisoner and a number were decorated for bravery. Some of those who went on to lead distinguished careers were lucky even to survive their time in Shropshire! Amongst them was F/O Harry Hardy, RCAF, who took to his parachute over Rednal airfield on 7 April 1944 following a mid air collision with another Spitfire. He went on to become a prominent 'tank-buster', piloting his Typhoon aircraft, '*Pulverizer*', over Normandy. F/O Idris Hassan Latif, who was to become the post-war Indian Chief of Air Staff, was another pilot trained at Rednal, who belly-landed near Tern Hill on 28 February 1944, after suffering an engine failure. P/O 'Bush' Parker, who had trained at Tern Hill and made a forced landing near Cheswardine on 26 January 1940, was subsequently shot down during the Battle of Britain and taken prisoner. He was a notorious escaper and consequently earned his place in the infamous Colditz Castle where he became the camp 'locksmith'. Post-war RAF Tern Hill's role turned to that of training helicopter pilots and a survivor of a particularly serious mid-air collision near Hinstock, in April 1970, was Keith Ifould, who is now one of the directors of the RAF Museum, responsible for the Cosford and Hendon sites.

A number of books have been written that have touched on the subject of aircraft crashes in Shropshire but none that have concentrated solely on the subject. Although this book tries to record as many accidents as possible, there are always going to be incidents for which no archive documentation has survived. Records of First World War accidents are particularly fragmentary, as are those incidents where aircraft force-landed with no damage to aircraft or injury to personnel. For the sake of keeping research to an acceptable length, accidents recorded here have been restricted to those that occurred outside the immediate vicinity of airfield boundaries, unless they were fatal or of particular interest. The book cannot, therefore, be described as a complete list, but it is as good a reference that can be found and I hope that it will serve to record an important part of our local history.

Many of the crash sites lie on private land and this must be recognized by readers. Map references for crash sites are provided for historical accuracy but are not there to encourage people to look for wreckage. It should be remembered that, in many cases, these accidents claimed the lives of the aircraft's crews and the sites should be treated with respect for those that died there. Removal of wreckage without permission is illegal as it is still considered the property of the Ministry of Defence.

Sadly, many of those involved in these accidents, or those who witnessed them, are no longer with us. I hope that this book will encourage those that do recall any incidents, or who had relatives involved in them, to come forward and add further details. Eye witness accounts have been particularly useful in providing crucial local information that has helped to identify crash sites. To those survivors of accidents, the eye witnesses and the relatives that have contributed to this work, I am incredibly grateful for your support in helping this book come to fruition, ensuring that the incidents are not forgotten over time.

Lastly, I must apologise for any inaccuracies that are found in the book, whether it be due to mistakes in the original sources, or through my own misinterpretation of them. Any corrections pointed out by readers shall be altered accordingly.

'Lest we forget'

Acknowledgements

Over the past few years I have received invaluable information from various individuals and institutes around the globe who are, quite simply, too numerous to thank individually. To all of you who have helped, no matter how brief or exhaustive your correspondence, I am sincerely grateful, for without your help this book would never have come into fruition.

In providing details and documents held in far flung archives which would otherwise remain unseen, I am particularly indebted to Errol Martyn (New Zealand), Hugh Halliday (Canada) and Craig Fuller (USA). Particular thanks should also be paid to Toby Neal at the *Shropshire Star* newspaper for running numerous articles which have led to new leads.

I am also particularly grateful to all those individuals and organisations who have generously allowed me to make use of their photographs of aircraft crashes and the crews involved. Some of these, having been taken in difficult circumstances, often with the barest minimum of photographic equipment, are not of the highest quality (particularly those sourced from the USAAF records). Whilst every effort has been made to enhance these pictures as much as possible, it was thought worthwhile to include them here as they are the only extant visual evidence of the incidents and / or personnel involved.

Abbreviations and Terminology

AACU – Anti Aircraft Cooperation Unit
AAF – Auxiliary Air Force
AFC – Australian Flying Corps (FWW) / Air Force Cross
AFM – Air Force Medal
AI – Airborne Interception (Radar)
AM – Air Medal (for USAAF personnel) or Air Ministry
Angels – RAF code word representing altitude in units of 1,000 feet.e.g. Angels 10 = 10,000 feet.
Anti-diver – patrols to intercept incoming V-1 bombs
AOC – Air Officer Commanding
AOP – Air Observation Post
AOS – Air Observers School
ARP – Air Raid Precautions
ATA – Air Transport Auxiliary
ATC – Air Training Corps
ATS – Armament Training Station / Advanced Training Squadron
BEM – British Empire Medal
BOAC – British Overseas Airways Corporation
Bullseye exercise – a bomber training exercise simulating operational conditions
Bunt – a manoeuvre where a pilot makes a half outside loop by pushing forward on the control column
CB – Companion, Order of the Bath
CBE – Commander of the Order of the British Empire
C de G – *Croix de Guerre*, a military decoration of both France and Belgium
CFI – Chief Flying Instructor
CFS – Central Flying School
CFS (H) – Central Flying School (Helicopter)
Chock – a wedge placed behind an aircraft's wheels to prevent it moving
CMG – Commander of the Order of St Michael and St George
CNCS – Central Navigation and Control School
CO – Commanding Officer
CWGC – Commonwealth War Graves Commission
Darky – a homing system for aircraft in distress
DCM – Distinguished Conduct Medal
D / F – Direction Finding
DFC – Distinguished Flying Cross
DFM – Distinguished Flying Medal
DSO – Distinguished Service Order
EFTS – Elementary Flying Training School
EKI/EKII – *Eiserne Kreuz I & II* (Iron Cross 1st & 2nd Class)
Erk – RAF slang for an aircraftman
FAA – Fleet Air Arm
FFAF – Free French Air Force (*Forces Aériennes Françaises Libres*)
FG – Fighter Group
FPP – Ferry Pilots Pool
FS – Fighter Squadron
FTC – Flying Training Command
FTG – Fighter Training Group
FTS – Flying Training School or Fighter Training Squadron (for US Air Force)
FTU – Ferry Training Unit
FWW – First World War
GCI – Ground Controlled Interception
GM – George Medal
GPR – Glider Pilot Regiment
GTS – Glider Training School
HGCU – Heavy Glider Conversion Unit
HQ – Headquarters
HQSFP – Headquarters Service Ferry Pool
IAF – Indian Air Force
ITS – Initial Training Squadron
ITW – Initial Training Wing
KG – *Kampfgeschwader* (a *Luftwaffe* bomber unit)
MBE — Member of the Order of the British Empire
MC – Military Cross
MID – Mentioned in Despatches
MP – Military Police
MTC – Mechanised Transport Corps
MU – Maintenance Unit
Navex – Navigation exercise
NCO – Non-commissioned officer
NFS – National Fire Service
(O)AFU – (Observers) Advanced Flying Unit
OBE – Officer of the Order of the British Empire
Oflag – *Offizierslager* (German prisoner of war camp for officers only)
OLC – Oak Leaf Cluster (to denote a second award)
Ops – Operations (against the enemy)
OTU – Operational Training Unit
PAF – Polish Air Force

(P)AFU – (Pilots) Advanced Flying Unit
Pancake – RAF slang for a landing (also used by USAAF to describe a belly landing)
POW – Prisoner of War
Prang – RAF slang for a crash
PR – Photo Reconnaissance
RAF – Royal Air Force
RAFVR – Royal Air Force Volunteer Reserve
RAFO – Reserve of Air Force Officers
RAAF – Royal Australian Air Force
RC – Recruit Centre
RCAF- Royal Canadian Air Force
RFC – Royal Flying Corps
RIrAF – Royal Iraqi Air Force
RJoAF – Royal Jordanian Air Force
RLG – Relief Landing Ground
RN – Royal Navy
RNAS – Royal Naval Air Service
RNoAF – Royal Norwegian Air Force
RNVR – Royal Naval Volunteer Reserve
RNZAF – Royal New Zealand Air Force
RNZNVR – Royal New Zealand Naval Volunteer Reserve
ROC – Royal Observer Corps
RPM – revolutions per minute
R/T – Radio Telephony
SAAF – South African Air Force
SFTS – Service Flying Training School
SofTT – School of Technical Training
SLG – Satellite Landing Ground
SS – Silver Star (USA)
TA – Territorial Army
TDS – Training Depot Station
TNA – The National Archives
TS – Training Squadron
USAAF – United States Army Air Force (post 1942)
USAAS – United States Army Air Service (to 1926)
USN – United States Navy
u/t – under training
WAAF – Women's Auxiliary Air Force
WARG – Wartime Aircraft Recovery Group, founded in 1978 to locate and recover crashed aircraft
WRAF – Women's Royal Air Force
W/T – Wireless Telephony

Abbreviated Ranks/Crew Positions

AB – Air Bomber (or Bomb Aimer)
AC1/AC2 – Aircraftman 1st and 2nd Class.
ACH/GD – Aircrafthand General Duties
ACW1/ACW2 – Aircraftwoman 1st and 2nd Class
AG – Air Gunner
AI Operator – Airborne interception (radar)
AM1/AM2 – Air Mechanic 1st and 2nd Class
App Tech – Apprentice Technician
Boy Ent – Boy Entrant
C/Chef – Caporal Chef, a Free French Air Force rank
Cpl – Corporal
Chief Tech – Chief Technician
Feldwebel – Luftwaffe rank equivalent to staff sergeant.
F/Eng – Flight Engineer
F/Sgt – Flight Sergeant
F/O – Flying Officer
F/Lt – Flight Lieutenant
Gefreiter – Luftwaffe rank equivalent to private
G/Capt – Group Captain
Junior Tech/Jnr Tech – Junior Technician
LAC – Leading Aircraftman
LACW – Leading Aircraftwoman
Lt – Lieutenant
2 Lt – Second Lieutenant
Lt Cdr – Lieutenant Commander
Master Pilot/Gunner/Navigator etc – warrant officer rank held by aircrew
Nav – Navigator
Oberfeldwebel – Luftwaffe rank loosely equivalent to flight sergeant
Obs – Observer
Pte – Private
Acting P/O – Acting Pilot Officer
P/O – Pilot Officer
PII – Pilot II (a short lived RAF NCO rank post 1945)
SAC – Senior Aircraftman
Sgt/Sjt – Sergeant/Serjeant
S/Sgt – Staff Sergeant
Sig II – Signaller II
S/Ldr – Squadron Leader
Sub Lt (A) – Sub Lieutenant (Air)
Togglier – operated the bomb release 'toggle-switch'
Uffz/Unteroffizier – Luftwaffe rank equivalent to corporal
W/AG – Wireless Operator/Air Gunner
W/Cdr – Wing Commander
W/O – Warrant Officer
W/Op – Wireless Operator

Airfields

Atcham (Station 342, USAAF)
Construction of the airfield began in late 1940 and by August 1941 it was chosen as the permanent station for 9 (Fighter) Group Sector HQ, which had previously been stationed at Tern Hill and was responsible for controlling and vectoring fighters as part of the air defence of the region. Its role as Sector HQ saw a number of fighter squadrons stationed at the airfield, but on 15 June 1942 the airfield was passed over to the USAAF and subsequently designated Station 342. Despite this, the Sector 'ops room', which was located adjacent to the Wroxeter turning on the Atcham road (at map reference 556093), continued to operate under RAF control until 1 November 1943.

The first American units to arrive in the summer of 1942 were 307th and 308th Squadrons, 31st Fighter Group, who immediately began converting from their P-39s to the Spitfire, which resulted in a number of accidents. On 1 August the Group was deemed combat ready and moved off south, while in their place arrived 49th Fighter Squadron, 14th Fighter Group and their unmistakeable twin boom P-38 Lightning fighters. Following their departure for combat in North Africa, 6th Fighter Wing arrived in November 1942 and Atcham's long association as an American training base began. Initially the pilots were trained on Spitfires and P-39s, but in the spring of 1943 these were replaced by the P-47 Thunderbolt, or 'Jug' (short for juggernaut in respect of its stout appearance) as it was known to pilots.

In the late summer of 1943 the 6th Fighter Wing was renamed 2906th Observation Training Group, then subsequently renamed again in December 1943 as 495th Fighter Training Group. Despite the name changes, the unit's role remained the same, in that it was responsible for preparing fighter pilots for combat in the European Theatre of Operations (ETO) and training was mostly carried out on P-47s (and some P-38s).

Atcham's association with the USAAF finally came to an end on 14 March 1945 when the airfield was handed back to the RAF and placed under control of Tern Hill, who used it as a Relief Landing Ground, prior to its closure in April 1946.

Bratton
Construction of Bratton airfield was completed in October 1940 but due to the threat of invasion the site was covered in obstructions and it was not until June 1941 that the airfield was brought into use as a Relief Landing Ground for RAF Shawbury's Oxford aircraft. Due to its small size and proximity to the Wrekin, however, the airfield was reserved for day flying only and, because of waterlogging, the grass

P/O Green standing in front of a Spitfire in dispersals at Atcham. [ww2images.com]

runways were frequently out of action during the winter months.

In January 1944 responsibility for the airfield was transferred to RAF Tern Hill, but it was used by aircraft from RNAS Hinstock until April 1944, before Tern Hill's Miles Masters began operating from the airfield. The airfield finally closed in the summer of 1945.

Bridgnorth

RAF Bridgnorth opened in November 1939 as a non-flying station with the responsibility of providing basic training to new recruits. It was primarily in this capacity that the station served until its closure in February 1963, although more specialised ground training was also provided during the latter half of the war.

During the war an RAF hospital was also established at the base, which was not only responsible for providing inoculations and health care for the recruits passing through, but also responded with its medical officer and ambulance to aircraft crashes across the south and south-east of the county.

Bridleway Gate

Approval was given for Bridleway Gate to be used as a Relief Landing Ground (RLG) by 11 SFTS, Shawbury, in September 1940, but it was not until 29 April 1941 that the airfield was put to use. Due to its grass runways the airfield was plagued with long periods of un-serviceability during the wetter months and it was also never used for night flying as 'the surface was too uneven and the approaches too poor'.

Following the move of 11 (P)AFU from RAF Shawbury to RAF Calveley in January 1944, Bridleway Gate became a fuel storage depot under the control of 245 Maintenance Unit and was also used for container dropping exercises by aircraft from 1665 HCU at RAF Tilstock. The site was abandoned after the war and subsequently reverted to agricultural use.

Brockton (30 SLG)

Designated as 30 Satellite Landing Ground (SLG), this small airfield was opened in June 1941 and used during the war to aid in the dispersal and storage of a wide variety of aircraft from 9 Maintenance Unit at RAF Cosford.

Buntingsdale Hall

Buntingsdale Hall was requisitioned by the RAF in July 1936 and served as the Headquarters of RAF Training Command until January 1940. The hall was subsequently used as HQ, 20 (Training) Group, until August 1943 and then HQ, 22 (Training) Group, until the unit's disbandment in January 1972. The hall remained under RAF Tern Hill's control for several more years before finally being sold off.

Chetwynd

Officially opened in September 1941 as a Relief Landing Ground (RLG) for 5 SFTS, Tern Hill, the grass airstrip was used for day and night flying by trainee pilots in their Miles Masters and Hurricanes.

Throughout its use the site suffered from waterlogging problems but,

A Free French pilot pictured at Chetwynd in March 1943. In the background can clearly be seen one of the open ended hangars which some pilots are purported to have flown through. [Pierre Magrot, via Bertrand Hugo]

nonetheless, the airfield continued to be used by RAF Tern Hill until 1976. Responsibility for the airfield then switched to RAF Shawbury and helicopters from Shawbury's Defence Helicopter Flying School continue to use the site to this day.

Condover

Work started on the airfield in late 1940 and in early 1941 it was earmarked as a possible site for the permanent station for the Sector HQ, 9 Group (based at Tern Hill at the time), but RAF Atcham was chosen instead and RAF Condover was relegated to the role of satellite airfield to Atcham. With the handover of RAF Atcham to the USAAF in the summer of 1942, Condover was assigned to RAF Shawbury in May 1942 as a satellite airfield but it was not until August 1942 that flying commenced. Due to its concrete runways the airfield could be used continually throughout the year, for both day and night flying, by the twin engine Oxford trainers of 11 (P)AFU.

In January 1944, 11 (P)AFU relocated to RAF Calveley and, as a result, Condover was taken over as a satellite airfield to 5 (P)AFU, Tern Hill, whose single engine Miles Masters (and subsequently Harvards) immediately began using the runways.

Following the departure of the USAAF from Atcham in March 1945, Tern Hill relocated its satellite there and RAF Condover was subsequently placed under care and maintenance and fell silent for the last time.

Cosford

Built as part of the RAF's 1930s expansion programme, the first unit to occupy the airfield was 2 School of Technical Training which formed there on 15 July 1938 to provide training for fitters, mechanics and armourers. Eight months later saw the arrival of 9 Maintenance Unit which was responsible for storing, maintaining, repairing and test-flying aircraft, and both units would remain at Cosford for the duration of the war and beyond.

Throughout the war the airfield also housed many varied and, mostly, non-flying units as well as being chosen as the site for an important regional RAF Hospital, which opened in June 1940. The hospital was responsible for treating airmen and women from all over the region and was home to various specialist departments, including a burns unit.

Post-war the station has continued its association with technical training to this day, including the training of boy apprentices, while 9 MU finally closed in 1956 and the RAF Hospital in 1977.

Harlescott

One of Shropshire's least known RAF stations, the site was acquired in 1917 as the 'North-western Aircraft Repair Depot' and appears to have performed a similar role to the Maintenance Units established during the Second World War.

Following the armistice the depot was established as a store for surplus MT vehicles and in July 1919 the station became the 'RAF Mechanical Transport Repair Depot' under the command of S/Ldr R H Verity, OBE. The role of the station was to act as a central overhaul and repair depot for RAF transport and, although the name was changed in 1926 by dropping 'motor' from its title, the depot continued to function at Harlescott until its closure on 31 March 1932.

High Ercall (Station 346, USAAF)

The airfield was first occupied on 1 October 1940 by 29 Maintenance Unit (MU), which was responsible for modifying and repairing aircraft and was manned, mostly, by civilian employees. Despite 29 MU remaining throughout the war and afterwards, the airfield was also to play a key part in the air defence of the Midlands and Liverpool between April 1941 and May 1943.

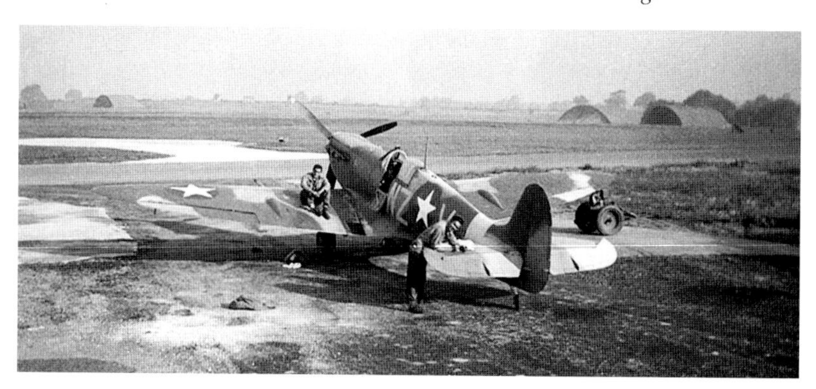

'Erks', taking a rest from work on an American 309th Squadron Spitfire at High Ercall in the summer of 1942. [Jim Earnshaw, via Mark Crame]

The first operational squadron to arrive was the Blenheim equipped 68 Squadron although, within a month, they re-equipped with the superior, radar-fitted Beaufighter to combat the German bombers. During their stay the squadron claimed several 'kills', although these victories did not come without loss and a number of the crews were killed in training accidents and one due to battle damage on 22 October 1941.

A series of operational squadrons followed, with 255 Squadron replacing 68 Squadron in March 1942 (also equipped with Beaufighters), then 257 Squadron arriving with 1456 (Turbinlite) Flight in June 1942 for a highly experimental innovation in night interception. This involved the Havocs of 1456 Flight attempting to illuminate enemy aircraft with a searchlight fitted to the nose, while an accompanying Hurricane from 257 Squadron would then make its attack. In practice the concept did not work and in July 257 Squadron began re-equipping with the Typhoon in preparation for a posting to the south coast and offensive sweeps over north-west Europe.

During 257 Squadron and 1456 Flight's stay at High Ercall, the airfield was also the temporary home of the American 309th Fighter Squadron, 31st Fighter Group, which had just arrived from the USA and was converting to the Spitfire in preparation for operations (the sister squadrons, the 307th and 308th, were stationed at Atcham at the same time).

In September 1942, 247 (China-British) Squadron arrived at High Ercall and, like their predecessor 257 Squadron, they were initially equipped with Hurricanes before converting to the Typhoon in January 1943. The squadron departed in March 1943 and in their place the Spitfire-equipped 41 Squadron arrived, briefly, until they too departed in April 1943.

Following the departure of the fighter squadrons at High Ercall, the airfield was to take on a whole new role, with the formation of 60 Operational Training Unit in May 1943 whose responsibility was to

F/Sgt Laurie Bush and his pilot, S/Ldr Geoffrey Matheson, pictured during their training at High Ercall in the summer of 1943. They would both lose their lives with 418 Squadron after leaving High Ercall. [Lorraine Eastcott]

train the next generation of Mosquito crews for operations.

The unit left High Ercall in March 1945, but the airfield continued to be used by 29 MU until 1957, then 99 MU until 1962, when it was placed under care and maintenance before being sold off.

Hinstock (originally Ollerton)

Originally designated 21 Satellite Landing Ground (SLG) and known as Ollerton, the airfield opened officially in October 1941 as a storage and dispersal airfield for 37 Maintenance Unit (MU) stationed at Burtonwood in Lancashire. By April 1942 the airfield was transferred under control of 27 Maintenance Unit at Shawbury but the following year the site was taken over by the Royal Navy, who had earmarked the site for an instrument training base.

In June 1943 the airfield was christened HMS *Godwit* and the airfield was used by 758 Squadron for training naval pilots in advanced instrument and blind flying techniques, while Hinstock Hall was taken over as the officers' mess. The squadron remained at Hinstock until early 1946 when it was disbanded and replaced by 780 Squadron, but soon afterwards the unit transferred to the larger airfield at Peplow and Hinstock was abandoned early the following year.

Oxfords and a Tiger Moth pictured at HMS Godwit *in 1943. [David Watson, via Lewis Wood]*

Hodnet

Designated as 29 Satellite Landing Ground (SLG), this small grass airstrip was opened on 12 June 1941 to store and disperse a wide variety of aircraft from 24 Maintenance Unit (MU), Tern Hill. On 20 April 1942 the landing ground was transferred to 37 MU, Burtonwood but, in June when Burtonwood was handed over to the USAAF, the airstrip was allocated to 27 MU, Shawbury. The airstrip continued to be used until February 1945 when it was finally closed down.

Ludlow

RAF Air Crew Camp, Ludlow, was one of Shropshire's least well known RAF sites and officially opened on 11 April 1942, to act as a holding camp for airmen awaiting postings to Initial Training Wings. Primarily a tented camp with only some permanent buildings and structures (including a rifle range and assault course), the airmen underwent physical training, lectures and parades during their time at the station.

During the winter months the camp was placed under 'care and maintenance' before re-opening in spring-time but, following the winter of 1943, it appears to have closed for use.

Monkmoor

Monkmoor is one of Shropshire's oldest airfields, established during the First World War in an area that has since been swallowed up by the expansion of Shrewsbury. Little is known of the airfield's early days, however, as contemporary records are scant, but by the time of the armistice the airfield was home to the Observers' School of Reconnaissance and Aerial Photography.

The airfield then appears to have been used as an Aircraft Acceptance Park, where newly manufactured aircraft were assembled and test flown before being allocated to their allotted squadron. The airfield was wound down soon afterwards and closed in the early 1920s, although some civilian flying continued to take place during the inter-war period.

Following the outbreak of the Second World War, the site was taken over again for military use and on 1 March 1940 the site reopened as the home of 34 Maintenance Unit, although there was no longer a landing ground attached to the site. The unit was responsible for recovering and repairing crashed or damaged aircraft and was the most important unit for salvaging crashes throughout Shropshire and the surroundings counties.

The unit left Monkmoor in August 1945 and the site was subsequently taken over as an industrial estate.

Montford Bridge

RAF Montford Bridge was first brought into use in April 1942 as the satellite airfield for 61 OTU at RAF Rednal and it was in this role that the airfield would continue to serve until June 1945. Despite its primary use as a Spitfire (and later Mustang) training airfield, the runways were also used briefly by two other units; first of these temporary lodgers were the Oxfords of 11 (P)AFU which used the runways in July 1942 while work was being completed on RAF Condover. Then, between December 1942 and November 1943, a detachment from 7 Anti-Aircraft Cooperation Unit (AACU) also used the airfield while working in conjunction with the trainee Royal Artillery gunners and searchlight troops at the nearby Park Hall army camp.

Following the move of 61 OTU to RAF Keevil in June 1945, Montford Bridge was assigned to 34 Maintenance Unit (which had spent the entire war at RAF Monkmoor) and the site was used to dismantle and scrap planes and gliders that were now surplus to requirements. The airfield finally closed in 1947.

Peplow (Child's Ercall)

Construction of the airfield began in 1939 but it was not until early 1941 that the grass runways were put into use as a Relief Landing Ground for the Miles Masters of 5 SFTS, Tern Hill. From September 1941 Oxfords from Shawbury also used the airfield for training flights but the following year it was closed so that the site could be enlarged and paved runways laid down.

The revamped airfield officially reopened on 15 July 1943 as the home of 83 Operational Training Unit and training flights began soon afterwards with Wellington bombers. Routine exercises included circuits and landings, cross-country flights and bombing exercises, mostly carried out at the nearby Cherrington bombing range, while a number of operational 'Nickel' (leaflet dropping) raids were also carried out over north-west Europe.

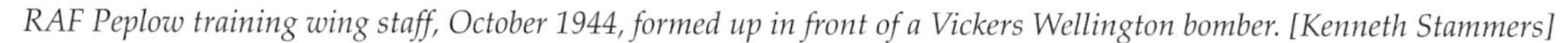

RAF Peplow training wing staff, October 1944, formed up in front of a Vickers Wellington bomber. [Kenneth Stammers]

In October 1944 83 OTU was disbanded but some of its personnel were used to form the nucleus of 23 Heavy Glider Conversion Unit, which trained pilots on Horsas and Hamilcars to replace losses suffered in the failed Arnhem operation. After the unit disbanded in December 1945, Peplow was used briefly by 21 (P)AFU, Wheaton Aston, then 1515 Beam Approach Training (BAT) Flight, before the site was taken over by the Royal Navy in February 1945 and used by aircraft from HMS *Godwit*. Following the navy's departure the airfield went into a state of care and maintenance before closing down in 1949.

Rednal

The airfield opened on 15 April 1942 as the home of 61 Operational Training Unit (OTU), training Spitfire (and later Mustang) pilots in prepar-ation for their operational postings. The unit remained at Rednal until the 21 June 1945, when they departed for RAF Keevil, and RAF Rednal was placed under care and maintenance.

A group of pilots (including a number of Polish pilots) pictured in front of Rednal control tower, December 1944. [www.ww2images.com]

During the airfield's first year, it also briefly housed two Anti-Aircraft Co-operation Unit (AACU) detachments, which worked in conjunction with the trainee Royal Artillery gunners and searchlight troops at the nearby Park Hall army camp. The first was a detachment of 6 AACU who stayed between 26 June and 2 August 1942 and then a detachment of 7 AACU between August and December, before they transferred to the satellite airfield at Montford Bridge.

Shawbury

Shawbury airfield began life in the summer of 1917 and was home to a number of different training units, instructing pilots on a wide variety of aircraft, until its closure in 1920.

As part of the RAF expansion scheme of the 1930s the site was selected for the construction of a new and enlarged airfield and the first occupants to arrive were the men of 27 Maintenance Unit, in February 1938. The unit, which was responsible for storing, maintaining, repairing and test-flying aircraft, remained at Shawbury with its mostly civilian work force until July 1972, but it was in its role as a flying training station that Shawbury would be most commonly remem-bered. It was in May 1938 that 11 Flying Training School arrived from RAF Wittering as one of the RAF's key training schools, instructing the next generation of pilots on Hawker biplanes and later the twin-engined Oxford. Renamed 11 (Pilots) Advanced Flying Unit in the spring of 1942, the unit continued training pilots on Oxford aircraft until January 1944 when it moved to Cheshire.

Two Airspeed Oxfords of 11 (P)AFU pictured at Shawbury. [RAF Museum]

A line up of Wellingtons (with a Short Stirling on the far right) belonging to the Central Navigation School at RAF Shawbury, 1944. [RAF Museum]

Following the departure of 11 (P)AFU, Shawbury's role changed to that of a navigation training establishment and it was in this capacity that it continued to serve into the post-war era, with the addition of Air Traffic Control (ATC) training from 1950. In 1963 the navigation wing departed Shawbury and the airfield became the home of the Central Air Traffic Control School (which remains to this day) but in 1976 the airfield also saw the arrival of helicopter pilot training in the form of 2 Flying Training School. Helicopter training continues to this day with the Defence Helicopter Flying School, which replaced 2 FTS in April 1997.

Sleap

Sleap airfield (pronounced Slape) was first brought into use in the spring of 1943 as a satellite airfield for 81 Operational Training Unit (OTU) at RAF Tilstock, which was responsible for training bomber crews on the twin engine Whitley.

In January 1944 1665 Heavy Conversion Unit was posted to RAF Tilstock and, as a result, 81 OTU relocated entirely to RAF Sleap. At the same time the unit transferred from Bomber Command to 38 Group, Allied Expeditionary Air Force, and its role of training bomber crews changed to that of training crews for glider towing operations in preparation for the forthcoming invasion of Europe. In December 1944 Wellingtons began to replace the Whitleys and at the same time glider towing training was wound down.

Following 1665 HCU's departure from Tilstock in March 1945, 81 OTU spread out again between Tilstock and Sleap but, by the end of the year, Sleap was placed into care and maintenance. Today the airfield is still in use as a civilian airfield and home of the Shropshire Aero Club.

Stoke Heath

A line up of Whitleys at Sleap in 1943. The first aircraft in the row is LA937, which crashed into the watch office at Sleap on 26 August 1943, killing two of the crew. [David Birrell]

Another view of Whitleys at Sleap in 1943. Again, the first aircraft in the row is LA937. [David Birrell]

A Horsa being towed into the air by a Whitley at Sleap. [Rob Cairns]

Although originally part of RAF Tern Hill, the Maintenance Unit site was subsequently referred to separately as RAF Stoke Heath.

Tern Hill

Established in late 1916 as one of Shropshire's earliest airfields, Tern Hill was home to a number of training units during the First World War before being sold off in 1920.

As part of the RAF's 1930s expansion plan, the airfield was re-opened in January 1936 as the home of 10 Flying Training School, training pilots on Harvards and Ansons until it departed for Canada and was replaced by 5 Service Flying Training School in November 1940. 5 SFTS was renamed 5 (Pilots) Advanced Flying Unit in 1942, but its responsibility for training pilots on single engine Miles Masters and Hurricanes remained throughout the rest of the war (although Harvards and Spitfires were also introduced later on).

In August 1940 Tern Hill was also chosen as the site for Fighter Sector HQ, 9 Group, controlling and vector-ing fighters onto enemy aircraft and, consequently, several fighter squadrons were stationed at Tern Hill between August 1940 and September 1941, when the Sector HQ was relocated to RAF Atcham.

Throughout the war the airfield's Stoke Heath site was also occupied by 24 Maintenance Unit (initially named 4 Aircraft Storage Unit when it was created in June 1937), which was responsible for storing, maintaining, repairing and test flying aircraft. The site, which was subsequently known separately from Tern Hill as RAF Stoke Heath, continued to operate as a maintenance unit long after the war.

Hurricanes of 306 (Polish) Squadron taking off from Tern Hill in the winter of 1940/41. [RAF Museum]

Tern Hill continued to train pilots after the war and was home to 6 Flying Training School from April 1946 until 1961, when it was replaced by helicopters from the Central Flying School (CFS). In 1976 the CFS moved and Tern Hill was largely taken over by the army, although the runways are still used to this day by helicopters from RAF Shawbury and fixed-wing aircraft for training Air Cadets.

Tilstock (Whitchurch Heath)

The airfield first opened in August 1942 under the name RAF Whitchurch Heath, but to avoid confusion with Whitchurch airfield in Gloucestershire the airfield was renamed RAF Tilstock the following year. The first unit to occupy the airfield was 81 Operational Training Unit (OTU) which was responsible for training crews in the twin-engined Whitley bomber. In January 1944 81 OTU was transferred to RAF Sleap and in its place arrived 1665 Heavy Conversion Unit (HCU) whose role was to train crews on four engine aircraft in preparation for the impending airborne operations during the invasion of Europe.

In March 1945, 1665 HCU departed Tilstock and the airfield returned to being used by 81 OTU as it had previously, although the Whitleys had now been replaced by Wellingtons. On 10 August 1945 81 OTU was re-designated 1380 (Transport) Conversion Unit but the following March the unit was disbanded and the airfield placed under care and maintenance.

Weston Park (33 SLG)

The small grass airfield at Weston Park officially opened on 18 April 1942 as 33 Satellite Landing Ground (SLG) and was used to store aircraft from 9 Maintenance Unit at RAF Cosford. Later, in the summer of 1944, the airstrip was also used by naval pilots from RNAS Hinstock but following the cessation of hostilities the airfield closed down and returned to agricultural farmland.

Westland Whirlwind helicopters, of the Central Flying School, in the snow at Tern Hill, January 1963. [TNA]

Military Aviation Accidents

1917

18 March (Sunday)
Training flight. 34 TS (Tern Hill aerodrome, Shropshire)
Sopwith 1½ Strutter (7807) crashed on the aerodrome when the pilot was attempting to pull out of a steep dive and the tail broke under the strain.

Lt (pilot u/t) Allan Wenman Smith, RFC, aged 20, the son of Frank Thomas and Jeanie B Smith of College Road, Crosby, Liverpool, is buried in Sefton (St Helen) Churchyard, Lancashire. Prior to joining the RFC he had fought at Ypres as a private in 1/6 King's (Liverpool) Regiment.

9 June (Saturday)
Training flight. 10 TS (Tern Hill aerodrome, Shropshire)
Airco DH2 (6008) crashed near the aerodrome at 19.00 hrs while attempting to reach the aerodrome after the engine had failed. The pilot turned with insufficient flying speed and the aircraft side-slipped and crashed, seriously injuring him. Despite being conveyed to Prees Heath Military Hospital for treatment, he succumbed to his injuries on 27 July.

2 Lt (pilot u/t) Edward Phillip Hughes, RFC, aged 24, was the eldest son of Edward James and Louise Ada Hughes (née Phillip) of Ellesmere, Knapdaar Station, in the Cape Province of South Africa. He came to England with the South African Contingent in 1915 but transferred to the Royal Flying Corps in August 1916. He is buried in Tilstock (Christ Church) Churchyard, Shropshire.

16 July (Monday)
Training flight. 10 TS (Shawbury aerodrome, Shropshire)
Airco DH2 (A2560) crashed near the aerodrome at approximately 10.00 hrs. Having climbed to 170 feet after taking off, the pilot was witnessed turning without banking, causing the aircraft to side-slip and nose-dive into the ground.

2 Lt (pilot u/t) George Everett Cayford, RFC, aged 21, was the only son of Ebenezer George and Charlotte Cayford of 71 The Mall, Wanstead. Educated at Bancrofts School in Wanstead, he was apprenticed to Messrs Broom & Wade Ltd, Admiralty Engineers & Co, of High Wycombe, but after completing his indentures he joined the Artists Rifles in February 1916. He subsequently transferred to the Royal Flying Corps and, according to *Flight* magazine, he was 'a somewhat skilful magician and very popular throughout the squadron he was attached to and greatly esteemed by numerous friends'. He is buried in the City of London Cemetery, Manor Park.

2 Lt Everett Cayford
[Jennie Leon]

27 July (Friday)
2 Lt E P Hughes died on this date from injuries received in an accident at Tern Hill on 9 June.

20 September (Thursday)
Training flight. 30 TS, AFC (Tern Hill aerodrome, Shropshire)
Sopwith 1½ Strutter (A6945) was involved in a ground accident at 07.00 hours. Cadet pilot Treadwell was standing on the left wing looking into the cockpit, as he wished to see the workings of the throttle control and instruments as a fellow pilot, Cadet pilot Benjamin, started the aircraft up. Having started the engine, Benjamin then

> ... throttled down preparatory to signalling for the chock to be removed. I then asked Cadet Treadwell to get down. A few seconds later I looked to see if he was standing clear of the machine and I saw him on the ground and his hand – right arm raised, and his hand pressed against his head. Apparently he stumbled, for almost simultaneously he was struck by the propeller and fell to the ground with blood streaming from his head. I stopped the engine and got out of the machine and assisted in putting him in the ambulance.

He died later in the day at Prees Heath Military Hospital.

Cadet (pilot u/t) Edward Jabez Cooper Treadwell (959), AFC, aged 22, was the son of Edward Cooper Treadwell and the late Mary Jane Treadwell of 32 York Street, St. Kilda, Victoria, Australia. Prior to enlisting he had worked as a printer and publisher. He is buried in Tilstock (Christ Church) Cemetery, Shropshire.

10 October (Wednesday)
Training flight. 34 TS (Tern Hill aerodrome, Shropshire)
Sopwith Camel (B6222) crashed near the aerodrome when the pilot was believed to have 'fainted in the air when at a height exceeding 3,000 feet contrary to the orders of his last medical board.'

2 Lt (pilot u/t) Clifford Ernest Rider, RFC, aged 20, was the son of John Ernest and Janet Christena Rider of 602 Ossington Avenue, Toronto. He is buried in Toronto (Mount Pleasant) Cemetery, Canada.

13 October (Saturday)
Training flight. 10 TS (Shawbury aerodrome, Shropshire)
Sopwith Camel (B5164) crashed near the aerodrome at 12.15 hrs. During an attempted spin, the pilot lost control and crashed as he was not experienced enough in the manoeuvre.

2 Lt (pilot u/t) Harold James Cryer, RFC, aged 19, was the son of Joseph Herbert and Sarah Annie Cryer of 24 Ferndene Road, Herne Hill, London. He is buried in West Norwood Cemetery, Lambeth.

15 October (Monday)
Training flight. 43 TS (Tern Hill aerodrome, Shropshire).
Airco DH5 (A9234) crashed 'two miles south of the aerodrome' (putting it roughly in the area of Ollerton and Hodnet) at 09.55 hrs. During the course of the training flight the upper right wing tip detached for unknown reasons, causing the aircraft to crash out of control.

2 Lt (pilot u/t) Herbert Frederick Meyer, RFC, aged 29, was born in Tokyo, on 8 February 1888, the son of Mrs F A Meyer. After returning to his native Canada, he grew up in Vernon, British Columbia and had worked as a chauffeur and book keeper before joining up. Prior to transferring to the RFC he had served for two years in 30 British Columbia Horse Militia and ten months in the Canadian Army Service Corps. He is buried in Stoke upon Tern (St Peter's) Cemetery, Shropshire.

23 October (Tuesday)
Training flight. 43 TS (Tern Hill aerodrome, Shropshire)
Avro 504A (B3105) crashed at Heath Field, Colehurst, to the north-east of the aerodrome at 11.15 hrs. The pilot was flying at 600 feet when a collision occurred with another of the squadron's aircraft, causing the two aircraft to crash out of control. The pilot of this aircraft was killed instantly in the crash, while the pilot of the Nieuport died of his injuries later that night in Prees Heath Military Hospital.

2 Lt (pilot u/t) Frank Jickling, RFC, aged 22, was the son of Mr and Mrs Jickling of 627 Home Street, in Winnipeg, Canada. Before enlisting in March 1916 he had worked as a 'druggist' and lived at De Salaberry, Provencher, Manitoba. He is buried in Stoke upon Tern (St Peter's) Cemetery, Shropshire.

Training flight. 43 TS (Tern Hill aerodrome, Shropshire)
Nieuport 20 (A6741) crashed at Heath Field, Colehurst after colliding in the incident described above.

2 Lt (pilot u/t) Leslie Thomas Hogben, RFC, aged 18, was the son of Charlotte and the late Walter James Hogben of 19 Albert Road, Canterbury. Before joining up he had been a pupil at Wye College, Ashford. He is buried in Canterbury (St Martin) Churchyard, Kent.

23 October (Tuesday)
Training flight. 43 TS (Tern Hill aerodrome, Shropshire)
Airco DH5 (A9467) crashed at the aerodrome. The pilot, who had almost completed his training and had just two more hours of flying to carry out before he would be posted to France, was flying near the aerodrome when the engine began missing and spluttering. In an endeavour to land at the aerodrome he began a turn at 150 feet but, with little flying speed, the aircraft stalled and crashed, fatally injuring the pilot.

2 Lt (pilot u/t) Sidney Harold Smith, RFC, aged 34, was the son of Sidney and Mary Thorpe Smith (née Bramwell) of St George, Manchester and the husband of Carrie Banks of 16 Cleveland Road, North Crumpsall, Manchester. Before joining up he had been a musical-instrument dealer. He is buried in Stoke upon Tern (St Peter's) Cemetery, Shropshire.

4 November (Sunday)
Training flight. 10 TS (Shawbury aerodrome, Shropshire)
Sopwith Camel (B6252) crashed near the aerodrome. After taking off for a morning flight, the engine began to splutter and smoke at 600 feet before failing altogether and, in an attempt to turn towards the aerodrome, the pilot allowed the aircraft to stall and crash.

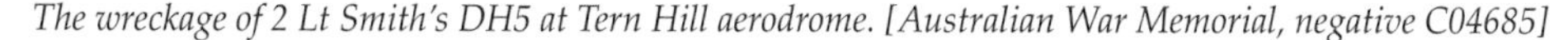

The wreckage of 2 Lt Smith's DH5 at Tern Hill aerodrome. [Australian War Memorial, negative C04685]

2 Lt (pilot u/t) Albert Charles Tallent, RFC, aged 21, was the only son of the late Albert Charles and Alice Maud Tallent of 37 Lordship Park, Stoke Newington, London. He is buried in Abney Park Cemetery, London.

17 November (Saturday)
Training flight (?). 30 TS, AFC (Tern Hill aerodrome, Shropshire)
Bristol Scout D (A1766) crashed at Abbey Foregate in Shrewsbury at 15.30 hrs. The pilot took off from Tern Hill at 14.45 hrs for a short flight to Shawbury but, due to the misty conditions he encountered en route, he overshot and found himself flying over Coton Manor in Shrewsbury, where his engine promptly failed at 1,000 feet. With little time to act, he tried to land in a railway goods yard but, due to a block of houses running at right angles to the yard, he was compelled 'to 'zoom' and thereby lost his engine, stalled and nose-dived to earth'.

Richard Henry Spencer of Frankwell, who gave evidence at the subsequent court of inquiry, described how,

> I saw an aeroplane manoeuvring in the air at about 600 feet. It was travelling in an unsteady condition. It flew for a matter of 300 yards on its side 'til it got over the station yard. The machine then turned over into an upright position and seemed to shoot into the air, after which it made for the ground as if to alight. Owing to a cement truck which the left wing struck, it was thrown into a level position, but the machine was crashed to pieces.

2 Lt Edmund Montgomery [RAeC Aviator's Certificate]

Evidence also given by Mr F W Nicholas, of Stanley Terrace, Castlefields, continued by adding that he

> ... found the pilot tangled up in the wreckage, the only part of his body which was free being the right leg. He was partly unconscious for a few minutes, and then made an effort to free himself. I helped to lift the pilot free from the machine after breaking away some wing and taking the belt off.

First aid was then rendered by railway officials and fifteen minutes later the pilot was on his way to the Royal Salop Infirmary, where he was treated for a fractured skull and left leg, numerous abrasions and superficial facial injuries.

2 Lt (pilot u/t) Edmund Montgomery (1322), AFC, was born in Manly, near Sydney, Australia on 26 December 1896, and had worked as a sail maker before enlisting in October 1916. Having arrived in the UK in January 1917 he initially served as an air mechanic before being accepted for pilot training. Following the accident in Shrewsbury he spent many months recuperating, firstly in Berrington War Hospital and then in the 3rd London General Hospital, before returning to Australia in March 1918 for a medical discharge.

6 December (Thursday)
Training flight. 30 TS, AFC (Tern Hill aerodrome, Shropshire)
Avro 504J (B4215) crashed near the aerodrome. During the course of the flight the engine began to fail and, while attempting to land in a field, the pilot allowed the aircraft to stall as he tried to clear some trees, lost control and crashed. One officer was killed instantly, while the instructor survived unhurt.

Capt (instructor pilot) Alfred William Leslie Ellis, AFC. Born in Victoria, Australia on 4 October 1894, he had undergone pilot training in Australia prior to being posted to Palestine to fly with 67 Squadron in June 1916. He served with the squadron until September 1917, when he sailed to the UK to take up instructor duties at Tern Hill. In January 1918 he was mentioned in despatches and awarded the Military Cross for his actions in Palestine. During the Second World War he served in the RAAF, rising to the rank of Group Captain. He died in Sydney in 1948.

2 Lt (pilot u/t) Alfred Edgar H Portlock, RFC, aged 22, was the son of Joseph Robert and Susie Annie Portlock of Vauxhall, London. Before transferring to the RFC he had served in France with the Scots Guards and then the Royal Fusiliers. He is buried in Lambeth Cemetery, London.

13 December (Thursday)
Training flight. 30 TS, AFC (Tern Hill aerodrome, Shropshire)
Sopwith Camel (B6445) crashed near the aerodrome. During the course of a training flight the pilot began a loop-the-loop at 500 feet, but misjudged his recovery and failed to pull up in time.

2 Lt (pilot u/t) Douglas Gordon Scott, RFC, was born on 26 April 1896 in Hawick, Scotland, the son of Mr Thomas B and Winifred B Scott. After emigrating to Canada, where his family settled at 64 Mountview Avenue, Toronto, Douglas was educated at Riverdale College before studying Applied Science at the University of Toronto. He joined the RFC in the spring of 1917. He is buried in Stoke upon Tern (St Peter's) Cemetery, Shropshire.

2 Lt Douglas Scott [University of Toronto, via Canadian War Memorial website]

18 December (Tuesday)
Training flight. 30 TS, AFC (Tern Hill aerodrome, Shropshire)
Sopwith Camel (B6268) crashed near the aerodrome. After accidentally choking the engine, the pilot tried to turn without banking, which caused the aircraft to enter a spin and crash.

2 Lt (pilot u/t) Robert Ernest Cleary, RFC, aged 22, was the son of Robert and Margaret Cleary of Dunedin, Ontario, Canada. He is buried in Stoke upon Tern (St Peter's) Cemetery, Shropshire.

1918

20 January (Sunday)
Formation training flight. 6 TS, AFC (Tern Hill aerodrome, Shropshire)
Sopwith Pup (B6089) crashed near the aerodrome at 14.30 hrs. The pilot had taken off at 14.00 hrs and made one circuit of the aerodrome at 1,000 feet when he got ahead of the formation and began a vertically banked turn into the wind, causing the aircraft to stall and enter a spin. Unable to regain control, the pilot was seriously injured in the resulting crash and was conveyed to Prees Heath Military Hospital, where he succumbed to his injuries on 16 February. Upon examination of the aircraft wreckage it was discovered that the pilot had been sick in the cockpit and therefore the court of inquiry concluded that the pilot 'became overcome by sickness and nausea in the air and lost control of the aircraft'.

2 Lt (pilot u/t) Reginald James Thomas Forsyth, AFC, aged 25, was the son of John Lile Lewis Forsyth and Elizabeth Christina Forsyth of Crow's Nest, North Sydney, Australia. After enlisting in 1 Light Horse in May 1915 he sailed to Egypt in January 1916, where the regiment was initially deployed in the Nile Valley to protect against bands of pro-Turkish Arabs. Following the regiment's re-deployment to protect the Suez Canal, in May 1916, Cpl Forsyth fought in the fierce Battle of Romani, where he received a gun shot wound to the chest and was admitted to hospital. It was during his time recuperating that he applied for a transfer to the Australian Flying Corps and, after an initial period as an air mechanic, was accepted for pilot training. He is buried in Tilstock (Christ Church) Cemetery, Shropshire.

12 February (Tuesday)
Training flight. 6 TS, AFC (Tern Hill aerodrome, Shropshire)
Sopwith Camel (B6442) crashed near the aerodrome. While turning in towards the aerodrome the pilot allowed the aircraft to stall and crash, injuring himself.

2 Lt (pilot u/t) Loren William Heseltine, RFC, was a Canadian. Following this accident he was discharged as permanently unfit for flying and returned to Ontario.

16 February (Saturday)
2 Lt R J T Forsyth died following an accident on 20 January 1918.

18 February (Monday)
Training flight. 10 TS (Shawbury aerodrome, Shropshire).
Sopwith Pup (B6083) crashed near the aerodrome at approximately 09.30 hrs. Ten minutes after taking off the pilot stalled during a turn at 100 feet and was unable to recover from the resulting spin.

2 Lt (pilot u/t) John Hardman Batten, RFC, aged 19, was the son of Thomas and Florence Batten of 71 Horace Street, St Helens. He is buried in Eccleston (Christ Church) Churchyard, Lancashire.

2 Lt Wilf McGinn [University of Toronto, via Canadian War Memorial website]

18 February (Monday)
Training flight. 34 TS (Tern Hill aerodrome, Shropshire)
Bristol Scout D (B716) crashed near the aerodrome at 16.15 hrs. The pilot had been in the air for approximately fifteen minutes when he attempted an intentional spin, during which he lost control and spun into the ground from several hundred feet. The subsequent court of inquiry concluded that it was 'impossible to state why the machine spun to the ground but is of the opinion that the pilot must either have fainted in the air or jammed his foot in the rudder controls'.

2 Lt (pilot u/t) Wilfrid Joseph McGinn, RFC, aged 20, was the son of James and Alice Gibbons McGinn of Dixon's Corners, Ontario, Canada. Born in Brinston, Ontario, on 30 September 1897, he had studied Applied Science at McGill University in Montreal prior to enlisting in the Royal Flying Corps in September 1917. He is buried in Stoke upon Tern (St Peter's) Cemetery, Shropshire.

21 March (Thursday)
Ground firing exercise. 67 TS (Shawbury aerodrome, Shropshire)
Sopwith Camel (B2521) crashed near the aerodrome. The pilot had just flown around the aerodrome and fired at the target on the ground twice, when he appeared to lose control and nose-dived into the ground.

2 Lt (pilot u/t) Charles McElroy Carpenter, RFC, aged 21, was the son of Frederick Albert and Beatrice Carpenter (née Wylie). Born in Hamilton, Ontario, on 17 November 1896, he was educated at Bishop Ridley College in St Catherine's, Ontario and was working for a brokerage business in Chicago before joining the RFC. He is buried in Shawbury (St Mary's) Churchyard.

22 April (Monday)
Unknown duty. 131 Squadron (Shawbury aerodrome, Shropshire)
Airco DH6 (C7215) crashed near the aerodrome at 10.10 hrs. The pilot (who it was is not specified) was flying at 600 feet and appeared to be in control when he throttled the engine back and gradually

descended to 50 feet, at which point it suddenly dived vertically into the ground. The subsequent inquest deemed the cause obscure, considering the experience of the pilot, but suggested that it was possible that 'the machine got up excessive speed on the glide and the reduction of elevator surface apparently rendered control insufficient to get out'.

Capt (pilot) Samuel Traherne Bassett Saunderson, RAF, aged 34, was the husband of Florence Saunderson who lived at The Groves, Shawbury. Born in Kingstown, Ireland, on 24 January 1884, he was educated in England at St Andrews School, Eastbourne and Cheltenham College. Briefly serving as a lieutenant with 3 Royal Dublin Fusiliers, he then transferred to the Northern Irish Horse before being seconded to the Royal Flying Corps in early 1915. After completing his pilot training in May 1915, he was posted to France in December and flew operationally over the Western Front. He is buried in Shawbury (St Mary's) Churchyard.

Capt (pilot) Norman Victor [although two sources state Vine] Harrison, RAF, aged 21, was the son of Robert Cecil and Alice Elizabeth Harrison of Bloomfield Road, Harpenden. Before the war he had been an articled clerk to a firm of chartered accountants and lived at Thornton Heath, Croydon. Following the outbreak of war he joined 15 London Regiment and served in France from August 1915, prior to transferring to the Royal Flying Corps in September 1916. He is subsequently believed to have served as an observer with 20 Squadron before beginning pilot training. He is buried in East Sheen Cemetery, Surrey.

5 May (Sunday)
Unknown duty. 131 Squadron (Shawbury aerodrome, Shropshire)
Airco DH6 (C6657) crashed near the aerodrome. The pilot was observed to take off badly and after reaching 100 feet is thought to have got 'his nose down on a right hand turn' and was unable to pull up in time before striking the ground. The two injured occupants were conveyed to Prees Heath Military Hospital, where the passenger succumbed soon afterwards, while the pilot is thought to have had a leg amputated but eventually recovered.

Lt (pilot) John Maurice Reid Miller, RAF, was born in Bearsden, on the outskirts of Glasgow, on 5 April 1898 and educated at Glasgow High School and Glasgow University before taking a commission in the army in 1915. Following his training he joined 1 King's Own Scottish Borderers in Gallipoli on 16 October 1915 and presumably remained there until the battalion's withdrawal on 8 January 1916. After transferring to the RFC he served with 22 Squadron as an observer/gunner on Bristol F2 fighters and, on 2 February 1917, was badly wounded when his aircraft was shot up over the Somme during a 'dogfight'. After several months recuperation in hospital he returned to 22 Squadron but was shot down once more on 14 February 1918, although this time he suffered only superficial injuries and a fractured nose when his aircraft crashed into a tree while landing. Following this second incident, however, he appears to have returned to England and begun pilot training.

Air Mechanic 1 (rigger, travelling as passenger) Charles Richard Clack (29412), RAF, aged 31, was married and lived in London. He is buried in Tilstock (Christ Church) Churchyard, Shropshire.

25 May (Saturday)
Training flight. 131 Squadron (Shawbury aerodrome, Shropshire)
Airco DH9 (D5163) crashed near the aerodrome at 16.45 hrs. A strong wind was blowing when the pilot began performing a bank close to the ground, and the aircraft was blown over into a spin from which he was unable to recover before crashing.

2 Lt (pilot) George Roper, RAF, aged 25, was the son of George A and Jean Roper of Steubenville, Ohio, USA. After studying mining and metallurgy at the Massachusetts Institute of Technology in Boston, he began a placement with the American Institute of Mining, Metallurgical and Petroleum Engineers in

2 Lt George Roper Jr.
[Inst. of Mining, Metallurgical & Petroleum Engineers' website]

1916, before joining the RFC in June 1917. He is buried in Shawbury (St Mary's) Churchyard.

8 June (Saturday)
Training flight. 13 TDS (Tern Hill aerodrome, Shropshire)
Maurice Farman S11 Shorthorn (B4733) crashed on the aerodrome at 22.05 hrs. The instructor pilot was coming in to land as light was fading, when it is believed that he made an error of judgement by allowing the aircraft's skids to catch the ground 'due to the bad light, long grass and a deceptive slope', flipping the aircraft onto its back. Despite help arriving quickly and the two occupants being conveyed to Prees Heath Military Hospital, the pupil pilot succumbed to his injuries the following day, while the instructor eventually recovered.

Capt (instructor pilot) David Leslie Nutt, RAF. Before joining the RFC he had served in France, from April 1915, as a private in the York Horse Yeomanry. He died in Leeds in 1962.

Cadet (pilot u/t) William Launcelot Corbett, RAF, aged 20, was the son of Sarah Bertha Corbett of 79 Walbrook Road, Derby. Prior to joining the RFC he had served as a private in the Seaforth Highlanders and was wounded in France in 1916. He is buried in Derby (Uttoxeter Road) Cemetery.

9 June (Sunday)
Cadet W L Corbett died of injuries received in a crash at Tern Hill the previous day.

23 July (Tuesday)
Test flight with chief mechanic. 9 TDS (Shawbury aerodrome, Shropshire)
Airco DH9 (C1321) crashed near the aerodrome at midday.

Frank Allsopp
[Roy Allsopp]

The pilot took off with the unit's chief mechanic on board, presumably to monitor the aircraft, but during the course of the flight the pilot pulled out of a steep dive and the resulting strain caused the aircraft to break up in mid-air.

Lt (pilot) Robert Bishop Slade, RAF, aged 26, was the son of Leonard Gillott and Maria Slade of Park Gate Farm, Donhead Saint Andrew, Dorset. Educated at Shoreham College, he enlisted in the Machine Gun Corps early in the war and served on the Western Front from September 1915, with 28 (North-west) Battalion, Canadian Expeditionary Force, before transferring to the RFC. He is buried in Aston Upthorpe (All Saints) Churchyard, Berkshire.

F/Sgt (mechanic) Frank Allsopp (11172), RAF, aged 19, was the son of Albert and Amy Allsopp of 1/11 Whitehead Street, Aston Manor, Birmingham. He is buried in Birmingham (Witton) Cemetery.

28 July (Sunday)
Fighting practice. 9 TDS (Shawbury aerodrome, Shropshire)
Royal Aircraft Factory BE2e (A1391) crashed near the aerodrome. After taking off and climbing to 300 feet, the pilot got into a spin from which he failed to recover. According to the subsequent inquest he had only flown solo for several hours before the fatal flight and had 'evidently lost his head and failed to shut off his engine when the machine descended'.

Flight Cadet (pilot u/t) Clarence Edwin Brown (100546), RAF, aged 18, was the son of Mrs E O Brown of 20 Oxford Street, Darlington. He is buried in Shawbury (St Mary's) Churchyard.

29 July (Monday)
Vertical turns practice. 9 TDS (Shawbury aerodrome, Shropshire)
Royal Aircraft Factory RE8 (C2397) crashed near the aerodrome at 09.15 hrs. The pilot, who had completed thirty-five hours of solo flying, took off from the aerodrome and soon afterwards lost control and entered a spin. The aircraft was witnessed to 'swing right over and descend wing over wing', before crashing behind a farm building.

2 Lt (pilot u/t) Joseph Arthur Freeman, RAF, aged 23, was the son of Joseph and Rose Freeman of Holly Street, Luton. He is buried in Luton General Cemetery.

30 July (Tuesday)
Airman being tested with a view to becoming a pilot. 13 TDS (Tern Hill aerodrome, Shropshire)
Avro 504K (D6361) crashed at Spoonley, to the west of Market Drayton, at 11.50 hrs. During the course of the flight the aircraft was observed to carry out a loop-the-loop, at the top of which it side-slipped and something was seen to fall out, before it crashed out of control. According to a contemporary article in the *Wellington Journal*,

> ... a number of people working near rushed to the spot and found the machine a complete wreck with the body of an RAF mechanic lying nearby. In a field on the opposite side of the road and several hundred yards from the scene, the remains of an RAF Officer were discovered.

In the subsequent inquest, evidence was given by Lt H J Murphy who stated that Maj Brisley and Pte Lythgoe were both strapped in the machine when they went up but, in his opinion, Maj Brisley's belt 'was not tight enough'. An examination of the wreckage also found that Maj Brisley's safety belt was still fastened and it was clear that he had slipped through the belt during the loop and fallen to his death, while his passenger, who had no flying experience, was unable to control the aircraft.

Maj (pilot) Cuthbert Everard Brisley, RAF, aged 32, was son of the late George C and Ella Brisley (née Gahagan) and the husband of Marjorie Beryl Dawson of Silverbeck, Stanwell, Middlesex. Born in Umzimkulu, South Africa, on 5 July 1886, he moved to England after his parents died and lived on the Isle of Wight with his grandmother, Eliza Gahagan, before moving to London and training as a lawyer. He joined the Royal Naval Air Service in November 1914 and, after gaining his wings, was briefly attached to 4 and then 2 Squadron, before being posted to the Dardanelles in August 1915 with 2 Wing. Here he flew a variety of aircraft over the Gallipoli front and, following the withdrawal from the peninsula in January 1916, continued to serve in the Aegean until April 1916. He subsequently returned to the UK by a somewhat roundabout route, via Romania and Petrograd in Russia, before finally arriving in the UK in January 1917 on a boat from Archangel. Upon his return he was given command of 13 TDS at Tern Hill. He is buried in Market Drayton Cemetery, Shropshire.

Pte Fred Lythgoe (155338), RAF, aged 18, was the son of George and Alice Jane Lythgoe of 41 Lovers Lane, Atherton. He is buried in Atherton Cemetery, Lancashire.

25 August (Sunday)
'Cat B test of pilot' carrying passenger. 9 TDS (Shawbury aerodrome, Shropshire)
Airco DH9 (D5587) crashed near the aerodrome at 18.00 hrs. The pilot had force-landed in a field owing to engine trouble but, after three mechanics went to the scene and overhauled the machine, he took off to return to the airfield. However, after reaching 200 feet, he turned with insufficient speed, stalled and the aircraft crashed, seriously injuring the two occupants. Both men were taken to Prees Heath Military

Cadet Arthur Dunn.
[Linda Fletcher]

Hospital but, sadly, Pte Baskerville died within twenty minutes of arriving, while Cadet Dunn succumbed the following day.

Cadet (pilot u/t) Arthur Dunn, RAF, aged 18, was the son of Hannah and the late Harry Dunn of 4 Royds Street, Longsight, Manchester. Born on 26 January 1899, he had worked as a solicitor's clerk before enlisting in the RFC in late 1917. He is buried in Manchester Southern Cemetery.

Pte (batman, travelling as passenger) Fred Baskerville (186648), RAF, aged 26, was the husband of Mrs R Baskerville of 17 Chandos Street, Holbeck, Leeds. He is buried in Leeds (Beeston) Cemetery.

26 August (Monday)
Cadet A Dunn died of injuries received in a crash near Shawbury the previous day.

30 August (Friday)
Turns and stalls practice. 13 TDS (Tern Hill aerodrome, Shropshire)
Royal Aircraft Factory FE2b (A9930) crashed near the aerodrome at 16.00 hrs. According to a report in the *Wellington Journal*, the pilot had taken off satisfactorily and climbed to 100 feet, at which point the engine began to splutter and 'pop back'. The pilot quickly turned towards the aerodrome and the engine appeared to be picking up again when, suddenly, it spluttered and the aircraft dived into the ground and burst into flames. The cause of the accident was subsequently attributed to an 'error of judgment on the part of the pilot, in that he was watching the ground when travelling down-wind, stalling the machine and spinning by holding the nose of the machine too high with too much rudder'.

2 Lt (pilot u/t) Howard Knight Stevens, RAF, aged 25, was the son of Edward S and Etta M Stevens of 95 Queen St, Sherbrooke, Canada. Prior to enlisting he had worked as an accountant and lived at Burwash Hall, West Toronto. He is buried in Market Drayton Cemetery, Shropshire.

1 October (Tuesday)
D Section, 262nd Aero Squadron, 9 TDS (Shawbury aerodrome, Shropshire)
A cadet pilot was sitting in the cockpit of an Avro 504K (D8979) preparing to take off, when a ground crew airman took hold of the propeller to help start the engine. As he did so, however, the cadet pilot accidentally knocked a switch in the cockpit and the engine fired up, striking the ground crew airman and killing him instantly.

Pte Louis Edwin Houseal (962953), USAAS [attached to RAF], aged 23, was the first of three sons to Louis J and Catherine A Houseal of 1729 State Street, Harrisburg and had been employed on the Pennsylvania railways as a brakeman before enlisting in December 1917. Initially buried in Shawbury (St Mary's) Churchyard, his body was disinterred in 1920 and reburied in the family plot at East Harrisburg Cemetery, Pennsylvania, USA.

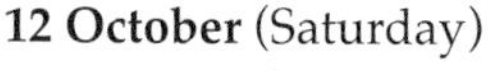

12 October (Saturday)
Training flight. 13 TDS (Tern Hill aerodrome, Shropshire)
Avro 504J/K (D4530) crashed near the aerodrome at 21.10 hrs. During the course of the flight the engine began to fail (probably 'due to choking') and, while attempting to turn the aircraft, the pilot allowed the aircraft to stall, lost control and crashed. The two seriously injured occupants were both

Pte Louis Edwin Houseal [Harrisburg Telegraph]

taken to Prees Heath Military Hospital but, sadly, the instructor died later the same day, while the pupil pilot succumbed to his injuries on 1 November.

Lt (instructor pilot) William Burt Bickell, RAF, aged 24, was the son of Mrs M J Hancock of 652 Manning Avenue, Toronto, Canada. Educated at Palmerston Avenue School, where he was a well-known athlete, he later worked for the Public Works Department in Toronto before enlisting in the RFC in April 1917. After arriving in the UK in August 1917, he was forced to return to Canada due to ill health but, after undergoing an operation, returned to the UK and was employed as an instructor at Tern Hill. He is buried in Tilstock (Christ Church) Churchyard, Shropshire. His brother, Pte G T Bickell, was killed in action at Passchendaele a year earlier on 30 October 1917.

Cadet (pilot u/t) George Lancaster Robinson, RAF, aged 21, was the son of John and Annie Robinson (née Lancaster) of 227 Strathearn Avenue, Montreal West. Prior to transferring to the RAF, he had served with the Princess Patricia's Canadian Light Infantry (Eastern Ontario Regiment). He is buried in Tilstock (Christ Church) Cemetery, Shropshire.

Lt William Bickell [The Toronto Star]

1 November (Friday)

Cadet G L Robinson, who was seriously injured near Tern Hill on 12 October 1918, died of his injuries.

11 November (Armistice Day)

17 December (Tuesday)

Circuits and landings training. 13 TDS (Tern Hill aerodrome, Shropshire)

Avro 504K (E9280) crashed near the aerodrome at 15.30 hrs. The pupil pilot had completed two circuits of the airfield and was then waved on by his instructor to carry out a third circuit, during which he collided with another aircraft and crashed into a tree, his aircraft bursting into flames. The two officers in the other aircraft, which also crashed, were both seriously injured and conveyed to Prees Heath Military Hospital where one died later that evening.

Flt Cadet (pilot u/t) John Francis Fox, RAF, aged 20, was the son of George and Ann Fox of 15 Edward Street, Bath. He is buried in Bathwick (St Mary the Virgin) Churchyard, Somerset.

Training flight. 13 TDS (Tern Hill aerodrome, Shropshire)

Avro 504K (E9285) crashed near the aerodrome after colliding in the incident described above.

Capt (pilot) Edgar Robert Hulme Beaman, RAF, aged 27, was the son of the late Surgeon-General Ardern Hulme Beaman (Indian Army Medical Service) and Isabel Sarah (née Deverall) and the husband of Dorothy Lewis of Eastbourne, Sussex. He had worked for HSBC for three years prior to enlisting in the Royal Engineers on the outbreak of war and served in France from December 1914, being mentioned in despatches in January 1916. After transferring to the RFC, he was appointed to various reserve squadrons in the UK from October 1916, before being posted to 51 (Training) Squadron in February 1917 as an instructor. Twelve months later he was posted to France with 102 Squadron and flew FE2 bombers between May and August 1918, when he was admitted to hospital and then subsequently posted to Tern Hill as an instructor. He is buried in Market Drayton Cemetery, Shropshire. His son, S/Ldr Robert Carleton Beaman, DFC, was shot down and killed on 31 December 1940 flying with 139 Squadron.

Capt (pilot, travelling as passenger) George Henry Harrison, DFC, RAF, was born on 14 May 1897 and served as an officer with 10 Middlesex Regiment before transferring to the RFC in August 1916. Posted to 23 Squadron in February 1917, he flew FE2s and Spad VII fighters over the Western Front and was wounded on 6 March by a gunshot wound to his arm and left hand. Following a long period of recovery in hospital and then service with 51 (Home Defence) Squadron, he returned to France in April 1918 to join 148 Squadron, flying FE2 bombers. He then flew operationally over the Western Front until August 1918, when he was admitted to hospital suffering 'flying sickness', and the following month was awarded the DFC for his gallantry on operations. After being declared fit for home flying only, in October 1918, he is believed to have been posted to Tern Hill as a flight commander, but the accident on 17 December is thought to have ended his flying career. Despite this, he remained in the RAF after the war and by the outbreak of the Second World War had attained the rank of wing commander. He was appointed an OBE in July 1940 and remained in the RAF until his retirement in March 1946.

1919

18 February (Tuesday)
Training flight. Observers School of Reconnaissance and Aerial Photography (Monkmoor aerodrome, Shropshire)
Airco DH9A (F1179) crashed adjacent to the aerodrome at midday. Shortly after taking off the aircraft's engine failed, causing the experienced pilot to stall the aircraft and dive into the ground from 400 feet. The *Shrewsbury Chronicle* reported how Mr Francis Price Edwards, licensee of the Hero of Moulton, was in the vicinity and

> ... hastened to the scene and saw Welch still seated in the broken machine, but apparently dead. Nothing could be seen of Lt Preece, that officer being buried beneath the wreckage. Mr Edwards endeavoured to reach Welch and whilst he was making the attempt the petrol tank, which contained upwards of 70 gallons of petrol, exploded and the machine was set ablaze. Mr Edwards had a miraculous escape. The burning petrol set his clothes on fire, but fortunately, he had the presence of mind to roll in the snow and thus put out the flames. The machine however was speedily destroyed and the occupants were burned almost beyond recognition.

Lt (pilot) Charles Evered Preece, RAF, aged 23, was the son of John and Ada Louisa Preece of The Ivy House, Hanley Castle. Mobilised in August 1914, in the Queen's Own Worcestershire Hussars (Worcester Yeomanry), Lt Preece had fought in the Gallipoli campaign and Palestine, prior to transferring to the RFC and serving in France. He is buried in Hanley Castle (St Mary) Churchyard extension, Worcestershire. His older brother, George Ernest Preece, had died of wounds on 23 August 1916, while serving with 8 Royal Fusiliers in France.

Air Mechanic 1 Harry Welch (249240), RAF, aged 20, was the son of William and Emma Welch of Osler Street, Ladywood, Birmingham. He is buried in Smethwick (Uplands) Cemetery, Staffordshire.

1936

23 March (Monday)
Cross-country flight. 10 FTS (RAF Tern Hill, Shropshire)
Hawker Hart I (K5017) crashed at Nagington Grange, between Child's Ercall and Hinstock, at 16.20 hrs. Having flown to RAF Bircham Newton in Norfolk on 20 March, as part of his training, the pilot was due to return to Tern Hill on 23rd and took off at 15.30 hrs. In a tragic turn of events, Tern Hill had sent a telegram to Bircham Newton at 15.07 hrs stating that there was now heavy rain and deteriorating

weather over Shropshire, but the message was not received until after the pilot had taken off. Unaware of the unfavourable conditions hanging over North Shropshire, the pilot continued on his flight until he was about four miles from Tern Hill, where he encountered a 'terrific thunderstorm' and attempted to force-land. Mr John Herbert Beddoes, who worked at Nagington Gate, and was interviewed by the *Shrewsbury Chronicle* newspaper, described how

> ... at the time the weather was very bad – it was dark and pouring with rain and thundering and lightening [sic] badly. The machine flew straight over the buildings and went out of sight, but two or three seconds later it came back again, flying in a circle. The engine appeared to shut off twice and then started up again. The machine went out of sight again but it returned and came down as if the pilot appeared to be landing. The machine, however, was straightened out again and then went on for a short distance. The engine then stopped completely and the machine dropped bodily for 30 or 40 feet. It went on for a short distance, but then the tail of the plane went up in the air and the machine dived into the ground.

The subsequent investigation concluded that the primary factor was the poor weather, but added that there was also an error of judgement on the part of the pilot by allowing his aircraft to stall, although it was possible that 'a vivid flash of lightening [sic] had temporarily blinded the pilot'.

Acting P/O Rowley Buchanan [Brian Powell]

Acting P/O (pilot u/t) George Rowland (Rowley) Buchanan, RAF, aged 24, was born in Dublin, on 7 May 1911, the son of Thomas Hardinge Buchanan and Anna Waggett (née Dunscombe). After the establishment of the Irish Free State in 1922, the family moved to Elstreet in Hertfordshire and Rowley was sent to prep school in Sidcup, while his father began work at Lloyds of London. Sadly, after discovering that his business partner had become hopelessly insolvent and the company was in financial difficulty, Thomas Buchanan took his own life in October 1923. Following his father's death, Rowley was able to complete his studies with financial assistance from the Professional Classes Aid Council and subsequently joined the RAF in 1935, while his mother moved to Dibden Purlieu, Hampshire. He is buried in Market Drayton Cemetery, Shropshire.

1937

13 May (Thursday)
Training flight. 10 FTS (RAF Tern Hill, Shropshire)
Hawker Hart I (K6492) aircraft landed heavily at the airfield at 10.00 hrs. On completion of their training flight, the instructor brought the aircraft in to land but, as he approached, he allowed the aircraft to stall and hit the ground heavily. The pupil pilot, who was in the front cockpit, received serious spinal injuries and was conveyed to the Shropshire Orthopaedic Hospital, where he sadly died six days later. As a result of the accident the instructor was 'posted to another unit for duties other than as an instructor'.

Sgt (instructor pilot) Charles Frederick Christopher Ridout (363713), RAF. Prior to becoming an instructor at Tern Hill, he had flown Vickers Virginia bombers with 7 Squadron, out of Worthy Down, in 1932. Following the accident he remained in the RAF (and was subsequently commissioned in February 1942) but was killed on 25 October 1942, piloting a Master (EM338), at the Glider Instructors'

School, RAF Thame. F/Lt Ridout, was the son of Edwin and Violet Ridout and the husband of Lydia Patti Budd of Haddenham, Cambridgeshire. He is buried in Cuddington (St Nicholas) Churchyard, Buckinghamshire.

Acting P/O (pilot u/t) Ormond Graham Thomson, RAF, aged 19, was the son of Robert and Sarah Thomson (née Gauger) of 16 York Street, Wakefield. Before joining the RAF he had gained a civilian pilot's licence in September 1936 with the Yorkshire Aeroplane Club. He is buried in Market Drayton Cemetery, Shropshire.

19 May (Wednesday)
Acting P/O O G Thomson died from injuries received six days earlier at Tern Hill

30 June (Wednesday)
Cross-country exercise. 90 Squadron (RAF Bicester, Oxfordshire)
Bristol Blenheim I (K7053) crashed at 'The Leath' (at map reference 585900), in the Corve Dale, between Stanton Long and Ditton Priors, at 11.20 hrs. 90 Squadron had only reformed in March 1937 as a bomber squadron and at the time of the accident the crews were re-equipping with the RAF's latest light bomber, the Blenheim Mark I. After taking off from Bicester the crew were ordered to fly in the direction of Gloucester, where they were to practice map reading locally, before returning to base. While flying over South Shropshire, as part of their map reading exercise, the aircraft was seen to dive into the ground with an almighty explosion. According to an article published in the Shrewsbury Chronicle newspaper, wreckage was spread over several hundred yards and

> ... two parachutes lodged in a high hedge at the top of the field and running parallel with the trail of wreckage left by the machine. Police of the Bridgnorth Division under Supt Ridgway, arrived shortly afterwards and about one acre of the field containing the bulk of the wreckage, was roped off to await Air Ministry inspection. The police remained on duty throughout the day and in the afternoon were joined by RAF officers and men from Tern Hill aerodrome.

Sgt (pilot) Edward Moorhouse (581832), RAF, aged 25, was born near Farnham in Hertfordshire on 17 November 1911, although at the time of his death his family had moved to Stafford. He is buried in Market Drayton Cemetery, Shropshire.

AC2 (electrical instrument tester) Alfred George Martin (528693), RAF, aged 20, was from Bedwellty, Monmouthshire. He is buried in Market Drayton Cemetery, Shropshire.

AC1 Sydney Herbert William (Sid) Coomber (514594), RAF, aged 24, was from Marsh Green, Kent. He is buried in Market Drayton Cemetery, Shropshire.

31 August (Tuesday)
Unknown flight detail 'from Debden to Sealand.' 80 Squadron (RAF Debden, Essex)
Gloster Gladiator (unknown serial) force-landed at Weir Farm, Montford Bridge. According to an article in the *Shrewsbury Chronicle* newspaper, the pilot force-landed because of bad visibility and then, 'after discovering his whereabouts and resting a while, was able to proceed on his way'.

P/O (pilot) Llewellyn Corrie Jones-Bateman, RAF. After joining the RAF in 1936 and completing his pilot training, he was posted to 80 Squadron in March 1937, flying Gladiator fighters. Following the outbreak of war he transferred to the Fleet Air Arm around 1941 and was reported missing during an anti-submarine patrol in the Mediterranean on 12 June 1943. Lt Bateman was the son of Revd Cecil and Mrs Sybil Rita B Jones-Bateman (née Corrie) of 10 Talbot Hill Road, Bournemouth. He is commemorated on the Lee-on-Solent Memorial.

9 September (Thursday)
Formation flying. 10 FTS (RAF Tern Hill, Shropshire)
Hawker Audax I (K7497) crashed near Hodnet railway station at 09.45 hrs. The pilot was cleared to take off in formation with two other aircraft led by Sgt Frank Bernard George Bacon. According to Sgt Bacon's account, which was provided for the court of inquiry,

> We took off due west and climbed steadily to about 1,000 feet, at which point we were approximately over Wollerton Station. I then noticed the machine on my left slightly break away from formation. It lost height slowly, 'til it was about 200-300 feet below me and slightly to my left. It remained in this position for some 20 seconds, with the engine still running. At this time I noticed flames from the port exhaust pipe. Deceased then commenced to carry out a forced-landing. He turned left and flew parallel with the Wollerton-Hodnet railway and at a low altitude turned left again over the railway. The machine then appeared to strike a bank. I could not tell exactly what it had struck, as I was 700 feet up. Immediately the plane turned over and caught fire, I returned to the aerodrome and reported what had happened.

William Hallmark, of Station Road in Hodnet, described for the *Shrewsbury Chronicle* how,

> I immediately ran towards the machine but when I was halfway across the field the machine burst into flames. As I got to the fence other people, including a railway porter named Whalley [Eric Whalley from Audlem, who was on duty at Hodnet] arrived along the railway line. We endeavoured to get the pilot out of the machine, but were unsuccessful. The pilot seemed to be pinned down by the weight of the machine and his parachute also appeared to be holding him in the cockpit. I cut two straps but the heat became too excessive and we were unable to release the pilot.

Acting P/O (pilot u/t) Danford Laycock Marsh-Smith, RAF, aged 19, was the son of Eric Cecil and Dorothy Violet Marsh-Smith (née Laycock) of Prestbury, on the outskirts of Cheltenham (although they also lived and worked in Ceylon). He is buried in Market Drayton Cemetery, Shropshire.

16 September (Thursday)
Delivery flight 'to packing depot Sealand'. 76 Squadron (RAF Finningley, Yorkshire)
Vickers Wellesley I (K7730) force-landed at the top of Crowmere Road, in Monkmoor, Shrewsbury. The pilot was flying on a triangular course from RAF Finningley to RAF Sealand when he became lost in poor visibility and circled around Monkmoor looking for somewhere to land. After spotting a sports field he touched down but the brakes failed to stop the aircraft from striking some iron railings, which badly damaged the undercarriage.

P/O (pilot) James Eric Riepenhausen (39127), RAF, was commissioned in September 1936, and was posted to the newly-reformed 76 Squadron in May 1937, flying the RAF's latest long-range bomber, the Wellesley. Although it is unclear if he flew operationally during the early stages of the war, he was subsequently posted to 10 OTU as an instructor. On 11 October 1940 he took off in a Wellington (N1526) to give instruction to a pupil crew, when a large area of fabric is thought to have stripped from the wing, causing the aircraft to crash. Ft/Lt Riepenhausen was twenty-eight years old and the son of James and Helen Hogarth Riepenhausen of Birkenhead. He is buried in Birkenhead (Flaybrick Hill) Cemetery.

1938

7 September (Wednesday)
Height test. 11 FTS (RAF Shawbury, Shropshire)

76 Squadron pilots standing in front of their newly-received Wellesleys, at RAF Finningley, April 1937. [Norman Hood]

Hawker Fury I (K8300) force-landed at Hordley Grange, near Ellesmere. After becoming lost during the flight the pilot overshot his forced landing and, as he opened up the throttle to gain height for another attempt, the wheels struck a hedge and the aircraft flipped onto its back.

Acting P/O (pilot u/t) Frank Brian Stiven, RAF, after completing his training, was posted to 3 Squadron and was killed on 18 April 1939 following a mid-air collision whilst piloting a Gladiator (K7962) near Kenley. Acting P/O Stiven was 20 years old and is buried in an unknown location.

11 October (Tuesday)
Air-to-air camera gunnery. 11 FTS (RAF Shawbury, Shropshire)
Hawker Audax I (K7435) crashed at Forton Heath, near Montford Bridge (at map reference 439172), at 11.00 hrs. The pilot took off at 10.30 hrs, in company with another aircraft, to carry out practice quarter-attacks on a drogue target being towed by a third aircraft. Having completed one attack, the pilot then dived on the target at approximately 2,000 feet to make a second attack but, after getting the target in his sights, he tried to straighten up and found that the aileron controls had jammed to the right of the central position. This caused the aircraft to roll over to the right until it was inverted, so the pilot undid his harness, fell out and parachuted to safety. According to witnesses, the pilot left the aircraft at approximately 300 feet and, unable to avoid a small copse, he landed in the branches of a tree overhanging the River Perry. The *Border Counties Advertizer* recorded that 'immediately help was forthcoming, but it was necessary to saw away some branches of the tree to release the pilot, who apart from bruises and sprains was little injured'. The article added that, 'another service plane landed in a nearby field, and the rescued pilot flew this machine home. Sgt MacPherson, Hanwood and PC Masters, Montford Bridge, and RAF personnel mounted guard over the wreckage which was immediately wired off with a barbed wire fence'. In the subsequent court of inquiry the cause of the accident was attributed to a

> ... structural failure of the starboard aileron, consequent upon the rigger having neglected to reattach it to its two inboard hinges after he had taken them off for repair, this omission passing unnoticed by the supervising NCO and not being discovered in the course of subsequent inspections. The aileron thus weakened, failed under stresses resulting from a somewhat coarse application of the controls by an inexperienced pupil.

Acting P/O (pilot u/t) John Douglas George Withers (40491), RAF. On completion of his training he was posted to 83 Squadron and completed forty ops, including two low-level attacks on the *Scharnhorst* battleship, for which he was awarded the DFC in November 1940. Soon after the award he was posted to 207 Squadron but did not survive his second tour and was killed when his Manchester (L7314) was mistakenly shot down by an RAF Beaufighter, on 22 June 1941, while returning from a night raid on Boulogne. F/O Withers, who was 25 years old, was the son of George Frederick and Nina Ethel Withers of Bromley, Kent. He is buried in Lincoln (Newport) Cemetery.

Police and RAF personnel inspecting the wreckage of Audax K7435
[The Border Counties Advertizer]

13 October (Thursday)
Advanced forced-landing practice. 11 FTS (RAF Shawbury, Shropshire)
Hawker Hart I (K4964) crash-landed at Caynton Manor, between Tibberton and Edgmond, near Newport. The pupil pilot was making a practice forced-landing approach when the engine failed suddenly and the instructor pilot, who according to the accident card had limited instructing experience, took over control too late, resulting in the wheels being torn off when the aircraft undershot into a field.

P/O (instructor pilot) Anthony Edward Robinson (39472), RAF, was born on 14 July 1914 in Wollongong, New South Wales, Australia. He was the son of Alfred Edward and Florence Emily Maria Robinson (née Crowther). After sailing to the UK to enlist in the RAF in 1936, little is known of his subsequent movements until his death on 10 February 1943, when he was shot down over Caen, in a Spitfire (EE767) while serving with 610 Squadron. S/Ldr Robinson, who was 28 years old was the husband of Joan Patricia Myrtle Robinson (née Leigh), from North Stoke, Oxfordshire. He is buried in Grandcourt War Cemetery, France.

The name of the pupil is unknown.

22 October (Saturday)
Return flight from RAF Penrhos. 10 FTS (RAF Tern Hill, Shropshire)
Avro Anson I (serial unknown) force-landed in the vicinity of Hadley, near Wellington. The pilot was returning from a practice bombing exercise when, due to fog and approaching darkness, he made a precautionary landing in a field between the railway line and the Donnington-Wellington road, coming to rest in the garden of a Mr G Cooper. The name of the pilot is unknown.

19 December (Monday)
Cross-country blind flying practice from Tern Hill to Woodesford, Chester and return. 10 FTS (RAF Tern Hill, Shropshire)
Hawker Hart I (K5795) crashed at Aychley Farm, just west of Bletchley, Market Drayton, at 11.40 hrs. Two pilots were detailed to carry out a cross-country flight, with Acting P/O Morgan in control under the hood (simulating night-flying conditions), while Acting P/O Jenns sat in the front cockpit and acted as his safety pilot. After taking off at 10.35 hrs the pair completed their flight and had returned to the vicinity of Tern Hill when it appears that Acting P/O Jenns began low-flying, during which he allowed the aircraft to strike the ground and crash, bursting into flames. For his gallant rescue of the seriously injured and trapped P/O Jenns, P/O Morgan's name was submitted to the Society for the Protection of Life from Fire 'as being considered worthy of reward'. Acting P/O Jenns' burns proved fatal and he

Acting P/O Winston Jenns [TNA]

Acting P/O Morgan [TNA]

died in the Royal Salop Infirmary at 03.00 hrs the following morning, while Acting P/O Morgan was treated for minor injuries in the station sick quarters.

Acting P/O (pilot u/t) Winston Alvanley Jenns, RAF, aged 20, was the son of Revd Percival Alvanley Jenns and Alice Rebecca Jenns of Vancouver, Canada (but presumably had family living at Easington on account of his burial). He is buried in Easington, Sunderland.

Acting P/O (pilot u/t) John Milne Morgan (40936), RAF, was born in Balham, London, on 8 December 1916. Little is known of his military service until he was posted to 92 (East India) Squadron in 1942, piloting Spitfires in support of Allied operations in the Mediterranean. In February 1943, by which time he had shot down five enemy aircraft, he was decorated with the DFC and around the same time he was given command of the squadron. By early 1944, he had been posted to 274 Squadron flying Spitfires in Italy, but on 28 February 1944 was shot down and taken prisoner. He spent the remainder of the war in *Stalag Luft III* and *Marlag und Milag Nord* camps until 9 April 1945, when he cut through the wire and went into hiding with two other RAF officers until the British army liberated the area. He continued to serve in the RAF after the war and eventually retired as a wing commander in December 1963.

20 December (Tuesday)
Acting P/O Jenns died from injuries received in a crash at Tern Hill the previous day.

1939

9 January (Monday)
Wind speed and direction-finding training and camera gunnery. 11 FTS (RAF Shawbury, Shropshire) Hawker Audax I (K5215) force-landed at Ellerton Hall, to the east of Hinstock, near Newport. The pilot was attempting to land (perhaps due to poor weather?) but came in too fast, so that when he touched

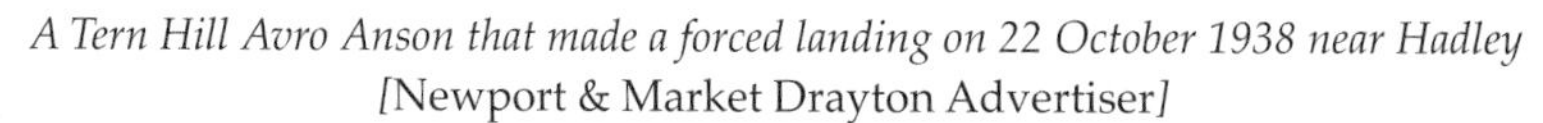

A Tern Hill Avro Anson that made a forced landing on 22 October 1938 near Hadley [Newport & Market Drayton Advertiser]

down the aircraft ran through some small trees and a fence on the edge of a field, causing the undercarriage to collapse.

LAC (pilot u/t) Douglas Stewart (517921), RAF. Little is known of his military service other than that he eventually flew operationally with 106 Squadron and was shot down and killed on 6 October 1944 piloting a Lancaster (PD214) on an op to Bremen. F/Lt Stewart was the son of John and Ada Mary Stewart and the husband of Vera Elizabeth Stewart (née Forgham) of Shrewsbury. He is commemorated on the Runnymede Memorial.

19 January (Thursday)
'Flying test'. 10 FTS (RAF Tern Hill, Shropshire)
Hawker Hart I (K5030) crashed at Longford, near Market Drayton. The instructor was behind the controls when he allowed the aircraft to stall on a gliding turn near the ground, lost control and crashed, although fortunately neither occupant was injured. In the subsequent court of inquiry the cause of the crash was attributed to the 'incompetence and carelessness of the instructor'.

P/O (instructor pilot) John Basil Wood (40653), RAF, was commissioned in March 1936 and gained his wings on 4 July 1938. He was eventually dismissed from the RAF following a General Court Martial in February 1941.

The name of the pupil pilot is unknown.

7 February (Tuesday)
Low-flying exercise. 10 FTS (RAF Tern Hill, Shropshire)
Hawker Hart I (K5031) crashed at Dodecote, between Bolas Heath and Child's Ercall, at 14.30 hrs. The pupil pilot was making a right hand turn at low level when it is thought that the attention of both himself and his instructor 'was taken up looking for other aircraft and not concentrating on flight path', and the aircraft collided with a tree, crashing in a field belonging to Mr Lea. The pupil, who was sitting in the front cockpit, was killed instantly in the crash while, amazingly, the instructor was 'thrown clean out of the cockpit, sustaining nothing worse than slight abrasions and shock'.

F/O (instructor pilot) Edward Reginald Berrill (34206), RAF, was born on 14 April 1914 and enlisted in the RAF in 1934. After completing his pilot training he was posted to 55 Squadron in June 1935, flying Wapiti bombers on policing duties in Iraq. Twelve months later he was attached to the Communications Flight, Iraq, but in October 1937 returned to the UK and subsequently underwent instructor training in the summer of 1938, following a brief spell at 3 Armament Training School. With war clouds looming, he was posted to 9 Squadron but did not survive his tour and was killed on 8 March 1940 when a Wellington (N3017), which he was tasked with ferrying from Weybridge to Honington, crashed during the flight. F/Lt Berrill was 25 years old and is buried in Brookwood Military Cemetery, Surrey.

Acting P/O Francis Hamell [TNA]

Acting P/O (pilot u/t) Francis Joseph Hamell, RAF, aged 23, had been educated at Dulwich College in London and served briefly as an officer in 55 Anti-Aircraft Brigade, before returning to his native Canada. He subsequently returned to the UK in July 1938 to join the RAF. He is buried in Prescott, Ontario, Canada.

16 March (Thursday)
Ferry flight from 6 MU, Reading to RAF Sealand, Flintshire. 2 FPP (Filton, Gloucestershire)
Miles Magister I (N5425) force-landed 1/4 mile west of Bettisfield railway station, on the north

Neech's force-landed Magister near Bettisfield [Border Counties Advertizer]

Shropshire border, at 13.00 hrs. Having encountered bad weather en route, the pilot became lost and decided to make a precautionary landing but, after touching down on the wet ground, the brakes failed to stop the aircraft and it crashed through a fence and came to rest overhanging the railway embankment. The accident was subsequently attributed to 'faulty airmanship by inexperienced pilot'.

Sgt (pilot) Thomas John Gordon Neech (522064), RAF, was born in Kent, on 22 December 1914, the son of Sydney J and Ruth Neech (née Gordon). After joining the RAF in the summer of 1937 he completed his pilot training and joined 7 Squadron in May 1938, flying the new Whitley bomber out of RAF Finningley. Six months later he was posted to 76 Squadron, flying the Wellesley bomber, before being attached to 2 FPP for ferry pilot duties the following March. Commissioned in October 1942, he never flew operationally and spent the entire war serving as a ferry and test pilot, for which duty he was graded as 'exceptional'. In January 1945 he was 'Commended for Valuable Services in the Air' and twelve months later was also awarded the King's Commendation for Valuable Services in the Air for his services as a test pilot at 9 MU, Cosford. Having survived the entire war, F/Lt Neech died on 18 October 1947 and is buried in Weston-super-Mare Cemetery.

23 May (Tuesday)
Drogue towing. 11 FTS (RAF Shawbury, Shropshire)
Hawker Hart Mk I (K4967) force-landed at Baschurch. After the pilot caused the engine to fail, due to 'mishandling', he force-landed on a downhill slope and applied the brakes to stop, causing the aircraft to overturn.

Acting P/O (pilot u/t) Ronald Alfred Rutherford Lee (41433), RAF, was born in Ilford, Essex, on 19 January 1919. Nothing further is known of his career other than that he resigned his commission on 10 June 1940 for unknown reasons. He died in Devon in 2005.

Hawker Hart (K4967) at Baschurch [David Lee]

Hawker Hart (K4967) at Baschurch [David Lee]

14 August (Monday)

Forced-landing practice. 10 FTS (RAF Tern Hill, Shropshire)

North American Harvard I (N7028) force-landed at High Ercall village. After becoming lost and with fuel running low, the pilot decided to make a precautionary landing in a field but, as he approached, he struck the branches of a tree. He then applied his brakes too harshly as he touched down, causing the aircraft to turn over, and injured himself slightly.

Acting P/O (pilot u/t) Pyers Arthur Worrall (42291), RAF, was born on 5 February 1921, the son of Col Percival Reginald Worrall, CBE, DSO, MC and Agnes Worrall of Avon Dasset, Warwickshire. On completion of his training he flew Hurricanes with 85 and 249 Squadron during the Battle of Britain and was shot down over Tunbridge on 31 August 1940, taking to his parachute and suffering slight injuries to his leg. Following the battle, he was posted to 136 Squadron as a flight commander, piloting Hurricanes as part of the air defence of the Calcutta region of India. He was killed on 8 June 1942 when his Hurricane (BM926) crashed on the edge of Alipore airfield while taking off. F/Lt Worrall was 21 years old and is buried in Calcutta (Bhowanipore) Cemetery.

Acting P/O Pyers Worrall [TNA]

30 August (Wednesday)

Cross-country flight 'to collect confidential documents' (presumably from RAF Tern Hill). 5 ATS (RAF Penrhos, Caernarfonshire)

Hawker Henley III (L3355) crashed at Longslow Farm, to the north west of Market Drayton, at 10.20 hrs. The pilot attempted to force-land 'due to over correction coming out of turn', but as he did so the aircraft 'spun slightly, stalled and [the] wing struck the ground' although, fortunately, he was unhurt.

Acting F/Lt (pilot) Edward Patrick Henley (40703), RAF, a native of Newfoundland, had travelled to the UK in the summer of 1938 to join the RAF. Little is known of his military service other than that he survived the war and attained the rank of squadron leader. He subsequently returned to Newfoundland, where he died in St John's in May 2002.

30 August (Wednesday)

Night circuits and landings. 11 FTS (RAF Shawbury, Shropshire)

Airspeed Oxford I (N4597) force-landed 'near Oswestry'. During the flight the pupil pilot was unable to locate the airfield due to low cloud and bad weather and decided to make a precautionary landing in a field, but when he touched down heavily on an upward slope, the undercarriage collapsed.

Cpl (pilot u/t) Cyril Haigh (566171), RAF, was educated at Mexborough Secondary School and joined the RAF as an apprentice in September 1932 (qualifying as a fitter before retraining as a pilot in 1939). On completion of his training he was posted to 604 Squadron, flying Blenheim night fighters during the Battle of Britain but was killed on 25 August 1940 when his Blenheim (L6782) crashed near Exeter during a night patrol. Sgt Haigh was 23 years old and is buried in Swinton (St Margaret) Churchyard in Yorkshire.

3 September – War declared

20 September (Wednesday)
Ferry flight from RAF Benson to an unknown airfield (but possibly Tern Hill's 24 MU). '6 Group Pool' (RAF Benson, Oxfordshire)
Fairey Battle I (L5220) force-landed at 'Hinton, Salop' (presumably Hinton, near Pontesbury) at 14.45 hrs. The pilot was ferrying the aircraft to an unknown airfield to have flame traps fitted when the engine failed and he was forced to land in a small field surrounded by trees, wrecking the aircraft but fortunately stepping out unhurt.

P/O (pilot) Peter Denis Brock Stevens (41329), RAF, was commissioned in September 1938 and survived the war, eventually retiring as a group captain in October 1972.

26 September (Tuesday)
Ferry flight to and from unknown airfields (but possibly to RAF Tern Hill's 24 MU). 2 FPP (Filton, Gloucestershire)
Westland Lysander II (N1317) crash-landed 'near Baschurch'. During the flight the pilot became lost and decided to make a precautionary landing as his fuel was running low. As he approached a field, the engine failed due to lack of fuel and, while attempting to glide in, the aircraft touched down in a small field, bounced and crashed through a hedge. Fortunately, the pilot was unhurt.

F/O (pilot) James Stewart Young (39362), RAF, was born in Saskatoon, Canada, on 5 August 1915. He had learned to fly with the Edmonton & Northern Aero Club during his last year at high school and subsequently travelled to the UK to join the RAF. On completion of his training he was posted to 10 Squadron in August 1936, flying Whitley bombers, after which he joined 2 FPP in September 1939 and then 7 AOS as a flight commander. In August 1940 he underwent a Spitfire conversion course and then flew with 234 Squadron during the latter stages of the Battle of Britain. In November 1940 he underwent instructor training, before spending the remainder of the war in a variety of non-operational roles, both in the UK and abroad. He transferred to the RCAF in July 1945 and eventually retired as a squadron leader in October 1962.

Cpl Watt [TNA]

14 October (Saturday)
Solo training flight. 10 SFTS (RAF Tern Hill, Shropshire)
North American Harvard I (N7102) force-landed at Church Stretton at 11.30 hrs. After losing his bearings in bad weather, the pupil pilot made a precautionary landing in a field but overshot slightly and the aircraft ran into a hedge.

Cpl (pilot u/t) George Thomas Watt (516242), RAF, was the son of John C and Agatha A Watt (née Van Hoytema) from Middlesex. He was killed on 17 October 1940 while serving with 15 OTU, when his Wellington (L4259) crashed during circuit practice at RAF Hampstead Norris. Cpl Watt, who was 25 years old, is buried in Harwell Cemetery, Oxfordshire.

19 October (Thursday)
Night circuits and landings. 10 SFTS (RAF Tern Hill, Shropshire)
North American Harvard I (N7101) crashed at Child's Ercall airfield (under construction) at 03.00 hrs. The pilot, who was a member of the Advanced Training Squadron (ATS), had just made a solo circuit of the airfield and landed successfully, despite having to correct after approaching too low and from behind some trees. He then took off for a second circuit but, after leaving the ground, made a wide circuit and mistook a flood-light used for excavation work at Child's Ercall Relief Landing Ground for the 'Chance-light' (used to light up the landing area during night flying) at RAF Tern Hill. Displaying a 'lack of experience' the pilot's 'one idea, forgetting entirely all night-flying procedure, seems to have been to land as quickly as possible, which he attempted to do', suffering concussion and mild shock in the resultant crash-landing. As a result of the accident he was 'considered for withdrawal from pilot training'.

Acting P/O (pilot u/t) Brendan Bernard Little (42241), RAF, was born on 23 October 1918. No further details are known of him other than that his commission was 'terminated on cessation of duty' on 12 July 1940.

30 October (Monday)
11 SFTS (RAF Shawbury, Shropshire)
This airman was on flarepath duty and was standing in the vicinity of N° 5 flare when an Airspeed Oxford (N4563) swung badly while landing, careered between N°s 4 and 5 flares and struck the airman, killing him instantly.

AC1 (ACH/GD) Thomas Gee (620845), RAF, aged 35, is buried in Sefton (St Helen) Churchyard, Lancashire. His next of kin are unknown.

7 November (Tuesday)
Local training flight. 11 SFTS (RAF Shawbury, Shropshire)

Airspeed Oxford I (P1845) crashed near Raven's Bowl, on the Wrekin, at 15.15 hrs. Two pupil pilots took off for a local flight, during the course of which the aircraft flew into the mist and cloud obscured hillside, killing the safety pilot and seriously injuring the pilot, who was thrown from the wreckage. The subsequent investigation concluded that the flight should not have been authorised considering the prevailing weather at the time.

Acting P/O (pilot u/t) William Oliver Cramer (42336), RAF, eventually recovered from his injuries and survived the war, attaining the rank of flight lieutenant.

Acting P/O (pilot u/t, but acting as navigator and safety pilot) George Hugh Hamilton Coates (42333), RAF, aged 18, was the eldest son of Ronald Assheton Coates and Dorothy Margaret Coates of Berkhamsted, Hertfordshire. He is commemorated at the Golders Green Crematorium.

10 November (Friday)
Ferry flight from RAF Perth to RAF St Athan. Station Delivery Flight, St Athan (RAF Perth, Scotland – satellite airfield to St Athan, South Wales)
Fairey Swordfish I (K8881) force-landed 'at Church Stretton'. After encountering bad weather en route, the pilot made a precautionary landing in a field, slightly damaging the lower mainplane, tailplane and tailwheel as it struck a hedge.

Sgt (pilot) George Milner Smith (563407), RAF. After joining the RAF in 1936, Smith was assessed as an 'above average' pilot during training, which is believed to be the reason why he was chosen to join the calibration flight (which required great accuracy) at the Aeroplane & Armament Experimental Establishment, RAF Martlesham Heath, in August 1937, working closely with the development of radar.

Sgt George Smith
[George Milner-Smith]

In September 1939 he was posted to the Wireless Development Unit in Perth and it was during his time there that the forced-landing at Church Stretton occurred. The following January he returned to Martlesham Heath, then subsequently Duxford and Fowlmere, and for the following three years was involved in further radar experiments and calibration flights, for which he was graded 'exceptional' and twice mentioned in despatches. In early 1943 he began training on twin-engine fighters and subsequently completed a tour of ops with 307 Squadron, flying Mosquitos, in the Mediterranean theatre. The following January he was posted to 256 Squadron, continuing to fly Mosquitos in the Mediterranean area, and in December 1944 was awarded the DFC for his actions with the squadron. Having nearly completed his second tour, he lost his life on 19 April 1945 when his Mosquito (HK508) was shot down over Copparo in northern Italy. Squadron Leader Smith is buried in Argenta Gap War Cemetery.

13 December (Wednesday)
Practice low-level bombing flight. 10 SFTS (RAF Tern Hill, Shropshire)
North American Harvard I (N7023) force-landed 'seven miles north-east of Market Drayton' (putting it roughly in the area of Woore). After becoming lost in poor visibility and with darkness approaching, the pupil pilot made a precautionary landing and the aircraft was slightly damaged by a barbed-wire fence.

Acting P/O Roy Bush.
[TNA]

Acting P/O (pilot u/t) Charles Roy Bush (42691), RAF, was born in Wellington, New Zealand, on 7 February 1918, the son of Charles and Margaret Rubina Bush (née Wilson). In June 1939 he sailed to the UK to join the RAF and, after completing his pilot training, was posted to 615 and then 242 Squadron, flying Hurricanes during the Battle of France and Battle of Britain. Later, he flew with 258, 610 and then 41 Squadron and, in October 1941, was awarded the DFC for having shot down three enemy aircraft during 48 operational sweeps over enemy territory. A period of instructing followed in the UK and then New Zealand, but in November 1943 he returned to ops as a flight commander with 15 Squadron in the Pacific theatre. The following February he was given command of 21 Squadron, flying Corsair fighters on ground-attack missions against the Japanese. After returning to the UK for a period of time he was given command of the General Purposes Communications Flight at Ohakea in New Zealand but, having survived so many operations during the war, lost his life on 30 November 1948 when his Oxford aircraft broke up in mid-air while carrying out a photographic reconnaissance in the Gisborne area. He was cremated at Wanganui. His brother, T N Bush, lost his life serving with the Fleet Air Arm in Orkney in December 1942.

1940

2 January (Tuesday)
Ferry flight from RAF Kemble, Gloucestershire, to RAF Sealand, Flintshire. Station Delivery Flight, RAF Depot Andover (RAF Andover, Hampshire)
De Havilland Tiger Moth I (K4901) force-landed 'near Much Wenlock' (believed to have landed at

Sheinwood Manor Farm, Sheinwood near Much Wenlock). Eight pilots were flown to 4 MU at Kemble with orders to deliver eight Tiger Moth aircraft to RAF Sealand in north Wales but, during the flight, the pilot of this aircraft became lost in bad weather and made a precautionary landing as darkness was closing in. Although unconfirmed, this accident is believed to have occurred on land belonging to the Pugh family of Sheinwood Manor Farm. Derek Pugh, whose account was passed on to the author by his niece in 2008, described how

> … the plane that crash-landed in foggy weather came down on the field called the Long Field, which was thirteen acres in size, sometime during 1940. The plane had one pilot named F/Lt Smithers who was flying back from Zeeland [sic]. The make of plane was a De Havilland Tiger Moth. F/Lt Smithers stayed at Sheinwood for three days. Granny Pugh put him up in the house'.

The name of the pilot is not recorded in official records; however, if this is the same accident remembered by Derek Pugh, then the pilot was 'F/Lt Smithers'.

16 January (Tuesday)
Height test and cross-country exercise from RAF Shawbury–RAF South Cerney, Gloucestershire. 11 SFTS (RAF Shawbury, Shropshire)
Airspeed Oxford I (N6425) force-landed 'near Bridgnorth'. After encountering a sudden snowstorm the pilot made a precautionary landing in a field.

The name of the pilot is unknown.

16 January (Tuesday)
Solo height test to 15,000 feet. 10 SFTS (RAF Tern Hill, Shropshire)
Avro Anson I (N5258) force-landed at Lee Brockhurst, to the south-east of Wem. After encountering a sudden snowstorm the pilot made a precautionary landing in a field.

The name of the pilot is unknown.

16 January (Tuesday)
High dive-bombing exercise. 11 SFTS (RAF Shawbury, Shropshire)
Hawker Audax I (K2011) force-landed 'one mile north of Shrewsbury' (putting it in the area of Harlescott and Mount Pleasant). After encountering a sudden snowstorm the pilot made a precautionary landing in a field, damaging the wheels in the process. A team from RAF Shawbury carried out repairs *in situ* and the pilot was able to fly back to the airfield later the same day.

Acting P/O (pilot u/t) Peter Gwavas Polsue (42641), RAF, was born in Leighton Buzzard on 29 June 1920. He survived the war and attained the rank of flight lieutenant. He died in September 2000 in Brighton.

17 January (Wednesday)
Height test to 15,000 feet. 11 SFTS (RAF Shawbury, Shropshire)
Airspeed Oxford II (N4724) force-landed near Ironbridge. The pilot made a precautionary landing in a field after becoming lost in poor visibility.

The name of the pilot is unknown

26 January (Friday)
Air-to-ground firing exercise. 11 SFTS (RAF Shawbury, Shropshire)
Hawker Audax I (K7492) force-landed at Cheswardine, to the south-east of Market Drayton. Having become lost in poor visibility the pilot made a precautionary landing in a field but, after touching down,

Vincent 'Bush' Parker
[Neil Anderson]

he had to swing the aircraft to avoid some sheep, causing it to tip up onto its nose.

Acting P/O (pilot u/t) Vincent 'Bush' Parker (42356), RAF, was born in Chester-le-Street, County Durham, on 11 February 1918, the son of Vincent and Lydia Wheatley, but was taken into care by his aunt and uncle, Edith and Jack Parker, after his mother died when he was young (his father was away serving in the Merchant Navy). In 1927, Edith and Jack Parker emigrated to Australia and, with the agreement of his father, Vincent and his two siblings went with them and at the same time adopted the Parker surname. Growing up in Townsville, where he became a keen horse-rider and magician, Vincent studied at Bohlevale State School and then worked as a magician in a travelling circus before sailing to the UK to join the RAF in 1939. On completion of his pilot training he was posted to 234 Squadron, flying Spitfires. During the Battle of Britain he was shot down into the sea off Dorset on 15 August 1940 and picked up by a German E-boat. After repeated escape attempts he was eventually sent to the infamous *Oflag IVc* (better known as Colditz Castle), where his skills as a magician were put to use entertaining his fellow inmates while also earning him the role of camp 'lock picker' (supposedly creating keys for all 100 doors in the castle!). Following the camp's liberation in 1945, Vincent returned to the UK where he was placed on a pilot refresher course at 56 OTU. Tragically, having survived so many years in captivity, he was killed on 29 January 1946 when his Hawker Tempest (EJ852) crashed during a training flight from RAF Millfield. F/Lt Parker was 27 years old and is buried in Harrogate (Stonefall) Cemetery.

23 February (Friday)
Ferry flight from RAF Tern Hill to the Westland Aircraft Company airfield, Yeovil, Somerset. 24 MU (RAF Tern Hill, Shropshire)
Westland Lysander I (L4736) force-landed near Bridgnorth at midday. The pilot, who was an instructor pilot with 10 SFTS on loan to 24 MU as a ferry pilot, force-landed in a ploughed field after the engine had failed during the flight.

Acting F/O (instructor pilot) Ronald Lee Jeffery (70861), RAF (RAFO), died on 21 March 1940 in a flying accident at Tern Hill and an entry for him can be found on that date.

23 February (Friday)
Ferry flight from 27 MU, RAF Shawbury, to RAF Northolt, Middlesex. 253 Squadron (RAF Northolt, Middlesex)
Fairey Battle I (N2256) force-landed 'one mile north of Oswestry' (putting it in the area just north of the Old Oswestry hill fort, near Pentre Clawdd) at 13.00 hrs. After taking off from Shawbury, the pilot became totally lost due to poor weather and tried to make a precautionary landing in a field, but the aircraft skidded on wet ground and crashed into a hedge, damaging a wing tip. The subsequent investigation concluded that, in view of the weather conditions, the flight 'should not have been allowed'.

P/O (pilot) John Kenneth Grahame 'Curly' Clifton (41902), RAF, was born in Plymouth, on 20 October 1918, the son of John Henry and Susie Dorothy Anderson Clifton. He grew up in Taunton, where he attended Taunton School. On completion of his pilot training he joined the newly-formed 253 Squadron and flew Hurricanes during the Battle of France, claiming two enemy aircraft shot down. He then flew during the Battle of Britain, claiming another aircraft shot down but was shot down and killed on 1 September, piloting a Hurricane (P5185) in combat over Dungeness. P/O Clifton was 21 years old and is buried in Staplegrove Cemetery, Somerset.

21 March (Thursday)
Unknown duty. 10 SFTS (RAF Tern Hill, Shropshire)
Avro Anson I (N5039) crashed at Tern Hill. The Commanding Officer of the Advanced Training Squadron (ATS) was approaching to land when a collision occurred with a Harvard (N7060) at 150 feet. Both pilots immediately tried to climb, but the two aircraft stalled and crashed, killing the occupants of the Harvard and seriously injuring S/Ldr Dale.

S/Ldr (pilot) Ivor Gordon Easton 'Daddy' Dale (19182), RAF, was born in Godstone, Surrey, in 1905. He was the son of Horace Easton and Frances Harriet Dale and was educated at Tonbridge School. After joining the RAF in 1925, little is known of his military service until 1930, when he travelled to the Middle East and spent ten months with 4 FTS before being posted to 47 Squadron in Khartoum, piloting Fairey III aircraft on air-policing duties over the Sudan. In March 1931 he was posted to 14 Squadron, flying Fairey IIIs and Fairey Gordons on air-policing and photo surveying duties in Palestine and Transjordan but, in June 1934, he returned to the UK and joined 501 Squadron briefly before being placed on the reserve in November. With war clouds looming, F/Lt Dale was recalled to service and spent the first few years of the war as an instructor before eventually being given command of 21 Squadron, flying Mosquito aircraft on daylight precision-bombing and night-bombing operations. In August 1944 he was awarded the DFC for his 'outstanding operational record' but was killed on 2 February 1945 when his Mosquito (PZ314) encountered engine trouble and crashed at Ophoven in the Netherlands, during a night intruder 'op'. W/Cdr Dale was 39 years old and is buried in Sittard War Cemetery, Netherlands.

21 March (Thursday)
Training flight. 10 SFTS (RAF Tern Hill, Shropshire)
North American Harvard I (N7060) crashed at Tern Hill following the collision described above.

F/O (instructor pilot) Ronald Lee Jeffery (70861), RAF (RAFO), aged 20, was the son of Thomas H Jeffery and Lily Lee of Sheffield. He is buried in Sheffield (Abbey Lane) Cemetery. He had been involved in an earlier accident on 23 February 1940 near Bridgnorth.

Sgt (pilot u/t) John George Stirling Kirkpatrick (741757), RAFVR, aged 20, was born in Hutchesontown, Glasgow. He is buried in Glasgow (Craigton) Cemetery.

21 March (Thursday)
Test flight. 27 MU (RAF Shawbury, Shropshire)
Hawker Hector I (K8123) force-landed in a field '1/4 of a mile from RAF Shawbury'. The pilot was taking off from the airfield when the aircraft's engine failed, forcing him to side-slip into a field ahead, slightly damaging the aircraft.

Sgt (Test pilot) John Henry Lowes (565123), RAF, was commissioned in June 1940 and spent the entire war serving as a test pilot, including a spell with 29 MU, High Ercall, between June and November 1942. He then returned to Shawbury and was involved in another forced landing on 11 January 1943 at Ellerdine but, soon afterwards, was posted to South East Asia where he commanded the Test and Dispatch Flight of 320 Maintenance Unit, Karachi. For his services with the unit he was awarded the AFC in the New Year's Honours List of 1945, by which stage he had completed over 5,000 test flights in 65 different aircraft types and made 54 forced-landings. He remained in the RAF after the war and was appointed an MBE in June 1957 in recognition of his distinguished service between October and December 1956 during the Suez Crisis. He died on 23 September 1965 while serving as a squadron leader at RAF Brawdy and is buried in Doncaster Cemetery, Yorkshire.

22 March (Friday)
Cross-country exercise. 12 SFTS (RAF Grantham, Lincolnshire)
Hawker Hart I (K5010) force-landed at Wellington at midday and then attempted to take off at 15.15 hrs. Having force-landed earlier in the afternoon because he was lost, the pilot decided to take off again but, as he taxied across the field to line up for his take off run, had to brake sharply to avoid a group of people that had gathered to watch and the aircraft tipped onto its nose.

F/O (instructor pilot?) Kenneth Howard Vivian Day (39076), RAF, was born on 27 May 1917. He was the son of John T and Janet F Day (née Mordecai) from south Wales and had joined the RAF in 1936. On completion of his training he was posted to 108 Squadron in May 1937 flying Hawker Hind light bombers and then, from September 1937, with 57 Squadron flying Hinds and Blenheims. Following his attachment to 12 SFTS he was posted to 9 Squadron flying Wellington bombers but, in November 1940, resigned his commission and left the RAF. He died in Cheshire in 2001.

31 March (Sunday)
Solo night circuits and landings. 11 SFTS (RAF Shawbury, Shropshire)
Airspeed Oxford II (N4840) crashed into trees on the north side of the airfield at 02.00 hrs. The pupil pilot was preparing to land when he approached far too low, undershot the runway and struck trees on high ground on the edge of the airfield, crashing further ahead.

Acting P/O (pilot u/t) Ronald Arthur Sims (42654), RAF, aged 19, was the son of Edward and May Sims of Peterborough. He is buried in Peterborough (Eastfield) Cemetery.

7 April (Sunday)
Cross-country exercise from RAF Sealand to RAF South Cerney, Gloucestershire. 5 SFTS (RAF Sealand, Flintshire)
Miles Master I (N7470) force-landed at Culmington Farm, in the Corve Dale, east of Craven Arms, at 11.30 hrs. After becoming lost in bad weather and low cloud, the pilot made a precautionary landing in a ploughed field, but when he touched down the aircraft tipped up on its nose when he applied the brakes to avoid running into a ditch.

Sgt (pilot u/t) Alan James McGregor (742543), RAFVR, was commissioned two months after the accident. He was mentioned in despatches both in June 1944 and again in the New Year's Honours list of 1945. In October 1945 he was also awarded the DSO for his services with 123 Squadron, flying Thunderbolts on fighter-bomber operations over Burma during the latter stages of the war. He remained in the RAF after the war and retired as a wing commander in November 1976.

8 April (Monday)
Night circuits and landings. 11 SFTS (RAF Shawbury, Shropshire)
Airspeed Oxford II (P1933) crashed into Actonlea Coppice, to the north west of the airfield, at 22.15 hrs. Due to the prevailing wind at the time, pilots of the Advanced Training Squadron (ATS) were required to take off towards Actonlea Coppice, which lay 300 yards from the airfield boundary on ground that rose 70 feet higher than the airfield. In between the wood and the airfield boundary there also stood an isolated oak tree, 50 feet high, which meant that pupil pilots had to climb away from the airfield rapidly.

F/Lt Alf Alexander had already completed several training flights with another pupil pilot earlier in the night, before taking off with his second pupil, LAC Houchin, to practice circuits and landings. According to LAC Houchin's statement given after the crash, the pair were taking off for their third circuit when, immediately after leaving the ground, witnesses heard 'a loud explosion accompanied by a flash'. The explosion was caused by the aircraft striking the isolated oak tree, which smashed the port propeller and sent the aircraft crashing into the wood beyond, seriously injuring the two occupants. The instructor's injuries proved fatal and he died at 03.00 hrs the following morning, while LAC Houchin eventually recovered from his injuries.

F/Lt (instructor pilot) Alfred (Alf) Alexander (36222), RAF, aged 27, was the husband of Marie Evelyn Alexander (née Chick). Born in Burnley, on 25 April 1913, he joined the RAF as an apprentice in 1928 and subsequently served as a wireless operator/mechanic in the UK and India before being accepted for pilot training in September 1934. On completion of his flying training he was posted to 30 Squadron in September 1935, flying Hawker Hardys in Iraq, before returning to the UK in August 1937 and becoming an instructor pilot. He is buried in Ash Cemetery, Surrey.

F/Lt Alf Alexander [Norman Ratcliffe & Ash Museum]

LAC (pilot u/t) Houchin, RAFVR, is believed to be Robert James Houchin (518421), although it is unconfirmed, who was killed on 30 January 1941 serving with 248 Squadron.

9 April (Tuesday)
F/Lt A Alexander died of injuries sustained the previous night at Shawbury

12 April (Friday)
Forced-landing practice and local air navigation. 11 SFTS (RAF Shawbury, Shropshire)
Hawker Audax I (K3091) crashed at High Hatton, near Peplow, at 10.15 hrs. The pupil pilot was flying low near a friend's house when he allowed the aircraft to stall and crash.

Sgt (pilot u/t) Denis Allen Hampton (741874), RAFVR, aged 23, was the second son of George Chudleigh and Kathleen Margaret Hampton of College Road, Epsom. Educated at Rugby School, he was a keen motorcyclist and had worked as an electrical engineer before joining up. He is buried in Ewell (St Mary) Churchyard, Surrey.

4 May (Saturday)
Formation flying as part of 12 Group exercise. 'B' Flight, 264 Squadron (RAF Wittering, Cambridgeshire)
Boulton Paul Defiant I (L6972) force-landed in a field 'near Shawbury'. The crew were taking part in a mass training exercise when the engine failed, due to a burst hydraulic pressure gauge. In the resultant forced landing, the pilot was partially blinded by spurting liquid from the broken gauge and the aircraft was slightly damaged when it ran through a hedge.

P/O (pilot) Gordon Emery Chandler (33559), RAF, was the son of Alfred Leonard and Mary Gertrude Chandler of Toddington, Bedfordshire. He was killed nine days later whilst piloting a Defiant (L6960) in combat with Me109s over the Netherlands. He is buried in Made en Drimmelen Protestant Churchyard, Netherlands.

Although unconfirmed, it is presumed that his gunner during the training exercise was LAC (AG) Douglas Leslie McLeish (581467), RAF. He was killed alongside his pilot nine days later and is buried in Werkendam Protestant Cemetery, Netherlands.

5 May (Sunday)
Cross-country exercise from RAF Tern Hill–RAF Brize Norton, Oxfordshire, via Worcester. 10 SFTS (RAF Tern Hill, Shropshire)
Avro Anson I (N5337) force-landed at Ellesmere. The pilot was returning from Brize Norton when he became lost and, as he searched for the airfield, the port engine failed due to a lack of fuel, forcing him to land in a field. The name of the pilot is unknown.

14 May (Tuesday)
Unknown flight detail. Unknown unit
Fairey Battle (serial unknown) force-landed at Shelvock, between Ruyton-XI-Towns and West Felton. Little is known of this accident other than that the pilot force-landed in a field and the aircraft was placed under guard by soldiers of 75 (Shropshire Yeomanry) Regiment, stationed at Oswestry. The name of the pilot is unknown.

23 May (Thursday)
Ground accident. 10 SFTS (RAF Tern Hill, Shropshire)
This airman was killed instantly when he was struck while turning a propeller.

LAC (ACH/GD) Arthur Maddy (536711), RAF, aged 23, was the son of Agnes Maddy (née McNiece) and the late Arthur Maddy (killed at Ypres in 1917, serving with 8 Loyal North Lancashire Regiment). He is buried in Market Drayton Cemetery, Shropshire.

7 June (Friday)
Air-to-ground firing exercise. 10 SFTS (RAF Tern Hill, Shropshire)
North American Harvard I (N7106) force-landed 'two and a half miles south-east of the airfield' (putting it roughly in the area between Wistanswick and Hinstock) at 12.20 hrs. As the pilot came out of a dive he opened up the throttle to increase power but there was no response and he was forced to land in a field. After touching down, however, the wheels struck a hedge and the aircraft flipped onto its back and caught fire but, fortunately, the pilot escaped uninjured.

Sgt Norman Taylor. [TNA]

Sgt (pilot u/t) Norman Taylor (742827), RAF, was born in Derby, on 23 October 1920 and had joined the RAF in January 1939 as an apprentice before being accepted for pilot training following the outbreak of war. On completion of his training he joined 601 Squadron in August 1940 and was credited with three enemy aircraft destroyed and two damaged while flying Hurricanes during the Battle of Britain, as well as being shot down once himself. Following the battle, the squadron began offensive sweeps over north-west Europe and Sgt Taylor claimed three further aircraft destroyed and two damaged, and in July 1941 was awarded the DFM. The following year he was posted to the Merchant Ship Fighter Unit (MSFU), piloting modified Sea Hurricanes (known as Hurricats), which were catapulted from a ship when an enemy aircraft was spotted approaching. On 1 November 1942, the now commissioned F/O Taylor was launched from his ship, the *Empire Heath*, as a Focke-Wulf Condor was seen approaching and, in the subsequent action, destroyed the aircraft before baling out into the sea and being picked up by a corvette. For his action he was awarded the DFC. Following his service with the MSFU he became a test pilot but,after surviving the entire war, was killed in a flying accident on 29 April 1948 while serving in Germany. F/Lt Taylor was 27 years old and is buried in Handorf Heath Cemetery, Germany.

16 June (Sunday)
Ferry flight to and from unknown airfields. 3 FPP (White Waltham, Berkshire)
Hawker Hurricane I (L1601) force-landed 'at Uffington' (although it is unclear if this is Uffington in Shropshire) at 13.15 hrs. During the flight the engine cut out after the pilot 'failed to concentrate on the petrol system due to trouble with aircraft' and he was forced to belly-land in a field. The subsequent court of inquiry added that a contributory factor may have been that the pilot was suffering from 'fatigue due to too much recent flying'.

First Officer (pilot) Philip James Grenside, ATA, was born in Paignton, Devon, on 6 December 1907 and gained his pilot's licence at Brooklands Flying Club in December 1935 while living in Godalming with his wife. He died in Godalming in July 1966.

20 June (Thursday)
Practice compass course and single-engine flying. 10 SFTS (RAF Tern Hill, Shropshire)
Avro Anson I (N5329) force-landed at Wappenshall, between Wellington and Kynnersley, at 19.00 hrs. After becoming lost the pilot made a precautionary landing in a field from where the aircraft had later to be recovered (only to be destroyed during the German bombing raid on RAF Tern Hill on 16 October 1940). The name of the pilot is unknown.

3 July (Wednesday)
Solo circuits and landings. 10 SFTS (RAF Tern Hill, Shropshire)
North American Harvard I (N7011) crashed 'near Tern Hill airfield' at 01.00 hrs. Having completed five dual circuits and landings with an instructor, the pupil pilot took off shortly before midnight and successfully completed two solo circuits and landings. He then took off normally for a third circuit but, after reaching 200 feet, reported that the angle of the bank pointer at the top of his Sperry horizon dial appeared to indicate a steep bank to the left. His own bodily sensations were that his bank was non-existent but, remembering that he should pin his faith on instruments rather than his own sensations, he moved his control column to the right to offset the supposed left bank. As he did so, he felt that the aircraft was banked steeply to the right and immediately afterwards the Sperry indicator gyro started to spin and the aircraft descended out of control, crashing through some trees and skidding 230 yards through a meadow before coming to rest against a bank. Incredibly, the pilot climbed out unhurt. The subsequent court of inquiry placed the blame on the pilot, stating that 'the accident was due to an error of airmanship on the part of the pilot in that he took off and attempted to fly by an instrument which was caged, i.e. out of action'.

Sgt Geoff Hardie [TNA]

Sgt (pilot u/t) Geoffrey Hardie (754673), RAFVR. On completion of his pilot training he was posted to 232 Squadron in September 1940, flying Hurricanes on defensive duties in the north of Scotland. Following a brief attachment to 4 Delivery Flight in June 1941, he returned to 232 Squadron and then proceeded with them to the Far East. As soon as the squadron arrived in the theatre, in January 1942, the pilots were thrown into extremely heavy fighting against the invading Japanese forces and, on 22 January, Hardie was shot down off Singapore and baled out into the sea while scrapping with Japanese Zero fighters. After being rescued by an Air-Sea Rescue launch, he returned to the squadron and over the next five weeks he was involved in further heavy fighting, during which the squadron suffered huge losses as it was forced to retreat in the face of the Japanese onslaught. Although the squadron's records were lost in the retreat, it was noted afterwards that Hardie had shot down three Japanese aircraft during the fighting and claimed two more probables. Little is known of his subsequent military service following the squadron's disbandment in February 1942 but, by 1944, he was back at Tern Hill serving as an instructor with 5 (P)AFU. He died on 7 April 1944 in a crash at Chetwynd airfield.

4 July (Thursday)
First night solo flight. 10 SFTS (RAF Tern Hill, Shropshire)
North American Harvard I (P5884) crashed at 'Northwood House Farm, Wollerton' (presumably Northwood Farm between Wollerton and Fauls), at 23.50 hrs. The pupil pilot had completed seven

Sgt James Mallinson [TNA]

dual circuits and landings with an instructor before taking off on his first solo night flight just before 23.50 hrs. However, almost immediately after he left the ground the aircraft was witnessed to bear away to the right before crashing a minute or so later into a mown hayfield, spreading wreckage over several hundred yards. The subsequent court of inquiry concluded that the pilot 'committed an error of judgment in losing control of his aircraft immediately after the take off in 'black out' conditions. He was very inexperienced and apparently was unable to fly by instruments'.

Sgt (pilot u/t) James Wilson Mallinson (754266), RAFVR, aged 21, was the son of Herbert Crosby Mallinson and Dorothy Mallinson of Shipley. He is buried in Shipley (Nab Wood) Cemetery, Yorkshire.

10 July (Wednesday)
Operational reconnaissance of Le Havre, on the north coast of France. 59 Squadron (RAF Thorney Island, Hampshire)
Bristol Blenheim IV (R3881, bearing the fuselage code TR-A), crashed into Titterstone Clee Hill (at map reference 591775), near Ludlow, at 03.15 hrs. The crew took off at 00.05 hrs with one other aircraft and were returning from the operation when the pilot of this aircraft became hopelessly lost and flew into the mist and cloud-covered hillside, striking an electricity pylon and crashing into a spoil dump. RAF Shawbury was quickly notified of the accident and dispatched their ambulance and crash crew to retrieve the bodies and also to neutralize four unexploded bombs. Following the subsequent investigation it was established that the wireless operator was unable to obtain wireless contact and, as a result, no direction-finding bearings could be transmitted to the aircraft to guide the crew to safety, resulting in the pilot becoming hopelessly lost.

P/O (pilot) James Rex (78982), RAFVR, aged 21, was the son of James Henry and Florence Martha Rex of Bristol. He is buried in Shawbury (St Mary's) Churchyard, Shropshire.

Sgt (Obs) John Samuel Jeffery (581226), RAF, aged 18, was the son of John James and Nellie Jeffery. He is buried in Greenwich Cemetery, London. His brother, Robert, also lost his life serving as a gunner with 69 Squadron on 25 March 1945.

Sgt (W/AG) James William Liddle (638666), RAF, aged 25, is buried in Sunderland (Bishopwearmouth) Cemetery. His next of kin are unknown.

11 July (Thursday)
Solo single-engine flying and powered approaches & landings. 11 SFTS (RAF Shawbury, Shropshire)
Airspeed Oxford II (P8927) crashed at Stanton upon Hine Heath at 19.00 hrs. During the flight the pilot stalled in a steep turn and entered a right-hand spin from which he was unable to recover.

Sgt (pilot u/t) John Cameron Johnston (748063), RAFVR, aged 25, was the son of John Matheson Johnston and Agnes Cameron Johnston of Newton Mearns, Renfrewshire. He is buried in Glasgow Necropolis.

18 July (Thursday)
Taking off from field following previous forced landing. 6 SFTS (RAF Little Rissington, Gloucestershire)
Avro Anson I (N5248) hit a hedge during take-off from field 'near Cosford' at 19.40 hrs. The aircraft had been force-landed by a pupil pilot a few days earlier and an instructor was brought in to fly the aircraft out. Before he could do so, several hedges had to be removed to provide a longer take-off run but, despite this being done, the aircraft struck a hedge during take-off which damaged the tailplane (although it appears the instructor still managed to fly it back to base).

F/O (instructor pilot) Frank John French (72120), RAF, was born on 5 February 1919 and had joined the RAF in early 1939 but little is known of his military service until March 1944 when he was awarded the DFC for sinking a U-boat while flying a Catalina flying boat out of Sullom Voe, in the Shetland Islands, with 210 Squadron. Six months later he was awarded the AFC for his part in rescuing the crew of a Liberator that had force-landed in the sea 540 miles north of the Shetland Islands on 21 July. He remained in the RAF after the war and was appointed an MBE in the New Year's Honours list 1958 while serving as a wing commander. He died in Ipswich in 1986.

31 July (Wednesday)
Solo night training flight. 10 SFTS (RAF Tern Hill, Shropshire)
Avro Anson I (N9680) crashed at Kenstone, one mile west of Hodnet, at 00.45 hrs. After taking off on his first solo night flight, the pilot climbed to 1,000 feet then turned across wind and began to lose height rapidly before striking a tree on high ground and crashing, suffering serious injuries.

Sgt (pilot u/t) Oscar Keith David Pulvermacher (742576), RAFVR. Born in Hampstead, London, on 28 February 1917, he was the son of Oscar and Marie Pulvermacher. He eventually recovered from his injuries, was commissioned in July 1943 and survived the war. He died in Cape Town, South Africa in September 1986.

Sgt Keith Pulvermacher [TNA]

1 August (Thursday)
Delivery flight from RAF Woodley, Berkshire, to RAF Shawbury, Shropshire. 3 FPP (White Waltham, Berkshire)
Miles Magister I (T9811) force-landed at Billingsley, six miles south of Bridgnorth, at 13.00 hrs. The aircraft was being ferried from the Miles Aircraft Ltd (at the time known as Philips & Powis Aircraft) airfield to RAF Shawbury when the pilot became lost and decided to force-land in a field as his fuel was running low. The name of the pilot is unknown.

15 August (Thursday)
Low-level bombing exercise at Fenns Moss bombing range. 11 SFTS (RAF Shawbury, Shropshire)
Airspeed Oxford I (N4595) force-landed in 'Long Meadow field', Moreton Corbet, at 15.50 hrs. Moments after leaving the ground, the starboard engine began to falter and fire intermittently at 200 feet and the pilot was forced to belly-land in a field ahead and was unhurt.

Sgt (pilot u/t) Henry Menary (748613), RAFVR. On completion of his training he was posted to 22 Squadron and flew Beaufort aircraft on anti-shipping strikes. In August 1941 he was awarded the DFM for his 'unquenchable enthusiasm for operations' and, in particular, for sinking a 5,000-ton ship off the Frisian Islands on 14 May in the face of heavy flak. He did not survive his tour and failed to return from a 'gardening' (mine laying) op to Brest on 27 August 1941 in a Beaufort (N1171). His body was later washed ashore on the Isles of Scilly where he was laid to rest.

17 August (Saturday)
Solo training flight. 5 SFTS (RAF Sealand, Flintshire)
Miles Master I (N7768) force-landed at Hordley, to the south-west of Ellesmere, at 12.15 hrs. The pilot force-landed, with wheels retracted, after the engine failed during the flight.

Sgt (pilot u/t) Arthur Ben Alfred Smith (742079), RAFVR, was commissioned in May 1942. Little is known of his military service other than that he is believed to have flown Mosquitos on night intruder operations with 239 Squadron later in the war. He survived the war, attaining the rank of flight lieutenant, and died in January 2000 in Newport.

18 August (Sunday)
Ferry flight to and from unknown airfields. 3 FPP (White Waltham, Berkshire)
Hawker Hurricane I (P3612) force-landed at Wooton, near Quatt, to the south-east of Bridgnorth, at 17.00 hrs. After the pilot allowed the aircraft's engine to fail due to 'mishandling', he was forced to make a belly-landing in a wheat field and, although uninjured, he was 'permanently suspended from flying duties' as a consequence.

First Officer (pilot) Leopold Frank Partridge, ATA. Born in Potters Bar, Hertfordshire on 14 June 1901, he was a notable footballer and athlete in his early life and had competed as a hurdler in the 1924 Paris Olympics. He gained his pilot's licence at the Airwork School of Flying in August 1931 while in business with his father running an antiques dealership. Following the outbreak of war, he volunteered for the ATA, but his contract was terminated in December 1940 on his being appointed a liaison officer. He died in Dublin in 1976.

5 September (Thursday)
Solo training flight. 11 SFTS (RAF Shawbury, Shropshire)
Airspeed Oxford I (R6296) force-landed at High Hatton, to the west of Peplow, at 12.30 hrs. After encountering a severe rainstorm, in which visibility was practically nil, the pupil pilot was unable to locate the airfield and made a precautionary landing in a field.

Sgt (pilot u/t) Peter John Walker (903305), RAFVR. On completion of his training he joined 107 Squadron, flying Blenheim bombers on anti-submarine and shipping patrols over the North Sea. He failed to return from an anti-shipping strike in a Blenheim (V6367) on 11 June 1941 and is commemorated on the Runnymede Memorial along with his crew.

5 September (Thursday)
Ferry flight to Burtonwood, Lancashire, via Woodford, Cheshire. RAF North Coates, Lincolnshire
Fairey Swordfish I (L7653) force landed at Shifnal at 13.15 hrs. The pilot force landed for unknown reasons and the tail wheel was damaged.

Sub Lt (A) Maurice Evelyn Sier, RNVR, was born in Camberwell in 1919. He survived the war and died in Surrey in 1973.

6 September (Friday)
Operational patrol. 64 Squadron (RAF Ringway, Cheshire – detached flight from RAF Leconfield)
Supermarine Spitfire IA (K9903) crashed 'near Tern Hill' at 08.30 hrs. Few details are known of this accident other than that five aircraft took off for an operational patrol and, possibly due to bad weather, one aircraft landed back at Ringway, three were diverted and landed at Tern Hill, while this aircraft crashed nearby and was written off, although the pilot was unhurt.

Sgt (pilot) Harry Walpole Charnock (901005), RAFVR, was born in Chorley, Lancashire on 20 June 1905. He had originally been commissioned in the RAF in 1925 but was cashiered by general court-martial for a low-flying offence and dismissed from the service in 1930. After re-enlisting as an NCO following the outbreak of war, he was posted to 64 Squadron, then 19 Squadron and in April 1942 was awarded the DFM after destroying four enemy aircraft. A further tour of operations was completed with 72 Squadron and, in April 1943, he was awarded the DFC, shortly after being commissioned. Little is known of his subsequent movements until August 1944 when he began a posting with 41 Squadron which lasted until the end of the war. He died in May 1974.

8 September (Sunday)
Low-flying training. 10 SFTS (RAF Tern Hill, Shropshire)
Avro Anson I (N5244) crashed at Springfields Farm, Ercall Heath, near Tibberton, at 18.30 hrs. The instructor

Sgt Vincent Brooke [TNA]

took off at 17.50 hrs, in excellent weather conditions, to give low-flying instruction to three pupil pilots but, during the flight, the aircraft was seen suddenly to climb steeply to 300 feet and then fall into a steep turning dive and crash. The accident investigation concluded that this was due to 'the instructor either allowing one of his pupils or himself to stall the aeroplane at a height from which normal recovery was not possible without striking the ground'. It does not explain why the pilot climbed steeply, but an explanation may come from John Handley, who was a child living at Spring Cottages at the time:

> One Sunday afternoon during the war, they were playing around and diving. There's a lot of woods around there, but there was a big tree in the hedge surrounding the wood and apparently they pulled back sharp on the joystick to miss a big tree and broke its back and crashed to the ground. I don't know why they were that low but it came back and broke its back and crashed to the ground.

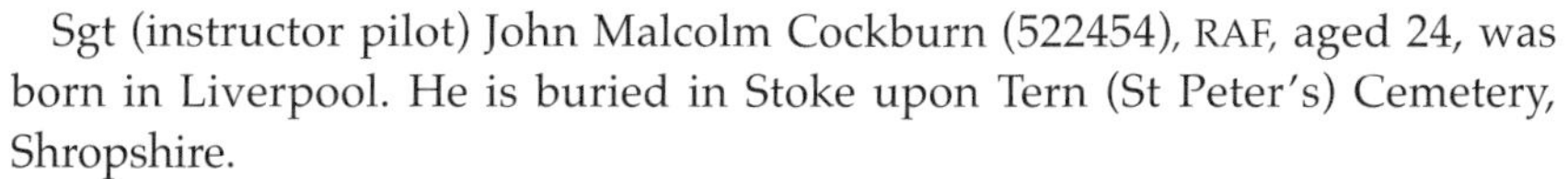

Sgt (instructor pilot) John Malcolm Cockburn (522454), RAF, aged 24, was born in Liverpool. He is buried in Stoke upon Tern (St Peter's) Cemetery, Shropshire.

Sgt Alexander Appleford [TNA]

A/Sgt (pilot u/t) Vincent Christopher Clanfergael Brooke (903461), RAFVR, aged 23, was born in Surrey on 14 October 1916, the son of Edward Arden and Lily Edith Evangeline Brooke (née O'Halloran). After gaining a scholarship to study at Strathcona Academy in Montreal, Canada (where he was awarded a Trustees' Medal for General Proficiency) he returned to the UK and worked as a life assurance rep. While living in Ealing he had also gained a civilian pilot's licence in May 1939 at the Airwork Flying Club. He is buried in Torquay Cemetery, Devon.

A/Sgt (pilot u/t) Alexander Horatio Nelson Appleford (901440), RAFVR, aged 24, was the son of Maj Walter Alexander Nelson Appleford and Lilian Mary Appleford of Bath and was a descendant of Admiral Nelson. His father, who was a serving officer in the Pioneer Corps, also died in the war on 27 June 1941, while his younger brother, Robin, flew Spitfires with 66 Squadron during the Battle of Britain and had been shot down in combat over the Thames Estuary on 4 September. He was recovering from his wounds at home when he learned of his elder brother's death at Tern Hill. Sgt Appleford is buried in Castle Combe (St Andrew) Churchyard, Wiltshire.

13 September (Friday)
Training flight. 5 SFTS (RAF Sealand, Flintshire)
Miles Master I (N7580) force-landed adjacent to Baschurch railway station at 13.30 hrs. After a ballast weight came adrift in flight, causing the elevator to jam, the pilot made a precautionary landing but could not get the tail down and the aircraft ran through a hedge before coming to a stop.

Sgt (pilot u/t) Walter Wilson (748084), RAFVR. On completion of his training he was posted to 222 Squadron and was, sadly, killed on 27 March 1941 when he collided with another of the squadron's Spitfires over Colton, to the west of Norwich. Sgt Wilson, who was 21 years old, was the son of Herbert W and Emily N Wilson. He is buried in Grimsby (Scartho Road) Cemetery.

15 September (Sunday)
Delivery flight from the Bristol Aeroplane Company, Filton, Gloucestershire, to RAF Shawbury, Shropshire. 3 FPP (White Waltham, Berkshire)

Bristol Beaufighter IF (R2093) force-landed in a field '1/2 mile east of Shawbury' at 11.25 hrs. While making a landing approach to RAF Shawbury from the east, one of the aircraft's engines failed and the pilot was forced to belly-land in a small field and was unhurt.

Capt (pilot) David Prowse, BOAC (on secondment to the ATA). Capt Prowse had served with the RAF in the early 1930s before joining British Airways Ltd in January 1936, flying DH86s and Lockheeds. During this pre-war period, he flew as second pilot on the aircraft that took Neville Chamberlain to Munich in September 1938 and also, in August 1939, was lucky to survive a serious incident on the London–Zurich service, when an engine fire resulted in his belly-landing in a French field. During the war Prowse served with BOAC and RAF Ferry Command (including time on secondment to the ATA) and was appointed an MBE in June 1941 for his services with BOAC. Little is known of his wartime movements other than that he was involved in the hazardous 'ball-bearing run' between Stockholm and Leuchars from 1943 onwards and flew numerous Ferry Command flights across the Atlantic. After the war he served with various companies and also flew converted Halifax freighters during the Berlin Airlift. He rejoined BOAC in 1967 and was involved in ground duties until his death in London, in August 1974.

22 September (Sunday)
Formation flying exercise. 13 OTU (RAF Bicester, Oxfordshire)
Bristol Blenheim IV (N6228) force-landed at Claverley, near Bridgnorth, at 14.15 hrs. While flying in bad weather the pilot became lost after separating from his formation and, rather than flying back towards better weather, or using his wireless transmitter to locate his position, he continued ahead. With his fuel running low and still unsure of his whereabouts, the pilot decided to make a precautionary landing in a small field and the aircraft ran through a fence and was badly damaged.

P/O (pilot u/t) Rothes John McKain Meek (41444), RAF, was native of Wellington in New Zealand. He had attended Wellington College and Victoria University in Wellington before travelling to the UK to join the RAF prior to the outbreak of war. He subsequently relinquished his commission in August 1941 on account of ill health and returned to New Zealand, where he died in 1984.

23 September (Monday)
Formation flying exercise. 11 SFTS (RAF Shawbury, Shropshire)
Airspeed Oxford I (N4637) crashed at Hadnall at 11.40 hrs. Three pilots from the ATS were flying in formation when a pilot from the ITS dived at them and collided with one of the aircraft. Sgt William Hall, who was piloting one of the ATS aircraft, recalled the incident in his memoirs:

> ... we took off again at 11.40. Flying side by side at about 700 feet with Alec on my starboard wing I saw an Oxford diving down towards us. As he neared us he started to pull up the nose of his plane but he appeared to sink down and trying to veer away he hit Alec's plane. Alec's plane seemed to hover for a moment and I can still see him getting out of his seat to go back to the door with the apparent intention of baling out. His plane disappeared under mine and as I swung round to see what had happened both planes were on fire on the ground. The other pilot was killed. Alec was too low to get out. What a waste of such a fine looking and talented person!

Sgt (pilot u/t) Alexander Glass Dunbar (968153), RAFVR, aged 23, was the son of Francis G and Mary Dunbar of Helensburgh. He is buried in Cardross Cemetery, Dumbartonshire.

AC2 (flight mechanic, travelling as passenger) Charles Marcel Gwynn (983903), RAFVR, aged 25, was the son of Albert and Maud Gwynn and the husband of Sarah Phyllis Gwynn of Uplands, Swansea. He is buried in Pontlliw (Carmel) Chapelyard, Glamorganshire.

Training flight. 11 SFTS (RAF Shawbury, Shropshire)
Airspeed Oxford I (N4769) crashed at Hadnall following the collision described above.

LAC (pilot u/t) Norman Henry Pulford (937486), RAFVR, aged 20, was the son of Harold Henry and Kathleen Pulford of Firth Park, Sheffield. He is buried in Sheffield (Shiregreen) Cemetery.

24 September (Tuesday)
Practice slow rolls and steep turns. 7 OTU (RAF Hawarden, Flintshire)
Supermarine Spitfire IA (N3166) force-landed at Hordley, to the south-west of Ellesmere, at 19.00 hrs. The pilot was forced to belly-land in a field after the engine failed during the flight.

P/O (pilot u/t) Norman McHardy Brown (84958), RAFVR, was born in Edinburgh on 27 July 1919 and educated at George Heriot's School. On completion of his training he was posted to 611 Squadron on 28 September 1940 and flew Spitfires during the closing stages of the Battle of Britain before transferring to 41 Squadron, at Hornchurch, two weeks later. On 1 November he overshot the airfield in poor visibility, entered the London barrage balloon area and had to force-land near Dagenham after seriously damaging his Spitfire on a balloon cable. He was involved in another forced landing on 7 February 1941 and, two months later, his commission was 'terminated on cessation of duty' and he left the RAFVR. He subsequently worked in the timber industry for the rest of the war and remained in the Forestry Commission until his retirement in 1979.

24 September (Tuesday)
Solo training flight. 10 SFTS (RAF Tern Hill)
Avro Anson I (N9547) force-landed at Ditherington, on the outskirts of Shrewsbury, at 19.50 hrs. After becoming lost the pilot made a precautionary landing in a small field and the aircraft ran through a hedge and into a ditch, causing the undercarriage to collapse.

LAC (pilot u/t) Harris Black (923087), RAFVR, on completion of his training, was posted to 10 Squadron, flying Whitley bombers on night raids over north-west Europe. He did not survive his tour and was killed on 8 July 1941 when his Whitley (Z6816) failed to return from an op to Osnabrück, Germany. Sgt Black and his crew are commemorated on the Runnymede Memorial.

25 September (Wednesday)
Instrument flying practice. 10 SFTS (RAF Tern Hill, Shropshire)
Avro Anson I (L7071) crashed at Eaton Constantine, near Cressage, at 15.30 hrs. While taking part in a routine training flight the pupil pilot began unauthorised low flying, during which he allowed the aircraft to strike a telegraph pole and wires, before crashing into a field. Incredibly, he escaped serious injury.

Sgt (pilot u/t) Hilton Jones (965692), RAFVR, on completion of his training,

Sgt Hilton Jones [TNA]

The wreckage of Anson L7071 pictured in a field at Eaton Constantine [Tom Yates via Edward Doylerush]

was posted to 220 Squadron flying Lockheed Hudsons on North Sea air patrols. On 19 October 1941, he failed to return from a reconnaissance flight between Stadlandet and Bergen in a Hudson (AM724). Sgt Jones was the 20-year-old son of Mabel Jones from Pontardulais, Glamorgan. He is commem-orated on the Runnymede Memorial.

4 October (Friday)
Training flight. 15 SFTS (RAF Kidlington, Oxfordshire)
North American Harvard I (P5796) force-landed at 'Morville Heath crossroads', one mile west of Bridgnorth, at 16.30 hrs. Little is known of the accident other than that the pilot force-landed in a field and the aircraft was placed under guard by RAF Bridgnorth.

P/O (pilot u/t?) Richard Keith Potter (81364), RAFVR, survived the war and was awarded the AFC in the New Year of 1946 for his services as a flying instructor at RAF Ambala, in India, during the latter stages of the war.

6 October (Sunday)
'Wind, speed and D/F flight.' 11 SFTS (RAF Shawbury, Shropshire)
Airspeed Oxford I (R6291) force-landed at 'Tibberton village near Ellesmere' (although no such village can be found of that name near Ellesmere). After encountering heavy rain and mist over Ellesmere the pilot tried to return to the airfield but, in the deteriorating weather, he was unable to find it and made a precautionary landing in a field.

Sgt (pilot u/t?) John Fosbroke Slatter (937676), RAFVR, was commissioned the following month and eventually joined 105 Squadron flying Mosquitos. He was killed during a training flight on 5 February 1944 when his Mosquito (DZ548) collided with a USAAF B-17 (42-97480) over St Ives in Cambridgeshire. F/Lt Slatter, who was the son of Henry John Brandis and Kathleen Norah Slatter of Stratford on Avon and the husband of Cynthia Dorothy Slatter, was twenty-four years old. He is buried in Salford Priors (St Matthew) Churchyard, Worcestershire.

Sgt (passenger) Walker.

18 October (Friday)
Transit flight to new base. 2 School of Air Navigation (RAF St Athan, Glamorgan)
Avro Anson I (K6155) force-landed at Ludlow at 16.30 hrs. At the time of the accident the unit was in the process of relocating to its new base at RAF Cranage in Cheshire and this aircraft was part of an advanced party making its way there. During the flight the pilot encountered bad weather and decided to make a precautionary landing. After touching down, the brakes failed to take full effect due to the wet ground and heavy load, causing the aircraft to bounce and crash through a hedge before coming to a stop.

F/O (pilot) Stevens.

23 October (Wednesday)
Unknown flight detail. Station Flight, Andover (RAF Andover, Hampshire)
Miles Magister I (N3908) force-landed at Cressage at 16.15 hrs. Little is known of this accident other than that the pilot force-landed in a field. The name of the pilot is unknown.

31 October (Thursday)
Steep turns, circuits and landings. 11 SFTS (RAF Shawbury, Shropshire)
Airspeed Oxford I (N4594) force-landed at 'Kings Bromley', near RAF Bridgnorth, at 10.20 hrs. After carrying out some steep turns the pilot found that he could not pinpoint his position and decided to

make a precautionary landing in a field near RAF Bridgnorth. He was subsequently conveyed back to RAF Shawbury while the aircraft was placed under guard by airmen from RAF Bridgnorth until it could be flown out by an instructor three days later.

LAC (pilot u/t) Reginald Alfred 'Dusty' Miller (928613), RAFVR, hailed from Sully, Glamorgan and was commissioned in May 1942. On completion of his training, he set sail for the Middle East on board the RMS *Laconia*. During the voyage the ship was torpedoed on 12 September 1942 and Miller spent several days in a life raft before being rescued by a Vichy cruiser and taken to North Africa. He eventually joined 89 Squadron flying Beaufighters in the Mediterranean theatre and shot down four enemy aircraft before being awarded the DFC in February 1943. Following his tour he was posted back to the UK and subsequently joined 604 Squadron, piloting Mosquitos over north-west Europe. During this second tour, he destroyed a further three enemy aircraft and, in October 1944, was awarded a bar to his DFC. Sadly, he would not survive the war and was killed on 26 April 1945 piloting a Mosquito (RS579) of the Night Fighter Development Unit, when it was shot down by flak over Austria. F/Lt Miller is buried in Klagenfurt War Cemetery in Austria.

3 November (Sunday)
Return flight to RAF Shawbury following previous forced landing. 11 SFTS (RAF Shawbury, Shropshire) Airspeed Oxford I (N4594) taking off from a field at 'King's Bromley' following forced landing.
In a letter written to the author in January 2010, the pilot, Bob Pugh, described how he was tasked with flying the aircraft out following a precautionary landing three days earlier.

> I was alone in the Flight Office when I received a telephone call about a student having force landed. I sought advice from the Flight Commander of another flight and he said he would fly me to the site to assess the situation. When we arrived there he said that the aircraft could be flown out. I suggested we land and I would collect the aircraft. He demurred and said his aircraft was underpowered and I should return the next day by road for the fly-out. I returned the next day with some ground crew and whilst they were doing a daily inspection I examined the field assessing the best take-off run. On a take-off run from rough ground the aircraft bounces and then settles down again until full flying speed is reached. In this case the aircraft was bouncing until it achieved rather a higher bounce but I felt if I tried to hold it off it would sink back on the hedge and I would crash. Therefore, I pushed the control forward and it bounced over and although the wheels went through the hedge and although I felt some contact, I became airborne, climbed away, beat up the small crowd and returned to base. On landing I found that a post hidden in the hedge had ripped a hole about twelve feet by one foot in the belly of the aircraft.

P/O (instructor pilot) Robert Michael (Bob) Pugh (42883), RAFVR, was born on 26 June 1921, the son of Thomas Garnet Pugh and Agnes Mary Pugh of Farnborough. His brother, Jack, had been killed on 21 May 1940 while serving as a pilot with the RAF. Before his posting to RAF Shawbury as an instructor, in October 1940, Bob had flown Ansons on anti-submarine patrols in Northern Ireland with 502 Squadron. He left Shawbury soon after the incident at Bridgnorth and served as an instructor in Canada until August 1942 when he returned to the UK to prepare for operations. On completion of his operational training he was posted to the Middle East flying Wellington bombers with 38 Squadron, but in August 1943 he returned to the UK at his mother's request after his other brother, Tom, was killed flying with 182 Squadron. He subsequently spent the remainder of the war as a flying instructor and, in the New Year of 1946, was awarded the Air Force Cross. He retired from the RAF as a squadron leader in September 1968.

16 November (Saturday)
Bombing raid on an aircraft factory on the outskirts of Coventry (a follow-up to the infamous Coventry

Parts of the Heinkel's fuselage at Derrington Farm. [Express & Star]

raids the previous night). *Kampfgeschwader 53 'Legion Condor'* (Lille Vendeville, France)

Heinkel He 111 (5509, bearing the fuselage code A1+LN), broke up and wreckage was scattered over a large area concentrated between Derrington and Callaughton, to the south of Much Wenlock, at 00.30 hrs. Twelve aircraft took off from their base at two minute intervals, starting at 22.00 hrs, on 15 November and then crossed the English coast at 10,500 feet over the North Foreland in Kent. Soon afterwards the crew of this aircraft, who were only on their second operational flight, saw six barrage balloons just below them, so they climbed to 17,000 feet as they skirted around the north of London and approached Coventry from the south. Despite bad icing being experienced on the approach, the crew managed to bomb their objective, but as they turned towards home the aircraft became completely uncontrollable due to further icing and the pilot ordered his crew to bale out as the aircraft plummeted out of control and began to disintegrate. The *Shrewsbury Chronicle* newspaper, which ran a dramatic account of the incident, described how

> … the tail of the plane and the rear part of the fuselage snapped off as cleanly as if cut by a knife and floated to earth to come to rest on an even keel in the centre of a ploughed field at Monkhopton. The rudderless craft then roared down to destruction in pastureland at Netchwood, Monkhopton, crashing about a mile and a half from where the tail of the plane had landed.
>
> During those last frantic seconds in the air the Germans released a cargo of incendiary bombs and it was the flares of these that ultimately led to the discovery of the plane and its crew. The crew in the central cabin of the plane would have little difficulty in baling out after the tail snapped off for the cabin was open wide.
>
> Two of the crew made more or less successful landings by para-chute, though one of them was injured. The uninjured man dragged his companion to the shelter of a hedge bottom where they lay throughout the night. They had descended at Callaughton, Much Wenlock, several miles from the wreckage, near the piggeries on Mr J W Milners farm. Early on Saturday morning in the garden of a cottage at Callaughton, occupied by Mr Rees, there was found an open parachute and the body of a young German with terrible head injuries. The youth must have been killed instantly.

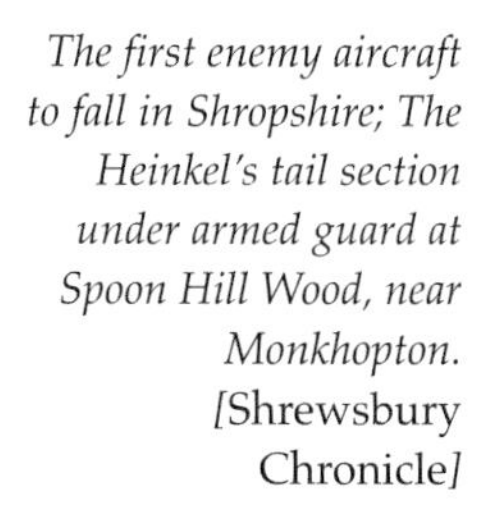

The first enemy aircraft to fall in Shropshire; The Heinkel's tail section under armed guard at Spoon Hill Wood, near Monkhopton. [Shrewsbury Chronicle]

Feldwebel
Alfred Achstaller
[Manfred Achstaller]

The fourth man, the pilot [incorrect, it was the bomb aimer], was not found, despite intensive search, until 11 o'clock on Saturday morning. His body was in a furrow, hidden by the foliage of rows of mangolds. He too, had been killed instantaneously, for his parachute had not opened and his body was barely 500 yards from the main part of the plane, it appears he baled out too late.

The wreckage of the aeroplane was found by a farmer and his son, who were looking for fires, following the shower of incendiary bombs and they immediately communicated with the police. The first body was discovered at Callaughton and later, when the police were scouring the district, the uninjured airman came across the fields and handed over his revolver to a police officer, indicating by gesture that he had a wounded man with him.

Both men were taken to hospital under guard and the search was intensified for the other member of the crew. Members of the Home Guard in the district worked from the early hours of the morning, assisting in the search, together with police and soldiers. Woods were surrounded and 'beaten' without success and it was only after a search lasting nearly seven hours that the body of the fourth man – the dead pilot [incorrect, it was the bomb aimer] – was discovered.

The bodies of the two airmen were subsequently taken to RAF Bridgnorth's morgue, while the two injured were treated in the station hospital before being interrogated. In the mean time, an armed guard was placed on the wreckage to stop any would-be souvenir hunters, although hundreds still came to catch a glimpse of the infamous swastika.

Lt (pilot) Karl Svata, *Luftwaffe*, aged 34, a native of Müllegg in Austria, had previously served in the Austrian Army, but following the annexation of Austria, volunteered to join the *Luftwaffe* in August 1938. On completion of his training he was posted to *KG*53 on 1 November 1940 and had only completed one operational flight with his crew on the night of 14/15 November (during the infamous Coventry raids). He spent the remainder of the war in a POW camp in Canada.

Feldwebel (Obs) Alfred Achstaller, *Luftwaffe*, aged 26, was a native of the Black Forest in southern Germany. He had served in the German army before the war and had marched into Austria in 1938 as part of its annexation by Germany, subsequently transferring to the *Luftwaffe* in August 1939. He was posted to *KG*53 on 1 November 1940 after completing his observer training. Following his capture, he was sent to Canada where he spent the remainder of the war in Camp 133, near Lethbridge, Alberta.

Unteroffizier (W/Op) Josef (Sepp) Mutzl, *Luftwaffe*, aged 23, was originally buried in Bridgnorth Cemetery but was later reinterred in the German War Cemetery at Cannock. He came from Augsburg in Bavaria and it was his body that was found in a garden at Callaughton.

Feldwebel (AB) Heinrich Engelken, *Luftwaffe*, aged 26, was also originally buried in Bridgnorth Cemetery but was later reinterred in the German War Cemetery at Cannock. He came from Ostendorf in Germany and it was his body that was found in the mangold field.

26 November (Tuesday)
Solo elementary flying practice. 5 SFTS (RAF Tern Hill, Shropshire)
Miles Master I (T8397) crashed at Uffington, near Shrewsbury, at 14.10 hrs. After allowing the aircraft to stall in a steep turn at approximately 1,000 feet, the pilot was unable to recover from the resultant spin and the aircraft dived into the ground.

LAC Alfred Bethell [Adrian Sillitoe]

LAC (pilot u/t) Alfred William Bethell (937701), RAFVR, aged 22, was the son of William Henry and Emila Rose Bethell (née Bate) of Shirley. He is buried in Shirley (St James) Cemetery, Solihull.

27 November (Wednesday)
Operational patrol. 306 (Polish) Squadron (RAF Tern Hill, Shropshire)
Hawker Hurricane I (L1717, bearing the fuselage code UZ-?) crash-landed 'three miles south of Shrewsbury' (putting it roughly in the area between Bayston Hill and Condover) at 16.00 hrs. While on patrol the engine caught fire suddenly, due to a mechanical defect, and the pilot immediately put the aircraft into a dive to put the flames out, but then had to belly-land when the engine failed. The injured pilot was taken to the Royal Salop Infirmary where he was kept under observation for three days before returning to his squadron.

P/O Aleksander Petruszka [TNA]

P/O (pilot) Aleksander Petruszka (P0319), PAF, served with 306 Squadron from 5 November 1940 until 10 March 1941, when he was posted to 60 OTU. Little is known of his subsequent military service until he was posted back to 60 OTU in early 1944 to undergo operational training on Mosquitos at RAF High Ercall. He did not survive his training and was killed on 10 March 1944 when his Mosquito (HJ933) crashed at Hankelow, Cheshire, during a training flight. F/Lt Petruszka was twenty-seven years old and is buried in Shawbury (St Mary's) Churchyard alongside his navigator, Sgt J W Burzynski.

2 December (Monday)
Night dual circuits and landings. 5 SFTS (RAF Tern Hill, Shropshire)
Miles Master I (N7597) crashed at 'Holme Farm, Hodnet' (although one source states Holme Farm, Peplow) at 02.00 hrs. Shortly after taking off the aircraft was seen to enter cloud momentarily before re-appearing in a nose-dive. The cause was believed to be that 'the pilot, having flown into cloud and lost touch with the flare path and the leading lights, allowed the aircraft to drop its nose and probably the starboard wing to such an extent as to put the blind flying instruments out of action and flew into the ground on a steep right hand turn'.

F/O (instructor pilot) Hubert Davenport Buswell (43366), RAF, aged 28, was the son of the late Cecil J Buswell and Mrs Ellen Elizabeth Buswell (née Bobart) of Warborough. He had served in the RAF before the war as an NCO and, in March 1939, his name had been published in *The Times* in recognition of 'distinguished services rendered in connection with the operations in the Aden Protectorate on April 29 and 30 1938 and from July 6 to September 4'. He is buried in Warborough (St Laurence) Churchyard, Oxfordshire.

LAC (pilot u/t) Richard Anthony (Tony) Chant (958288), RAFVR, aged 23, was the son of Maurice George and Alice Margaret Hall Chant of Moor Park, Hertfordshire. He is buried in Stoke upon Tern (St Peter's) Cemetery, Shropshire.

2 December (Monday)
Solo training flight. 5 SFTS (RAF Tern Hill, Shropshire)
Miles Master I (N7875) force-landed at Brandwood, between Sleap and Burlton, to the south-west of Wem. After becoming lost when thick fog obscured the ground, the pilot made a precautionary landing, during which the undercarriage collapsed on rough ground.

LAC (pilot u/t) Michael Charles Folkard (1160839), RAFVR, who was commissioned in July 1942, survived the war and attained the rank of flight lieutenant.

9 December (Monday)
Dual night training flight. 11 SFTS (RAF Shawbury, Shropshire)
Airspeed Oxford I (R6287) crashed at 'Park Farm, Shawbury', at 03.55 hrs. The pupil pilot, of the ITS, was in control when he is believed to have turned the aircraft downwind, parallel to the flare path, and then, either deliberately or accidentally, put the aircraft into a steep left hand turn, which increased before hitting a tree and crashing.

F/O (instructor pilot) William John Boston Wadie (73050), RAFVR, aged 23, was the son of William Boston Wadie and Agnes Kate Wadie of Teddington, Middlesex, and the husband of Moya Molshee Gillow Wadie (née Sweeney). He had been posted to the unit as an instructor exactly three months earlier. He is buried in Leaton (Holy Trinity) Churchyard, Shropshire.

LAC (pilot u/t) Reginald Basil Wright (999008), RAFVR, aged 23, was the son of Joseph Henry and Florence Anne Wright of Copmanthorpe, Yorkshire. He is buried in Shawbury (St Mary's) Churchyard.

14 December (Saturday)
Cross-country exercise. 17 OTU (RAF Upwood, Cambridgeshire)
Bristol Blenheim IV (L4835) crashed into Clee Hill (at map reference 605761), near Ludlow, at 12.45 hrs. The trainee crew were flying at 1,200 feet in deteriorating weather conditions when the aircraft crashed into the side of the hill, which was totally obscured by cloud.

Sgt (pilot) Ian Munro Curror (754790), RAFVR, aged 19, was the son of Finlay Munro Curror and Dorothy May Curror (née Ellis) of Highfield, Southampton. He is commemorated at the Cambridge Crematorium.

Sgt (Obs) Alfred James Victor Secker (40743), RNZAF, aged 27, was the son of Maj Victor Hart Secker and Lorna Marjorie Secker of Te Awanga, in the Hawkes Bay region of New Zealand. He is buried in Bury Cemetery (near Upwood airfield).

Sgt (W/AG) John Pinchard (759021), RAFVR, aged 20, was the son of Walter and Annie Pinchard of Walker, Newcastle-upon-Tyne. He is buried in Newcastle-upon-Tyne (Byker and Heaton) Cemetery.

15 December (Sunday)
Training flight. 11 SFTS (RAF Shawbury, Shropshire)
Airspeed Oxford I (L9682) force-landed near Baschurch. After becoming lost in poor visibility the pilot made a successful precautionary landing in a field.

LAC (pilot u/t) George Edmund Betts (928338), RAFVR, was commissioned on 9 July 1943 and survived the war. He died in St Albans in 1999.

17 December (Tuesday)
Dual training flight. 5 SFTS (RAF Tern Hill, Shropshire)
Miles Master I (N7691) crashed at Tern Hill airfield at 09.50 hrs. While taking off from the airfield the instructor found that the controls were very sluggish. As soon as the wheels left the ground, the aircraft side-slipped and crashed, killing the pupil and seriously injuring the instructor. The subsequent investigation found that the frost covers had not been fitted the previous night and, as a result, frost had accumulated on the mainplanes, reducing their effectiveness and causing the sluggish handling on take-off.

Acting F/O (instructor pilot) William Norman Basson (78539), RAFVR, was born in Hemel Hemstead, on 29 June 1912. He gained his pilot's licence in October 1938 at the Elementary and Reserve Flying Training School in Luton. Commissioned in February 1940, little is known of his military service other than that he was mentioned in despatches in June 1944 and again in January 1945, both while ranked as an acting squadron leader. He eventually relinquished his commission as a squadron leader, in October 1948, due to medical unfitness. He died in Chelmsford in 1980.

LAC (pilot u/t) Harold Walter Harris Joseph (956834), *RAFVR*, aged 24, was the son of Clifton Hyman Joseph and Vera Rachel Joseph of Armadale, Melbourne, Australia. He is buried in Stoke upon Tern (St Peter's) Cemetery, Shropshire.

17 December (Tuesday)
Ferry flight from RAF Hooton Park, Cheshire (although one source states Ringway)–RAF Cardiff. 8 AACU (RAF Cardiff, Clamorgan)
DH-89A Dragon Rapide (G-AFME) force-landed at Newport. The aircraft was being flown back to its base, after having night-flying equipment fitted at Carlux Ltd, when the pilot encountered thick fog and decided to make a precautionary landing in a field. As he did so, however, he allowed the aircraft to hit the branches of a tree, damaging it slightly, which meant that it could not be flown out until 28 December after it had been repaired *in situ*.

Sgt (pilot) Ian Neil MacLaren (1181220), RAFVR, was commissioned in June 1943 and remained in the RAF after the war. He was awarded the Queen's Commendation for Valuable Service in the Air in June 1955. He died in 2005.

19 December (Thursday)
Solo steep turns and precautionary landings practice. 11 SFTS (RAF Shawbury, Shropshire)
Airspeed Oxford I (L4599) force-landed at More, near Bishops Castle, at 13.10 hrs. After visibility deteriorated suddenly during the flight, the pupil pilot decided to make a precautionary landing but misjudged the size of the field. The aircraft ran through a hedge and down a bank, tearing the undercarriage off.

LAC (pilot u/t) Cyril John Simmonds (1375437), RAFVR, was commissioned in December 1941 and subsequently joined 466 Squadron but was killed on 30 January 1943, when his Wellington (HE397) was shot down on an 'op' to Emden. F/Lt Simmonds, who was 27 years old, was the son of William David and Alice Rosina Simmonds of New Barnet, Hertfordshire. He and his crew are commemorated on the Runnymede Memorial.

20 December (Friday)
Day solo training flight. 5 SFTS (RAF Tern Hill, Shropshire)
Miles Master I (N7581) force-landed at 'Ashford Grange, 2½ miles from Tern Hill' (presumably between Fauls and Bletchley) at 14.30 hrs. During the course of the flight the engine failed and the pilot 'acted well under the circumstances' and belly-landed in a field.

LAC (pilot u/t) Peter William Crump (908977), RAFVR. On completion of his training he was posted to 274 Squadron flying Hurricanes over the Western Desert but did not survive his tour. On 3 June 1941 he is believed to have been shot down in a Hurricane (Z4369) when his section was attacked by Me109s while covering a fleet sailing towards Tobruk. Sgt Crump, who was 21 years old, was the son of Charles F and Agnes Crump of Horsham, Sussex. He is commemorated on the Alamein Memorial.

22 December (Sunday)
Solo cross-country flight. 11 SFTS (RAF Shawbury, Shropshire)
Airspeed Oxford I (N4630) crashed taking off after a forced landing at Eaton, near Bishops Castle, at 12.40 hrs. After making a precautionary landing in a field a little earlier, the pupil pilot decided to take off to return to the airfield without first gaining authorization. As he attempted a crosswind take-off the aircraft failed to gain height, struck a hedge and crashed, badly injuring him.

LAC (pilot u/t) Cyril Gethin Thomas (929131), RAFVR, was born on 30 January 1921. He died in Waveney, Suffolk, in 1995.

24 December (Tuesday)
Practice dawn flying. 306 (Polish) Squadron (RAF Tern Hill, Shropshire)
Hawker Hurricane I (V6992, bearing the fuselage code UZ-?) crashed at Hopton, to the south-west of Hodnet, at 08.05 hrs. Little is known of this accident other than that the aircraft dived into the ground in very poor weather conditions.

F/Lt (pilot) Harold Wray Tennant (37431), RAF, aged 25, was the son of Harold Cecil and Alice Mary Tennant of Ferring, Sussex, and the husband of Margot Tennant. F/Lt Tennant had joined the RAF in 1935 and, after completing his training, was posted to 22 (Torpedo) Squadron at Donibristle in November 1936, flying Vickers Vildebeest. He served with the squadron until at least March 1938, following which he was posted to 100 (Torpedo) Squadron in October 1938, flying Vildebeest aircraft in Singapore and Malaya. He then appears to have returned to the UK in 1940 and joined 306 (Polish) Squadron in September 1940 as 'B' Flight's English commander. He is buried in Little Stanmore (St Lawrence) Churchyard, Middlesex alongside his brother, W/Cdr Eric Tennant, DFC, who was also killed whilst serving in the RAF.

30 December (Monday)
Solo training flight. 5 SFTS (RAF Tern Hill, Shropshire)
Miles Master I (N7542) force-landed at Calverhall, to the north west of Market Drayton, at 11.15 hrs. After the engine failed in flight the pupil pilot was forced to belly-land in a field and was unhurt.

LAC (pilot u/t) Anthony Herbert Foord (915323), RAFVR. After completing his training, he was commissioned in January 1941 and posted to 99 Squadron flying Wellington bombers. He was awarded the DFC in October 1941. Little else is known of his military service other than that he survived the war and was mentioned in despatches in the New Year's Honours of 1946 while ranked as an acting squadron leader. He died in October 1997.

LAC Anthony Foord [Fenella Holt]

31 December (Tuesday)
Solo forced landings practice. 5 SFTS (RAF Tern Hill, Shropshire)
Miles Master I (T8442) crashed at Longford Grange, to the west of Market Drayton, at 15.35 hrs. After taking off, the flight leader decided that the weather was unsuitable for the exercise and ordered the formation to break away but, as the pilot of this aircraft did so with insufficient power, his aircraft stalled and dived into the ground.

LAC (pilot u/t) James Docherty (910187), RAFVR, aged 19, was the son of John and Jane Docherty of Dunnville, Ontario, Canada. He is buried in Market Drayton Cemetery, Shropshire.

1941

4 January (Saturday)
Delivery flight from RAF Sywell, Northamptonshire, to RAF Tern Hill. 24 MU (RAF Tern Hill, Shropshire)
Gloster Gauntlet II (K5279) force-landed at Cheswardine at 12.45 hrs. The pilot was en route to Tern Hill

when he was forced to land in a field after the engine failed and the aircraft ran into a hedge.

P/O (pilot) Leslie Arthur Bale (82166), RAFVR, the son of Alderman William Henry Bale, JP, and Mabel Ada Bale of Caversham, Reading, was educated at Reading School and then worked in his father's wholesale tobacco and confectionary business before joining up after the outbreak of war. On completion of his pilot training he appears to have been posted to 24 MU as a test pilot and served there until November 1941, following which he underwent operational training. In mid 1942, he was posted to 272 Squadron, flying Beaufighters over north Africa but, sadly, failed to return from a strafing attack on El Taqa airfield on 14 November 1942, aged 29. He is commemorated on the Malta Memorial.

9 January (Thursday)
Unknown flight detail. 32 Squadron (RAF Middle Wallop, Hampshire)
Hawker Hurricane I (V7125) force-landed at Kenley, between Acton Burnell and Hughley, at 10.40 hrs. Few details are known of this accident other than that the unknown pilot force-landed near Kenley searchlight site after running out of fuel. Soldiers from the battery (manned by 505 Searchlight Battery) were quickly on the scene and checked the pilot was alright before mounting guard on the aircraft.

14 January (Tuesday)
Ferry flight from RAF Aston Down, Gloucestershire, to RAF Sealand, Flintshire. 3 FPP (RAF Hawarden, Flintshire)
Fairey Battle I (L5534) force-landed at Quatford, five miles south-east of Bridgnorth, at 16.30 hrs. After the engine failed in flight the pilot was unable to choose a suitable landing site due to low cloud and, as a result, he touched down in a small field and the aircraft ran into some trees.

First Officer (pilot) Michael Bruce-Porter, ATA. Nothing further is known of this pilot other than that he survived the war.

15 January (Wednesday)
Solo cross-country exercise from Tern Hill–Worcester–Upper Heyford–Tern Hill. 5 SFTS (RAF Tern Hill, Shropshire)
Miles Master I (N7807) force-landed 'five miles north west of Oswestry' (putting it roughly in the area of Selattyn) at 16.00 hrs. The pilot had completed his first leg and landed at Worcester, where he misunderstood instructions that were relayed to him second-hand, stating that he was not to take off on the next leg as the weather conditions were too poor. As he returned towards Shropshire he ran into the bad weather and, after becoming lost and with fuel running low, made a precautionary landing in a snow-covered, ploughed field which caused the wheels to collapse.

LAC (pilot u/t) Peter John Anson (960345), RAFVR. On completion of his training he was posted to 81 Squadron and flew Spitfires in the UK, then north Africa, where he shot down one enemy aircraft. Later in the war he joined 135 Squadron, flying Thunderbolts on ground-attack and offensive operations over Burma, during which he shot down another aircraft. He was subsequently awarded the DFC in October 1945 and remained in the RAF until his retirement as a wing commander in July 1958.

4 February (Tuesday)
Local formation flying exercise. 5 SFTS (RAF Tern Hill, Shropshire)
Miles Master I (T8328) force-landed at Gobowen, near Oswestry, at 16.30 hrs.

P/O Leslie Bale [Roger Bale]

After becoming lost during the flight the pupil pilot made a forced landing in a snow-covered field and was subsequently 'admonished and told to be more careful'.

LAC (pilot u/t) Norman Francis Clarke Williams (920701), RAFVR. On completion of his training he was posted to 123 Squadron and failed to return from a training flight over the North Sea in a Spitfire (X4919) on 31 July 1941. Sgt Williams, aged 21, was the husband of Phyllis Audrey Williams of Watlington, Oxfordshire. He is commemorated on the Runnymede Memorial.

13 February (Thursday)
Operational night patrol. 306 (Polish) Squadron (RAF Tern Hill, Shropshire)
Hawker Hurricane I (V6946, bearing the fuselage code UZ-Q), crashed just north of the airfield at 20.30 hrs. The pilot was returning to land after an hour and forty-five minutes in the air when he encountered thick fog and haze shrouding the area. As he approached from the north he failed to see a tree in the prevailing conditions and crashed after colliding with it, suffering minor injuries.

Sgt (pilot) Wawrzyniec Jasiński (784725), PAF, was killed on 26 January 1943 flying a Spitfire (BS459) of 306 Squadron, when he collided with another Spitfire over the Channel while returning from an offensive sweep. Warrant Officer Jasiński was 27 years old and is buried in Dunkirk Town Cemetery.

13 February (Thursday)
Operational night patrol. 306 (Polish) Squadron (RAF Tern Hill, Shropshire)
Hawker Hurricane I (P3069, bearing the fuselage code UZ-Y), crashed at 24 MU's No. 5 Site, at Buntingsdale, at 21.10 hrs. Similarly to Sgt Jasiński, the pilot of this aircraft was returning to land after 55 minutes in the air but approached too low in the foggy conditions, struck a tree and crashed.

P/O (pilot) Bohdan Bielkiewicz (P-0687), PAF, aged 27, had been involved in 306 Squadron's only combat while based at Tern Hill when a section of three aircraft intercepted a Heinkel He111 south of Worcester on 13 November 1940. The three pilots scored numerous hits, silencing the rear gunner and reducing the starboard engine to a tick-over speed, but Bielkiewicz took the brunt of the Heinkel's return fire, suffering a number of bullet holes, including one on the right side of his cockpit and one through his seat! Unfortunately, the Heinkel escaped into a layer of cloud and was not seen again, so the three pilots were credited with a 'shared probable' after landing safely at Tern Hill. He is buried in Market Drayton Cemetery, Shropshire.

16 February (Sunday)
Forced landings practice. 5 SFTS (RAF Tern Hill, Shropshire)
Miles Master I (N7932) crashed at Ollerton, between Hodnet and Hinstock, at 11.45 hrs. The pupil pilot was attempting to force-land after the engine failed. As the aircraft descended and lost flying speed it developed a left-hand spin, from which the pilot could not recover, and crashed.

LAC (pilot u/t) Arthur Spencley (1252430), RAFVR, aged 28, was the son of Frederick and Annie Spencley and the husband of Doreen Valentine Spencley (née Gleening) of Raynes Park, London. He is buried in Morden Cemetery, London.

16 February (Sunday)
Ferry flight from RAF Brize Norton, Oxfordshire, to RAF Shawbury. HQSFP (RAF Kemble, Gloucestershire)
Fairey Battle I (L5750) force-landed 'one mile north west of Whittington', near Oswestry (putting it in the area of Great Fernhill), at 12.05 hrs. After the engine failed in flight the pilot force-landed in a field, striking a hedge in the process.

P/O (pilot) Allan James Farie (42825), RAF, was born in Worthing, Sussex, on 26 April 1920. Little is known of his military service other than that he transferred to the Administration and Special Duties

Branch in August 1943 and attained the rank of flight lieutenant by the war's end. He died in West Sussex in August 1996.

28 February (Friday)
Ferry flight from 24 MU, Tern Hill, to RAF Hawkinge, Kent. HQSFP (RAF Kemble, Gloucestershire)
Supermarine Spitfire IIA (P7929, a presentation aircraft named *The Transport Men-Ace*) belly-landed at 'Beeston Farm, Bletchley,' to the south-west of Market Drayton, at 16.45 hrs. Soon after take-off from the airfield the aircraft's engine failed and the pilot managed to belly-land in a field, despite his being partially blinded by smoke and oil.

Sgt (pilot) Zbigniew Kleniewski (P781414), PAF, was born on 7 February 1917. He went on to serve with 307 Squadron piloting Mosquitos on intruder operations and survived the war with the rank of flight lieutenant. He died in Deux-Montagnes, Canada, in July 2004.

3 March (Monday)
Operational bombing raid on the French coastal port of Brest. 58 Squadron (RAF Linton-on-Ouse, North Yorkshire)
Armstrong Whitworth Whitley V (Z6465, bearing the fuselage code GE-U) crashed 'at Sutton upon Tern' (believed to be near Rock Cottage, at map reference 670327), just south of Market Drayton, at 01.55 hrs. Eight aircraft took off at 18.05 hrs the previous evening to bomb the important coastal port but, due to dense cloud cover, only five aircraft located and bombed the target. Of the remaining three aircraft, one dumped its bombs at sea and returned to Linton, the second returned with its bomb load on board, while this aircraft, for unknown reasons, attempted to land at Tern Hill with its bombs still on board. As the pilot approached, however, he lost height while making a half-circuit of the airfield and, when he turned the aircraft into the wind for his final landing approach, it was very low and still had some miles to go to reach the runway. Shortly afterwards the aircraft rose suddenly, presumably as the pilot tried to avoid a tall tree, and the aircraft stalled and crashed, killing the entire crew. In the subsequent investigation it was noted that this was only the pilot's second night-time flight as first pilot on this type of aircraft. This indicated a lack of experience but it was also added that his judgment would, undoubtedly, have been affected by fatigue brought on by a long operational flight.

Sgt (pilot) Stanley Victor (Stan) Bunn (748368), RAFVR, was born on 24 February 1919, the son of Stanley Philip and Zillah Carry Bunn of 17 Broughton Road, Hockley, Birmingham. He was educated at Handsworth Grammar School and then worked as a clerk in a local business before joining up. He is buried in Birmingham (Handsworth) Cemetery.

Sgt (pilot) Thomas James Thurling (754631), RAFVR, aged 20, was the only son of Thomas William and Florence May Thurling of Mile Cross, Norwich. He is buried in Norwich Cemetery.

Sgt (Obs) Harold Gordon (747861), RAFVR, aged 23, was the son of Mr and Mrs H Gordon of 16 Downing Street, Chippenham. He is buried in Hardenhuish (St Nicholas) Churchyard, Wiltshire.

Sgt Bunn (second from left) and Tom Thurling (second from right) are the only two identified on this crew photo taken after landing from their first operation [Chris Bunn]

Sgt (W/AG) Herbert Frederick Jennings (509138), RAFVR, aged 29, was the son of Frederick and Ellen Jennings of Frimley Road, Camberley. He is buried in Frimley (St Peters) Churchyard, Surrey.

Sgt (W/Op) Kenneth Wright (975751), RAFVR, aged 22, was the son of Alfred and Mary Ellen Wright of Brook House, Cogshall. He is buried in Great Budworth (St Mary and All Saints) Churchyard, Cheshire.

Sgt Stan Bunn [Chris Bunn]

13 March (Thursday)
Local solo flying practice. 5 SFTS (RAF Tern Hill, Shropshire)
Miles Master I (N7934) crash-landed at 'Old Dudleston', near Ellesmere, at 11.20 hrs. After becoming lost during the flight and with fuel running low, the pilot attempted to force-land in a ploughed field and was seriously injured as the aircraft crashed to a halt. The subsequent inquiry commented that he was 'lacking experience due to frequent changes of instructor'.

LAC (pilot u/t) John Michael Dixon (1171227), RAFVR, was subsequently killed in action on 16 September 1944, whilst flying Spitfires with 145 Squadron in Italy. He is buried in Ravenna War Cemetery.

15 March (Saturday)
Solo local flying practice. 5 SFTS (RAF Tern Hill, Shropshire)
Miles Master I (T8572) force-landed at Upper Battlefield, north of Shrewsbury, at 13.00 hrs. After encountering bad weather during the flight the pilot attempted to make a precautionary landing in a field which had ridges running at right angles to his landing path. When he applied the brakes the aircraft nosed over.

LAC (pilot u/t) C Austin (754533), RAFVR. Nothing further is known of this airman other than that he survived the war.

21 March (Friday)
Navigation training exercise. 2 School of Air Navigation (RAF Cranage, Cheshire)
Avro Anson I (K6248) crashed at Hawkswood Farm, near Hordley (at map reference 370299), at 11.05 hrs. The pilot was initially believed to have been carrying out an unauthorised practice forced landing when he saw a tall oak tree in his path, pulled up in an attempt to clear it and struck the branches with his tail. This sent the aircraft crashing into the wood beyond. However, further investigation by the court of inquiry added that evidence, although conflicting, 'tended to support the fact that the undercarriage was lowered and therefore considers that the pilot was, for some obscure reason, attempting to land'.

F/O (pilot) Eric Walwyn Padfield (33480), RAF, aged 22, was the son of Wilfrid Walwyn Padfield and Priscilla Sophia Padfield of Bath, Somerset. He had initially served for three years as a Halton aircraft apprentice before being accepted for a cadetship and pilot training at RAF College Cranwell in February 1938. He is buried in Byley (St John) Churchyard, Cheshire (near Cranage airfield).

P/O (pilot) James Frederick Minett (62330), RAFVR, aged 26, was the son of Frederick Harold and Leonora May Minett (née Pearce), of London Road, Slough. Educated at the King's School, Canterbury and London School of Economics, he had worked as the editor of the trade paper *Store* prior to joining the RAFVR. He is buried in Hackington (St Stephen) Churchyard, Canterbury.

Sgt (pilot) Frederick Ralph Percival Burgess (1162683), RAFVR, aged 21, was the son of Percy Alfred and Marguerite Helen Burgess of Alstonefield. He is buried in Alstonefield (St Peter's) Churchyard, Staffordshire.

Sgt (W/Op) Wilfred Hewish (538041), RAF, aged 23, was the son of William and Ellen Hewish from Shepherdswell, Kent and the husband of Lydia Evelyn Blanch from Pontyclun, near Llantrisant. He is buried in Llantrisant (Cefn-y-Parc) Cemetery, Glamorgan.

Sgt (? u/t) Peter Rowland Hill (1153385), RAFVR, aged 20, was the son of Cyril Rowland Hill and Joy Hill (née Gunter). He is buried in Byley (St John) Churchyard (along with the pilot).

28 March (Friday)
Homing exercise. 57 OTU (RAF Hawarden, Flintshire)
Supermarine Spitfire IA (L1030) force-landed at Great Ness, near Nesscliffe, at 14.30 hrs. During the course of the training flight the pilot became lost and was forced to belly-land the aircraft in a field as the fuel was running low, suffering injuries in the process. The subsequent investigation attributed the cause of the crash as a 'lack of common sense and airmanship' on the part of the pilot and added that he had disobeyed orders by not carrying a map with him (having lent it to another pilot).

Sgt (pilot u/t) Bradley Smith (R.6755), RCAF. Born in the USA, on 7 December 1913, Smith had travelled to Canada in July 1940 to volunteer for the RCAF. On completion of his operational training in the UK he was posted to 121 'Eagle' Squadron which was in the process of training up to an operational standard with Hurricanes. During training he was extremely lucky to survive a mid-air collision over Lincoln on 26 July 1941. After re-equipping with Spitfires and beginning operations, little is known of Sgt Smith's military service other than that he was commissioned in August 1941 and transferred to the USAAF in February 1943.

30 March (Sunday)
Circuits and landings. 11 SFTS (RAF Shawbury, Shropshire)
Airspeed Oxford II (P8965) crashed on the edge of Shawbury airfield at 17.15 hrs. The pupil pilot had made only his first solo flight earlier in the day and, after receiving some further dual instruction, was ordered up to practice his solo circuits and landings. Having completed four circuits he was carrying out a fifth when the port engine failed, due to a technical failure of number 2 cylinder. The pilot immediately turned to land on the airfield but, because another aircraft was taxiing across the runway, was forced to attempt a single-engine overshoot. As he did so he allowed the aircraft to stall during a steep turn to port and the aircraft crashed onto the edge of the airfield.

LAC (pilot u/t) Alastair McKenzie Stott (1078584), RAFVR, aged 19, was the son of David and Jane Milne Stott (née McKenzie) of Aberdeen. He is buried in Aberdeen (St Peter's) Cemetery.

1 April (Tuesday)
Bombing raid on Birmingham. *Kampfgeschwader* 1 (KG1) '*Hindenburg*' (Nijmegen, Netherlands)
Junkers Ju88 A-5 (6245, bearing the fuselage codes V4+BS), crashed near the Wicket on Brown Clee Hill (at map reference 604859), at 09.50 hrs. The bomber was first plotted by Royal Observer Corps personnel entering the county from the south-west, passing over Bridgnorth at a height of 1000 feet, and was designated as 'Raid 73'. 306 (Polish) Squadron, which was stationed at Tern Hill, was immediately informed and P/O Edward Jankowski took off to intercept the aircraft. Soon after becoming airborne he was recalled, due to the low cloud shrouding the south of the county. It was this low cloud, in fact, that would cause the crash of the *Luftwaffe* bomber as the crew were believed to have been off course and flying low to establish their bearings when they flew into the cloud-obscured hillside, cutting a swathe through the trees and exploding on impact. News of the crash quickly spread and a group of soldiers from the local searchlight station, along with members of the Home Guard and local police, were soon on the scene to set up guard. Once the wreckage had cooled down an inspection of the site revealed that there were four unexploded bombs, which had to be defused. The remains of the crew

were taken to RAF Shawbury and buried with full military honours on 4 April.

Uffz (pilot) Heinrich Ewald, *Luftwaffe*, aged 25, was buried in Stoke on Tern (St Peter) Cemetery before being reburied in Cannock Chase German Military Cemetery during the 1960s.

Uffz (W/Op) Werner Lehnhardt, *Luftwaffe*, aged 21, was buried in Stoke on Tern (St Peter) Cemetery before being reburied in Cannock Chase German Military Cemetery during the 1960s.

Feldwebel (Obs) Erich Wels, *Luftwaffe*, aged 28, was buried in Stoke on Tern (St Peter) Cemetery before being reburied in Cannock Chase German Military Cemetery during the 1960s.

Uffz (engineer) Heinz Prochnow, *Luftwaffe*, aged 20, was buried in Stoke on Tern (St Peter) Cemetery before being reburied in Cannock Chase German Military Cemetery during the 1960s.

6 April (Sunday)
Solo night circuits and landings. 5 SFTS (RAF Tern Hill, Shropshire)
Miles Master I (T8569) crashed at Tern Hill airfield at 03.10 hrs. The pilot was taking off from the airfield when his aircraft was seen suddenly to lose height from 100 feet and strike a hangar before crashing. The crash was subsequently attributed to the pilot having failed to concentrate on instruments, but there seems to have been some disagreement as another officer stated that there was no evidence to support this theory.

LAC (pilot u/t) Geoffrey Allan Stanford Blake (1259650), RAFVR, aged 18, was the son of Dr Henry Edward Blake and Gwendoline May Blake (née Stanford) of Marylebone, London. He is buried in Stoke upon Tern (St Peter's) Cemetery, Shropshire.

7 April (Monday)
Sector reconnaissance. 605 (County of Warwick) Squadron (RAF Tern Hill, Shropshire)
Hawker Hurricane IIA (Z2318) collided with a Spitfire in mid-air at 11.43 hrs and wreckage scattered over a wide area about half a mile west of the airfield, between the railway line and the Hodnet Road. 605 Squadron had only arrived at Tern Hill on 31 March to take over from 306 Squadron in the defence of the West Midlands and the pilots were sent out on sector reconnaissance flights to familiarise themselves with the local area. Having completed one such flight the pilot was making a right-hand circuit of the airfield (rather than the correct left-hand circuit) in preparation for landing. At the same time, a Spitfire from Tern Hill's Maintenance Unit was making a correct left-hand circuit. Evidently, neither pilot was aware of their converging courses until it was too late and both aircraft collided head-on, disintegrating in mid-air.

Oldřich Kestler. [Pavel Vancata]

Sgt (pilot) Oldřich Kestler (787527), RAFVR, was born at Čižice, near Klatovy, Czechoslovakia, on 18 March 1913. Prior to joining 605 Squadron, on 4 December 1940, he had flown Hurricanes with 111 Squadron during the latter stages of the Battle of Britain. He is buried in Market Drayton Cemetery, Shropshire.

Test flight. 24 MU (RAF Tern Hill, Shropshire)
Supermarine Spitfire IIB (P8315) collided with a Hurricane in the incident described above and wreckage spread over a wide area about half a mile west of the airfield, between the railway line and the Hodnet Road.

Sgt (pilot) Josef Martinec (787683), RAFVR, was born in Doudleby nad Orlicí, Czechoslovakia, on 19 July 1915. After the fall of Czechoslovakia he made his way to France, where he was wounded in a German air raid on Chateauroux airfield on 10 May 1940 while serving with the French Air Force. He

Josef Martinec
[Pavel Vancata]

subsequently escaped to the UK, after recovering from his injuries, and was eventually posted to 24 MU as a test pilot. He is buried in Market Drayton Cemetery, Shropshire.

10 April (Thursday)
Solo training flight. 5 SFTS (RAF Tern Hill, Shropshire)
Miles Master I (T8439) crashed at Helshaw Grange, to the south-west of the airfield, at 13.15 hrs. The pupil pilot was taking off from the airfield when, for unknown reasons, he collided with another Master (T8827) which was approaching to land. Both aircraft crashed out of control onto marshy ground near the airfield. Assistance was called for from 34 MU, Monkmoor, to help in the recovery of the wreckage but, despite their best attempts, the body of LAC Carr could not be recovered. In fact, it was not until the Shropshire Wartime Aircraft Recovery Group excavated the site in the late 1970s that his body was finally recovered and laid to rest.

LAC (pilot u/t) Denis Michael Whittam Hartley (1178785), RAFVR, aged 19, was the son of John Whittam Hartley and Eva Althea Hartley. He is buried in Basildon (St Bartholomew) Cemetery, Berkshire.

Solo training flight
5 SFTS (RAF Tern Hill, Shropshire). Miles Master I (T8827) crashed at Helshaw Grange (at map reference 632289) following the collision described above.

LAC (pilot u/t) John Toplis Carr (1252426), RAFVR, aged 19, was the son of Charles Watson and Elsie Margaret Carr (née Toplis) of Eastbourne, Sussex. Prior to enlisting he had worked as an articled clerk to Mr Francis H Busby's law firm in Eastbourne. He is buried in Brookwood Military Cemetery, Surrey.

17 April (Thursday)
Solo formation flying. 11 SFTS (RAF Shawbury, Shropshire)
Airspeed Oxford I (L9682) crashed at Moreton Corbet, just north of Shawbury airfield, at 16.35 hrs. After the pilot failed to switch from his main fuel tank to reserve tank, resulting in the failure of the port engine, he attempted an emergency single-engine landing at the airfield. However, while making a left-hand circuit of the airfield at 1,000–1,200 feet he displayed a 'lack of experience and judgment' by turning across wind into his 'dead' engine, causing the aircraft to stall and dive into the ground. Despite being rushed to the Royal Salop Infirmary, he died there three hours later.

LAC (pilot u/t) Kenneth Robert Moseley (1166145), RAFVR, aged 19, was the son of Robert Thomas Moseley and Annie Moseley of King's Heath, Birmingham. He is buried in Birmingham (Brandwood) Cemetery.

18 April (Friday)
Dual night circuits and landings. 5 SFTS (RAF Tern Hill, Shropshire)
Miles Master I (N7823) crashed at 'Stoke Grange Farm, Stoke on Tern', at 00.55 hrs. The pupil pilot completed a circuit of the airfield before climbing to approximately 500 feet and beginning a right-hand turn, from which he failed to pull up before flying into the ground.

Sgt (instructor pilot) Jack Proctor (741471), RAFVR, aged 24, was the son of William and Fanny Proctor of Coventry and the husband of Audrey Louise Proctor (née Thomas) of Stoke, Coventry. He is buried in Stoke (St Michael) Churchyard, Warwickshire.

LAC (pilot u/t) Fred Taylor (1006784), RAFVR, aged 23, was the son of Thomas and Nancy Alice Taylor of Bolton and the husband of Elsie Mary Taylor of Radcliffe, Lancashire. He is buried in Breightmet (St James) Churchyard, Lancashire.

20 April (Sunday)
Solo night flying practice. 5 SFTS (RAF Tern Hill, Shropshire)
Miles Master I (T8824) crashed on Gallantry Hill (at map reference 653295), Stoke on Tern, at 22.30 hrs. The pupil pilot was making his first solo night flight when he began to lose height, after making a turn, and failed to correct his mistake before flying into the ground. According to John Taylor, who lives at Gallantry House, the accident was witnessed by Jim Ward, who was cycling back from his job at the airfield canteen to Stoke on Tern. He told John that

> ... the plane lost height, clipped the cottage thatch, demolished the headgear of the garden well and gouged a line out of Gallantry Hill. It then crashed through the hedge and barbed wire defences, narrowly missing the anti-aircraft gun and disintegrated spilling its fuel load. The body of the unfortunate Belgian pilot was recovered from the garden of Gallantry House.

Sgt (pilot u/t) Gaston Jean C Vandebos (1299894), RAFVR, aged 20, had been accepted for pilot training in Belgium but, after the German invasion, escaped to the UK and joined the RAFVR. Initially buried in Market Drayton Cemetery, his body was later repatriated to Belgium and interred in Cimitière du Sud, Tournai.

22 April (Tuesday)
Solo night circuits and landings. 5 SFTS (RAF Tern Hill, Shropshire)
Miles Master I (N7712) crashed at 'Wood Lane, Wollerton' (presumably Wood Lane Farm, between Wollerton and Fauls), at 01.05 hrs. After realising that he was overshooting a landing the pilot opened up the throttles to go around again but, as he did so, allowed the aircraft to turn to the left, due to 'faulty instrument flying', and flew into the ground.

LAC (pilot u/t) Michael Edward Frankish (1259896), RAFVR, aged 19, was the son of Capt John Raven Frankish, MBE and Dorothy Edith Frankish (née Whitehead) of Kingsgate, Kent. He was educated at King Edward VI School in Bury St Edmunds (where he was head boy) and had joined the RAFVR after leaving school (his twin brother, John, joined the Royal Navy). He is buried in Stoke upon Tern (St Peter's) Cemetery, Shropshire.

22 April (Tuesday)
Cross-country flight. 5 SFTS (RAF Tern Hill, Shropshire)
Miles Master I (T8843) crash-landed at Kenwick, between Cockshutt and Ellesmere, at 11.00 hrs. After encountering bad weather during the flight the pilot decided to make a precautionary landing but, as he touched down, the undercarriage struck a hedge and collapsed.

LAC (pilot u/t) George Charlton Jobling (1054474), RAFVR. On completion of his training he was posted to 150 Squadron, flying Wellingtons on night-bombing operations over north-west Europe. He failed to return from an operation on 21 February 1942 piloting a Wellington (X9830). Sgt Jobling, aged 25 at the time of his death, was the son of John Sharp and Ella Beatrice Jobling of Forest Hall, Northumberland. He is commemorated on the Runnymede Memorial.

26 April (Saturday)
Dual instructional flight. 5 SFTS (RAF Cosford, Shropshire – detached flight from RAF Tern Hill)
Miles Master I (T8757) crashed 'three miles east of Cosford' (putting it in the area between Albrighton and Codsall Wood) at 14.10 hrs. In order to relieve congestion at Tern Hill, the crew were operating out

of RAF Cosford and had just taken off from the airfield when the engine failed at 500 feet. While endeavouring to reach a suitable field to force-land, the instructor lost control due to a 'whipstall' at 150 feet and the aircraft crashed. In the subsequent court of inquiry it was remarked that the prevailing conditions at the time were very bumpy and that there were strong winds, which contributed to the 'whipstall'.

F/O (instructor pilot) Cyril George William Moore (84000), RAFVR, aged 22, was the son of Guy G and Vera H M Moore and the husband of Josephine Phyllis Marie Moore (née Rice) of Bournemouth. He is buried in Bournemouth East Cemetery.

LAC (pilot u/t) Arthur Naylor (1191778), RAFVR, aged 20, was the son of Arthur and May Lilian Naylor of Newthorpe. He is buried in Eastwood Cemetery, Nottinghamshire.

4 May (Sunday)
Solo circuits and landings. 11 SFTS (RAF Shawbury, Shropshire)
Airspeed Oxford I (N4563) crashed at Moreton Corbet, just north of the airfield. The pilot was only on his second solo flight in an Oxford aircraft when he took off, climbed to 700 feet and then allowed the aircraft to fall into a steep right-hand turn and dive into the ground. The cause of the crash was uncertain, with three different possibilities provided by various reports. Firstly, that the starboard engine failed while climbing away and the pilot got into a spin, although a strip examination of the engines seemed to reveal no indication of technical defect. Secondly, that the pilot may have experienced a period of irregularity in the running of the starboard engine (rather than a complete failure) and swung off to the right, or lastly, that the pilot entered the slipstream of an aircraft taking off at the same time and lost control.

LAC (pilot u/t) Colin Glynn Eustace Crouch (1202561), RAFVR, aged 28, was the son of Frederick Benjamin and Ethel May Crouch (née Berridge) of Woodford and the husband of Doris Margaret Crouch (née Jarvis). He is buried in Woodford (St Mary) Churchyard, Northamptonshire.

5 May (Monday)
Precautionary landings and single engine forced landing practice. 11 SFTS (RAF Shawbury, Shropshire)
Airspeed Oxford I (L4575) crashed on the edge of the airfield at 17.15 hrs. The pilot was witnessed practicing single-engine flying, during which he made a steep turn to port at approximately 1,000 feet over the airfield, lost control and dived into the ground under power. The cause was subsequently attributed to the pilot losing control while single-engine flying, although there was a suggestion that the pilot may have been trying an 'aileron turn'. This had formed part of a lecture given on 23 April, in which it had been stressed by the lecturer that the manoeuvre applied to fighters only, but the night before the accident the pilot had remarked to a friend that he intended to try the manoeuvre.

LAC (pilot u/t) John Neville Watson (1266787), RAFVR, aged 19. His parents lived at 35 Homewood Road, Kingston-upon-Thames and he had been educated at Selhurst Grammar School, Croydon. He is buried in Shawbury (St Mary's) Churchyard.

14 May (Wednesday)
Solo steep climbing turns and gliding approaches. 5 SFTS (RAF Tern Hill, Shropshire)
Miles Master I (N7927) crashed at Ellerton Hall, to the south-east of Hinstock, at 12.05 hrs. The pupil pilot had just made a low pass over Chetwynd airfield with wheels down and engine throttled back, as part of his gliding approach training, when he opened up the throttle to climb away. During the climb, however, the pilot is thought to have stalled, as the nose of the aircraft was seen to drop and then descend in a semi-stalled condition before diving into the ground.

LAC (pilot u/t) Denis Layton (937443), RAFVR, aged 20, was the son of William Cuthbertson and

Jennie Layton of Gosforth. He is buried in Stoke upon Tern (St Peter's) Cemetery, Shropshire.

Sgt Geoffrey Morris [TNA]

14 May (Wednesday)
Solo general revision flight. 5 SFTS (RAF Tern Hill, Shropshire)
Miles Master I (N7779) crashed at Goldstone Common, between Cheswardine and Hinstock, at 17.20 hrs. During the course of the routine training flight, the pupil pilot began unauthorised low flying over his cousin's farm and allowed the aircraft to stall while performing a steep right-hand turn at 500–600 feet, flicked over into a spin and crashed.

Sgt (pilot u/t) Geoffrey Morris (758256), RAFVR, aged 21, was the son of Frederic William and Josephine Anne Morris of Eaton Hill, Norwich. He is buried in Eaton (St Andrew) New Churchyard, Norfolk.

18 May (Sunday)
Non-operational 'local night-flying practice'. 68 Squadron (RAF High Ercall, Shropshire)
Bristol Blenheim IF (L8675) crashed behind the sugar beet factory at Allscott, between Withington and Wellington (at map reference 603120) at 00.20 hours. While flying at low altitude in the vicinity of his parents' house the pilot allowed the aircraft to stall and crashed. Colin Thompson, who was a schoolboy living at Walcot Mill at the time, remembers his parents saying how they heard the aircraft going over. The next morning Colin went down to look at the wreckage with some friends:

> There was a gang of us kids peering across from the railway line. One of these Cole's cranes was arriving and the ambulance was there. The crane was lifting the wreckage in places. I think they recovered the bodies there and then as we saw them being put into the ambulance.

P/O Geoff Butcher [Rebecca Farr]

P/O (pilot) Geoffrey Robert Butcher (60825), RAFVR, aged 21, was the son of George Henry and Edith Louisa Butcher of The Compasses Inn, Beveley (in modern-day Telford). Before the war he had studied at The Priory School, Shrewsbury before receiving a classics scholarship to Christchurch College, Oxford. He is buried in Wombridge (SS Mary and Leonard) Cemetery, Shropshire.

Sgt (W/Op) Irwin Harold Wiskar (1107254), RAFVR, aged 32, was the son of Frank Marshall and Agnes Martha Wiskar and the husband of Dorothy Emily Wiskar (née Wedge) of Penrith, Cumberland. He is buried in Eston Cemetery, Yorkshire.

20 May (Tuesday)
Ciné-gun practice attacks. 605 (County of Warwick) Squadron (RAF Tern Hill, Shropshire)
Hawker Hurricane II (Z2318) crash-landed 'one mile north west of the airfield' (putting it roughly in between the airfield and Bletchley) at 16.30 hrs. The pilot was returning to land in a section of three aircraft when the formation was obliged to make another circuit of the airfield as there was an aircraft blocking the runway. However, as they did so, the pilot of this aircraft failed to switch to his reserve fuel tank when the main tank ran dry and his engine failed at 300–500 feet. In the ensuing forced landing, the pilot's Sutton harness (safety belt) cable broke and he was fatally injured when he struck the instrument panel, and died on his way to hospital.

Sgt Bernard Samp [neibieskaeskadra.pl]

Sgt (pilot) Bernard Samp (783611), PAF, aged 23, is buried in Market Drayton Cemetery, Shropshire. His death was recorded in the squadron's war diary as 'a sad loss for the squadron, he was a very promising pilot and well liked'.

21 May (Wednesday)
Engine trials flight. Rolls-Royce Flight Test Establishment (Hucknall, Nottinghamshire)
Avro Manchester I (L7295) crashed on approach to RAF Tern Hill. The aircraft was being tested by one of the company's experienced test pilots when the cooling system failed and one of the engines caught fire. Despite attempting to reach RAF Tern Hill to make an emergency landing, the pilot was unable to maintain height and the port wing struck a tree causing him to crash short of the runway, killing him instantly. The three remaining occupants were slightly injured.

Mr (pilot) Reginald Edward Kirlew, AFM, a Rolls-Royce employee, was the husband of Alice Elizabeth Kirlew of Plumtree, Nottinghamshire. Born in Dorset, on 17 September 1895, he joined the Dorset Regiment in August 1914 and served with the regiment for three years (presumably in France) before transferring to the Royal Flying Corps in September 1917 and becoming an air mechanic. Following the armistice he underwent wireless operator training and subsequently served with 58 Squadron, 208 Squadron and 'M' Section, 6 FTS, in Egypt, between August 1919 and October 1922. After being accepted for pilot training and gaining his wings, he then joined 12 Squadron, which was in the process of developing their bombing techniques at Northolt (and then Andover) with the DH9A. In September 1927 he was posted to the Middle East and over the next ten years he served as an instructor with various training establishments, for which he was awarded the Air Force Medal in June 1938. The recommendation for the award read:

> Since completing his training as a pilot in October, 1922, this airman pilot has been employed continuously on flying duties and has completed 3,585 hours flying. For six of the last ten years he was instructing at 4 Flying Training School, Abu Sueir, and for the remainder at 3 Flying Training School and the Central Flying School. Throughout this long period, during which he has trained an exceptionally large number of pupils and flying instructors, his work has been of the highest standard and of greatest value to the Royal Air Force.

He is buried in an unknown location.

Mr (observer) Derek H Broome was born in Derby. He joined Rolls-Royce as an apprentice (where his father was a well-known engineer) at the age of 16 shortly before the outbreak of war. Following his recuperation from the accident he joined the Fleet Air Arm and flew Swordfish bi-planes and later Corsairs in the Far East. At the end of the war he studied at Oxford University before beginning a career in the engineering industry. He died in 2009.

Mr (fitter) Douglas Healey.

Mr (fitter) Charles Poole.

26 May (Monday)
Ferry flight from RAF Ringway, Cheshire, to RAF Northolt, Middlesex. 1 FPP (White Waltham, Berkshire)
De Havilland Tiger Moth II (T6112) crashed on the river bank at Highley (at wartime map reference 743834), at 13.15 hrs. The pilot was flying at low altitude when he failed to observe high-tension power

cables ahead, collided with them and was injured in the resultant crash. The accident, which was witnessed by members of the local ARP post, cut off the village power supply and also meant that a shift was lost at Highley Colliery before power could be restored. Upon questioning, the pilot explained that he had lost height while unfolding a map and struck the power lines, but the court of inquiry rejected this excuse and attributed the crash to deliberate 'low flying in breach of regulations'.

First Officer (pilot) George Henry Wood (PL77469), ATA, was an American pilot and survived the war.

27 May (Tuesday)
Dual training flight. 5 SFTS (RAF Tern Hill, Shropshire)
Miles Master I (T8851) force-landed '1/2 mile south-east of Lilleshall' at 09.10 hrs. The instructor belly-landed in a field after the engine failed in flight and both occupants were unhurt.

F/Lt (instructor pilot) William Arthur Toyne (39140), DFC, RAF, was born on 1 September 1917. He joined the RAF in 1936 and flew Gauntlets (and later Hurricanes) with 213 Squadron from May 1937 until the outbreak of war. He then joined 17 Squadron and flew Hurricanes during the Battle of France and over the beaches at Dunkirk, shooting down two enemy aircraft and damaging another, for which he was awarded the DFC in June 1940. Following his return to the UK after the capitulation of France, he presumably began instructor duties as he did not take part in the Battle of Britain. Little else is known of his military service other than that he survived the war, retired as a group captain in September 1967 and died in Spalding, Lincolnshire, in April 1994.

The name of the pupil pilot is unknown

5 June (Thursday)
Dual training flight. 5 SFTS (RAF Cosford, Shropshire – detached flight from RAF Tern Hill)
Miles Master I (T8663) force-landed 'one and a half miles north of Cosford' (putting it in the area around Tong village), at 16.15 hrs. The instructor and his pupil were operating out of RAF Cosford to relieve congestion at Tern Hill and had just taken off from the airfield when the engine failed and the instructor was forced to belly-land in a field ahead.

P/O (instructor pilot) Norman Arthur Kynaston (89810), RAFVR. Little is known of his military service until he was given command of 91 Squadron in August 1943, flying Spitfire XIIs on offensive sweeps over north-west Europe, and was awarded the DFC in November. He continued to command the squadron throughout 1944 and, between June and August, was heavily involved in 'diver' operations (intercepting V1s). He was killed on 15 August 1944 after baling out over the sea following flak damage to his aircraft during a fighter sweep to St Trond. His final tally stood at four enemy aircraft destroyed, one shared, one probable, one damaged and 22 V1s shot down, for which he was awarded a posthumous bar to his DFC. S/Ldr Kynaston, who was 29 years old, was the husband of Kathleen Marian Kynaston of Hereford. He is commemorated on the Runnymede Memorial.

The name of the pupil pilot is unknown.

14 June (Saturday)
Training flight. 5 SFTS (RAF Tern Hill, Shropshire)
Hawker Hurricane I (P3219) force-landed at Cheswardine at 12.30 hrs. During the course of the training flight the engine failed and, due to smoke obscuring his vision, the pilot slightly damaged the aircraft on the branches of a tree as he made his landing approach.

Sgt (pilot u/t) Georges François Désiré Deltour (1299923), RAFVR, was born in Liège, Belgium, on 16 December 1919 and had joined the Belgian military before the war. At the time of the German invasion, he was undergoing pilot training. He subsequently escaped to England, via Morocco, in July 1940 and joined the RAFVR. On completion of his training he was posted to 131 Squadron in August 1941 and then, three months later, transferred to 350 (Belgian) Squadron (which was formed from a nucleus of airmen from 131 Squadron) and flew Spitfires with the squadron until February 1943. Following his tour he spent the remainder of the war in a number of non-operational instructing roles before leaving the military. He died in January 2005.

22 June (Sunday)
Formation flying. 5 SFTS (RAF Child's Ercall, Shropshire – Relief Landing Ground to RAF Tern Hill) Hawker Hurricane I (P5170) force-landed 'one mile north west of Child's Ercall' (putting it roughly in the area just north of Ollerton), at 14.50 hrs. During the course of the flight the pilot caused the engine to fail due to 'mishandling' and was forced to belly-land in a wheat field.

LAC (pilot u/t) Cyril John Moffat (1059152), RAFVR, was commissioned in October 1942. He survived the war and transferred to the Royal Naval Volunteer Reserve (Air Branch) in January 1953, retiring as a lieutenant-commander in February 1966.

AC1 Bill Beardmore [Kate Dudley]

24 June (Tuesday)
5 SFTS (RAF Child's Ercall, Shropshire – satellite to RAF Tern Hill)
Two airmen were on flare-path duty when a pupil pilot, on his first solo night flight in Master N7999, touched down at 01.15 hrs too far along the runway, lost control and struck the two men, killing them both instantly.

AC1 (ACH/GD) William (Bill) Frederick Beardmore (940687), RAFVR, aged 22, was the son of Bert and Lily Beardmore (née Turley) of Vicar Street, Wednesbury. Educated at St Bartholomew's Church School, he had worked in the office of F H Lloyd (steelworks) prior to joining the RAF and was due to be married in August 1941 to a girl named Dilys. He is buried in Wednesbury Cemetery, Staffordshire.

AC1 (ACH/GD) Kenneth Ollier (1105089), RAF, aged 21, was the son of Arthur and Minnie Ollier (née Astles). He is buried in Over Tabley (St Paul's) Churchyard, Cheshire.

LAC David Kenward [TNA]

25 June (Wednesday)
Force-landings and navigation practice. 5 SFTS (RAF Tern Hill, Shropshire)
Miles Master I (T8760) force-landed '3/4 mile from Wellington' at 20.25 hrs. The pupil pilot belly-landed in a field after the engine failed in flight.

LAC (pilot u/t) David Robert Kenward (1268239), RAFVR, was born in Kent, on 30 August 1922. He was commissioned in August 1941 but little is known of his military service other than that he flew Typhoons with 257 Squadron during 1942. He continued to serve in the RAF after the war but was killed on 28 August 1962 when a Valetta (WJ480) crashed during a single-engine overshoot near Chippenham, Wiltshire. F/Lt Kenward is buried in London Road Cemetery, Chippenham.

LAC Charles Booth [TNA]

26 June (Thursday)
Solo circuits and landings. 5 SFTS (RAF Tern Hill, Shropshire)
Miles Master I (N7925) crashed at the east boundary of Tern Hill airfield, at 01.30 hrs. The pupil pilot was approaching to land when he made his final turn into the wind too late and allowed the aircraft to stall and crash on the edge of the airfield.

LAC (pilot u/t) Charles Henry Booth (1375075), RAFVR, aged 21, is buried in the City of London Cemetery, Manor Park. His next of kin are unknown.

27 June (Friday)
Test flight. 27 MU (RAF Shawbury, Shropshire)
Fairey Battle I (K7634) struck by another aircraft at RAF Shawbury. The test pilot had just landed and was still on the runway when a pupil pilot from 11 SFTS came in to land in an Oxford (L9687) and touched down at 90 degrees to the correct 'landing T'. The pupil pilot then saw the Fairey Battle directly in his path and tried to bounce over it, but his undercarriage and fuselage smashed into the side of the Battle's cockpit, killing the test pilot and injuring his civilian MU passenger.

F/Sgt (test pilot) Frederick Herbert Dennis McCuan (550079), RAF, aged 23, was the son of Walter Frederick and Elsie McCuan (née Prowse) of Acocks Green, Birmingham. He is buried in Birmingham (Yardley) Cemetery.

Mr (fitter) A Cribb.

30 June (Monday)
Solo training flight. 11 SFTS (RAF Shawbury, Shropshire)
Airspeed Oxford I (T1045) crashed at RAF Shawbury at 15.35 hrs. The Free French pupil pilot was approaching to land when he was witnessed to open up his port engine, climb and then spin upside down into the ground. The subsequent court of inquiry found it impossible to ascertain the cause of the crash with any certainty, although it was evident that 'during the approach the starboard engine was not giving any power, but whether this was due to engine failure or to the fact that Cpl Desgrés had set the throttles unevenly was obscure'.

Cpl (pilot u/t) Gabriel Desgrés, FFAF, aged 19, was born in St Malo, on 7 July 1921. He was undergoing pilot training with the French Air Force in Brittany at the time of the German invasion and managed to escape to England on 19 June with a group of French airmen aboard *Le Trébouliste* (a lobster fishing boat). He was buried in Shawbury (St Mary's) Churchyard prior to his body being repatriated to France after the war for reburial in St Malo.

7 July (Monday)
'Non-operational flight' (possibly to gain firsthand knowledge of the aircraft type and sector for which the pilot was responsible). 68 Squadron (RAF High Ercall, Shropshire)
Bristol Beaufighter IF (R2264) crash-landed at Betton Strange, near Bayston Hill, at 17.00 hrs. The aircraft was being piloted by the commanding officer of the Fighter Sector HQ, 9 Group (based at RAF Tern Hill), who was a very experienced pilot with 2,097 flying hours to his name. Despite this experience, however, he had only flown four hours in Beaufighters and it was this lack of familiarity with the aircraft that resulted in his neglecting to switch over fuel tanks when the first had run dry, which caused the engines to fail. In the subsequent crash-landing the pilot was badly injured and woke up in the Royal Salop Infirmary, while his navigator was unhurt.

W/Cdr (pilot) James Winter Carmichael 'Hank' More (26161), DFC, RAF, was born on 4 June 1910, the eldest son of Dr John and Mrs Mabel Winter More of Blewbury, Berkshire. He was educated at Haileybury and Imperial Service College. After joining the RAF in the late 1920s, he completed his pilot training and was posted to 54 Squadron in July 1930, flying Siskin fighters. Following a spell in the UK he was posted to 403 Flight in February 1932 (a naval fleet fighter unit), flying from the aircraft carrier HMS *Hermes* in the South China Sea, then in late 1934 he returned to the UK to join the instructing staff at Cranwell. The following year he was posted to 43 Squadron, piloting Hawker Furys, and then, in 1936, he returned to fleet fighters with 800 Squadron, flying from the aircraft carrier HMS *Courageous* (which was sailing in home waters) and RAF Southampton. On 30 April 1937, while flying from Southampton, he was extremely lucky to survive a mid-air collision between three aircraft, which claimed the life of one of the other pilots. Between 1938 and 1939 he served at RAF Cottesmore and then, in April 1940, he was given command of 73 Squadron, which had been sent to France to combat the German onslaught. In the fierce fighting that followed S/Ldr More claimed a total of four aircraft destroyed, one probably destroyed and two shared destroyed, and was awarded the DFC in July 1940. Upon his return to the UK, he was promoted to wing commander and given command of Fighter Sector HQ, 9 Group, which was responsible for the defence of the West Midlands and Liverpool. Following the accident at Betton Strange, he was posted to the Far East as the Senior Air Staff Officer (SASO) of 224 Group in Burma and appointed OBE in the New Year's Honours list 1942. On 22 January 1943 he went to Maungdaw airfield to brief crews for a raid on the Japanese at Prome River and, always keen to lead by example, he decided to accompany the men and took off in a Hurricane belonging to 615 Squadron. Whilst over the target area, however, his aircraft was shot down by ground fire and he was taken prisoner by the Japanese and sent to a POW camp in Burma (and later Thailand). In September 1944, with the Allies pushing the Japanese forces back, G/Capt More was put onto the transport ship *Rakuyo Maru* with a large number of POW's, to be transported to Japan. Tragically, on 12 September the ship was torpedoed by an American submarine and, although G/Capt More survived the attack and was last seen alive on a raft, he was never recovered. He was 34 years old and is commemorated on the Singapore Memorial to the Missing.

P/O (Nav/AI Op) John Rushworth Juleff (82717), RAFO, was born in Barnet, in 1916. He served as an aircrafthand with 601 Squadron, Auxiliary Air Force, before the war then, following the outbreak of hostilities, remustered as an air gunner and subsequently flew on night-fighter operations with 600 Squadron during the Battle of Britain. Commissioned in June 1940, little else is known of his military service other than that he was posted to 68 Squadron sometime during 1941 and survived a serious car crash near Wellington on 1 September 1941 (which killed another passenger). He eventually retired from the RAF as a squadron leader in 1946 and died in 1977.

11 July (Friday)
Civilian employee of British Runways Ltd (Employed at RAF Tern Hill, Shropshire)
A pupil pilot of 5 SFTS was landing in a Master (N7567) when he lost control and collided with a roller being driven by a civilian employee, who was killed instantly.

Robert Leonard Johnson, aged 16, was the son of John and Edith Johnson (née Kelly) of 2 Hill Side, Grinshill. He is buried in Drayton Rural Cemetery, Shropshire.

Cpl Robert Hénaux [TNA]

14 July (Monday)
Solo formation flight. 5 SFTS (RAF Tern Hill, Shropshire)
Miles Master I (N7474) force-landed 'at Bridle Gate, Shawbury' (presumably Bridleway Gate, between Preston Brockhurst and Lee Brockhurst), at 17.15 hrs. During the course of the training flight the engine failed and, due to smoke obscuring his vision, the pilot slightly damaged the aircraft on the branches of a tree as he made his landing approach.

Cpl (pilot u/t) Robert J Hénaux, FFAF, was born in Paris XII, on 9 February 1920 and was undergoing pilot training in France at the time of the German invasion. He managed to escape to England on board the lobster-fishing boat, *Le Trébouliste*. After completing his training with 5 SFTS, he was posted to 56 OTU to undergo operational training but was killed on 16 August 1941, when his Hurricane crashed during a training flight.

16 July (Wednesday)

Section formation training. 403 (Wolf) Squadron, RCAF (RAF Tern Hill, Shropshire)

Supermarine Spitfire IIA P7355 force-landed '1/2 mile south of the airfield' (putting it in the area of Helshaw Grange), at 16.20 hrs. The squadron had been stationed at Tern Hill for over a month as part of the defence of the West Midlands, and, on the day of the accident, the pilot was carrying out a routine training flight. Having completed the flight, he was preparing to land when the engine failed, due to a lack of fuel (the gauge was giving a faulty reading), and he was forced to belly-land in a field.

F/Lt (pilot) Edmund Charles (Ted) Cathels (37905), RAF, was born in Victoria, Canada, on 1 June 1917 and had enlisted in the RAF in 1936. Following his training, he joined 47 Squadron in Khartoum, in April 1937, flying Vickers Vincents in support of the British forces in the Sudan.
He continued his service in the Middle East, until 1940 when he returned to the UK and was posted to 403 Squadron. Following his accident he moved south to Hornchurch with the squadron and began operations over north-west Europe but, on 27 August 1941, he was shot down in a Spitfire (P8726) during an offensive sweep and taken prisoner. He spent the remainder of the war as a POW before being liberated by the Allies at the end of the war.

17 July (Thursday)

Medium turns practice. 5 SFTS (RAF Tern Hill, Shropshire)

Miles Master I (T8853) force-landed at 'Quarry Farm, Newport' (possibly Quarry Farm at Howle, near Newport), at 11.30 hrs. Whilst the instructor was giving dual instruction to a pupil pilot, the aircraft's engine failed (presumably due to a technical defect) and he was forced to belly-land in a field.

F/Sgt (instructor pilot) Bernard James Jennings (516308), DFM, RAF. Before his posting to Tern Hill as an instructor he had flown Spitfires with 19 Squadron during the Battle of Britain and destroyed two enemy aircraft and claimed six more probable. His DFM was awarded in April 1941, the citation for which explained that his high number of probables was 'due to his unselfish conduct in protecting less experienced members of the squadron when in action instead of confirming his own probables'. Little is known of his subsequent military service other than that he survived the war and is thought to have flown Mustangs with 168 Squadron in 1944. He remained in the RAF after the war and was awarded the AFC in 1953 before retiring as a wing commander in March 1962.

C/Chef (pilot u/t) René Royer, FFAF was born in Gennevilliers, Paris, on 2 August 1920 and was undergoing pilot training in France when the Germans invaded. He escaped to England on board *Le Trébouliste* (a lobster fishing boat). On completion of his training he joined 154 Squadron, briefly, before being posted to 19 Squadron on 26 April 1942, flying Spitfires on offensive sweeps over north-west Europe. In March 1943 he was posted to 340 (French) Squadron and was killed on 3 September 1944 when his Spitfire suffered engine failure at low altitude and crashed at Bernay, in northern France.

18 July (Friday)

Solo training flight. 5 SFTS (RAF Tern Hill, Shropshire)

Miles Master I (T8546) force-landed at Lilleshall at 16.05 hrs. During the course of the training flight the engine failed due to a loss of pressure and, according to the pilot's memoirs on the *BBC's Peoples War* website, he 'scraped under some power cables and managed to land wheels up in a field of corn. The farmer was not pleased! This was a salutary lesson after only 83 hours' flying!'

LAC (pilot u/t) Alfred Gordon Conway (1295392), RAFVR, was born in London, on 18 March 1923. He attended University College School and then worked for Kodak before joining the RAFVR in November 1940. On completion of his training he was posted to 136 Squadron flying Hurricanes (and later Spitfires) in the Far East, and subsequently became one of the leading fighter aces in Burma (with seven aircraft credited to his name). In September 1943 he was forced to bale out of his Spitfire, after the hood

LAC Conway [TNA]

detached and jammed the tailplane. Two months later he was awarded the DFC. Following a brief spell of leave in September 1944 he was given command of 155 Squadron in May 1945 and flew Spitfires over Burma until the end of the war. He remained in the RAF after the war, retiring as a wing commander in March 1977. He died in January 2003.

18 July (Friday)
Solo steep and climbing turns. 5 SFTS (RAF Tern Hill, Shropshire)
Miles Master I (T8381) crashed on Cherrington Moor, to the south-west of Tibberton (at map reference 673183), at 20.25 hrs. The pilot was carrying out slow rolls and was in an inverted position when flames were seen emitting from the port centre section of the aircraft. Moments later, the pilot was seen to abandon the aircraft but, tragically, his parachute had been burnt in the flames and he was killed instantly as he hit the ground, leaving a noticeable imprint in the boggy ground. In the subsequent examination of the site, the petrol filler cap was found in another field and it was concluded that it had not been correctly fitted prior to the flight and had worked loose owing to vibration. When the pilot was inverted in the roll, the engine spluttered and a flame from the exhaust ignited the fuel pouring out of the fuel tank, causing the aircraft to catch fire.

Sous Cadet (pilot u/t) Xavier Hahn, FFAF, was born in Marseille, on 31 March 1914. He appears to have served as an observer in the French Air Force before escaping to England after the German invasion. Initially buried in Market Drayton Cemetery, his body was repatriated to France in July 1949.

Cadet Xavier Hahn [TNA]

20 July (Sunday)
Dual spinning practice. 5 SFTS (RAF Tern Hill, Shropshire)
Miles Master I (N7939) force-landed at Holmer Farm, Stirchley (at map reference 710068), at 06.50 hrs. After the engine failed in flight the instructor belly-landed in a large sloping field where 'it went skidding across the field and into a hedge', according to local schoolboy, Warwick Tart.

Acting F/Lt (instructor pilot) Roy Bailey (43828), RAF, was born in Gillingham, on 1 October 1914 and joined the RAF as a Halton apprentice in January 1930. He served with a number of different squadrons before being accepted for pilot training in 1938. Gaining his wings in January 1939, he was subsequently selected for instructor training and spent the majority of the war as a flying instructor, for which he was awarded the AFC in June 1944. In November 1944 he finally underwent operational training before being posted to 692 Squadron in January 1945, flying Mosquitos on night bombing strikes until the end of the war. He remained in the RAF after the war and eventually retired as a squadron leader in December 1968.

The name of the pupil pilot is not known.

21 July (Monday)
Engine test (to 'obtain data on modified connecting rod bearings with negative-G carburettor programme'). Rolls-Royce flight test establishment (Hucknall, Nottinghamshire)
Hawker Hurricane IIA (Z2316) crashed at Sutton Grange Farm, Sutton-upon-Tern, to the north-east of Tern Hill. The pilot is believed to have been trying to land at Tern Hill (perhaps due to engine trouble) when he allowed the aircraft to stall and crash.

Mr (test pilot) David Robert McCartney, an employee of Rolls-Royce, aged 32, was the husband of

Kathleen B McCartney (née Wood). He was born in Church Stretton on 24 May 1909 and had lived and worked in Worcestershire as a 'maltster' during the 1930s, gaining his pilot's licence with the Worcestershire Flying Club in 1935. He is buried in Church Stretton (Cunnery Road) Cemetery, Shropshire.

David McCartney [RAeC]

25 July (Friday)
Practice single engine flying. 11 SFTS (RAF Shawbury, Shropshire)
Airspeed Oxford I (V3885) crashed near Admaston, Wellington (at wartime map reference 627129), at 10.15 hrs. The pilot had been in the air for just ten minutes when he entered a spin while climbing to 1,500 feet to carry out single-engine flying. According to witnesses, the pilot was seen to close the throttles when the plane stalled, rather than opening them, which contributed to his loss of control.

LAC (pilot u/t) Victor Edward George Burt (1192945), RAFVR, aged 20, was the son of Frederick Henry and Beatrice Hilda Burt (née Bartlett) of Wimborne, Dorset. He is buried in Wimborne Minster Cemetery, Dorset.

26 July (Saturday)
Non-operational searchlight co-operation flight. 68 Squadron (RAF High Ercall, Shropshire)
Bristol Beaufighter IC (T3354) crashed into the south side of the Wrekin (possibly near Hell's Gate) at 01.32 hrs. The crew were on a local training exercise with Buildwas searchlight site (BG064), when the weather unexpectedly turned for the worse, with the cloud base dropping down to just 750 feet. All crews airborne at the time were immediately recalled to base and landed safely but the crew of this aircraft were unable to gain a visual fix of the airfield due to the cloud. Tragically, as the pilot continued to circle while searching for the landing lights, he flew straight into the cloud-obscured hillside at full power and the aircraft was totally destroyed. Following the crash, soldiers from Buildwas searchlight site set off to search for the aircraft, followed swiftly by a search party from RAF High Ercall, assisted by the Wellington Home Guard and local policemen. The scene that met the men was one of utter devastation and it was a while before the bodies were discovered by S/Ldr Jackson, the Medical Officer from High Ercall. As a direct result of the crash, it was decided that a red beacon should be installed to warn pilots of its presence and a beacon has marked the hilltop ever since.

F/O (pilot) Oliver Bertram 'Tiny' Morrogh-Ryan (40979), RAF, aged 22, was the son of Leonard and Laura Morrogh-Ryan of Dunboyne Castle, County Meath, Ireland, and husband of Emily Ord Vaux of Brettanby Manor, Yorkshire. Born on 19 March 1919, he joined the RAF in 1938 and, after completing his training, was posted to 41 Squadron on 15 April 1939, flying Spitfires. He flew with the squadron during the Dunkirk evacuations and the Battle of Britain and claimed two enemy aircraft destroyed and one damaged, as well as being shot down once himself on 7 September. In December 1940 he was posted to 96 Squadron on its formation at Cranage and began night-fighter training, but in June 1941 he was posted to 68 Squadron, teaming up with his radar operator, Sgt Willis. He is buried in Barton (St Cuthbert) Churchyard, Yorkshire.

F/O Oliver Morrogh-Ryan [Jeremy Morrogh-Ryan]

Sgt (AI Operator) Horace Robert Willis (942245), RAFVR, aged 24, was the son of Horace Henry and Ellen Christabel Willis (née Sharp) of Rushden. He is buried in Rushden Cemetery, Northamptonshire.

LAC Vincent Nuttall [Mick Irving]

26 July (Saturday)
Night training flight. 11 SFTS (RAF Shawbury, Shropshire)
Airspeed Oxford II (N4779) struck by a landing aircraft at the airfield. After the pilot made a heavy landing and caused his undercarriage to collapse, the aircraft lay obstructing the runway. The Airfield Control Pilot (ACP) therefore ordered a floodlight to be switched on to illuminate the wreckage and make it visible for other aircraft preparing to land. Unfortunately, an instructor pilot and his pupil, who were preparing to land in an Oxford (P8930), thought that the light had been switched on to aid their landing and touched down on the runway. No sooner had they done so than they saw the wrecked Oxford ahead, opened up the throttles and tried to bounce over the wreckage but their wheels smashed into the side of N4779, fatally injuring the pilot who was still inside the cockpit.

LAC (pilot u/t) Vincent Nuttall (1375912), RAFVR, aged 28, was the son of James Thomas and Johanna Nuttall of Higher Openshaw, Manchester. He is buried in Droylsden Cemetery, Lancashire.

30 July (Wednesday)
Formation cloud flying practice. 403 (Wolf) Squadron, RCAF (RAF Tern Hill, Shropshire)
Supermarine Spitfire IIA (P7825, presentation aircraft bearing the name *Tyrone*) crashed 'one mile north west of Cosford' (putting it in the area between Cosford and Shifnal), at 10.55 hrs. The pilot had only been with the squadron two days and was flying a routine training flight when he became separated from his formation in cloud, lost control and crashed (although there was also a suggestion that he may have been knocked unconscious flying in bumpy conditions).

Sgt (pilot) Lou Lesa German (R.71250), RCAF, aged 22, was the son of Russian-born Joseph German and Polish-born Esther Goretski of Winnipeg. Born on 15 August 1918, he had worked in various jobs, including time as a garage helper, chauffeur, cattle buyer and labourer before enlisting in September 1940. He is buried in Birmingham (Witton) Cemetery.

30 July (Wednesday)
Solo training flight. 11 SFTS (RAF Shawbury, Shropshire)
Airspeed Oxford II (P1938) crashed at Bomere Heath, at 15.40 hrs. After entering heavy rain and cloud at about 1,800 feet the pilot 'started to glide but the aircraft started a turn to the right which the pupil was unable to control'. With the aircraft out of control, the pilot left by the emergency escape hatch, opened his parachute while still in cloud and landed safely in a field near Bomere Heath, while his aircraft crashed nearby. The cause of the crash was subsequently attributed to a loss of control due to 'inexperience of the pupil'.

LAC (pilot u/t) John Duncan White (1027455), RAFVR, was born on 15 July 1916 and lived in Kingsway, Manchester. He had worked as a 'master printer motor engineer' before enlisting in January 1941. Commissioned in June 1942, he eventually joined 207 Squadron but was shot up on 19 December 1944, piloting a Lancaster (LM671) on an mission to Gdynia in Poland, and forced to ditch in the Baltic. After skilfully putting the aircraft down the crew spent nine hours in a dinghy before being picked up by the Germans and spending the remainder of the war as POWs.

31 July (Thursday)
Circuits and landings. 5 SFTS (RAF Child's Ercall, Shropshire – Relief Landing Ground to RAF Tern Hill)
Miles Master I (T8432) crashed at Steppes Farm, Child's Ercall ('300 yards from the airfield'), at 01.45 hrs. An instructor and pupil pilot were taking off on a dark night when the 'comparatively

inexperienced' instructor failed to ensure that his pupil had set the propeller to fully fine pitch. With the aircraft failing to gain height, the port wing struck the top of a fifty foot tree and crashed near the airfield boundary.

Sgt (instructor pilot) Allan Cyril Mew (1109747), RAFVR, aged 21, was the son of J William and Sarah Mew (née Pyle) of Stretford. He is buried in Stretford Cemetery, Lancashire.

LAC (pilot u/t) John Kenneth Young (1191569), RAFVR, aged 18, was the son of David Charles and Jessie Margaret Young of Moseley, Birmingham. He is buried in Birmingham (Yardley) Cemetery.

LAC John Young [TNA]

3 August (Sunday)

Solo night training flight. 5 SFTS (RAF Child's Ercall, Shropshire – Relief Landing Ground to RAF Tern Hill)

Miles Master I (T8850) crashed into a tree near Child's Ercall airfield, at 02.15 hrs. The pilot was approaching to land when he turned too late to line up with the flare path. This necessitated his making an 'S' turn to get back in line with the runway. As he did so, however, he allowed the aircraft to undershoot, struck some trees and crashed some distance from the perimeter, injuring himself.

LAC (pilot u/t) Barrett Christison (1311836), RAFVR. On completion of his training he joined 155 Squadron in April 1942, flying Mohawks on ground attack, recce and escort flights over the Burma front. Commissioned in January 1944, he was awarded the DFM in September 1944 for his actions with 155 Squadron but, sadly, he would never learn of his award. On 4 September 1944, he is thought to have been killed in a Spitfire (LV747) while on a test flight with 166 Wing. F/O Christison, who was 23 years old and the son of James Moodie and Florence Lucy Veronique Christison of Alton, Hampshire, is buried in Chittagong War Cemetery, Bangladesh.

4 August (Monday)

Training flight. 5 SFTS (RAF Tern Hill, Shropshire)

Hawker Hurricane I (L1684) force-landed 'two miles north west of Lilleshall' (putting it in the Longford Moors area to the south-west of Edgmond) at 13.00 hrs. The pilot belly-landed in a field after the engine failed and was unhurt.

LAC (pilot u/t) Ronald David Emery (1375732), RAFVR. After leaving Tern Hill, he was posted to 60 OTU to undergo advanced training but was killed on 30 August when he crashed into high-tension power cables at Scremerston while low flying in a Miles Master (T8627). Sgt Emery, who was 19 years old, was the son of Charles Herne Emery and Ethel Ada Emery of Kenton, Middlesex. He is buried in Streatham Park Cemetery.

7 August (Thursday)

Steep turns, single-engine flying and precautionary landings. 11 SFTS (RAF Shawbury, Shropshire)

Airspeed Oxford II (V3689) crashed into trees just off the western boundary at 16.15 hrs. Having undershot his approach and bounced heavily near the perimeter track, the pupil pilot opened up the throttles to make another circuit of the airfield and attempt another landing. As the aircraft passed the lamella hangars on the western edge of the airfield he is thought to have 'committed an error of judgment in that he failed to gain sufficient height before reaching the aerodrome boundary and that he probably raised his flaps too soon and too fast, causing the aircraft to drop into some trees and stall'.

LAC (pilot u/t) George Edward Pyper (1380753), RAFVR, aged 21, was the son of Edward and Emma Pyper of Shefford. He is buried in Campton and Shefford Cemetery, Bedfordshire.

Jim Currie [Ian Currie]

8 August (Friday)
Formation flying. 5 SFTS (RAF Tern Hill, Shropshire)
Hawker Hurricane I (L1769) force-landed at Sambrook, to the south-east of Hinstock, at 20.05 hrs. After the engine failed during the flight the pupil pilot made a successful belly-landing in a field 'under difficult conditions' and was unhurt.

LAC (pilot u/t) James Hogan (Jim) Currie (1365319), RAFVR, was born in Ayr, Scotland, on 26 December 1920 and educated at St Margaret's High School and St Aloysius College in Glasgow. Commissioned on 20 August 1941, he eventually joined 4 Squadron, Indian Air Force, flying Hurricanes (and later Spitfires) on operations over Burma. For his services with the Squadron, he was awarded the DFC in October 1945 while ranked as an acting squadron leader. He remained in the RAF after the war and eventually relinquished his commission as a flight lieutenant in September 1956, after which he became a Roman Catholic priest.

20 August (Wednesday)
Solo training flight. 5 SFTS (RAF Tern Hill, Shropshire)
Miles Master I (N7825) crashed at Sheriffhales, near Shifnal, at 15.10 hrs. The French pupil pilot was on a routine training flight, during which he is believed to have met with another French pilot at a prearranged rendezvous and begun unauthorised low flying. After manoeuvring onto the tail of the other aircraft, at a height of 1,700 feet, it is thought that he hit the aircraft's slipstream, lost control and crashed. Following an investigation, the AOC expressed his recommendation that the 'authorities are exposed to this accident with views to improvement and to ensure Allied personnel comply with regulations', as he considered that the 'flying discipline of the Free French [was] poor'.

Cpl (pilot u/t) Émile Laurent [who also went under the alias of Davis Garbutt] (30090), FFAF, aged 20, was born in Quimperlé, on 22 March 1921. He was undergoing pilot training in France when the German invasion occurred and escaped to England on board *Le Trébouliste* (a lobster fishing boat). He was buried in Market Drayton prior to being repatriated for burial in Quimperlé in Brittany, in 1949.

21 August (Thursday)
Cross-country exercise. 9 SFTS (RAF Hullavington, Wiltshire)
Hawker Hurricane I (R4194) force-landed 'one mile north of Ludlow' (presumably between Whitbatch and Fishmore Farm), at 15.00 hrs. After running into very poor weather conditions, and knowing that he was entering an area of hilly ground obscured under a blanket of low cloud, the pupil pilot decided to make a precautionary landing. He unfortunately touched down too far along the field and crashed through a hedge, causing the aircraft to tip onto its nose.

LAC (pilot u/t) Alec Brees (1360722), RAFVR, was commissioned in September 1941 and eventually joined 268 Squadron, flying Mustangs on tactical reconnaissance, intruder and escort missions over north-west Europe (for which he was awarded the DFC in January 1944). In 1945, he was given command of 245 Squadron (which was part of the first jet-fighter wing in the RAF) but, sadly, did not survive his command and was killed on 23 August when he was involved in a mid-air collision and crashed into the sea near Weston-super-Mare flying a Meteor (EE280). S/Ldr Brees, aged 25, is commemorated on the Runnymede Memorial. Five months after his death he received a posthumous mention in despatches.

21 August (Thursday)
Cross-country exercise. 9 SFTS (RAF Hullavington, Wiltshire)

Hawker Hurricane I (N2402) crashed on the runway at RAF Shawbury, at 17.30 hrs. The pilot was presumably flying the same cross-country route as LAC Brees (see above) when he became lost in poor weather and decided to make a precautionary landing at the nearest airfield (RAF Shawbury). As he touched down, however, the aircraft bounced badly. As it touched down a second time he applied the brakes too hard and the aircraft skidded, overturned and slid along the ground on its back. The seriously injured pilot was conveyed to RAF Hospital, Cosford where he succumbed to his injuries later that evening.

LAC (pilot u/t) Norman Charles Herbert Clout (1330092), RAFVR, aged 18, was the son of Maj Charles William Clout, MBE and Mary Clout of Chislehurst, Kent. He is buried in Chislehurst Cemetery.

23 August (Saturday)
Force-landing approaches and local map reading. 5 SFTS (RAF Tern Hill, Shropshire)
Miles Master I (T8855) crashed at Alveley, to the south-east of Bridgnorth, at 09.40 hrs. The pilot was flying in bad weather conditions when he lost control in low cloud and spun into the ground.

Sgt (pilot u/t) René Le Bian [under the alias Ralph Sayers], FFAF, aged 21, was born in Le Havre, France on 19 August 1919 and joined the French Air Force in December 1939. He was undergoing pilot training when the Germans invaded and, along with several other trainee pilots, managed to escape to St Jean de Luz in the south of France, where they boarded the *Arandora Star* for England. Initially buried in Market Drayton Cemetery, his body was repatriated to France in 1949.

28 August (Thursday)
Training flight. 5 SFTS (RAF Tern Hill, Shropshire)
Miles Master III (W8571) force-landed at Apley Castle, near Wellington, at 09.50 hrs. Little is known of the incident other than that the pilot made a precautionary landing in a field and that the aircraft was undamaged. The name of the pilot is unknown.

30 August (Saturday)
Aileron control test flight (following delivery to the unit from the Hawker Aircraft Company). 29 MU (RAF High Ercall, Shropshire)
Hawker Hurricane IIC (BD786) crashed at Longdon on Tern, between Wellington and High Ercall, at 14.50 hrs. While flying at 2,300 feet, the pilot found that the control column could be moved from side to side without having any effect on the aileron movement and therefore took to his parachute, slightly injuring his right leg in the process. The cause of the loss of control was subsequently found to have occurred when 'the aileron (lower) chain on the starboard side of the control column became detached from the tie-rod end due to failure of the connecting link or rivet.'

Sgt (Test pilot) Leonard Stanley Loveridge (754958), RAFVR, was born in Porth, Glamorgan on 21 January 1918 and joined the RAF in August 1939. After gaining his wings he was posted to 23 Squadron during the Battle of Britain, flying Blenheims on night-fighter operations, shipping protection and intruder operations. Following the squadron's conversion to Havocs in October 1940, he continued to fly intruder operations but, on 22 December 1940, he had to bale out over the Isle of Wight when his aircraft ran out of fuel returning from an operation. Tragically, his two crew members drowned in the sea. In June 1941 he was posted to 29 MU for twelve months as a test pilot (during which time he was also commissioned) and spent the remainder of the war as an instructor for which he was awarded the AFC in September 1945, while serving at 3 EFTS, Shellingford. He remained in the RAF after the war and was awarded the Air Efficiency Medal in 1946, before transferring to the reserve and finally retiring as a squadron leader in the early 1950s.

30 August (Saturday)
Ferry flight from RAF Sywell, Northamptonshire, to RAF Tern Hill. 24 MU (RAF Tern Hill, Shropshire)
Hawker Hector I (K9779) crash-landed at Child's Ercall at 13.40 hrs. The two pilots were both members of 131 Squadron, which was based at Tern Hill, but had been loaned to 24 MU to help ferry aircraft. At the time of the accident they were returning to Tern Hill when the engine failed, due to the pilot having omitted to switch to the gravity tanks when the main fuel tank ran dry (he was no doubt unfamiliar with this type of aircraft). Despite an attempt to land at Child's Ercall airfield, the approach was affected by some trees and the pilot crashed into a cornfield, completely writing off the aircraft and injuring both men, who were conveyed to RAF Hospital, Cosford.

Sgt (pilot) James Victor McIvor (402884), RNZAF, was born in Hastings, New Zealand on 15 February 1920 and enlisted in the RNZAF in September 1940. After serving with 131 Squadron, he was subsequently posted to 135 Squadron and flew Hurricanes over Burma.

Sgt (pilot, but travelling as passenger) Raymond Ignatius Phillips (402893), RNZAF, had joined 131 Squadron on 15 July 1941 and was posted out on 22 September after recovering from his injuries. He then spent a brief period with 132 Squadron before joining 486 (New Zealand) Squadron but was killed on 2 October 1942 on his nineteenth operation, when he was shot down in a Typhoon (R8683) while escorting Bostons on a bombing raid on Le Havre. P/O Phillips, aged 30, was the son of Daniel Paul Phillips and Mary Imelda Phillips (née Maher) of Wellington, New Zealand. He is commemorated on the Runnymede Memorial.

7 September (Sunday)
Cross-country exercise. 17 OTU (RAF Upwood, Cambridgeshire)
Bristol Blenheim IV (R3875) crashed at Bull Farm (at map reference 559013), Kenley, near Acton Burnell, at midday. The trainee crew were flying on the Worcester–Shrewsbury leg of a cross-country flight when the aircraft was witnessed making at least four turns before diving out of control from a height of 2,500 feet and crashing into trees. The loss of control was believed to be due to an accidental stall, while flying on instruments in overcast conditions, and the pilot having insufficient height to recover before striking the ground.

Sgt Elias Brearley [Anne Coleman]

Sgt (pilot) Mathew Francis Fox (1014018), RAFVR, aged 25, was the son of the late Richard Fox and Anne Fox (née Nolan) of Hough Green, Widnes. Educated at Ditton St Mary's Roman Catholic School and St Mary's College, in Strawberry Hill, London, he had returned to Widnes to become an assistant school master at St Marie's School before enlisting. He is buried in Widnes Cemetery.

Sgt (Obs) Bruce Adams Coukell (R.162788), RCAF, aged 25, was the son of John Edward Coukell and Mary H Coukell of High Bridge, in New Jersey, USA (although he had been born in Canada). He is buried in Shawbury (St Mary's) Churchyard, Shropshire.

Sgt (W/AG) Elias Cyril Brearley (1177594), RAFVR, aged 29, was the son of William and Eliza Brearley of Alfreton and the husband of Lily Holmes. Educated at Old Swanwick Hall School, near Alfreton, he had married Lily in 1934. He is buried in Alfreton Cemetery, Derbyshire.

10 September (Wednesday)
'Taxi flight to satellite airfield for air test.' 9 MU (RAF Cosford, Shropshire)
De Havilland DH90 Dragonfly (X9390) crashed near Cosford waterworks, to the west of the airfield, at 14.30 hrs. The pilot had just taken off when the port engine cut suddenly at 50 feet. While attempting

to force-land ahead, the pilot was unable to avoid striking a line of trees, causing the aircraft to crash, seriously injuring himself and slightly injuring his passenger. The cause of the engine failure could not subsequently be determined with any certainty, although it was considered most likely that an airlock developed in the petrol system, possibly due to incorrect setting of the fuel cocks.

F/Lt (test pilot) Charles William Francis (44048), RAF, had evidently served in the RAF for a considerable time before the war as he was awarded the Long Service and Good Conduct medal in January 1940 while ranked as a warrant officer. He was posted to 9 MU on 9 October 1939 as a test pilot and is believed to have spent the entire war serving with the unit before finally being posted out on 12 October 1945 to 22 MU. He eventually retired from the RAF with the rank of squadron leader.

F/Lt (test pilot, travelling as passenger) Alfred Keith Holdsworth (70314), RAF. After joining the RAF in 1937, he qualified as a bomber pilot and by the beginning of 1940 was serving with 149 Squadron flying Wellington bombers. He completed seven ops with the squadron but, on 24 May 1940, he was returning from a bombing raid on the battle area around Givet, in northern France, when his aircraft crashed for unknown reasons at Barton Mills, in Suffolk. Three of the crew were killed in the crash while the other three, including Holdsworth, were seriously injured. It appears that he left the squadron as a result of his injuries and later became a test pilot. He was involved in another crash while stationed at Cosford, on 10 December 1941, but survived the war and attained the rank of squadron leader.

14 September (Sunday)
Cross-country exercise from Shawbury–Sealand (Flintshire)–Shawbury. 11 SFTS (RAF Shawbury, Shropshire)
Airspeed Oxford II (P1876) force-landed at Market Drayton. The pupil pilot was returning to Shawbury when he lost his position in poor visibility and made a precautionary landing in a field of standing barley.

LAC (pilot u/t) Brendan Massey (1125506), RAFVR, was commissioned in April 1943 and subsequently became a test pilot on Meteor jets at the Gloster aircraft company. After leaving the service he returned to the RAF in February 1950 and was killed on 20 December 1952 when his Brigand (RH823) disintegrated during a shallow dive while flying from RAF Tengah, Singapore. F/Lt Massey was 30 years old and is buried in Kranji Military Cemetery, Singapore.

15 September (Monday)
Solo training flight. 11 SFTS (RAF Shawbury, Shropshire)
Airspeed Oxford I N4634 crashed into Acton Lea Coppice, to the north west of the airfield, at 15.45 hrs. The pilot was only on his second solo flight when he overshot a landing approach and then failed to open up the throttles quickly enough, causing him to pull back sharply on the control column to avoid a belt of trees two hundred yards from the airfield boundary. As he did so, however, the aircraft lost air speed, stalled and then crashed into a small coppice, injuring the pilot, who was taken to RAF Hospital, Cosford.

P/O Edgar Charlesworth [Alan Charlesworth]

P/O (pilot u/t) Edgar Richard Charlesworth (52413), RAFVR, was born in 1910, the son of Percy H and Sarah Charlesworth, and brought up on Percy Street, Liverpool and educated at Liverpool College. After leaving school he joined 5 King's (Liverpool) Regiment, in August 1931 and by the time war was declared had reached the rank of captain. In early 1941 he applied for a transfer to the RAF to train as a pilot, but following the accident at Shawbury retrained as a navigator and was posted to 427 Squadron, RCAF. He did not survive his tour and was killed on 15 November 1943 when his Wellington

(BK364) was shot down in the target area during a bombing op to Lorient in France. P/O Charlesworth is buried in Guidel Communal Cemetery, France, along with the rest of his crew.

23 September (Tuesday)
Dual training flight. 5 SFTS (RAF Tern Hill, Shropshire)
Miles Master I (N7572) force-landed at Whixall, to the west of Prees, at 18.20 hrs. After allowing the aircraft to run low on fuel the instructor was forced to belly-land in a stubble field.

F/Lt (instructor pilot) George Patrick Hall (48840), AFM, RAF, was born in Ashton-under-Lyne in 1907, the son of George Henry and Laura Ann Hall. His AFM was awarded during an investiture at Buckingham Palace in March 1941, but little is known of his military service until his death on 3 April 1943, while still serving as an instructor at Tern Hill, when a Master (W8057) crashed near Calveley in Cheshire. F/Lt Hall, the husband of Doris Florence Hall (née Poulton), is buried in Chester (Blacon) Cemetery.

The name of the pupil is unknown.

24 September (Wednesday)
Ferry flight from RAF Farnborough, Hampshire, to RAF West Freugh, Scotland. 'E' Flight, 1 AACU (RAF West Freugh, Wigtownshire, Scotland)
Hawker Henley III (L3270) force-landed at Selattyn, to the north west of Oswestry, at 17.00 hrs. The pilot was returning to base when he became lost in extremely bad weather conditions and decided to force-land. Due to the small size of the field, the aircraft was slightly damaged when it struck a fence.

F/Sgt (pilot) Leslie William (Bill) Rookley (566056), RAFVR, was commissioned in October 1942 and eventually joined 63 Squadron. He was killed on 22 October 1944 when he lost control of his Spitfire (BL235) during a training flight and crashed at Kelvedon, Essex. F/Lt Rookley, who was 28 years old, was the husband of Elizabeth Brown Rookley of Stranraer. He is buried in Stranraer (Glebe) Cemetery.

25 September (Thursday)
Night solo flight. 5 SFTS (RAF Tern Hill, Shropshire)
Miles Master I (N7628) crashed near 'Peplow Bridge, Hodnet', at 22.05 hrs. The French pupil pilot was approaching to land when another aircraft took off from the airfield, causing him to veer slightly and begin another landing circuit at 500 feet. During this second circuit, however, he displayed a 'lack of airmanship' by entering a shallow dive from which he failed to pull out before striking the ground. Amazingly, he was only injured.

Cpl Marcel Renaud [TNA]

Cpl (pilot u/t) Marcel Renaud [who also went under the alias of William Reynold], FFAF, was born in Paris VI, on 16 July 1920. He was undergoing pilot training in France when the Germans invaded and had escaped to England on board the lobster-fishing boat, *Le Trébouliste*. On completion of his training he was posted to 124 Squadron and then 340 (*Ile de France*) Squadron, with whom he was credited with an Fw190 probably destroyed on 12 December 1942. Sadly, he failed to return from a fighter sweep over northern France on 13 March 1943 piloting a Spitfire (EN475).

25 September (Thursday)
Training flight. 5 SFTS (RAF Cosford, Shropshire – detached flight from RAF Tern Hill)
Hawker Hurricane I (L1571) crash-landed south-south-west of RAF Cosford, at 16.05 hrs. The pilot was flying out of Cosford as part of a detached flight, to relieve congestion at Tern Hill, and had just taken

off when the engine cut out at a height of 150 feet. With little time to react, he force-landed in a field directly ahead. The aircraft was slightly damaged when it struck a hedge as he tried to pass under some telephone wires.

Cpl (pilot u/t) Pierre Bourgeois, FFAF, was born in Paris XVII, on 25 November 1922. He had managed to escape to Gibraltar, via the south of France, with help from his parents, and eventually arrived in England, where he enlisted in the FFAF. After completing his training he joined 340 (*Ile de France*) Squadron in November 1941 but was killed on 4 May 1942 when he is believed to have been shot down in a Spitfire (W3947) over the Channel while returning from an operation.

25 September (Thursday)
Solo aerobatics practice. 5 SFTS (RAF Tern Hill, Shropshire)
Miles Master Mk I (N7765) crashed at 'Goldstone Lane, Hinstock' at 17.59 hrs.
The pupil was authorised to carry out aerobatics at a height of 8,000 feet, during which he is believed to have deliberately induced a spin and then 'allowed the aircraft to reach too low an altitude before commencing recovery action.'

LAC George D'Silva. [TNA]

LAC (pilot u/t) George John Howard D'Silva (129367), RAFVR, aged 18, was the son of George Thomas and Rita Alice D'Silva of 125 Canterbury Road, Herne Bay, Kent. He was born in India, where his father was working as professor of surgery at the Veterinary College in Madras, and the family did not return to England until the 1930s. Educated at Balham Grammar School and Herne Bay College, he was a noted rugby and hockey player. He is buried in Herne Bay Cemetery, Kent.

28 September (Sunday)
Training flight. 5 SFTS (RAF Cosford, Shropshire – detached flight from RAF Tern Hill)
Hawker Hurricane I (P3395) force-landed near Chadwell and Weston, to the north-east of Sherrifhales, at 19.15 hrs. The pilot was flying from Cosford as part of a detached flight, to relieve congestion at Tern Hill, when he became lost in bad visibility and made a precautionary landing on rough ground, causing the wheels to collapse.

Sgt (pilot u/t) Pierre Gallay, FFAF, had served in north Africa with the French military before the war and, following the German invasion of France in 1940, escaped to England aboard the *Arandora Star*. He enlisted in the FFAF and, on completion of his training, was posted to 130 Squadron, then out to the Middle East to join *Groupe de Chasse I* before returning to the UK to join the newly-formed 341 (Alsace) Squadron in March 1943. Flying on fighter sweeps over north-west Europe, he shot down an Me109 on 28 September 1944. The following month he was forced to crash-land a Spitfire (PT996) near Oisterwijk, on 22 October, after suffering flak damage. After evading capture for nine days he managed to reach Allied lines and subsequently returned to his squadron. Following the war he became a test pilot but lost his life on 7 April 1950 test-flying the French prototype SNCAC NC1080 carrier-based jet fighter.

28 September (Sunday)
Return flight from RAF Hucknall, Nottinghamshire. 131 Squadron (RAF Atcham, Shropshire)
Miles Magister I (R1977) was struck by a Spitfire on the runway, at 16.40 hrs. The squadron had only arrived at Atcham the previous day, having spent the last few weeks flying from RAF Tern Hill. Two of the squadron pilots were returning from a flight to RAF Hucknall (although it is unclear what they were doing there). The accident that followed was witnessed by one of the squadron's ground personnel, whose account appears on the excellent 350 Squadron website (the squadron was born out of 131 Squadron's 'B' Flight):

Whilst at Atcham, 131 'B' flight had a bad day. A flying accident in the true sense of the word. I have never forgotten this day. I had obtained permission from Flying Control for P/O Picard [Henri Picard] to take-off on sector recce (remember the Belgian aircrew had just joined 131 and had started their programme). I can remember him taxying past our flight HQ to take up position on 1 runway. In the mean time 'A' flight's Magister had just landed and was taxying down the runway when P/O Picard took off. I grabbed the Very pistol and ran out to the perimeter, I think Corporal Redman had seen this too, took the pistol from me and ran towards the runway firing red warning shots towards P/O Picard's Spit, too late for him to see the Magister, he was at full throttle by now and the tail had just come up, he collided with the Magister at midships, an absolute tragedy. P/O Chubb was already dead when we arrived on scene and Sgt Lee was badly injured, he died later that day. Remember we had no such thing as 'Airfield Control' in those days and during the court of enquiry, the question of 'permission for take-off' was mentioned. I think this might have been the start of 'Airfield Control', as we came to know them as the war went on.

P/O (pilot) Peter Chubb (65521), RAFVR, aged 20, is buried in Mount St Mary's College Churchyard, Derbyshire. His death notice in *The Times* newspaper described him as 'an old mountaineer' and asked for correspondence to be sent to 59 Westfield Drive, Loughborough.

Sgt (pilot, but travelling as passenger) Stanley Douglas Lee (927861), RAFVR, aged 21, is commemorated at the South London Crematorium, Mitcham. His next-of-kin are unknown.

30 September (Tuesday)
Circuits and landings. 5 SFTS (RAF Child's Ercall, Shropshire)
Hawker Hurricane I (L1788) crashed on the outskirts of Tern Hill airfield, at 09.10 hrs. The pilot had been driven over to Child's Ercall in the morning to begin his circuits and bumps training on Hurricanes and had then taken off and flown to Tern Hill, where he made a successful landing. He then took off again but, as he reached 100 feet, the engine failed due to a glycol leak and, according to the diary of his fellow course member and friend, 2 Lt David Greville-Heygate,

Lt Neville Day [TNA]

he had not jammed the nose down and consequently it had stalled and done a quarter spin straight into the ground. It immediately caught fire and was burned out. Neville was thrown clear, his harness breaking, but his neck was broken and he was killed instantaneously. It was the beginning of a series of misfortunes in quick succession ...

Lt (pilot u/t) Neville Lawrence Winkworth Day (124767), RAFVR, aged 23, was the son of Major Sam and Maria Elsie Day of Great Missenden. Commissioned into the Monmouthshire Regiment in March 1940, he transferred to the RAFVR the following year. He is buried in Great Hampden (St Mary Magdelene) Churchyard, Buckinghamshire. His brother, Capt G L Day, died whilst serving in Burma in 1945.

30 September (Tuesday)
Training flight. 5 SFTS (RAF Cosford, Shropshire – detached flight from RAF Tern Hill)
Hawker Hurricane I (V7722) force-landed at Blythbury Farm, one mile west of Shifnal, at 18.00 hrs. The pupil pilot was flying from Cosford as part of a detached flight, to relieve congestion at Tern Hill, and was near the airfield when the engine failed and he was forced to belly-land into a grazed field.

LAC (pilot u/t) Aksel Andreas Svendsen (1314900), RAFVR, was born in Copenhagen, Denmark, on 21 September 1922. He had moved to live in Devon in 1928, where his stepfather, Svend Iversen, was the managing director of a Danish bacon company in Exeter. After completing his training he was posted to 32 Squadron, piloting Hurricanes, before transferring to 234 Squadron on 1 April 1942, flying

Spitfires on operational sweeps over north-west Europe. Three days after his twentieth birthday, he was shot down piloting a Spitfire (BL924) during combat with Fw190s over the French Coast.

9 October (Thursday)
Solo training flight. 11 SFTS (RAF Bratton, Shropshire – Relief Landing Ground to RAF Shawbury)
Airspeed Oxford II (T1278) crashed near the Gate House pub on the edge of the airfield. The pupil pilot had taken off across wind from the small grass airfield, not realising that another Oxford (P1860) was also taking off, correctly, into the wind and therefore on a converging course. As the two aircraft began to pick up speed and lift off, the instructor pilot in P1860 saw the other aircraft and tried, in vain, to avoid it and the two aircraft collided 20 feet off the ground. The pilot of this aircraft was thrown twenty yards from the cockpit in the resultant crash and died of his injuries two days later in the Royal Salop Infirmary. The occupants of P1860, which belly-landed in a field directly ahead, were slightly injured.

LAC (pilot u/t) Ronald Henry Hughes (1387751), RAFVR, aged 19, was the son of Thomas George and Lily Hughes of St Neots, Cambridgeshire. He is buried in Shawbury (St Mary's) Churchyard.

Training flight. 11 SFTS (RAF Bratton, Shropshire – Relief Landing Ground to RAF Shawbury)
Airspeed Oxford I (P1860) collided with the above mentioned aircraft and belly-landed by the airfield.

P/O (instructor pilot) James Morley Randall (67074), RAFVR, survived the war and attained the rank of flight lieutenant.

LAC (pilot u/t) Godfrey Harry Grantham (1310307), RAFVR, who was the 30-year-old son of the late Capt Frederick William Grantham and Alexandra E Grantham of Abingdon, Berkshire, was commissioned in December 1941. He was killed on 21 June 1942, serving as an instructor at 16 EFTS, when a Magister (L8227) crashed at Dalbury Lees in Derbyshire. He is buried in Repton (St Wystan) Churchyard. His father had lost his life serving with the Royal Munster Fusiliers in France in 1915 and his elder brother, 2 Lt H F Grantham, had died at Gallipoli in 1915 whilst serving with the Essex Regiment.

11 October (Saturday)
LAC R H Hughes died today from injuries received in a crash two days earlier at Bratton.

11 October (Saturday)
Solo training flight. 5 SFTS (RAF Tern Hill, Shropshire)
Miles Master I (T8389) force-landed 'three miles north-east of Wellington' (putting it in an area roughly around Preston on the Weald Moors) at 13.10 hrs. The pupil pilot made a forced landing after the engine failed and was unhurt.

LAC (pilot u/t) Herbert Robert Johnson (56146), RAFVR. He was to be killed just twelve days later in a crash at Chetwynd.

12 October (Sunday)
Solo training flight. 5 SFTS (RAF Tern Hill, Shropshire)
Miles Master I (N7867) force-landed at 'Castle Hotel, Bletchley', to the west of Market Drayton, at 15.30 hrs. During the course of the flight the engine failed and, in the resultant forced landing, the aircraft struck a hedge and crashed to a stop. The pilot was fortunately unhurt.

Sgt (pilot u/t) François Henri Guinamard (30088), FFAF, was born in Douai in September 1919. Following the German invasion of France, he had escaped to England aboard the lobster-fishing boat, *Le Trébouliste*. On completion of his training he was posted to 130 Squadron, then out to the Middle East to join *Groupe de Chasse I*, before returning to the UK to join the newly formed 341 (Alsace)

Squadron in March 1943. He remained in the French Air Force after the war, attaining the rank of *capitaine* and completed 65 missions against the Vietminh in French Indochina. He was shot down and killed on 29 July 1952 piloting a Bearcat on a mission to attack a Vietminh-held bridge.

14 October (Tuesday)

Solo circuits and landings. 5 SFTS (RAF Tern Hill, Shropshire)

Miles Master I (T8759) force-landed at New House Farm, just west of Wollerton, near Hodnet, at 13.30 hrs. The pupil pilot was making a circuit of the airfield when the engine failed and he was forced to land in a field.

LAC (pilot u/t) André Emile Eid (1383977), RAFVR, was a Belgian citizen who had been born in Cairo, on 1 November 1920 and had lived in Egypt until 1940 when he travelled to the UK to join up. After completing his training he served with 501, 130, 349 (Belgian) and 272 Squadrons before finally joining 601 Squadron in September 1943, flying Spitfires on ground-attack operations in support of the advancing Allied armies in Italy. During his time with the squadron he shot down two Me109s but was killed on 15 May 1944 while test-flying a Spitfire (JG258). He was buried in Monte Cassino Military Cemetery and his body was repatriated and reinterred in Brussels City Cemetery after the war.

17 October (Friday)

Solo night circuits and landings. 5 SFTS (RAF Chetwynd, Shropshire – Relief Landing Ground to RAF Tern Hill)

Miles Master III (W8562) crashed on approach to Chetwynd airfield at 01.50 hrs. The pupil pilot was approaching to land, at a very low altitude on a dark night, when he struck a large tree and crashed. Reg Brown, who was on fire-tender duty that night, recalled the incident to the author in 2007:

> The ambulance nearly always went off together [with the fire tender]. It wasn't a very nice experience. One aircraft was coming in to land at night. He was coming in from this direction I think [from the north] and he came in too low and hit a tree. So, on the flare path there would be a vehicle with some crew on it. Now if anything went wrong they would flash us with an Aldis lamp. So, we could see this fire in the distance so we went chasing round the country lanes until we could get to it across a wheat field. The farmers were there as usual and of course it was a complete wreck. It was almost completely burnt away, it was all molten.

LAC Bill Vocking [Bert Vocking]

LAC (pilot u/t) William Charles (Bill) Vocking (656391), RAFVR, aged 26, was the son of William and Jessie Harriet Vocking. Born in Acton, West London, on 24 January 1915, he had grown up in Chiswick and attended Chiswick County School, where he was both academically gifted and a good athlete (winning quite a few races whilst competing for the Thames Valley Harriers). After leaving school he became an accountant and office manager for a local scrap-metal firm before being called up and serving in the Royal Welch Fusiliers, prior to transferring to the RAFVR. He is buried in Chiswick New Cemetery, Middlesex.

22 October (Wednesday)

Bombing raid on a 'grain elevator at Birkenhead', Merseyside. *Kampfgruppe* 606 (Amsterdam Schiphol airfield, Netherlands)

Junkers Ju88 A4 (1376, bearing the code 7T + CH) crashed on the edge of Woore reservoir (at map reference 722423), to the north-east of Market Drayton, at 21.33 hrs. The crew took off at 18.57 hrs as part of a force of nine aircraft tasked with attacking a grain elevator on Merseyside and flew across the North Sea before turning west and making landfall near Spurn Head, in Yorkshire. In order to avoid heavily defended areas the pilot then passed to the south of Sheffield and approached the target from the south-east, during which time he had to take evasive action twice after being picked up by searchlights. Due to the prevailing weather conditions the target could not be identified and their bombs were consequently dropped in the general area from a height of 11,800 feet. Soon after setting course for home, a violent explosion rocked the aircraft, wounding the bomb aimer and damaging the starboard engine, which immediately began losing revs. Moments later, a second anti-aircraft shell exploded below the nose of the aircraft and is believed to have seriously wounded the pilot as he was observed 'crouching in a very tense attitude over the control column'. The order was then given to bale out but only the wireless operator and observer were able to get out before the aircraft entered a spin and crashed out of control on the edge of the reservoir. According to a contemporary report in the *Newport & Market Drayton Advertiser*, one of the survivors walked to a keeper's cottage where Mr and Mrs Peter Farnell had just retired to bed.

> My husband went to the window and asked who was there. A voice replied in perfect English 'German airman wishes to give myself up to the military or the police.' My husband went downstairs and opened the front door. He searched the German but he was unarmed. He came into the house and asked if we had a telephone. He seemed a decent sort of a chap. He said he was 24 years old and was married with two children. He said he had been over England eight times but that the war had now finished for him. He stated that he had been on a raid on Liverpool and that his machine had been struck by 'flak'. My husband thought that the man was wearing the Iron Cross. After a short time my husband took the man to the police station ...

The other survivor, in the meanwhile, had walked to the house of Mr and Mrs B Jones where he knocked at the door.

> My husband, who is in the Home Guard, went downstairs and opened the door. He saw a man standing there. The man could not speak English, but he put out both his hands and my husband felt his pockets but he had

The funeral of the two Luftwaffe *airmen Herbert Dätzert and Erich Neukirchen pictured en route for burial with full military honours in Stoke upon Tern Cemetery. [TNA]*

got no arms. We then asked the man to come into the house and by various signs the German indicated that he wanted to wash his hands and have a glass of water. He then sat down and smoked some of his own cigarettes. My husband then called his father from next door, while he went to telephone the police. The German, who looked about 28 or 29, had a nasty weal on his neck as if he had struck something when he was coming down. He was very quiet and gave no trouble at all. He had no flying helmet nor any gloves and he wore an ordinary airman's uniform with black laced-up boots. When the police arrived the German shook hands with his before he left.

The two men were taken to Market Drayton Police Station, where they were interrogated by an RAF intelligence officer, while the bodies of their two comrades were taken to RAF Tern Hill. The follow-ing day the joint funeral was accorded full military honours, the coffins draped in a swastika.

Oberfeldwebel (pilot) Herbert Dätzert, EKI, EKII, *Luftwaffe*, aged 26, was born on 29 June 1915 and lived at *Strasse 4* in *Berlin Südwest* and had joined the *Luftwaffe* in 1935. After completing his pilot training he was posted to *Kampfgruppe* 606 and subsequently completed 140 'war flights' prior to his death. He was buried in Stoke on Tern (St Peter) Cemetery before being reburied in Cannock Chase German Military Cemetery during the 1960s.

Gefreiter (Obs) Karl Hennemann, *Luftwaffe*, who was born on 2 February 1919 and joined the *Luftwaffe* in February 1940, was making his first war flight with *KG*606, having only been posted to the unit two months previously. He spent the remainder of the war as a POW, presumably in Canada.

Uffz (W/Op) Josef Kolar, EKI, EKII, *Luftwaffe*, a native of Austria, had joined the Austrian Army in October 1937 and served as a 'W/T operator of the flying personnel'. Following the annexation of the country by Germany, his regiment was transferred to Berlin and trained 'in German discipline'. In September 1938, he was posted to *KG*76 then, three months later, transferred to *KG*606 with whom he subsequently completed 92 'war flights' (including a number during the Polish and French campaigns). He spent the remainder of the war as a POW, presumably in Canada.

Feldwebel (AB) Erich Neukirchen, *Luftwaffe*, aged 24, was a resident of 'Kromberg Tannes, near Berlin' and had completed 35 'war flights' before his death. He was buried in Stoke upon Tern (St Peter) Cemetery before being reinterred in Cannock Chase German Military Cemetery during the 1960s.

F/O Josef Kloboučník [Pavel Vancata]

Sgt Josef Klváček [Pavel Vancata]

23 October (Thursday)

Operational patrol. 68 Squadron (RAF Valley, Anglesey – detachment from RAF High Ercall, Shropshire)

Bristol Beaufighter IF (R2099, bearing the fuselage codes WM-Y) crashed near Poynton Green, one mile south-west of High Ercall, at 00.05 hrs. The Czech crew had been in the air for approximately an hour and a half when they requested permission to land at RAF High Ercall but were refused as the runway was temporarily obstructed by another aircraft. Six minutes later the pilot contacted the Sector HQ (at RAF Atcham) but, after the initial message, RAF High Ercall was unable to make contact with the crew again. At about the same time an enemy aircraft was plotted in the vicinity and when the wreckage of the Beaufighter was examined it was found to have bullet holes in it, indicating that it had crashed as a result of battle damage.

F/O (pilot) Josef Kloboučník (83971), RAFVR, aged 30, was a Czechoslovakian citizen, but had been born in Vienna on 10 March 1911. Following the outbreak of war, he escaped to France where he served as a pilot with the French Air Force at Chartres (although it is unknown if he flew in combat while based there) before escaping to England. Upon his arrival in the UK he underwent further training before joining 312 Squadron on 5 September 1940 and then 96 Squadron, at Cranage, in February 1941. Following a brief spell with the squadron, he was posted to 54 OTU for training on twin-engine aircraft before joining 68 Squadron. He is buried in Wellington General Cemetery, Shropshire.

Sgt (AI operator) Josef Klváček (787848), RAFVR, aged 25, was born in Hodolany, Czechoslovakia, on 1 March 1916. He escaped to England after his country's collapse and enlisted in September 1940. He is buried in Wellington General Cemetery, Shropshire.

24 October (Friday)
Formation flying. 17 OTU (RAF Upwood, Cambridgeshire)
Bristol Blenheim IV (V6004) crashed at Grafton, on the edge of Montford Bridge airfield at 10.15 hours. The trainee crew were on a routine training flight during which the pilot failed to change over fuel tanks correctly and one of the engines began to fail due to a lack of fuel. After presumably spotting Montford Bridge airfield nearby (which was still under construction) the pilot made a landing approach but overshot (possibly due to obstructions) and crashed.

Sgt (pilot) Peter Desmond Thompson (1181167), RAFVR, aged 19, was the son of Leonard Robert and Hilda Hetty Thompson of Edgware, Middlesex. He is buried in Luton General Cemetery.

Sgt (W/AG) Allan Ian Wilson Fairbairn (1375034), RAFVR, aged 25, was the son of John Wilson Fairbairn and Lucy Ellen Fairbairn (née Slatter) and the husband of Georgina Florence Fairbairn (née Stone) of Buena Vista, Gibraltar. He is buried in Streatham Park Cemetery, Surrey.

28 October (Tuesday)
Delivery flight from the Bristol Aeroplane Company airfield at Filton, Gloucestershire, to RAF Sealand, Flintshire. 2 FPP (Whitchurch, near Bristol)
Bristol Beaufighter IIF (T3045) crashed south-east of Norton crossroads (at map reference 571093), between Atcham airfield and Wroxeter, at 11.48 hrs. The pilot was coming in to land at RAF Atcham when he 'lost flying speed on approach and became out of control'. However, eyewitness, Joe Dorsett, who lived at Cross Houses and was working for the Air Ministry at RAF Atcham, saw the crash and believes that one of the engines was out as he approached.

> I was right on Norton crossroads, not very far away from it. My father drove a tanker which carried water. Well I was with him. We had to take water around the site, taking water to the concrete mixers and all that. We just happened to be down at Norton crossroads. I had just got out of the vehicle, and I was going across to the shop, [to] get some cigarettes or something for someone. I saw this plane coming in and the port engine was feathered. You could see it turning round. It was coming in and it came nearly to the road and fell to the left and turned on its back and hit the ground.
>
> Now I didn't do anything, but I can see it now. The RAF had got this short-wheeled Bedford lorry with a tank of water on it. They come round the corner off the 'drome' onto the main road. I remember the driver's door was still open with the driver's overcoat hanging off it, swinging about. The lorries that were all on the road stopped when they saw the crash. Some ran across to it but of course the poor lad had gone.

First Officer (pilot) Harry Wolff, ATA, aged 34, was the son of Joseph and Bessie Wolff and the husband of Ruth Wolff of New York City, USA. He was cremated at the Birmingham (Perry Bar) Crematorium and his ashes returned to his widow.

Wreckage of the Hampden lying in the fields near Llynclys – the starboard undercarriage and wheel are the only recognizable pieces of wreckage. [TNA]

30 October (Thursday)
Cross-country exercise from Cottesmore–Selby–Lincoln–Bicester–Lechlade–Whitchurch– Cottesmore. 14 OTU (RAF Cottesmore, Leicestershire)
Handley Page Hampden I (P1294) crashed onto the eastern slopes of Llynclys Hill, near the White Lion Crossroads, four miles south of Oswestry, at 12.39 hrs. The trainee crew took off from their base at 09.45 hrs and were flying on the Lechlade to Whitchurch leg, during which the pilot increased height from 3,000-7,000 feet as he passed over Kidderminster. At this point, the pilot diverged from his course slightly and flew towards Oswestry, where it is believed that he lost control while flying through cloud and entered a steep dive. It is then believed that the pilot, 'who was not strapped in, was thrown forward onto the controls, this causing the aeroplane to bunt when in a high speed dive and the wings [to] fail in the download owing to overstressing'. This conclusion was made following interviews with other pilots at 14 OTU who explained that they frequently flew with their Sutton harness (safety belt) clipped together and thrown over the back of their seat, which is how the harness was found in the wreckage of this aircraft.

F/O (pilot) George Donald Kerr (87062), RAFVR, aged 26, was the son of Richard and Isabella Kerr of Liverpool and the husband of Phyllis Kerr (née Hales) of Nottingham. He is buried in Liverpool (Allerton) Cemetery.

Sgt (Obs) Ivor Morgan Williams (927803), RAFVR, aged 19, was the son of Arthur Morgan Williams and Charlotte Elizabeth Williams of Newport, Monmouthshire. He is buried in Cardiff (Cathays) Cemetery. His brother, Stanley Rhys Williams, was also killed whilst serving with the RAF as a trainee navigator, on 5 March 1943.

Sgt (W/AG) Douglas Tatton (1355405), RAFVR, aged 21, was the son of William Caldicott Tatton and Lily Florence Winifred Tatton of Erdington, Birmingham. He is buried in Erdington (St Barnabas) Churchyard, Warwickshire. His brother, Cyril Tatton, was killed serving with 405 Squadron, on 24 July 1941.

Sgt (W/AG) Herbert Playforth (1052823), RAFVR, aged 21, was the son of James Henry and Portia Reed Playforth of York. Educated at Brompton Grammar School, he had worked as a clerk for the North Riding County Council before joining the RAF. He is buried in Brompton Cemetery, Northallerton.

3 November (Monday)
Search flight for missing aircrew of a Defiant (T4008). 96 Squadron (RAF Wrexham, Denbighshire)
Boulton Paul Defiant I (T3997) force-landed at 'Seehall Farm', 'south-east of Whitchurch' (although this is thought to be Lea Hall Farm near Ash Magna), at 10.25 hrs. The crew were searching for another of the squadron's aircraft, which had crashed in mid Wales the previous night and whose crew was still

missing. During the search, however, the weather began to close in and the pilot discovered that his R/T receiver was unserviceable and that he therefore had no way of contacting Wrexham to gain a homing signal. With a passenger who had never received instruction in using a parachute, the pilot decided to fly east until he reached low ground and then made a forced landing. As the aircraft was coming to a rest he applied too much pressure on the brakes and an undercarriage component broke, causing the wheels to collapse.

Sgt (pilot) Alfred Enoch Scott (815013), RAFVR. Before the war he had served as an aircrafthand with 504 Squadron, AAF, before being remustered as a pilot. He subsequently flew Hurricanes with 73 Squadron during the Battle of France and Battle of Britain. On 15 October 1940 he joined 422 Flight on its formation at Shoreham (as a Hurricane-equipped night-fighter unit) before moving north to Cranage, where it was re-designated as 96 Squadron and re-equipped with Defiants in February 1942. Following the accident at Whitchurch he was posted to 245 Squadron, flying Hurricanes on daylight fighter sweeps over north-west Europe. He was killed on 19 August 1942 flying a Hurricane (HL669) as part of the covering force for the Dieppe raid, when his aircraft was hit by flak while making a strafing run along the sea front. P/O Scott, who was the son of Harry and Elizabeth Scott and the husband of Gladys Crowther of Nottingham, was 25 years old and is commemorated on the Runnymede Memorial.

An unknown ground-crew corporal who was acting as an observer.

18 November (Tuesday)

Aerobatics training. 57 OTU (RAF Hawarden, Flintshire)

Supermarine Spitfire IA (R7058, presentation aircraft bearing the name *R J Mitchell*) force-landed at Belton Farm, on the south-western edge of Whitchurch, at 15.00 hrs. The pilot made a belly landing in a field after the engine failed during the training flight.

Sgt (pilot u/t) Alfred Coghlan Moore (1384277), RAFVR. On completion of his training he was posted to north Africa to join 92 Squadron, but due to a lack of aircraft the squadron was non-operational and several of the pilots were consequently attached to 80 Squadron. While on attachment to 80 Squadron, Sgt Moore was shot down and mortally wounded on 24 July 1942, during combat with a group of Me109s. Aged 26, he was the son of the Chief Inspector of the Shanghai Municipal Police, Christopher William Moore and Esther H Moore. He is buried in Heliopolis War Cemetery, Egypt.

26 November (Wednesday)

First solo flight on type. 5 SFTS (RAF Chetwynd, Shropshire – Relief Landing Ground to RAF Tern Hill)

Hawker Hurricane I (P3607) crashed 100 yards from the airfield, near Puleston Common, at 13.20 hrs. The pupil pilot was taking off on his first solo flight in a Hurricane when he neglected to put the propeller into fine pitch and, as the aircraft failed to gain height, had to pull the nose up sharply to avoid obstructions at the end of the runway, causing the aircraft to stall and crash. LAC Reg Brown was on ambulance duty that day and recalled the event in a conversation with the author in 2007 (even remembering the pilot's name):

> ... we were sitting again in that ambulance watching this one. Now I think he was taking off down that one there [pointing to the north/south runway]. It wasn't a runway you know, it was just a grass field. He was taking off along there and he couldn't take off because he was in the wrong pitch. His nose was up and tail down and he couldn't climb. He wasn't very high, just house height or so, so he only just got over the hedge and crashed in a field.

Having quickly driven to the scene, Reg found the seriously injured pilot 'was slumped over the front of the cockpit and he said something to the effect of 'I don't know what I did wrong Mr Howarth'. He [Mr Howarth] was one of the instructor's there.

LAC John Price [TNA]

Sadly, despite being rushed to the station sick quarters, the pilot died at 16.15 hrs the same day.

LAC (pilot u/t) John Basil Price (1076998) RAFVR, aged 29, was the son of John Edmund Victor Price and Emily Bessie Price of Ilford, Essex. He is buried in City of London Cemetery, Manor Park.

7 December (Sunday)
Cloud formation flying. 57 OTU (RAF Hawarden, Flintshire)
Supermarine Spitfire IA (P9446) tipped over during forced landing at Bratton airfield at 11.25 hrs. Sunday, 7 December 1941 was to prove the worst day in the history of Shropshire air accidents, with a total of six crashes caused by an extremely bad weather front moving in over the region. The pilot of this aircraft was an Australian named Jack Turbill whose memoirs, *One Life at a Time*, describe the situation he found himself in:

> John (Upward), and I were ordered up to do some formation with Sgt. Philpots (an instructor). We did this over the Welsh mountains which were covered in snow and it was very cold. After about an hour we came down and tried to return to base but found absolutely foul weather had closed right in. Visibility was bugger all even at a few feet caused by a snowstorm. The formation broke up and I decided to turn on a reciprocal course and eventually flew out into the clear again. The others made forced landings at Wrexham. I was hopelessly lost and tried to get a D/F bearing on my radio back to base but as there were so many aircraft lost in the same snowstorm this became hopeless and as the weather was rapidly moving south I soon got out of R/T touch with base. I then decided to land somewhere to find where I was and to wait for the snowstorm to pass over. I found a nice green paddock [the grass aerodrome at Bratton] by a mountain [The Wrekin] and made a successful landing before the storm hit. A little later two aircraft (one a Spit) lost in the storm, crashed into the mountain killing both pilots.
>
> Unfortunately the small paddock I had landed on was very soft and boggy and while taxiing to the boundary both wheels sank and the aircraft stood up on its nose leaving me dangling from my straps in mid-air. Very bad luck actually but the only damage was a bent airscrew. (I later got fined ten shillings for a repairable prang and a pat on the back for saving the aircraft and myself).
>
> I telephoned base and received orders to go to Shrewsbery [sic] aerodrome [most probably Shawbury] nearby and a dual seat Master was sent to pick me up. Sgt. Philpots arrived and we flew around squalls and murk all the way back to base and found another snowstorm was moving in to cover our aerodrome. We got down luckily before it set in properly but others were not so fortunate and six pilots were killed. We sat in our aircraft and listened on the R/T and heard them trying to get in roaring overhead, in all directions through the sleet...it was bloody awful.

P/O (pilot u/t) Jack Ashby Turbill (403016), RAAF, was born on 7 October 1915 in New South Wales.

Jack Turbill's Spitfire lying upside down in the snow at Bratton. [RAF Museum]

Following the accident he completed a tour of ops flying Spitfires with 501 Squadron between April and August 1942. Posted to 55 OTU in May 1943, he was discharged from the RAAF on medical grounds three months later and repatriated to Australia.

7 December (Sunday)
Ciné-gun and aerobatics practice flight. 131 Squadron (RAF Atcham, Shropshire)
Supermarine Spitfire IIA (P7746, presentation aircraft bearing the name *City of Bradford I* and fuselage codes NX-K) crashed into woodland at Rushton Cottage, on the western end of the Wrekin (at map reference 614076), between 11.00 hrs and 12 noon. A number of the squadron's pilots were ordered up in the morning for a training flight but, between 11 and 12 o'clock, the weather took an unexpected turn for the worse and a violent snowstorm moved into the area. The pilots were immediately recalled to land at the airfield but the pilot of this aircraft found it impossible to locate and radioed base requesting a vector to another airfield. As he did so, however, he suddenly saw the Wrekin emerge from the gloom in front of him and, in a desperate attempt to avoid it, he pulled the nose up sharply, causing the aircraft to stall. Despite quickly opening his canopy and baling out, there was insufficient height for his parachute to open and his body was found at 13.56 hrs by soldiers from Buildwas searchlight station.

Sgt (pilot) Horace Albert Metcalfe (402962), RAAF, aged 24, was the son of Albert and Edith Mabel Metcalfe and the husband of Margaret Metcalfe of Shortland, New South Wales. He is buried in Atcham (St Eata) Cemetery, Shropshire.

7 December (Sunday)
Ferry flight from Brockworth, Gloucestershire, to 48 MU, RAF Hawarden, Flintshire. 2 FPP (Whitchurch, Bristol)
Hawker Hurricane IIB (Z5663) crashed at Button Oak in the Wyre Forest, just inside the Shropshire border (at map reference 747779), at 12.20 hrs. The pilot had been flying towards north Wales when he crashed for reasons that are not stated on the accident card, although, considering the other fatal accidents that occurred on this day, the weather undoubtedly played a major part.

First Officer (pilot) Ernest Edward Gasser, ATA, aged 32, was a resident of Chevy Chase, in Maryland, USA. According to research by Ross McNeill, he was born in the USA to Swiss-American parents and had spent his childhood moving between Europe and the USA. During the great depression his parents moved back to Switzerland but Ernest joined the United States Marine Corps and served from May 1931 until May 1935, specialising in radio operation. He is subsequently thought to have learned to fly as a 'barnstormer' before the war, but when he travelled to the UK to join the ATA is unknown. He is buried in Wribbenhall (All Saints) Churchyard, Worcestershire.

7 December (Sunday)
Training flight. 57 OTU (RAF Hawarden, Flintshire)
Supermarine Spitfire IA (L1005) crash-landed at Pontesbury.
Unfortunately, no accident card survives for this incident and all that is known is that the pilot force-landed due to extremely poor weather conditions. The name of the pilot is unknown.

7 December (Sunday)
Practice dogfighting. 57 OTU (RAF Hawarden, Flintshire)
Supermarine Spitfire IA (R6963) force-landed on Montford Bridge airfield at 17.30 hrs. After becoming totally lost in a very heavy snowstorm, the pilot spotted an airfield under construction and made a belly landing on the incomplete runway.

P/O (pilot u/t) Leendert Carel Marie van Eendenburg (1149981), RAFVR, was born in the Dutch East Indies, on 29 December 1914 but had returned to the Netherlands in the 1930s to study at the University of Leiden. Following the outbreak of war he served with the Dutch army during the German invasion and in August 1940 was awarded the Dutch Bronze Cross for bravery in the face of the enemy while serving as an officer in the artillery. After escaping to England, he joined the RAFVR and subsequently flew with 41, 118 and 322 (Dutch) Squadrons. During his final tour he was shot down by flak on 1 September 1944, crash-landing his Spitfire near St Omer, and spent the following ten days on the run before reaching Allied lines. He survived the war and returned to the Netherlands, where he died in September 1966.

7 December (Sunday)
Ferrying pilots from RAF Litchfield, Hampshire to RAF Hawarden, Flintshire. 3 Delivery Flight (RAF Hawarden, Flintshire)
De Havilland DH.89 Dominie I (X7354) crashed at Hordley near Tetchill, to the south-west of Ellesmere, at 17.30 hrs. No. 3 Delivery Flight was responsible for delivering fighter aircraft to units of both 9 and 12 Groups, and the Dominie was used to deliver and pick up the unit's pilots for wherever they were required for flying duties. On the day of the accident, the pilot had picked up three airmen from RAF Litchfield to return them to Hawarden, and was en route back to north Wales when an appalling snowstorm enveloped them. The aircraft was then struck by lightning, rendering the blind-flying instruments unserviceable. The pilot immediately ordered his passengers to bale out but, tragically, neither he nor his co-pilot (who is thought to have been acting as wireless operator on the flight) were wearing their parachutes and they both lost their lives when the aircraft crashed out of control.

P/O (pilot) John Ernest Moodie (60527), RAFVR, aged 24, was the son of Benjamin Cecil and Gertrude Emily Moodie and the husband of Mildred Moodie of Howick, Auckland, New Zealand. He is commemorated at Birkenhead (Landican) Crematorium. His brother, Sgt William Adamson Moodie, was killed just two months later, serving with the RNZAF in Singapore.

P/O (pilot, but acting as W/Op for the flight) George Kingston Eaton (101066), RAFVR, aged 20, was the son of Frederic Ray and Ruth Evangeline Eaton of Eaton, Norwich. At the time of the accident he was on attachment to 3 Delivery Flight from 256 Squadron. He is buried in Eaton (St Andrew) Churchyard, Norfolk.

F/Lt (pilot, travelling as passenger) Austin. He was the flight commander of 3 Delivery Flight.

Sgt (pilot, travelling as passenger) Brookes. At the time of the accident he was on attachment to 3 Delivery flight from 74 Squadron.

AC (travelling as passenger) Cameron. He was a ground crew airman from 57 OTU, RAF Hawarden.

9 December (Tuesday)
Dual instructional flight. 5 SFTS (RAF Tern Hill, Shropshire)
Miles Master III (W8578) crashed 'one mile south of Cheswardine' (putting it in the area of Little Soudley), at 14.45 hrs. The aircraft was seen to spin and crash vertically into the ground under full power but the cause seems to be obscure, with the accident card stating that there was 'no evidence of defects, but possibly [there] was some aerodynamic or technical defect'.

F/O (instructor pilot) Noel Inglis Chalmers Francis (40817), RAF, aged 23, was the son of James Bernard and Margaret Edith Chalmers Francis of Brighton and the husband of Margaret Hazel Chalmers Francis (née Lock) of Brighton. He had joined the RAF in April 1938 and, after completing his training, was posted to the Fighter Flight, Sumburgh, in the summer of 1940, flying Gladiator bi-planes in the air defence of the Shetland Islands. On 21 June 1940, while flying on a routine patrol, his engine failed and his aircraft flipped over onto its back after he touched down for a forced landing on a beach on the island of Unst, although he was fortunately unhurt. The following month the Fighter Flight was moved to Plymouth and, on 1 August, was re-designated 247 Squadron. He flew with the squadron throughout the Battle of Britain before being posted to 5 SFTS as an instructor. He is buried in Stoke upon Tern (St Peter's) Cemetery, Shropshire.

LAC Reginald Hinde [TNA]

LAC (pilot u/t) Reginald William Hinde (1384280), RAFVR, aged 20, was the son of George and Ethel Hinde and the husband of Cecile L Hinde (née Kendall) of Hampstead. He is buried in Highgate Cemetery, London.

10 December (Wednesday)
Return flight to base following forced landing. 9 MU (RAF Cosford, Shropshire)
De Havilland Tiger Moth II (T5622) crashed in Burwarton Park, on the eastern slopes of Brown Clee Hill, at 12.30 hrs. The aircraft had been force-landed in the park at an earlier date and, according to Wartime Aircraft Recovery Group records, a more experienced pilot was requested to fly it out. After taking off, the aircraft was caught in a sudden downdraught at 50 feet, causing the aircraft to drop 20 feet and strike the top of a tree before crashing and slightly injuring the pilot. Ron Pearce, who was a teenager living at Banbury Farm at the time, recalled how

> … it came down and it landed ok. I don't know if it was the same pilot or not, but they left him a day or two as the wind was the wrong way. The bloke ran out of patience and started her up and he tore off up the park and he stalled and he come down in a tree. I believe the words he said were unprintable and then he walked away. He just had a slight cut above his one eye. I saw the aircraft after it had crashed but I didn't see it taking off. It would only be about a mile from my house. He was meant to wait for the wind to change so that he could have taken off downhill. He didn't though and he stalled into an oak tree.

F/Lt (test pilot) Alfred Keith Holdsworth (70314), RAF, had been involved in another accident at Cosford on 10 September 1941 and further details on him can be found under that date.

10 December (Wednesday)
Ground accident. 68 Squadron (RAF High Ercall, Shropshire)
A ground-crew airman was removing a 'chock' (a wooden wedge placed either side of the wheel to prevent the aircraft from moving) from the wheels of one of the squadron's Beaufighters when he stumbled and fell into one of the rotating propellers, killing him instantly.

AC2 (ACH/GD) David John Davies (1239491), RAFVR, aged 37, was the son of Thomas and Elizabeth Ann Davies and the husband of Gwyneth Davies of Galon Uchaf, near Merthyr Tydfil. He is buried in Merthyr Tydfil (Pant) Cemetery, Glamorganshire.

11 December (Thursday)
Training flight. 5 SFTS (RAF Tern Hill, Shropshire)
Hawker Hurricane I (V6824) force-landed at Alkington Hall, two miles south-west of Whitchurch, at 12 noon. During the course of the flight the pupil pilot displayed 'sheer carelessness' in neglecting to switch over to the main fuel tank when his reserves had run dry and the engine failed, forcing him to belly land in a field.

2 Lt (pilot u/t) Robert John Heugh Drummond (P130385), RAFVR, was born in Masterton, New Zealand, on 4 November 1913, the son of Robert Crawford Drummond and Agnes Cecilia Mary

Drummond (née Telford). Educated at Wairarapa High School, where he excelled in sports, he attended Balliol College, Oxford, before returning to New Zealand to become a teacher at Wellesley College. Following the outbreak of the war he spent a brief period with the New Zealand military before sailing to the UK, where he enlisted in the York and Lancaster Regiment in May 1940, prior to transferring to the RAF. On completion of his pilot training he was posted to 26, 171 and finally 152 Squadron, flying Spitfires in the north African campaign. He was shot down by flak and killed in a Spitfire (JG725) while strafing ground targets on 24 April 1943. F/O Drummond, who was 29 years old and the husband of Vera Jane Carter, is buried in Massicault Cemetery.

1942

3 January (Saturday)
Cross-country exercise. 17 OTU (RAF Upwood, Cambridgeshire)
Bristol Blenheim IV (P6959) crashed at Hermitage Farm (at map reference 576267), between Lee Brockhurst and Hodnet, at 11.45 hrs. The trainee crew were on a routine training flight when the aircraft was seen to dive out of cloud from a height of 2,000 feet and crash. The precise cause of the accident is unknown.

F/O (pilot) Melville John (Mel) Kingshott (400278), RAAF, aged 25, was the son of Harry Julian and Elsie May Kingshott of West Brunswick, Australia. Before the war he had worked as an accountant with the City of Brunswick sustenance department. A keen sportsman, he enjoyed horse riding and was also an accomplished pianist with a very good singing voice. He is buried in Shawbury (St Mary's) Churchyard, Shropshire.

F/O Mel Kingshott [Alan R Kingshott]

Sgt (Obs) Wilfred Jowett (1058855), RAFVR, aged 21, was the son of Harry and Emmeline Jowett of Lidget Green, Bradford. He is buried in Bradford (Thornton) Cemetery, Yorkshire.

Sgt (W/AG) Robert Macauley Masson (1058546), RAFVR, aged 21, is buried in Aberdeen (Allenvale) Cemetery, Scotland. His next of kin are unknown.

3 January (Saturday)
Low-flying formation practice. 131 (County of Kent) Squadron (RAF Atcham, Shropshire)
Supermarine Spitfire VB (AD544) belly-landed at Cruckton, near Hanwood, at 14.55 hrs. After the engine failed due to a faulty carburettor valve, the pilot belly-landed in a field and the aircraft slid along the ground until it hit a small ridge which swung it around and brought it to a stop.

Sgt (pilot) Francis David Colin Brown (404330), RNZAF, was born in Christchurch, New Zealand, on 26 October 1921 and had worked as a tractor driver before joining up in November 1940. Following his spell with 131 Squadron, he was posted to 3 Photo Reconnaissance Unit in December 1942 (re-designated 681 Squadron in January 1943) and flew Spitfires on photo reconnaissance operations over Burma. On 8 June 1943, he was returning from his 23rd operation, flying a Spitfire (AB318), when he ran into a huge thunderstorm over the Arakan Mountains and, with no other option, continued to fly straight through it. After 20 minutes of worsening conditions, the aircraft disintegrated suddenly at 23,000 feet and Sgt Brown was thrown out of the wreckage unconscious. Amazingly, he came to at 3,000 feet and was able to pull his parachute cord but was so badly injured in the accident that he was repatriated to New Zealand, never to fly again.

LAC John Tomlinson [TNA]

3 January (Saturday)
R/T training exercise. 5 SFTS (RAF Tern Hill, Shropshire)
Hawker Hurricane I (L1695) crashed near Eaton Constantine, to the south-west of the Wrekin, at 16.05 hrs. During the course of a routine training flight the pupil pilot began unauthorised low flying outside the designated low-flying area, collided with some power lines and crashed.

LAC (pilot u/t) John Robert Tomlinson (656503), RAFVR, aged 20, was the son of James and Marion Tomlinson of Elderslie, Renfrewshire, Scotland. He is buried in Stoke upon Tern (St Peter's) Cemetery, Shropshire.

9 January (Friday)
Unauthorised flying detail. 5 SFTS (RAF Tern Hill, Shropshire)
Hawker Hurricane I (P3055) crashed at Middle Farm, Chetwynd Aston, near Newport, at 11.20 hrs. Two instructors were performing 'unauthorised flying and air fighting practice contrary to regulations', during which the pilot of this aircraft collided with the other aircraft while making a mock attack from astern at a height of 2,000 feet, causing both aircraft to crash out of control.

Acting F/Lt (instructor pilot) Michael George Pascalis (91067), RAF (AAF), aged 29, was born in Athens on 26 July 1912, the only son of Alexander and Lucy Arabella Pascalis. Educated at Pembroke College, Cambridge, during which time he learned to fly with the Cambridge University Air Squadron, he had subsequently joined 610 Squadron, Auxiliary Air Force, in August 1939, although little else is known of his military service. He is commemorated at Golders Green Crematorium, London, having moved to live in Marylebone, in London.

Unauthorised flying detail. 5 SFTS (RAF Tern Hill, Shropshire)
Hawker Hurricane Mk I (P3668) crashed at Middle Farm, Chetwynd Aston, near Newport, following the accident described above.

F/O (instructor pilot) Douglas Frank Newsham (89811), RAFVR, aged 22, was the son of Frank and Bertha Newsham of Dore and the husband of Jessie Newsham (née Love). He is buried in Dore (Christ Church) Churchyard, Yorkshire.

13 January (Tuesday)
Local map reading exercise. 5 SFTS (RAF Tern Hill, Shropshire)
Miles Master I (N8051) force-landed at Kinlet near Highley, to the south of Bridgnorth, at 17.15 hrs. The pilot was on the last leg of his flight when he became lost in bad weather and decided to make a precautionary landing as visibility was deteriorating. However, as he approached a field, he held off too high and allowed the aircraft to drop, causing the undercarriage to collapse.

Cpl (pilot u/t) Ferdinand Hardy (30699), FFAF. On completion of his training he served with 93 and then 340 Squadron, flying Spitfires on fighter sweeps over north-west Europe. He survived the war and died in 2007.

14 January (Wednesday)
Ferry flight from 22 MU, RAF Silloth, Cumbria, to RAF Lichfield, Staffordshire. 16 FPP (RAF Kirkbride, Cumbria)

Bell P-39 Airacobra AH693 – Force-landed near 'Roberts Farm, Edgmond', west of Newport, at 11.40 hrs. After encountering poor weather conditions in the vicinity of Lichfield, the pilot diverted to RAF High Ercall, where he spent the night. The following morning he took off for the short flight to RAF Lichfield and, according to the pilot's account in his memoirs *We Flew Without Guns*:

I was cruising at eight hundred feet, just under the clouds, and had nothing but plowed fields, a scattering of trees, and the few buildings of a crossroads town below me when the steady roar of the Airacobra's Allison engine suddenly broke into a series of racking coughs and then abruptly cut out. Thinking I might be out of gas, I hastily opened the valves on the auxiliary fuel tanks, but that did no good. At cruising speed I had only about 130 miles per hour with the gear up – and speed diminishes quickly at that altitude in a light fighting plane. There was only one thing to do in the few second I had to work with: I pushed the stick forward, nosing the plane into a dive to keep it from stalling.

Diving from eight hundred feet doesn't give you much time to pick a landing place. Wherever it was, it had to be almost directly below me – and the only smooth spot around which was unimpeded by ditches or trees or plow furrows was a field about fifty yards wide running back from the main street of a crossroads town and fading into a willow grove some two hundred yards back of the two frame buildings it separated. Behind the building on the right a bunch of children were playing, and paralleling the street at the front end of the vacant lot was a multiple row of telephone wires. With the gear up I thought I had a chance of clearing the wires – but I was wrong: the propeller chewed a path right through them. However, this didn't affect the speed of the plane, and I landed with gear up, hard on the 'Cobra's belly, and slid a hundred yards straight down the lawn. The impact of the landing was terrific; it threw me forward and my head smashed against the gun sight, giving me a deep gash on the forehead, but the shoulder straps prevented more serious injury. The straps wouldn't have done any good at all, of course, if the armored glass plate had been in its normal position about twelve inches in front of my face. I would probably have hit that hard enough to break my neck.

I wouldn't have guessed beforehand that I would be so observing of my surroundings while trying to crash land an Airacobra between two buildings fifty yards apart; but when I loosened the straps and climbed out of the plane I knew with absolute certainty that the building on my left was a pub; that even on my shaking legs it was within quick walking distance; and that what I needed more than anything else at that moment was a drink. Among the scores of people who swarmed around me and the slightly damaged 'Cobra in the next minute or two was one old fellow with a round red face who wore a short white apron over his big bay window. He was the tavern keeper, and I gave him my undivided attention.

First Officer (pilot) Joseph Genovese (AM6551), ATA, was an American citizen who had volunteered for the ATA in July 1941. After completing his year-long contract he returned to the USA where he volunteered for the China National Aviation Corporation (CNAC) and subsequently flew supply runs over the Himalayas between India and China (a route known as 'The Hump'). He returned to the USA in 1943 and joined Republic Aviation as a test-pilot. He died in 2010.

5 February (Thursday)
Navigation exercise. 3 AOS (RAF Bobbington, Staffordshire)
Avro Anson I (K6628) force-landed at Waen Wen to the east of Pant, near Oswestry, at 11.40 hrs. While flying in bad weather conditions the pilot encountered problems with his starboard engine and tried to make a precautionary landing but, in the poor visibility, he overshot and went through a hedge, striking some telegraph poles and slightly injuring two of the crew.

Sgt (staff pilot) Wallace Russell King (405810), RNZAF, was born in Reefton, New Zealand, on 28 August 1920. He had joined the RNZAF in December 1940 and sailed to the UK where he became a staff pilot at RAF Bobbington. He continued to serve at the unit until December 1943 and, for his inspiring service, he received a King's Commendation for Valuable Service in the Air in January 1944. After leaving RAF Bobbington he was posted to 490 Squadron, RNZAF, flying Catalina (and later Sunderland) flying boats, and completed 55 maritime patrols flying out of west Africa. In February 1945 he was seconded to BOAC before being demobbed in December 1946.

The names of the other crew members are unknown.

11 February (Wednesday)

Steep turns, climbing turns, aerobatics and navigation training. 5 SFTS (RAF Atcham, Shropshire – detached flight from RAF Tern Hill)

Miles Master II (W8785) crashed at Leighton Bank (at map reference 616053), near Cressage, at 15.45 hrs. The pupil pilot was flying from RAF Atcham as part of a detached flight to relieve pressure on RAF Tern Hill's runways, when the sun is thought to have obscured his vision and he clipped some power lines while approaching to land from the north-east. He immediately gained some height, presumably to look for a suitable field to force-land in, but, for unknown reasons, tried to bale out at 300 feet and his parachute failed to open. His body was discovered near a hedgerow, on land belonging to Sheinton Hall Farm on the south side of the river Severn. As a consequence of the accident it was suggested by the investigating officers that the cables should be removed; however, it was agreed by the Air Ministry that obstruction lights would be fitted on the pylons instead. Whether this was ever done is unclear, as a section of several hundred yards of the cables to the north-east of the airfield is still buried to this day.

LAC (pilot u/t) Cuthbert Earl Douglass (1079608), RAFVR, aged 18, was the son of William and Edith Annie Douglass of Dormanstown. He is buried in Coatham (Christ Church) Churchyard, Yorkshire.

LAC Cuthbert Douglass [TNA]

17 February (Monday)

Dual training flight. 5 SFTS (RAF Tern Hill, Shropshire)

Miles Master I (N7891) force-landed at 'Northwood Farm, Shropshire' (presumably Northwood Farm, between Fauls and Wollerton). After the engine failed, due to an internal coolant leak, the instructor belly-landed in a field.

F/Sgt (instructor pilot) Edward Howard 'Jeny' Marsh (758002), RAFVR, was born in Dudley, on 20 February 1917. He enlisted in the RAFVR just prior to the outbreak of the war and subsequently flew Spitfires during the Battle of Britain with 152 Squadron. He damaged a number of enemy aircraft during the battle and then, in the months that followed, claimed a further two destroyed, one shared destroyed and one damaged. In October 1941, he left the squadron and underwent instructor training before being posted to 5 SFTS. Little is known of his military service after leaving Tern Hill other than that he survived the war and reached the rank of flight lieutenant. He died in March 2001.

The name of the pupil pilot is unknown.

17 February (Monday)

Dual night flying training. 5 SFTS (RAF Chetwynd, Shropshire – Relief Landing Ground to RAF Tern Hill)

Miles Master III (W8571) crashed at Chetwynd Heath, near Newport, at 10.10 hrs. The pilot was carrying out a steep climbing manoeuvre at 1,500 feet when he spun off the turn and dived into trees.

W/O (instructor pilot) Nathaniel Arnold (745549), RAFVR, aged 25, was the son of Louis Edgar and Mary Arnold of New Lenton, Nottingham, and the husband of Nora Arnold (née Tunneycliff). He is buried in Nottingham Southern Cemetery.

Lt (pilot u/t) Thomas Foster-Barham (126992), RAF, aged 22, was the son of Hugh Garratt and Margaret Moore Foster-Barham of Nelson, New Zealand. Born in Lausanne, Switzerland, where his father was working as

W/O Nathaniel Arnold (James Greenhalgh)

Lt Thomas Foster-Barham [TNA]

a civil servant, his family had returned to their native New Zealand while he was still young. He was educated at Nelson College and then Oundle School in the UK and, following the outbreak of war, was commissioned into 1 Black Watch and had survived the Dunkirk evacuations before applying for a transfer to the RAF. He is buried in Stoke upon Tern (St Peter's) Cemetery, Shropshire.

14 March (Thursday)
Practice bombing exercise at 500 feet. 3 AOS (RAF Bobbington, Staffordshire)
Avro Anson I (N9750) crashed on the lower slopes of Brown Clee Hill (at map reference 572848) near Clee St Margaret, at 18.30 hrs. The crew were practicing low-altitude bombing when both engines failed simultaneously and the pilot prepared for a crash-landing. However, as he was gliding in towards a field, both engines picked up again but, by this stage, the aircraft had lost too much height and, despite trying to gain altitude, clipped a tree, stalled and crashed into a field. Two of the crew were killed in the crash while the remaining three were conveyed to the RAF Hospital at Bridgnorth and treated for their injuries.

Temporary F/Sgt (pilot) Oris Earl Wilson (R.67946), RCAF, was born in the USA, on 9 January 1917, and brought up in St Louis, Missouri. He volunteered for the RCAF in November 1940 and on completion of his pilot training in Canada, sailed to the UK and was posted to 3 AOS. Little else is known of his military service other than that he transferred to the USAAF in November 1943 and survived the war.

LAC (Obs u/t) George Edward Morris Glassman (640791) RAF, aged 27, was the husband of Emily Glassman (née Wilson) of Davyhulme, Urmston. He is buried in Urmston Cemetery, Lancashire.

LAC (Obs u/t) Roy Ian Gilbert (1382516), RAFVR, aged 33, is buried in Lancing (St James the Less) Churchyard, Sussex. His next of kin are unknown.

The names of the other two crew members are unknown.

16 March (Saturday)
Navigation exercise. 3 AOS (RAF Bobbington, Staffordshire)
Avro Anson I (N4906) force-landed 'two miles east-north-east of Bridgnorth' (putting it between Claverley and Bridgnorth, although another source states the location as Swancote), at 15.40 hrs. The pilot was flying through low cloud and heavy rain, which 'prevented him from seeing through windscreen', so he dropped below the cloud and tried to open his window to improve his vision. As the navigator struggled to secure the window for him (as it would not stay open) he accidentally knocked the petrol switches off, causing both engines to fail. The pilot was forced to belly-land into a field, slightly injuring the entire crew.

Sgt (pilot) Bruce Irvine Crofts (405745), RAAF, was born in Nambour, Queensland, on 28 February 1921. He survived the war having attained the rank of flight lieutenant.

The names of the three other crew members are unknown.

16 March (Saturday)
Cross-country exercise from Shawbury–Church Stretton–Stanton Harcourt, Oxfordshire. 11 SFTS (RAF Shawbury, Shropshire)
Airspeed Oxford II (W6558) flew into 'Nills', a small spur above Ashes Hollow on the Long Mynd near Church Stretton (at map reference 433927), at 09.30 hrs. Two pupil pilots took off together (with one acting as navigator) and were flying on the first leg of their flight, when they ran into very bad weather

conditions with cloud down to approximately 800 feet. Rather than return to base, which is what their flight commander had ordered them to do should they run into adverse weather, the pilot flew on at a height of 1,500 feet and the aircraft crashed into the side of the hill, which was totally obscured by cloud. It did not catch fire after striking the ground but was totally destroyed and parts of the wreckage tumbled down the slope to the brook below. Due to the weather conditions the wreckage was not discovered for 24 hours.

LAC (pilot u/t) James Gardner (1106766), RAFVR, aged 19, was the son of Mr and Mrs James Gardner of Leven. He is buried in Scoonie Cemetery, Fifeshire.

LAC (pilot u/t, acting as navigator) Paul Anthony McArdle (1034137), RAFVR, aged 19, was the son of Harold and Gertrude Cecilia McArdle of Waterloo, Liverpool. He is buried in Great Crosby Churchyard, Lancashire.

1 April (Wednesday)
Bombing exercise. 3 (O) AFU (RAF Bobbington, Staffordshire)
Avro Anson I (R3584) force-landed at Ightfield, to the south-east of Whitchurch, at 10.45 hrs. After encountering bad weather the pilot made a precautionary landing in a field but, as he touched down, he had to swing the aircraft to avoid a hedge and the undercarriage collapsed.

Sgt (pilot) Howard John Corre (655445), RAFVR, was born in Holborn, London, on 7 December 1921. After joining the RAFVR he was commissioned and posted to 264 Squadron, flying Mosquitos on night-defence patrols and intruder operations over north-west Europe. During his tour he claimed four enemy aircraft and one doodlebug destroyed, for which he was awarded the DFC in August 1944. Having survived the war, he was killed serving with 85 Squadron on 18 May 1951, when a Tiger Moth (DF211) crashed near RAF West Malling. F/Lt Corre was 29-years old and is buried in Kingswinford, West Midlands.

5 April (Sunday)
Cross-country exercise. 57 OTU (RAF Hawarden, Flintshire)
Miles Master I (T8364) force-landed at Manor Farm, Withington (possibly at map reference 584126, where a Master I was witnessed in a field), near Wellington, at 11.15 hrs. After the engine failed in flight the pilot made an emergency landing, during which the undercarriage collapsed on soft ground.

Sgt (pilot u/t) John Murray Lock (404967), RAAF, was born in Australia, on 19 February 1919. He was living in Brisbane and working as an audit clerk at the time he enlisted. On completion of his training he was posted to 81 Squadron in April 1942, flying Spitfires over north-west Europe, before sailing to the Middle East in July 1942. Following some brief desert training, he was attached to 33 Squadron and flew Spitfires in the Mediterranean theatre. He returned to the UK in August 1944 and served as an instructor at 57 OTU until December, when he joined 131 Squadron and sailed for India. However, following the squadron's arrival it was disbanded, in June 1945. F/Lt Lock therefore returned home and was discharged from the RAAF.

13 April (Monday)
Solo cross-country exercise. 16 EFTS (RAF Derby, Derbyshire)
Miles Magister I (N3953) crash-landed at Gobowen, to the north of Oswestry, at 17.50 hrs. The pilot was undergoing elementary flying training, as part of his glider pilot course, when he became lost during the flight and decided to make a precautionary landing in a field. After overshooting his approach, however, the pilot opened the throttles to gain height and make a second attempt but, as he did so, the aircraft caught some telegraph wires, which ripped off the pitot head (airspeed indicator). Unable to judge his airspeed, the pilot then lost control of the aircraft and crashed, fracturing his right arm and suffering facial injuries.

Cpl Roland Sunter [Linda Turner]

Cpl (pilot u/t) Roland Davies Sunter (4446357), GPR, was born in Scotland Gate, Northumberland, on 14 August 1910, the son of James and Jane Sunter. Educated at Bedlington School, where he was a keen footballer, he susequently worked on the railways for a while before becoming a lorry driver. Following the outbreak of war he joined 1 Durham Light Infantry, but in 1942 volunteered for the Glider Pilot Regiment. On completion of his training he was posted to 1 GPR but lost his life on 16 May 1943 when a Halifax (DG390) crashed while transporting men to RAF Holmsley. Sgt Sunter, who was aged 32, was the husband of Mary Fawcus. He is buried in North Sunderland Cemetery.

14 April (Tuesday)
Cross-country exercise. 'E' Flight, 21 OTU (RAF Moreton-in-Marsh, Gloucestershire)

Vickers Wellington IC (R1085) crashed at Wollerton, to the south-west of Tern Hill airfield, at 15.31 hrs. During the course of the training flight one of the aircraft's propellers fell off, causing the aircraft to enter a steep turn to the left and stall, before crashing out of control. The remains of the six crew members were subsequently recovered by RAF Tern Hill's ambulance and taken to the station morgue in preparation for their burial.

Sgt (pilot) John Martin Smith Millar (1126135) RAFVR, aged 21, was the son of Hugh and Jean Martin Millar of Dumbarton. He is buried in Dumbarton Cemetery, Scotland.

F/Sgt Lew Sheffler [Anne Douglass]

F/Sgt (pilot) Lew Wallace Sheffler (R.83056), RCAF, aged 24, was the son of Mr H R and Mrs Ada I Sheffler of Berkley, West Virginia, USA. He had been educated at Woodrow Wilson High School and the University of Alabama before volunteering for the RCAF. He is buried in Stoke upon Tern (St Peter's) Cemetery, Shropshire.

Sgt (Obs) Graham Douglas Lindsay (1078148), RAFVR, aged 19, was the son of Ralph Morgan Lindsay and Margery Lindsay of Kirk Ella, Yorkshire. He is buried in Stoke upon Tern (St Peter's) Cemetery, Shropshire.

P/O (W/AG) Richard Bloor (111785), RAFVR, aged 24, was the son of John and Elizabeth Bloor of Thurrock, Essex. Born in Karachi, India, on 21 August 1917, he had joined the British Bata Shoe Company in 1933 and spent four years in Czechoslovakia between 1934 and 1938, before returning to take up an appointment as manager at the East Tilbury factory. He is buried in Stoke upon Tern (St Peter's) Cemetery, Shropshire.

P/O Richard Bloor [John Gothard]

Sgt (W/AG) Trevor Victor Yde (41626), RNZAF, aged 21, was the son of Samuel Emil and Frances Yde (née Harris) of Turiwhati, Westland, New Zealand. He is buried in Stoke upon Tern (St Peter's) Cemetery, Shropshire.

Sgt (AG) Lionel Leslie Bennett (1330697), RAFVR, aged 21, was the son of Lilian Bennett and the husband of Joan Constance Bennett (née Bianco) of Golders Green, Middlesex. He is buried in Stoke upon Tern (St Peter's) Cemetery, Shropshire.

2 May (Saturday)
Single engine landings practice. 11 (P)AFU (RAF Shawbury, Shropshire)
Airspeed Oxford II (AS766) crashed at 'Hardwick Wood, Hadnall', between Hadnall and Grinshill, at 19.00 hrs. The pilot was flying in the circuit when he made a steep right-hand turn to avoid another aircraft and allowed the aircraft

to enter a spin, from which he did not have enough height to recover.

Sgt (pilot u/t) Arthur Rex Whitington (416028), RAAF, aged 27, was the son of Arthur Onslow Whitington and Elsie Adeline Whitington and the husband of Muriel Whitington of Glenside, South Australia. He is buried in Shawbury (St Mary's) Churchyard.

4 May (Monday)
Instrument flying. 61 OTU (RAF Rednal, Shropshire)
Miles Master III (W9003) crashed at Melverley Hall Farm, near Kinnerley, at 17.00 hrs. The pilot is thought to have entered a spin during unauthorised aerobatics (although one source suggested a spin during instrument flying) and, while he attempted to pull out of the resulting high speed dive, the port wing detached under the stress and the aircraft crashed out of control.

P/O Tony Pensa. [Mary Leigh]

P/O (pilot) Anthony (Tony) Pensa (J9461), RCAF, aged 21, was the son of Peter and Annetta Pensa of London, Ontario. His father had emigrated from Italy in 1905 and settled in London, where Tony attended St Peters Elementary School and then De La Salle High School. After graduating from high school in 1939 he began a year studying aerial navigation at the University of Toronto, before joining the RCAF in 1940 and subsequently sailing to the UK in February 1942. He is buried in Oswestry General Cemetery, Shropshire.

F/Sgt (passenger) Peter Reginald Wright (655986), RAF, aged 26, was the son of Edward Walter and Fanny Wright of York. He is buried in Fulford Cemetery, Yorkshire. His brother, Laurence Walter Wright, also died in the war, serving with a bomb disposal unit in the Far East.

8 May (Friday)
Formation flying. 57 OTU (RAF Hawarden, Flintshire)
Supermarine Spitfire IIA (P8594) belly-landed at Gadlas Farm, Dudleston Heath near Ellesmere, at 09.15 hrs. After his engine failed to respond when he opened up the throttles, the pilot was unable to maintain height and belly-landed in a field.

Sgt (pilot u/t) Eric Herbert Moore (656753), RAFVR, hailed from Ruislip in Middlesex and after completing his training, on 25 May 1942, was posted to 501 Squadron flying Spitfires. In November 1942 he sailed to the Western Desert where he continued to fly operationally until the following March, when he was posted to 601 Squadron, flying Spitfires over the Mediterranean theatre. He survived the war attaining the rank of flying officer.

15 May (Friday)
Formation flying. 61 OTU (RAF Rednal, Shropshire)
Supermarine Spitfire IA (X4177) belly-landed 'south of Wykey' to the north of Ruyton-XI-Towns, at 16.25 hrs. The pilot force-landed in a field, with wheels retracted, after the aircraft's engine failed due to an unknown cause.

F/Lt (pilot u/t) William Henry Alexander Wright (70834), RAF (RAFO). Little is known of his military service until January 1944 when he was given command of 548 Squadron, which was being formed in Australia in preparation for its involvement in the Pacific theatre. On 19 April 1944 he took off for a training flight from Strathpine airfield, near Brisbane and, shortly after leaving the ground, his aircraft collided with another of the squadron's Spitfires and crashed. Squadron Leader Wright, who was 26 years old, was the son of William Henry Wright, MRCS, FRCP and Sadie Ann Wright of Helensburgh, Scotland. He is buried in Brisbane (Lutwhyche) Cemetery.

17 May (Sunday)
Steep turns, precautionary landings and single-engine flying. 11 (P)AFU (RAF Bridleway Gate, Shropshire – Relief Landing Ground to RAF Shawbury)
Airspeed Oxford I (L4603) crashed just outside the boundary of the airfield at 11.00 hrs. The pilot was approaching to land when, unknown to him, another pilot in an Oxford (X7062) made a 'tight circuit and failed to keep a proper lookout for other aircraft' and came in to land below and behind his aircraft. Despite the airfield control pilot spotting the danger and desperately firing off red Very flares, a collision occurred at 200 feet and both aircraft crashed out of control.

Sgt (pilot u/t) Maurice Daniel Duggan (405578), RAAF, aged 21, was the son of John Stephen and Charlotte Duggan of Toowoomba in Queensland, Australia. He is buried in Shawbury (St Mary's) Churchyard.

Cross-country flight. 11 (P)AFU (RAF Bridleway Gate, Shropshire – Relief Landing Ground to RAF Shawbury)
Airspeed Oxford II (X7063) crashed just off the airfield boundary after colliding in the incident described above.

Sgt (pilot u/t) Orville Norman Elwell (R.106525), RCAF, aged 27, was the son of Oscar Wilde Elwell and Mary Francis Elwell of Pittsburg, Texas, USA. He is buried in Shawbury (St Mary's) Churchyard.

21 May (Thursday)
Steep turns and precautionary landings practice. 11 (P)AFU (RAF Shawbury, Shropshire)
Airspeed Oxford II (N4798) force-landed at Winsbury Farm near Chirbury, at 20.00 hrs. The pilot was carrying out local flying practice when he lost his position in deteriorating weather and decided to make a precautionary landing in a field after finding himself surrounded by hilly country. After touching down, however, he applied too much pressure on the brakes and the aircraft turned over onto its back, seriously damaging the aircraft but fortunately not injuring the pilot. In the subsequent investigation the pilot was deemed to have been 'too hasty in choosing to land, but considering his limited experience, was not found to be careless or negligent'.

Sgt (pilot u/t) William Morris Arnold (416140), RAAF. On completion of his training he was posted to 279 Squadron flying air sea rescue flights but was lost without trace on 7 January 1943, in a Hudson (V9031), when it failed to return from a sortie off the Lizard. F/Sgt Arnold, who was 22 years old, was the son of William Turner Arnold and Nellie May Arnold of Glenelg, South Australia. He is commemorated on the Runnymede Memorial.

21 May (Thursday)
Dual instruction training flight. 5 (P)AFU (RAF Tern Hill, Shropshire)
Miles Master III (W8830) force-landed 'two miles north-east of the airfield' (putting it in the area between Stoke Grange and Pell Wall), at 20.30 hrs. The aircraft had been in the air for 35 minutes when the engine backfired briefly and then failed, forcing the instructor to belly-land in a field.

Sgt (instructor pilot) Gerald William Guy Buckland (1376006), RAFVR, was born on 19 October 1915. He was commissioned in April 1943 and survived the war, attaining the rank of flight lieutenant. He died in Oxfordshire in July 2005.

Sgt (pilot u/t) Alexander G MacGibbon (1367161), RAFVR. Nothing further is known of this pilot other than that he survived the war.

26 May (Tuesday)
Ferry flight. 3 Delivery Flight (RAF High Ercall, Shropshire)
Miles Magister I (R1822) crashed at Burgess Farm, High Ercall, at 15.50 hrs. The pilot had just taken off

from the airfield and was waiting for another aircraft to join him, when he began performing unauthorised aerobatics and lost control during a roll at low height.

Sgt (pilot) Jerzy Stanislaw Zieliński (P782403), PAF, aged 21, was born in Topola, near Inowroclaw, in Poland. Having joined the Polish Air Force in 1936 he fought in the 1939 campaign with the 114th Fighter Escadrille, before escaping to France and joining the *Groupe de Chasse Polonaise I/145* (a French unit comprising of mostly Polish pilots). He fought with the *Groupe* in the latter stages of the Battle of France but, following the collapse of the country, fled to the UK, where he joined the reconstituted Polish Air Force. On completion of refresher flying training he was posted to 308 (Polish) Squadron in June 1941 and flew Spitfires on offensive sweeps over north-west Europe. He completed his tour, claiming three aircraft destroyed and three damaged, for which he was awarded the Polish Cross of Valour with three bars. It was following this tour that he was posted to 3 Delivery Flight, on 12 May 1942, for a period of rest. He is buried in Leconfield Cemetery, Yorkshire.

15 June (Monday)
Anti-aircraft co-operation flight. 6 AACU (RAF Shawbury, Shropshire)
Miles Master I (N7428) crashed at Aston Hall, between West Felton and Oswestry, at 15.05 hrs.
6 AACU was based at RAF Shawbury as a lodger unit and was working in co-operation with 210 Heavy Anti-Aircraft Training Regiment at Park Hall Camp near Oswestry, towing targets for the trainee Royal Artillery gunners stationed there. On the day of the accident the pilot of this aircraft had just completed his co-operation exercise and was being relieved of duty by the pilot of Master N8014. Both pilots were experienced airmen but, according to the investigation, the pilot of N8014 'flew dangerously' while changing over and allowed his aircraft to strike the back of N7428, severing the tail completely and sending both aircraft crashing out of control.

Sgt (pilot) Tadeusz Pacahan (P-792154), PAF, aged 20, was born in Poland, on 30 July 1921. He is buried in Shawbury (St Mary's) Churchyard.

Anti-aircraft co-operation flight. 6 AACU (RAF Shawbury, Shropshire)
Miles Master I (N8014) crashed at Aston Hall between West Felton and Oswestry, after colliding in the accident described above.

Sgt (pilot) Edward Powloka (P-792548), PAF, was born on 24 July 1919. He is buried in Shawbury (St Mary's) Churchyard.

16 June (Tuesday)
Cloud flying and low flying training. 61 OTU (RAF Rednal, Shropshire)
Supermarine Spitfire IA (X4329) crash-landed at 'Grobe Farm, Dudleston Heath' near Ellesmere, at 13.12 hrs. Following engine failure, due to a 'break in the connecting rods', the pilot attempted to force-land, but, as he did so, the aircraft clipped a tree, crashed and caught fire. The seriously injured pilot was rushed to RAF Hospital, Cosford where, sadly, he succumbed to his injuries three days later.

Sgt (pilot u/t) Edward Douglas Featherstone-Wilson (1331603), RAFVR, aged 19, was the son of Harry Samuel and Grace Elizabeth Mary Wilson (née Featherstone) of Ickenham, Middlesex. He is buried in Donington (St Cuthbert's) Churchyard, Shropshire.

19 June (Friday)
Sgt E D Featherstone-Wilson died of injuries received in a crash three days earlier.

20 June (Saturday)
Dual navigation training. 5 (P)AFU (RAF Tern Hill, Shropshire)
Miles Master I (N8051) force-landed at Stoney Stretton, between Yockleton and Westbury, at 09.50 hrs.

After the engine failed, due to an unknown cause, the instructor belly-landed in a field.

F/O (instructor pilot) John William Emslie Rawle (111954), RAFVR, was born in Epsom, on 7 April 1922. He survived the war and attained the rank of flight lieutenant. He died in Salisbury in May 1996.

Sgt (pilot u/t) Leslie Martin Lack (1384774), RAFVR. On completion of his training he was posted to 118 Squadron, flying Spitfires on offensive sweeps over north-west Europe. He was killed on 18 March 1943, flying a Spitfire (EP228), when it was shot down into the sea by British anti-aircraft fire while returning from an op. Sgt Lack, aged 22, was the son of James George and Daisy Mary Lack of Clerkenwell, London. He is commemorated on the Runnymede Memorial.

28 June (Sunday)
Evasive manoeuvres and aerobatics practice. 308th Fighter Squadron, 31st Fighter Group (Atcham airfield, Shropshire)
Supermarine Spitfire VB (BM454) crash-landed near the airfield at 16.25 hrs. The American squadron had only arrived in the UK earlier in the month and was in the process of converting from the P-39 Airacobra to the Supermarine Spitfire, in preparation for its deployment in combat. While returning to the airfield to land, the pilot came across another aircraft and began 'dogfighting' for approximately ten minutes, until he realised that his fuel was nearly out. Despite just managing to reach the airfield with the engine spluttering, the pilot overshot his landing, due to problems lowering his undercarriage, and the aircraft flipped onto its back after he was forced to touch down in a cornfield nearby.

1 Lt (pilot) Elmon Redell Cobb (O-421604), USAAF, remained with the squadron after it was posted to the Mediterranean and was credited with one enemy aircraft destroyed on 15 March 1943. He survived the war and is known to have remained in the USAAF/USAF until at least the mid 1950s.

29 June (Monday)
Training flight. 308th Fighter Squadron, 31st Fighter Group (Atcham airfield, Shropshire)
Supermarine Spitfire VB (66-847 – previously EN847 with the RAF) crashed 'one mile east of the airfield', at 12.50 hrs. The pilot had only been in the air for ten minutes when he was witnessed returning to land. As he approached the airfield from the east, with wheels and flaps down, he made a rather steep turn to line up with the runway and the aircraft stalled. He immediately gave a good burst of throttle to try and regain control but the aircraft crashed into a potato patch, fatally injuring the pilot (who became the first casualty to be suffered by the American 8th Air Force in Europe). In the subsequent investigation it was revealed that he was an experienced pilot, with over 440 hours on all types, but his experience on Spitfires was limited to just three hours. This lack of experience undoubtedly contributed to the stall, although the Engineering Officer added that there was the possibility of engine trouble (although no evidence of this could be found).

1 Lt Al Giacomini [Patty Trout]

1 Lt (pilot) Alfred William (Al) Giacomini (O-421595), USAAF, was born on 11 January 1918 and grew up on the family ranch just outside Sterling, Colorado. After attending the local high school he studied mechanical engineering at the University of Colorado, before joining the US Army Air Corps. He subsequently learned to fly at Randolph Field in Texas and was then posted to 308th Fighter Squadron, flying P-39s. He is buried in Sterling (St Anthony's) Churchyard, Colorado.

4 July (Saturday)
Transit flight to RAF Bridleway Gate. 11 (P)AFU (RAF Bridleway Gate, Shropshire – Relief Landing Ground to RAF Shawbury)

Airspeed Oxford I (L9688) crashed at Hopton House Farm (at map reference 598277), near Hodnet, at 09.07 hrs. The instructor had flown to Shawbury from Bridleway Gate for a brief visit but, while he was there, the weather deteriorated rapidly. Nonetheless, he thought it was safe enough to take off for the short hop back to Bridleway Gate but, in terrible weather conditions, he flew into the side of the cloud-covered hill soon after taking off. The cause of the crash was subsequently attributed to 'inexperience on the part of a young but capable instructor'.

P/O (instructor pilot) Joseph Jenks (119565), RAFVR, aged 28, was the son of James and Maggie Jenks of Birmingham and the husband of Greta Anna Jenks (née Schafer) of Totnes, Devon. He is buried in Birmingham (Yardley) Cemetery.

10 July (Friday)
Training flight. 61 OTU (RAF Rednal, Shropshire)
Supermarine Spitfire IA (X4644, a presentation aircraft named *Sarkar-I-Tirhut*) crashed at 'Gadlas Farm, Elson' to the west of Ellesmere near Dudleston Heath, at 10.05 hrs. The aircraft crashed after the engine had caught fire in flight, killing the pilot instantly.

Sgt (pilot u/t) Donald John Mackenzie (127161), RAFVR, aged 22, was the son of Murdo C Mackenzie and C C Mackenzie of 10 Newton Street, Stornoway. Although born on the Isle of Lewis, he was working in London as a qualified draughtsman when war broke out and initially attempted to join the Royal Navy, only to be rejected due to his reserved occupation, before later trying for the RAFVR. He is buried in Sandwick Cemetery, on the Outer Hebridean Isle of Lewis.

Sgt Donald John Mackenzie [Stornoway Gazette, *via Malcolm MacDonald*]

12 July (Sunday)
Training flight. 61 OTU (RAF Rednal, Shropshire)
Supermarine Spitfire IIA (P8577) belly-landed at 'Henbarns, Haughton', to the south-east of the airfield, at 10.15 hrs. After the engine failed, due to a glycol leak, the pilot belly-landed in a field and was slightly injured.

Sgt (pilot u/t) L K Johnson (R.98440), RCAF. Nothing further is known of this pilot other than that he is thought to have survived the war.

13 July (Monday)
Cloud flying and camera gunnery practice. 257 (Burma) Squadron (RAF High Ercall, Shropshire)
Hawker Hurricane IIA (Z2629) crashed into Wytheford Wood, between Muckleton and Shawbury, at 15.40 hrs. The squadron had been stationed at High Ercall for just over a month, during which time the pilots occupied their time mostly with training flights. It was during one such flight that the pilot stalled, while making a tight turn at 400 feet, and crashed. In the subsequent investigation it was concluded that the flight commander should not have authorised the flight, as the weather conditions did not permit the minimum safe height requirements.

Sgt (pilot) Robert Henry Smith (1181158), RAFVR, aged 20, was the son of William James Smith and Elizabeth Ann Smith of St John's Wood. He had joined 257 Squadron on 26 August 1941 and, according to the war diary, was 'one of the best NCO pilots of the squadron and a very popular member'. He is buried in St Marylebone Cemetery, London.

14 July (Tuesday)
Training flight. 61 OTU (RAF Rednal, Shropshire)
Supermarine Spitfire IA (R6980) belly-landed 'two miles south of Rednal' (putting it in the area around

Elbridge) at 12.10 hrs. After 40 minutes in the air the pilot noticed the oil and glycol coolant temperatures were getting high (due to a glycol leak), so he throttled back and began to return to the airfield. No sooner had he done so than the engine failed but he 'kept his head and chose a good field' into which he belly-landed.

Sgt (pilot u/t) George Roland Wilson (414711), RNZAF. Little is known of his military career other than that he had arrived in the UK in February 1942 and survived the war.

19 July (Sunday)
Dual night training, 11 (P)AFU (RAF Shawbury, Shropshire)
Airspeed Oxford II (P1928) crashed at Yeaton Peverey, Walford, near Baschurch, at 02.45 hrs. The pupil is believed to have been in control of the aircraft when it was seen to overshoot the airfield and climb too steeply. The pilot then 'failed to correct drift to starboard and stalled due to faulty instrument flying'.

P/O Frank Alston
[Francesca Crook]

P/O (instructor pilot) Francis Desmond (Frank) Alston (118062), RAFVR, aged 31, was the son of Joseph Andrew Olsen Hafstad, a master mariner of Norwegian descent, and his wife Marie Louise Jeffreys. Born in Calcutta, on 24 April 1911, he and his family returned to England the following year and, it was while living in the UK during the First World War, that they changed their surname to avoid any animosity toward them. Educated at St Francis Xavier College in Liverpool, he worked for the Penrith and then the Liverpool branch of the Westminster Bank before the war. He married Mildred Mary Wiseman on 16 May 1939 and, according to his family, is believed to have been selected as an instructor because of his easy temperament and his interest in flying. He is buried in Liverpool (Yew Tree) Roman Catholic Cemetery.

Sgt (pilot u/t) Andrew McAlpine Begg (R.103136), RCAF, aged 22, was the son of Andrew and Elizabeth B Begg of Hamilton, Ontario, Canada. He is buried in Shawbury (St Mary Borland) Churchyard.

Sgt Andrew Begg
[Toronto Star]

19 July (Sunday)
Solo training flight. 61 OTU (RAF Rednal, Shropshire)

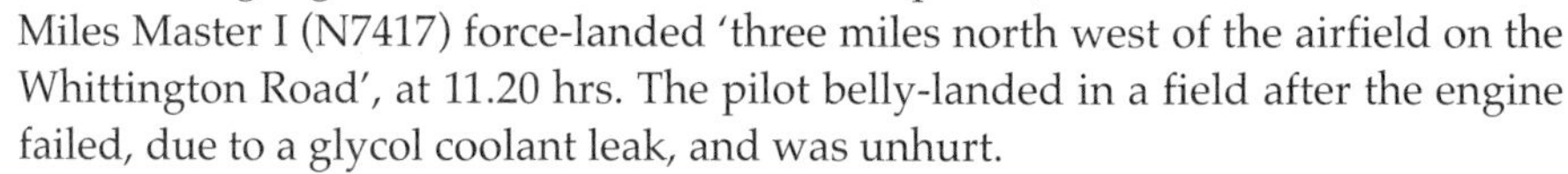

Miles Master I (N7417) force-landed 'three miles north west of the airfield on the Whittington Road', at 11.20 hrs. The pilot belly-landed in a field after the engine failed, due to a glycol coolant leak, and was unhurt.

Sgt (pilot u/t) Robert Jansen Evans (R.103806), RCAF. Nothing further is known of his military service other than that he survived the war.

20 July (Monday)
Training flight. 61 OTU (RAF Rednal, Shropshire)
Supermarine Spitfire IA (X4852) belly-landed at Morda near Oswestry, at 11.15 hrs. The pilot was flying over Oswestry at 1,000 feet and had just checked his gauges, which were giving normal readings, when the engine suddenly failed. Despite opening and closing the throttle and changing pitch, the engine would not restart and the pilot was forced to belly-land in a field, slightly damaging the wings and underside of the fuselage and shock-loading the engine. Considering that this was only his second flight in a Spitfire, the pilot was deemed to have 'kept his head in an exemplary manner' according to his Commanding Officer.

Sgt (pilot u/t) John Michael (Mike) Kassaneff (R.98300), RCAF. He was killed on 13 September in a crash near Ellesmere and further information can be found on that date.

24 July (Friday)
Training flight. 5 (P)AFU (RAF Tern Hill, Shropshire)
Hawker Hurricane I (L1592) belly-landed 'two miles north-east of Atcham aerodrome' (putting it roughly in the area between Walcot and Isombridge near Allscott), at 18.15 hrs. During the course of the flight the pilot was forced to belly-land in a field when his engine failed, after he neglected 'to maintain check of fuel contents and improper changing over to reserve'. As a result, the pilot's logbook was endorsed for 'carelessness'.

Sgt (pilot u/t) Duncan Miles McGrath (1385182), RAFVR. Commissioned in March 1945, he survived the war and attained the rank of flying officer. He died in Greenwich in 1982.

26 July (Sunday)
Training flight. 61 OTU (RAF Rednal, Shropshire)
Supermarine Spitfire IA (X4478) crash-landed '1/4 mile east of West Felton', near Oswestry, at 11.20 hrs. After the engine failed during the flight the pilot was unable to reach the airfield and belly-landed in a field, totally wrecking the aircraft but only slightly injuring himself.

P/O (pilot u/t) Bertie Walter Sharpe (121374), RAFVR, subsequently served with 126 Squadron and was killed on 29 March 1945 when his Mustang (KH489) crashed off the Dutch coast. F/Lt Sharpe, who was the husband of Olive Rosemary Sharpe of Kilburn, London, is commemorated on the Runnymede Memorial.

29 July (Wednesday)
Aerobatics practice. 257 (Burma) Squadron (RAF High Ercall, Shropshire)
Hawker Typhoon IB (R8633) crashed at Sugdon (at map reference 603153, while the tail section came down at 609139), between Rodington and Longdon on Tern, at 16.45 hrs. The squadron was in the process of converting from the Hurricane to the Typhoon at the time of the crash and the pilot was putting one of the new aircraft through its paces when the port elevator suddenly detached. The resultant stresses caused the entire tail section to break away and the aircraft was sent into an uncontrollable dive, which was witnessed by local schoolboy Colin Thompson, who was camping by the River Tern with several schoolmates.

> This Typhoon came out the sky and he sort of whipped over on his back and the whole tail unit broke off. I shouted 'Hey lads look at this, look at this'. Of course he was on his back then spinning down. He was going down and down and down, the pilot never got out. We just saw it disappear on the horizon. We went, we didn't go right to the crash, but it crashed at a place called Sugdon, near High Ercall.

F/O William McDunnough [Library and Archives Canada]

F/O (pilot) William Ralph McDunnough (J.5137), RCAF, aged 24, was the son of Mr R B McDunnough of Quebec, and had been educated at McGill University, Montreal. According to the squadron diary his death was 'keenly felt by the whole squadron, for he was always cheerful and full of life – an excellent pilot with real ability.' He is buried in Ercall Magna Churchyard, near the airfield.

30 July (Thursday)
Aerobatics training. 61 OTU (RAF Rednal, Shropshire)
Supermarine Spitfire IIA (P7289) force-landed 'two miles south of the airfield' (putting it in the area around Elbridge), at 17.15 hrs. The New Zealander pilot was returning to land when his engine failed through lack of fuel, which he was unaware of as the fuel gauge was giving a faulty reading because a

plug had become detached from its socket during aerobatics. The pilot, who was contacted by the author in 2008, recalled how:

> I was sent up to practise aerobatics at the conclusion of which I prepared to return to base. I glanced at the fuel gauge which registered a satisfactory fifteen gallons. On approaching base [at below 1,000 feet], however, the engine cut out at the very point that I had reached the circuit perimeter and was preparing to land. There was no alternative but to attempt a belly-landing. By more of luck than good judgement I tore into some rough ground between two lines of posts but the aircraft was not beyond repair. Afterwards I just hung around with some locals present until transport arrived from Rednal.
>
> I was subsequently called up to the Station Commander's office and interviewed by the Group Captain who reminded me that the reason for the crash-landing was a lack of fuel and proceeded to reprimand me for carelessness at not monitoring the fuel situation, this continued until I reminded him that I had done exactly that, and there was probably a fault in the fuel gauge system. At this he virtually leaped to the telephone and rang the Engineering Officer and enquired about the reading on the petrol gauge; when told that the reading was fifteen gallons, the cheeky station commander turned to me and said, and I quote – 'Spitfire's are easy to "force-land" aren't they Frewer? Dismiss!'. So no sanction for the event! It appeared that the gauge was faulty. There had probably been only one or two gallons rather than fifteen in the tank at the time I turned for home.

Sgt (pilot u/t) Alan Vernon Frewer (413053), RNZAF, was born on 2 August 1921 and brought up in Christchurch by his aunt, following the death of both his parents when he was a young boy. After attending Christchurch Technical College he took an electrical engineering apprenticeship with Woof & Salvesen in Christchurch, but following the outbreak of war joined the RNZAF. On completion of his training he was posted to 485 Squadron in September 1942, flying Spitfires on operational sweeps out of Tangmere, before being posted out to the Mediterranean to join 232 Squadron in early 1943. He subsequently completed 175 sorties flying Spitfires in support of the advancing Allied armies in the Mediterranean, during which time he was forced to bale out over Sicily on 17 July 1943 when his engine failed due to flak damage. He was credited with one Me109 destroyed near the south of France on 12 August 1944. He returned to New Zealand after the war and with his wife, set up his own electrical appliance firm, which they ran until their retirement.

8 August (Saturday)
Dual instructional flight. 5 (P)AFU (RAF Tern Hill, Shropshire)
Miles Master III (DL614) force-landed at 'Rudds Farm, Wollerton', between the airfield and Hodnet, at 15.00 hrs. Soon after taking off from the airfield the French pupil pilot cut the engine at 500 feet and, despite his immediately being ordered by the instructor to restart it, there was a delay 'owing to language difficulty' and he was forced to belly-land in a field.

Sgt (instructor pilot) Harold Meadowcroft Hargreaves (1016742), RAFVR, was born in Lancashire on 12 September 1916. He was commissioned in November 1943 and eventually retired as a flight lieutenant in September 1960. He died in Carlisle, in September 1992.

Sgt (pilot u/t) Jean Jacques André Camus (35013), FFAF, was born in Thiers in central France, on 4 July 1921. He escaped to Spain following the German occupation of France and was interned for a while before being released and making his way to the UK in May 1942. On completion of his training, he was posted to 329 (French) Squadron but was shot down and killed on 30 October 1944 while attacking enemy ground positions in the Netherlands, in a Spitfire (PT673).

11 August (Tuesday)
Night navex. 3 (O)AFU (RAF Bobbington, Staffordshire)

Avro Anson I (N9614) crashed into 'high ground near Batchcott Hall' near Picklescott (presumably on the northern slopes of the Long Mynd), at 22.45 hrs. After the pupil navigator made a mistake in pinpointing during the flight the pilot decided to reduce height to 1,500 feet in an attempt to get below cloud and find out where they were. As he did so, however, he was unaware that he was approaching an area of high ground and in the dark and cloudy conditions, the aircraft struck the side of the hill. Incredibly, it came sliding to a stop with no serious injuries suffered by any of the crew.

F/Sgt (staff pilot) Grahame Perry Armstrong (404163), RAAF, was born in Brisbane, on 29 March 1917 and had worked as a bank officer in that city before enlisting in 1940. After completing his pilot training he sailed to the UK in August 1941 and, the following month, was posted to 3 (O)AFU (at the time still known as 3 AOS), where he remained as a staff pilot until February 1943. He then underwent operational training and in April 1943 was posted to 165 Squadron, flying Spitfires on offensive operations over north-west Europe and 'diver' patrols (intercepting V1s). During one such patrol, on 1 July 1944, his Spitfire was badly damaged by an exploding Doodlebug (which he had just shot down) but, amazingly, he managed to return to base and land, despite his tail being very badly shredded. He completed his tour of ops in December 1944 and spent the remainder of the war serving as an instructor (including a time at RAF Rednal) before returning to Australia in April 1946.

The names of the other crew members are unknown

14 August (Friday)
Training flight. 28 EFTS (Penderford, Staffordshire)
De Havilland Tiger Moth II (T5698) crashed, or crash-landed, at 'Pool House Farm, Newport', at 19.00 hrs. Very few details of this accident are known as the accident card simply states 'awaiting further information', although it is believed that the pilot was injured in the accident.

LAC (pilot u/t) Albert Eccleston (1199330), RAFVR. No further details are known of this airman other than that he survived the war.

15 August (Saturday)
Formation flying. 61 OTU (RAF Rednal, Shropshire)
Supermarine Spitfire IA (X4815) belly-landed at Bagley to the east of the airfield, at 09.00 hrs. While flying in formation, at 8,000 feet, the engine failed suddenly due to a lack of fuel and, despite his attempting to glide back, the pilot was unable to reach the airfield and belly-landed in a field. Following an investigation it was discovered that the airman in charge of re-fuelling the aircraft had failed to do so correctly and he was disciplined accordingly.

Sgt (pilot u/t) Alpine Rae Lebans (R.55973), RCAF. Little is known of this pilot other than that he was subsequently commissioned and survived the war. He died in Guelph, Ontario in 1998.

22 August (Saturday)
Navex. 9 (O)AFU (RAF Penrhos, Caernarfonshire)
Avro Anson I (R9639) crash-landed at Onston Farm, Tetchill to the south of Ellesmere, at 11.30 hrs. While flying at an unauthorised low height the aircraft's starboard engine cut out due to a lack of fuel after the pilot failed to switch over from his empty tank, forcing him to crash-land in a field. All four occupants were injured in the landing and, sadly, one of them succumbed to his injuries the following day in the Agnes Hunt Orthopaedic Hospital, Oswestry. In the subsequent investigation it was remarked that the pilot could have remained airborne on one engine long enough to switch to his full tank and, as a result of his actions, his logbook was endorsed for 'carelessness'.

Sgt (pilot) Ernest Clifford Foster (1212909), RAFVR. Nothing further is known of this pilot other than that he survived the war.

Sgt (Nav) Kenneth Arthur Wilson (1219671), RAFVR, aged 21, was the son of Arthur and Edith Ann Wilson of Erdington, Birmingham. He is buried in Birmingham (Witton) Cemetery.

The names of the other two crewmen are unknown.

23 August (Sunday)
Sgt K A Wilson died in hospital from injuries received in a crash the previous day

2 September (Wednesday)
Training flight. 61 OTU (RAF Rednal, Shropshire)
Supermarine Spitfire IIA (P8472) belly-landed 'at Ellesmere'.
After the engine failed, due to a glycol coolant leak, the pilot made 'a good force-landing', with wheels retracted.

Sgt (pilot u/t) Clarkson. No further details available.

5 September (Saturday)
Operational scramble. 49th Fighter Squadron, 14th Fighter Group, USAAF (Atcham airfield, Shropshire)
Lockheed P-38F Lightning (41-7659, bearing the fuselage artwork *Legs*), crashed at Woodhouse Farm, near Priorslee (at map reference 729100) at 12.20 hrs. The aircraft was the personal mount of Lt Bob Carlton and bore a cartoon pair of women's legs in recognition of his nickname, which he had earned in the USA after his drill instructor referred to him as 'legs' when he had fallen behind during a training march. Bob, who lives in California and is still a member of the P-38 association, recalled the accident in an e-mail to the author in 2009:

The artwork on the port boom of Carlton's P-38 (41-7659) [Bob Carlton]

To start with, I was not scheduled to fly on that day. Not having any duties to perform, I got on my bicycle and rode out to the flight line to talk to my friend, Oscar Bluer, who was standing alert. I believe this was the first day that the squadron had stood alert duties. It was almost noon time, and Oscar asked me if I would take his place while he went to eat lunch. He said it had been quiet and if anything happened the tower would fire off a flare. Another P-38 was also standing alert. So I agreed to relieve him and got into my P-38. Since I did not expect anything to happen, I did not put on my life vest, but I did strap on my parachute.

It wasn't but a short time later that the control tower fired off a flare, and my wing-man and I started up our engines and took off. The weather was overcast with a ceiling of about 1000 feet. As soon as we were airborne I contacted the ground control and was given a vector and told to climb to 10,000 feet. Shortly I entered the overcast and reported to ground control that I was 'Popeye' [in cloud] and gave my heading and altitude. When I reached 10,000 feet I reported in and was told to climb to 15,000. I advised ground control that I was still 'Popeye', and that was about the last contact that I was able to make with ground control, although I made several calls and attempts to contact them. I realized then that my radio was out. Also at that time I lost all of my gyro instruments. My gyro compass and my artificial horizon stopped working.

On a previous occasion, one of our pilots had lost the antenna on his P-38 during a training flight, and I believed that had happened due to my loss of contact with ground control. I couldn't figure out why I had lost my gyro instruments. I still don't know why unless there was some moisture that froze the instruments.

Without my radio and primary instruments, I decided to try and get above the clouds, so I continued to climb, using my magnetic compass and my needle, ball, and bank and turn instruments to try to maintain the last course that ground control had given me. I finally broke out of the clouds at 32,000 feet. The outside temperature was -40 degrees C.

Well, I flew around up above the overcast for some time, hoping that someone would come up and help me, but no one came up. Finally I decided to let down and see if I could find a place to land. I didn't know if I was over land or water, and I was concerned that if I got below the clouds I might run into some barrage balloons; however I decided I had to try to get back down. So I picked up a reciprocal heading on my magnetic compass and started to descend. My magnetic compass was swinging back and forth and I was trying to keep it within about 15 degrees of the course I had selected. I was so intent on trying to maintain somewhat of a course I had selected that I took my eyes off the airspeed indicator momentarily. When I glanced at it I was surprised to see it read 550 mph!

At that time I tried to bring the nose of the plane up, but when I pulled back on the control, it just buffeted. I had chopped the throttles and rolled back on the trim tab, but nothing I did helped. At that time I decided to bail out. I think that I was about 20,000 feet when I pulled the ripcord on my parachute--and nothing happened! I looked down and my ripcord was just hanging there. So I gave it another tug, and my chute opened. About that time I saw my mae west [life jacket] go floating past me, and I just hoped that I wouldn't need it. When my chute opened the jerk pulled off one of my shoes and I thought my foot would freeze.

I finally broke out of the overcast and found that I was over a farmer's back yard. The farmer was out in his yard and came over and helped me get out of my chute. He helped me get into his house, then called the local constabulary to make sure I wasn't a German spy. I was in the hospital for about a week with a dislocated shoulder and injuries to my knees and other injuries.

In the subsequent investigation the accident was attributed to icing, but Bob, who had never read the report and always thought it was due to his own error, disagrees. He said, 'I really don't think the ice on my wings really had much of an effect on the plane going into compressibility. It was just the characteristic of that model P-38'.

1 Lt Bob Carlton pictured at Atcham with his dislocated arm in a sling [Bob Carlton]

1 Lt (pilot) Robert N Carlton (O-43117), USAAF, was born on a farm in Morgan Hill, California, on 20 October 1917. He and his family moved to San Jose in the 1930s, where Bob gained an associate degree in aeronautics at San Jose State College. After graduating, he joined the US Army Air Corps (following a brief period working for the Lockheed Aircraft Company) and passed out of flying school four days after the Japanese attack on Pearl Harbour. He was then assigned to 49th Fighter Squadron, flying P-40 and P-66 fighters, before the squadron re-equipped with the P-38 and travelled to the UK in July 1942. Following the accident at Atcham Bob completed 42 combat missions with the squadron in north Africa, destroying three enemy aircraft (two in the air and one on the ground) and was awarded the DFC with two Oak Leaf Clusters and the Air Medal with two Oak Leaf Clusters. In January 1943 the 14th Fighter Group was reorganized and many of the pilots, who had completed their required number of missions (including Bob), were sent home. On his return to the USA, Bob was assigned to the 330th Fighter Squadron and was responsible for instructing pilots in preparation for postings to the European and Pacific theatres. He remained in the US Air Force after the war and retired as a lieutenant-colonel in 1966.

8 September (Tuesday)
Training flight. 61 OTU (RAF Rednal, Shropshire)
Supermarine Spitfire IIA (P7963) crashed at Haughton Farm next to the airfield (at map reference 373271). The pilot was taking off along runway 16 when a swing became uncontrollable and, as the aircraft began to leave the ground, it veered off the side of the runway, struck the roof of a barn and

crashed into the yard behind. Despite the airfield medics' arriving swiftly on the scene, the seriously injured pilot died within a few minutes of the accident.

Sgt (pilot u/t) Stanley Paul Lister (657692), RAF, aged 20, was the son of Mr and Mrs Charles E Lister of Sandgate, Folkestone. He is buried in Shorncliffe Military Cemetery, Kent.

8 September (Tuesday)
Ferry flight from RAF Sealand, Flintshire, to RAF Shawbury. 30 MU (RAF Sealand, Flintshire)
Bristol Beaufighter II (T3445) crashed '1/2 mile east of RAF Shawbury', at 14.15 hrs. The pilot was making a landing approach when the aircraft 'spun into the ground' and caught fire.

Sgt (pilot) Stanisław Jednaki (P793700), PAF, aged 21, is believed to have been born in Auschwitz, as was his brother, Jozef, who also died serving with 300 (Polish) Squadron on 15 January 1943. He is buried in Shawbury (St Mary's) Churchyard, Shropshire.

8 September (Tuesday)
Bombing and navigation exercise. 16 OTU (RAF Upper Heyford, Oxfordshire)
Vickers Wellington IC (DV830) crash-landed 'near Rednal airfield' at 14.50 hrs. Having completed their bombing detail the trainee crew were flying on a course to Worcester when the port engine cut and, despite the pilot's best attempts in operating the balance cocks, the engine would not restart. With the aircraft losing height rapidly, the pilot ordered his crew to prepare for a belly-landing but, as the aircraft neared the ground, its port wing clipped the top of a tree, causing the aircraft to stall and crash. The injured crew members immediately scrambled out of the wreckage as the aircraft caught fire but, sadly, the rear gunner was unable to free himself and lost his life.

P/O Harry Larkins [Mary Allan]

P/O (pilot) Harry William Larkins (122145), RAFVR. Two weeks after the accident he was posted to 115 Squadron and was killed on 6 December 1942 piloting Wellington BJ898 on an op to Mannheim, in Germany. He was the son of Charles Thomas James and Mary Ann Alice Larkins of Dalston, London and is buried in Rheinburg Cemetery along with his crew.

Sgt (AG rear) James Herbert Hall (970800), RAFVR, aged 23, was the son of Herbert Henry and Christina Simpson Hall of Motherwell, Lanarkshire. He is buried in Oswestry General Cemetery, Shropshire.

Although unconfirmed, the other three crew members are believed to be those that joined 115 Squadron along with P/O Larkins and also lost their lives on 6 December: F/O (Nav) Jack Sydney Abel (120353), RAFVR; Sgt (AB) Richard Edwards Hayman (1262068), RAFVR; F/Sgt (W/AG) Ernest Frank Stammers (R.59841), RCAF.

10 September (Thursday)
Dogfighting practice. 61 OTU (RAF Rednal, Shropshire)
Supermarine Spitfire IIB (P8530, a presentation aircraft named *The Clan*), crashed at Bomere Heath. Few details are known of this accident other than that a collision took place with Spitfire P8268 and this aircraft crashed while the pilot of P8268 managed to remain in control and landed back at the airfield.

Sgt (pilot u/t) Douglas Arthur (Dougie) Camm (537646), RAF, aged 24, was the son of George and Sarah Elizabeth Camm (née Lawton). Educated at Green Lane School in Wortley, Leeds, he was more studious than sporting and, after leaving school, worked as a bookkeeping clerk at A Whyman Ltd, where he met his future wife, Alice Pickering. He joined the RAF in January 1937 and served in the UK as an aircrafthand until February 1939, when he was posted to India and served on the North-west Frontier as an office clerk. In December 1940 he was posted to Rhodesia, where he was accepted to undergo pilot training before returning to the UK to complete his operational training. He is buried in Horsforth Cemetery, Leeds.

Dogfighting practice. 61 OTU (RAF Rednal, Shropshire)
Supermarine Spitfire IIA (P8268) collided in the incident described above and landed safely back at the airfield.
Sgt (pilot u/t) W V Jones (service number unknown), RAFVR.

Sgt Dougie Camm.
[Sharney Camm-Hoza]

11 September (Friday)
Training flight. 28 EFTS (Penderford, Staffordshire)
De Havilland Tiger Moth II (T5716) force-landed at Redhill Farm between Sheriffhales and Oakengates, at 11.20 hrs. While flying at 5,000 feet the pilot performed a slow roll, during which the float stuck in the spin position and the engine filled up with fuel, causing it to fail. Unable to restart it the instructor attempted a forced landing but overshot his chosen field. The aircraft then struck a hedge and turned onto its back but, fortunately, neither occupant was hurt.
Sgt (instructor pilot) Robert Joseph Cavanagh (R.94905), RCAF. Commissioned in April 1944, he survived the war and retired from the RCAF in May 1945.
LAC (pilot u/t) Alec Bridgewater Broadbent (1335321), RAFVR. Commissioned in August 1943, he was killed two months later serving with 50 Squadron when his Lancaster (ED483) crashed during an op to Kassel, on 22 October 1943. Pilot Officer Broadbent, aged 20, was the son of Reginald Bridgewater Broadbent and Ethel Broadbent and the husband of Joyce E Cottrell of Furze Platt, Maidenhead. He is buried in Hanover Cemetery.

13 September (Sunday)
Flight to provide air experience for a prospective aircrew candidate. 61 OTU (RAF Rednal, Shropshire)
Miles Master III (DL611) crashed at Sandyhill, one mile north of Ellesmere, at 16.40 hrs. One of the OTU pilots was giving a prospective aircrew candidate a flight in one of the unit's Masters when he collided with a tree and crashed while performing unauthorised low flying. The accident was witnessed by Don Stokes, who gave the following account in an interview with Toby Neal of the *Shropshire Star* newspaper, in 2007:

> There were actually two planes on that day who came down over Ellesmere Mere. They were both flying at about 400-500ft and the Miles Master was slightly in front of the other one, and when it came over my farm, right over our house, it went straight up, did a half roll at the top, obviously trying to come behind the other aircraft as if it was having a bit of a dogfight.
>
> In coming down he obviously misjudged it and hit the top of an oak tree, and the plane broke into hundreds of pieces and with a great big explosion.
>
> I jumped on my bike, telling them (my parents) to ring the police and ambulance. This is at the farmhouse where my mother and father lived. I jumped on the bike and was probably down on the site within three to four minutes.
>
> The American who was the pilot had been thrown out and had actually crawled to a hedge and was lying very badly injured at the bottom of a hedge. When I went to him I said, 'Are you alright'? All he said was 'Don't touch me, go away'. Then I said 'There's help coming, so hang on if you can'.
>
> The other person had been thrown out of the plane and was lying probably 100 metres away in the field. There was another man who had run across from another direction and he was kneeling down looking at him. And then he came to where I was and said 'Good gracious, is this one alive?' He said 'The other one is dead, unfortunately.' He took his jacket off and put it round this very badly injured American.

Sadly, he succumbed to his injuries shortly afterwards.
Sgt (pilot) John Michael (Mike) Kassaneff (R.98300), RCAF, was the husband of Virginia Houdek of

Sgt Mike Kassaneff [Sue Pawlak]

Chicago, USA. Born in Chicago, on 21 November 1914, he had trained as a draughtsman before the war but then worked as a salesman instead due to the lack of work in the pre-war years. He crossed the border to join the RCAF in May 1941 and gained his wings in Canada before sailing to the UK in May 1942 to continue his operational training. He is buried in Oswestry Cemetery, Shropshire.

AC1 (ACH/GD) Kenneth George (Ken) Bowler (1384791), RAFVR, aged 21, was the son of Sam and Alice Bowler of Harrow and the husband of Mary Kathleen Bowler (née Ewart). He is buried in Harrow (Pinner) New Cemetery, Middlesex.

16 September (Wednesday)
Flying training. 5 (P)AFU (RAF Tern Hill, Shropshire)
Miles Master I (N7413) crashed at Child's Ercall. The pilot was performing a slow roll when, according to him, the aircraft became uncontrollable and he took to his parachute. The subsequent investigation deemed it more likely that he had stalled and lost control.

F/Sgt (pilot u/t) Jacques Jean-Marie Ghislain Désiré A Fromont (1424871), RAFVR. Born in Binche, Belgium on 3 July 1917, he had joined the Belgian Air Force in September 1938 and flew Fairey Fox fighter bombers with the *5e Escadrille* during the German invasion. Following the collapse of France he returned to Belgium but, the following autumn, he escaped to Spain and eventually reached the UK in March 1942. On completion of his refresher training, he was posted to 349 (Belgian) Squadron in June 1943 and flew Spitfires on operational sweeps over north-west Europe. He then completed a second tour between August 1944 and February 1945, flying Typhoons on armed reconnaissance sweeps over the advancing Allied armies in north-west Europe with 609 Squadron. He survived the war and died in 1984.

22 September (Tuesday)
Ferrying pilot to RAF Rednal. 61 OTU (RAF Montford Bridge, Shropshire – Satellite to RAF Rednal)
Miles Master III (W8939) force-landed at Ensdon to the west of the airfield, at 15.30 hrs. Immediately after becoming airborne from the airfield the engine failed, due to an unknown cause, and the pilot turned the aircraft to port and made an 'excellent forced landing', with wheels retracted, in a ploughed field.

Sgt (pilot) David Edwin Cooke (548410), RAFVR, was commissioned in March 1944. He remained in the RAF after the war and eventually resigned his commission as a flight lieutenant in March 1955.

The name of the passenger is unknown.

6 October (Tuesday)
Ferry flight to and from unknown airfields. 3 FPP (RAF Hawarden, Flintshire)
Bristol Beaufighter VI (V8468) force-landed 'near Bridgnorth' at 16.25 hrs. After one engine failed, due to an unknown cause, the pilot continued to fly on until his second engine started to lose power and he was forced to land in a field, striking some trees as he did so.

First Officer (pilot) Dennis Gerald Brinjes, ATA. Little is known of this pilot other than that he was from Maidenhead and that he survived the war.

15 October (Thursday)
Unknown flight detail. Unknown unit (but presumably an operational Polish squadron)
Vickers Wellington (serial unknown) crash-landed to the south-west of Chetwynd airfield at night.

While night flying was being carried out at Chetwynd airfield, a Wellington aircraft unexpectedly attempted to force-land but, after touching down halfway along the small grass airstrip, at 120 mph, the aircraft overshot the end of the runway. LAC Tom Gatward, who was on duty that night, recalled the incident for Toby Neal's book, *Shropshire Airfields*:

> For night flying we used paraffin flares. All of a sudden this huge aircraft appeared and tried to land. It was a Wellington and landed on our flare path. It could not pull up in the length of the field and so it went over the road across the Sambrook road, into a potato field and stopped just short of the Meese [river]. All the fuselage was piled up with potatoes. I think they were Free Frenchmen. They asked: 'Are we in France?' We said, 'No, you're not – you're in Shropshire.' They were from a base in Yorkshire and were loaded with incendiaries and were supposed to be on an incendiary raid to Germany. I was on duty and we went there and rushed across. They were alright.

The names of the crew are unknown but they are recorded as having completed 23 operational sorties.

18 October (Sunday)
Test flight. 29 MU (RAF High Ercall, Shropshire)
De Havilland Tiger Moth II (R5210) crashed at Rowton Halt to the north-east of the airfield, at 11.30 hrs. The aircraft was being put through an intentional spin, as part of an air test, when the pilot left his recovery too late and allowed the aircraft to crash through some high tension power cables and hit the ground, injuring both occupants.

W/O (test pilot) John de Little (745291), RAFVR, was born in Gosforth, Newcastle in 1919. He had served as a test pilot with 41 Group (of which 29 MU was a part) since June 1942 and was awarded the Air Force Cross in the New Year Honours list of 1945 for his services. After the war, Jock (as he was known) became a civilian test pilot and was killed on 15 February 1951 when he was struck by an aircraft taking off at RNAS Lossiemouth (where he was based). He was 31-years old and is buried in York Cemetery.

'A Gregory C44'. The identity of this airman has yet to be confirmed.

18 October (Sunday)
Training flight. 5 (P)AFU (RAF Tern Hill, Shropshire)
Miles Master I (T8571) force-landed at 'New House Farm, Hatton' (presumably at Hungry Hatton, near Hinstock), at 16.10 hrs. After the engine failed in flight the pupil pilot force-landed in a field and was subsequently admitted to RAF Hospital, Cosford, suffering a fractured 'horizontal ramus'.

Lt (pilot u/t) H Budan, Turkish Air Force. Despite Turkey's neutrality during the war, several hundred Turkish airmen underwent pilot training at RAF establishments, including RAF Tern Hill.

9 November (Monday)
Formation training. 61 OTU (RAF Rednal, Shropshire)
Supermarine Spitfire IA (R6993) belly-landed at 'Burton Mill Farm, Ellesmere', at 10.23 hrs. The pilot was flying in formation when his engine began to run rough, due to a glycol leak. Unable to maintain height, he dropped away from the other aircraft and belly-landed in a field.

Sgt (pilot u/t) Arthur James Adams (1238963), RAFVR, was born in Coventry, on 8 December 1917. He was posted to 111 Squadron on completion of his training and flew Spitfires over the advancing Allied forces in Sicily and Italy. In January 1944 he was awarded the DFC for his actions with the squadron and, in particular, 'on one occasion, when shot down by anti-aircraft fire over enemy territory, he evaded capture and trapped and held three German parachutists until our ground forces arrived on the scene'. He survived the war having attained the rank of flight lieutenant in May 1945.

13 November (Friday)
D/F homing practice. 247 (China-British) Squadron (RAF High Ercall, Shropshire)
Hawker Hurricane II (Z5220) overturned on the airfield at 20.45 hrs. The pilot, who had only been with the squadron a month, was landing at the airfield when he allowed the aircraft to swing off the runway onto soft ground. When he applied the brakes the aircraft flipped over onto its back, killing him instantly.

Sgt (pilot) Desmond Terence (Des) Gale (1333476), RAFVR, aged 21, was the son of Arthur Terence and Hannah Gale of Walthamstow, Essex and the husband of Joan Ivy Hollyer, also of Walthamstow. According to the squadron war diary he had 'shown himself a steady, reliable and pleasant personality'. He is buried in Ercall Magna Churchyard near the airfield.

21 November (Saturday)
Ferry flight. 1 FPP (White Waltham, Berkshire)
Hawker Typhoon IB (DN251) crashed into trees at Banbury Cottage (at map reference 603844) and came to rest by Boyne Water Pool on the eastern slopes of Brown Clee Hill, near Burwarton, at 13.47 hrs. While flying through very poor weather conditions the pilot failed to see rising ground, which was obscured by thick mist, and the aircraft struck the hillside under full power. Ron Pearce, who lived at Banbury Farm and worked in the woodland on the hill, recalled the accident in a conversation with the author in 2008:

> I left school in the middle of the war on 21 September 1942. On the 24th I was signed on by what is now known as the Forestry Commission and I worked one of our horses timber tushin'. My father had three horses timber tushin' and I was on my way back from the sawmill one Saturday morning and there was a mist on the hill above me, which we were quite used to. I heard this aircraft coming from behind me, so I stopped the nag and turned around, I was riding her home, too lazy to walk, and this Hawker Typhoon come tearing up past me about a hundred yards away climbing up the hill and he disappeared in the mist and, of course, he crashed about a mile further on from where I was. I got the nag home and tied her to the local wicket post and dashed into the house to my mother and said, 'there's a plane crashed back up by the Ways' (who were some of our neighbours) and she went ghostly white and I said, 'oh, what's the matter?'. She said, 'oh, your brothers have just gone up there to fetch some sheep.' Anyway I dashed up the hill and I met them coming through the field at the top of the hill with the sheep and they'd heard the bang but they didn't know anything about it, so we went and found the aircraft. By the time we got there, my line of country wasn't quite spot on, there were about a dozen people there and the pilot was dead on the ground. He was an ATA pilot and I found his watch in the bottom of the hedge in a rabbit hole. It was the first watch I'd ever seen with a sweep second hand. The second hand had come off and was crossed under the glass which wasn't broken and naturally the watch had stopped, so I wondered as a kid like, 'bout 14, I couldn't afford a gold watch, so who can I give it to, to get it back to his family, so I gave it the estate agent, on the Burwarton Estate, a man named Mr Edwards. He took it away and he traced it back to the family.

Captain (pilot) Walter 'Wally' Mason, ATA, aged 50, was born in Bury St Edmunds, on 18 May 1892, the son of Ezra and Martha Maria Mason. He had served in the Royal Artillery during the First World War and left the army in 1927 as a regimental sergeant-major, after which he settled in Catterick with his wife, Edith Irene Mason, and ran a shoe repair business. While living there he also learned to fly at the Yorkshire Air Services in 1934 and, with the Nazi threat escalating, he joined the Civil Air Guard in 1938 and then, following the outbreak of war, was one of the first entrants into the ATA. He is buried in Otford (St Bartholomew) Churchyard, Kent.

30 November (Monday)
First night solo flight. 81 OTU (RAF Whitchurch Heath, Shropshire)

Armstrong Whitworth Whitley V (EB339) crashed '450 yards short of the airfield' at 01.03 hrs. The pilot took off at 00.55 hrs for his first solo night flight and was flying in the circuit when an isolated patch of poor visibility, or smoke, drifted across the airfield and, probably, caused him 'to panic and approach too low without waiting for permission to land'. As he neared the end of the runway the aircraft struck a tree and crashed, bursting into flames and killing all onboard except the rear gunner. It was the first major accident suffered by the unit since its formation and, following an investigation, it was considered that it would have 'been wiser to wait for results of air test before sending pupil on his first night solo'.

Sgt John Evans [John Drew]

Sgt (pilot) Thomas John Terrence Evans (1270758), RAFVR, aged 26, was born in Tonypandy, South Wales, the youngest son of Morgan and Ann Rowena Evans. Educated at school in Rhondda, he had trained as a motor mechanic after leaving school but, following the outbreak of war, travelled to London to join the RAF. It was whilst living in London that he met his wife-to-be, Ruth Agnes Milne, whom he married on 20 November 1942, just ten days before he was killed. He is buried in Ash (Christ Church) Churchyard, Shropshire.

Sgt (AB) Laurence Cecil Lawson (1558325), RAFVR, aged 21, was the son of Thomas and Frances Gertrude Lawson of Darlington. He is buried in Darlington West Cemetery, Durham.

Sgt (W/AG) Jack Overend (1126642), RAFVR, aged 31, was the son of Harry and Ellen Overend of Bradford and the husband of Esme Olga Overend (née Ackroyd) of Stanningley. He is buried in Bradford (Scholemoor) Cemetery.

Sgt (AG rear) Roy Edward Whitebeard (778992), RAFVR, was born in Broken Hill, Northern Rhodesia, on 1 February 1924. He joined 156 Squadron after surviving the accident and recovering from his injuries. He was killed on 24 February 1944 when his Lancaster (ND454) was shot down near Sarrebourg during an op to Schweinfurt. Sgt Whitebeard is buried in Schalbach Roman Catholic Cemetery, France, alongside his fellow crew members.

12 December (Saturday)
Night navex from Base–'Occult Vee' (a flashing beacon north west of Shrewsbury)–Pershore–DF position on the River Severn–Base. 6 AOS (RAF Moreton Valance, Gloucestershire – Satellite airfield to RAF Staverton)
Avro Anson I (EF932) flew into the northern slopes of Brown Clee Hill, 90 feet from the summit, at 19.55 hrs. Having taken off at 18.30 hrs, with a wireless operator and two pupil navigators on board, the pilot reached the first turning point, where LAC Spilsbury gave him the next bearing to Pershore. This second leg would put the aircraft in line with Brown Clee Hill but, according to the pilot's statement following the accident, he was aware of this and had deliberately flown at 2,000 feet knowing that the highest point of the hill was 1,800 feet. Whether he lost height to fly underneath a patch of cloud is unclear (although this was the conclusion of the investigation) but the aircraft flew into the hill, striking a small mound, which ripped the port wing off, before sliding thirty yards to a halt and badly injuring all on board. The second pupil navigator, LAC Coles, who was acting as a wireless operator on the exercise, provided the following account for the subsequent investigation:

> Everything in the aircraft was normal, as far as I knew, and the crash came as a complete surprise to everybody in the crew. After the crash I got out by the door. I had no torch. I saw LAC Spilsbury in the nose of the aircraft. W/O Fuller and the pilot Sgt Anthony had been thrown about ten yards ahead of the aircraft. My left arm was

> broken. I saw a house about 100 yards away and stumbled to it. I found it was only a shell. I came back and helped W/O Fuller to the house and afterwards Sgt Anthony part of the way. I dragged Spilsbury by his feet about 30 yards in case the aircraft caught fire. Two civilians arrived after about half an hour. I did not touch the first-aid kit. I did not like to give the other man morphine as I thought they would go to sleep and freeze.

LAC Coles was subsequently awarded the BEM for his part in the rescue. The citation stated that,

> LAC Coles although suffering intense pain and being very weak, having sustained a compound fracture of the left arm with multiple abrasions and severe shock, dragged one of his helpless comrades out of the aircraft and clear of the wreckage. He then assisted the remaining two airmen to safety. During the whole of this time there was a grave danger of fire due to escaping petrol. LAC Coles displayed courage and devotion to duty of a very high standard.

Following the crash, the injured men were taken to RAF Hospital, Bridgnorth, where Sgt Anthony was diagnosed as having a dislocated right hip and head injuries, LAC Spilsbury a crushed third lumbar vertebra and W/O Fuller a cracked rib close to his lung. LAC Spilsbury, Sgt Anthony and LAC Coles were subsequently transferred to RAF Hospital, Cosford, where they received more specialized treatment, but W/O Fuller could not be moved at the time due to the proximity of the cracked rib to his lung and remained at RAF Bridgnorth until it was safe to transfer him.

LAC Douglas Spilsbury [Kathryn Lockwood]

Sgt (staff pilot) Thomas Wilkinson Anthony (401481), RAAF. After recovering from his injuries he went on to fly Halifax bombers with 640 Squadron and was awarded the DFC in November 1944. He survived the war and returned home to Australia, where he died in Melbourne in 1980.

W/O (staff W/Op) John Edward Fuller (581445), RAF. Commissioned in May 1943, he survived the war and eventually retired as a squadron leader in November 1966.

LAC (Nav u/t) Douglas Spilsbury (1508456), RAFVR. Born in Newbould, Worcestershire, on 3 October 1920, he and his family moved to Sheffield when he was young and after leaving school he worked in the laboratory of the George Senior steelworks at Ponds Forge, Sheffield.

Following the accident he underwent some groundbreaking surgery and his torso and right leg were encased in plaster. However, as a result of his injuries, he was declared unfit for operational flying and spent the rest of the war instructing. He returned to Sheffield after the war and went back to work for George Senior but, according to his family, suffered back problems for the rest of his life. He died in 1994.

LAC Ken Coles [Mike Perry]

LAC (Nav u/t) Kenneth George (Ken) Coles (1318594), RAFVR, was born in Abergavenny, Monmouthshire, on 15 January 1923, the only child of George and Florence Coles (née Winstone). According to his family he spent the remainder of the war in India, where he flew in Mosquito aircraft, before returning to the UK and being demobbed. Following a brief period in civilian employment, he re-enlisted in the RAF and served during the Berlin Air Lift in 1948. Later in his career he went on to serve on Air Sea Rescue helicopters in Singapore and, shortly before his retirement, narrowly missed out on the chance of flying on the first Concorde flight, in 1969. He died in Tiverton in 1999.

21 December (Monday)
Navex. 3 (O)AFU (RAF Bobbington, Staffordshire)
Avro Anson I N5089 force-landed at Folly Farm, to the east of Broseley (at map reference 687017), at 11.15 hrs. After both engines failed in flight, due possibly to a misuse of controls, the pilot was forced to land in a field with wheels down and the aircraft was slightly damaged when the wing struck a tree. The accident soon attracted great attention from the local schoolchildren, one of whom later recalled how

> … there were four occupants and they got out alright. It came down over the river, whether it was having trouble rising back up, I don't quite know what happened. It kind of ditched. It was more like a crash-landing. I think there was an Australian and a Canadian in the crew. I went to see it later, in the evening. We went down on our pushbikes but they wouldn't let us go down right near to the aircraft. It was there for a day or two days and then it was taken away on a low-loader. I wasn't near enough to see whether the wheels were up or down. I think it came to rest in a hedge though.

F/O (pilot) John Charles Jeffery (J.15199), RCAF, was born in Canada on 29 May 1916. He enlisted in November 1940 and gained his wings in Canada before sailing to the UK in August 1941. Little is known of his movements after arriving in England, but he appears to have served as a staff pilot at Bobbington from at least October 1942. Following the landing at Broseley, he was involved in another incident on 17 April 1943, when he was seriously injured after misjudging his approach and crashing into the station gymnasium in an Anson (AX234). He was eventually repatriated to Canada in September 1944 and demobbed the following January.

The names of the other crew members are unknown.

28 December (Monday)
Routine training flight. 122nd Observation Squadron (Station 342, Atcham, Shropshire)
Bell P-39L Airacobra (42-4544) crashed 'three miles south of Much Wenlock' (putting it in the area of Callaughton and Spoonhill) at 11.30 hrs. The aircraft was witnessed flying into cloud at very low altitude and, soon afterwards, dived out of the cloud in a right-hand turn from which the pilot failed to pull up in time to clear the top of a hill. Following an investigation the crash was attributed to 'pilot error both in judgement and technique' due to his decision to proceed into conditions requiring instrument flying with 'no RT and without sufficient altitude to provide any margin of safety for unforeseen occurrences'.

2 Lt (pilot) Robert Morris Trulock (O-791353), USAAF, aged 21, was the son of Paul Hines Trulock and Helen Christine Trulock (née Morris) of Decatur County, Georgia. After leaving school, he worked as a news photographer before enlisting in the US Army Air Corps in December 1941. He is buried in Cambridge (Madingley) Cemetery.

The smashed wreckage of the P-39 near Much Wenlock [USAAF]

1943

9 January (Saturday)
Night circuits and landings. 11 (P)AFU (RAF Condover, Shropshire – satellite to RAF Shawbury)

Sgt Glenn Raby
[Library & Archives Canada]

Airspeed Oxford II (AP500) crashed at Acton Burnell at 01.55 hrs. The pupil pilot had just taken off on his fifth circuit, when the aircraft was witnessed climbing to 1,000 feet and turning 270 degrees to the left before diving vertically into the ground under full power. The inquiry that followed found that the pilot had been to a dance on the evening of 7 January and had only had four and a half hours' sleep in the previous forty-four hours. It was, therefore, concluded either that he had fallen unconscious onto the control column or, more likely, that his reactions to the blind flying instruments had been impaired due to his lack of sleep.

Sgt (pilot u/t) Glenn James Raby (R.103541), RCAF, aged 20, was the son of James and Myrtle Raby of Banff, in Alberta, Canada. He is buried in Shawbury (St Mary's) Churchyard.

11 January (Monday)
Test flight. 27 MU (RAF Shawbury, Shropshire)
Armstrong Whitworth Albermarle I (P1447) force-landed at Ellerdine Grange, near Muckleton, at 15.40 hrs. The aircraft was being flown by one of the unit's experienced test pilots when the starboard propeller went into fully fine pitch, due to a failure of the feathering motor, and he was forced to switch it off as it began to overheat. Unable to maintain height on only one engine, he then belly-landed in a field but was unhurt.

F/Lt (Test pilot) John Henry Lowes (43936), RAF. For further details on this officer see the entry for 21 March 1940, when he was involved in another forced landing near Shawbury.

11 January (Monday)
Night navigation exercise. 16 OTU (RAF Upper Heyford, Oxfordshire)
Vickers Wellington III (Z1669) crashed on the Long Mynd, 'near All Stretton' (according to one witness it came down near Robin Hood's Butts on the north end of the hill), at 22.05 hrs. A trainee crew were being instructed by a staff pilot when they became lost due to 'poor navigation' and were ordered to descend below cloud to establish their position. As the pilot did so the aircraft flew into the hillside which was obscured by cloud. Fortunately, due to the low cruising speed and angle at which the aircraft struck, it came to rest with no serious injuries to any of the crew.

P/O (staff pilot) Roger William Manuel (133030), RAFVR, survived the war, attaining the rank of flight lieutenant and was twice mentioned in despatches, in June 1944 and January 1946.

Sgt (pilot) Nunez, RAFVR. Although unconfirmed, he is believed to be P/O George Albert Nunez (146436), from Trinidad, who was killed on 1 May 1943 piloting a Lancaster (ED838) of 9 Squadron.

The names of the other crew members are unknown.

11 January (Monday)
Night cross-country exercise from Base–Priors Hardwick–Cambridge–Goole–Northampton–Base. 22 OTU (RAF Wellesbourne Mountford, Warwickshire)
Vickers Wellington III (HZ104) crashed near Bobbington airfield (at wartime map reference 818922), to the west of Halfpenny Green, at 23.06 hrs. The trainee crew were on their final flight at OTU and were

flying on the Goole to Northampton leg when the navigator obtained a 'Gee' fix which showed the aircraft was south of track. The pilot adjusted his course accordingly but, when a second fix was taken a short while later, high winds had put the aircraft off course again and south of Birmingham. Finding that the wireless set was not working, the pilot began a square search pattern to try to locate Wellesbourne Mountford airfield and, at the same time, put out a 'Darky' (homing) call. Soon afterwards he saw some airfield lights and entered the circuit while he requested permission to land. Once that was granted, however, he 'erred in his method of approach', allowing the aircraft to sink too soon before reaching the runway and the aircraft crash-landed after striking some telegraph poles. The following account was given by the navigator during a conversation with the author in 2007:

> Well, we hit something. I don't know what it was but it made a big bang! We were just sitting as normal in preparation for a landing, so we weren't braced for anything. I remember a bloody great crash and getting my leg trapped and it was all very unpleasant, as any accident is. We just had to wait until help arrived. Ha, ha. Now I remember our bomb aimer was a very young chappy, I don't think he knew much of what was going on. When I managed to get out I found him knocking on the side of a haystack asking for a telephone! But anyway, they eventually turned up and got us all into hospital.

P/O Ernie Fisher [Library & Archives Canada]

The crew were, in fact, taken to RAF Hospital, Bridgnorth, suffering various broken bones and crush injuries, but the pilot, who had suffered serious head injuries, died three days later after being transferred to RAF Hospital, Cosford.

P/O (pilot) Ernest Edward (Ernie) Fisher (J.22786), RCAF, aged 19, was the son of Ernest and Mary Fisher of Toronto, Canada. Educated in architectural drafting, he had worked as a draughtsman for four months before enlisting in August 1941. He is buried in Donington (St Cuthbert's) Cemetery, Shropshire.

P/O (Nav) John Robert Alfred (Bob) Huxstep (127927), RAFVR, was born in Rye, Sussex, in 1921. He was posted to 624 Squadron after the accident, despite suffering back injuries,subsequently completing seventy special-duty ops, dropping supplies and secret agents, for which he was awarded the DFC in November 1944. Following the war he returned to his home town and became a schoolteacher.

Sgt (AB) Frank William Robert Frost (1320288), RAFVR.

Sgt (W/AG) William Stephen 'Bill' Yates (1295363), RAFVR.

Sgt (AG rear) F E Fry (R.129752), RCAF.

P/O Bob Huxstep, DFC [Bob Huxstep]

13 January (Wednesday)

Test and delivery flight. 9 MU (RAF Cosford, Shropshire)

Airspeed Horsa I (DP518) force-landed at 'Lillihurst steelworks, Priorslee' (in what is now part of Telford) at 15.15 hrs. During the course of the flight the glider developed a left wing low attitude which the pilot was unable to correct. He therefore cast off from the tug, spiralled down and crash-landed, injuring the three occupants. In the inquest that followed, no technical defect was found with the glider but a possible explanation was offered in that hot air from the steel furnaces may have aggravated the problem and 'reduced aileron efficiency in an unstable attitude'.

Sgt (pilot) John Bernard Coulson (1207579), RAFVR, was commissioned two months after the accident and remained in the RAF after the war, relinquishing his commission as a flight lieutenant in February 1958.

Sgt (pilot) W C Woods (100111), GPR.
One unnamed GPR soldier.

14 January (Thursday)
P/O E E Fisher, RCAF, died in RAF Hospital, Cosford, following an accident on 11 January 1943.

14 January (Thursday)
Low-level sortie of the Wem area. 41 OTU (RAF Hawarden, Flintshire)
North American Mustang I (AG515) crashed at the Waymills, on the north-east outskirts of Whitchurch (concentrated in the area around wartime map reference 554414), at 15.10 hrs. Two pilots were instructed to carry out similar exercises in adjacent areas, during the course of which they met up and, 'in wilful disobedience of orders, carried out weaving and/or formation at low altitude'. Numerous witnesses, including pilots from 81 OTU who were training in the area, described seeing the aircraft flying from west to east at approximately 100 feet and weaving close to one another. Harold Rolfe, a local Home Guard who was in his garden at 78 Dodington, saw the aircraft approaching at low altitude and gave the following account in the subsequent investigation:

> The leading aircraft banked to starboard and the following aircraft which was to his starboard struck the leader's starboard mainplane. The leading aircraft fell immediately and the second aircraft carried on a short distance, struck the ground and exploded.

Wreckage from the two aircraft was scattered over a considerable area and one of the .50 calibre machine guns smashed through the roof of W H Ashley's garage and funeral furnishers business at Waymills, wrecking a motor hearse. Mrs D McLellan, of 6 Ash Magna, who was in the garage at the time, was seriously injured (suffering a fractured skull) and had to be rushed to Whitchurch Cottage Hospital.

P/O (pilot u/t) Raphael Rex Heathcote (406850), RAAF, aged 21, was the son of Albert Edward and Ivy Gertrude Heathcote of Bridgetown, Western Australia. Before enlisting in April 1941 he had worked as a bank clerk. He is buried in Hawarden Cemetery, Flintshire.

Low-level sortie of Whitchurch. 41 OTU (RAF Hawarden, Flintshire)
North American Mustang I (AP199) crashed at Waymills after colliding in the incident described above.

P/O (pilot u/t) Richard George Beevers (127994), RAFVR, aged 20, was the son of Harold Edgar Greaves Beevers and Ebba Emily Agneta Beevers (née Hasselhuhn) of Lee. He is buried in Lewisham (Hither Green) Cemetery, London.

16 January (Saturday)
Test flight. 109th Observation Squadron, 6th Fighter Wing (Station 342, Atcham, Shropshire)
Supermarine Spitfire VB (EN772) crashed at Roden, near High Ercall, at 11.15 hrs. The aircraft had been involved in a minor taxiing accident the previous day and the pilot was ordered to take off at 10.59 hrs to conduct a test on the aircraft to ensure its serviceability. However, soon after it left the airfield, a local farmer, Mr W Foulkes, heard a whining sound of increasing volume and, seconds later, the aircraft emerged from cloud in a spin at approximately 500–800 feet. The pilot was seen to try and bale out at 100–150 feet but, at such a low altitude, his parachute failed to deploy and his body was found lying in a field close by. In the subsequent RAF investigation the accident was attributed to 'a loss of control', although it was added that there was insufficient evidence to say whether this was due to 'a fault in the aircraft or due to a fairly inexperienced pilot flying in cloud'. Rather contradictorily, the American report states that the pilot had 'compiled a fine record while training at Atcham' and 'displayed all the desired qualities of a young officer pilot plus excellent flying abilities', attributing the accident to '50% pilot error and 50% undetermined'.

2 Lt (pilot) George Parker Toms Jr (O-885475), USAAF, aged 21, was the son of George Parker Toms and Marion Toms (née Fagan) of Santa Barbara, California. He is buried in Golden Gate National Cemetery, California.

20 January (Wednesday)
Formation flying exercise. 61 OTU (RAF Rednal, Shropshire)
Supermarine Spitfire IA (P9329) crashed at Gaerstone Farm (at map reference 473936), on the edge of Hope Bowdler Hill, to the east of Church Stretton, at 11.15 hrs. Two pupil pilots took off from Rednal with orders to rendezvous with an instructor over the airfield, who would then lead them in formation. However, after leaving the ground it is believed that they joined up with the wrong aircraft and followed it instead. After realising their mistake the two pilots found themselves over unfamiliar countryside in very poor weather conditions and, as they flew down the valley towards Church Stretton at 800 feet, they decided to turn left to fly out of the valley. They were unfortunately not to know that, through the gap in the hills into which they had turned, were yet more hills shrouded in cloud, and the two aircraft ploughed into a hillside several hundred yards from one another.

Sgt Donald Moulds [Library & Archives Canada]

Sgt (pilot u/t) Donald Lawrence Moulds (R.125851), RCAF, aged 20, was the son of Ernest and Ethel Smith Moulds of Ottawa, Canada. He is buried in Oswestry General Cemetery, Shropshire.

Formation flying exercise. 61 OTU (RAF Rednal, Shropshire)
Supermarine Spitfire IA (X4852) crashed into woods on Helmeth Hill (at map reference 472937) to the east of Church Stretton, in the incident described above.

Sgt (pilot u/t) Howard King Adams (R.136079), RCAF, aged 19, was the son of Joseph R and Jessie E Adams of Toronto, Canada. Before enlisting in October 1941 he had worked as a youth counsellor. He is buried in Oswestry General Cemetery, Shropshire.

23 January (Saturday)
Training flight. 61 OTU (RAF Rednal, Shropshire)
Supermarine Spitfire IIB (P8569) crash-landed at Webscott, between Myddle and Harmer Hill, at 16.40 hrs. The pilot was flying at low level when the engine suddenly failed due to a glycol leak and, with little height to choose a suitable field and with smoke fumes blinding him, he touched down in a ploughed field. The aircraft then cart-wheeled, tearing off both wings. RAF Shawbury were quick to respond and the injured pilot was taken to the station sick quarters to be treated for a fractured left clavicle and bruising of the left arm before being transferred to RAF Hospital, Cosford.

Sgt (pilot u/t) Donald Boulton Wilson (1230168), RAFVR, was born on 20 April 1920, and died in Dewsbury, Yorkshire, in 1974.

30 January (Saturday)
Cross-country and bombing exercise. 16 OTU (RAF Upper Heyford, Oxfordshire)
Vickers Wellington III (X3890) crashed at Abdon Burf on Brown Clee Hill (at map reference 595868), at 00.55 hrs. Having completed an evening cross-country flight the staff pilot, trainee crew and two screened aircrew (who had operational experience and were on board to help instruct the trainee crew) received orders to carry out another shorter cross-country flight without first landing. During this next leg, however, the navigator became lost in deteriorating weather conditions and the aircraft strayed

well west of its intended track. Unaware that he was now approaching an area of high ground, the pilot continued at a low altitude (although there was a suggestion that he may have been descending through cloud to pinpoint their location) and the aircraft crashed into the hillside. The navigator's account of the accident, which appeared in an article written by Glyn Warren for the *Aviation Archaeologist Magazine*, adds:

My specific reason for being on board that night was to demonstrate the new 'Gee' navigation aid to members of the crew. Unfortunately not long out of base at Upper Heyford, it packed in completely, so I had to relatively sit back and enjoy the ride. It was, in fact, our second cross-country of the night. On return to base, we had been ordered to go around again. None of us were very amused! I am not sure of the reason, but it was probably to get in the flying hours for the five members of the OTU crew, who would be passing to a front line squadron very shortly.

After a few hours' flight, I checked with the navigator, who admitted he was lost. I was standing in the cockpit area, engaged in getting a radio 'fix' with base, when a terrible shuddering was felt. Unknown to us, we had struck the top of the Brown Clee. The aircraft was torn apart and soon caught fire. Lapsing into unconsciousness, I could see that the bottom of my trousers had been torn away, and flames from one of the engines, under which I was trapped, were lapping up my legs. Underneath, the ground was soft, so I literally burrowed my way out to safety. The three of us who survived, Sergeant Tait, Sergeant Adair and myself, huddled together in the dinghy, which had opened, for some protection against the elements. It was lashing down with rain, and terribly cold. One of the lads had lost a leg, the other a hand. Several hours went by before we saw the lights of the search party coming up the hill. In the torn wreckage around us lay five dead colleagues.

F/Sgt George Hosford, GM *[Philip Wilson, Dundonald Primary School]*

Following initial treatment in RAF Hospital, Bridgnorth, the three injured men were transferred to RAF Hospital, Cosford, with P/O Boucher suffering chest injuries and burns, Sgt Tait a fractured pelvis and scalp wounds, and Sgt Adair burns to his legs, foot and both hands, lacerations of his scalp and injuries to his right leg.

F/Sgt (staff pilot) George Lynas Hosford (1283824), GM, RAFVR, aged 22, was the son of Charles Maxwell Hosford and the late Eleanor Whitely Hosford. Born in India, where his father was serving with the Inniskilling Fusiliers, he returned to Ireland aged three and attended Dundonald Primary School. After his mother died in 1935 the family moved to Wood Green in London, where George worked for HM Stationery Office in Kingsway, before joining up in August 1940. After finishing his training he was posted to 104 Squadron and completed 42 ops flying Wellingtons in the Mediterranean theatre. He was awarded the George Medal in December 1942, the citation for which read:

Sgt Hosford was in charge of a party which laid a flare path and loaded bombs on to a squadron of aircraft when they were operating from an airfield one night in June 1942. The bombers had taken off from a nearby landing ground and soon afterwards, enemy aircraft commenced to drop flares and bombs in the neighbourhood. The attack continued throughout the night. At 23.00 hours our bombers commenced to arrive back, landing at the airfield to be refuelled and reloaded for a second sortie. One of the aircraft when taking off on its second operation, received a direct hit by an enemy bomb: a terrific explosion occurred and the aircraft burst into flames. Three members of the crew escaped through the pilots escape hatch, whilst the rear gunner, who was badly injured but had managed to free himself from his turret was assisted by Sergeant Hosford to get clear of the aircraft. The bombs on the aircraft began to explode but, despite the great danger, Sergeant Hosford returned to the blazing wreckage for the wireless operator, who was lying seriously injured close to it and dragged him to a nearby vehicle. The vehicle was badly damaged and, although Sergeant Hosford had not driven before, he succeeded in driving the vehicle away from the danger area. During the whole of this time, enemy aircraft were overhead bombing and machine gunning the blazing aircraft. Afterwards to enable our bombers to land when returning from operations, Sergeant Hosford helped to relay a flare path, which he managed for the rest of the night. He displayed courage and devotion to duty of a very high standard and undoubtedly saved two lives.

He is buried in Dundonald (St Elizabeth) Church of Ireland Churchyard, County Down.

Sgt (pilot) Bruce Alexander Tait (409252), RAAF. After recovering from his injuries, he was posted to 467 Squadron but failed to return from an op to Berlin on 29 December 1943, in a Lancaster (ED547). P/O Tait, who was 22-years old and the son of James and Mabel Isabel Tait from Melbourne, is buried in Berlin War Cemetery.

F/O (screened Nav) Jack Stewart Boucher (119892), DFM, RAFVR. Before joining 16 OTU he had served as a navigator on Hampden bombers with 144 Squadron. His DFM was gazetted just two weeks before the accident and was awarded for the part he had played in a daylight attack on the German battle cruisers in the port of Brest, during which he had been wounded in the face. Little else is known of his military career following the accident, other than that he survived the war and died in Dacorum, Hertfordshire, in 2001.

Sgt (Nav) Kenneth Lawson (1029770), RAFVR, aged 22, was the son of Redvers S and Elizabeth Lawson of Levenshulme, Manchester. He is commemorated at the Manchester Crematorium.

P/O (AB) France Louis Farla (132184), RAFVR, aged 23, whose next of kin are unknown, is buried in Bridgnorth Cemetery, Shropshire.

F/Sgt (screened W/AG) George Wartnaby (581545), RAF, aged 30, was the son of William Edward and Gertrude Mary Wartnaby of Loughborough and the husband of Peggy Wartnaby (née Smith) of Syston. He is buried in Seagrave Cemetery, Leicestershire.

Sgt (W/AG) Edmond Adair (1083270), RAFVR, who was born in Northern Ireland on 2 November 1922, had worked as a baker before the war and lived at 11 Woodburn Drive, Belfast. After recovering from his injuries he joined a new crew and was posted to 630 Squadron. On 22 May 1944 he was shot down in a Lancaster (JB546) during an op to Brunswick in Germany and spent the remainder of the war as a POW.

Sgt David Skinner
[Library & Archives Canada]

Sgt (AG) David Beatty Evans Skinner (R.92454), RCAF, aged 26, was the son of Joseph and Florence Maud Skinner of Ladner, in British Columbia, Canada. He is buried in Bridgnorth Cemetery, Shropshire.

1 February (Monday)

Training flight. 61 OTU (RAF Rednal, Shropshire)

Supermarine Spitfire IIA (P7609) belly-landed in a field at Bagley Marsh, to the east of the airfield, at 14.50 hrs, after the engine failed due to 'obscure reasons'.

Sgt (pilot u/t) Stanley Payne (1272701), RAFVR. Born in London, on 11 May 1920, he was the son of Frederick and Marion Payne. On completion of his training he was posted to 129 Squadron flying Spitfires (and later Mustangs) and was killed on 17 June 1944 piloting a Mustang (FB165), which crashed at Coolham in Sussex after the engine failed, while taking off. F/O Payne, who was 24 years old, was the husband of Peggy Mary Payne (née Lawrence) of Wood Green, Middlesex. He is buried in Horsham (Hills) Cemetery.

4 February (Thursday)
Dual instructional training. 11 (P)AFU (RAF Condover, Shropshire – Satellite to RAF Shawbury)
Airspeed Oxford I (R6286) crashed between Wroxeter and the Southern Dale Nursery (on the Cressage road) at 11.15 hrs. The aircraft was being flown by Sgt Smith, with another pupil pilot also on board, when the pair ran into a heavy rainstorm. While trying to fly below the storm cloud they failed to see some high-tension power cables and collided with them. The subsequent investigation concluded that the pilot was 'justified by the weather conditions in flying low, but was actually lower than was necessary'. However, it was also noted that power lines should have been marked on the maps.

Sgt (pilot u/t) Norman John Gow Smith (1342102), RAFVR, aged 21, was the son of William George and Jeannie Cowie Smith (née Gow) of Glasgow. He is buried in Glasgow (Riddrie Park) Cemetery.

Sgt (pilot u/t) Thomas John Ruff (1390378), RAFVR, aged 22, was the son of Frederick Thomas Ruff and Annie Elizabeth Ruff of Felpham, near Bognor Regis. He is buried in Felpham Churchyard, Sussex.

5 February (Friday)
Dual steep turns and feathering exercise. 81 OTU (RAF Whitchurch Heath, Shropshire)
Armstrong Whitworth Whitley V (EB409) belly-landed 'two miles north of Wellington' (putting it in the area around Eyton-upon-the-Weald Moors) at 09.23 hrs. After feathering the starboard engine as part of the exercise the pilot found that the propeller would then not un-feather. He therefore carried out a 'skilful emergency landing' in a field as he was unable to maintain height. Despite his skilful handling of the situation it was considered that, had the pilot carried out the exercise in the vicinity of the airfield (as ordered), he would have been able to make an emergency landing on the runway.

W/O (pilot) Ernest Wilfred (Wilf) Woodley (742120), RAFVR, was born in Heston, Middlesex on 15 April 1917, the son of James William and Emily Woodley (née Bucknall). Commissioned in August 1943, he was mentioned in despatches in January 1944 and posted to 214 Squadron in December 1944, piloting Flying Fortress aircraft on electronic countermeasure operations, for which he was awarded the DFC in July 1945. He remained in the RAF after the war and eventually relinquished his commission as a flight lieutenant in June 1955. He died in January 2003.

5 February (Friday)
Dual instructional navigation flight. 5 (P)AFU (RAF Tern Hill, Shropshire)
Miles Master III (W8964) crashed at Grug Hill Farm near Ruyton-XI-Towns, at 16.40 hrs. During the course of the training flight the pilot began unauthorised low flying and struck a 40 foot tree, crashing in flames.

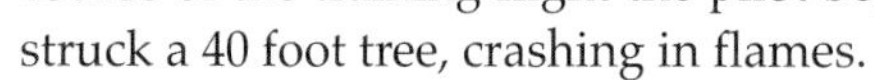

Sgt Ken Clithero
[Brindle Historical Society]

Sgt (instructor pilot) Thomas James Symons (1317038), RAFVR, aged 31, was the son of Edwin John and Elizabeth Symons and the husband of Olive Laura Symons (née Price) of Torquay. He is buried in Torquay Cemetery, Devon.

Sgt (pilot u/t) Kenneth Clithero (1537024), RAFVR, aged 25, was the son of the late John Thomas Clithero and Elizabeth Ann Clithero of Gregson Lane, near Hoghton. Before joining up he had served as a policeman with the Widnes Division of the Lancashire Constabulary. He is buried in Brindle (St James) Churchyard, Lancashire.

10 February (Wednesday)
Cross-country exercise, practice bombing and infrared photography. 81 OTU (RAF Whitchurch Heath, Shropshire)
Armstrong Whitworth Whitley V (LA769) crashed on the edge of the

runway at approximately 02.40 hrs. The instructor and trainee crew were carrying out a routine training exercise when a broken con rod caused the starboard engine to fail and then catch fire. The instructor immediately gave the order for the crew to bale out, which they all did, except for the pupil pilot who had to return to the controls and attempt a forced landing after his parachute opened while he was still inside the aircraft. Tragically, despite successfully reaching the airfield, he was killed when he lost control and crashed on the edge of the runway.

P/O (instructor pilot) Kenneth Winton Dunlop (137278), DFM, RAFVR, was born in Wandsworth, London on 7 November 1920 and had worked as a bank clerk before the war. He gained a private pilot's licence in May 1939 flying with the Midland Bank flying club. Following the outbreak of war he volunteered for the RAFVR and subsequently completed a tour of ops, flying Hampdens with 144 Squadron, for which he was awarded the DFM 'for continuous gallantry and devotion to duty.' Commissioned in December 1942, he remained an instructor at 81 OTU for a considerable time, being mentioned in despatches in January 1945 and then awarded the Air Force Cross in September 1945. He remained in the RAF after the war and eventually relinquished his commission as a flying officer in April 1956.

F/O (pilot u/t) Dennis Paul Reginald Wild (122767), RAFVR, aged 21, was the son of Paul Arthur Eric and Ida Mildred Kathleen Wild of Northwood. Before joining up he was an undergraduate at Oxford University. He is buried in Northwood Cemetery, Middlesex.

According to *Bomber Command Losses*, volume 4 (by W R Chorley), the remainder of the crew were: Sgt N E Legge; P/O Todd; Sgt E Sheppard; Sgt Bucklitach; Sgt J L Webb.

12 February (Friday)

Night training flight (presumably circuits and landings). 61 OTU (RAF Montford Bridge, Shropshire – Satellite to RAF Rednal)

Supermarine Spitfire IIA (P7757, a presentation aircraft named *Sayles*) crashed into a small coppice on the edge of the airfield. After having made a successful landing, the pilot opened up the throttle to carry out another circuit but, as he climbed away from the ground, the aircraft stalled and spun into a coppice, seriously injuring him. Dennis Diggory, a schoolboy living at Montford Bridge at the time, gave an account of the accident which appears in the Shropshire Wartime Aircraft Recovery Group files.

> One such incident occurred during night flying when the only airfield lighting consisted of aptly named 'glim' lamps placed as runway markers. In the early hours of the morning, Dennis and his family were woken by a loud banging on the door. Their visitor was a serviceman from Montford Bridge, who told them that a Spitfire was missing and asked if they had heard the noise of an aircraft in difficulty. As the weather was extremely bad, with high wind and lashing rain, no such sound had been heard. About an hour later a large party of airmen arrived at the house and were helped by the family to search the surrounding fields, without success.
> The missing aircraft was, in fact, found in a small wood on the edge of the airfield early in the morning. The unconscious pilot was in the cockpit with both clavicles broken, but not otherwise seriously injured.

Sgt (pilot u/t) R Dunne (Service No. unknown), RAFVR. Nothing further is known of this NCO other than that he survived the war.

14 February (Sunday)

Formation flight. 109th Observation Squadron, 6th Fighter Wing (Station 342, Atcham, Shropshire)

Supermarine Spitfire VB (W3797, a presentation aircraft named *Hendon Endeavour*) crashed near Chetwynd at 14.35 hrs. A section of three Spitfires was being led in formation by Flight Officer Warburton, when the group encountered another formation of Spitfires and made an unauthorised attack. Flight Officer Warburton immediately went after the lead aircraft of the other flight (which was being flown by Atcham's chief flying instructor) but, due to the attitude and direction in which he made his 'attack', he was unaware of the position of the CFI's number two (piloted by Lt Lambert), who provided the subsequent accident investigation with the following report:

> As I was close up under the CFI's tail, I was too intent on watching him and did not see any aircraft to my port. Our section turned sharply to starboard. There was a flash and I evidently became unconscious. On coming to I was covered in oil, glycol and petrol. The cockpit was folded over the lower part of my body and the sliding hatch was jammed into the cockpit over me. I kicked my way free, stepped onto the wing and jumped from there. I saw my aircraft falling flat with no spin, hitting the ground some fifty yards from a farm house. I still saw no evidence of another aircraft. I came to earth in an oak tree, unhurt and with only a small scratch on my face.

Flight Officer Warburton was less fortunate and his aircraft crashed out of control following the collision.

On ambulance duty that day, at nearby RAF Chetwynd, was LAC Reg Brown, from Lichfield, who gave evidence at the original investigation and also recalled the incident in a conversation with the author in 2007:

> Now we went chasing off down the lanes onto there, went up there [pointing to the A41 northbound on a map] and, I reckon, the first one that had parachuted out had landed in that wood [Chetwynd Heath]. I'm a hundred per cent sure that's where he crashed, so we went up there [up one of the tracks leading off the north of the A41 onto the heath] and found the plane. We checked there was nobody in it. Now I've got an idea, I don't know where he made his way to, but he made his way somewhere, so we went further along the road [A41], somewhere and I can't exactly remember where, and the other plane had crashed in a field. We had to climb over this fence and go up this ploughed field and there were all these farmers. Farmers always arrived on the scene first! He [the pilot] was still in the plane, so we got him out.
> I do remember getting him out and carrying him across the field as he was bloomin' heavy. Actually he had a wallet sticking out of his back pocket; you know, it was half out of his back pocket. I just left it as it was. It took the two of us to carry him across the field. So we carried him down this field and put him in the ambulance and took him off to Tern Hill.

Flight Officer (pilot u/t) Joseph R Warburton (10600459), USAAF, aged 30, was the son of Joseph and Sarah E Warburton of Pawtucket, Providence County, Rhode Island. He is buried in Long Island National Cemetery, New York.

Formation flight. 109th Observation Squadron, 6th Fighter Wing (Station 342, Atcham, Shropshire)

Spitfire W3505, which crashed near Chetwynd, still bearing RAF roundels rather than the USAAF star. [USAAF]

Supermarine Spitfire VA (W3505, bearing the fuselage code WD-I) crashed near Chetwynd after colliding in the incident described above.

2 Lt (pilot u/t) Donald E Lambert (O-885189), USAAF.

17 February (Wednesday)

Circuits and landings. 11 (P)AFU (RAF Condover, Shropshire, satellite to RAF Shawbury)

Airspeed Oxford II (P8973) crash-landed at Eaton Constantine, at 17.50 hrs. The pupil pilot was carrying out unauthorised low flying when he allowed the aircraft to strike the brow of a hill, damaging one of the airscrews and forcing him to crash-land in a field ahead. Following the accident, the pilot was placed under close arrest and subsequently pleaded guilty to 'two charges of low flying' at a court martial, although the punishment he received is unknown.

Sgt (pilot u/t) John Claude Western (1318803), RAFVR. Nothing further is known of his military service other than that he survived the war.

21 February (Sunday)

Test flight. 109th Observation Squadron, 6th Fighter Wing (Station 342, Atcham, Shropshire)

Bell P-39M Airacobra (42-4834) crashed near Shawbury village ('behind some trees towards Edgebolton'), while the pilot landed near Shawbury School by parachute, at 15.00 hrs. The pilot's account, which was provided for the accident investigation, describes how he climbed to 7,000 feet and made three rolls.

> The control in these rolls was very good so I decided to try a roll in which I could gain a little altitude. I pulled the nose up to about 20 degrees and did a very slow roll, when I got into an inverted position I pushed forward on the stick to maintain my gradual climb. I had approximately 210 mph airspeed in the inverted position when, without warning the aircraft stalled and started in an end over end spin. The manoeuvre was very violent and the turns were quite rapid accompanied with jerks, which seemed to come when the ship was on its back. I tried to kick the aircraft into a normal spin by using right stick and rudder. I had the stick in both fore and aft positions. I pulled the throttle back to see if the aircraft would regain normal flight without power. I repeated this several times, and suddenly it snapped into a right-hand spin from which I made a normal recovery. It seems that the aircraft did two turns of a flat spin before it dropped into a normal spin. During these manoeuvres I tried all the control combinations I could think of. I recovered at 3,000 [feet].
>
> After I had gained control of the aircraft, I noticed that it was very badly out of trim with a tendency to be right wing heavy. I climbed it slowly and straight at about 200 mph. After reaching 8,000 feet, I levelled off, and after a time I got the ship in fair trim. The stick had a tendency to become immovable in a neutral position at times. I decided to lower my wheels and if I could handle the ship at all reduced speeds, I thought I would try a landing.
>
> The airplane, although not quite normal, handled fairly well so I raised my wheels with the intention of coming in for a landing. Just after the wheels had come up, the aircraft came very badly out of trim

The tailplane of the Airacobra (42-4834) is the only recognizable piece in this photo taken following the crash. [USAAF]

Maj Albert DeFehr [Jeff DeFehr]

again, with a tendency to want to fall out to the right. I could not trim the ship satisfactorily this time. I tried some coordin-ation exercises and the controls seemed to vary with the main tendency of right wing heaviness and a tendency for the stick to become immovable in a neutral position.

I was fully convinced that it would be unwise to land the aircraft, fearing that the sudden changes in the trim would result in a spin at slow speeds, so I flew to 10,000 feet and baled out. I switched off the engine upon leaving the aircraft.

Maj (pilot) Albert Roger DeFehr (O-417010), USAAF. Born in Corn, Oklahoma, on 8 April 1918, he had attended the local high school and then South-western College, Weatherford, where he was president of the student body. After enlisting in October 1940 and completing his pilot training, he was posted to the UK in September 1942 with the 109th Observation Squadron. Later in the war he transferred to the 314th Fighter Squadron, flying P-40 Warhawks in the Mediterranean. He was killed on 15 March 1944 when his aircraft was hit over Anzio and crashed into the sea. Maj DeFehr's body was never found and his name is inscribed on the tablet of the missing at Sicily-Rome American Cemetery.

28 February (Sunday)
Night circuits and landings. 11 (P)AFU (RAF Shawbury, Shropshire)
Airspeed Oxford I (DF344) crashed 'three miles south of the airfield' (putting it roughly in the area of Haughton on the northern side of Haughmond Hill), at 18.40 hrs. After overshooting the airfield on a very dark night the pilot climbed to 500–600 feet to make another circuit and is thought to have lost control, 'either through faulty instrument flying or because he raised the flaps of the aircraft too quickly'. Following further investigation it transpired that he had been 'considerably shaken by a previous bad landing and had expressed to an airman at the marshalling post some reluctance to continue flying'. This nervousness possibly contributed to the overshoot.

P/O (pilot u/t) Dennis Alfred Phillips (133115), RAFVR, aged 21, was the son of Edward Campbell Phillips and Ethel Gertrude Phillips of Northolt, Middlesex. He is buried in Shawbury (St Mary's) Churchyard.

3 March (Wednesday)
Night cross-country training exercise from Base–Cambridge–Worcester–St Tudwal's Island (Llŷn peninsula)–St David's–Land's End–Taunton–Oxford–Base. 460 Squadron, RAAF (RAF Breighton, Yorkshire)
Avro Lancaster I (W4864, bearing the fuselage code UV-?) crashed in the grounds of Acton Reynolds Girls' School (at map reference 534236), between Grinshill and RAF Shawbury, at 00.07 hrs. The crew, who had only joined the squadron on 27 February and were getting in some final training before being declared ready for ops, had reached Oxford, at which point the pilot steered the wrong course. This mistake is thought to have happened either after the pilot practised evasive action, causing the compass unit to become hung up on its guard rails, or due to the pilot's setting a course other than that given to him by the navigator. Whatever the reason, the aircraft was subsequently plotted by the Observer Corps flying over Kidderminster and, as it became clear that the aircraft was lost, a 'Darky' (homing) call was put out by RAF Wheaton Aston. The pilot continued to fly on, however, until he reached the vicinity of RAF Shawbury, where he made a low pass over the south/north runway (presumably in preparation for landing). Unaware of the high ground to the west of the runway, the pilot turned towards it and the aircraft struck the hillside at over 200 mph, spreading flaming wreckage over a wide area and killing the entire crew instantly. In the subsequent investigation it was revealed that the aircraft could not be

contacted at any stage during the flight, indicating that the wireless transmitter was unserviceable. This would explain why the 'Darky' call went unheard.

Sgt (pilot) Edgar Claude Fulton (411890), RAAF, aged 23, was born in Penrith, New South Wales, on 22 July 1919, the son of Edgar Glendenning Fulton and Mabel Augusta Fulton. Educated at Penrith Public School and Telopea Park Intermediate High School, where he was a prefect, he and his parents later moved to Kingston, in Canberra, where he completed his studies at Canberra High School. According to his family he was a passionate musician and his piano playing was put to good use during the long voyage on the troop ship to the UK. After joining 460 Squadron, along with his crew, he completed one operational flight as 'second dickie' (with one of the squadron's veteran crews), on 28 February, to provide him with experience in captaining an aircraft on ops. He is buried in Shrewsbury General Cemetery, Shropshire.

Sgt (F/Eng) Thomas Patrick Gore Milledy (1321984), RAFVR, aged 20, was born in Bury St Edmunds, the son of Thomas Joseph Gore Milledy and Edyth R Thomas. He is buried in Shrewsbury General Cemetery, Shropshire.

Sgt (Nav) Roderick Watson Kerr (979213), RAFVR, aged 24, was the son of James and Katherine Flucker Greig Kerr of Glasgow. He is buried in Glasgow (Riddrie Park) Cemetery.

F/Sgt (AB) Edward Francis Murphy (401457), RAAF, aged 25, was the son of Edward William and Fanny Charlotte Murphy of Somerville, Victoria. He is buried in Shrewsbury General Cemetery, Shropshire.

Sgt (W/AG) Ross Clive Graham (411312), RAAF, aged 27, was the son of Albert James and Ellen Graham of Braidwood, New South Wales. He is buried in Shrewsbury General Cemetery, Shropshire.

Sgt (AG mid upper) Peter Frederick Bacon (1392379), RAFVR, aged 20, was the son of Walter Frederick and Adelaide Dolamor Bacon of Enfield. He is buried in Enfield (Hartford Road) Cemetery, Middlesex.

Sgt (AG rear) Ronald (Ron) Oldfield (1438969), RAFVR, aged 21, was the son of James and Mabel Oldfield of Boythorpe, Chesterfield. Educated at Christ Church School, Stonegravels, he had worked as a carpenter for the local borough council before enlisting and was engaged to local girl, Peggy Andrews, at the time of his death. He is buried in Chesterfield (Boythorpe) Cemetery, Derbyshire.

5 March (Friday), although one source states 6 March (Saturday)
Training flight. 61 OTU (RAF Rednal, Shropshire)
Supermarine Spitfire IIA (P8391, presentation aircraft named *City of Carlisle*) belly-landed at 'Haughton Hall, Shropshire' (presumably Haughton near the airfield), at 14.50 hrs. After the engine failed, due to a technical fault, the pilot belly-landed in a field and was unhurt.

Top–bottom:Sgt Edgar Fulton; [Meredith McNay]; Sgt Roderick Kerr [Peter Kerr]; Ross Graham [Tim Maddrell]; Sgt Sgt Ron Oldfield [Maureen Spooner]

P/O (pilot u/t) Edmund D Whalen (130627), RAFVR, was an American citizen serving with the RAFVR. He was posted to 222 Squadron, flying Spitfires on offensive sweeps over north-west Europe, after completing his training. In November 1943 he transferred to the USAAF and flew P-47 Thunderbolts (and later P-51 Mustangs) with the 334th Fighter Squadron, 4th Fighter Group, out of Debden, during which time he claimed three enemy aircraft shot down. His last victory, on 6 March 1944, also claimed his life when his Mustang (43-6899) was hit by exploding debris from the Me110 he had just destroyed over Nienburg and crashed out of control. 1 Lt Whalen, who came from Gouverneur in New York, is buried in the American Cemetery at Margraten, Netherlands.

11 March (Thursday)
Cross-country dual instruction. 5 (P)AFU (RAF Tern Hill, Shropshire)
Miles Master I (T8679) force-landed at Racecourse Farm, on the western outskirts of Bridgnorth, at 12.50 hrs. Having become lost during the course of the flight and with fuel gauges reading empty, the instructor decided to force-land in a field but overshot on his first attempt. After climbing back up to 100 feet to try again, the engine failed while the wheels and flaps were down, and the instructor had no choice but to put down directly ahead.

Sgt (instructor pilot) Derek Vaughan Joyes (1293477), RAFVR, was killed on 8 October in a crash near Tern Hill.

Sgt (pilot u/t) James Alexander Christie (1318326), RAFVR. Nothing further is known of this pilot other than that he survived the war.

19 March (Friday)
Flight to RAF Middle Wallop, Hampshire. 247 (China-British) Squadron (RAF High Ercall, Shropshire)
Hawker Typhoon IB (DN444) crashed at Windmill Farm, Madeley (at map reference 700058, in modern-day Telford), at 16.10 hrs. Four pilots were instructed to fly to their new base at RAF Middle Wallop (to which the squadron was in the process of re-locating) and had been told that, although local weather was very poor, conditions would improve further south. After taking off, however, the four pilots found the conditions were far worse than expected and two pilots turned back to High Ercall, one managed to reach RAF Defford in Worcestershire, while the fourth lost control in cloud and crashed. Fred Jones, who was a young boy living in Ironbridge at the time, had just been to visit his cousin at the butcher's shop in Madeley when he stopped on the railway bridge near the station:

> ... [I was] talking to the driver and the fireman of the engine that was shunting underneath. It was a miserable day, all cloudy, but we could hear this plane. Silence, then it would accelerate, then silence, then accelerate. Then we got a slightly bigger silence. The first I saw of the plane, it was about 10 or 15 foot off the ground, nose down when he hit. He was fully loaded and there was cannons going off in all directions.

Sgt (pilot) Quentin Macphail Shippee (R.132528), RCAF, aged 22, was the son of Frederick Earl and Elda MacVagh Shippee of Pointe Claire, Province of Quebec, Canada. He is buried in Donington (St Cuthbert's) Churchyard, Shropshire.

26 March (Friday)
Bombardier training. 3 (O)AFU (RAF Bobbington, Staffordshire)
Avro Anson I (N9642) force-landed in a field 'two miles from Bridgnorth', at 20.00 hrs. After failing to switch over from outer to inner fuel tanks, when the fuel in one had run dry, the pilot was forced to land in a field and, as a result of his actions, his logbook was endorsed for 'gross carelessness'.

Sgt (pilot) Samuel Morlais Jones Lloyd (655451), RAFVR, was born in Llanelli in 1913. He was commissioned in June 1944 and eventually transferred to the administration and special duties branch in March 1945. He remained in the RAF after the war and relinquished his commission as a flying officer in November 1958.

The names of the trainee bomb aimers are unknown.

27 March (Saturday)

Aerobatics training. 109th Observation Squadron, 6th Fighter Wing (Station 342, Atcham, Shropshire)

Supermarine Spitfire VA (X4669, presentation aircraft named *Sir Walter*) crashed at Kingsnordley, between Quatt and Tuckhill to the south-east of Bridgnorth, at 14.40 hrs. The pilot was attempting a forced landing, after the engine began to falter due to a glycol leak, when he is believed to have been overcome by fumes on the approach and crashed through a hedge, ripping off both wings and skidding across a narrow lane, before coming to rest inverted and on fire. The accident was witnessed by Bombardier W D Allen, who was manning the local searchlight site. He gave the following account for the investigation:

> I heard an aeroplane flying low and approaching the site BG041b. I looked up and identified a Spitfire flying at about 100–150 feet, this plane was approaching the site in a circular movement from the southwest and receded in the same direction. The pilot 'revved' his engine two or three times which appeared to sound normal but emitting several large clouds of white smoke from the region of the base of the engine. From the unusual amount of smoke coming from the plane, I deduced that it was on fire and gave the alarm telling the detachment to bring the fire extinguisher. Following the direction of the plane, I heard it crash and shortly afterwards saw a column of black smoke appearing. When I reached the plane, it was blazing fiercely and I saw the blackened remains of the pilot who was beyond hope. After putting the fire out, I posted a guard and then notified the police at Bridgnorth and Battery headquarters.

Flight Officer (pilot u/t) John L Becker (T-190561), USAAF, aged 25 (?), was the son of Louis and Sigrib Becker of 40 Garden Street, West Englewood, New Jersey. Educated at Teaneck High School, he had served with the RCAF before transferring to the USAAF in February 1942. He is buried in Cambridge (Madingley) Cemetery.

Spitfire X4669's wings, still bearing RAF roundels, pictured on the edge of the lane after being torn off by the impact. [USAAF]

29 March (Monday)

Sector reconnaissance flight. 109th Observation Squadron, 6th Fighter Wing (Station 342, Atcham, Shropshire)

Supermarine Spitfire VA (P7849) crashed near the Cross Keys Pub, Hadley (in what is now part of Telford), at 15.40 hrs. Lt Scott was flying in the vicinity of Wellington when he made several unauthorised 'attacks' on another Spitfire piloted by Lt Smith. During his last attack, however, he made a series of slow barrel rolls around Lt Smith's aircraft and a collision occurred. This resulted in the severing of the tail assembly of Lt Smith's aircraft and sent it crashing into a field, while the tail section fell near the REME work-shop. Lt Scott managed to remain in control of his aircraft for a further ninety

The wreckage of Lt Scott's aircraft lies strewn in a garden in Hadley. [USAAF]

seconds but, according to another pilot who was flying nearby, '... seemed to be descending to orbit Lt Smith's aircraft with me, but when he reached between 1,000 and 1500 feet his aircraft went into a spin and crashed into the front yard of a house.' In fact, he attempted to bale out of the aircraft shortly before it hit the ground but, with insufficient height, his parachute failed to open in time.

2 Lt (pilot) Daniel Ray Scott (O-885500), USAAF, aged 23, was the son of Asa Ray and the late Cleo Stewart Scott of Coleman City, Texas. Educated at Center Point High School and the University of Texas, he dropped out in May 1941 to volunteer for the RCAF. He is buried in Fort Sam Houston National Cemetery, Texas.

2 Lt Ray Scott [Maribeth Impson]

Transition flight. 109th Observation Squadron, 6th Fighter Wing (Station 342, Atcham, Shropshire)
Supermarine Spitfire VB (BL660) crashed at Leegomery Farm (at map reference 665128, while the tail section fell a little distance away at map reference 672128), following the collision described above.

2 Lt (pilot) Edward D Smith (O-660206), USAAF, was the son of Rupert Webster Smith and Annie Balmforth of Wilton, New Hampshire. He is buried in Cambridge (Madingley) Cemetery.

The wreckage of Lt Smith's Spitfire (BL660) lies inverted in a field near Leegomery Farm. [USAAF]

30 March (Tuesday)

Formation flying training. 5 (P)AFU (RAF Tern Hill, Shropshire)
Miles Master III (DL686) crash-landed at Hopton Farm, to the south-west of Hodnet, at 15.00 hrs. The instructor was preparing to force-land, after the engine failed at 1,800 feet, when he noticed some posts in the field ahead. He was forced to undershoot and crash-land into a different field, fortunately escaping uninjured.

Sgt (instructor pilot) Donald Edmund Hinchley (1085173), RAFVR, was born in Lancashire in 1921. He died in the London borough of Waltham Forest in 2003.

F/O (pilot u/t) Mieczyslaw Galicki (P1337), PAF. On completion of his training he was posted to 318 (Polish) Squadron flying Hurricanes (and later Spitfires) on ground attack and tactical reconnaissance operations in support of 8 Army in Italy. After completing his tour he was posted to 74 OTU as an instructor and on 10 November 1943 became a member of the 'Caterpillar Club' when he had to bale out of a Spitfire. He returned to 318 Squadron after his posting at 74 OTU and survived the war.

3 April (Saturday)
First night solo flight. 11 (P)AFU (RAF Shawbury, Shropshire)
Airspeed Oxford I (DF465) crashed 'one mile north of the airfield' (putting it roughly in the area around Preston Brockhurst) at 03.40 hrs. Shortly after leaving the ground the pilot is thought to have failed to 'concentrate on his instrument panel while doing his vital actions after take off' and commenced a right-hand turn that developed into a dive from which he failed to recover. The seriously injured pilot was rushed to the station sick quarters suffering from 'extensive head injuries, petrol burns, injuries to both ankles, shock and exposure' but died later in the day after being transferred to RAF Hospital, Cosford.

Sgt (pilot u/t) Edward Trevor Dawson (1504557), RAFVR, aged 20, was the son of Edward Philipson Dawson and Gertrude Mabel Dawson of West Denton, Newcastle-upon-Tyne. He is buried in Newcastle-upon-Tyne Cemetery.

8 April (Thursday)
Formation flying. 61 OTU (RAF Montford Bridge, Shropshire – satellite airfield to RAF Rednal)
Supermarine Spitfire IIA (P8429, presentation aircraft named *Frimley and Camberley*) crashed at Broomfields, on the north edge of the airfield, at 16.03 hrs. While practising close formation flying the pilot 'failed to keep a good lookout' during a manoeuvre and crashed after his tail was severed in a collision with Spitfire P7921. The pilot of P7921 was, fortunately, able to maintain control and made an emergency landing on the airfield. The incident was witnessed by local schoolboy Dennis Diggory, whose account can be found in the Wartime Aircraft Recovery Group files in the Shropshire archives:

> At about 4.00 pm on a warm, fine afternoon I saw four Spitfires flying in close 'box' formation on a westerly heading towards Montford Bridge at an altitude of about 1,500 feet. As the aircraft came within about a quarter of a mile of where I was standing, they commenced a formation change. The two outer aircraft changed places safely, and the upper one of the inner pair decreased altitude to take up its new position as the lowest aircraft in the formation. To the onlooker, the whole manoeuvre seemed faultless as the four machines flew on in very close formation, and I was impressed by the skills of the pilots. Suddenly, the lower of the centre pair climbed slightly and struck the propeller of the upper aircraft, fell away from the formation, shedding fuselage debris, and dived, inverted, into a field, just about two hundred yards from where I stood. The tail unit fell into the Knowles Coppice, about half a mile from the main wreckage.

Sgt (pilot u/t) Paul Huart Rowland Moody (758126), RAFVR, aged 27, was the son of Charles Rowland and Clara Fanny Moody of Southampton and the husband of Leonie Margaret Mary Moody (née Cargill). He is commemorated at the Southampton Crematorium.

Formation flying training. 61 OTU (RAF Montford Bridge, Shropshire – Satellite airfield to RAF Rednal)
Supermarine Spitfire IIA (P7921) landed at the airfield following the incident described above.

Sgt (pilot u/t) Leslie Stanley Clarke (1390697), RAFVR, was commissioned in July 1945 and survived the war.

10 April (Saturday)
Training flight. 81 OTU (RAF Whitchurch Heath, Shropshire)
Armstrong Whitworth Whitley V (LA771) crashed just outside the airfield at 10.23 hrs. While climbing away from the airfield the starboard propeller flew off without warning and, despite the pilot's

Sgt Leslie Garnham
[James Currie]

managing to keep the aircraft in the air for a further 400 feet, it stalled and crashed just outside the airfield perimeter. The pilot was killed instantly and the rest of the crew were injured. Sadly, the wireless operator succumbed to his injuries two days later in RAF Hospital, Cosford.

Sgt (pilot) Walter Berry (1081914), RAFVR, aged 22, was the son of James and Effie Berry of Bolton. He is buried in Bolton (Heaton) Cemetery, Lancashire.

Sgt (W/AG) Leslie Henry Garnham (1295534), RAFVR, aged 21, was the son of Elizabeth Ethel Garnham and stepson of John Samuel Malton of Romford, Essex. He is buried in Romford Cemetery.

Sgt G B Whalley, RAFVR.

Sgt B H Stedman, RCAF.

12 April (Monday)

Practice precautionary landings. 11 (P)AFU (RAF Bratton, Shropshire – Relief Landing Ground to RAF Shawbury)

Airspeed Oxford II (AB707) crash-landed 'half-a-mile to the east of Bratton airfield' at 17.15 hrs. The pupil pilot was trying to open up the throttles, after undershooting a landing at the airfield, when the starboard engine failed to respond, probably due to the fact that it had been throttled back for some time. Unable to reach the runway he force-landed in a field, suffering some superficial injuries, while the aircraft was badly damaged.

Sgt (pilot u/t) Cedric Banner (1451951), RAFVR, was commissioned in May 1944. He remained in the RAF after the war and relinquished his commission as a flying officer in July 1950.

12 April (Monday)

Sgt L H Garnham succumbed to his injuries received in a crash at Whitchurch Heath on 10 April.

19 April (Monday)

Local aerobatics training. HQ Squadron, 6th Fighter Wing (Station 342, Atcham, Shropshire)

Republic P-47C Thunderbolt (41-6257, bearing the fuselage code VM-E) belly-landed 'two miles south-west of the airfield' (putting it in the area around Atcham village and Cross Houses) at 21.00 hrs. The pilot took off at 20.15 hrs and had been in the air for nearly forty-five minutes when he changed over from auxiliary to main fuel tanks, before diving and then climbing steeply to approximately 5,000 feet. At this point the engine cut and, after checking his instruments, the pilot

> … called control and told them I had to crash-land and tried to locate the field. The engine caught twice and over revved each time so I selected manual and attempted to decrease the revs, but the engine quit again, so I could not determine whether this worked. I was losing height rapidly and in my final turn the engine caught, making my turn too wide, thereby not being able to make the field. I shut off all switches and the gas selector to off, tightened my harness, opened the hood and landed wheels up at 110 mph, dodging trees as best I could and ducking under high tension wires. I saw a slight incline and decided to try and land uphill, but I bounced off and lost control stopping in a ditch after dragging along the ground.

The subsequent investigation concluded that the accident was due to 'pilot error' as, 'prior to the change over [of fuel tanks], the pilot allowed the auxiliary tank to run dry and in doing so an airlock developed. During the change over there is a possibility that the selector switch did not properly 'sit', although there was no malfunctioning of the selector switch'.

Flight Officer (pilot u/t) Conrad Christie 'Connie' Ingold (T-190565), USAAF, was a resident of New

Thunderbolt 41-6257 seen as it came to rest near Atcham [USAAF]

Flight Officer Connie Ingold pictured whilst serving with the 336th Fighter Squadron [Peter Randall]

York City. He joined the 336th Fighter Squadron, 4th Fighter Group, in May 1943 and flew P-47 Thunderbolts out of Debden. On 22 September 1943 he was lucky to survive a crash while taking off for a mission but, after the accident was blamed on poor sight, it is believed that he was taken off flying duties. Sources are then a little unclear, but it appears that he became 4th Fighter Group's Personnel (Flying) Equipment Officer and later the 334th Fighter Squadron's Intelligence Officer.

20 April (Tuesday)
Training flight. 5 GTS (RAF Shobdon, Herefordshire)
Miles Magister I (L8090) crashed at Lower Ledwyche Farm, one mile east of Ludlow, at 16.00 hrs. The pilot was performing unauthorised low flying when the aircraft struck high tension power cables and crashed. Fortunately, the pilot was only injured and after three days in Ludlow RAF Air Crew Camp's sick quarters (suffering from concussion and lacerations to his leg), he was transferred to RAF Shobdon, where he was subsequently found guilty of breaching flying regulations and 'reduced to the ranks and detained for 56 days'.

Cpl (pilot u/t) Edgar Raspison (S/3131992), GPR, was born in Wigan on 29 May 1919. He went on to fly gliders during the D-Day and Arnhem landings and was awarded the DFM in August 1945. He died in Northumberland in July 2000.

Cpl (passenger) Hunter (6153101), GPR.

28 April (Wednesday)
Night navigation flight from Base–Newport Reservoir–Andover–Evesham–Tern Hill–Base. 3 (O)AFU (RAF Bobbington, Staffordshire)
Avro Anson I (N5379) crashed into Brown Clee Hill (at map reference 599842) above Banbury Farm, near Burwarton, at 00.35 hrs. The staff pilot was instructed to take off at 22.16 hrs, with a wireless operator and three trainee aircrew to carry out the training flight below the forecasted cloud base of 2,500 feet (but no lower than 2,000 feet). The last call received from the aircraft was at 00.12 hrs and several minutes later the aircraft was seen, with navigation lights on, flying north west (on the Evesham–Tern Hill leg) towards Clee Hill. By this stage the pilot was 'flying below the minimum height detailed for the flight' and this, 'coupled with either a navigational error, compass error, or the pilot failing to make good the courses given to him', had put the aircraft on a collision course with the high ground. Ron Pearce, who lived at Banbury Farm, recalled the event in a conversation with the author in 2008:

Sgt William Sprowell [Library & Archives Canada]

> We heard this aircraft roar overhead full throttle and then bang, bang and then silence as the engine died out. There was a neighbour, who had a little bit of land tacked on to the bottom of our farm. Like all farmers, he was leaning on the gate one day and he looked up the field and, 'what the hell's that tree doing up there'? About seven or eight feet of this fir tree had been taken off up the field about 70 or 80 yards away. He went up the field and there was an aluminium door halfway up the field. It was below our house and not quite in line for our house but the aircraft must have sort of stooped past the house about 50 yards away and this was the first time we knew that it had hit a tree below the house. There were five of them on board, all killed, and I think they were from Bobbington, near Wolverhampton.

First on the scene after the crash were soldiers from 353 Searchlight Battery, stationed at Blackford, who had turned their searchlight around to illuminate the crash site, before rushing up to search for survivors. Sadly, they found none and, after the arrival of RAF Bridgnorth's ambulance, they helped load the bodies on board to be taken away.

Sgt Keith Stratton [Library & Archives Canada]

Sgt (staff pilot) William Michael Richardson Lloyd (1278603), RAFVR, aged 27, was the son of William Edgar and Edith Lloyd of Thornton Heath, Surrey, and the husband of Isabel Lloyd (née Kirby) of East Croydon. He is buried in Bridgnorth Cemetery, Shropshire.

Sgt (staff W/Op) Eric Frank Banks (1132835), RAFVR, aged 32, was the son of Frank and Clara Edith Banks and the husband of Itala Florence Mary Banks (née Lisle) of Wednesfield. He is buried in Wednesfield (St Thomas) Churchyard, Staffordshire.

F/Sgt (Nav u/t) William Sprowell (R.144996), RCAF, aged 27, was the son of William and Elizabeth Manion Sprowell of Montreal, Canada. Born in England on 27 February 1916, he spent three years in the UK before he and his family emigrated to Canada. Before enlisting in December 1941 he had worked as an office and sales clerk for the Robert Simpson Company. He is buried in Warrington Cemetery, Lancashire.

F/Sgt (Nav u/t) Keith Robinson Stratton (R.140944), RCAF, aged 20, was the son of Mr A K Stratton of Stonewall, Manitoba. He had enlisted in November 1941, following in the footsteps of his brother, Sgt Ronald Grant Stratton, who also lost his life, on 5 July 1941, while undergoing pilot training in the UK. F/Sgt Stratton is buried in Bridgnorth Cemetery, Shropshire.

Sgt (W/AG u/t) Kenneth Arthur Hammond (1335656), RAFVR, aged 21, was the son of Arthur Harry and Edith May Askew Hammond of Forest Gate, London. He is buried in City of London Cemetery, Manor Park.

1 May (Saturday)
Training flight. 5 (P)AFU (RAF Tern Hill, Shropshire)
Miles Master II (W8560) force-landed at Showell Grange, near Sambrook, at 15.30 hrs. After the pupil pilot mishandled the controls the engine failed in flight, and the instructor was forced to belly-land in a field.

Sgt (instructor) Kenneth Gordon Tormey (1336578), RAFVR. Born on 5 October 1922, he lived at 66 Westfield Avenue in North Watford, and had worked as a draughtsman before joining up. Following the accident at Tern Hill he was posted to 12 Air Gunners' School and, on 23 September 1943, had to force-land in the Irish Sea after his engine failed during a target-towing flight. Fortunately, he was picked up by a passing boat. Nothing further is known of his military service other than that he survived the war and gained a civilian pilot's licence in 1947. He died in Cambridge in 2003.

P/O (pilot u/t) Leslie Ernest Laws (135737), RAFVR, survived the war and eventually relinquished his commission as a flight lieutenant in June 1962.

3 May (Monday)
Night navigation exercise
81 OTU (RAF Sleap, Shropshire – satellite airfield to RAF Tilstock)
Armstrong Whitworth Whitley V (EB405) crashed near Loppington, to the west of Wem, at 04.20 hrs. Having taken off at 22.35 hrs the previous evening the crew had completed their exercise and were preparing to land, when the pilot overshot and had to make another circuit. After overshooting on his second attempt he opened up the throttles to go around yet again but on this occasion failed to clear some trees near the airfield and the aircraft crashed in flames.

Sgt (pilot) Harry James Spiers (1319678), RAFVR, aged 20, was the son of Henry and Bessie Spiers of Teddington, Middlesex. He is buried in Ash (Christ Church) Churchyard near Tilstock.

Sgt (Nav) Harold Leather (1456975), RAFVR, aged 22, was the son of William and Jane Leather of Whiston. He is buried in Prescott Cemetery, Lancashire.

Sgt (AB) John James Brown (1482424), RAFVR, aged 23, was the son of John James and Margaret Brown of Jarrow. He is buried in Jarrow Cemetery, Durham.

Sgt (W/AG) James William Scott (1369058), RAFVR, aged 20, was the son of James and Catherine Scott of Crieff. He is buried in Crieff Cemetery, Perthshire.

Sgt (AG) William Arthur Cadel (1411702), RAFVR, aged 25, was the son of Charles Robert and Sarah Annie Cadel of Ely, Cardiff. He is buried in Cardiff Western Cemetery.

4 May (Tuesday)
Training flight. 8 (Coastal) Operational Training Unit (RAF Dyce, Aberdeenshire)
Supermarine Spitfire PR.IV (X4499) crash-landed at 'Middle [Myddle?] Hill, Wem' (while another source states 'at Sleap'), at 12.30 hrs. Following an engine failure, caused by a glycol (coolant) leak, the pilot overshot on an attempt to force-land at RAF Sleap and belly-landed in a field nearby.

P/O (pilot u/t) Edward Herrick Knatchbull-Hugessen (J.13590), RCAF. Born on 4 June 1923, the son of the Honourable Adrian Norton Knatchbull-Hugessen and Margaret Cecilia Duggan, he had lived in Canada but was educated at Eton in England. He enlisted in the RCAF in September 1941 and, on completion of his operational training in the UK, joined a photographic reconnaissance squadron flying in the Mediterranean theatre. He survived the war and died in 1955.

14 May (Friday)
Fighter affiliation exercise with a Wellington bomber from 22 OTU. 61 OTU (RAF Rednal, Shropshire)
Supermarine Spitfire IIA (P8268) crashed at Whittingslow near Little Stretton, at 11.20 hrs. The exercise involved practice attacks on a Wellington (BK186), the purpose of which was both to improve the proficiency of the bomber crew in performing evasive manoeuvres and to coordinate air gunners, whilst also giving the Spitfire pilot practice in deflection attacks. However, during his third pass at the bomber, the Spitfire pilot displayed 'bad judgment' and a 'disregard for instructions' by closing to less than 150 yards and collided with the Wellington's rudder and fin. The Spitfire was immediately sent spiralling out of control and crashed, while the Wellington pilot, S/Ldr L K Smith, skilfully brought his damaged aircraft back to its base at Pershore in Worcestershire.

F/Sgt (pilot u/t) Alfred James Webb (413297), RAAF, aged 21, was the son of Alfred James and Eva Jessie Webb of Randwick, New South Wales. He is buried in Oswestry General Cemetery, Shropshire.

His brother, P/O J W Webb, also lost his life serving with the RAAF in England, in December 1944.

16 May (Sunday)
Delivery flight. 9 MU (RAF Cosford, Shropshire)
Airspeed Horsa (LG672 or LG692) force-landed at Beckbury, three miles south-west of the airfield, at 11.30 hrs. After the tug pilot accidentally released the tow rope in flight the glider pilot managed successfully to force-land in a field, despite his approach being hampered by high-tension power cables. As a result of the accident the commanding officer of 9 MU suggested that the tow-release lever be painted red and labelled DANGER to avoid any future recurrences.

Sgt (pilot) John Reid Hebden (5393603), GPR, was born in Worcestershire on 10 May 1924. He subsequently fought at Arnhem and survived the war, attaining the rank of staff sergeant. He died in Yorkshire in 2011.

28 May (Friday)
Training flight. 3 GTS (RAF Stoke Orchard, Gloucestershire)
Miles Magister I (T9739) crashed at 'Moor House Farm, Alveley', to the south-east of Bridgnorth, at 15.45 hrs. While performing unauthorised low flying the aircraft struck high-tension power cables and crashed, killing the pilot and seriously injuring his glider pilot passenger. RAF Bridgnorth was notified and immediately dispatched their ambulance and the injured pilot was taken to the station hospital, where he remained for several weeks undergoing surgery.

Sgt (pilot) Basil William Gill (1129713), RAFVR, aged 22, was the son of Reginald and Mary Gill of 36 Uplands Road, Harehills, Leeds. He is buried in Leeds (Harehills) Cemetery.

Cpl (glider pilot pupil, travelling as passenger) R G Brims, GPR. No further details are known.

29 May (Saturday)
Night flying test. 11 (P)AFU (RAF Shawbury, Shropshire)
Airspeed Oxford I (LB478) crashed at 'Little Wollascott crossing' to the south of Bomere Heath, at 15.40 hrs. An instructor pilot took off for a test flight, with a ground crew airman as passenger, during the course of which he began performing unauthorised low flying and, due to 'an error of judgment', allowed the wing to strike the ground during a right-hand turn and crashed.

P/O (instructor pilot) Hugh Dymoke Francis (141137), RAFVR, aged 21, was the son of Cecil and Janie Moody Francis of Pinchbeck. He is buried in Pinchbeck Cemetery, Lincolnshire.

AC2 (W/Op, travelling as passenger) William Ralph Whitehouse (1579798), RAFVR, aged 18, was the son of David Thomas and Winifred Whitehouse of Coseley. He is buried in Coseley (Providence) chapel yard, Staffordshire.

30 May (Sunday)
High altitude training flight. 6th Fighter Wing (Station 342, Atcham, Shropshire)
Republic P-47D Thunderbolt (42-7964) crashed at 'Roden near High Ercall' (although an eye witness puts it at map reference 590138, on the River Roden near Rodington), at 16.40 hrs. The pilot was cruising at 35,000 feet along with his wingman, Lt Howitz, when they both entered a steep dive. As the two aircraft picked up speed Flight Officer Buck's aircraft began to disintegrate, before falling into a flat spin and crashing out of control. Lt Howitz, realising the danger as they picked up speed, had tried to pull out of the dive but 'too high a velocity in the prolonged dive did not give the pilot enough altitude to recover' and his aircraft dived into the ground to the south-east of P-47 42-7964.

Flight Officer (pilot u/t) Shelby Othello Buck (T-190615), USAAF, aged 25, was one of six sons of Oscar and Minnie Buck of Crosbyton, Texas, who were known as the 'Battling Bucks.' Educated at the

University of Texas, he had played for the university 'Longhorns' team and was a prospective All-American football player as well as being a good boxer. In fact, both he and his brother, John Quinn Buck, had defeated the 1930s heavyweight world boxing champion, Max Baer, during training bouts in the early 1940s. While studying at university he was selected for a Rhodes Scholarship to Oxford University but, following the outbreak of war, he volunteered (along with five other 'Longhorn' players) to join the RCAF, later transferring to the USAAF. He is buried in Cambridge (Madingley) Cemetery.

High altitude training flight. 6th Fighter Wing (Station 342, Atcham, Shropshire)
Republic P-47D Thunderbolt (42-2932) crashed onto Overley Hill, near Uppington (at map reference 615106), at 16.40 hrs. The pilot crashed in the circumstances described above and the accident was witnessed by many people, who particularly remembered the 'boom' as it struck the ground. Technical Sergeant Wayne Scholer, USAAF, who was serving as a ground mechanic at Atcham at the time, recalled the incident in a conversation with the author in 2008:

> I heard a noise and we looked up and we could barely see an aeroplane coming straight down. This was after we'd switched over to P-47s - the Thunderbolts. Apparently this fella was up flying formation at about 30,000 feet. His oxygen had quit and he had blacked out and the aircraft was headed straight to the ground. When he had got down to about 10,000 feet we could see him sort of falter a bit as if he was trying to pull it out of the dive and then it just came right straight on down and we dug it out of the top of the Wrekin [sic]. So he buried himself up there. The P-47, from what we were told, was a tough old bird. One of them had supposedly dived at 750 mph, which is in the area of supersonic and compressibility, as we called it at the time, and it had not come apart! But this one was coming to pieces before it hit the ground, so he must have gone at over 750. I can remember the ailerons and control surfaces coming off of it before it hit the ground. At least I think that's what was coming off, because this was up over the Wrekin and we were down at the base.

2 Lt (pilot u/t) Morris Howitz (O-2044425), USAAF, aged 23, was the son of Russian-born Aaron and Fannie Howitz of Harrisburg Village, Franklin County, Ohio. Before enlisting in the Air Corps, in March 1941, he had worked as an actor after leaving college. He is buried in Mount Olive Cemetery, Cleveland, Ohio.

31 May (Monday)
Familiarisation flight. 60 OTU (RAF High Ercall, Shropshire)
De Havilland Mosquito T.III (HJ881) crashed at Berwick on the northern outskirts of Shrewsbury, at 12 noon. Four Spitfires from RAF Montford Bridge were flying in line astern formation when their flight leader suddenly noticed the Mosquito aircraft approaching from behind. The Mosquito's pilots, who were thought to have been 'too preoccupied with their conversion course', failed to notice the Spitfires ahead and, despite the Spitfire flight leader diving away in an attempt to lead his flight out of danger, the Mosquito rammed his number two and both aircraft crashed out of control.

W/O (instructor pilot) Victor Alfred Clouder (740712), AFM, RAF, aged 24, was the son of Alfred Thomas Clouder and Rosie May Clouder of Wanstead, and the husband of Gertrude Bick, also of Wanstead. He had joined the RAF before the war and was awarded the Air Force Medal in March 1942 for his services as an instructor at 9 SFTS. The recommendation read:

> This Non-Commissioned Officer has been a flying instructor at this school since 13 November 1939. During this period he has carried out his duties conscientiously and efficiently despite the fact that he has always wanted to become an operational pilot. During his period of service at this school he has flown 884 instructional hours by day and 117 instructional hours by night.

F/Lt Gordon Mason [Library & Archives Canada]

His wish for operational flying had eventually been granted and he completed a tour of operations with 151 Squadron (one of the first Mosquito armed night-fighter squadrons in the UK) before being posted to 60 OTU in May 1943. He is buried in Wanstead (St Mary) Churchyard, London.

F/Lt (pilot u/t) Gordon Ward Mason (J.4105), RCAF, aged 27, was the son of Allan James Mason and Harriet Mason and the husband of Grace Margaret Pettigrew Mason of Toronto. He is buried in Ercall Magna Cemetery, near the airfield.

Formation flying exercise. 61 OTU (RAF Montford Bridge, Shropshire – satellite to RAF Rednal)
Supermarine Spitfire IA (X4930) crashed at Berwick on the northern outskirts of Shrewsbury, after colliding in the incident described above.

Sgt (pilot u/t) John Francis Cameron McPherson (413013), RAAF, aged 21, was the son of Robert and Myra McPherson of Mittagong, New South Wales, Australia. He had previously been involved in a very serious accident on 26 February while flying a Tiger Moth (N9384) of 2 EFTS, when a Spitfire collided with his aircraft over Worcestershire, forcing him to take to his parachute. He is buried in Oswestry General Cemetery, Shropshire.

8 June (Tuesday). Training flight
61 OTU (RAF Rednal, Shropshire)
Supermarine Spitfire IA (K9824) crash-landed 'near Ellesmere' at 08.34 hrs. The Norwegian pilot is considered to have 'acted well' after his engine failed and he was forced to belly-land in a field.

Sgt (pilot u/t) Otto Grieg Tidemand (5386), RNoAF. On completion of his training he was posted to 332 (Norwegian) Squadron and flew Spitfires on offensive sweeps over north-west Europe, during which he was credited with one Fw190 destroyed and one Me410 shared. He survived the war and returned to his native Norway, where he became a politician and served as Minister of Defence 1965–70. He died in 2006.

9 June (Wednesday)
Air test. 3 (O)AFU (RAF Bobbington, Staffordshire)
Avro Anson IV (AX363) force-landed at Hampton Loade to the south-south-east of Bridgnorth, at 17.20 hrs. After accidentally knocking the port engine switches off, while trying to retract a very stiff undercarriage, the pilot was forced to land in a field but had to swerve to avoid a telegraph pole, causing the undercarriage to collapse.

Sgt (staff pilot) Kenneth Norman Sanders (1318752), RAFVR, was involved in another accident near Wroxeter on 23 September 1943. Commissioned in January 1944, little else is known of his military service other than that he is believed to have flown Liberators later in the war and reached the rank of flight lieutenant. He died in Surrey in 2005.

11 June (Friday)
Cross-country training exercise from RAF Dunsfold to Hawarden, Flintshire. 430 'City of Sudbury' Squadron, RCAF (RAF Dunsfold, Surrey)
North American Mustang I (AP171) crashed at The Toot (at map reference 594835), on the south end of Brown Clee Hill, at 11.30 hrs. Two pilots took off in formation and were flying through thick cloud at 2,500 feet when F/O Watts (who was flying number two position) heard a distorted message from F/O

Brouillette signalling to return to base, which he did. Soon afterwards F/O Brouillette also turned but, as he did so, he is believed to have lost height and flew into the cloud-obscured hillside.

F/O (pilot) Sidney (Sid) Philippe Richard Brouillette (J.13030), RCAF, aged 24, was the eldest of five sons of Romeo and Eva Reynolds Brouillette of Knowlton, Quebec. He is buried in Bridgnorth Cemetery, Shropshire. His brother, Flying Officer J R E Brouillette, was also killed serving with the RCAF on 14 October 1944.

F/O Sid Brouillette [Suzanne Brouillette]

11 June (Friday)
Sector reconnaissance and D/F homings exercise. 52 OTU (RAF Aston Down, Gloucestershire)
Supermarine Spitfire IA (AR221) crashed into the Long Mynd near Church Stretton (at wartime map reference 411923), at approximately 13.00 hrs. Having taken off at 11.30 hrs with instructions to remain in R/T contact throughout the exercise (because of poor visibility), the pilot failed to do so, possibly due to a faulty R/T set. He is thought to have become lost during the course of the flight and, while flying through thick cloud and mist, he struck the hillside which was totally obscured by the conditions. Following the discovery of the crash, RAF Condover's medical orderly was dispatched in the station ambulance and the pilot's body was collected and taken to RAF Shawbury for burial.

F/O (pilot u/t) John William Grant (J.20159), RCAF, aged 22, was the son of John P and Grace I Grant of Ymir, British Columbia. Before enlisting in July 1941 he had worked as a clerk and truck driver. He is buried in Shawbury Cemetery, Shropshire.

F/O John Grant [Library & Archives Canada]

12 June (Saturday)
Formation flying and dogfighting practice. 61 OTU (RAF Montford Bridge, Shropshire – Satellite airfield to RAF Rednal)
Supermarine Spitfire IIB (P8505, presentation aircraft named *Stamford*) crashed 'at Bomere Heath' (although the wartime map reference 487197 equates to a position near Preston Gubbals), at 08.30 hrs. Twenty minutes after taking off, in formation with four other Spitfires, the pilot of this aircraft spotted a formation of three Spitfires flying below at 5–6,000 feet and dived towards them to make a simulated attack. As he did so, two of the unsuspecting Spitfires chose that moment to pull up into a steep right-hand climb and a collision occurred, sending this aircraft crashing out of control. Fortunately, the pilot of one of the Spitfires (P8195) was able to remain in control, despite damage to his propeller and oil tanks, and made an emergency landing at RAF Sleap.

F/O (pilot u/t) Terrence Blachford O'Reilly (402535), RAAF, aged 23, was the son of Bernard John and Iris Osborne O'Reilly of Pymble, New South Wales, Australia, and the husband of Joyce Gwenda O'Reilly of South Brisbane. He is buried in Oswestry General Cemetery, Shropshire.

Training flight. 61 OTU (RAF Montford Bridge, Shropshire – Satellite airfield to RAF Rednal)
Supermarine Spitfire IIA (P8195, presentation aircraft named *Gold Coast II*) force-landed at RAF Sleap following the collision described above.

Sgt (pilot u/t) Arthur Henry Exelby (658251), RAFVR, was commissioned in October 1944. He survived the war.

19 June (Saturday)
Air firing exercise. 61 OTU (RAF Rednal, Shropshire)
Supermarine Spitfire IIB (P8677, presentation aircraft named *Colchester & District*) force-landed 'near Ellesmere' at 14.57 hrs. After the engine began to smoke badly and then fail, due to a glycol leak, the pilot displayed 'coolness and judgment' by successfully belly-landing in a field.

F/O (pilot u/t) Lionel Sydney Frost (113435), RAFVR. On completion of his training he was posted to 74 Squadron and flew Spitfires over the Mediterranean and later over north-west Europe (from May 1944). He was credited with one enemy aircraft destroyed and two damaged during his tour and was awarded the DFC in September 1945, before retiring as a squadron leader in January 1947. The following year he was awarded the American DFC in recognition of his services while on attachment to the 358th Fighter Squadron, USAAF, piloting P-51s during the latter stages of the war.

21 June (Monday)
Training flight. 11 (P)AFU (RAF Condover, Shropshire – Satellite to RAF Shawbury)
Airspeed Oxford I (BG589) crashed near Condover airfield at 14.50 hrs. Having touched down on the runway the pilot decided to carry out an overshoot after a swing began to develop but, as he crossed the airfield boundary, he had to pull the aircraft up to avoid some trees, causing it to stall and crash. The aircraft immediately burst into flames but, fortunately, the pilot managed to escape from the wreckage suffering only relatively minor injuries.

Sgt (pilot u/t) Alfred George Henriquez (1800848), RAFVR, the son of Alfred St Elmo Henriquez and Linda May Henriquez, and the husband of Essie Adeline Henriquez (née Silvera) of Buff Bay, Jamaica, was born in the West Indies. After recovering from his injuries and completing his training, he was posted to 630 Squadron but was killed on his twentieth op on 17 August 1944, when his Lancaster (LL972) was shot down during a raid on Stettin. F/Lt Henriquez is buried alongside his crew in Poznan Old Garrison Cemetery, Poland.

25 June (Friday)
Solo navigation exercise. 5 (P)AFU (RAF Tern Hill, Shropshire)
Miles Master I (T8767) crash-landed at Church Farm, Adderley, to the north of Market Drayton, at 14.00 hrs. The pilot was attempting to stretch-glide back to the airfield after the engine had failed, due to a coolant leak. Unable to reach it, he tried to force-land in a field and allowed the aircraft to stall just before touching down, injuring himself in the resultant crash-landing.

Sgt (pilot u/t) Egil Hagen (2036), RNoAF. On completion of his training he was posted to 332 (Norwegian) Squadron and flew Spitfires in support of the advancing armies in north-west Europe. On 8 April 1945 he was forced to bale out of his Spitfire (NH59) after being hit by ground fire near Oldenburg, but managed to evade capture and reached the Allied lines. He survived the war.

29 June (Tuesday)
Ciné-gun exercise. 61 OTU (Believed to have taken off from RAF Montford Bridge, Shropshire – satellite airfield to RAF Rednal)
Supermarine Spitfire IA (X4941, presentation aircraft named *Swansea II*) crashed at Pound Lane, Great Hanwood. Two pilots had completed their ciné-gun exercise and the pilot of this aircraft then suggested that they practise deflection attacks, during the course of which he lost control of his aircraft and crashed. According to local resident, Arthur Jones, the Spitfire clipped the chimney pot of his mother's bungalow before crashing into a hayfield and exploding.

P/O (pilot u/t) Gordon Edward Anthony Grey (150204), RAFVR, aged 19, was the son of Mr and Mrs John A Grey of Chelsea, London. He is buried in Oswestry General Cemetery, Shropshire.

13 July (Tuesday)
Night navigation exercise. 16 OTU (RAF Upper Heyford, Oxfordshire)
Vickers Wellington III (Z1743) crash-landed at Shropshire Farm, Alveley, to the south-east of Bridgnorth, at 05.00 hrs. The trainee crew had been airborne for three-and-a-quarter hours when the pilot turned onto a new course for base and the starboard engine suddenly began to lose revs, at a height of 7,500 feet. He immediately tried various techniques to increase power but the engine continued to lose power and, with the aircraft now down to 2,500 feet, he tried to gain a little height, using his one good engine, so that his crew could bale out. Unable to do so, he ordered them into their crash positions and prepared for a crash-landing but, as he approached a field, the port wing clipped a tree and the aircraft spun through 180 degrees before crashing a hundred yards further on and catching fire. All but one of the crew were quick to get out of the wreckage and were taken to RAF Hospital, Bridgnorth to have their injuries treated but the bomb aimer was unable to get out and perished in the blaze.

F/O (pilot u/t) David Francis McLauchlan (409573), RAAF, was born in Perth, Western Australia, on 27 October 1913. He joined 467 Squadron on 23 April 1944 and completed 34 ops flying Lancaster bombers over north-west Europe, following which he was awarded the DFC in January 1945. He survived the war.

P/O (Nav) Michael Ward (134564), RAFVR, was posted to another trainee crew after recovering and eventually joined 83 Squadron as a navigator on Lancaster bombers. He was killed on 25 July 1944 when his Lancaster (ND922) was lost on an op to Stuttgart. F/Lt Ward was twenty-two years old and the son of William and Isabel Ward of York. He is buried alongside his crew members in Durnbach War Cemetery and was posthumously awarded the DFC.

Sgt (Nav) Hugh Fulton (1559794), RAFVR, was posted to another trainee crew after recovering and eventually joined 207 Squadron as a navigator on Lancaster bombers. He did not survive his tour and was killed on 22 September 1943 when his Lancaster (ED442) was lost on an op to Hamburg. Sgt Fulton, who was twenty-one years old and the son of David Jack and Margaret P Fulton of Hamilton, Lanarkshire, is buried in Hanover War Cemetery, Germany.

F/O (AB) Robert John (Bob) Martin (136815), RAFVR, aged 29, was the son of William Henry and Annie Catherine Martin (née Wilkinson). He is buried in Henbury (St Mary) Churchyard, Gloucestershire.

F/O Robert Martin [Kurt Martin]

Sgt (W/Op) James John Bromfield (1078967), RAFVR, was posted to another trainee crew after recovering and eventually completed a tour of ops with 158 Squadron (on Halifax bombers) between July 1944 and March 1945.

Sgt (AG) Howard Burn (1812636), RAFVR. Nothing further is known of this airman.

14 July (Wednesday)
Night cross-country flight and bombing exercise at Fenns Moss bombing range. 81 OTU (RAF Tilstock, Shropshire)
Armstrong Whitworth Whitley V (LA831) crashed at Bridge Farm, Quina Brook, near Prees, at 04.15 hrs. The crew had taken off at 22.50 hrs the previous evening, along with a screened navigator who had operational experience and was on board to provide advice and instruction to the trainee crew during the exercise. Having completed the five-hour cross-country flight the pilot was descending from 10,000 feet to 5,000 feet (at which height the bombing exercise was to take place) when it is believed that he 'lost control of the aircraft during the descent through cloud'. The aircraft was then seen by members of the Royal Observer Corps in a 'screaming dive' in which the wings broke off ('probably during an

Sgt Les Bugg [Phil Bugg]

F/O Alan Kelly [Brian Tutty]

Sgt David Waite [Kevin Murray]

attempt at recovery') and struck the tail assembly, causing the whole rear fuselage to disintegrate.

Sgt (pilot) Leslie William (Les) Bugg (1247330), RAFVR, aged 23, was the son of William and Daisy Bugg of Chipping Hill, and was engaged to WAAF Doreen A Polhill (who is thought to have been a cook at RAF Tilstock). Just two weeks before his death, on 1 July, he had survived a very serious crash while taking off at Tilstock. He is buried in White Notley Churchyard, Essex.

F/O (screened Nav) Frank Bird (142562), RAFVR, aged 32, was the son of Peter R and Priscilla Bird of Chadderton and the husband of Lucille Bird (nee Staziker), also of Chadderton. He is buried in Chadderton (St Mathew) Churchyard, Lancashire.

Sgt (Nav) Stanley Vine Stephens (1601045), RAFVR, aged 22, was the son of Ernest John and Eliza Ann Stephens of Illogan. He is buried in Illogan (St Illogan) Churchyard, Cornwall.

F/O (AB) Alan Douglas Kelly (J.22193), RCAF, aged 22, was the son of George Douglas and Daisy L Kelly of Bridgewater, Nova Scotia. He is buried in Chester (Blacon) Cemetery.

Sgt (W/AG) David Waite (1531151), RAFVR, aged 20, was the son of Agnes and the late Horace Waite, and the husband of Corporal Margaret Mary Burns, WAAF, whom he had only married on 22 May. He is buried in Ossett (Holy Trinity) Churchyard, Yorkshire.

Sgt (W/AG) Donovan Munt (1803564), RAFVR, aged 19, was the son of Alfred John and Dorothy Ella Munt of Cranford, Middlesex. He is buried in Chester (Blacon) Cemetery.

14 July (Wednesday)

Training flight. 6 (P)AFU (RAF Little Rissington, Gloucestershire)

Airspeed Oxford I (EB748) force-landed at Pipe Gate, near Woore to the north-east of Market Drayton, at 12.45 hrs. The pilot belly-landed the aircraft in a field after an engine failed but neither occupant was hurt.

Sgt (pilot) Douglas Milton Bridges (1387810), RAFVR. Commissioned in February 1944, he was one of only two survivors from a Lancaster (LL903) of 166 Squadron, which was shot down on a bombing op to Friedrichshafen on 27 April 1944. P/O Bridges spent the rest of the war as a POW before returning to the UK and serving in the RAF until January 1955.

Sgt John Darby (986428), RAFVR. Commissioned in April 1945, nothing further is known of his military service other than that he survived the war.

19 July (Monday)

Target towing flight. 61 OTU (RAF Rednal, Shropshire)

Miles Martinet TT.I (HP328) crashed at Middleton to the east of Oswestry, at 13.20 hrs. During the course of the flight the pilot began unauthorised low flying over his drogue operator's wife's house, lost control in a tight turn at 200 feet and crashed out of control.

Sgt (pilot) John William (Jack) Twelftree (1436774), RAFVR, aged 32, was the son of Owen and Alice Maud Twelftree and the husband of Rose Elizabeth Nurish of 30 Scarborough Street, Irthlingborough. Educated at Stanwick School, he then worked for the Walker & Gunn Factory in Higham Ferrers and, in his spare time, was a section leader with the Irthlingborough Auxiliary Fire Service. After joining the RAF he underwent his pilot training in the USA, where he gained his wings, before returning to the UK to complete his operational training. He is buried in Irthlingborough Cemetery, Northamptonshire.

AC1 (drogue operator) Herbert Alexander Peters (1243490), RAFVR, aged 36, was the son of Alfred Alexander and Alice Peters and the husband of Sarah Elizabeth Peters (née Fletcher) of Walthamstow. He is buried in the City of London Cemetery, Manor Park.

Sgt Jack Twelftree [Irthlingborough Historical Society]

21 July (Wednesday)
Practice R/T homings. 60 OTU (RAF High Ercall, Shropshire)
De Havilland Mosquito T.III (HJ892) crashed between Neen Savage Farm and Catherton Farm, near Cleobury Mortimer, at 12.10 hrs. The pilot was flying solo at 2–3,000 feet when he is thought to have lost control in cloud, either due to 'instrument failure' or 'inexperience', and entered a high-speed stall from which he did not have enough height to recover.

F/O (pilot u/t) Claude Neil Wilcox (J.9496), RCAF, aged 22, was the son of Edward E and Estella Wilcox of Fort Meade, Florida, USA. He is buried in Chester (Blacon) Cemetery.

25 July (Sunday)
Training flight. 11 (P)AFU (RAF Condover, Shropshire – satellite to RAF Shawbury)
Airspeed Oxford I BF934 crashed on the edge of the airfield at 15.25 hrs. When a swing began to develop as he landed, the pupil pilot tried to carry out an overshoot procedure but left it too late and the aircraft struck trees on the edge of the runway and crashed. Fortunately, the pilot was unhurt.

Sgt (pilot u/t) Dennis William Ryan (1323539), RAFVR. On completion of his training he was posted to 9 Squadron but did not survive his tour and was killed piloting a Lancaster (LL785) on an op to Creil in France on 5 July 1944. P/O Ryan, who was 21 years old and the son of William G and Marguerite I Ryan of Edgware, Middlesex, is buried in Creil Communal Cemetery.

27 July (Tuesday)
Night dual training . 11 (P)AFU (RAF Condover, Shropshire – satellite to RAF Shawbury)
Airspeed Oxford I (LW791) crashed near Moat Farm, Stapleton (at map reference 460039), at 02.50 hrs. Shortly after taking off, the instructor noticed that his airspeed was only 80 mph and, in an attempt to pick up speed, he moved the control column forward and put the aircraft into a dive. The aircraft soon reached 140 mph but, due to an 'error of judgement', he had left it too late to pull up and the aircraft hit the ground horizontally at high speed next to the Stapleton–Pulverbatch road. Incredibly, due to the shallow angle at which it struck, the aircraft bounced back into the air before striking a large V-shaped willow tree (growing by a small brook), which tore off both the wings. The fuselage came to rest in a potato field a little further on. At the time Mike Bradbury's family farmed in Stapleton and he recalled how, after the crash, RAF Condover's ambulance driver stopped on New House Lane, near Pulverbatch, where he heard faint cries from the injured pupil pilot. He was wandering in the fields looking for help, while his instructor was trapped in the cockpit. Both crewmen eventually recovered from their injuries.

Sgt (instructor pilot) Roy Churton Paine (655997), RAF, was born in Croydon on 5 March 1920. He died in Bromley, Kent, in 1996.

Sgt (pilot u/t) Leslie Torry (1575250), RAFVR.

27 July (Tuesday)
Ferry flight. 27 MU (RAF Shawbury, Shropshire)
Douglas Havoc II (AH470) force-landed at Moreton Corbet to the north of the airfield, at 14.30 hrs. While taking off from the airfield the pilot experienced vibrations in the controls and decided to belly-land the aircraft directly ahead. Following an inspection of the aircraft by the station Engineering Officer, the cause was thought to be the pilot's 'faulty cockpit drill' as the 'upper cowlings [were] in open position'.

F/Lt (test pilot) Peter Frederick McDonald Davies (40088), RAF, was born in Wellington, Shropshire on 11 August 1919. He joined the RAF in July 1937 and was posted to 56 Squadron in July 1939 after completing his training. Following the outbreak of war he flew during the Battle of France and Battle of Britain but, on 13 August 1940, was shot down in a Hurricane (N2429) during combat over Sheppey and suffered serious burns. As a result of his injuries he was declared fit only for non-operational flying and began ferry flying duties in December 1940. Posted to 29 MU, High Ercall in April 1941 as a senior test pilot, he was subsequently posted to 27 MU in November 1942 and continued test flying until the end of the war. He remained in the RAF after the war and eventually retired as a squadron leader in 1958. He died in Chichester in 1993.

27 July (Tuesday)
Ferry flight. 5 FPP (RAF Hatfield, Hertfordshire)
Fairey Swordfish II (LS220) force-landed at 'East Underton Farm' to the south-west of Bridgnorth, at 17.20 hrs. The pilot was flying to and from an unknown airfield (perhaps High Ercall?) when the engine failed and he tried to force-land in a field but crashed through a hedge, slightly damaging the aircraft.

Sgt (pilot) John Maurice Mahon (R.107558), RCAF. Little is known of this pilot other than that he was later commissioned and survived the war.

27 July (Tuesday)
Low flying training. 6th Fighter Wing (Station 342, Atcham, Shropshire)
Republic P-47D Thunderbolt (42-7953, bearing the fuselage code VM-L) crashed at Wiston Farm, Tetchill, near Ellesmere, at 17.50 hrs. Having taken off at 17.30 hrs the pilot (call sign Sinbad 156) flew to the low-flying area and began his exercise, during which he made 'too steep a turn at a dangerously low altitude' and struck a hedge, 'throwing the aircraft completely out of control and causing it to crash.' Charles Wynn, a local farmer, stated in the accident investigation that he

> ... first saw the plane approaching very low from the south. Upon nearing the house, he started a turn to the left around the house. As he came around from the north, he seemed to be considerably lower. The tip of his left wing struck a hedge which seemed to throw the plane out of control. As he crossed the road in front of the house, he seemed to recover for a second, then crashed into a wheat field in front of the house. The plane burst into flames and rolled two hundred yards through the wheat. After phoning the Sergeant at Ellesmere Police station, I went at once and found the pilot dead.

Thunderbolt 42-7953's tail fin in a wheatfield at Tetchill. [USAAF]

Flight Officer (pilot u/t) Robert Edward Eble (T-190657), USAAF, aged 20 (?), was the son of Harold Albert and Ruth M Eble of Newark, New Jersey, USA. He is buried in Cambridge (Madingley) Cemetery.

28 July (Wednesday)
Camera-gun exercise. 60 OTU (RAF High Ercall, Shropshire)
De Havilland Mosquito NF.II (HJ643) crashed at Uckington Farm to the south-east of Atcham airfield (while the tail unit fell nearby at map reference 583097), at 16.30 hrs. The pilot was authorised to carry out camera-gun attacks on a drogue target towed by Sgt Shields (in a Martinet aircraft), who was ordered to fly along the railway line between Shrewsbury and Atcham at a height of 5,000 feet (with instructions not to descend below 3,000 feet). Sgt Shields carried out several runs at a height of 5,500 feet, above a cloud layer, but, as he could not see the Mosquito and had no radio to contact its pilot, he descended below cloud to 3,000 feet (although witnesses claimed it to be no more than 2,000 feet) where he was 'attacked' several times by the Mosquito. As the Martinet passed in the vicinity of Atcham, however, the attacking Mosquito collided with a Spitfire, which was approaching Atcham airfield. The two aircraft crashed out of control and the Mosquito set fire to farm buildings (which were fortunately saved by the airfield fire squad). Technical Sergeant Wayne Scholer, USAAF, who was serving as a ground mechanic at Atcham at the time, remembered seeing the

> ... Mosquito scooting along just underneath this ceiling [of cloud] and a Spitfire dropped out through the ceiling and they hit head-on. There were pieces of the aircraft landing on the base if I remember. I remember one part of the aircraft, the wheel and some other structure, it landed on the base over by the rifle butts.

Joe Dorsett, who worked for the Air Ministry under contract to the USAAF at Atcham, also described what he saw:

> I think the Spitfire pilot tried to get out, but he got caught on the tail. I'm pretty sure the Spitfire took off, turned into a bit of cloud and collided head-on with a 'Mozzie' that had gone in the other side. Boom! I just looked up and I just heard the bang and saw them falling down on fire. They came down in Marsh's stackyard.

Following an investigation, neither pilot was found to be at fault, but it was recommended that 'If it is essential on a particular occasion to do this exercise below 5,000 feet, a specific warning should be given to any airfields in the vicinity.' It was also stated that R/T sets should be fitted in drogue-towing aircraft.

W/O (pilot) Rupert Anthony Hodges (1167828), RAFVR, aged 22, was the son of Winifred B Hodges of Caversham, Reading. He is buried in Reading (Henley Road) Cemetery.

F/O (Nav) William Hemmings (131555), RAFVR, aged 37, was the son of William Charles and Laura Eveline Hemmings and the husband of Rosalind Alice Mary Hemmings (née Jones) of Enfield, Middlesex. He is buried in Chester (Blacon) Cemetery.

Test flight. 6th Fighter Wing (Station 342, Atcham, Shropshire)
Supermarine Spitfire VB (AA924) crashed at Ravenswood on the edge of the airfield, after colliding in the incident described above.

Major (pilot) Henry Ovila Asselin (O-399769), USAAF, aged 27, was the son of Henry Cyprien Asselin and Elizabeth Asselin (née Beattie) of

Maj Henry Asselin [Ancestry.com]

Left: The tailplane of Mosquito HJ643 lying in a field near Atcham airfield. [USAAF]

Right: The wreckage of Major Asselin's Spitfire with the Wrekin in the background. [USAAF]

Allston, Boston, Massachusetts. Before the war he had studied at the Boston Mechanic Arts High School. He is buried in Cambridge (Madingley) Cemetery. His father subsequently died in Normandy on 9 January 1945, serving with the Merchant Marine.

3 August (Tuesday)
Night cross-country training exercise. 467 Squadron, RAAF (RAF Bottesford on the Leicestershire/ Lincolnshire border)
Avro Lancaster III (ED500) crash-landed at Park Farm, between Coxbank and Adderley, to the north west of Market Drayton, at 02.30 hrs. The crew had only joined the squadron a week earlier and were undergoing a training flight, prior to beginning operations, when the port outer-engine failed, followed quickly by the port inner and then the starboard inner. Despite the flight engineer carrying out all the correct actions, the engines failed to restart and, unable to keep the aircraft airborne, the pilot ordered his crew to bale out, while he remained at the controls to make a forced landing. In the ensuing crash-landing he suffered mild concussion, abrasions and lacerations to the leg, arms, face and hands and was taken to RAF Tilstock's sick quarters before being transferred to RAF Hospital, Cosford. The remainder of the crew, who had landed further to the north, were all uninjured and stayed the night at Hack Green GCI station before being returned to their base.

F/Sgt (pilot) Jack Willoughby Nancarrow (408867), RAAF, was born in Perth, Western Australia, on 12 June 1917. He joined 467 Squadron on 28 July 1943 and completed two ops on 30 and 31 July as 'second dickie' (to gain experience before captaining his own crew on operations). Following the accident, he was posted back to the squadron on 18 August with the newly-commissioned rank of pilot officer, but it appears that he did not fly any more operations with the squadron. He was then posted to 463 Squadron on 25 November, but only took part in one op on 21 January 1944. He survived the war and was discharged in February 1945 with the rank of flying officer.

Sgt (F/Eng) Thomas Forsyth Preston (965739), RAFVR. Following the accident he joined 61 Squadron but, on 20 February 1944, was shot down in a Lancaster (HK538) during an op to Leipzig and taken prisoner. He spent the remainder of the war in *Stalag Luft IV*, until 10 April 1945, when he managed to escape from a marching column and spent six days in hiding before being picked up by the British Army.

P/O (Nav) Harold Leonard Fry (130595), RAFVR, remained with the squadron after the accident but was killed on 29 January 1944 in a Lancaster (ED867) which was shot down on an op to Berlin. Initially commemorated on the Runnymede Memorial for the missing, his body was discovered during an excavation of the crash site in 2003 and his remains were interred in the Berlin 1939–45 War Cemetery, Germany. P/O Fry was twenty-one years old and the son of Leonard and Daisy May Fry of Ilford, Essex.

Sgt (AB) William Cullen (1515485), RAFVR. No further details are known of this NCO other than that he survived the war.

Sgt (W/AG) Wilfred Sydney Millar (1487423), RAFVR, transferred to 463 Squadron following the accident and was killed on 23 April 1944 in a Lancaster (LL892) which was lost over the Netherlands during an op to Brunswick. F/Sgt Millar is buried in Nieuwolda General Cemetery, Netherlands along with other members of the Lancaster's crew.

Sgt (AG) Gavin Carfrae Borradaile (1332645), RAFVR, transferred to 463 Squadron following the accident and was killed on 30 January 1944 in a Lancaster (ED772) which was shot down by a night fighter on an op to Berlin. Sgt Borradaile was twenty years old and is buried in Berlin 1939–45 War Cemetery, Germany.

12 August (Thursday)
Training flight. 5 (P)AFU (RAF Tern Hill, Shropshire)
Miles Master I (N7537) force-landed at Colehurst Farm to the north-east of the airfield, at 14.30 hrs. The pilot was presumably taking off, or preparing to land, when the engine failed due to a coolant leak. He was forced to belly-land the aircraft in a field and was unhurt.

Sgt (pilot u/t) Richard Allan Shannon (R.156972), RCAF, was born on 17 May 1921. He enlisted in March 1942 and gained his wings in Canada before sailing to the UK in May 1943. On completion of his training he was posted to 417 Squadron, RCAF, flying Spitfires over the advancing armies in Italy. He was killed on 10 December 1944, piloting a Spitfire (JG243) which collided with another Spitfire while circling a ground target at Ravenna, Italy. P/O Shannon, who was twenty-three years old and the son of George Richard and Ettie White Shannon of Hamilton, Ontario, is buried in Forlì War Cemetery, Italy.

13 August (Friday)
Training flight. 61 OTU (RAF Rednal, Shropshire)
Supermarine Spitfire IIA (P7508) belly-landed at 'Morton Vicarage, Maesbury', to the south of Oswestry, at 13.34 hrs. Immediately after take-off the engine lost power due to a 'constant speed control failure' and the Norwegian pilot put up 'a good show' (according to his CO) by belly-landing the aircraft in a field.

Sgt (pilot u/t) Wrold Emil Wroldsen (829), RNoAF, was killed on 3 October 1943, flying Spitfire R7986 out of Rednal, when he collided with another aircraft during an interception exercise over Leicestershire. He was twenty-four years old and it is presumed that his body was repatriated to Norway.

13 August (Friday)
Night test flight. 60 OTU (RAF High Ercall, Shropshire)
De Havilland Mosquito II (DD630) crashed on High Ercall airfield at 21.05 hrs. After being ordered to test an aircraft, prior to its being used later that night by a pupil, the instructor used the opportunity to take his wife up in the aircraft and perform some aerobatics. Shortly after taking off the pilot made a low dive across the airfield before returning to make another low pass, travelling from east to west, during which he completed a perfect roll. Moments later he began a similar roll but this time his initial speed was slower and it is thought that the engines cut while upside down, due to 'upsetting of the mixture by the attitude of the aircraft'. The aircraft consequently lost speed, completing the roll in a

stalled condition, and then 'flicked over into a spin from a height of less than 1,000 feet. After completing little more than one turn it struck the ground on the tarmac and burst into flames'.

F/O (instructor pilot) Peter William Stokes (46735), DFC, RAF, aged 22, was the son of William Edward and Catherine Stokes of Upminster, Essex. Prior to joining 60 OTU as an instructor he had flown Mosquitos in the Mediterranean theatre with 23 Squadron, for which he had been awarded the DFC in April 1943. The citation read:

> F/O Stokes has completed 47 sorties involving attacks on airfields, marshalling yards and factories. On one occasion in November 1942, he attacked a factory at St Dizier, starting fires. More recently he has undertaken intruder sorties over Sicily and Italy. One night in March 1943, he made two sorties on the Tripoli-Gabes Road. In the face of heavy AA fire, he pressed home his attacks, destroying many vehicles, starting many fires and causing much confusion on the road, thus enabling following aircraft to bomb with destructive effect. Two nights later over the airfield at Castel Vetrano, F/O Stokes destroyed an enemy aircraft. This officer has displayed courage and determination worthy of high praise.

He is buried in Wellington General Cemetery, Shropshire.

Mrs Daphne Joan Stokes (née Pegram), aged 20, is buried in Wellington General Cemetery, Shropshire. She had married F/O Stokes the previous year.

22 August (Sunday)
Training flight. 61 OTU (RAF Rednal, Shropshire)
Supermarine Spitfire IIA (P7304) crashed into Hincks Plantation near Lilleshall, at 17.25 hrs. Whilst 'dogfighting' the two Belgian pilots collided head-on due to an 'error of judgement', by failing to realise the 'converging speed of head-on attacks' and also due to 'inexperience in forward view from Spitfires and disregard of personal danger due to excessive keenness'. The collision threw this aircraft out of control and it crashed into a wooded plantation, killing the pilot. The other pilot was able to maintain control, and made an emergency landing at RAF Bobbington, Staffordshire.

P/O (pilot u/t) Jean Joseph Albert Noizet (143485), RAFVR, aged 28, was born in Florenville, Belgium, on 3 March 1915. He had joined the Belgian Air Force in 1936 and, by the outbreak of war, was serving as an instructor with the *1er Escadrille École*. Following the German invasion he escaped to French Morocco, where he served until December 1942 before travelling to the UK to join the RAFVR. His body was repatriated to Belgium after the war and buried in the Air Force section of Brussels Cemetery.

Training flight. 61 OTU (RAF Rednal, Shropshire)
Supermarine Spitfire IIA (P7444) landed at RAF Bobbington following the collision described above.

P/O (pilot u/t) Henri Maurice Goldsmit (151928), RAFVR, was born in St Gilles on the outskirts of Brussels, on 29 March 1916. He escaped to the UK in June 1940, following the German invasion, and joined the *1er Bataillon de Fusiliers* in September 1940. He subsequently volunteered for the RAFVR in January 1942 and, after completing his training, joined 349 (Belgian) Squadron. He was shot down by flak near Klundert on 3 November 1944, piloting a Spitfire (PT963) and is buried in Evere Cemetery, Belgium.

25 August (Wednesday)
Instrument flying training. 11 (P)AFU (RAF Shawbury, Shropshire)
Airspeed Oxford II (AS870) force-landed at Linley near Bishops Castle, at 11.10 hrs. An instructor was giving instrument flying instruction to his pupil at 4,000 feet when the starboard wing began to vibrate severely and the aircraft started to lose height. After taking control the instructor found that 'the aircraft was not controllable at under 140 mph and required full left rudder and an application of considerable

left bank to be maintained on an even keel'. He therefore belly-landed the aircraft in a field and it skidded for some 200 yards before crashing into a hedge and coming to a halt. A subsequent examination of the wreckage found no obvious defect other than a fracture in the starboard engine mounting. However, it 'could not be established if this happened in the air or during the crash-landing'.

Sgt (instructor pilot) Douglas Haig Gordon (R.10448), RCAF. Born on 9 October 1915 in Borne, Quebec, he settled in Shropshire after the war and died in Shrewsbury in 1970.

F/O (pilot u/t) Geoffrey Francis Snow (127254), RAFVR, had been commissioned in August 1942 and survived the war attaining the rank of flight lieutenant.

F/O Keith Laing [Library & Archives Canada]

26 August (Thursday)
'Bullseye' exercise and practice bombing. 81 OTU (RAF Sleap, Shropshire – satellite to RAF Tilstock)
Armstrong Whitworth Whitley V (LA937, bearing the fuselage code EZ-J) crashed into the airfield watch office at 03.20 hrs. The trainee crew had taken off at 21.10 hrs the previous evening and were approaching the airfield, after completing their exercise, when the pilot decided to land without first gaining permission as he suspected they were nearly out of fuel. As he made his final turn to line up with the runway, however, both engines failed in quick succession, due to a lack of fuel, and the pilot ordered the crew into crash positions before trying to touch down. Unfortunately, the aircraft had overshot the flare path slightly and was travelling at an angle across it. After it had bounced twice the pilot tried to raise the undercarriage to bring it to a halt but, by this stage, it was too late. The aircraft then bounced into the air a further time and, as it did so, the port wing struck a Nissen hut, which wrenched off the wing and swung the fuselage around, causing it to smash into the watch office. Two crew members in the front of the aircraft were killed instantly in the crash, while the remainder of the crew and numerous staff in the watch office were injured, including the station commander. The two most seriously injured (a WAAF and one airman), were subsequently taken to RAF Hospital, Cosford, while the remaining injured were treated in the station sick quarters. The subsequent investigation found that the pilot had been too hasty in changing over his fuel tanks during the flight, as the wing tanks still had fuel inside them when examined. It was decided that, to prevent another similar accident happening, 'a red obstruction light should be placed on the watch office when flying is in progress'. Whether this was done is unclear but, just twelve days later, an almost identical accident happened.

F/O (pilot) Keith Nesbitt Laing (J.23273), RCAF, aged 20, was the son of Thomas Nesbitt Laing and Annie May Laing of Saskatoon. Before joining up in December 1941 he had worked as a clerk for T Eaton Company. He is buried in Chester (Blacon) Cemetery.

Sgt (Nav) Thomas Worthington Fair (R.139965), RCAF. After recovering from his injuries he joined 463 Squadron but was killed on 25 April 1944 when his Lancaster (LL848) was shot down by a night fighter during an op to Munich. P/O Fair, who was twenty-seven years old and the son of Thomas Worthington Fair and Anne Fair, is buried in Durnbach War Cemetery, Germany.

Sgt (AB) Thomas Reginald Armstrong (R.161129), RCAF, aged 22, was the son of Fredrick James and Clarie Grace Armstrong of Kemptville, Ontario.

Sgt Thomas Armstrong [Library & Archives Canada]

Sgt Ron Guile
[Phil Guile]

He is buried in Chester (Blacon) Cemetery.

Sgt (W/Op) Robert Godfrey Henderson (1365032), RAFVR, was commissioned in November 1944 and was subsequently awarded the DFC in May 1945 while serving with 405 (RCAF) Squadron.

Sgt (AG) Ronald (Ron) Guile (1675093), RAFVR. Following the accident he joined 463 Squadron along with Sgt Fair, and was lost on the same aircraft on 25 April 1944. His brother, James Guile, was killed just thirteen days later while serving with 106 Squadron.

The three seriously injured in the watch office were:

W/Cdr (pilot) David Stewart Robertson (40141), DFC, RAF, was the commanding officer of RAF Sleap and had flown Whitley bombers earlier in the war with 51 and 78 Squadrons, following which he had been awarded the DFC in November 1940. After a spell as an instructor, he completed a second tour of ops with 149 Squadron before being posted to 81 OTU in March 1943. He was mentioned in despatches in January 1945 and, at about the same time, was appointed to the RCAF before returning to his native Canada after the war.

AC1 (ACH/GD) Ferguson, RAFVR.

ACW2 (R/T operator) Jean M Viney, WAAF. She emigrated to Australia after the war and died in June 2008.

29 August (Sunday)
Unauthorised flight by suspended pilot. 5 (P)AFU (RAF Tern Hill, Shropshire)
Miles Master II (AZ248) crashed at 24 MU's Heath Site, just north of Tern Hill airfield, at 15.23 hrs. An airman, who had been suspended and had not flown since 19 March, approached an aircraft at dispersal with a parachute and told the airman standing there (LAC Shelley) that he had come to taxi the aircraft across to the night-flying dispersal area. Despite noticing that the airman was not wearing wings, LAC Shelly believed that a pilot had got into the rear cockpit to accompany him (in fact he had leant in to release the brake), so he removed the chocks from the wheels and the aircraft began to taxi quickly away. By this stage it was clear that there was no other pilot in the back cockpit and, despite attempts by a couple of NCOs to stop the aircraft, the suspended pilot proceeded to taxi to the end of the runway and took off at once. The aircraft was seen to take off in a normal manner but, after reaching 300 feet, the pilot turned left and proceeded to 'shoot up' the Maintenance Unit site before climbing to 1,500 feet and commencing a slow roll to the left. As the aircraft came out of the roll it appeared that the pilot lost control and it made a steep diving turn into the ground and burst into flames. In the subsequent investigation it was concluded that the suspended pilot was 'not competent to carry out such a slow roll' but also added that the chocks should not have been removed without permission from the pilot in charge of the aircraft and the brake also should not have been released.

AC1 Frederick Walter Johns (339602), RAF, aged 27, had evidently undergone a fair amount of pilot training as he is recorded as having 97 hours of flying to his name, of which 22 hours were on Masters. He is buried in Southend-on-Sea (Sutton Road) Cemetery, Essex.

31 August (Tuesday)
Altitude interception exercise. 2908th Observation Squadron, 2906th Observation Training Group (Station 342, Atcham, Shropshire)
Republic P-47D Thunderbolt (42-7917) crashed at Woore to the north-east of Market Drayton, at 18.18 hrs. Two pilots took off at 17.15 hrs for a training exercise but, soon after becoming airborne, the pilot of this aircraft, with call sign Sinbad 192, noticed a 'slight roughness in his engine'. He had, however, noticed it several times in the past and decided to continue. While waiting to be intercepted by his

wingman Lt Woodrow W Anderson, the pilot manipulated his controls to try and reduce the vibration, to no avail and after Lt Anderson 'attacked', the two pilots began a series of steep, climbing turns. Having completed four or five of these turns, however, the pilot experienced a sudden increase in vibration. He therefore broke off combat and signalled for Lt Anderson to take lead position and return towards the airfield, while he tried various settings to reduce the vibration. The two aircraft then made a shallow diving turn towards base but, about thirty seconds after levelling off, at 10,000 feet, the pilot described how

Thunderbolt 42-7917's engine pictured at Atcham for a technical examination following the accident. [USAAF]

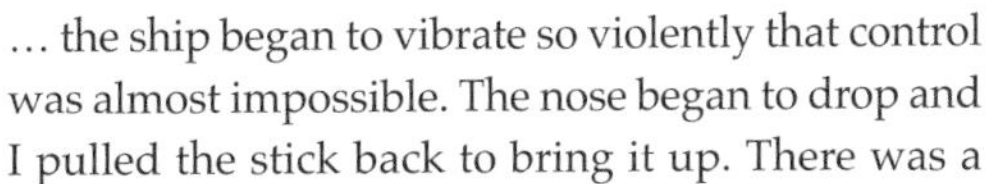

> ... the ship began to vibrate so violently that control was almost impossible. The nose began to drop and I pulled the stick back to bring it up. There was a sudden loud noise and the windshield clouded over with oil. I glanced at my left wing and noticed the leading edge was broken inside the number one gun, the skin being open over about a foot of the leading edge and back to the main spar. At the same time, the ship began to tumble and buck violently. I cut the switches immediately and tried to control the ship, thinking I might be able to make a crash-landing. However, I was being thrown violently about in the cockpit and movements of the stick and rudder had no effect other than slight elevator control. I was able to change a nose-down motion to a nose-up motion, but the ship immediately went off on a wing. (In this change, the attitude of the ship changed about 45 degrees in about three seconds, but seemed to be caused more by slopping of the ship than be response to the controls.) The ship was still tumbling, completely out of control and knowing that the ship falls fast, I got out as fast as possible. I went out of the cockpit and fell flat on the wing. At that time the ship was inverted. I scrambled clear and pulled the rip cord. The chute worked. Altitude at the time of bailing out was less than 1,000 feet.

A subsequent examination of the wreckage concluded that one of the propeller blades had broken off due to 'excessive wear' and the resulting vibration caused the engine to break away from its mountings.

1 Lt (pilot u/t) Richard L Altschuler (O-661174), USAAF, was a native of Chicago, USA. He joined the 62nd Fighter Squadron, 56th Fighter Group, after finishing his training at Atcham and completed sixty-nine missions. He survived the war and was awarded the Distinguished Flying Cross with two Oak Leaf clusters.

2 September (Thursday)
Transition training flight. HQ Squadron, 2906th Observation Training Group (Station 342, Atcham, Shropshire)
Republic P-47D Thunderbolt (42-7976) crashed at Billingsley to the south of Bridgnorth, at 18.38 hrs. The pilot was flying at 8,000 feet when he made a shallow diving turn to port and the engine suddenly lost power. According to the pilot's statement, the aircraft:

> ... immediately regained normal flight and the engine seemed to pick up slightly and then resumed its former status of reduced power. I am fully sure I was on the main tank as I changed over only five minutes previous. At this time, I radioed my difficulty and checked all instruments, except the boost and RPM. All other instruments were on the green line. During my conversation over R/T and while looking for a suitable forced landing field, I advanced and closed the throttle several times with no result on the performance of the engine.

> I believe at this time my boost was very low and my RPM about 800. With this loss of power, I was unable to keep altitude. I believe the failure was due to insufficient gas coming into the carburettor. That is, the setting was set and I could not increase or reduce my engine speed. The controls were probably jammed or disengaged and the carburettor assumed a position giving the low power. I bailed out at 600 feet by order of the Flying Control. After the chute opened, I observed the plane to continue flight and go into a wide turn to the right and finally, it went in at a shallow angle and blew up.

After landing safely the pilot was taken to RAF Bridgnorth, where he spent the night in the officers' mess before returning to Atcham, while the crash site was placed under an RAF guard. A subsequent inspection of the wreckage found it impossible to identify the cause of the accident, but it was stated that the failure was 'in the engine controls'.

Flight Officer (pilot u/t) Howard N Pearson (T-190927), USAAF.

4 September (Saturday)

Towing training. 5 GTS (RAF Shobdon, Herefordshire)

General Aircraft GAL.48 Hotspur II glider (HH303) force-landed at Clungunford at 17.45 hrs. After the R/T set broke during the flight the tug pilot released the glider, whose pilot was forced to land in a field as he was unfamiliar with the countryside and could not locate the airfield. As a result of the accident the pilot of the tug aircraft had his logbook endorsed for failing to release the glider in a suitable position.

Cpl (pilot u/t) W Gordon (5391601), GPR.

7 September (Tuesday)

Circuits and landings. 81 OTU (RAF Sleap, Shropshire – satellite to RAF Tilstock)

Armstrong Whitworth Whitley V (BD257, bearing the fuselage code EZ-U) crashed into the airfield watch office at 00.25 hrs. While taking off, the aircraft began to swing to the left (which the Whitley had a tendency to do) but, when the pilot tried to correct it, he overcompensated, causing a swing to the right. He then attempted a further correction, but this time the aircraft swung violently to the left, recrossed the runway and headed across the grass with engines running at full power and the tail wheel leaving the ground. Moments later the starboard wing tip struck the wind sock and the fuselage ploughed into the watch office, bursting into flames and engulfing the building, station fire tender, a Hillman van and a Fordson 30 cwt. truck (which were all parked alongside the building). On board the aircraft the rear gunner was the sole survivor, while two WAAFs inside the watch office and an airman on duty on the fire tender (Cpl Peate) were also killed. Two further WAAFs were seriously injured in the watch office and were taken to RAF Hospital, Cosford, to be treated at the hospital's burns centre. The subsequent investigation again recommended that a red light be placed on the watch office along with an escape door (a similar recommendation had been made following the accident on 26 August), but the Commander-in-Chief responded that there was no need for these measures as, 'the chances of the building being hit are 1 in 1,000,000 and when it does happen, there's no warning. It is just part of the risk everybody runs on airfields'. Whether he was aware that an almost identical crash had occurred just two weeks earlier is unclear.

F/O (pilot) Richard William Browne (55102), RAF, aged 20, was the son of Major Theophilus Coxon Browne, SAAF and Ethel May Browne of Rietondale, Pretoria, South Africa. He is buried in Chester (Blacon) Cemetery.

F/O (Nav) Everlyn Leonard Ware (J.22431), RCAF, aged 31, was the son of Martin Alfred and Gertrude Augusta Ware and the husband of Clara Elizabeth Ware of Guelph, Ontario. Born and raised in Niagara Falls City, he had worked in a number of jobs before enlisting in January 1942. He is buried in Chester (Blacon) Cemetery.

F/O Everlyn Ware [Library & Archives Canada]

Sgt (AB) William Dyson Kershaw (1580784), RAFVR, aged 22, was the son of Leonard and Ellen Kershaw of Whitworth. He is buried in Heywood Cemetery, Lancashire.

Sgt (W/AG) Eric Young (1515649) RAFVR, aged 22, was the son of David R and Gladys Young of Rochdale. He is buried in Rochdale Cemetery, Lancashire.

Sgt (AG) S Williams (1608989), RAFVR. Little is known of this airman other than that he survived the war.

The ground staff killed, or seriously injured, were:

Cpl (ACH/GD) Norman Walter (Jack) Peate (1739039), RAFVR, aged 20, was the son of James and Alice Peate of New Marton, St Martin's, Shropshire. Before joining up he had been on the permanent staff at Derwen Training College, Gobowen. He is buried in St Martin's Churchyard, Shropshire.

ACW2 Kitty Ffoulkes [Margaret Steele]

ACW2 (MT driver) Kathleen Megan (Kitty) Ffoulkes (476799), WAAF, aged 21, was the daughter of Mr A E Ffoulkes of Abbotsway, Newcastle-under-Lyme, Staffordshire. Educated at Orme Girls' School, where she was 'a very popular girl', she had worked at her father's florist's shop in Newcastle before joining up earlier in 1943. She is buried in Newcastle-under-Lyme Cemetery.

ACW2 (MT driver) Vera Hughes (470079), WAAF, aged 21, was the daughter of Mr and Mrs R W Hughes of Parr, St Helens, Lancashire. She is buried in Rainhill (St Anne) Churchyard, Lancashire.

LACW (Met staff) A B Jowett (2050867), WAAF, was serving in the meteorological section at the airfield and survived the war.

ACW2 (Met staff) H Hall (474855), WAAF, was serving in the meteorological section at the airfield and was under training at the time of the accident.

8 September (Wednesday)

Cross-country and bombing exercise from Base–Somerton–Port Isaac–Somerton–Chipping Norton–Conwy Castle–Leominster–Base (680 miles). 12 OTU (RAF Chipping Warden, Oxfordshire)

Sgt Norman Wachter [National Archives of Australia]

Vickers Wellington II (BJ621) crashed at Eudon Mill (at map reference 687896) to the south-west of Bridgnorth, at 00.29 hrs. The trainee crew took off from their base at 21.50 hrs the previous evening and were, presumably, on the Chipping Norton–Conwy leg when the pilot is believed to have lost control 'due to atmospheric conditions' and fatigue ('due to the amount of recent flying'). The force of the crash was such that only three bodies were recovered by RAF Bridgnorth's medical officer.

Sgt (pilot) William Shepherd (1551889), RAFVR, aged 21, was the son of William and Janet Gillespie Shepherd of Edinburgh. He is commemorated on the Runnymede Memorial, Berkshire.

Sgt (Nav) Francis George Wells (953542), RAFVR, aged 26, was the son of George and Elizabeth Wells and the husband of Iris Wells (née Watkins) of Hall Green, Birmingham. He is commemorated on the Runnymede Memorial, Berkshire.

Sgt (AB) George Donald Morrow (R.163708), RCAF, aged 26, was the son of Gilbert R and Dollina Morrow of Big Beaver, Saskatchewan, Canada. He is buried in Chester (Blacon) Cemetery.

Sgt (W/AG) Walter Henry Lawrence (1388668), RAFVR, aged 19, was the son of John Thomas and Susan Lawrence of Walthamstow, Essex. He is buried in Chester (Blacon) Cemetery.

Sgt (AG) Norman Leslie Wachter (425911), RAAF, aged 19, was the son of Leslie Harry Otto and Ivy May Wachter of Kenmore, Queensland, Australia. He is buried in Chester (Blacon) Cemetery.

12 September (Sunday)
Bombing exercise. 61 OTU (RAF Rednal, Shropshire)
Supermarine Spitfire IA (R7127, presentation aircraft named *Plymouth*) crashed on the airfield at 17.21 hrs. Two pilots were practising bombing in the vicinity of Rednal airfield when the pilot of this aircraft 'disobeyed orders given by his CO and approached the target area from incorrect angle', colliding with a Spitfire (X4173) which was 'cutting in and out of turn.' The aircraft was immediately sent crashing out of control onto the airfield, while the pilot of Spitfire X4173 was able to maintain control and made an emergency landing.

Sgt (pilot u/t) Donald Gordon Keith (1337715), RAFVR, aged 22, was the son of David Harold and Florence Sarah Keith of Walthamstow, London. He is buried in Walthamstow (Queen's Road) Cemetery.

Bombing exercise. 61 OTU (RAF Rednal, Shropshire)
Supermarine Spitfire IA (X4173) landed at the airfield following the collision described above.

Sgt (pilot u/t) Trygve Marthinsen (1742), RNoAF. After completing his operational training he flew Spitfires with 331 (Norwegian) Squadron and survived the war.

13 September (Monday)
Cross-country exercise from Base-Reading-Conway-Reading-Base and practice bombing on the local range. 12 OTU (RAF Chipping Warden, Oxfordshire)
Vickers Wellington III (BJ664) crashed on Burrow Hill (at map reference 382831), near Aston on Clun, at 15.45 hrs. The trainee crew took off at 13.50 hrs with an additional three 'screened' crew members, who had operational experience and were on board to help instruct and pass on their experience. While flying from Conwy to Reading the crew ran into a severe thunderstorm over south Shropshire and, as the aircraft passed over Lydbury North at a fairly low level, a vivid flash was seen to strike the aircraft. From that point onwards it was observed on fire and losing height, before cutting a swathe through the trees on the hilltop and disintegrating.

F/Lt (screened pilot) John Edwin Fairchild (129115), RAFVR, aged 28, was the son of Edwin C and Ethel M Fairchild of Kensington, London, and the husband of Alice Doreen Fairchild (née Langley). He is buried in Chester (Blacon) Cemetery.

Sgt (pilot) Clifford Stanley Walters (1415639), RAFVR, aged 21, was the son of Harry Trevor and Clara Elizabeth Walters of Monmouth. He is buried in Monmouth Church Cemetery, Monmouthshire.

F/Lt (screened navigator) Raymond Thomas Bowen (109017), RAFVR, aged 22, was born in Willesden, Middlesex. He is buried in Chester (Blacon) Cemetery.

Sgt (Nav) Eric Gates (1446136), RAFVR, aged 21, was the son of Harry Gates, DCM and Gertrude L Gates of St Ives, Huntingdonshire. He is buried in St Ives Public Cemetery.

Sgt (AB) Edward Alan Opie (R.131859), RCAF, aged 30, was the son of Edward Trevose Opie and Margaret Opie of Red Deer, Alberta. He is buried in Chester (Blacon) Cemetery.

F/Sgt (screened W/AG) Bernard Green (944129), RAFVR, aged 23, was the son of Joseph and Gertrude Green and the husband of Margaret Alice Green of Lenton, Nottingham. He is buried in South Kilworth (St Nicholas) Churchyard, Leicestershire.

Sgt (W/AG) Ellis Davies (1578847), RAFVR, aged 21, was the son of Lawrence and Elizabeth Davies. He is buried in Rhondda (Trealaw) Cemetery, Glamorganshire.

Sgt (AG) Tom Johnston (533353), RAF, aged 24, was the son of William and Anne Johnston of St John's, Surrey. He is buried in Chester (Blacon) Cemetery.

15 September (Wednesday)
'DM flying'. 5 (P)AFU (RAF Tern Hill, Shropshire)
Miles Master I (T8453) crash-landed at 'Low Farm, Ash', near Whitchurch, at 15.00 hrs. During the course of the flight the engine failed, due to a glycol leak, and the instructor was forced to crash-land while trying to avoid trees. Both occupants were slightly injured and taken to Tern Hill sick quarters by RAF Tilstock's ambulance.

Sgt (instructor pilot) Leslie Steele Raven (R.139445), RCAF, was born in Canada, on 1 March 1915. He enlisted in December 1941 and had sailed to the UK in March 1943. Little is known of his military career other than that he was repatriated to Canada in November 1944 and demobbed in March 1945.

P/O (pilot u/t) Colin Osborne Bibby (152363), RAFVR, was born on 30 November 1922 and lived at 40 Canterbury Avenue in Sheffield and was studying at university when he enlisted. On completion of his training, he flew Mustangs with 19 Squadron but, on 18 September 1944, was shot down over Tilburg in the Netherlands and taken prisoner. After receiving treatment for a dislocated shoulder in Utrecht Hospital, he spent the remainder of the war in various POW camps. He returned to the UK at the end of the war and died in Sheffield in September 1985.

16 September (Thursday)
Formation flying and R/T homings. 60 OTU (RAF High Ercall, Shropshire)
De Havilland Mosquito II (DD678) crashed at Stone House Farm near Bings Heath, to the south of Shawbury, at 18.52 hrs. The pilot finished formation flying with another Mosquito and then began 'throwing the aircraft about as though with the intention of starting a dogfight'. It was during a tight turn at 1,000–1,500 feet, while trying to get onto the other aircraft's tail, that the pilot entered a high-speed stall and crashed out of control. In the subsequent court of inquiry the crash was attributed to the pilot's performing unauthorised manoeuvres, adding that 'pilot boys being pilot boys, the temptation to throw the aircraft about became irresistible'.

F/O (pilot u/t) Peter Royce Wilmot (421953), RAAF, aged 21, was the son of Harold Royce and Hilda Annie Wilmot of Canberra, Australia. He is buried in Chester (Blacon) Cemetery.

F/O Peter Wilmot [TNA]

17 September (Friday)
Cine-gun exercise. HQ Squadron, 2906th Observation Training Group (Station 342, Atcham, Shropshire)
Republic P-47D Thunderbolt (42-7978) crashed at Shirlett Farm, two miles east of Much Wenlock, at 13.45 hrs. Two aircraft took off together for a routine cine-gun exercise, with the pilot of 42-7930 (Flight Officer Reese) acting as the target aircraft and the pilot of this aircraft making astern attacks. According to Flight Officer Reese's account provided for the investigation,

> I was stooging for Zollinger flying straight and level doing about 200 mph. All of a sudden there was a terrific shock and the next instant I was in a left-hand spin and my engine was burning. Up until this time, my aircraft was functioning perfectly.
>
> When I finally got the hood back and my safety harness undone, the aircraft had made a turn or a turn-and-

The smouldering remains of one of the P-47s at Shirlett Farm, near Much Wenlock. [USAAF]

a-half. I bounced off the wing and waited until I thought I was clear, then pulled the rip cord. Upon landing I ran directly to the other aircraft, but it was a blazing inferno and a few minutes after I arrived, it exploded.

Ernest G Evans of Marsh Brasley, who also witnessed the crash and gave an account for the investigation, described how

> ... one was slightly behind the other and all at once the one in the rear picked up speed and came up under the other. Then they separated and I saw one man out on the wing. He jumped and I saw him fall and his parachute opened. Next the two planes crashed and caught fire. I went to the scene to do what bit I could. I went to the pilot that jumped and he said he wasn't hurt but wanted to get the other chap. We went to the plane but couldn't do nothing because the flames were too fierce. The pilot wanted to get to this chap but I held him away because the flames were too bad. We then rolled up his parachute and the ambulance came up. We got him to get in the ambulance, put his parachute in with him and the ambulance took him somewhere.

Flight Officer (pilot u/t) Ernest T Zollinger (T-190899), USAAF, aged 24, was the son of Swiss-born Theodore John Zollinger and his Irish wife, Margaret, of St Matthews, Jefferson County, Kentucky. He is buried in Cambridge (Madingley) Cemetery. His brother, Henry Theodore Zollinger, was killed on 27 November 1944, serving as an aviation radioman in the Pacific.

Cine-gun exercise. HQ Squadron, 2906th Observation Training Group (Station 342, Atcham, Shropshire)
Republic P-47D Thunderbolt (42-7930) crashed at Shirlett Farm, two miles east of Much Wenlock, following the incident described above.

Flight Officer (pilot u/t) William H Reese (T-190895), USAAF. After completing his training he was posted to the 83rd Fighter Squadron, 78th Fighter Group and was killed on 11 April 1944 piloting a P-47 (41-6210) over Germany. His body was repatriated to America after the war for burial in Arlington Cemetery, Virginia.

17 September (Friday)
'Canopy' searchlight co-operation exercise. 7 AACU (RAF Montford Bridge, Shropshire)
Airspeed Oxford I (X6864) crashed at West Farm, one mile south of Montford Bridge airfield, at 21.20 hrs. While approaching the airfield to land, on a very dark night, the pilot allowed the aircraft to strike the top of a tree and a barn before crashing into an orchard.

Sgt (pilot) William Richard John Spry (1162047), RAFVR, aged 32, was the son of Mr and Mrs William Spry and the husband of Jane Lilian Spry (née Kent). He is buried in Horsley (St Martin) Cemetery, Gloucestershire.

18 September (Saturday)
Practice night attacks. 60 OTU (RAF High Ercall, Shropshire)
De Havilland Mosquito NF.II (HJ703) belly-landed at 'The Hill', between Longdon on Tern and Isombridge, at 02.40 hrs. Moments after taking off from the airfield the aircraft's port engine failed due

to the pilot's 'not changing over from outer to main [fuel] tanks' and he was forced to belly-land in a turnip field.

P/O (pilot) John Humphrey Curwin Cockton (135715), RAFVR. Born in Cambridge on 25 April 1917, he survived the war and relinquished his commission as a flight lieutenant in 1949. He died in Whitehaven in 1985.

Sgt (Nav) Eric Edward Jenner (1321918), RAFVR. He was killed while still undergoing training at High Ercall on 14 October, when his Mosquito (HJ617) crashed in Leicestershire during a cross-country flight. Sgt Jenner was twenty years old and is buried in Burton-on-the-Wolds Cemetery.

22 September (Wednesday)
Circuits and landings. 83 OTU (RAF Peplow, Shropshire)
Vickers Wellington X (LN530) crashed near Ellerton Hall, Hinstock, at 10.30 hrs. The trainee crew had just taken off from the airfield when the starboard engine seized due to a mechanical failure and, as the pilot attempted to avoid some trees, the aircraft stalled and crashed, killing both pilots instantly. The three remaining crew members were treated for their injuries but Sgt Whyte succumbed later that day in RAF Hospital, Cosford.

Sgt (pilot) David Lambert Spence (1559800), RAFVR, aged 26, was the son of George and Jean Spence (née Lambert) of Knightswood, Glasgow. After leaving school he followed his father into the shipyards and worked as a sheet metal worker before volunteering for the RAFVR. According to his daughter he was a keen golfer, swimmer and amateur boxer (which he had to give up at his wife's insistence!). He is buried in Renfrew (Arkleston) Cemetery.

P/O (pilot) Andrew Mather McBride (152200), RAFVR, aged 21, was the son of Robert and Jeanie McBride of Jerviston, Motherwell. He is buried in Dalziel (Airbles) Cemetery, Lanarkshire.

Sgt Robert Whyte (1345028), RAFVR, aged 21, is buried in New Stevenston (St Patrick's) Roman Catholic Cemetery, Lanarkshire. His next of kin are unknown.

Sgt (AG) Charles Winton (1571247), RAFVR. Little is known of this NCO other than that he survived the war and visited Sgt Spence's widow twice after the accident.

The name of the other crew member is unknown.

22 September (Wednesday)
Training flight. 5 (P)AFU (RAF Tern Hill, Shropshire)
Miles Master II (AZ790) force-landed at Lynn Farm near Great Chatwell, between Newport and Sheriffhales, at 14.20 hrs. The pilot was performing a slow roll when the engine failed, possibly as a result of water contamination of the fuel (caused by condensation in the fuel system), forcing him to belly-land in a field.

A collage of what is thought to be Sgt Spence's crew of the Wellington LN530 at Peplow – Sgt Winton is seen on the right of the picture with Sgt Spence over his shoulder. The other three remain unidentified. [Billie Spence]

F/O (pilot u/t) James Joseph King (131039), RAFVR, was killed on 5 January 1944 in a mid-air collision over the Wrekin and further information on him can be found under that date.

23 September (Thursday)
Navigation exercise. 3 (O)AFU (RAF Halfpenny Green, Staffordshire)
Avro Anson I (DJ669) crash-landed near Wroxeter at 11.45 hrs. The crew had been in the air for two hours and fifty minutes when the pupil bomb aimer released a practice bomb while the bomb doors were still closed, causing it to 'hang up' in the bomb bay. In an attempt to release the bomb safely the pilot followed the River Severn as he tried to jettison it but, as he did so, he failed to notice some high tension power cables spanning the river. The resulting collision, which plunged the nearby Atcham Sector HQ ops room into darkness, caused such damage to the aircraft that the pilot had to crash-land in a field ahead. Fortunately, the entire crew survived, although the wireless operator was treated for minor burns to his face in RAF Hospital, Cosford. As a result of the accident, disciplinary action was taken against the bomb aimer and the pilot also received a logbook endorsement for 'gross carelessness'.

Sgt (staff pilot) Kenneth Norman Sanders (1318752), RAFVR, had force-landed an Anson near Bridgnorth on 9 June 1943 and further information on him can be found under that entry.

Sgt (W/AG u/t) John George Frederick Toll (1324335), RAFVR. After recovering from his injuries and completing his training he was posted to 78 Squadron. He was killed on 13 August 1944, in a Halifax (LV957) which was lost on an op to Braunschweig. Sgt Toll was the husband of Irene L Bidnell and is buried in Becklingen Cemetery, Germany.

The name of the bomb aimer is unknown.

26 September (Sunday)
Altitude formation training. HQ Squadron, 2906th Observation Training Group (Station 342, Atcham, Shropshire)
Republic P-47D Thunderbolt (42-7971, bearing the fuselage code DQ-G) force-landed at Beslow Farm, south of the airfield, at 15.25 hrs. The flight had taken off at 14.10 hrs and, twenty minutes into the exercise, the flight leader called for a fuel check, which was carried out. At that point, the pilot of this aircraft, who was flying in number four position, decided to switch to his main fuel tanks, despite still having approximately twenty gallons left in his reserve tanks. Having completed their training exercise, the flight returned towards the airfield but, as they did so, the engine of this aircraft began cutting due to a shortage of fuel. The pilot immediately switched to reserve tanks and operated the boost pump (not realising that this only worked on the main tank), but the engine cut completely. By now, at only 800 feet, he quickly

... decided to turn into the field and try an approach. I called the Control on my R/T but got no response. When I finished my turn, I saw that I could not make a normal glide approach and as I was on the side of the field where there is a power line among other obstruc-

Thunderbolt 42-7971 pictured as it came to rest in a field at Beslow Farm. [USAAF]

tions, I decided it was better to overshoot the airport than to undershoot. I kept my speed well up so that I could manoeuvre into a clear field. After turning to miss a few trees and a house, I tried to get into a field but dropped about 10 feet short went through a hedge and across a road into a potato field.

The subsequent investigation concluded that the pilot showed poor technique, due to inexperience, but added that his flight leader showed bad judgment in calling a fuel check so soon into the flight.

Staff Sgt (pilot u/t) Evan DeVon 'Mac' McMinn (10601326), USAAF. On completion of his training he was posted to the 61st Fighter Squadron, 56th Fighter Group and, flying P-47s over north-west Europe, was credited with five enemy aircraft destroyed and one damaged. He was killed on D-Day, piloting a P-47 (42-8458), which was shot down by flak over Normandy. Lt McMinn, who was the son of Mr and Mrs William T McMinn, is buried in Pittsburgh.

28 September (Tuesday)
'Bullseye' exercise. 81 OTU (RAF Tilstock, Shropshire)
Armstrong Whitworth Whitley V (EB404) landed at RAF High Ercall following a mid-air collision. The crew took off at 20.10 hrs, under the supervision of a screened navigator, for a 'Bullseye' exercise, which involved Beaufighters from 406 Squadron intercepting a formation of aircraft and making mock attacks. At 23.15 hrs, whilst coned by searchlights approximately ten miles west of Shrewsbury, the Whitley crew noticed a 'slight bump' which, in fact, proved to be one of the attacking Beaufighters (call sign Snooker 17) clipping the Whitley's port engine with its own port wing tip. A short while later the port engine failed, as a result of a severed oil pipe, and the pilot requested a 'Darky' (homing) signal to direct him to the nearest airfield, before telling his crew that they could bale out if they wished. This they did, at approximately 7,000 feet, except for Sgt Scott, who remained with the pilot to assist in the emergency landing, which was carried out without incident at RAF High Ercall. For his 'calmness, judgement and skill in [the] emergency' the pilot was recommended for a 'green' logbook notation. Meanwhile, the remainder of the crew had parachuted to safety except for the navigator who, tragically, is thought to have suffered a spill, or struck some trees, before landing and broke his neck. His body was discovered at 08.30 hrs the following morning on the north-west corner of Bridleway Gate airfield.

Sgt (pilot) Dudley Charles Gibbons (1317212), RAFVR, was commissioned in February 1944 and subsequently posted to 166 Squadron. He was shot down on 13 July 1944 piloting a Lancaster (LM388) on an op to Revigny, France. After parachuting to safety, along with two of his crew, P/O Gibbons managed to evade capture for the following weeks, before eventually reaching Allied lines.

P/O (screened Nav) James McGregor Freckleton (149671), DFM, RAFVR. His DFM was awarded in October 1943 for services with 100 Squadron. Following his rest period as a navigator instructor at Tilstock he was posted to 49 Squadron for a second tour of ops, but was killed on 22 June 1944 when his Lancaster (ME808) was lost during an op to Wesseling, Germany. F/O Freckleton is buried in Schoonselhof Cemetery alongside his crew.

F/O (Nav) George Albert Wallace (J.22912), RCAF, aged 32, was the son of George Wellington Wallace and Lucy Copping Wallace and the husband of Doris Audrey Irwin Wallace of Hamilton, Ontario. He is buried in Chester (Blacon) Cemetery.

F/O George Wallace [Library & Archives Canada]

Sgt (AB) C T Rose (1557436), RAFVR. Posted to 166 Squadron along with P/O D C Gibbons, he too was shot down on 13 July 1944, survived and evaded capture until reaching Allied lines.

Sgt (W/AG) Reginald Frederick Scott (1392909), RAFVR. Posted to 166

Squadron along with P/O D C Gibbons, he was killed on 13 July 1944 in Lancaster LM388. F/Sgt Scott, who was 20 years old and the son of Herbert William and Phoebe Scott, is buried in Vitry-le-Croise Churchyard, France.

Sgt (AG mid upper) A C Summers (1135092), RAFVR. Nothing further is known of this airman other than that he survived the war.

Sgt (AG rear) Edwin Ashton (1892578), RAFVR. Posted to 166 Squadron along with P/O A C Gibbons, he was killed on 13 July 1944 and lies alongside F/Sgt Scott in Vitry-le-Croise Churchyard, France. Sgt Ashton was nineteen years old and the son of Henry and Gertrude Emma Ashton of Rainham, Kent.

1 October (Friday)
Practice forced landings. 5 (P)AFU (RAF Tern Hill, Shropshire)
Miles Master I (T8486) crashed at Holmer Farm, Stirchley (at map reference 706066, in modern-day Telford), at 14.30 hrs. After allowing his pupil pilot to carry out a practice forced landing outside the allocated low-flying area, the instructor then let the pupil descend too low before opening up the throttles to climb away and the aircraft struck some high tension power cables and crashed. Local schoolboy, Warwick Tart, who lived in Stirchley, recalled:

> I was sitting on a hill called Grange Mound with my mate Dennis Dabbs from Aqueduct. We were looking in a southerly direction when we saw this flash in the distance. Apparently the plane had been flying around all morning. There was an instructor and a young pilot and he went under the cables of, you know, those large pylons and I think the tail just caught the cable and there was a big flash. My friend [Walford Phillips] wasn't far off and he was first to it. According to him the ambulance arrived and took away the two crew, and he learned later that one of them had died.

F/Sgt (instructor pilot) Edwin Fairclough (1217962), RAFVR, aged 22, was the son of Alfred Gregory and Hannah Fairclough of Sheffield. He had been posted to the unit as an instructor on 26 May 1943. He is commemorated at the Sheffield Crematorium.

Sgt (pilot u/t) Alan John Harris (1585528), RAFVR, recovered from his injuries and remained in the RAF after the war, receiving the Queen's Commendation for Valuable Service in the Air in June 1955 and the Air Force Cross in January 1960. He retired as a flight lieutenant in January 1963.

3 October (Sunday)
Air Ministry civilian employee (RAF Shawbury, Shropshire)
This civilian contractor is believed to have been trimming a hedge on the southern edge of Shawbury airfield, near the Carradine Road, when an aircraft came in at hedge height for an emergency landing and struck him as he warned his workmates to jump clear.

Walter Henry (Harry) Edgerton, aged 61, was the son of Samuel and Elizabeth Edgerton of Barkers Green and the husband of Martha Edgerton (née Huxley) of Fir Tree Cottage, Lower Road, Myddle. Born in Wem, in 1882, he had previously worked for McAlpines (who helped to build the hangars at RAF Shawbury in 1936) but, after construction finished, he started work for the Air Ministry as a general labourer at the airfield. He is buried in Wem (Rural) Cemetery.

4 October (Monday)
Training flight. 7 (P)AFU (RAF Peterborough, Cambridgeshire)
Miles Master II (DK812) force-landed on 'Walton [or Worthen?] Hill, 4 1/2 miles south-east of Welshpool', at 17.00 hrs. Having encountered an unexpected area of bad weather the pilot continued to fly on despite his having been told to return to base or land at the nearest airfield if bad weather was encountered. As the weather continued to deteriorate he decided to belly-land on a hillside and, as a

result of his disobedience of orders, his logbook was endorsed for 'carelessness'.

Sgt (pilot u/t) Ashton Irving Cohen (R.161592), RCAF, was born in Canada on 24 August 1923 and was posted to the UK in June 1943. After completing his training he was posted to 419 Squadron but was killed on 9 October 1944 when his Lancaster (KB754) was shot down by a night fighter on an op to Bochum, Germany. P/O Cohen is buried in Reichswald War Cemetery alongside six of his crew.

8 October (Friday)
Formation flying. 5 (P)AFU (RAF Tern Hill, Shropshire)
Miles Master II (AZ799) crashed at 'Moreton crossroads', near Bletchley, to the west of Market Drayton, at 14.33 hrs. A formation of eight aircraft, each piloted by an instructor and pupil, had taken off at 13.40 hrs to practise formation flying. After fifty minutes in the air, during which several changes of formation took place, the aircraft formed into 'squadron echelon port' at 1,500 feet and continued in this manner for three minutes. A correction of position was then made by number three, who banked to the left, and this bank was performed by each aircraft in turn until reaching number seven, who found that number eight was too close to him. To avoid number six banking into the side of him, he climbed but, at the same time, number eight also climbed and allowed his front fuselage and then wing tip to strike the canopy of number seven. The collision sheared three feet of wing tip off and sent the aircraft crashing out of control. Fortunately, number seven was able to maintain control, and carried out an emergency landing at the airfield with his front hood and windscreen badly damaged.

Sgt (instructor pilot) Derek Vaughan Joyes (1293477), RAFVR, aged 21, was the son of Archibald and Gladys Joyes of Maida Vale, London. He is buried in Kensall Green (All Souls) Cemetery, London.

F/Sgt (pilot u/t) Frederick John Linden (425174), RAAF, aged 22, was the son of Frederick George and Annie Linden of Bardon, a suburb of Brisbane, and the husband of Cicely Linden of Calgary, Canada (whom he had presumably met during training there). He is buried in Chester (Blacon) Cemetery.

Formation flying. 5 (P)AFU (RAF Tern Hill, Shropshire)
Miles Master II (AZ661) landed at Tern Hill airfield following the incident described above.

F/Lt (instructor pilot) Miroslav Kopecky (107246), RAFVR, was a Czechoslovakian national who had flown Hurricanes during the Battle of Britain with 111 and 253 Squadrons. After completing his posting at Tern Hill he was posted to 310 Squadron, flying Spitfires, and ended the war with the rank of flight lieutenant.

P/O (pilot u/t) Richard Walter Vokey (J25397), RCAF. On completion of his training he was posted to 439 (RCAF) Squadron but was killed on his third op on 24 September 1944, piloting a Typhoon (PD465) on a ground attack sortie over Holland. F/O Vokey, who was twenty-one years old and the son of John Philip and Catherine Vokey of Montreal, is buried in Bergen-op-Zoom Canadian War Cemetery, Netherlands.

10 October (Sunday)
Dual instructional training. 11 (P)AFU (RAF Condover, Shropshire, satellite to RAF Shawbury)
Airspeed Oxford II (T1097) force-landed at Battlefield on the northern outskirts of Shrewsbury, at 10.35 hrs. After being ordered by his flight commander to carry out the training flight in the vicinity of the airfield, the instructor disobeyed the order, became totally lost and had to make a precautionary landing in a field. The aircraft was undamaged but the field was deemed too small to risk taking off and, as a consequence, it had to be salvaged, while the instructor was 'disciplined' for disobeying orders.

Sgt (instructor pilot) J H Telford (R.139019), RCAF.

The name of the pupil pilot is unknown.

15 October (Friday)
Glider towing training. 5 GTS (RAF Shobdon, Herefordshire)
Miles Master II (EM302) force-landed at Moat Farm, Alcaston, to the north of Craven Arms, at 17.20 hrs. While towing a glider on a routine exercise, the pilot became lost in bad weather and, after failing to use his radio to get directions back to the airfield, decided to force-land when his fuel began running low. Local schoolboy, Henry Hand, who lived in the village at the time, recalled:

> I was in the garden and we heard the aeroplane coming over. It was the time of the flying bombs, you know, so I got taken indoors. There was a glider being towed and then they separated. The glider landed separately but the plane, it just missed the electric cables and then he landed through a hedge. It came to a halt, with leaves and branches from the hedge that he had crashed through in the engine.
>
> There was a debate amongst the grown-ups as to whether he'd done the wrong thing. He got down safely, so I should imagine that he hadn't put his wheels up. The four airmen were brought in, two in each plane. They came in and I remember they had bacon and eggs, but the one, he kept being ill because he was suffering from shock.

Sgt (pilot) Basil Herbert Silverthorne (1339959), RAFVR. Born in Wilton, Wiltshire, on 27 August 1924, he died in London in 1993.

The name of the second crew member is unknown.

15 October (Friday)
Towing training. 5 GTS (RAF Shobdon, Herefordshire)
General Aircraft GAL.48 Hotspur II glider (HH520) force-landed south-west of Alcaston following the incident described above.

F/Sgt (instructor pilot) Richard Ian Trotter (953581), RAFVR. He emigrated to the USA after the war to live in Alabama with his wife whom he had met whilst undergoing pilot training there in 1942.

Cpl (pilot u/t) J Nunn (1871217), GPR.

19 October (Tuesday)
Cross-country exercise. 11 (P)AFU (RAF Shawbury, Shropshire)
Airspeed Oxford II (V3671) force-landed near Broseley at 17.35 hrs. After becoming lost in deteriorating weather conditions the pilot made a precautionary landing in a field, from which the aircraft had to be salvaged.

Sgt (pilot u/t) Leonard Latham (1534009), RAFVR. Nothing further is known of this pilot other than that he survived the war.

20 October (Wednesday)
Aerobatics training. HQ Squadron, 2906th Observation Training Group (Station 342, Atcham, Shropshire)
Republic P-47C Thunderbolt (41-6619, bearing the fuselage code VM-I?) crash-landed at Baschurch at 09.30 hrs. The pilot had completed his training and was returning to the airfield when, at 6,000 feet, his engine began to run rough due to a lack of fuel. According to his statement he changed from auxiliary to main fuel tanks but the engine continued to run rough, so he

> ... called control and told them I was going to attempt a forced landing. I turned back to more open country. I was gliding at 150 mph when I hit telephone wires. I did not see the wires or I could have pulled up. I hit the ground and bounced over the tops of two adjoining hedges on a corner of a field. I took the tops off these two hedges. I landed again in the next field and came to a stop upon hitting a third hedge.

Following the subsequent inspection of the aircraft it was concluded that the pilot 'either did not change tanks or did not turn the selector tank to the proper position' as the main tank was found to be full and fuel flowed freely when selected.

1 Lt (pilot u/t) Boyd W Sorenson (O-886086), USAAF. On completion of his training he flew P-47s out of Duxford with the 83rd Fighter Squadron, 78th Fighter Group and was credited with one enemy aircraft shared destroyed on 25 April 1944.

Thunderbolt 41-6619 pictured as it came to rest in a hedgerow at Baschurch. [USAAF]

4 November (Thursday)
Unknown flight detail. 7 AACU (RAF Montford Bridge, Shropshire – detached flight). Airspeed Oxford (V387?) force-landed at Weston Farm on the southern outskirts of Oswestry.
After encountering very bad weather conditions the pilot carried out a precautionary landing, for which he was commended for 'superior airmanship'.

W/O (pilot) Jerzy Jablonowski (783184), PAF. Born in Chrostowo Zalesie, Poland on 20 January 1919, he was undergoing pilot training at the time of the German invasion of Poland and was involved in evacuating aircraft from Warsaw to various landing grounds. Following the fall of his country he fled to France, where he was stationed at St Jacques, near Rennes, before escaping to the UK, via North Africa. On completion of his pilot training, in the UK, he was posted to 309 Polish Army Cooperation Squadron and served with the unit in Scotland until the spring of 1942. He then served with various units, including 7 AACU, before being posted to 305 (Polish) Squadron in April 1944 and completing a tour of ops flying Mosquitos over north-west Europe. In October 1944 he was attached to 577 Squadron (which had formed from the amalgamation of Nos. 6, 7 and 8 AACUs) flying anti-aircraft co-operation flights before being sent on a Lancaster conversion course. In May 1945 he joined 300 (Polish) Squadron and was involved, among other things, in the repatriation of British POWs. He continued to serve in the Royal Air Force after the war and died in Stroud, Gloucestershire, in 1996.

W/O Jerzy Jablonowski [Marian Jablonowski]

4 November (Thursday)
Visit to Towyn, Merionethshire. 'Q' Flight, 61 OTU (RAF Rednal, Shropshire)
Gloster Gladiator I (K8004) force-landed at Park Hall Farm to the north-east of Oswestry, at 17.00 hrs.
On 13 October 1943 the film company, Independent Producers, arrived at RAF Rednal to begin shooting a film adaptation of the book *Signed with their Honour* (by James Aldridge), which chronicled the air war over Greece between 1940 and 1941. Ten Gladiators and one Wellington were assigned to 61 OTU and designated as 'Q' Flight, with the Wellington used as a filming platform while the aircraft flew over Shropshire and mid Wales. The unit remained at Rednal until January 1944 but, for unknown reasons, the film was never completed. This flight appears to have been unconnected with any filming and occurred when the pilot was caught up in 'exceptional weather conditions' and attempted to make a

One of 'Q' Flight's Gladiators pictured at RAF Rednal during filming of Signed with their Honour. *F/Lt 'Dutch' Kleimeyer (who survived a mid air collision over mid Wales) is pictured in the cream flight suit, standing fifth from left, and S/Ldr Richard Acworth is standing to his left wearing a cap. [Ian Simpson]*

precautionary landing. As he approached to land, he failed to see some high-tension power cables through the thick fog and collided with them, crashing into a field and suffering injuries.

F/Lt (pilot) Hugh Dudley Wanklyn 'Twinstead' Flower (41390), AFC, RAF. Born in Kensington, London, on 5 March 1914, he had joined the RAF in 1938 and was commissioned on the day war was declared. Posted to Egypt with 80 Squadron in December 1939, he flew Gladiators as part of air defence duties against the Italians and was credited with a probable on 8 August 1940 over El Gobi. After moving to Greece later in the year he destroyed an Italian CR.42 on 28 November and, following the squadron's conversion to Hurricanes, in February 1941, he claimed a further one destroyed and one shared. After the fall of mainland Greece and then Crete, he succeeded in escaping to the Middle East where he was posted to 71 OTU, Ismailia, as an instructor in June 1941. The next two years were spent instructing at Ismailia and, in January 1943, he was awarded the Air Force Cross for his services with the unit. In early 1943 he was posted back to the UK but little else is known of his subsequent movements other than that he survived the war and attained the rank of squadron leader. He died in Essex in 1988.

4 November (Thursday)

Low flying cross-country exercise. 11 (P)AFU (RAF Shawbury, Shropshire)

Airspeed Oxford I (BG554) force-landed 'one mile north west of Nesscliffe' (putting it in the area around Wolfshead) at 17.45 hrs. This was the unit's last accident before its move to RAF Calveley in Cheshire and occurred when the instructor became lost during an exercise for which he had 'taken off without being authorised to do so'. Unable to establish his position, due to the foggy weather and failing light, the instructor belly-landed the aircraft in a field. The occupants stepped out unhurt.

F/Sgt (instructor pilot) Wallace Fred Woodman (1315088), RAFVR, was born in Devon in 1921. He survived the war and died in Taunton, Somerset in 2001.

Sgt (pilot u/t?) James Hope Laidlaw (1391356), RAFVR. Born in Dumfriesshire in 1914, he was commissioned in December 1944 and survived the war, resigning his commission as a flying officer in April 1948.

P/O (pilot u/t?) William Swindburne Bateson (153085), RAFVR, remained in the RAF after the war, receiving the King's Commendation for Valuable Service in the Air in August 1946. He eventually relinquished his commission as a flight lieutenant in May 1959.

7 November (Sunday)
Ground-Controlled Interception (GCI) exercise. 5 (P)AFU (RAF Tern Hill, Shropshire)
Avro Anson I N4934 crashed at Longford Farm (at wartime map reference 645335) to the north west of the airfield, at 14.05 hrs. P/O Rothwell took off at 13.55 hrs, with two pupil pilots accompanying him to gain navigational experience and one ground crew NCO riding as passenger. After leaving the ground the pilot began a normal climbing turn away from the airfield but, unknown to him, he was flying into the path of a Miles Master, which was making a circuit of the airfield 900 feet above him. The two pilots continued converging until a collision occurred, which tore off the Anson's port wing and the Master's starboard wing tip, sending the two aircraft crashing out of control. Mr Martin, who was a schoolboy at the time, recalled in a conversation with the author that

> ... they hit one another above 11-acre field and crashed in it. We found one's gold watch six months after and we handed it in back up at Tern Hill. It's up Fordhall lane. One crashed at the top end of the field, the other crashed at the bottom of the same field. I think they were there for about a week or so getting rid of it.

F/Lt Verdun McDonald [Phyllis Marie Smyth]

P/O (instructor pilot) John Rothwell (413990), RNZAF, aged 24, was the son of Thomas Green Rothwell and Agnes Rothwell, and the husband of Nancy Ethel Dorothy Rothwell of Orakei, Auckland. Before his posting to Tern Hill in February 1943 he had completed two ops in May 1942 while on a brief attachment to 12 Squadron. He is buried in Chester (Blacon) Cemetery.

F/Sgt (pilot u/t) Clement James Walsh (425470), RAAF, aged 21, was the son of Adam and Amelia Walsh of Sandgate, Queensland. He is buried in Chester (Blacon) Cemetery.

F/Lt (pilot u/t) Verdun Frederick McDonald (J.3711), RCAF, aged 27, was the son of Robert Donald and Mary McDonald and the husband of Phyllis Marie McDonald of Saskatoon, Saskatchewan. Having enlisted in the RCAF in June 1940 he had been selected for instructor duties after gaining his wings. He subsequently instructed at various units, between September 1941 and June 1943, before being posted to the UK to prepare for operations. He is buried in Chester (Blacon) Cemetery.

Cpl ('WE Mechanic' riding as passenger) Lawrence Allan Manners (1485911), RAFVR, aged 22, was the son of Arthur and Elsie Manners of Bramhall, Cheshire. He is buried in Stand (All Saints) Churchyard, Lancashire.

P/O John Rothwell. [Auckland Museum Cenotaph]

Circuits and landings
5 (P)AFU (RAF Tern Hill, Shropshire). Miles Master II (EM281) crashed at Longford Farm (at wartime map reference 644334) after colliding in the incident described above.

F/O (instructor pilot) James Orville Cross (J.24116), RCAF, aged 27, was the son of George V and Gertrude A Cross of Windsor, Ontario. He had been posted to the unit as an instructor on 29 September 1943. He is buried in Chester (Blacon) Cemetery.

F/Sgt (pilot u/t) Denis Frank Carter (658594), RAF, aged 24, was the son of Arthur and Lois Hannah Carter of Guilden Morden, Cambridgeshire. This was only his first dual flight in a Miles Master but he was 'an experienced bomber pilot who had acted as first pilot on Lancasters both over Germany and Italy and on operational flights'. He was presumably re-training for fighter aircraft duties. He is buried in Braintree and Bocking (Braintree) Cemetery, Essex.

10 November (Wednesday)
Training flight. 5 (P)AFU (RAF Tern Hill, Shropshire)
Miles Master I (T8452) belly-landed at Soulton Hall between Wem and Prees Green, at 11.00 hrs. The pilot belly-landed in a field after the engine began to smoke and then failed during the flight.

Sgt (pilot u/t) Dennis A L Coles (1323112), RAFVR, was born in Chipping Sodbury, in 1922. Nothing is known of his military service other than that he survived the war.

11 November (Thursday)
Training flight. 5 (P)AFU (RAF Tern Hill, Shropshire)
Miles Master II (AZ251) force-landed at Longford Farm to the north west of the airfield, at 12.45 hrs. The pilot force-landed after the engine failed, due to a blown plug adaptor. According to Mr Martin, who was the farmer's son, the aeroplane came across the Longford Road and crashed through a hedge, just missing a tree.

P/O (pilot u/t) Ronald Winston Woolford (51127), RAFVR, survived the war and attained the rank of flight lieutenant.

12 November (Friday)
Transit flight back to base. 1659 HCU (RAF Topcliffe, North Yorkshire)
Handley Page Halifax II (BB326) crashed at Bobbington village on the Shropshire/Staffordshire border, at 13.15 hrs. Having landed at RAF Halfpenny Green the previous evening, after encountering engine problems during a cross-country flight, the crew stayed the night before preparing to fly back to Topcliffe. The starboard inner engine was looked over and still showed signs of overheating as the aircraft was 'run up', but the pilot decided nonetheless to continue with the return journey. However, immediately after leaving the ground, the engine belched black smoke and the aircraft lost height, struck some trees with its starboard wing tip and crashed, killing all but the rear gunner. The gunner, who was thrown from the wreckage, was subsequently taken to RAF Hospital, Cosford, to be treated for 'shock and injury to right shoulder and left lower ribs and minor abrasions to the scalp'.

P/O (pilot) George Keith Patman (J.18941), RCAF, aged 26, was the son of Rollo and Blanche Patman of St Thomas, Ontario. He is buried in Chester (Blacon) Cemetery.

F/Sgt Frank Fearneley [Mike Mellor]

Sgt (F/Eng) David Sharp (1566236), RAFVR, is buried in Glasgow Western Necropolis. His next of kin are unknown.

Sgt (F/Eng) Robert Trevor Gibson (1036711), RAFVR, aged 21, is buried in Belfast City Cemetery. His next of kin are unknown.

F/Sgt (Nav) Francis Newton Salisbury (Frank) Fearneley (R.154156), RCAF, aged 25, was the son of Ellis and Iris Fearneley of East Angus, Quebec. Born on 6 July 1918 in Bermuda, where his father was an inspector with the island police, he and his family moved in the early 1920s to East Angus, where Frank grew up. He is buried alongside his English grandparents in Pendlebury (St John) Cemetery, Lancashire.

F/O (AB) David Michael Blair (132995), RAFVR, aged 22, was the son of Archibald and Catherine Blair of Campbeltown. He is buried in Campbeltown (Kilkerran), Cemetery, Argyllshire.

Sgt (W/AG) Godfrey Purdon Fuller (1318951), RAFVR, aged 21, was the son of Frederick George and Bridget Fuller of West Ealing, Middlesex. He is buried in Stourbridge Cemetery, Worcestershire.

F/Sgt (AG) Keith Douglas Ross (R.129274), RCAF, aged 23, was the son of Robert A and Sarah Ross of Oshawa, Ontario. He is buried in Chester (Blacon) Cemetery.

P/O (AG rear) Thomas Martin Murdock (J.27606), RCAF, was born on 13 January 1914. He enlisted in Montreal on 16 September 1942 and sailed to the UK in July 1943. He made a full recovery after the accident and was repatriated to Canada in March 1945.

13 November (Saturday)
Return flight from RAF Ingham, Lincolnshire–Peplow. 83 OTU (RAF Peplow, Shropshire)
Airspeed Oxford II (P8926) crash-landed at 'Hollins Farm [presumably The Hollings], Woodseaves,' between Market Drayton and Hinstock, at 17.45 hrs. The pilot was returning to Peplow when he ran into a severe snowstorm and made a precautionary landing. After touching down, however, the aircraft flipped onto its back and was badly damaged.

S/Ldr 'Kay' Stammers [Kenneth Stammers]

Acting S/Ldr (instructor pilot) Kenneth Searby 'Kay' Stammers (65989), DFC, DFM, RAF, was born in Carshalton, Surrey on 22 June 1914, the son of Archibald and Katherine Stammers (née Searby). Before the war he had worked as an insurance clerk and lived in Beddington with his wife, Elizabeth Stanford, whom he had married in June 1938. In July 1939 he enlisted in the RAF and, on completion of his training, was posted to 106 Squadron for a brief period before joining 44 Squadron and completing thirty ops piloting Hampden bombers. Commissioned in April 1941, he was awarded the DFM three months later for his services with 44 Squadron and spent the following year-and-a-half in a variety of non-operational postings. In November 1942 he was posted to 12 Squadron and completed a second tour of ops piloting Lancaster bombers, for which he was awarded the DFC in May 1943. Following this second tour he was given command of 93 Group Instructors School (later renamed Group Screened Pilots School) at Church Broughton until October 1943, when he was posted to Peplow as an instructor. For his outstanding instructing abilities at Peplow he was subsequently awarded the AFC in September 1944. After the war Squadron Leader Stammers married Adrian Joan Twigge-Molecey in February 1946, following the death of his first wife from a brain haemorrhage. He was killed three months later, on 10 May 1946, while test flying a Halifax (PP349) of 1665 HCU, at Linton-on-Ouse. S/Ldr Stammers was 31 years old and is buried in Harrogate (Stonefall) Cemetery.

15 November (Monday)
Searchlight homing exercise. 60 OTU (RAF High Ercall, Shropshire)
De Havilland Mosquito II (DZ701) crashed at Broadstone (at wartime map reference 545894) in the Corve Dale, at 19.25 hrs. The trainee crew were on a routine training flight, during which the pilot is believed to have lost control due to 'faulty instrument flying and/or trying to fly on an obscured or non-existent horizon'.

F/O (pilot) Albert Horn (J.23089), RCAF, aged 26, was the son of Mr and Mrs Thomas Horn of Hamilton, Ontario, and the husband of Dorothy Stock, of Waterdown. After graduating from Hamilton Technical Institute he worked for the Dominion Foundries & Steel Company, before enlisting in November 1940. After completing his pilot training he was selected for instructor duties, and subsequently served as an instructor in Canada, until June 1943, before being posted to the UK. He is

F/O Albert Horn
[TNA]

F/O 'Duke' Abelson
[Alan Abelson]

buried in Chester (Blacon) Cemetery.

F/O (Nav) Lawrence Balfour 'Duke' Abelson (J.9152), RCAF, aged 21, was the son of Jess Hyman and Molly Abelson of 96 Marlborough Avenue, Ottawa. After attending Lisgar Collegiate, where he excelled in sports, 'Duke' enlisted in the RCAF in November 1940 and underwent his training in Canada (graduating top of his class). He was then selected for instructor duties and served in Canada until the autumn of 1942, before sailing to the UK to begin operational training. Prior to his death he had actually finished his training and completed two ops with 418 Squadron. However, his pilot was killed during an air test and he was sent back to High Ercall to crew up with a new pilot, F/O Horn. He is buried in Chester (Blacon) Cemetery.

15 November (Tuesday)
Training flight (?). 21 (P)AFU (RAF Wheaton Aston, Staffordshire)
Airspeed Oxford I (LX487) force-landed at Redhill Farm, Crackley Bank, between Priorslee and Sheriffhales, at 21.40 hrs. Very few details are known of this accident as the war diary simply records that the aircraft 'crashed on landing, sustaining Cat[egory] E damage', while the accident card states that 'the card for this accident is "secret" and is kept in Secret folder in cupboard.'
Sgt (pilot u/t) Samuel Cadman (954080), RAFVR, was commissioned in September 1944 and survived the war.

16 November (Tuesday)
Circuits and landings. 83 OTU (RAF Peplow, Shropshire)
Vickers Wellington X (HF465) belly-landed 'one and a half miles north west of Hatton village' (presumably between Hungryhatton and Stoke upon Tern) at 12.27 hrs. The instructor made a forced landing, with wheels retracted, when the port engine failed immediately after taking off from the airfield.

F/Lt (instructor pilot) Sydney Crozier Robinson 'Dingle' Bell (42785), DFC & Bar, RAF. Born in Armagh, Northern Ireland in 1914, he was educated at the Royal School and lived in Belfast. He joined the RAF in 1939 and was awarded his first DFC in November 1941, following a tour of ops flying Hampden bombers with 144 Squadron. His bar to the DFC was awarded in August 1943, during a second tour of ops piloting Lancaster bombers with 619 Squadron, following which he was posted to Peplow as an instructor. He remained in the RAF after the war and served at least into the 1950s.

Sgt (pilot u/t) Richard William Miller (R.225010), RCAF. On completion of his training he was posted to 166 Squadron and shot down and taken prisoner on 23 September 1944 piloting a Lancaster (ME829) on an op to Neuss. He spent the remainder of the war as a POW before being repatriated to the UK and then Canada in December 1945.

23 November (Tuesday)
Cross-country exercise. 105 (Transport) OTU (RAF Bramcote, Warwickshire)
Vickers Wellington IC (T2840) crashed at Abdon Burf (at map reference 590865) on Brown Clee Hill, at 16.30 hrs. During the course of the flight the pilot strayed 25 miles off course and descended to an unsafe height, possibly due to engine trouble as the starboard airscrew was found to be coarser than the port one and witnesses had described hearing an engine 'backfiring' (the subsequent investigation however deemed this evidence 'not conclusive'). The pilot, now flying low and in very poor weather

conditions, was unaware of the high, mist-shrouded ground ahead, and the aircraft ploughed into the hillside, killing two of the crew and seriously injuring the third. Maud Massey, who lived in Clee St Margaret, was told by her father that an aircraft had supposedly crashed on the hill yet, despite going to search in the dark on her pony, she was unable to find anything due to the fog and strong wind. The following morning she set off again at first light and her account of the day can be read on the BBC WW2 People's War website:

> Lo, I looked around and I saw this big object, it looked like a crash of some sort — a plane or something that hadn't been there before. I quickly ran down the tracks that the sheep make- down towards this object I could see and lo and behold it was a Wellington Bomber that had crashed!
>
> It had come down from the direction of Ashfield on an angle over an old well — it's still on the Common, it's called Elsie's well. It had caught the fence which divided the meadows. I came quietly past the plane; I gave the plane a fair distance because in those days you had to be careful you didn't know whether there was any leftover shells or bombs they'd been carrying.
>
> I went pretty cautiously along the tracks where it had crashed into the fence and I came across one gentleman, poor man, he was face-down in a pit and I could see blood in the water where the rushes were growing. It was very sad; I knew I was too late to help him.
>
> Further on there was a man with his arm up. He'd got his arm reared up with his watch on and I quickly sped along thinking probably he was alive. I got hold of his arm and it was stiff and cold, the watch was on his arm but I left it there. The watch had stopped though, the time read twenty minutes past four.
>
> I carried on around the plane and I could see a man underneath the one wing. He'd been sheltered, I think, as he'd been there all through the night and it was wet and cold. I thought 'that was a good thing, you know'. I quickly pulled off an old top I had on and put it under his head. He was unconscious, but he wasn't absolutely out – he could tell someone was with him and he gave a little moan. I said 'I'll be back; I'm going to go and get you some help. Don't worry.' I ran off – right the way down on to a flat bit of the land, and Father was down on the road – I called and called, and waved and it wasn't long 'til he and Tom Price heard me and came up and brought a flask of tea (with whisky in it) to give the gentleman a drink.
>
> We gave him little sips so as not to choke him but to warm him a bit; I remember we were very careful. Meanwhile father went to get help from other areas – the Air Force and what have you, and it wasn't long before we were surrounded by many, many people. Eventually the gentleman was brought down carefully on a stretcher.
>
> That gentleman's name was Linley [sic] James, and the one with his arm raised was called Harold Jessop. Harold's family have been to see me since and thank me for what I did to try and help him, which was very, very nice. I've never seen Linley [sic] James again. I'd love to see him one day if I can.

Sgt Kenneth Imeson [Christine Milburn]

Sgt James was taken to RAF Bridgnorth to be treated for a fractured right femur, fractured left fibula and tibia and facial abrasions, before being transferred the following day to RAF Hospital, Cosford, for further treatment.

Sgt (pilot) Kenneth Frank Charles (Ken) Imeson (1392791), RAFVR, aged 25, was the son of Frank and Annie Elizabeth Imeson of Brockley, and the husband of Louisa Jessie Rhoda Imeson (née Northam) of Crofton Park. He is buried in Lewisham (Ladywell) Cemetery, London. His brother, F/O Ronald Henry Imeson, had been killed serving as a flying instructor at 6 FTS on 15 May 1942.

Sgt (Nav) Harold Jessup (1081074), RAFVR, aged 22, was the son of John Harold and Edith Jessup of Bury, Lancashire. Born in Parr, near Whitefield, on 27 December 1920, Harold spent his childhood in Bury and attended Bury Municipal High School where he was a keen rugby player. After leaving school he worked in Manchester as a sorting clerk and telegraphist

Sgt Harold Jessup
[Peter Jessup]

in the Newton Street Post Office, before volunteering for the RAFVR. He is buried in Chester (Blacon) Cemetery.

Sgt (W/AG) Leonard James (1577588), RAFVR. Nothing further is known of this NCO other than that he survived the war.

26 November (Friday)
Training flight. 61 OTU (RAF Rednal, Shropshire)
Supermarine Spitfire IIA (P7855, presentation aircraft named *Bengal Railway I*) belly-landed at 'Parry's Farm [almost certainly Perry Farm], Whittington', to the east of Oswestry, at 15.00 hrs.
After the engine failed (presumably due to a mechanical defect) the pilot belly-landed in a field and was unhurt.

Sgt (pilot u/t) Zbigniew Bezwuklo (794841), PAF. Born in Poland on 16 February 1920, he was posted to 306 Squadron in February 1944 piloting Spitfires (and later Mustangs) on ops until June 1944. Following a six week detachment to 84 Group Support Unit, he was posted back to 306 Squadron in August and flew with them again until January 1945, when he was posted to Blackpool Polish Depot. He spent four months there before again returning to 306 Squadron in May 1945. He survived the war and appears to have remained in the UK until at least 1950.

2 December (Thursday)
Altitude training mission. 552nd FTS, 495th FTG (Station 342, Atcham, Shropshire)
Republic P-47D Thunderbolt (42-7955) crashed at Teakins Farm (at map reference 522266), between Wem and Preston Brockhurst, at 12.17 hrs. The pilot was flying at 25,000 feet when he sent his last radio message, at 12.14 hrs, stating that he was 'at Angels 25 and letting down.' By the tone of his voice it was evident that everything was alright but, just three minutes later, several witnesses described seeing the aircraft in a screaming dive before it hit the ground with a loud thud and exploding. The subsequent investigation concluded that it was most likely that the pilot entered a terminal velocity dive from which he was unable to recover (this aircraft was notoriously difficult to recover from a high-speed dive) and discounted the possibility of oxygen supply problems because of the short time which elapsed between his radio message and the dive.

2 Lt (pilot u/t) Arvil J Foster (O-686735), USAAF, aged 22, was the son of Hyrum and Jane C Foster of Eight Mile, Idaho. Educated at Soda Springs High School, he had also helped run the family farm in Eight Mile Canyon before attending university at Ricks College, Rexburg. He is buried in Cambridge (Madingley) Cemetery.

4 December (Saturday)
Cross-country exercise. 105 (Transport) OTU (RAF Bramcote, Warwickshire)
Vickers Wellington IC (DV925) crashed 'in open country near Tilstock' at 04.40 hrs after the starboard engine caught fire in flight over Madley Heath in Staffordshire. The entire crew baled out, with only the pilot and F/Sgt Walton suffering slight injuries to their ankles on landing.

W/O (instructor pilot) Morton Edgar MacDonald (1365777), RAFVR, survived the war and was awarded the King's Commendation for Valuable Service in the Air in June 1945.

F/O (pilot) Charles Alexander George (413057), RNZAF, survived the war and attained the rank of flight lieutenant.

F/Sgt R H Walton (507809), RAFVR. Nothing further is known of this airman other than that he survived the war.

Two unknown crew members.

9 December (Thursday)
Training flight. 61 OTU (RAF Rednal, Shropshire)
Supermarine Spitfire IIA (P8237) crashed at 'Rhosfach Farm, one mile north of Oswestry Racecourse', between Selattyn and Rhydycroesau, at 11.10 hrs. Shortly after taking off for a routine training flight the weather deteriorated very rapidly and, in the bad visibility, the pilot flew into high ground and was killed instantly.

P/O (pilot u/t) Jan Heilman-Rawicz (P2312), PAF, aged 22, was born in Grodno, Poland (now in the Belarus Republic), on 20 November 1921, the son of Kazimierz and Józefa Heilman-Rawicz. Records show that he was with British Command in the Middle East during the late summer of 1940 before arriving in the UK in December 1940 and joining the PAF. Over the following months he is thought to have served as ground crew with 315 and then 301 (Polish) Squadrons before beginning pilot training in August 1941. He is buried in Shawbury (St Mary's) Churchyard, Shropshire.

P/O Jan Heilman-Rawicz [neibieskaeskadra.pl]

13 December (Monday)
W/T exercise. 4 Radio School (RAF Madley, Herefordshire)
Percival Proctor III (HM349) force-landed 'one mile east of Bedstone', near Leintwardine, on the Shropshire/Herefordshire border, at 12.05 hrs. After losing his bearings during a training flight, and with his fuel running low, the pilot decided to force-land the aircraft, which ran onto soft ground and overturned.

F/O (pilot) Geoffrey Harold Banks-Smith (133450), RAFVR, survived the war, attaining the rank of flight lieutenant. He died in Hitchin, Hertfordshire, in 1978.

18 December (Saturday)
Cross-country exercise and fuel consumption test. 311 Ferry Training Unit (RAF Moreton-in-Marsh, Gloucestershire)
Vickers Wellington III (BK132) crashed on the end of the south runway at Atcham airfield (at map reference 571098), at 14.08 hrs. The crew were awaiting a posting to the Middle East when they were cleared to take off at 11.47 hrs for one final training flight. An hour after leaving the ground an amendment to the weather forecast was received and instruction was given for the crew to divert and land at RAF High Ercall, however, at 14.08 hrs the aircraft was seen plummeting out of cloud. The cause of the crash was obscure, but it was suggested that the pilot may have lost control either due to icing, or while flying in cloud, despite his being considered a 'very efficient captain'. Joe Dorsett, who lives in Shrewsbury and recalls the event clearly, was working for the Air Ministry, under contract to the Americans at Atcham at the time.

> There was always an MP [Military Policeman] at the end of the runway, stopping traffic if there was anything coming in or taking off. This Wellington bomber, they thought he was just buzzing the field, but he just came straight down in and into the end of the runway. This bloody MP, it blew him far enough away! It blew him over! He was alright though. Now I didn't actually see that crash, but my father gave my son a penny out of that crash that was all bent. I helped clear up bits and pieces. The main part of it had gone, but the engines were left in the ground and were just covered over. I tell you what, there was a hell of a stench there for a good time after.

Technical Sergeant Wayne Scholer, USAAF, who was a ground mechanic at Atcham and now lives in the south of England, also recalled the day.

The crew of Wellington BK132 pictured not long before the crash at Atcham that claimed their lives. From left: David Wright, 'Tubby' Semmens, Neil Ross, Ron Halliday and Lance Phillips. [Nora Morgan]

One time a Wellington was crossing over the base and for some reason – I suppose he had been at 5,000 feet or so, I don't know how high, but not terribly high – it suddenly peeled over and came straight down onto the end of the runway. It dug a hole in the runway, well, three holes actually; centre hole was the fuselage and the two holes either side were where the engines went in. [He] crashed on the intersection of the perimeter track and the end of the runway. That was on the end towards the A5 at the end of the main runway. We never knew exactly why this one crashed. We were on the runway and we could hear these engines whining as it came down. I was on the ramp outside the hangar, working on an aircraft, just outside the hangar.

F/Sgt (pilot) Neil Colin Ross (410852), RAAF, aged 30, was the son of Donald and Louisa Margaret Ross of Maryborough, Victoria. Before joining up he had been a farmer in Maryborough. He is buried in Chester (Blacon) Cemetery.

Sgt (Nav) Edwin Roylance Phillips (1801951), RAFVR, aged 33, was the son of Edwin Gittoes Phillips and May Phillips, and the husband of Whynne Phillips of Upminster. He is buried in Cranham (All Saints) Churchyard, Essex.

F/Sgt (AB) Ernest Jack William Semmens (419344), RAAF, aged 27, was the son of Ernest Henry Fulton Semmens and Nora Eurimbla Semmens of Bendigo, Victoria. Known as 'Tubby' to his family, he had worked for the Bendigo Butter Factory after leaving school. He is buried in Chester (Blacon) Cemetery.

Sgt (W/AG) Kenneth Roland Halliday (1335256), RAFVR, aged 33, was the son of Louis and Helen Halliday and the husband of Launa J Halliday (née Tomkins) of Letchworth. He is buried in Norton (St Nicholas) Churchyard, Hertfordshire.

Sgt (AG) David Hartnoll Wright (1622986), RAFVR, aged 20, was the son of Robert and Maude Wright of York. He is buried in Stockton-on-the-Forest (Holy Trinity) Churchyard, Yorkshire.

21 December (Tuesday)
Training flight. 61 OTU (RAF Rednal, Shropshire)
Supermarine Spitfire IA (K9871) crashed on the edge of the airfield at 15.06 hrs. The Polish pilot was taking off but failed to gain height and the aircraft struck a raised railway embankment on the edge of the airfield and crashed, fortunately without causing him serious injuries. In the subsequent inquiry it was discovered that the pilot had concealed a 'bad eye defect' in his keenness to become a pilot and was consequently taken off the course.

P/O (pilot u/t) Konstanty Dowbór-Musnicki (P2308), PAF. Born in Terjoki, Finland, on 5 May 1918, he transferred to the Polish army following the accident and survived the war.

27 December (Monday)
Training flight. 61 OTU (RAF Rednal, Shropshire)
Supermarine Spitfire IIA (P7501) belly-landed at Spoonley, near Market Drayton, at 15.35 hrs, due to 'negligence', the pilot having allowed his aircraft to run out of fuel.

Sgt (pilot u/t) Birger Tidemand-Johannessen (5548) RNoAF, was born in the Oslo suburb of Bærum, Norway, on 19 June 1918, the son of Reidar Torfinn and Ingeborg Marie Tidemand-Johannessen (née

Steen). In early 1940 he volunteered to serve in Finland with a Swedish volunteer battalion during the Soviet invasion and, on his return to Norway, saw further action during the German invasion in April 1940. Remaining in Norway during the occupation, he joined the resistance in June 1941 before escaping to the UK, along with 60 other men, aboard a fishing vessel five months later. On his arrival he joined the RNoAF and was sent to Canada to train, before returning and joining 331 (Norwegian) Squadron in March 1944, flying Spitfires over north-west Europe. He completed his tour in January 1945 and was credited with one enemy aircraft destroyed and one damaged. He returned to Norway at the end of the war and died in December 2005.

27 December (Monday)
Training flight. 5 (P)AFU (RAF Tern Hill, Shropshire)
Miles Master II (DM450) crash-landed at Sutton Grange Farm, south of Market Drayton, at 19.25 hrs. The pilot was flying in the circuit when the engine failed. For his resultant belly-landing, in which he suffered facial injuries, the instructor was 'commended'.

F/Lt (instructor pilot) Charles Beagley Chisholm (414960), RNZAF. Born in New Zealand, on 6 October 1917, he had enlisted in September 1941 and underwent pilot training in New Zealand before sailing to the UK in May 1942. He appears to have become an instructor soon after his arrival, but nothing further is known of his military service other than that he survived the war and returned to New Zealand. He died in New Plymouth in June 2003.

'F/O Bradley'. His identity has yet to be confirmed.

28 December (Tuesday)
Ground-Controlled Interception (GCI) exercise. 125 (Newfoundland) Squadron (RAF Valley, Anglesey)
Bristol Beaufighter VI (V8751, bearing the fuselage code VA-D) crashed at Crudgington, to the east of High Ercall, at 20.16 hrs. A detailed account of the accident, written by the pilot, appears in Chaz Bowyer's *Beaufighters at War*:

> I was acting as a target aircraft for another machine of 'A' Flight under control of Hack Green GCI Station when at about 20,000 feet my starboard motor failed. A 'Mayday' call resulted in a homing flight over 100 miles on one engine to a master airfield at High Ercall. We made a normal single engine approach and circuit, turning into the final approach at about 500 feet, when the port motor faltered and then also failed. The situation was depressing to say the least. A strange airfield, black as the inside of a cow, and the realisation that I was not going to make the runway. My Navigator was leaning over my shoulder trying to pump the wheels back into the 'wheels up' position so that we could make a belly-landing. I hadn't a clue as to what I was going to land on, so I did the only thing left for me to do, fly her as slowly and safely as possible and descend as gently as I could. Fortunately she landed in the only open space, a large field, in an otherwise built-up area. Completing a perfect 360-degree cartwheel, the starboard wing struck first and fractured at the wing root, the port engine (white hot by then) was catapulted 150 yards away well clear of the aircraft and the fuselage snapped like a carrot behind the trailing edge of the wings. Fuel was pouring out of the tanks, but we both got away without a scratch!

The navigator also recorded his account of the accident after the war and passed a copy on to the pilot's family, which adds:

> We were taken to the Station Sick Quarters and examined for damage. We both appeared to be in good shape considering what we had been through. Peter had to get one foot out of the boot before we could release him. After a return visit he managed to release his boot and hobble away. I was sore all over, I had been thrown to the floor behind Peter's seat on impact and was wedged behind the seat with my right arm twisted under my

body. Of course pride being what it is, and fear of being listed LMF [Lack of Moral Fibre], and being discharged accordingly, can keep one going on for a long time.

Next afternoon we obtained transport and went to the scene to retrieve our personal effects, parachutes, dinghy's, torches, maps etc. There were two officers from the Maintenance Unit at High Ercall at the scene. They were very surprised to know that the two crew had survived.

F/O (pilot) Peter Geldart (128070), RAFVR, was born in Bangalore, India on 2 September 1917, the son of Walter and Janet Geldart. Having joined the Territorial Army in 1937 he was sent to France with the British Expeditionary Force following the outbreak of war but, after developing trench foot, was sent home to recuperate just weeks before Dunkirk. It was whilst convalescing in hospital that he saw a poster calling for volunteers for the RAF, and decided to join. After the war he had another lucky escape while serving with 611 Squadron, Auxiliary Air Force, when he ran into trouble piloting a Spitfire (NM814) out of RAF Woodvale and was forced to bale out over the Pennines on 3 July 1948. He died in Lancashire in October 2004.

P/O (Nav) Howard S Kilpatrick (J.21639), RCAF, survived the war and died in St John's, Newfoundland in 2006.

P/O Gerald Dawson [Library & Archives Canada]

29 December (Wednesday)
Single engine flying, steep turns and stalling practice. 11 (P)AFU (RAF Shawbury, Shropshire)
Airspeed Oxford II (W6648) crashed into Harnage Wood (at map reference 561035), near Cressage, at 10.45 hrs. Twenty minutes after taking off for a morning training flight the pilot lost control, during a deliberate stall, and entered a vertical dive from which he had insufficient height to recover.

P/O (pilot u/t) Gerald Obenauf Dawson (J.28728), RCAF, aged 30, was the son of Thomas W and Emma A Dawson of Peterborough, Ontario, and the husband of Edna Mae Dawson, also of Peterborough. He is buried in Chester (Blacon) Cemetery.

29 December (Wednesday)
Dual night training. 11 (P)AFU (RAF Condover, Shropshire – Satellite to RAF Shawbury)
Airspeed Oxford I (LW730) crashed at Ryton Farm, near Dorrington (at map reference 492034) to the south-west of the airfield, at 23.00 hrs. Shortly after taking off from the airfield the instructor requested permission over the R/T to leave the circuit. It was considered that this 'may have possibly distracted the pilot's attention' (although this could not be confirmed with any certainty). Moments later the aircraft crashed, adjacent to some farm buildings, and the two occupants were killed instantly.

F/Sgt Glen Gerow [Library & Archives Canada]

F/Sgt (instructor pilot) Glen Thomas Gerow (R.121602), RCAF, aged 22, was the son of Clifford and Jessie Gerow of Edmonton, Alberta. Born in Lloydminster, Saskatchewan, on 17 October 1921, he had enlisted in August 1941 and gained his wings in Canada, before sailing for the UK in March 1943. Following his arrival in the UK he was selected for instructor training and posted to 11 (P)AFU in October 1943. He is buried in Chester (Blacon) Cemetery.

Sgt (pilot u/t) Terence Frank Henry Mills (1337341), RAFVR, aged 21, was the son of Frank Frederick Sylvester Mills and Emily Mills of Hastings. He is buried in Hastings Cemetery, Sussex.

30 December (Thursday)
Night training flight. 11 (P)AFU (RAF Shawbury, Shropshire)
Airspeed Oxford II (X6946) crashed into trees just off the perimeter track, '1/4 mile south-west of the airfield', at 05.00 hrs. During the course of a training flight the pilot notified the airfield controller that the engines were giving trouble and permission was given for him to land immediately. After making a low and fast approach the aircraft bounced as it touched down on the runway and the pilot began to carry out an overshoot procedure. As the aircraft passed the airfield boundary it lost height and crashed into some trees, seriously injuring the pilot, who was conveyed to RAF Hospital, Cosford and treated for a fractured right femur and shock. In the subsequent investigation an examination of the engines found no defect and concluded that 'an absence of proof of engine failure make it appear that [the] pilot became anxious about his ability to land, made a poor approach, panicked and probably messed up cockpit drill'.

Sgt (pilot u/t) Douglas Lloyd Stewart Martin (427719), RAAF, was born in Bruce Rock, Western Australia on 20 January 1922. He enlisted in the Australian Army in September 1940 but transferred to the RAAF in September 1942. He survived the war and was discharged in December 1945 with the rank of warrant officer.

1944

1 January (Saturday)
Circuits & landings and single-engine flying practice. 11 (P)AFU (RAF Condover, Shropshire – satellite to RAF Shawbury)
Airspeed Oxford I (LW914) crashed in the area known locally as 'The Wilderness' (at map reference 483953), on the north-east of Caradoc Hill, between Church Stretton and Cardington, at 14.35 hrs. The pilot took off at 13.30 hrs and was subsequently plotted, by the Craven Arms Royal Observer Corps post, travelling north-east at 14.30 hrs. Soon after he was witnessed flying northwards between Caer Caradoc and Willstone Hill at a height of 2,000 feet. According to the accident investigation the pilot is believed to have lost height while practising single-engine flying, and when he tried to open up the throttle of the starboard engine it only partially responded. He then turned towards his good engine and 'described a full circle which was necessarily steep owing to the configuration of the ground'. The aircraft then stalled and dived into the hillside. A contributory factor in the accident may have been 'violent air currents between the hills'. Betty Pennington, who lived at Willstone Farm and whose family owned the land on which the crash occurred, recalled that:

> It must have been about two o'clock, January time. We heard a noise and one of the neighbours at the next farm said that a plane had crashed. My father went to see it, but I didn't go up until a couple of days later. It had crashed in a very wet area of the field and there was wreckage spread about. They were there for about a fortnight before they'd fetched it. They couldn't get one of the engines out. I think they were looking for something the family wanted as well. A watch, or a bracelet, that the pilot had been given on his birthday. They never found it. There were two people there at a time. They would come to the farm for cups of tea in front of the fire. It was very cold at the time, with snow on the ground. They used to drink their tea and then say 'We better go in case one of the head folks comes.'

Sgt Donald Robertson [Library & Archives Canada]

Sgt (pilot u/t) Donald Stuart Robertson (R.179340), RCAF, aged 20, was the son of James Boyd Robertson and Annie Helen Robertson of Outremont, Quebec. Before enlisting in August 1942 he had worked as a telephone installer. He is buried in Chester (Blacon) Cemetery.

2 January (Sunday)
Beam approach and instrument flying exercise. 758 Squadron, HMS *Godwit* (RNAS Hinstock, Shropshire)
Airspeed Oxford II (MP299) crashed in Limekiln Wood (at map reference 648092), Steeraway, north east of the Wrekin, at 11.35 hrs. The Deputy Chief Flying Instructor and his trainee instructor took off at 11.05 hrs and, a short while later, were witnessed approaching the Wrekin from a northerly direction at a height of approximately 2,000 feet. As the aircraft emerged from a thin layer of cloud, it suddenly entered a spin and crashed into the ground at high speed. The subsequent investigation concluded that there was not enough evidence to determine the precise cause of the crash, although wind turbulence may have contributed as

> … the aircraft was flying at a height only 700-800 feet higher than the summit of the Wrekin and in a region where the air would be extremely turbulent in the conditions of wind prevailing at the time of the accident. It is considered possible, therefore, that the pilot lost control of the aircraft in these difficult conditions and that a spin followed at a height which made recovery impossible. It is likely that a severe downdraught existed on the east side of the Wrekin and this may have been a contributory factor.

Lt Cdr James Watson [David Watson, via Lewis Wood]

Lt Cdr (instructor pilot) James Christian Victor Kiero Watson, RNVR, aged 39, was the son of Lt Colonel James Kiero Watson, CMG, DSO and Katherine Emelia Kiero Watson of 21 Sheffield Terrace, Kensington. At the time of his death he was living at Hatton Lodge, Hinstock, with his wife, Miriam Constance Kiero Watson, of Tunbridge Wells in Kent. He is buried in Hinstock Church burial ground.

Sub Lt (instructor pilot u/t) Robert Charles (Bob) Reeder, RNVR, aged 22, was the son of Charles Edward and Clara Reeder of Wilmot Way, Banstead. Born on 4 November 1921, he was educated at Sutton County School and had worked for the Civil Service and then the Ministry of Economic Warfare prior to enlisting. Having previously served at Lee-on-Solent with 781 Squadron, FAA, he was undergoing training in the use of the 'Lorenz' beam approach technique at the time of his death, in preparation for becoming an instructor. He is buried in Banstead (All Saints) Cemetery, Surrey.

Sub Lt Bob Reeder [Lewis Wood, Banstead History Research Group]

5 January (Wednesday)
Formation flying exercise. 5 (P)AFU (RAF Chetwynd, Shropshire – Relief Landing Ground to RAF Tern Hill)
Miles Master II (AZ726) crashed at Wrekin Farm, Aston, to the south-west of Wellington, at 15.50 hrs. After twenty-five minutes in the air a formation change, from line astern to line abreast, was ordered by the pilot of number one aircraft (Master, AZ726). However, the pilot had unwittingly lost a little

height so, when he ordered the change, he could not see the other aircraft behind. In an attempt to locate their position he made a turn but, as he did so, he struck the top of number four aircraft (Master, DM314) which was in his blind spot and both aircraft crashed out of control. Only the instructor pilot managed to bale out. According to an article in the Wartime Aircraft Recovery Group magazines, held in the Shropshire Archives, a local farm worker recalled how

> ... the Masters collided near the Ercall, a hill to the immediate north-east of the Wrekin. Large portions of wreckage fell from the aircraft as they flew locked together, on a south-easterly heading. One or possibly both aircraft crashed near buildings at Wrekin Farm, near Aston. The witness was unable to recall whether the aircraft separated before impact as his attention was taken by a horse which bolted towards him after being struck by falling wreckage.

F/Sgt (instructor pilot) Raymond Phillips (1330411), RAFVR, was commissioned in December 1944. He survived the war and eventually retired as a flight lieutenant in August 1966.

F/O (pilot u/t) Naresh Kumar Srivastava (1871), IAF (seconded to the RAF), aged 26, was born in Bareilly, in Uttar Pradesh, India, the son of Dr Gaya Prasad Srivastava, medical officer for WIMCO Ltd in Bareilly, and his wife Prem Pujari. Brought up in Clutterbuck ganj, on the outskirts of Bareilly, Naresh attended the local school before studying for an MSc in chemistry and zoology at Allahabad University (one of the foremost Indian universities). Cremated at Manchester Crematorium in accordance with traditional Hindu custom, his ashes were returned to his parents in India in 1944.

Formation flying exercise. 5 (P)AFU (RAF Chetwynd, Shropshire – Relief Landing Ground to RAF Tern Hill)
Miles Master II (DM314) crashed at Wrekin Farm, Aston, following the incident described above.

F/O (pilot u/t) James Joseph King (131039), RAFVR, aged 21, was the son of Mrs B M King of Kilburn, Middlesex. He is buried in Chester (Blacon) Cemetery.

5 January (Wednesday)
Formation flying exercise. 61 OTU (RAF Rednal, Shropshire)
Supermarine Spitfire IA (X4606, presentation aircraft named *Ceylon V*) crashed at 'Lightwood Farm near Tern Hill' (thought to be Lightwood, near Woodseaves). Two Spitfires were emerging from cloud in formation when the pilot of P7906 ran into the back of this aircraft, severing its tail and sending it crashing out of control. Fortunately, the pilot managed to bale out and survived. The pilot of P7906 remained in control and was able to make an emergency landing at RAF Tern Hill.

Lt (instructor pilot) Johan Bernhard Gilhuus, RNoAF, born in Oslo on 4 December 1915, was the son of Per Gilhuus and had been an architect in Norway before the war. Before arriving at 61 OTU, he had completed a tour of ops, flying Spitfires with 332 (Norwegian) Squadron, and was credited with one enemy aircraft destroyed, one probable and one damaged. Following his rest period as an instructor at 61 OTU he was posted to 80 Squadron but was killed on 17 December 1944 piloting a Tempest (EJ746) which was shot down by flak over Raesfeld, in Germany.

Formation flying exercise. 61 OTU (RAF Rednal, Shropshire)
Supermarine Spitfire IIA (P7906) landed at RAF Tern Hill after colliding in the incident described above.

F/Sgt (pilot u/t) Godfrey Tate (574580), RAFVR, was born in Haslingden, Lancashire. He had originally joined up as a Halton apprentice before being accepted for pilot training. On completion of his training he was posted to 1 Squadron and was killed on 30 July 1944 when his Spitfire (MJ422) developed engine trouble and crashed into the Channel while returning from a 'diver' (doodlebug) patrol. F/Sgt Tate, who

Thunderbolt 41-6217 had previously been in service with the 82nd Fighter Squadron but is pictured here after running out of fuel on 23 January [USAAF]

was 21 years old, is commemorated on the Runnymede Memorial.

23 January (Sunday)
Altitude formation training mission at 30,000 feet. 551st FTS, 495th FTG (Station 342, Atcham, Shropshire)
Republic P-47C Thunderbolt (41-6217, bearing the fuselage code VM-U) crash-landed '3$^{1}/_{2}$ miles north-east of the airfield' (putting it roughly near Longden on Tern) at 11.17 hrs. While returning to the airfield, following a two-hour training flight, the pilot (call sign Yapper 151) made too wide a landing approach and was forced to carry out another circuit. As he did so Flying Control told him to stand by, while another section took off from the airfield, and he continued to circuit. Soon afterwards, however, he informed Flying Control that he was almost out of fuel and was told to land immediately. Rather than make an emergency approach he carried out a normal peel-off during which the engine failed, forcing him to belly-land in a field.

2 Lt (pilot u/t) Benton C Grayson (O-682634), USAAF. Nothing further is known of his military service other than that he survived the war.

27 January (Thursday)
Circuits and landings. 5 (P)AFU (RAF Tern Hill, Shropshire)
Miles Master III (DL898) crashed at Weobley Farm, to the south-east of Hodnet, at 11.14 hrs. The pupil pilot had just completed two landings and one overshoot practice, with an instructor, after which he was ordered up alone to carry out a circuit and landing. However, after overshooting his landing approach, the pilot opened up the throttle and climbed to 500 feet to begin another circuit. Moments later the aircraft is believed to have stalled, during a left-hand turn, and dived out of control.

Sgt (pilot u/t) John Francis Richards (1338721), RAFVR, aged 21, was the son of Herbert and Lilian Richards of Alston. He is buried in Sydenham Damerel (St Mary) Churchyard, Devon.

30 January (Sunday)
Local map reading, circuits & landings and aerobatics. 5 (P)AFU (RAF Condover, Shropshire – satellite to RAF Tern Hill)

W/O Andrew Taylor [Janice Holborow]

Miles Master II (AZ611) crashed on the northern edge of the airfield at 14.35 hrs. During the course of the flight one of the propeller blades broke off 'due to metal fatigue' and the instructor attempted to reach the airfield to make an emergency landing. As he approached the airfield from the north, at 100 feet, the vibration resulting from the broken airscrew caused the engine bearings to fail and the engine dropped out. The aircraft immediately rose sharply before dropping vertically and crashing onto the runway, while the engine struck the ground and bounced for 100 yards before coming to rest. The station ambulance was immediately dispatched and arrived just before the medical officer but the Norwegian pupil pilot died before he could be removed from the wreckage, while the instructor died of his injuries at 20.15 hrs in the Royal Salop Infirmary.

W/O (instructor pilot) Andrew Edward Taylor (414275), RAAF, aged 22, was the son of Benjamin and Christina Tulloch Taylor of Mount Larcom, Queensland. Born in Longreach, Queensland, on 19 February 1921, he had worked as a dairy farmer and fruit grower before enlisting in the RAAF. He is buried in Chester (Blacon) Cemetery.

Sgt (pilot u/t) Lars Albert Scharning, RNoAF, aged 28, was born in Oslo, Norway on 12 August 1915. Before arriving at 5 (P)AFU, in December 1943, he had undergone pilot training in Canada. He is buried in Oslo (Ullern) Cemetery, Norway.

Unknown date in January
Towing exercise. 81 OTU (RAF Sleap, Shropshire)
Airspeed Horsa (aircraft serial unknown) force-landed at Longden Common (at map reference 450042), near Longden, at approximately 14.30 hrs. During the course of the training flight the tug aircraft entered cloud 'which caused a state of affairs such that neither the glider nor the tug knew in which direction the other was flying' and the tow rope snapped. The glider pilot was forced to land in a field, damaging the front wheel slightly, and a Queen Mary low-loader had to retrieve the glider (only to become stuck in a ditch on the narrow Stapleton road). The names of the crew are unknown

2 February (Wednesday)
Aerobatics training mission. 551st FTS, 495th FTG (Station 342, Atcham, Shropshire)
Republic P-47C Thunderbolt (41-6206, bearing the fuselage code VM-?) crashed '1 mile east of Condover' (although later in the crash report it states 'in the vicinity of Cressage, or near Harley Bank,' at 14.35 hrs. The pilot was returning to Atcham at 2,000 feet, in poor weather conditions, when he radioed in and was given his final vector directing him towards the airfield. Moments later, it is believed, 'a detonation caused by the accumulation of gases in the cockpit or thereabouts or some intense heat on the pilot's person' caused him to lose control and crash. The accident was witnessed by RAF Condover's Airfield Controller, who immediately dispatched the medical orderly in an ambulance but, on his arrival, it was apparent that nothing could be done for the pilot. He waited for the American medics to arrive before leaving.

The tailplane of S/Sgt Griffin's Thunderbolt lying in a field following the accident. [USAAF]

Staff Sgt (pilot u/t) Charles Robert Griffin Jr. (10601316), USAAF, aged 24,was the son of Charles Robert and Helen N. Griffin of Seattle. He is buried in Cambridge (Madingley) Cemetery.

8 February (Tuesday)
Training flight. 81 OTU (RAF Sleap, Shropshire)
Airspeed Horsa (LH319) force-landed at Battlefield, just north of Shrewsbury. The pilot force-landed in a field after the tow rope came adrift during a training flight. The glider came to rest undamaged (only to be lost later during the Arnhem landings, in September).

The names of the crewmembers are unknown.

10 February (Thursday)
Ferry flight from 9 MU, RAF Cosford, to 39 MU, RAF Colerne, Wiltshire. 12 FPP (RAF Cosford, Shropshire)

Supermarine Spitfire IX (MK616) crashed on the edge of Tong Lake, two miles north of Cosford airfield, at 10.22 hrs. Soon after leaving the ground the engine cut twice, before failing completely. The female pilot, who had only flown three hours on Spitfires, allowed the aircraft to stall at 600 feet while attempting to line up for a forced landing.

Second Officer (pilot) Jane Winstone, ATA, aged 31, was the daughter of Arthur George and Lina Storme Winstone of Wanganui, Wellington, New Zealand. According to *For Your Tomorrow*, by Errol Martyn, she had gained her pilot's licence with the Wanganui Aero Club before the war and had been engaged to Angus Carr MacKenzie, RNZAF, who was killed on 9 June 1942 flying with 35 Squadron. She is buried in Maidenhead Cemetery.

12 February (Saturday)
Ferry flight to and from unknown airfields. 5 FPP (Thame, Oxfordshire)
Miles Martinet I (NE361) force-landed at 'Upton House Farm, Upton Cressett', to the west of Bridgnorth, at 16.00 hrs. The ferry pilot was flying in poor weather conditions when he became lost and decided to force-land in a field. He was subsequently taken to RAF Bridgnorth where he spent the night in the officers' mess while the aircraft was placed under guard.

Second Officer (pilot) Hobart Howard Steely, ATA, was an American citizen. He was born on 8 November 1901 in Pocatello, Idaho and had served as an officer in the US Coast Artillery in 1918, before becoming a reserve officer in the Air Corps between 1922 and 1930. He left the ATA in March 1944 and died in 1978. His son, Hobart Jr, completed a tour of duty as a navigator on B-17s with the 303rd Bomb Group.

F/Sgt Ronald Broun [John Broun]

15 February (Tuesday)
Cross-country glider towing exercise. 81 OTU (RAF Sleap, Shropshire)
Armstrong Whitworth Whitley V (BD420) crashed into Mytton Dingle (at map reference 373005), on the Stiperstones, at 17.25 hrs. The trainee crew took off at 17.10 hrs and were on the first leg of their journey which took them over the high ground in South Shropshire. According to the account of the glider pilot,

> … we were passing over some flat-topped high ground at about 200 feet above the ground; the tug was still behaving quite ok. We were now approaching a valley which had its closed end on our port. Suddenly, the Whitley whipped over into an almost vertically banked left turn and it became very obvious that a crash was imminent as the tug was now turning into the closed end of the valley at the same time slipping in. I therefore pulled the tow release and my co-pilot made a steep turn to the right down the valley. As I was sitting in the first pilot's seat in the left of the cockpit, I had a good view of the Whitley whilst we were turning and I observed that it exploded in the air.

W/O Ted Creber [Jill Upton]

A subsequent examination of the wreckage and interviews with numerous witnesses concluded that there was insufficient evidence to deduce the exact cause of the accident and the glider pilot's account of an explosion in the air was discounted. The conclusions reached were either that of 'a bird striking the windscreen and blinding or injuring the pilot' or, more likely, that the pilot encountered a 'downdraught on crossing the top of the hill', causing him to lose control. The investigation report also states that the pilot was 'very unwise to give this high and broken ground such small clearance when weather conditions did not make this necessary', while the commanding officer's report added that 'no explanation can be offered as to why the pilot unnecessarily flew at a low height over high ground, other than that F/Sgt Broun (although an above average pilot) was inclined to over-confidence'.

F/Sgt (pilot) Ronald Richmond Broun (417013), RNZAF, aged 21, was the only son of the late Richmond Thomas Broun and Frances Caroline Broun (née Boxall) of 31 Maungawhau Road, Mount Albert, Auckland. Posted to 81 OTU in April 1943, he had been seriously injured in a car crash on 18 June and was off flying duty for a considerable time before resuming his training. He is buried in Chester (Blacon) Cemetery.

Sgt Reginald Hodges [Library & Archives Canada]

W/O (Nav) Edward Alan (Ted) Creber (936235), RAFVR, aged 24, was the son of William and Annie Louise Creber of Mousecroft Lane, Shrewsbury. Educated at the Priory Boys' School and Heralds College, London, he had joined the RAFVR soon after the outbreak of war. Following a brief period in Northern Ireland, he spent 2 1/2 years as an instructor in South Africa before returning to the UK to prepare for ops. He is buried in Shrewsbury General Cemetery, Shropshire.

Sgt (AB) Reginald Frederick Hodges (R.170348), RCAF, aged 19, was the son of Edgar and Selina Hodges of Kamsack, Saskatchewan. He is buried in Chester (Blacon) Cemetery. His brother, W/O R B Hodges, had been killed serving as a W/AG with 238 Squadron on 7 June 1943.

Sgt Jack Brownhill [Connie Hall]

Sgt (W/AG) Jack Thomas Brownhill (1715949), RAFVR, aged 21, was the son of John Thomas and Edith Madge Brownhill of Whitton, Twickenham, and was engaged to Connie Edmondson. He is buried in Twickenham parochial cemetery, Middlesex.

Sgt (AG rear) Henry Little (1593467), RAFVR, aged 20, was the son of Henry and Lauraetta Little (née Hunter) of Killinghall. He is buried in Harrogate (Stonefall) Cemetery, Yorkshire.

Cross-country towing exercise. 81 OTU (RAF Sleap, Shropshire)
Airspeed Horsa (HA443) force-landed between Snailbeach village and the Waterwheel at 17.25 hrs. Having made a successful landing in a field belonging to Mr T Evans of West View, Snailbeach, following the incident described above, the pilot 'went by car to the scene of [the] crash and took possession of one note book and a magazine of .303 ammunition.'

Staff Sgt (pilot) William Colin McLaren (1604219), GPR, the son of John William and Maud McLaren of Leeds, was involved in another forced landing four weeks later. He was killed in action at Arnhem on 19 September 1944 and is buried in Arnhem Oosterbeek War Cemetery.

Staff Sgt (pilot) J Howe (1077879), GPR.

27 February (Sunday)
Cross-country flight from Base to Warton, Lancashire. HQ Squadron, Station 112 (Bovingdon, Hertfordshire)
Fairchild UC-61A Forwarder (43-14483) force-landed at Craven Arms at 16.00 hrs. The crew had been cleared for take-off with special instructions that, if bad weather was encountered en route, they were to return to base or land at the most convenient airfield. However, this order was ignored after snow

Forwarder (43-14483) pictured after it flipped onto its back during a forced landing at Craven Arms. [USAAF]

L–R: Capt John Castle [303rd Bomb Group Assoc] and 1 Lt 'Fuzz' Colthorpe [Randy Colthorpe]

squalls were encountered. The pilot's account describes how

> ... east of Worcester we encountered snow at 1,000 feet, circled in a clear area climbing to 4,000 and continued on course above 6 to 8/10 cumulus. Located our position east of course at the rail junction near Craven Arms and let down to less than 1,000 feet with intention of following the railroad to the area around Atcham. North and east of Craven Arms encountered snow again, so returned along the railroad track looking for a field to land in to wait the snowstorm out. Circled a field near Craven Arms that showed green and was of suitable size. Flew over the field low to view the ground and obstructions and decided the area was suitable. On the approach for landing, the snowstorm had reached the area. Approached from downwind, let down full flaps and came into the field at lowest possible speed. The aircraft tended to balloon in the gusty air, and a variable cross wind from the left was encountered due to the slope of the adjoining hill. On touching down at a very slow ground speed, the wheels struck in soft ground and the aircraft slowly nosed down and came to rest on its back with no violent jar. The occupants released their safety belts and left the aircraft by the left-hand door. injury to personnel.

British soldiers based in the town were quickly on the scene, and arrangements were made with Atcham (being the nearest American base) to pick up the crew, while a guard for the aircraft was organized by the local British military traffic officer in Craven Arms.

Capt (pilot) John Arlo Castle (O-435855), USAAF. Prior to serving at Bovingdon, he had completed seven missions flying B-17s with 360th Bomb Squadron, 303rd Bomb Group, between November 1942 and April 1943 (it is unclear why he did not complete a full tour). He died in Santa Clara, California in October 1983.

1 Lt (Nav) Sidney Ernest 'Fuzz' Colthorpe (O-801060), USAAF. Born in Montreal, Canada, in 1920, he had completed 25 missions with the 385th Bomb Group between October 1943 and January 1944 (including the infamous Schweinfurt and Marienburg raids). Posted to Bomber Command after completing his tour, he remained in the Air Force after the war and was the navigator on board the first USAAF aircraft to fly over the North Pole. During the Korean War he completed a further 59 combat missions and eventually retired from the USAF as a Lt Colonel in 1970. He died in May 2000.

2 Lt (passenger) Jerry A Kennedy (O-748676), USAAF.

28 February (Monday)
Formation flying exercise. 61 OTU (RAF Rednal, Shropshire)
Supermarine Spitfire VA (W3118, presentation aircraft named *Kirklands*) belly-landed 'in field at Tern Hill' at 14.45 hrs. While flying at 900–1,000 feet the aircraft's engine began to splutter and smoke (due to a glycol leak). The flight leader instructed the pilot to feather his engine and he carried out a belly-landing in a field, suffering some slight injuries.

F/O (pilot u/t) Idris Hasan Latif (1804), IAF (seconded to the RAF), was born in Hyderabad on 9 June 1923, the son of the Chief Engineer of Hyderabad state and was educated at Nizam's College. Before being seconded to the RAF to train on high-performance aircraft, he had learned to fly in India and flew obsolete biplanes with 2 Coastal Defence Flight in Karachi. On completion of his training in the UK he was posted to 3 Squadron, IAF, flying Hurricanes over the Burma front. He remained in the IAF after the war, eventually rising to become Chief of Air Staff in 1978 before retiring in 1981. He then spent seven years as Indian Ambassador to France, before settling back in his home city of Hyderabad in 1988.

1 March (Wednesday)
Cine-gun training mission. 552nd FTS, 495th FTG (Station 342, Atcham, Shropshire)
Republic P-47C Thunderbolt (41-6538, bearing the fuselage code DQ-Q) crash-landed at 'Aston Farm, near Uppington', to the north west of the Wrekin, at 17.15 hrs. The pilot was returning to land, after completing his flight, when the fuel in his auxiliary tanks ran dry, so he throttled back and changed to the main tank. According to his statement he then opened the throttles and

> … the engine caught momentarily, but then started losing RPM until after about 30 seconds no power was available. Thinking the prop had gone out, action was taken to rectify the trouble. As no results were obtained, the fuel cock was moved to different positions and reset on 'main' at the same time using emergency fuel pressure system. At no time did the engine give signs of starting. A wheels up landing was made in the best area available.

Following an examination of the aircraft it was concluded that a break in the emergency boost pump caused a slight delay in the flow of fuel but, as the pilot was 'not too experienced in this type of aircraft, [he] immediately had visions of propeller and engine failures and started manipulating controls' which further delayed the flow of fuel and, by this stage, the aircraft was so low that the pilot had to concentrate on a forced landing.

1 Lt (pilot u/t) Gilbert W Hunt (O-886265), USAAF, subsequently flew with the 336th Fighter Squadron, 4th Fighter Group and was credited with one enemy aircraft destroyed on 12 September 1944. He retired from the USAF as a colonel and died in 2002.

Thunderbolt 41-6538 had previously been the mount of Capt Walter Hollander of the 334th Fighter Squadron and bore the nose art Wela Kahao! *(meaning 'Strike while the iron is hot!' in Hawaiian), but is seen here with the snow-covered Wrekin in the background after its accident near Atcham. [USAAF]*

3 March (Friday)

Night training exercise. 83 OTU (RAF Peplow, Shropshire)

Vickers Wellington X (LN164) crashed into a barn at Cherrington Manor (at map reference 667202), near Tibberton, at 02.35 hrs. The pilot had just taken off and was climbing away from the airfield when the port engine failed at low altitude. As he struggled to maintain control to carry out a forced landing, the aircraft smashed into some farm buildings in the dark. Sid Watkins, who was a schoolboy living in Cherrington at the time, recalled how it

> … came from an easterly direction. There was a row of Dutch barns. He took a six inch circular piece out of the top row, top of the arch of the barn. The next row of Dutch barns, which would be about 15 yards apart, well, he demolished three bays and then came down on a brick cowshed, where they keep the cows, and the granary. The wheel was hanging through the roof into this cowshed and they [the cows] all bolted and broke the retainer.

In the minutes that followed, the bomb aimer displayed great bravery in trying to rescue his crewmates and, as a result of his actions, was subsequently awarded the BEM. The citation described how

> Sgt Rumsby, although badly bruised and shaken, managed to extricate himself from the wreckage and fell off the roof of the building into the midst of many pedigree bullocks in a stall below. After releasing the animals, who were wild with fear, Sergeant Rumsby climbed back on the roof to search for his companions. He found the pilot of the aircraft injured and with his clothes on fire. Sergeant Rumsby put out the flames and assisted the pilot from the roof and to the farmhouse. He then returned to the blazing wreckage and made a further search, disregarding the danger from the explosion of fuel tanks in the aircraft and the collapse of the roof of the building. He displayed great gallantry and undoubtedly saved the life of his pilot.

Despite the entire crew surviving the crash, the navigator was killed when he jumped from the rafters and struck his head on a mobile whitewash container. His body was discovered by Sid Watkins' father, a member of the Home Guard, who had rushed to the scene to try and help.

F/Sgt (pilot) John Jardine Graham (1349145), RAFVR, was commissioned in July 1944 and was killed on 11 September 1944 piloting a Wellington (MF337) of 34 Wing Support Unit, which was lost without trace during a ferry flight. P/O Graham, who was 29 years old and the son of John and Margaret Graham of Hawick, Roxburghshire, is commemorated on the Runnymede Memorial.

Sgt (Nav) Arthur Draper (1522838), RAFVR, aged 24, was the son of Hugh Dobson Draper and Katrina Draper (née Quinn) of Gateshead and the husband of Emily Draper of High Felling, Gateshead. Born

Sgt Arthur Draper (far right) pictured after crewing up at Peplow. Although the names have not been written on the photo, it can be assumed that F/Sgt Graham is seated in front of Sgt Draper (wearing pilot's brevet) and Sgt Rumsby is to his right, while the two other survivors are either of the three remaining airmen. [Tony Draper]

in Gateshead on 17 October 1919, he had attended primary school there before gaining a scholarship to St Cuthbert's Grammar School in Newcastle. He is buried in Heworth (or Windy Nook) (St Alban) Churchyard, Durham.

Sgt (AB) John Noel Rumsby (1586158), RAFVR, was born on 25 December 1916 and had served with the Essex County Constabulary in Romford and Upminster before the war. He was also killed along with F/Sgt Graham on 11 September 1944 and his name is inscribed on the Runnymede Memorial.

Sgt(?) Norman Oates Sutcliffe (Service No. unknown), RAFVR, was born in Yorkshire. Nothing further is known of his military service. He died in Grantham in 1984.

The name of the fifth crew member is unknown.

6 March (Monday)

Day flying training. 11 (P)AFU (RAF Calveley, Cheshire)

Airspeed Oxford I (V4160) crashed 'one and a half miles south-west of Ellesmere' (putting it in the area of Tetchill and Welsh Frankton), at 10.15 hrs. The pupil pilot was practicing steep turns, with wheels down and 20 degrees of flap ('a practice he stated had been shown to him by his SFTS instructor in Canada') when he allowed the aircraft to stall. Having failed to regain control by 3,000 feet he took to his parachute and the aircraft crashed a short distance away. The subsequent investigation concluded that, as the pilot 'was practicing this experience in all good faith, although not authorised to do so, no disciplinary action was taken'.

F/O (pilot u/t) Erwin Henry McKeown (J.26476), RCAF. Born in Acton, Ontario, in 1924, he had worked as a garage attendant before enlisting in January 1942. On finishing his training he completed a tour of ops piloting Halifax bombers with 420 Squadron, RCAF, for which he was awarded the DFC in May 1945.

11 March (Saturday)

Dual instruction flight. 83 OTU (RAF Peplow, Shropshire)

Vickers Wellington X (HE635) belly-landed at Tyrley Castle Farm, on the south-eastern outskirts of Market Drayton, at 09.27 hrs. The instructor pilot was demonstrating feathering procedure at 8,000 feet when he found that the airscrew would not un-feather when selected to do so. The aircraft began to lose height and, unable to reach the airfield, the instructor force-landed in a field, with wheels retracted. Ken Goodwin, whose family were living at the farm at the time, recalled how

> … it was early one morning and my father, my brother and me, we were standing out by the back of the house and we heard this tremendous roar and looked up and saw this thing! You know we were looking right up underneath its belly sort of thing. How he missed us, God only knows. Well, he missed the farm house by, well, I wouldn't say feet, more like inches! He missed an ash tree in what we called the 'front field' and he was about halfway down that and he just skipped over the hedge, which was just further along beyond it, and then skidded up the grass field to the top of the high ground … the fellas were all getting out when we got there. There was no fire or anything, fortunately. They all survived and they all came back down to the house and my mother gave them tea and biscuits or whatever and then they made a phone call and that's the last we saw of them really. I don't know where it came from. We understood from the fellas, or the pilot, that they were following the river, hoping that there would be some flat ground along the riverside, you see. They were very, very lucky. They all survived, I think there was five of them.

F/Lt (instructor pilot) Owen Leonard Hawes, (118907), DFM, RAFVR, was born in Suffolk on 1 July 1919. He had been awarded the DFM in May 1942 following a tour of ops with 38 Squadron, flying Wellington bombers in the Mediterranean theatre. Commissioned in February 1942, he survived the war and died in 2002.

F/O 'Joe' Tilley
[Jill Humphreys]

Sgt (pilot u/t) Hagerty (service number unknown).
The names of the other crew members are unknown.

11 March (Saturday)
Formation flying exercise. 5 (P)AFU (RAF Condover, Shropshire – satellite to RAF Tern Hill)
Miles Master II (AZ596) crashed at Hunger Hill, one mile west of Condover village, at 10.00 hrs. During the course of the training exercise, the formation flight leader signalled for the pilots to descend through cloud but, moments after entering cloud, the pilot of this aircraft broke away, stalled and entered an uncontrollable spin. Unable to regain control, he took to his parachute and was slightly injured, while the aircraft dived into the ground nearby. In the subsequent investigation it was concluded that the flight leader had 'disobeyed and disregarded all his briefing instructions and showed a complete lack of airmanship' by leading the pupil pilots into conditions of instrument flying.

F/O (pilot u/t) Harry Ambrose Tilley (127203), RAFVR. Born in Battle, Sussex, on 2 November 1915, he and his family moved to Ashford in Kent when he was four and 'Joe', as he was known to his family, attended the local secondary school there. After leaving school he worked for a short time in the local flour mills, before joining the local constabulary prior to the war. Following the accident at Condover he never flew operationally and relinquished his commission on account of ill health in August 1944 (presumably as a result of the injuries suffered in the accident). He rejoined the police after the war and died in Brighton in 1977.

15 March (Wednesday)
Night training flight. 61 OTU (RAF Montford Bridge, Shropshire – Satellite airfield to RAF Rednal)
Supermarine Spitfire IA (R7022) crashed on the edge of Montford Bridge airfield, at 20.35 hrs.
Little is known of this accident (no accident card survives) other than that the aircraft crashed adjacent to the communal site while night flying.

Sgt (pilot u/t) Jack Reginald Newman (658762), RAF, aged 22, was the son of Reginald John and Elsie Mabel Newman of Oxford. He is buried in Oxford (Rose Hill) Cemetery.

15 March (Wednesday)
Night circuits and landings. 81 OTU (RAF Sleap, Shropshire)
Airspeed Horsa II (LH349) force-landed at Tilley Park, to the east of the airfield, at 20.42 hrs. The pilot made an emergency release for unknown reasons and landed undamaged in a field (the glider was subsequently lost on D-Day).

Staff Sgt (1st pilot) William Colin McLaren (1604219), GPR, had been involved in a serious incident on 15 February at Snailbeach and further details can be found for him on that date.

Sgt (2nd pilot) J Cutler (912610), GPR. He subsequently fought at Arnhem with 1 Wing and survived the war.

18 March (Saturday)
Single-engine flying practice. Central Navigation School (RAF Shawbury, Shropshire)
Vickers Wellington XIII (JA304) belly-landed at Ightfield Farm, to the east of Tilstock airfield, at 11.30 hrs. After taking off from Shawbury the pilot feathered his propeller, while flying at only 1,000 feet, and then, 'as speed [was] lost, pilot kept nose up and [the] aircraft lost height rapidly', causing him to belly-

land in a field. Upon coming to rest the aircraft burst into flames and the pilot suffered serious burns to his face and hands while trying to get out. He was consequently taken to RAF Hospital, Cosford, for treatment in its burns centre. In the subsequent investigation it was stated that the pilot should not have practiced single-engine flying at such a low altitude and, also, that the pilot's instructor should not have authorised the flight in view of the low cloud at the time.

F/Sgt (pilot u/t) Roger Fletcher Crankshaw (1532538), RAFVR. Born in Gateshead, in 1920, nothing further is known of this NCO other than that he survived the war.

19 March (Sunday)
Aerobatics practice. 758 Squadron (HMS *Godwit*, RNAS Hinstock, Shropshire)
De Havilland Tiger Moth II (DE197) crashed at an unknown location, assumed to be in the vicinity of the airfield. Little is known of the accident other than that the pilot stalled the aircraft while performing aerobatics at low level and crashed in a field.

Sub Lt (A) Charles E S Minshaw, RNVR, survived the war and became a commercial pilot in the 1950s.

20 March (Monday)
Day flying training and aerobatics. 5 (P)AFU (RAF Tern Hill, Shropshire)
Hawker Hurricane I (V6678) force-landed at Helshaw Grange, to the south of the airfield, at 12.55 hrs. The pilot was flying in the vicinity of the airfield when he failed to turn on his reserve fuel tanks when his main tanks ran dry. This caused the engine to fail and forced him to belly-land in a field. As a result of his actions the pilot's logbook was endorsed for 'gross carelessness'.

Sgt (pilot u/t) Karel Lamberton (788101), RAFVR. Born in Prague on 9 February 1922, he was posted to 310 (Czechoslovak) Squadron in July 1944 and flew Spitfires on armed reconnaissance operations until October. He was then posted to 312 (Czechoslovak) Squadron and continued to fly until the end of the war.

20 March (Monday)
Dual glider lifting exercise. 81 OTU (RAF Sleap, Shropshire)
Airspeed Horsa I (LH442) force-landed in a field '1/2 mile south-west of Myddle', near Wem, at 09.24 hrs. During the course of the exercise the tug aircraft developed engine trouble and the glider pilot 'got out of position in slipstream causing a jerk on the rope'. He therefore cast off and landed undamaged in a field (the glider was subsequently lost on D-Day).

Staff Sgt (1st pilot) Sydney Augustus Wilkinson (186344), GPR, was killed at Arnhem on 25 September 1944 serving with 1 Wing and is buried in Arnhem Oosterbeek War Cemetery. He was 30 years old and the son of Frederick Augustus and Marian Edith Wilkinson.

Sgt (2nd pilot) J Dolling (6293697), GPR, subsequently served at Arnhem with 1 Wing and survived the war.

Two unknown passengers.

29 March (Wednesday)
Night flying training. 5 (P)AFU (RAF Condover, Shropshire – Satellite to RAF Tern Hill)
Miles Master III (DL852) crashed 'near Condover' at 00.30 hrs. The pilot was approaching the airfield, at low level and in deteriorating weather conditions, when he struck a tree, which was obscured by fog, and crashed. The seriously injured pilot was rushed to the Royal Salop Infirmary but died later that day.

F/O (pilot u/t) Anthony Boyre Brentnall (49595), RAF, aged 23, was the son of Sam Boyre Brentnall and Ellen Meredyth Brentnall (née Lowe) of Didsbury, Manchester. Prior to joining the RAF in August 1942 he had served as a 2 Lt in 6 Lancashire Fusiliers and is believed to have survived the Dunkirk evacuation. He is commemorated at the Manchester Crematorium.

29 March (Wednesday)
Ferry flight from RAF High Ercall–RAF Worthy Down, Hampshire. 29 MU (RAF High Ercall, Shropshire)
Fairey Swordfish III (NF262) force-landed 'four miles south-south-west of Shifnal' (putting it in the area around Brockton and Kemberton). The female ferry pilot was flying at 200 feet when the engine failed and, in the resultant forced landing, the aircraft ran into a hedge and overturned.

Second Officer (pilot) Molly Daphne Rose (née Marshall), ATA. Born in 1921, she was the daughter of the founder of the famous Cambridge-based Marshall Group aviation company, David Gregory Marshall and his wife Maude Edmunds Marshall. She married Bernard William George Rose (who later became a well-known post-war musician) in 1939 and served with the ATA throughout the war.

4 April (Tuesday)
Altitude formation training mission. 552nd FTS, 495th FTG (Station 342, Atcham, Shropshire)
Republic P-47C Thunderbolt (41-6395, bearing the fuselage code DQ-W) crashed at Yell Bank (at map reference 426146), Montford, between Montford Bridge and Ford, at 14.55 hrs. The pilot was flying at 20,000 feet, in number three position of an eight aircraft section, when smoke was observed coming from his turbo exhaust and, although this was a common occurrence and not deemed to be of great concern, the flight leader decided to turn towards base. As they did so, however, sight was lost of number three aircraft and when the flight leader called the pilot up over his R/T set, the aircraft had already fallen off into a vertical dive. This dive was subsequently attributed to the pilot's experiencing 'an undetermined unconscious condition'. The possibility of anoxia was discounted and no mention was made of possible smoke inhalation. The accident was witnessed by local schoolboy Dennis Diggory, whose account was published in the Wartime Aircraft Recovery Group magazines:

> Suddenly, it went into a steep dive and soon the high-pitched noise of the engine could be heard, followed by silence for a few seconds and then a double 'boom'. The aircraft continued to dive, emitting a loud 'screaming' noise at an altitude of about 500 feet before crashing with a terrific explosion at Yell Bank, Montford. A recovery team from the 495th FTG, USAAF airfield at Atcham, presumably the aircraft's unit, spent almost two weeks at the site.

2 Lt (pilot u/t) William E Witte (O-815448), USAAF, aged 23, was the son of Mr & Mrs William Witte of Nebraska City. Born in Hot Springs, South Dakota, he and his family moved to Nebraska in 1924 where he attended the local high school and Peru State Teachers' College. He then began civilian pilot training at Midland College, Fremont and Omaha University, Nebraska, before enlisting in July 1942. He is buried in Wyuka Cemetery, Nebraska City.

6 April (Thursday)
Training flight. 60 OTU (RAF High Ercall, Shropshire)
De Havilland Mosquito FB.VI (HX865) crashed on approach to the airfield at 19.18 hrs. The trainee crew were approaching to land on one engine after the other had failed, when the pilot made a tight turn away from his good engine, causing the aircraft to stall, crash and cartwheel along the ground.

F/Lt (pilot u/t) Clifford Birkett Rigg (42579), RAF, aged 28, was the son of Percival Birkett Rigg and Winifred Rigg and the husband of Joan Gertrude Rigg (née Thomas) of Baron's Court, London. He is buried in Weston-super-Mare Cemetery.

F/Sgt (Nav) Thomas Waddell (1368228), RAFVR, aged 22, was the son of Alexander and Euphemia Waddell of Dunoon. He is buried in Dunoon Cemetery, Argyllshire.

7 April (Friday)
Formation flying and cine gun exercise. 61 OTU (RAF Rednal, Shropshire)
Supermarine Spitfire IIB (P8509, presentation aircraft named *The Old Lady*) crashed near RAF Rednal. Although no accident card survives for the incident, the pilot's account is available online and describes how he was tail-chasing in the vicinity of the airfield when he,

> ... dropped a little flap to tighten up my turn. He [the other pilot] wasn't watching and he flew right into me. My Spitfire exploded. His was still flyable so he got it down. I was just left there in the seat and there was no Spitfire. I got rid of the seat and opened my parachute. I remember how quiet it was going down. There was fog on the ground. I went down through it and landed in a farmer's field. I wasn't hurt at all. They put the two of us in a hospital and checked us all over. They endorsed my logbook and said it was partially my fault.

F/O (pilot u/t) Harry James Henry Hardy (J.20841), RCAF. Born in Virden, Manitoba in 1922, he was living in Vancouver when he enlisted in November 1941. On completion of his operational training in the UK he was posted to 440 Squadron and then 438 Squadron, with whom he became a distinguished tank buster, piloting his personalized Typhoon *Pulverizer I* (and later *II*, *III* and *IV*). He survived the war, despite having to bale out of stricken aircraft twice more, and was awarded the DFC in recognition of his courage and ground-attack skills, particularly during the Ardennes offensive.

Formation flying and cine gun exercise. 61 OTU (RAF Rednal, Shropshire)
Supermarine Spitfire IIA (P7672) crash-landed on the runway at Rednal following the collision described above.

P/O (pilot u/t) John David Andrew Beal (421349), RNZAF. Born in Glasgow on 28 December 1919, he and his parents, Fred and Catherine Rennie Beal (née Gibson), emigrated to New Zealand when he was a child and settled in Wellington. After attending Wanganui College he worked as a motor mechanic and also served in the TA before enlisting in the RNZAF in February 1942. On completion of his operational training in the UK he was posted to 66 Squadron in July 1944 and flew Spitfires on operations over north-west Europe. Sadly, he did not survive his tour and was killed on 22 September 1944 when his Spitfire (MJ981) was hit by flak while dive-bombing gun positions near Dunkirk. F/O Beal was 24 years old and is buried in Dunkirk Town Cemetery.

9 April (Sunday)
Circuits and landings. 83 OTU (RAF Peplow, Shropshire)
Vickers Wellington X (HE589) belly-landed at Eaton on Tern at 14.50 hrs. Immediately after taking off from the airfield the port engine failed, at 50 feet, and the instructor took control and belly-landed in a field ahead. For his swift actions, he was subsequently recommended for a 'green endorsement' in his logbook. On board the aircraft was Les Landells, who was on his first training flight at the unit, while his newly-formed crew stood on the tarmac to judge his flying skills. He described the events of that day in a series of letters to the author in 2008:

> F/Sgt James Price was the training instructor pilot. F/O Spurrs was alongside him as pupil under instruction. The wireless operator of F/O Spurrs' crew was also aboard and one other of his crew if I recall correctly. I was seated, I think, in the navigator's seat or nearby.
>
> When F/O Spurrs had completed his circuit and bumps instruction he was then to leave the aircraft. Then it was my turn to be given circuit and bumps instruction. However, as it happened, the accident intervened. I, at the time of impact, was behind the main spar facing the rear of the aircraft with my feet nearly on the floor. On impact with the ground I held on tightly. I was thrown about somewhat as some soil entered the floor, but managed to hold on.

Sgt Les Landells
[Les Landells]

We all escaped serious injury but the aircraft was in pieces spread over two to three fields. Fortunately, very muddy, therefore it softened the impact, which reduces the chances of fire. Actually there was mud and fuel spraying all over the place. We went through two to three hawthorn hedges, lost at least one engine, part of a wing and the rear turret. So you can imagine the spectators' reaction. Some thought we had had it, as Wellington bombers, a good aircraft, were still very vulnerable to crashing on landings (they caught fire fairly easily). Flight Sergeant Price's alertness and skill helped save all our lives. After 24 hours in Sick Bay, I was asked to fly on 'circuits and bumps' again. It was standard practice to see whether or not you could face up to it again.

F/Sgt (instructor pilot) James Price (1058736), RAFVR. After finishing his instructor duties at Peplow he was posted to 214 Squadron and completed a tour piloting Flying Fortresses on radio counter-measure ops, for which he was awarded the DFC in July 1945.

F/O (pilot u/t) Joseph Harold Spurrs (152591), RAFVR. Born in Tynemouth on 23 November 1915, he joined 12 Squadron after his training and was taken prisoner of war on 29 August 1944 when his Lancaster (PD273) was shot down on an op to Stettin. He was repatriated to the UK in May 1945 and died in 1987.

Sgt (pilot u/t) Leslie (Les) Landells (1004562), RAFVR. Born in South Benwell, Newcastle upon Tyne on 21 April 1921, he was brought up by his cousin and her husband in Distington, Cumbria after his parents died when he was young. After leaving school at 14, he followed in the footsteps of his older brother and joined the RAF in 1939 as an aircraftman, eventually being posted to RAF Bassingbourn for general duties. He was employed at the airfield in a number of roles, such as guard duty, but, during his spare time, began studying to enable him to apply for aircrew selection, for which he was eventually accepted. On completion of his training he was posted to 626 Squadron on 16 September 1944 and flew Lancaster bombers with the squadron until the end of the war. He currently lives in Stockport.

The names of the other two airmen are unknown.

10 April (Monday)
Instrument flying and aerobatics. 5 (P)AFU (RAF Tern Hill, Shropshire)
Miles Master II (AZ725) crashed '50 yards south of Chetwynd airfield' (at wartime map reference 728232) at 11.50 hrs. The instructor and his pupil had taken off at 10.50 hrs for a 1-hour training flight, nearing the end of which the instructor landed at Chetwynd airfield for unknown reasons. He then taxied fast, displaying 'slipshod aerodrome procedure', before taking off without waiting for the green light, and at an angle to the runway, as 'he was so close to the No. 1 flare that it would have been dangerous to take off parallel to the flarepath'. The instructor, who was in control for take-off, was unfamiliar with the airfield and also 'short of stature'. Consequently, as the aircraft rumbled down the runway, he could not see the airfield windsock directly ahead. As he lifted off at the end of the airstrip the aircraft collided with the windsock, tearing off a three foot square section of the leading edge and undersurface of the starboard mainplane. This caused the pilot to lose control and crash.

P/O Thomas Rutherford
[Library & Archives Canada]

F/O (instructor pilot) Geoffrey Hardie (156938), RAFVR, aged 22, was the son of John Charles and Josephine Hardie of Levenshulme, Manchester. He had been involved in an accident on 3 July 1940 while undergoing training at Tern Hill and further information can be found for him on that date. He is buried in Stockport (Willow Grove) Cemetery, Cheshire.

P/O (pilot u/t) Thomas Rutherford (J.35668), RCAF, aged 28, was the son of John and Agnes Rutherford and the husband of Margaret M Rutherford of New Westminster, British Columbia. Born in Hodgeville, Saskatchewan on 29 September 1915, he was educated to senior matriculation level in Saskatchewan and had a variety of jobs before enlisting in June 1942. He is buried in Chester (Blacon) Cemetery.

11 April (Tuesday)
Circuits. 81 OTU (RAF Sleap, Shropshire)
Airspeed Horsa I (LH449) crash-landed at Leaton Knolls, two miles south of Bomere Heath, at 12.40 hrs. The glider was being towed by a Stirling tug when the 'tow rope came adrift in extremely difficult country'. The glider was written off in the resultant forced landing (although none of the crew was injured).

Capt (1st pilot) Stanley Galland Cairns (164161), GPR. Born in Nottingham on 28 January 1919, he was training to be an accountant when he decided to join the army in July 1939. On completion of his training with the Survey Regiment, Royal Artillery, he was posted to Belgium during the 'Phoney War' and was subsequently evacuated from Dunkirk after the German invasion. Commissioned in December 1940, he served in the UK for the following two years before volunteering for the Glider Pilot Regiment in May 1942. Due to his being struck on the head by a propeller during training, he missed taking part in the glider-borne assault on Sicily in July 1943. Promoted to captain, he was then posted to Sleap and placed in command of three officers and 30 glider pilots to begin training in preparation for the D-Day landings. He subsequently took part on D-Day and in the airborne assault on Arnhem, where he was one of those fortunate enough to escape back to Allied lines. The remainder of the war was spent with the Independent Airborne Brigade in Italy where he was promoted to major before leaving the army in 1946 and returning to the UK to complete his accountancy training. He died in Canada in September 2007.

Capt Stanley Cairns
[Rob Cairns]

Staff Sgt (2nd pilot according to Captain Cairns logbook) Kendrick (service number unknown), GPR.

Staff Sgt (2nd pilot according to the accident card) Desmond Ryans (4694484), GPR, was from High Wycombe and had already taken part in the invasion of Sicily in July 1943. Following the accident he took part in the D-Day landings, Arnhem and the crossing of the Rhine in March 1945, for which he was awarded the DFM for his 'marked determination and coolness in times of adversity'.

Two unknown RAF passengers.

13 April (Thursday)
Non-operational photo reconnaissance training flight to Liverpool docks. 31st Photo Reconnaissance Squadron, 10th Photo Reconnaissance Group (Station 465, Chalgrove, Oxfordshire)
Lockheed F-5B Lightning (42-68254) crashed at Brookhouse Farm, behind the Lady Forester Hospital, Much Wenlock, at 10.00 hrs. On the day of the accident the pilot had been scheduled to fly an operational mission over north-west Europe but, after that was cancelled, he was instructed to carry out a training mission to photograph Liverpool docks from a height of 5,000 feet. Having taken the photos, the pilot was instructed to climb to 35,000 feet for the return flight. It was during this leg that he is believed to have 'lost control of the aircraft while flying on instruments and, after realising he could not recover or that the plane was coming to pieces, decided to leave it'. The accident was witnessed by Mr D N Hill, who lived at Brookhouse Farm and whose account is recorded on the BBC People's War website:

Lt Wallace Haywood in the cockpit of an F-5B aircraft. [via David J Smith]

I was ploughing in the next field and I saw the crash and the aeroplane burst into flames. Although I was quite close I did not approach the plane because I was worried that it may have bombs, or live ammunition on board and that it would blow up. Fortunately there was neither bombs nor ammunition on the plane. The pilot baled out, but his parachute failed to open and he fell to his death some distance from the plane. In a very short time a fire engine and an ambulance appeared on the scene together with Doctor Bigley, the local doctor, who certified that Wallace [the pilot] was dead.

In the subsequent investigation it was noted that members of the accident committee, 'have experienced instrument flying in this type of aircraft and realize the tendency of this type of aircraft to get out of control, especially at high speeds, when flying under instrument conditions'. It was, therefore, recommended that special emphasis be put on instrument flying and let-downs through overcast in this type of aircraft.

1 Lt (pilot) Wallace Murray Haywood (O-736204), USAAF, aged 24 (?), was the son of Leonard Ellis and Lucy Haywood of Danville City, Virginia. He is buried in Highland Burial Park, Danville City.

14 April (Friday)

Solo cross-country exercise. 3 Tactical Exercise Unit (RAF Annan, Dumfriesshire, Scotland)

Miles Martinet I (MS732) force-landed at 'Green House Farm, Alveley', to the south of Bridgnorth, at 18.25 hrs. After allowing his inner fuel tanks to run dry in flight the pilot switched to both outer tanks but was unable to restart the engine due to a petrol feed failure and, subsequently, belly-landed in a field. According to the accident card, the pilot should have selected only one of the outer tanks and it was obvious that he 'did not know the petrol system' and showed 'carelessness and stupidity'. Blame was also placed on the officer who authorised the flight, as he did not ensure that the pilot knew his petrol system.

W/O (pilot) Eddie Richardson (1023596), RAFVR. Born in Hunslet, Yorkshire on 19 April 1921, he had previously flown Typhoons operationally with 193 Squadron, during which time he shared in the destruction of a Me 110 on 10 February 1944. His posting to 3 TEU was probably to undergo training prior to 193 Squadron's change in role to a fighter-bomber unit, as he returned to the squadron in the autumn of 1944 and was commissioned at the same time. He survived the war and died in June 2004.

15 April (Saturday)

Circuits, landings and pinpointing exercise

5 (P)AFU (RAF Tern Hill, Shropshire). Miles Master II (AZ501) force-landed at Leaton (at wartime map reference 475187), near Bomere Heath, at 14.30 hrs. After throttling back the engine to descend through cloud, the pilot found that the throttle would not then open up again at 2,500 feet. He was forced to belly-land in a field as he was unable to maintain height.

F/Sgt (pilot u/t) Donald Peter Drummond (426325), RAAF. Born on 25 April 1921, he was the son of Peter and Elsie May Drummond of Wooloowin, Brisbane and had worked as an apprentice wood machinist before enlisting in June 1942. On completion of his training at Tern Hill he was posted to RAF Fayid in Egypt where he served from June–October 1944, before returning to the UK to undergo operational training. He was then posted to 183 Squadron in March 1945 (flying Typhoons) but was killed on 1 April when his Typhoon (DN248) was shot down by flak while attacking ground targets near Deventer in Holland. W/O Drummond was 23 years old and is buried in Hardenburg Protestant Cemetery, Overijssel, Holland.

Sub Lt Allen Lee [Auckland Museum Cenotaph]

16 April (Sunday)
Ferry flight from RNAS Lee on Solent, Hampshire to RNAS Stretton, Lancashire. 798 Squadron (HMS *Daedalus*, Lee-on-Solent, Hampshire)
Fairey Barracuda II (BV721) crashed at Leebotwood, near Church Stretton. 798 Squadron was a training unit formed at Lee-on-Solent in October 1943 to train crews for the newly-equipped Fleet Air Arm Barracuda squadrons. On 20 April 1944 a detached flight was to begin operating out of RNAS Stretton and it is believed that this aircraft was flying to the airfield, as part of the new establishment, when it crashed for unknown reasons.

Sub Lt (A) Allen Stephen Lee, RNZNVR, aged 22, was the son of John Kiljay and Jessie Renfrew Lee of Waipukurau, in the Hawkes Bay region of New Zealand. He is buried in Chester (Blacon) Cemetery.

17 April (Monday)
Local weather check. 552nd FTS, 495th FTG (Station 342, Atcham, Shropshire)
Republic P-47C Thunderbolt (41-6363, bearing the fuselage code DQ-E) crashed by the airfield, on the banks of the River Tern at Duncote Farm (at map reference 570114), at 16.50 hrs. Two of the unit's instructors, Captains Kirby Tracy and Howard Askelson, took off at 15.45 hrs for a local weather check and climbed to 8,000 feet where they did some aerobatics before returning to the airfield. After circling the airfield once, the two pilots peeled off at 450 feet with flaps and wheels down. Realising that his turn was too tight, Capt Askelson decided to go around again. Captain Tracy, on the other hand, who was flying approximately 75 feet behind Capt Askelson, tightened his turn to try and land, but his aircraft stalled and made a half-turn spin before crashing to the ground. Local schoolboy, Colin Thompson, who was helping out on Duncote Farm at the time, recalled the incident in 2008:

> We [Harley Griffiths and himself] just saw him side-slip behind some trees and then we saw the smoke. We both shouted 'Let's go'. We were down on the River Tern, so we left the tractor and we ran down across the railway and, of course, by the time we got there the crash crew had arrived at the scene and this Yankee was shouting 'Get back, get back, these cannons are loaded'. He'd hit the right-hand bank and slewed over and the nose was just in the river with the tail sticking up. If I remember, the wings had broken off.

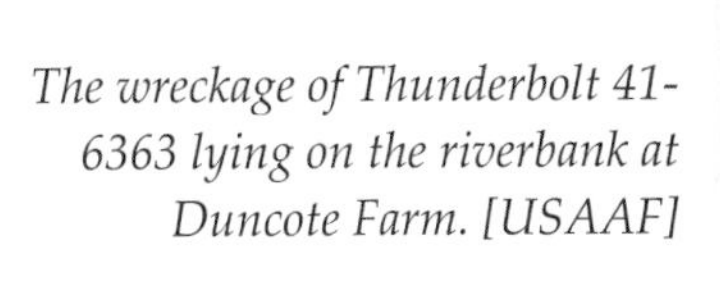

The wreckage of Thunderbolt 41-6363 lying on the riverbank at Duncote Farm. [USAAF]

Capt Kirby Tracy
[Peter Randall]

The cowman at the farm was Harley's uncle. He was the first to it. He reckons that Capt Tracy, they say, would have lived if apparently he hadn't loosened his harness straps and banged his head on the instrument panel when he hit the deck. He died on the way to the American base hospital.

Colin eventually got to see the wreckage close-up when it was pulled from the riverbank and clearly remembers the nose art; 'It was by the cockpit – a cartoon of a priest. In one hand he was holding a Bible out in front of him and in his left-hand by his side was a truncheon. It had *Topper* written above it and underneath, *So be it*.' By an amazing coincidence, the aircraft had been the personal mount of none other than Captain Askelson when he had flown out of Duxford with the 83rd Fighter Squadron, prior to his posting to Atcham. In a letter to the author in 2008, Colonel Askelson confirmed that he had had the nose art painted on when he was stationed at Duxford and also that he had shot down two enemy aircraft while flying it. The aircraft had been retired from front-line service around the same time that he was posted to Atcham as an instructor.

Capt (instructor pilot) Kirby N Tracy (O-387676), AM, USAAF, aged 27 (?), was the son of Jacob Nathaniel and Retta Tracy (née Pardue) of Pulaski County, Arkansas (but had later moved to Orleans Parish, Los Angeles). Prior to serving at Atcham as an instructor he had completed 17 missions with the 61st Fighter Squadron, 56th Fighter Group, and was considered to be a very good pilot by his colleagues, although also a daredevil. He was remembered with affection by the ground staff, including Technical Sergeant Wayne Scholer, who recalled in 2008 how 'he was a favourite amongst most of the people as he never went up in a two-seat aircraft with the back seat empty. He always took one of the ground staff with him, treat 'em to a ride as we didn't get many of them. I remember having one ride with him in what we called an AT-6 (a Harvard) and he turned the aeroplane every which way but loose! There's me in the back seat trying to stop myself vomiting my socks off!' Capt Tracy is buried in Cambridge (Madingley) Cemetery.

21 April (Friday)
Steep turns practice. 5 (P)AFU (RAF Tern Hill, Shropshire)
Miles Master II (DL127) crashed at Isombridge Farm, south of Longdon on Tern, at 15.50 hrs. While performing a steep turn to the left, at 1,100 feet (despite a briefing to do so only above 5,000 feet), the aircraft entered a spin from which the pilot was unable to regain control.

W/O (pilot u/t) Robert Emery Stewart (R.113645), RCAF, aged 23, was the son of George Perley Stewart and Ellen Stewart of Chatham Hill Street, New Brunswick, Canada. He is buried in Chester (Blacon) Cemetery.

22 April (Saturday)
Dogfighting practice. 61 OTU (RAF Rednal, Shropshire)
Supermarine Spitfire IA (R6623) crashed near Selattyn, to the north west of Oswestry. A section of Spitfires, led by F/Lt Raymond Baxter (who became the well-known commentator and TV presenter of *Tomorrow's World*), was engaged in a practice dogfight during which one Spitfire (W3364) struck the tail of this aircraft, causing it to crash out of control. The pilot of W3364 was able to make an emergency landing at the airfield.

Sgt (pilot u/t) Leslie James Friend (1318189), RAFVR, aged 20, was the son of George Lowen Friend and Agnes Friend of Gipsy Hill, London. He is buried in Oswestry General Cemetery, Shropshire.

Dogfighting practice. 61 OTU (RAF Rednal, Shropshire)
Supermarine Spitfire VA (W3364) landed at RAF Rednal following the collision described above.

Sgt (pilot u/t) Adriaan Jacob Bary (1649905), RAFVR. Born in Zevenaar, Holland on 1 May 1921, he had escaped to England in May 1940 as a member of the Dutch Army Air Force but, due to unknown circumstances, did not join the RAFVR until April 1942. Injured in a previous accident, on 5 January 1944, when he force-landed in Herefordshire, he was eventually posted to 322 (Dutch) Squadron in December 1944. On 13 February 1945 he was shot down by flak and wounded, while piloting a Spitfire (RK921) and taken prisoner of war. He was liberated from Enschede Hospital by Allied soldiers in April 1945.

23 April (Sunday)
Practice stalling, spinning and steep turns. 5 (P)AFU (Although it is unconfirmed it is believed to have been flying from RAF Condover, Shropshire – satellite to RAF Tern Hill)
Miles Master II (DL447) crashed at Eyton on Severn (at wartime map reference 575060), between Wroxeter and Cressage, at 12 noon. The pilot had just completed some aerobatics and was climbing to gain altitude when he failed to see an approaching P-47 (due to his 'short stature'). The two aircraft collided and crashed out of control, although the American pilot was able to take to his parachute.

Sgt (pilot u/t) Arthur Goddard (1473916), RAFVR, aged 20, was the son of Horace and Alice Goddard of Shiregreen, Sheffield. He is buried in Sheffield (City Road) Cemetery.

23 April (Sunday)
Training flight. 552nd FTS, 495th FTG (Station 342, Atcham, Shropshire)
Republic P-47C Thunderbolt (41-6585, bearing the fuselage code DQ-O) crashed at Eyton on Severn (at map reference 578074), near Wroxeter, after colliding in the incident described above.

2 Lt (pilot u/t) Ed Lyons (service number unknown), USAAF, hailed from Long Beach, California.

25 April (Tuesday)
Experimental flight. Telecommunications Flying Unit (RAF Defford, Worcestershire)
Bristol Beaufighter VI (EL167) crash-landed near Woofferton railway station, to the south of Ludlow. During the course of the flight the starboard engine failed and caught fire. While attempting to crash land, the pilot misjudged his approach, due to an inability to lower the flaps, causing the aircraft to strike trees and crash. Sadly, the navigator died of his injuries while the pilot suffered lacerations of the nose and abrasions of knees, and was admitted to Ludlow Cottage Hospital.

F/O (pilot) Cornelius Sipkes (124180), RAFVR, returned to his native Holland after the war and subsequently became a colonel in the Netherlands Air Force.

P/O (Nav) John Herbert Silvester (159721), RAFVR, aged 22, was the son of Herbert William and Gertrude May Silvester of Peckham Rye, London. He is buried in Camberwell New Cemetery.

27 April (Thursday)
Training flight. 61 OTU (RAF Rednal, Shropshire)
Supermarine Spitfire IIA (P7608) crashed at Maesbrook, near Oswestry. Very little is known of this incident (no accident card survives) other than that a collision occurred causing both aircraft involved to crash.

Sgt (pilot u/t) Marian Lis (792046), PAF, aged 23, was born in Splawie, a suburb of Poznań, in Poland on 5 September 1921 and had escaped to the UK in June 1940. He is buried in Lancaster Cemetery, Lancashire.

Training flight. 61 OTU (RAF Rednal, Shropshire)
Supermarine Spitfire IIA (P8079) crashed at Maesbrook following the collision described above.

W/O (pilot u/t) Eugeniusz Jaworski (784055), PAF, aged 22 was born in Luniniec, Poland (now part of Belarus) on 24 November 1921 and had escaped to the UK in June 1940. He served under the ID of his close friend, Jozef F Jaworzyn, at the time of his death and is buried in Market Drayton Cemetery, Shropshire.

F/O William Alexander [Library & Archives Canada]

28 April (Friday)
Night circuits and landings. 5 (P)AFU (RAF Condover, Shropshire – satellite to RAF Tern Hill)
Miles Master III (DM108) crashed at Grove Farm (at wartime map reference 488055), Condover, at 02.15 hrs. The pilot took off at 02.05 hrs and was making a circuit of the airfield when he ran into a patch of cloud through which he continued to fly, 'not entirely on instruments', while turning in an attempt to find the flare path. As he came out of the cloud, however, he realised that he had lost height and, by pulling back sharply on the control column to gain height, caused the aircraft to stall and crash.

F/O (pilot u/t) William Wilson Alexander (J.11082), RCAF, aged 26, was born in Pittsburgh, on 9 October 1917 and had worked in the city as a clerk prior to the war, living at 334 Birmingham Avenue. He volunteered for the RCAF in July 1941 and, on completion of his pilot training in Canada, was chosen for instructor training and remained there as an instructor until November 1943, when he sailed for the UK to prepare for operational flying. Initially buried in Chester (Blacon) Cemetery, his body was repatriated to Pittsburgh, USA after the war.

28 April (Friday)
Training flight. 61 OTU (RAF Rednal, Shropshire)
Supermarine Spitfire IIB (P8535) belly-landed 'one mile north of Rednal' (at wartime map reference 371302, near Hawkswood Farm, Hordley) at 11.50 hrs. The pilot was taking off from Rednal when the engine failed at 200 feet, due to a glycol leak, and he was forced to belly-land the aircraft in a field ahead.

F/O (pilot u/t) Marc George Rivet (J.25402), RCAF. Born on 2 March 1921, he had enlisted in the RCAF in March 1942 and underwent pilot training in Canada before sailing to the UK in May 1943. He had some lucky escapes during his training, including a crash at 7 (P)AFU which seriously injured him and killed his instructor, and a belly-landing on Rednal airfield in December 1943. Eight days after this, on 6 May 1944, he was involved in a mid-air collision with a Spitfire (X4821) while flying at 12,000 feet over Isycoed, Flintshire. F/O Rivet took to his parachute on that occasion, while the other pilot went down with his aircraft. Nothing further is known of his military service other than that he was repatriated to Canada in July 1944 and released from military service in November 1944.

30 April (Sunday)
Training flight. 83 OTU (RAF Peplow, Shropshire)
Vickers Wellington X (LN836) crash-landed at 'Manor Farm, Child's Ercall', at 20.15 hrs. The trainee crew were returning to the airfield when the aircraft ran out of fuel on the final approach and the pilot was forced to land in a field. This caused the port undercarriage to collapse and brought the aircraft to a stop. As a result of his carelessness the pilot was 'withdrawn from training'.

F/Sgt (pilot u/t) Audley Vincent Black (1253522), RAFVR. Nothing further is known of this airman other than that he survived the war.

The names of the five other crew members are unknown.

5 May (Friday)
Formation training. 552nd FTS, 495th FTG (Station 342, Atcham, Shropshire)
Republic P-47C Thunderbolt (41-6345, bearing the fuselage code DQ-?) crashed 'two and a half miles north-east of the airfield' (almost certainly at map reference 607133, between Isombridge and Walcot, where a crashed P-47 was seen) at 15.40 hrs. Lt Zumwalt was leading a flight of four P-47s when he noticed fuel streaming out of the belly of his number four and immediately called him up to inform him, while setting a course back to the airfield. No sooner had the flight turned than the pilot of number four called up over his R/T saying that fumes were entering his cockpit. Moments later, during an echelon turn to the left, he was overcome by fumes and his aircraft crashed out of control, hitting the ground in an inverted position.

2 Lt (pilot u/t) Gray A Mashburn (O-1300191), USAAF, aged 24, was the son of the former Attorney General for Nevada, Arthur Gray Mashburn, and his wife Ruby Mashburn (née Frick) of Carson City, Nevada. Born in Reno on 22 March 1920, he and his family subsequently moved to Carson where he was educated at the local high school before studying law at the University of California. He is buried in Mountain View Cemetary, Reno, Nevada.

5 May (Friday)
Night circuits and landings. 1665 HCU (RAF Tilstock, Shropshire)
Short Stirling III (EF117, bearing the fuselage code OG-L) crash-landed on 'Ash Hill', Ash Magna, to the north of the airfield, at 23.29 hrs. While this aircraft was making a circuit of the airfield its starboard inner engine suddenly caught fire. The pilot immediately feathered the propeller, retracted the undercarriage and carried out a belly-landing in a field. As the aircraft touched down the three remaining engines caught fire and the flames quickly spread through the fuselage but, fortunately, the crew were able to escape with, mostly, slight injuries. The two most seriously hurt between them suffered burns to the hands, face and a fractured left leg, and were conveyed to RAF Hospital, Cosford. The remaining crew were taken to the station sick quarters and checked over, before being sent to their

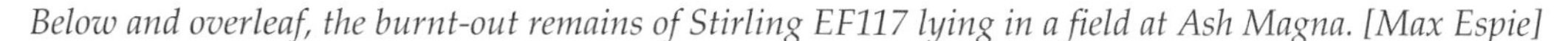

Below and overleaf, the burnt-out remains of Stirling EF117 lying in a field at Ash Magna. [Max Espie]

quarters to rest. For his 'coolness and initiative in getting his crew out of the machine' the pilot was subsequently commended by the station commander.

F/Sgt (pilot) Walter James Jennings (422058), RNZAF, was born in Palmerston North, New Zealand, on 24 April 1915 and had enlisted in the RNZAF in March 1942, arriving in the UK in June 1943. After recovering from his injuries he completed his HCU course at Tilstock and was posted to 570 Squadron in late 1944, flying Stirlings on special ops (including SOE drops and the Rhine crossing in March 1945). In recognition of his 'distinguished service and devotion to duty' he was mentioned in despatches in January 1945. He returned to New Zealand in December 1945 and died in Shannon, North Island, in January 1976.

Sgt (W/Op) W Bernard Meaten (1566821), RAFVR. Following the accident he completed his HCU course and was posted to 570 Squadron as part of F/Sgt Jennings' crew.

The names of the other four crew members are unknown.

6 May (Saturday)
Air test. 60 OTU (RAF High Ercall, Shropshire)
De Havilland Mosquito NF.II (HJ699) crashed '200 yards from the runway', at High Ercall, at 10.40 hrs. The aircraft was being piloted by a staff pilot, with an NCO from the training wing orderly room riding as passenger, when engine trouble was experienced after taking off. The pilot indicated that he was returning to the airfield to carry out a single-engine landing, but then 'failed to carry out set drill' by feathering the propeller which was out of action, causing the aircraft to stall and crash.

Sgt (staff pilot) James Lambert Terence Hinchliffe (1088305), RAFVR, aged 23, was the son of Ernest and Greta Hinchliffe of Scawthorpe, Doncaster. Prior to his posting as an instructor at 60 OTU on 3 April 1944, he had completed a tour of ops with 23 Squadron, flying Mosquitos in the Mediterranean. He is buried in Ardwick-le-Street Cemetery, Yorkshire.

Sgt (passenger) Percy George Orman Reynolds (743245), RAF, aged 25, was the son of Thomas George Archie and Maude Elise Jennie Reynolds of Southampton. He is commemorated at the Southampton Crematorium.

7 May (Sunday)
Dual instructional training flight. 5 (P)AFU (RAF Condover, Shropshire – satellite to RAF Tern Hill)
Miles Master II (DK880) force-landed at Longnor (at wartime map reference 493007), near Dorrington, at 10.45 hrs. Shortly after taking off, the engine failed at 500 feet and the instructor pilot took control and belly-landed the aircraft in a field.

F/Sgt (instructor pilot) Charles Smith Fraser (1346731), RAFVR. Nothing further is known of this airman, other than that he was commissioned in September 1944 and survived the war.

Sgt (pilot u/t) Carsten Henning Selvik Langeland (5831), RNoAF. On finishing his training he was posted to 332 (Norwegian) Squadron in November 1944 and completed a tour of ops flying Spitfires over north-west Europe.

7 May (Sunday)
Simulated instrument training mission. 551st FTS, 495th FTG (Station 342, Atcham, Shropshire)

Republic P-47C Thunderbolt (41-6627, bearing the fuselage code VM-?) crashed on Benthall Bank (at map reference 668022), Broseley, at 10.50 hrs. Two pilots took off at 10.30 hrs and climbed to 7,000 feet, where Lt Finney lowered his seat as far as possible and began simulated instrument flying while his wingman, Lt Jack F Flaitz, observed. In the subsequent accident investigation, Lt Flaitz stated that:

> ... [Lt Finney] proceeded to do climbing spirals to an altitude of 9,000 feet when I saw his plane snap roll one and one half times to the right. He affected a good recovery and started climbing again on instruments. At an altitude of 9,000 feet the plane again snapped rolled one and one half times and passed under me and out of my line of vision. When I saw the plane again, it was in a spin, with the nose at a shallow angle as in a flat spin. I followed the plane down to 2,000 feet and levelled off but it never recovered from the spin. I advised Lt Finney over the radio to bail out and we had good radio contact but he did not bail out.

2 Lt David Finney [Western Ellington Alumni Association]

In fact, Lt Finney had tried to bale out but had only managed to open his canopy and step onto the wing by the time the aircraft struck the ground. He was killed instantly.

2 Lt (pilot u/t) David Akers Finney (O-813138), USAAF, aged 23, was the son of Charles A and Edna Linn Finney of 2115 Pennsylvania Avenue, Washington DC. Educated at the Western High School in Washington DC, he had worked as a 'purchasing agent' for Weaver Bros (Washington realtors) before joining up. He then gained his wings in the USA and served as an instructor for a short while before sailing to the UK to prepare for operations. He is buried in Cambridge (Madingley) Cemetery.

8 May (Monday)
Training flight. 1665 HCU (RAF Tilstock, Shropshire)
Airspeed Horsa (LJ496) crashed 500 yards north of RAF Tilstock, at 15.11 hrs. A glider carrying two of 1665 HCU's pilot instructors as passengers, cast off from its tug aircraft and made a steep diving turn to port to line up for a landing on N°. 1 runway. However, as the pilot began to level off, the glider was still in a turning attitude with its port wing very low. The wing struck some power cables and the ground, flipping the glider onto its back as it crashed 100 yards further on.

Staff Sgt (1st pilot) John Charles Dyer (4924917), GPR, aged 22,was the son of Charles and Dilys Dyer of King's Norton, Birmingham. He is buried in Whitchurch Cemetery, Shropshire.

Sgt (2nd pilot) Gordon Dennis Coe (6898359), GPR, aged 23. was the son of William and Ivy Mabel Coe of Westcliff-on-Sea, Essex. He is commemorated at the Golders Green Crematorium, London.

F/Lt (instructor pilot) Alan Austin (123302), DFC, RAFVR, aged 22, was the son of Samuel and Ellen Austin of Levenshulme, Manchester. Commissioned in May 1942, his DFC was awarded in February 1943 while he was serving with 1651 HCU. The citation reads:

> Pilot Officer Austin has at all times displayed outstanding determination in operations against the enemy. He has participated in many successful sorties, on which excellent photographs of the target area have been obtained, often in the face of intense enemy opposition. While flying as captain of aircraft, Pilot Officer Austin's courage and keenness have provided an example of the highest order.

He is buried in Manchester Southern Cemetery.

F/Lt (instructor pilot) Sidney Godfrey Falconer (129233), DFC, DFM, RAFVR, aged 23, was the son of William and Annie Falconer of South Shields. His DFM was awarded for actions while serving with 218 Squadron, the citation for which read:

F/Lt Sidney Falconer, DFC, DFM [Ian Falconer]

> Temporary Sgt S G Falconer was captain of a Stirling aircraft which set out to raid Bremen on the night of 27/28 June 1942. About two miles over the Dutch coast, in the light of a full moon, the aircraft was attacked by a Ju88, which climbed suddenly from about 3000 feet below on the port bow, passed underneath and then came in on the port quarter. At the same time Sgt Falconer saw a second Ju88 coming in from the starboard bow and, immediately afterwards, the rear gunner reported an Me110 approaching from dead astern. The Me110 and the rear gunner opened fire simultaneously at about 350 yards, the Stirling's rear turret being rendered useless at once. The mid upper gunner took over fire control but a burst from the Messerschmitt, which was now coming in from the starboard and above, put that turret out of action. In the mean time the first Ju88 had shot away the British bomber's rear turret pipe lines and the second JU88 had been pumping her with tracer. The first JU88 attacked from dead ahead and, although the front gunner returned fire, his turret was rendered unserviceable after the first burst. During the whole of the combat, Sgt Falconer had been taking violent evasive action. Just when it seemed like he had shaken off his three attackers, a single engined unidentified enemy fighter appeared and raked the Stirling from nose to tail. The complete battle lasted for nearly 20 minutes and was fought from 15,000 feet down to sea level (the Stirling's trailing aerial was actually whipped off over the Zuider Zee). With two of his crew wounded, his front mid upper turrets useless, his astrodome, blind flying panel and oxygen system shot away, flying controls and control stick damaged, brake system, intercom and TR9 out of action, Sgt Falconer set course for home and weaved his way through strong concentrations of light flak over the Dutch coast. Sgt Falconer showed daring and adroitness of a very high order. His cool courage and command of the situation were remarkable. His expert and stout hearted captaincy undoubtedly saved the lives of his crew. He has now taken part in 20 operational sorties embracing 101 operational hours. His loyalty, fearlessness and sense of duty are outstanding.

Commissioned in June 1942, he was awarded the DFC in October 1943 for services with 214 Squadron, the citation reading:

> A first class operational pilot and captain of aircraft, Flight Lieutenant Falconer has successfully completed many operational sorties of a varied nature. He has set a high example of keenness and courage in his squadron and been unfailing in his devotion to duty.

He is buried in South Shields (Harton) Cemetery, Durham.

8 May (Monday)

Camera-gunnery and evasive-flying practice. 83 OTU (RAF Peplow, Shropshire)

Vickers Wellington X (LP568) crashed at the Sydnall (at wartime map reference 686308), Woodseaves, to the south of Market Drayton, at 15.35 hrs. Having taken off at 15.00 hrs, the pilot was practising a 'corkscrew' manoeuvre, which involved a steep diving turn to port followed by a sharp climbing turn to starboard and was a procedure intended for evading attacking night fighters. During the manoeuvre the starboard engine failed and the pilot tried to force-land. However, as he approached a field, his wing clipped a tree, causing the aircraft to crash. Of the eight crew on board, three were seriously injured and conveyed to RAF Hospital, Cosford (where the rear gunner died of his injuries), three were less seriously injured and conveyed to RAF Tern Hill station sick quarters by local farmer, Richard Gough, while the remaining two were unhurt.

Sgt (instructor? pilot) William Thomas Cake (551017), RAFVR, was commissioned in January 1945 and retired from the RAF as a flight lieutenant in January 1965.

Sgt (pilot u/t) Norman Laird Pegg (R.149993), RCAF. Born on 1 March 1920, he had enlisted as a radio mechanic in February 1942 but remustered as a pilot in December 1942 and began his pilot training in Canada. After sailing to the UK in September 1943 little is known of his military service other than that he survived the war and was released from service in March 1945.

Sgt Albert Wedin [Library & Archives Canada]

Sgt (AG) Albert Ormond Wedin, (R.221579), RCAF, aged 21, was the son of Albert O and Lillian S Wedin of Yreka, California. Born in Weyburn, Saskatchewan on 6 December 1922, he had worked as a truck driver before enlisting in February 1943. He is buried in Chester (Blacon) Cemetery.

The names of the other five crew members are unknown (although two of them are known to be RCAF and the remaining three were RAFVR).

13 May (Saturday)
Training flight (presumably formation flying). 61 OTU (RAF Rednal, Shropshire)
Supermarine Spitfire VA (R7343, presentation aircraft named *Hexham and District*) crashed at Five Ways (at map reference 413110), Ford Heath, near Yockleton. Little is known of the accident other than that the Polish pilot was joining formation at low altitude when the aircraft spun into the ground.

W/O (pilot u/t) Stefan Gruszczak (P-794547), PAF, aged 26, was born in Tropiszów, on the outskirts of Kraków, in Poland, on 19 March 1918. He is buried in Market Drayton Cemetery, Shropshire.

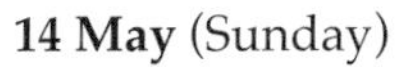
14 May (Sunday)
Steep turns and aerobatics. 5 (P)AFU (RAF Tern Hill, Shropshire)
Miles Master II (EM391) force-landed at 'The Chain House, Alkington' (at wartime map reference 532417), south of Whitchurch, at 09.50 hrs. After the engine failed, during a slow roll, the pilot belly-landed the aircraft in a field and was later conveyed to Tern Hill by RAF Tilstock's ambulance, having suffered slight injuries.

F/Sgt (pilot u/t) Jack Alexander Clyde Kennedy (427805), RNZAF. Born on 22 March 1922, he had enlisted at Waipapakauri in July 1942 and underwent pilot training in New Zealand before sailing to the UK in October 1943. Nothing further is known of his military service other than that he survived the war.

18 May (Thursday)
Navigation instruction. 81 OTU (RAF Sleap, Shropshire)
This officer was giving navigation instruction to a trainee crew and was not wearing his parachute, when the front escape hatch of a Whitley (LA924) gave way as he walked over it and he fell to his death from 1,400 feet. His body was found at 14.15 hours the same day at Cotonwood, between Tilstock and Whixall. A subsequent inspection of the escape hatch found the hinges worn and the airman in charge of maintaining the aircraft was consequently found 'blameworthy for not notifying the wear and tear on the hinges'.

P/O (navigation instructor) Robert Leonard Double (175954), DFM, RAFVR, aged 22, was the son of Albert Edward and Kate Double of Stowmarket. His DFM was awarded in August 1943 following a tour of ops on Stirling bombers with 199 Squadron. The recommendation read:

> Since October 1942, Sergeant Double has taken part as Bomb Aimer in 27 operational sorties over enemy territory and has completed 154 hours operational flying. These operations include a daylight attack on Essen and night attacks on Duisburg (2), Hamburg (2), Stuttgart and Mannheim as well as numerous sorties on other targets in Germany and France and the laying of mines in enemy waters. Under calm and quiet manner, he

hides a fine offensive spirit. He has always pressed home his attacks with the utmost determination, frequently in the face of strong enemy opposition. This action has inspired his crew and contributed in a large measure to the success of his operations.

He is buried in Stowmarket Cemetery, Suffolk.

18 May (Thursday)
Training flight. 83 OTU (RAF Peplow, Shropshire)
Vickers Wellington X (HE830) crash-landed near Child's Ercall village (at wartime map reference 676236). The pilot was carrying out overshoot procedure after a swing developed on landing but, as the aircraft passed over the airfield boundary, the starboard engine failed. The instructor immediately took control and just managed to clear some houses and trees before crash-landing the aircraft in a field directly ahead. The pupil pilot was slightly injured in the process.

W/O (instructor pilot) Ronald Edward Brown (748253), RAFVR.

Sgt (pilot u/t) Noel John Crane (1316063), RAFVR. Born in Poole, Dorset, on 15 October 1921, he subsequently flew Lancaster bombers with 153 Squadron and was awarded the DFC in July 1945. He died in Poole in 1996.

The names of the other five crew members are unknown.

19 May (Friday)
Day flying training. 83 OTU (RAF Peplow, Shropshire)
Vickers Wellington III (BJ662) crashed 'two miles from the airfield' at 12.25 hrs. While taking off, the pilot mishandled his pitch controls, causing the port engine to run with excessive revs. He immediately began a circuit and requested permission to make an emergency landing. Permission was granted but, as the pilot approached with flaps and wheels down, he realised that he was overshooting and began to make another circuit of the airfield. After crossing the boundary at 1,000 feet, he turned into his dead engine, causing the aircraft to stall and crash. The rear gunner was killed and the five remaining crew were badly injured.

Sgt (pilot) Gordon John Bradbury (R.152357), RCAF. Born on 7 December 1922, he had enlisted in January 1942 and underwent pilot training in Canada before sailing to the UK in June 1943. He was subsequently released from service in February 1945 and returned to Canada.

Sgt Rannie McKinnon [Library & Archives Canada]

F/O (Nav) Joseph Edouard Gerard Leblanc (J.28914), RCAF. Born on 16 March 1921, the son of Albert and Rose Leblanc of Montreal, he had enlisted in June 1942. After recovering from his injuries he was posted to 432 (RCAF) Squadron but was killed on 16 September 1944 when his Halifax (NP719) was lost during an op to Kiel. F/O Leblanc was 23 years old and is buried in Aabenraa Cemetery, Denmark.

Sgt (AB) Joseph Jean Roland Lanctot (R.164779), RCAF. Born on 19 April 1921, he had enlisted in Montreal in June 1942 and survived the war.

W/O II (W/AG) Peter Noel Leveille (R.163579), RCAF. Born on 19 December 1922, he had enlisted in Regina in April 1942 and survived the war, returning to Canada in August 1945.

Sgt (AG) Owen Sidney Thetford Clarke (R.200657), RCAF. Born on 28 August 1922, he lived in Hamilton, Ontario and had enlisted there in November 1942. After recovering from his injuries, he was posted to 433 (RCAF) Squadron and was awarded the DFC in November 1945 for his 'courage and devotion to duty' (and also for downing an enemy night fighter during one op).

Sgt (AG) John Ronald McKinnon (R.62951), RCAF, aged 24, was the son of Dougal and Mary McKinnon (née McPhee) of Glace Bay, Nova Scotia. Known as Rannie to many, he had attended MacKay's Corner School, after which he worked at Shore's Marketeria before enlisting in the RCAF. He is buried in Harrogate Cemetery, Yorkshire.

19 May (Friday)
Instrument and aerobatics training. 552nd FTS, 495th FTG (Station 342, Atcham, Shropshire)
Republic P-47D Thunderbolt (42-7926, bearing the fuselage code DQ-K) crash-landed at 'Sondern Estate [Sundorne Castle Estate which covered a large area around Haughmond Hill], 1,000 yards from the end of runway 01,' at 15.27 hrs. The pilot, with call sign Yapper 23, was approaching the airfield at approximately 3,000 feet, when he called airfield control to say that his propeller was not functioning properly and revs would not increase. Permission was given for him to land immediately. In the pilot's own account:

> I let my wheels down and came in but came in too hot and had to go around. I pulled up my wheels and went around. The tower said to lower my wheels on down wind leg and come on in. I came in too hot again and gave it full throttle but couldn't get enough power from the prop so gave it supercharge but it still didn't have enough power. I pulled up my wheels and bellied it in a field just off the runway.

The subsequent examination of the aircraft showed that the 'propeller blades were at a 45-degree angle, indicating that this pilot neglected to manually select increase RPM for some reason or another'. The report added that newly-arrived pilots should be advised on the importance of brushing up on emergency procedures as, in most cases, 'pilots become nervous and neglect to carry out minor details. As a result they get into predicaments such as this pilot'.

2 Lt (pilot u/t) Leonard R Bennett (O-818326), USAAF. On finishing his training he completed 101 missions with the 10th Fighter Squadron, 50th Fighter Group.

25 May (Thursday)
Low-altitude navigational training mission to the Bristol Channel. 552nd FTS, 495th FTG (Station 342, Atcham, Shropshire)
Republic P-47C Thunderbolt (41-6367, bearing the fuselage code DQ-?) crashed at Lower Treverward Farm (at map reference 273777), to the south west of Clun, at 12.15 hrs. Two pilots took off at 11.45 hrs for the training flight but, after encountering bad weather over the high ground in south Shropshire, the leader of the element, 1 Lt Thomas Guerrero Jr, decided that the pair would return to base. Lt Guerrero's account continues:

> The weather was getting lower at approximately 12.00 hrs and I noticed that Lt Carson fell back about 100 yards. Immediately after, we ran into a solid wall and we made a quick turn to the left to a heading of 0 degrees. After flying for several minutes I was uncertain of my position and I called Starglow several times for a homing--with no answer. I rocked my wings wanting Lt Carson to come into close formation to go into the clouds. Our altitude was approximately 800 feet. I called Lt Carson by ship number with no answer. Soon after I heard R/T from Lt Carson but could not read his message. His voice was not excited and his ship did not seem to be in trouble. On the course back I kept turning slightly to the left to stay in sight of the hills and fly in the valley where the overcast had not yet reached. At approximately 12.05 hrs I turned to a heading of 40 degrees still flying up a valley. Lt Carson was at this time about 50 yards to the rear not quite in trail. As I could not see the tops of the hills I went into the overcast at about 1000 to 1200 feet. As I entered the overcast I looked back and Lt Carson was not there. I climbed to 2500 to 3000 feet, got a homing and flew back to the field.

It was subsequently concluded that Lt Carson had either been 'caught in the slipstream of his element

1 Lt Frank Melkush Jr [Alan Bucari]

leader in cloud and lost control or, having entered cloud, he lost his number one and, not being on instruments, fell off in a spiral dive', striking a tree and then cartwheeling along the ground.

2 Lt (pilot u/t) Gale E Carson (O-686818), USAAF, aged 24, was the son of Jess C and Frances E Carson of Spokane City, Washington. He is buried in Arlington National Cemetery, Virginia.

26 May (Friday)
Aerobatics training. 552nd FTS, 495th FTG (Station 342, Atcham, Shropshire)
Republic P-47D Thunderbolt (42-75186, bearing the fuselage code DQ-?) crashed on the edge of Shawbury village, to the north-east of Shawbury airfield, at 19.14 hrs. The aircraft was witnessed, by RAF Shawbury's Airfield Controller, performing aerobatics at approximately 5,000 feet, during which time the aircraft entered a flat spin. After a few seconds the aircraft straightened out but, at approximately 2,000 feet, it started to spin again. The pilot called up base over the R/T and reported that he was 'spinning and could not recover' but, for unknown reasons, made no attempt to bale out.

1 Lt (pilot u/t) Frank O Melkush (O-668483), USAAF, aged 24, was the son of German-born Frank and Olive North Melkush and was educated at Springfield High School and Brown's Business College, after which he was employed in the general offices of C & IM railroad. Enlisting six days after the attack on Pearl Harbour, he was subsequently chosen for instructor duties and served at Moore Field, Texas, before travelling to the UK to begin operational training. He was initially buried in Cambridge (Madingley) Cemetery before being repatriated to Oakridge Cemetery, Springfield, Illinois, after the war.

The wreckage of Lt Melkush's Thunderbolt near Shawbury. [USAAF]

26 May (Friday)
Altitude formation training. 552nd FTS, 495th FTG (Station 342, Atcham, Shropshire)
Republic P-47D Thunderbolt (42-8562, bearing the fuselage code DQ-U) crashed 'near Newport' at 20.25 hrs. A flight of four pilots climbed away from the airfield in close formation to 23,000 feet, at which point they spread out into battle formation and were 'bounced' by another flight. The engagement lasted for just a few turns, following which the flight re-formed and made a few further turns at 18,000 feet, before beginning a spiral dive to the left. After one turn of this spiral, aircraft No. 4

(piloted by 2 Lt White) overtook N°. 3 and collided with the wing tip of N°. 2 (piloted by 2 Lt Lowers). Lt White's aircraft was so badly damaged that he baled out but, tragically, his parachute was 'spilled' by a gust of wind as he prepared to land and he was thrown into the dried branches of a tree and killed. In the meanwhile, Lt Lowers managed to maintain control of his aircraft and, according to his account,

> I called N°. 1 and he could not understand me. Then N°. 3 man called him and told him that my right wing tip was battered in. My radio seemed very poor at times. I followed N°. 3 man until we found N°. 1 man and proceeded back to the field. While circling the field, I checked my flaps, then followed N°. 1 man on into the pattern and planned it big so as not to stall.

2 Lt (pilot u/t) Robert S White (O-818496), USAAF, was from Massachusetts. He is buried in Cambridge (Madingley) Cemetery.

2 Lt Lower's Thunderbolt pictured after landing at Atcham with its right wing tip bent downwards. [USAAF]

Altitude formation training. 552nd FTS, 495th FTG (Station 342, Atcham, Shropshire) Republic P-47C Thunderbolt (41-6203, bearing the fuselage code DQ-H) landed at Atcham airfield after colliding in the incident described above.

2 Lt (pilot u/t) Daniel E Lowers (O-821741), USAAF. Nothing further is known of this pilot other than that he was from Hamilton, Ohio.

2 June (Friday)
Instrument flying and navigation training. 551st FTS, 495th FTG (Station 342, Atcham, Shropshire) Republic P-47D Thunderbolt (42-7929, bearing the fuselage code VM-Q) crashed at Walford Manor, to the south-east of Baschurch, at 08.50 hrs. Two pilots had taken off in formation at 07.55 hrs and climbed to 15,000 feet, where they levelled off and took it in turns to practise instrument flying while the other observed. Having completed the exercise, Captain William D Smith broke away and departed, while his wingman, Captain White, is believed to have remained in the area to 'execute a deliberate spin to satisfy himself as to his ability to recover'. Soon afterwards, the aircraft was seen spinning out of control and the pilot baled out at an altitude between 2 and 3,000 feet. It is believed that he may have been temporarily knocked unconscious as he failed to pull the ripcord until it was too late.

Capt (pilot u/t) George O White (O-393595), USAAF, aged 25, was the son of Augustine Withers White and Columbia Malo White of Huntsville, Alabama. He is buried in Maple Hill Cemetery, Huntsville, Alabama.

The smouldering wreckage of Thunderbolt 42-7929 pictured in a field at Walford Manor. [USAAF]

2 June (Friday)
Tail chase. 61 OTU (RAF Rednal, Shropshire)
Supermarine Spitfire IIA (P8443, presentation aircraft named *Molukken*) crashed at Meadow Farm (at wartime map reference 438244), between Weston Lullingfields and Marton, to the north of Baschurch, at 10.30 hrs. The instructor pilot was leading a 'tail chase' at 7,000 feet when his aileron jammed during a diving turn and he was forced to take to his parachute. In the subsequent investigation it was discovered that the aircraft had recently had new left and right ailerons fitted and, although no evidence could be found to explain why the aileron had jammed, the problem was presumed to be related to the recent alterations.

F/O (instructor pilot) Ross Kenneth Whitney (J.16287), RCAF, retired from the RCAF in March 1945 and returned to his native Canada. He died in British Columbia in 1989.

3 June (Thursday)
Single-engine approach and overshoot practice. 81 OTU (RAF Sleap, Shropshire)
Armstrong Whitworth Whitley V (LA770) crashed at 'Belton Farm, Myddle', near Harmer Hill, at 16.10 hrs. After overshooting his landing approach, the pilot opened up the throttles to make another circuit but, as the aircraft passed over the airfield at 200 feet, the port engine failed due to a possible failure of the supercharger. Because the aircraft was unable to maintain height, its starboard tailplane struck a tree, causing the aircraft to crash and catch fire, seriously injuring two of the crew (one of whom died five days later in RAF Hospital, Cosford) and injuring the remaining two.

F/O (pilot u/t) Kenneth William Wright (152177), RAFVR, survived the war and eventually relinquished his commission as a flight lieutenant in January 1957.

F/Sgt (W/AG) Clarence Stephen (Steve) Nickson (1120869), RAFVR, aged 23, was the son of Clarence and Ethel May Nickson of Lupset, Wakefield. He is buried in Wakefield Cemetery, Yorkshire.
The names of the two remaining crew members are unknown.

8 June (Thursday)
F/Sgt C S Nickson, RAFVR, died in RAF Hospital, Cosford as a result of injuries sustained on 3 June.

8 June (Thursday)
Formation training. 551st FTS, 495th FTG (Station 342, Atcham, Shropshire)
Republic P-47D Thunderbolt (42-7913, bearing the fuselage code VM-P) belly-landed at Eyton House Farm, to the east of Bratton airfield, near Wellington, at 18.00 hrs. The pilot was flying in number three position of a four aircraft formation when he began to experience engine problems and asked his flight leader to head back towards the airfield. As they did so, the engine failed and, according to the pilot's statement,

I looked around and discovered I was over a town. Since the plane was at 1,500 feet, I decided not to bail out because of the town and started looking for a field. Up ahead I saw a large green field and started for it. It

Thunderbolt 42-7913 lying in a field near Wellington. [USAAF]

became apparent that I was not going to make it so I went into a big brown field. The flaps came down normally and I cut the switches, slowing the plane up, trying to lift it over a hedge. My tail dug through a grain field for about 20 yards and then I hit the hedge. I bounced for about 10 yards and settled back to earth. The plane slid forward for 143 steps and came to a halt. The time was 18:00 hours.

I checked the cockpit, unbuckled and crawled out. The engine was very hot. A farmer came running up and I told him to stand back. A fire engine from the RAF field across the road [RAF Bratton] came up within a quarter of a mile of the plane and brought fire extinguishers. They stood by for about 45 minutes.

2 Lt Claude Chinn [Peter Randall]

The subsequent examination of the aircraft showed that it was a technical failure that had caused the problem and that the pilot 'was fully justified in handling his aircraft the way he did'.

2 Lt (pilot u/t) Claude Allen Chinn (O-702766), USAAF. Born in Independence, Missouri, on 3 August 1923, he was the son of Arthur W and Gwen Chinn (née Brewer). After leaving school he worked in a steel mill before joining up in February 1942 and being accepted for pilot training. Soon after the accident in Shropshire he joined the 63rd Fighter Squadron, 56th Fighter Group and was credited with seven enemy aircraft shot down by the time he completed his tour in December 1944. Soon after, he returned home where he eventually married and had three children. He died in March 2006.

10 June (Saturday)
Local flight. 758 Squadron (HMS *Godwit*, RNAS Hinstock, Shropshire)
De Havilland Tiger Moth II (BB857) crashed 'into the River Severn' (although unconfirmed, it is believed to have crashed into the river near Ironbridge). According to the pilot, who recalled the event in a conversation with the author in 2009, every Saturday the instructors were allowed to 'vent their spleen' on a small aeroplane and he had taken off, alongside a fellow instructor, to do just that. Soon after leaving the airfield the other pilot indicated that he was descending and

> ... started going down and levelled off at about 500 feet and I'm afraid I went down to almost zero. I then followed the Severn and then hit some high tension cables and stopped all the local farmers doing anything for a few days! I was in hospital for about a fortnight.

Midshipman (instrument instructor pilot) Maurice H C Such, RNVR. Born in Salford in 1924, he had undergone his pilot training in Canada, after which he returned to the UK and was selected for instructor training prior to being posted to HMS *Godwit*. Following the accident he left the Fleet Air Arm, was subsequently called up into the army and served in 4 Royal Tank Regiment during the closing stages of the war.

12 June (Monday)
Training flight. 5 (P)AFU (RAF Tern Hill, Shropshire)
Miles Master II (DL418) force-landed at Wollerton, between Hodnet and the airfield, at 16.40 hrs. Immediately after the aircraft took off, the engine cut at 150 feet and, with little time to react, the Indian pilot belly-landed in a field and was slightly injured.

P/O (pilot u/t) R S Sandhu (18006), IAF. His identity has yet to be confirmed.

13 June (Tuesday)
Formation flying. 5 (P)AFU (RAF Tern Hill, Shropshire)

Miles Master II (DL194) crash-landed at Harnage Grange Farm (at wartime map reference 581018), between Harley and Acton Burnell, at 17.20 hrs. The pilot had been in the air for an hour and was flying at 3,000 feet when the engine cut, possibly as a result of 'violent movement of controls'. In the resultant forced landing the pilot was seriously injured.

F/O (pilot u/t) Leonard Vernon Chambers (158018), RAFVR. He survived the war attaining the rank of flight lieutenant.

14 June (Wednesday)
Day dual training flight. 60 OTU (RAF High Ercall, Shropshire)
De Havilland Mosquito T.III (HJ863) crashed on the airfield at 10.59 hrs. The instructor and his pupil were returning to the airfield, after 25 minutes in the air, when the port engine failed, due to a glycol leak, during an overshoot. The aircraft stalled and crashed in flames.

F/Lt (instructor pilot) Antony Trelawney Wickham (103011), DFC, RAFVR, was the son of the late Colonel Thomas Edward Palmer Wickham, DSO and Betty Wickham (née Grieve) of Averys, Rusper. His DFC had been awarded in February 1943, while serving with 105 Squadron. The group citation read:

> On 30 January 1943, two forces of bombers were detailed to attack Berlin, one during the morning and the other in the afternoon. To reach the German capital necessitated a flight of more than 500 miles, mostly over heavily defended territory. Close coordination and precise timing were essential, but such was the skill exhibited, that the target was reached and the attacks delivered within seconds of the specified time. That complete success was achieved despite opposition from the ground forces, is a high tribute to the calm courage, resolution and endurance displayed by the following officers and airmen who, in various capacities, acted as members of the aircraft crews.

Before arriving at 60 OTU in May 1944, he had completed a second tour of ops flying Mosquitos with 21 Squadron. He is buried in Rusper (St Mary Magdalene) Churchyard, Sussex.

F/Lt (pilot u/t) Kenneth Eric Evans (40619), RNZAF, aged 34, was the son of Somerville Walter Robert Evans and Caroline Evans (née McCarthy) of Palmerston North, New Zealand. Before being posted to 60 OTU for pilot training, he had completed 55 ops as a navigator with a number of units, including a tour with 75 Squadron, RNZAF. He is buried in Chester (Blacon) Cemetery.

16 June (Friday)
Navigational training mission. 551st FTS, 495th FTG (Station 342, Atcham, Shropshire)
Republic P-47D Thunderbolt (42-7890, bearing the fuselage code VM-K) crashed near the Bluebell crossroads (at map reference 597103), just north of Uppington, at 09.12 hrs.The pilot, with call sign Honey 28, had been in the air for an hour and fifty minutes when his engine began to lose power and he prepared to make an emergency landing at the airfield. After overshooting his approach, however, the pilot was forced to make another circuit. As he lined up for his second attempt, the engine failed and he was forced to put the aircraft down in a field. Local schoolboy, Colin Thompson, visited the scene soon afterwards and recalled how

> ... there was a line of poplars by Uppington, known as the Uppington Avenue. He clipped the top of those trees, carried on, hit a power pole and then came to rest in a field pretty near to the Bluebell crossroads. Its wings had come off and all you could see was the fuselage lying on its side.

The subsequent investigation concluded that the engine problem was caused by 'failure of a bolt which connected the control rod to the bell crank' although, it added, the pilot would still have been able to operate the propeller by using the manual selector. In the opinion of the accident investigators, the pilot 'did run into a good deal of difficulty and, upon applying himself, became a bit confused, thereby getting into a situation which pretty near cost his life'.

Thunderbolt 42-7890 had previously served with the 4th Fighter Squadron, 334th Fighter Group and bore the nose art Boise Bee, *but is pictured here after being written off near Uppington. [USAAF]*

2 Lt (pilot u/t) Alfred A Garback (O-700252), USAAF. On completion of his training he was posted to the 84th Fighter Squadron, 78th Fighter Group and shared in the destruction of an enemy aircraft on 5 August 1944. He returned to the USA in November 1945 and died in Southgate, Michigan, in 1998.

16 June (Friday)
Low-level navigation training. 551st FTS, 495th FTG (Station 342, Atcham, Shropshire)
Republic P-47D Thunderbolt (42-22543, bearing the fuselage code VM-L) crash-landed 'half a mile from the end of runway 30' (approximate map reference 56017) at 15.27 hrs. The pilot was returning from a training mission when his engine RPM's suddenly increased. He notified his flight leader, who told him to return to the airfield and land immediately. After overshooting his approach, however, the pilot experienced a sudden decrease in power as he passed over the end of the runway and was forced to belly-land in a field ahead. In the subsequent investigation it was concluded that

> ... the speed he was travelling [at] and the diving attitude coming in to land was the reason for his RPM's to be around 2,400 RPM; when, upon applying power and raising his nose to go around, the engine load imposed upon the engine – which was actually in a coarser position than the pilot believed – caused it to lose power.

Above & left: Lt Parmelee's Thunderbolt lying in a cornfield following the crash-landing near Atcham. [USAAF]

2 Lt (pilot u/t) Charles Edmund Parmelee (O-700211), USAAF. On completion of his training he was posted to 84th Fighter Squadron, 78th Fighter Group, piloting P-47s over north-west Europe. During his tour he was credited with three enemy aircraft destroyed (and two on the ground) but he did not survive the war and was killed on 10 September 1944, in a P-47 (43-25593) which was shot down over Luxembourg. His body was repatriated to the USA after the war for burial in Arlington National Cemetery.

19 June (Monday)
Camera-gunnery training mission. 551st FTS, 495th FTG (Station 342, Atcham, Shropshire)
Republic P-47C Thunderbolt (41-6225, bearing the fuselage code VM-M) crash-landed near the Manor Stone, on Cothercott Hill (at map reference 413996), near Picklescott, at 15.10 hrs. The pilot was flying at 5,000 feet when his engine began cutting out due to a 'failure of the oil line connection' and, according to his account, he

> … immediately put the prop control switch into manual increase RPM but there was no reaction shown on the tachometer. I tried then to increase the throttle setting but I couldn't change the manifold pressure with the throttle. At that time my engine spluttered a bit and completely stopped. I then read the cylinder head temperature at 200°C and while looking for a field I called the base and gave them my altitude and told them I was going to make a belly-landing. They then gave me my position as 8 miles south of the field. After changing fields due to the presence of workers I had to land cross-wind going south in a plowed [sic] field, wheels up. Before landing I cut off the gas and ignition switches lowered my seat and made sure my harness was locked. I dropped my flaps a few seconds before hitting the ground and noticed no abnormal jar on landing which took place at 1510 hours.

Above: Thunderbolt 41-6225 pictured after it came to rest on Cothercott Hill, near Picklescott. [USAAF]

Left: A portrait photo of Warren Huber. [Paul Huber]

Local farmworker, Tom Morris, of the Outrack, near Pulverbatch, was working nearby and visited the scene soon afterwards. He clearly recalled how the aircraft had touched down in a potato field (the heather-covered hilltop had been planted with potatoes as part of the war effort) near the old 'Lostwithin Mine' workings and had skidded some distance across the hilltop, leaving a furrow in its wake. While inspecting the aircraft, he found that the military guard was most relaxed and even let him look inside the cockpit.

2 Lt (pilot u/t) Warren Elmer Huber (O-815341), USAAF. Born in Minnesota on 11 February 1922, the son of John and Nellie Huber, he and his family eventually moved to Milwaukee, Wisconsin. On completion of his training he was posted to the 509th Fighter Squadron and flew P-47s during the latter stages of the Normandy campaign. On 9 August 1944 he made another forced landing after his engine failed,

but this time he was forced to land in an area still occupied by the enemy and spent the following two days evading capture before returning to the Allied lines. Sadly, he was killed on 12 December 1944 when his P-47 was shot down during a mass dogfight over the Kaiserslautern area of Germany. His body was repatriated for burial in Pinelawn Cemetery, Milwaukee, after the war.

20 June (Tuesday)
Navigation and instrument training mission. 552nd FTS, 495th FTG (Station 342, Atcham, Shropshire) Republic P-47C Thunderbolt (41-6381, bearing the fuselage code DQ-M) crashed at Dawley Bank (at map reference 683084), in what is now part of Telford, at 14.26 hrs. Lt Jensen and 2 Lt Dwight W Johnson took off from Atcham at 14.00 hrs, circled the field and then climbed to 3,000 feet, where they made a simulated attack on two P-47s. In the ensuing 'dogfight', Lt Jensen attempted to shake off one of the P-47s and 'executed a violent half wing-over and half split S' at 2,000 feet, from which he failed to recover. As a consequence of the accident, it was stated that pilots should be cautioned on the dangers of 'dog-fighting' at low altitude, especially when engaged on other missions.

The wreckage of 2 Lt Jensen's Thunderbolt on the village green at Dawley Bank. [USAAF]

2 Lt (pilot u/t) Clifford Wallace Jensen (O-766541), USAAF, aged 21, was of mixed Danish-German parentage, the son of George and Christina Jensen of Lane County, Oregon. Born on 4 October 1922, he and his family later moved to Alameda, California, where he enlisted in March 1943. He is buried in Golden Gate National Cemetery, California.

20 June (Tuesday)
Tactical reconnaissance exercise. 41 OTU (RAF Poulton, Cheshire – satellite to RAF Hawarden, Flintshire)
Hawker Hurricane IIC (LF359) crashed at Moreton Hall Farm (at wartime map reference 631349), Moreton Say, to the west of Market Drayton, at 14.20 hrs. After losing control, while flying in cloud at 2,000 feet, the pilot 'made incorrect recovery' and the aircraft spun into the ground. The loss of control was subsequently attributed to an 'error of judgement' and 'the comparative inexperience of the pilot on modern aircraft'.

Capt (pilot u/t) Lars Trygve Heyerdahl-Larsen (5882), RNoAF, aged 31, was the son of Captain Trygve Heyerdahl-Larsen and the late Kirsten F. Rolson of Oslo. Born on 12 September 1912, he married Else Holst in 1938 and lived in Oslo. He joined the Norwegian Army Air Service before the war and fought during the German invasion. Following the capitulation of Norway, he served as a member of the resistance, before escaping to the UK, via Sweden, to join the RNoAF. Cremated at Honour Oak Crematorium, London, his ashes were returned to Norway and interred at Vestre Gravlund, Oslo.

22 June (Thursday)
Transition training. 552nd FTS, 495th FTG (Station 342, Atcham, Shropshire)
Republic P-47D Thunderbolt (42-8397, bearing the fuselage code DQ-S) crash-landed at Duncote Farm, on the north edge of the airfield, at 11.09 hrs. Immediately after take-off the engine began cutting out due to a suspected carburettor problem and the pilot (call sign Yapper 32), turned back towards the airfield to make an emergency landing. By this stage another aircraft had taxied onto the runway to take off and Yapper 32 was forced to open up the throttle and attempt another circuit. As he did so, the engine lost power again and he was forced to belly-land in a field ahead.

1 Lt (pilot u/t) Norman Horace Frisbie (O-26336), USAAF. Born in Montana on 9 January 1922, he flew P-47s with the 397th Fighter Squadron, 368th Fighter Group, on completing his training. He subsequently served in both the Korean and Vietnam wars before retiring as a colonel. He died in Holden, Louisiana in January 2000.

25 June (Sunday)
Formation training. 551st FTS, 495th FTG (Station 342, Atcham, Shropshire)
Republic P-47C Thunderbolt (41-6231, bearing the fuselage code DQ-B) crashed along New House Lane (at map reference 435037), near Pulverbatch, at 19.45 hrs. A flight of four P-47s, led by Captain Joe H Powers, took off from Atcham at 18.30 hrs and flew in close formation for about an hour until they were 'bounced' by another flight of between two and four aircraft. According to the subsequent investigation, a 'general rat race' developed, in which considerable altitude was lost by all aircraft but, after a short while, the 'rat race' broke off and the pilots 'flew around at random in an attempt to regain their positions'. Local belief, however, is that the pilots had been to a party at Wrentnall House the previous night (where the Holcroft family frequently entertained American flyers) and were now putting on 'a bit of a show'. Numerous local witnesses describe how the aircraft were seen 'stunting' and just moments before the crash the aircraft passed low over the church, where people were coming out of an evening service. According to an eyewitness account, provided for the investigation:

> I observed the third aircraft in line come extremely close to a low church tower. He seemed to take evasive action at the last moment which just cleared the steeple and lifted his star plane. He righted this and was only a few feet from the trees.
>
> The next action was somewhat indistinct, as he was a little distance away, but it appeared that he attempted a bank to port. Port wing came down striking some obstruction causing him to come in contact with the ground.

The obstruction was, in fact, a large tree on the edge of the lane, which was scythed down as the aircraft exploded in a mass of flames, spreading wreckage northwards across a cornfield. The subsequent investigation concluded that the pilot had either 'just begun a roll off the deck and slipped out of it', 'executed a turn too close to the ground and misjudged his distance', or 'could have been caught in another aircraft's slipstream while in a turn and lost control'.

2 Lt (pilot u/t) Arthur David Brody (O-767100), USAAF, aged 20, was the son of Joseph and Edna Brody of 930-29 Street, Des Moines, Iowa. He is buried in Cambridge (Madingley) Cemetery.

Lt Brody's Jewish headstone at Cambridge Cemetery. [Author]

26 June (Monday)
Gunnery exercise. 5 (P)AFU (RAF Tern Hill, Shropshire)
Miles Master II (DL343) force-landed at Helshaw Grange (at wartime map reference 633295), south-west of the airfield, at 14.15 hrs. After developing engine trouble during the flight, the pilot came in for an emergency landing but overshot the airfield and was forced to belly-land in a field, as he was unable to maintain height.

F/O (pilot u/t) David McClymont (150598), RAFVR. He survived the war and retired as a flight lieutenant in November 1956.

28 June (Wednesday)
Instrument and navigation training. 551st FTS, 495th FTG (Station 342, Atcham, Shropshire)
Republic P-47C Thunderbolt (41-6385, bearing the fuselage code VM-M) crashed at Dorrell's Farm, near Leighton (at map reference 617069), at 14.29 hrs. The pilot was climbing away from the airfield through thick cloud, using his gyro horizon (artificial horizon), when he found that his airspeed was dropping. He therefore levelled off to gain a little speed. Shortly afterwards he continued his climb but, at approximately 6,500 feet, he noticed the needle (in his turn and bank indicator) wobbling badly and the aircraft suddenly fell off into a spin. Despite his regaining control, the aircraft fell off into yet another spin at 3,500 feet and the pilot, realising that he was in the vicinity of the Wrekin, decided to bale out. His account of the accident continues:

> I don't believe a recovery could be made at that altitude and in the position I was in. I pulled the safety belt catch and immediately crumpled up against the canopy. Being upside down, I fought for seconds to get it open, succeeded and fell out, pulled the rip cord and chute opened. Immediately I heard the plane explode but couldn't see it as I was still in solid cloud. I then emerged and looked around and saw I was just over the right side of the Wrekin, about one thousand feet up as near as I could judge. I saw the plane burning on the left side of the Wrekin. I landed in a thick patch of trees. Only one farmer in that immediate area came to see if I was alright. The farmer took me towards my home station in his car until I met a jeep that was looking for me.

In the pilot's opinion, the cause of the accident was a faulty gyro horizon, but the accident investigation committee blamed the pilot's poor instrument flying abilities.

Flight Officer William Nellis [Wikipedia]

Flight Officer (pilot u/t) William Harrell Nellis (T-62148), USAAF. Born in New Mexico on 8 March 1916, he and his family relocated to Searchlight, Nevada, when he was still a child. After attending Las Vegas High School, he worked in the city for a while, during which time he married Shirley R Fletcher. He enlisted in the Reserve Corps in December 1942 and began pilot training in March 1943, before being posted to the UK in May 1944. On completion of his training at Atcham, he joined 513th Fighter Squadron on 9 July 1944 and flew 70 missions in support of General Patton's 3rd Army. Sadly, on 27 December 1944, he was shot down in his P-47 (44-19570) while strafing a German convoy over Luxembourg. Lt. Nellis is buried in Henri-Chapelle American Cemetery, Belgium.

4 July (Tuesday)
Battle formation training. 552nd FTS, 495th FTG (Station 342, Atcham, Shropshire)
Republic P-47D Thunderbolt (42-7950, bearing the fuselage code DQ-?) crashed at Lawley (at map reference 668092), near Wellington, at 20.17 hrs. A flight of four P-47s, led by Captain Kenneth W

Dougherty, took off at 19.30 hrs and climbed to 20,000 feet, where they spread out into battle formation. After completing the training exercise, the flight began to descend, doing 'hammerhead turns', before pulling up and starting a climbing turn to the left. During this climbing turn, the pilot of No. 3 aircraft (Lt Haycock) described how he, apparently,

> ... lost track of No. 2 man under my right wing (I was turning to left) when suddenly something seemed to catch my right wing tip and throw it down. I looked out and my right wing had been badly broken [in fact his entire tail assembly had been severed also].
>
> I immediately opened my canopy and started to prepare for a jump. The plane fell into a violent spin. I kept trying to crawl out of the cockpit but could not make it. After several attempts I began to think that I was going in with the plane. The plane suddenly did a violent snap and I was thrown out. I lost consciousness immediately on leaving the cockpit.

2 Lt Robert Haycock [Kathleen Fenton]

The subsequent investigation concluded that, in fact, Lt Haycock's parachute had opened before he left the aircraft. In the resulting jerk, as it pulled him from the aircraft, his pelvis was dislocated and he was rendered unconscious. He awoke lying on the ground, with his right leg doubled up underneath him, and was taken to the US 16th General Hospital at Penley, near Ellesmere. The pilot of No. 2 aircraft (Lt Buttram), which lost its port wing, also managed to bale out but, as he left the aircraft, he fractured his left leg when he struck the tail assembly.

2 Lt (pilot u/t) Robert Howard Haycock (O-767220), USAAF. Born in Salt Lake City, Utah, on 7 July 1924, he was the son of Benjamin and Emilie Karen Bertha Haycock (coincidentally his father was born in Leighton, near Atcham). Following the accident he is believed to have been repatriated to America where he left the Air Force in January 1945 and subsequently studied at the University of California, before becoming an engineer. He died in August 1989.

Battle formation training. 552nd FTS, 495th FTG (Station 342, Atcham, Shropshire)
Republic P-47D Thunderbolt (42-7971, bearing the fuselage code DQ-G) crashed at Lawley (at map reference 666091), near Wellington, following the collision described above.

2 Lt (pilot u/t) Thomas J Buttram (O-767110), USAAF. He was repatriated to the USA the following month and, presumably, discharged from the Air Force.

11 July (Tuesday)
Training flight. 1 Heavy Glider Servicing Unit (RAF Netheravon, Wiltshire)
Airspeed Horsa I (LH323) force-landed at Huntington Farm, Ashford Carbonell, to the south of Ludlow, at 12 noon. Having cast off from the tug aircraft in cloud, the pilot tried to land in a field but the port wing struck a tree, causing it to swing around and suffer a little damage.

Staff Sgt (1st pilot) A F Holliday (177067), GPR.
Sgt (2nd pilot) D Gray (2719253), GPR.

12 July (Wednesday)
Navigation exercise. Central Navigation School (RAF Shawbury, Shropshire)
Vickers Wellington XIII (HF127) crashed on the perimeter track at Shawbury airfield, at 11.00 hrs. The trainee crew were just becoming airborne when their aircraft collided with a De Havilland Mosquito, which was being towed along the perimeter track by a tractor driven by a maintenance unit employee.

The two aircraft immediately burst into flames. The Wellington crew scrambled free, although three of them were badly burned, but the two civilian employees in the Mosquito (Bancroft and Musson) and the tractor driver (Taylor) were trapped and could not get free. Five civilian employees (Trew, Bull, Humphrey, Howard and Clarkson), who were working nearby, immediately rushed to the scene and 'showed gallantry in rescuing the civilians concerned'. Bull and Trew were subsequently awarded the BEM and Fred Humphreys received a commendation for bravery. The joint citation for the BEM read:

> Trew tried to release an injured man, who was pinned beneath the wrecked tractor, but was unable to do so unaided. He was then joined by Bull and together they made a second attempt. This too, was unsuccessful. Other helpers approached the wreckage but a petrol tank exploded and the heat became so intense that they had to give up their attempt. Trew and Bull, however, held their ground and eventually the man was released.
>
> A second injured man was seen struggling to get out of the burning cockpit of the stationary aircraft. Trew tried at once to reach him but was forced back by the flames. The man then fell through the burning floor of the cockpit and Trew and Bull, without thought for their own safety, went through the flames and carried him to safety. Both men showed great bravery in going to the rescue of their fellow workers.

Following the accident, the injured airmen were promptly treated by the airfield medics, while the three badly-burned crewmembers of the Wellington (F/Lt Bean, W/O Fussell and F/Sgt Goodfellow) were conveyed to the specialist burns centre at RAF Hospital, Cosford. RAF Shawbury, being unable to cope with the large number of casualties, sought outside medical help from RAF Sleap and Tern Hill, whose ambulances helped to convey Bancroft and Musson to Cosford, while Taylor was taken to the Royal Salop Infirmary and treated for shock. Sadly, although all the casualties arrived at Cosford burns centre within two hours of the accident, Bancroft succumbed to his injuries two days later, while F/Sgt Goodfellow died on 3 August.

F/Lt (pilot) William Reginald Bean (109370), RAFVR.

F/Sgt (2nd pilot) Thomas Tapner Anderson Goodfellow (1531713), RAFVR, aged 28, was the son of Abel and Rachel Catherine Cooper Anderson Goodfellow of Sunderland. He is buried in Sunderland (Bishopswearmouth) Cemetery.

F/O (Nav) Banting.

F/O (Nav) G E Treleaven (J.21764), RCAF.

Sgt (Nav) Roberts.

W/O (W/Op) Arthur Charles Fussell (914594), RAFVR, was commissioned in December 1944 and survived the war.

In tow towards compass swing area (to calibrate the aircraft's compass). 27 MU (RAF Shawbury, Shropshire)

De Havilland Mosquito FB.VI (PZ233) burst into flames on the perimeter track at RAF Shawbury following the collision described above.

Mr Albert Victor Bancroft, Maintenance Unit employee, aged 37, was the husband of Dorothy Kate Bancroft (née Morris) of 39 Alfred Street, Shrewsbury. He is buried in Shifnal Rural Cemetery.

Mr C Musson, Maintenance Unit employee.

Mr Taylor, Maintenance Unit employee.

The rescuers, who were all civilian employees of 27 MU, were:

Mr George Frederick Bull. Born at 7 Elm Street, in Shrewsbury, on 13 January 1897, he was the son of Charles Eugene and Lucy Bull (née Roberts). After serving as a driver in the Army Service Corps in Mesopotamia during the First World War, he settled back in Shropshire and worked as a driver-mechanic. During the Second World War he lived at English Bridge Court in Shrewsbury, with his wife,

Ivy Slaymaker. He died in January 1955 and is buried in Shrewsbury Cemetery.

Mr (Fitter) Alexander Wesley (Wes) Trew. Born on 17 April 1903, he was the son of Joseph Alexander and Cordelia Trew (née Wright) of 5 Luxor Street, West Derby, Liverpool. Before the war he had worked as a chauffeur and mechanic for Barker & Dobson in Liverpool, followed by a period in Llandrindod Wells, where he met his future wife, Lily. After marrying in Wem, on 13 December 1926, the couple settled in Liverpool, but following the outbreak of war moved in with Lily's parents at Shrubbery Gardens, Wem, to escape the bombing. Wes subsequently worked as a fitter, specialising in hydraulics, at RAF Shawbury and continued to serve after the war, eventually retiring on grounds of ill health. He died in Wem in March 1973.

Mr (Fitter) Fred Humphreys.

Mr Howard.

Mr Clarkson.

12 July (Wednesday)

Battle formation training mission. 552nd FTS, 495th FTG (Station 342, Atcham, Shropshire)

Republic P-47D Thunderbolt (42-7981, bearing the fuselage code DQ-?) crashed 'eight miles south-west of airfield' (believed to have crashed at Pitchford, near Acton Burnell) at 16.50 hrs. A flight of four aircraft, led by Maj J R Bertrand, took off at 16.00 hrs and was flying in close formation at approximately 5,000 feet when the flight leader signalled for the formation to open up. Lt Porter, who was flying in N°. 3 position, described what happened next for the accident investigation:

> ... we were flying on our leader's left wing when the leader fish-tailed for string formation. I repeated the fish-tail for my wing man's benefit, at the same time noticing that he recognized the signal and was apparently moving out of close formation. The leader started a turn to the left, his wing man following out, and I started my turn. At this time I felt a jar in the ship and saw that my wing was crumpled, also that N°. 4 airplane was flipping violently in the air, beating my cowling, fuselage and plane in general with his wing. I immediately went into a dive from 5,000 feet, which was our altitude at the time and I managed to pull it out at around 2,000 feet.

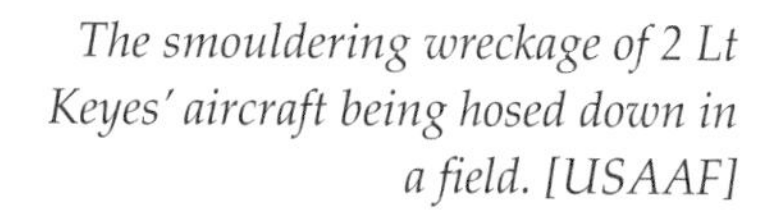

The smouldering wreckage of 2 Lt Keyes' aircraft being hosed down in a field. [USAAF]

2 Lt Porter's aircraft, pictured on the tarmac after belly-landing on the runway at Atcham, had previously been in service with the 63rd Fighter Squadron, 56th Fighter Group and bore the nose art Michigan Mauler. *[USAAF]*

In fact, what had happened was that Lt Keyes (flying No. 4 position) had become 'out of position on the turn and in an attempt to get out of danger threw his aircraft into a vertical bank. While in this attitude he mushed into the other aircraft which was turning toward him.' His aircraft was immediately thrown off into a steep dive and he was killed in the ensuing crash. Lt Porter managed to maintain control and belly-landed on the airfield.

2 Lt (pilot u/t) Roman H Keyes (O-820508), USAAF, aged 27 (?), was the son of Stephan and Bertha Keyes of Utica City, Oneida County, New York. He is buried in New York State.

Battle formation training mission. 552nd FTS, 495th FTG (Station 342, Atcham, Shropshire)
Republic P-47D Thunderbolt (41-6362, bearing the fuselage code DQ-I) belly-landed on the airfield following the collision described above.

2 Lt (pilot u/t) Jimmie D Porter (O-701802), USAAF. Born in Tennessee on 14 January 1921, he went on to serve with the 512th Fighter Squadron, 406th Fighter Group and died in October 1965.

14 July (Friday)
Mr A V Bancroft died in RAF Hospital, Cosford, from injuries received at Shawbury two days earlier.

16 July (Sunday)
Camera-gunnery training. 551st FTS, 495th FTG (Station 342, Atcham, Shropshire)
Republic P-47C Thunderbolt (41-6237, bearing the fuselage code VM-J) belly-landed on Baggy Moor, between Bagley and Rednal airfield, at 17.15 hrs. The pilot was briefed to take off at 16.30 hrs and undertake his training mission at no less than 8,000 feet but, whilst climbing up to altitude, he engaged a flight of P-47s in a simulated dogfight and descended to 1,000 feet. After breaking off the engagement he was orbiting to find his wing man when the engine suddenly failed and, according to his statement, he checked his fuel gauge which

> … read 30 gallons in the auxiliary and approximately 150 gallons in the main. For a moment I could not understand the failure and headed for a field. Then I realized the auxiliary gas gauge had stuck and I immediately changed to the main tank. The engine failed to catch. I then spun the emergency boost on, but it was too late and I bellied in a field, with wheels up and flaps down.

Interestingly, the pilot gives a slightly different account in his recollections on the 313th Squadron website, stating that he had been mixing it up with a Spitfire piloted by one of the ATA's blond-haired female pilots rather than a flight of P-47s! However, his description of the subsequent engine failure and forced landing do tie in with his original statement, which continues:

Gil Burn's Thunderbolt, pictured lying in a field on Baggy Moor, had previously been in service with the 61st Fighter Squadron, 56th Fighter Group and bore the nose art Idaho Spud. *[USAAF]*

I hit the ground tail first and crash-slid to a stop. Releasing my oxygen connection, radio cable and safety belt, I jumped out and started running in case the plane decided to blow. I looked back over my shoulder at the plane while I was running and what was chasing me but a bull! I kept running and came to a barbed wire fence that surrounded the field. With the bull coming up fast, I jumped over the fence. Going over the barbs ripped the seat of my flying suit and drew blood on my behind. This was to be my only 'wound' of the war.

2 Lt (pilot u/t) Gilbert C (Gil) Burns Jr (O-824407), USAAF. On completion of his training he flew P-47s with the 313th Fighter Squadron, 50th Fighter Group, until the end of the war.

Sgt Robert Ives [Library and Archives Canada]

17 July (Monday)
Instrument flying, recovery from spins and 'unusual manoeuvres'
5 (P)AFU (Believed to have taken off from RAF Bratton, Shropshire – Satellite to RAF Tern Hill)
Miles Master II (DL246) crashed at Ashes Farm (at wartime map reference 672287), Wistanswick, at 15.28 hrs. Ten minutes after taking off, the aircraft was witnessed in level flight at approximately 1,000 feet, when its engine was heard to throttle back and the aircraft was seen to stall and dive into the ground. On subsequent examination of the wreckage it was concluded that the fabric on the leading edge of the starboard wing had come away in flight as 'the glue exhibited signs of poor adhesion' and the resulting structural failure caused the pilot to lose control.

Sgt (instructor pilot) Robert Owen Gregory Ives (R.161444), RCAF, aged 21, was the son of William C and Mary Theresa Ives of St Catharine's, Ontario. Prior to his posting to 5 (P)AFU, in April 1944, he had undergone his pilot training in Canada before sailing to the UK and being selected for an instructor's course. He is buried in Chester (Blacon) Cemetery.

Sgt (pilot u/t) Richard George Foster (R.121320), RCAF, aged 22, was the son of Donald Pollock Foster and Rose Ann Foster of Calgary, Alberta, and the husband of Gertrude Margaret Foster, also of Calgary. He is buried in Chester (Blacon) Cemetery.

20 July (Thursday)
Local flying training. 21 (P)AFU (RAF Wheaton Aston, Staffordshire)
Airspeed Oxford II (X7278) crashed at Pool Farm, Adderley (although another source states Coxbank), to the north of Market Drayton, at 09.15 hrs. A pupil pilot was performing unauthorised low flying, with a flight engineer under training as a passenger, when the port wing struck a tree, causing the plane to crash.

Sgt (pilot u/t) John Murray Wilson (R.212664), RCAF, aged 20, was the son of John J and Grace Wilson of Oshawa, Ontario. He is buried in Chester (Blacon) Cemetery.

AC2 (F/Eng u/t) Thomas William Davies (2203359), RAFVR, aged 19, was the son of Henry and Jane Davies of Withington, Manchester. He is buried in Llanfihangel-ar-Arth (Pencader) Cemetery, Carmarthenshire.

27 July (Thursday)
Tactical reconnaissance of the Wellington-Warrington road. 41 OTU (RAF Hawarden, Flintshire)
Hawker Hurricane IIC (LF327) crashed at Ollerton Park (at map reference 641252), near Peplow, at 12.45 hrs. F/O Skelton took off at 12.15 hrs, with F/O B V Genge as his wingman, and flew in open formation until reaching Wellington, where they were instructed to begin their training exercise. According to F/O Genge's account,

> … we had covered about twelve miles of the road, from Wellington and I was flying at a height of approximately 2,400 feet about 300 feet below base of cloud and 300 yards on F/O Skelton's port in line abreast formation, when an aircraft at first I took to be a Typhoon with black and white stripes around the fuselage, crossed in front and above right in the cloud base. As it passed I saw it had no radiator scoop, and decided it must be a Hurricane. This aircraft disappeared in cloud momentarily, turning to port. Watching for an attack I saw the aircraft again appear starting an attack of F/O Skelton's aircraft. In order to avoid having F/O Skelton meeting the attacking aircraft in the hanging cloud, I gave the order to 'break port' and immediately myself broke hard to port, maintaining height and turned through three complete 360 degree turns and having seen nothing of F/O Skelton or the other aircraft called F/O Skelton on the R/T to straighten out. I continued to call him orbiting this position, however, I received no reply and saw nothing of F/O Skelton's aircraft. I received a call from base saying they would attempt to contact him – which they did, without success.

The subsequent investigation revealed that F/O Morrison, in a Hurricane (PG536), had just completed an affiliation flight with a Wellington bomber and was returning to the airfield when he 'found himself behind F/O Skelton or decided to make a dummy attack'. During this manoeuvre F/O Skelton's port wing struck F/O Morrison's aircraft in the fuselage and both aircraft crashed out of control. F/O Morrison was killed instantly in the crash, while F/O Skelton attempted to bale out at low altitude but his parachute only partially opened and he died at the scene before RAF Peplow's ambulance could arrive.

F/O William Skelton [Library and Archives Canada]

F/O (pilot u/t) William Hugh Skelton (J.28994), RCAF, aged 28, was the son of John Moore Skelton and Ethel Henderson Skelton of Toronto. Born on 10 May 1916, he trained at the Michigan College of Mining and Technology, following which he was employed at two mines between 1936 and 1940, prior to enlisting in January 1941. After gaining his wings in Canada he was selected for instructor training and subsequently remained in Canada as an instructor until September 1943, when he sailed to the UK to prepare for operations. He is buried in Chester (Blacon) Cemetery.

Fighter affiliation flight. 83 OTU (RAF Peplow, Shropshire)
Hawker Hurricane IIC (PG536) crashed near Peplow Grange following the collision described above.

F/O (pilot) Hew Morrison (127904), RAFVR, aged 21, was the son of James Douglas and Jean Mackay Mackenzie Morrison of Helensburgh. He is buried in Faslane Cemetery, Dumbartonshire.

F/O Hew Morrison. [Marjorie Morrison]

28 July (Friday)
Formation flying. 5 (P)AFU (RAF Tern Hill, Shropshire)
Miles Master III (DL828) force-landed at Cherrington (at wartime map reference 666198), near Tibberton, at 09.45 hrs. The instructor and his pupil were returning to the airfield when the engine cut at 1,500 feet and the instructor was forced to belly-land the aircraft in a field.

W/O (instructor pilot) N F Cottrill (R.89961), RCAF, was commissioned in September 1944. He survived the war and returned to Canada in June 1945.

Sgt (pilot u/t) Jacques van Liefland (1424983), RAFVR. Born in Mechelen, Belgium on 25 March 1922, he was posted to 350 (Belgian) Squadron on 13 April 1945 and flew Spitfires on ground attack operations during the closing stages of the war.

29 July (Saturday)
Low-level formation training. 552nd FTS, 495th FTG (Station 342, Atcham, Shropshire)
Republic P-47D Thunderbolt (42-7962, bearing the fuselage code DQ-F) crashed into the River Severn at Tophouse Farm, Uffington, at 09.40 hrs. Four aircraft took off in loose formation, led by Lt M V Marlowe, and were flying on a course from Ironbridge when one of the aircraft collided with some high tension power cables. According to the flight leader's account,

> I pulled our flight up to gain altitude over transmission wires which were clearly visible to rest of flight. N°. 3 man obviously tried to remain low instead of following his leader. I did not see Lt Ernst when latter hit transmission wires. Lt Greer, who was flying N°. 4 position, saw Lt Ernst when latter hit wires. However, he gave leader no knowledge of it at the moment it happened. Shortly after pulling up, I observed that my N°. 3 man had disappeared and called Lt Greer over the intercom for information about N°. 3 man. Lt Greer simply stated that Lt Ernst had hit the transmission wires we had just passed over. He gave no inkling that Lt Ernst had crashed. Consequently, I, not knowing Lt Ernst had crashed, circled once waiting for N°. 3 man to rejoin, and when he did not, went back to fly over the area of the transmission wires to investigate. After circling the vicinity 2 or 3 times, seeing no smoke or signs of mishap and thinking N°. 3 had returned to field to land, we continued on training flight 3A. It was not until the flight landed that I was informed of what actually happened.

2 Lt (pilot u/t) Thomas Andrew Ernst (O-770217), USAAF, aged 19, he was the son of half-German Hilmar Furst Ernst and Irene C Ernst of Albany, Georgia. He is buried in Marietta National Cemetery, Georgia.

30 July (Sunday)
Navigation training flight. 552nd FTS, 495th FTG (Station 342, Atcham, Shropshire)
Republic P-47 D Thunderbolt (42-7937, bearing the fuselage code DQ-?) crashed at Asterley (at map reference 376072), near Pontesbury, at 10.08 hrs. Having completed his scheduled navigation exercise the pilot began practising spins, as he wished to become acquainted with the spinning characteristics of the P-47. According to his account,

> I had done one power off spin to the left and made a normal recovery at 7,000 feet. I climbed back to 11,000 feet and made a normal entry into another power off spin. After the first half turn, the nose still remained well above the horizon. I tried normal recovery but the spin continued and became faster, the nose remaining at the horizon. Then I tried blasting out with full power. Still unsuccessful and spin became faster with controls becoming stiff. At this time I was at 7,000 feet and decided to bail out. I pulled emergency canopy release and tried to open the canopy; it seemed jammed. Then I continued to try to open canopy by placing feet against instrument panel with no success. Again tried to recover from spin but was unable to move controls to recovery position. At this time my altimeter read 1,000 feet. Again I tried to open canopy by pulling emergency release as hard as possible at which time canopy opened. I stood up and attempted to dive over right wing. I hit the wing and was partly knocked out, however was able to pull the rip cord. The 'chute opened and I landed in a farm field.

2 Lt Jerry Barnard [Gini Seeley]

The subsequent investigation highlighted the fact that over the previous few months the station had suffered a number of similar accidents (the majority of which had ended fatally) and it was emphasized that pilots should be 'instructed to refrain from intentionally putting the Thunderbolt into a spin.'

2 Lt (pilot u/t) Gerald Butler (Jerry) Barnard Jr (O-770136), USAAF. Born on 9 March 1925, he was the son of Gerald Butler Barnard and Virginia Lee Barnard (née Turner) of California. On completion of his training, he went on to serve with the 53rd Fighter Squadron, 36th Fighter Group, flying P-47s in support of the advancing armies. He died in Rockwall, Texas, in January 1997.

3 August (Thursday)
F/Sgt T T A Goodfellow (1531713) died in RAF Hospital, Cosford, from injuries sustained at Shawbury on 12 July.

4 August (Friday)
Training flight. 61 OTU (RAF Montford Bridge, Shropshire – Satellite airfield to RAF Rednal)
Supermarine Spitfire VA (W3118, presentation aircraft named *Kirklands*) belly-landed at Preston Montford Farm (at map reference 426136, between Ford and Preston Montford), at 15.50 hrs.
The pilot was returning to the airfield after his throttle control broke but, after overshooting his approach, was unable to maintain height and belly-landed in a field.

P/O (pilot u/t) Tadeusz Szlenkier (P2493), PAF. On completion of his training he was posted to 308 (Polish) Squadron and credited with one Fw190 shot down during the *Luftwaffe's* famous last-ditch effort to destroy the Allied air forces on 1 January 1945 (Operation *Bodenplatte*).

8 August (Tuesday)
Navigation and aerobatics training mission. 551st FTS, 495th FTG (Station 342, Atcham, Shropshire)
Republic P-47D Thunderbolt (42-8584, bearing the fuselage code VM-?) crashed at Home Farm, Cruckton, near Hanwood, at 08.17 hrs. Having taken off at 07.30 hrs and climbed to 16,000 feet to practice aerobatics, the pilot executed an 'Immelmann turn', which involved his putting the aircraft into a steep climb and completing a half loop, at the top of which he would roll the aircraft into an upright position. After entering the manoeuvre with insufficient airspeed, however, the aircraft reached the top of the loop in a stalled state and fell off into a spin. The pilot's account continues:

Lt Charles Bond
[Peter Randall]

The smouldering wreckage of 2 Lt Bond's Thunderbolt lies in a field near Cruckton. [USAAF]

> After a turn or two of normal spin, I applied full right rudder and immediately afterwards, forward stick and slight opposite aileron. This didn't have much effect and after a couple more turns, I tried a violent normal spin recovery. About this time the plane stopped oscillating in the spin and flattened out level. The rate of turn increased to about twice what it was. When I tried to push the stick forward in the recovery, it wouldn't go. I put my foot behind it and just did get it to go to the neutral position. There was no noticeable effect on the plane from either the stick or opposite rudder. I tried this a couple more times along with cutting my throttle which had no effect. At 9,000 feet I decided to bail out. I had little trouble getting untangled and then got out on the outside of the spin, which was the right side.

2 Lt (pilot u/t) Charles R Bond (O-711927), USAAF. On finishing his training at Atcham, he completed 52 missions with the 61st Fighter Squadron, 56th Fighter Group.

11 August (Friday)
Combat and instrument training. 552nd FTS, 495th FTG (Station 342, Atcham, Shropshire)
Republic P-47C Thunderbolt (41-6532, bearing the code DQ-?) crashed at Shelcott Farm, Montford Bridge (at map reference 431155), at 08.33 hrs. A flight of four aircraft took off at 07.45 hrs and were just about to enter a 'Lufberry' when they were 'bounced' by two white-nosed P-47s. During the ensuing dogfight, Lt Barrett (flying number two position) noticed:

> … the last aircraft that bounced us having made a left turn, was coming around on my tail. I steepened my climb and sharpened my turn to make a greater deflection shot for him. The plane fell over gently on its back between about 7 and 9,000 feet without any warning of a stall. I at once pulled the stick back in my stomach to pull the nose through the horizon, at the same time the ship started a fast spin. Since the nose did not drop I put the controls with the spin, trying to get it in a normal spin, retarding my throttle as I did this. The ship continued its spin and after no response to the controls, around five turns, I opened the canopy and dropped out somewhere around 5,000 feet or a little less.

The subsequent investigation established that, from Lt Barrett's own admission that he 'pulled the stick back into my stomach', it could be concluded that he 'over controlled on his first attempt to recover and, as a result, the aircraft was thrown into a violent flattish spin'.

2 Lt (pilot u/t) Fred H Barrett (O-711911), USAAF. On completion of his training, he flew P-47s with the 61st Fighter Squadron, 56th Fighter Group and survived the war. He subsequently served in Korea, flying F-86 Sabres with the 16th Fighter Interceptor Squadron, during which time he was credited with a MiG-15 shot down on 6 June 1952.

12 August (Saturday)
Cross-country flight from base to Burtonwood, Lancashire. 598th Bombardment Squadron, 397th Bombardment Group, 9th Air Force (Station 492, Hurn, Dorset)
L-5H Stinson (42-98658) force-landed at 'St James, Bridgnorth', at 19.35 hrs. The squadron was a B-26 Marauder-equipped unit which normally flew bombing missions over north-west Europe but, on the day of the accident, one of the squadron pilots was flying to Burtonwood with a passenger (the purpose of the visit is unknown). After experiencing engine trouble en route over Shropshire, the pilot landed at Atcham, where the engine was checked over and given the all clear to continue. Ten minutes later, the engine again began cutting out and the pilot was forced to land at RAF Tilstock where an RAF engineer looked it over and also found it to be functioning normally. However, the pilot decided to return to Atcham, while his passenger caught a train the rest of the way to Burtonwood. Returning from Tilstock, the pilot found the aircraft to be in normal working order and, after stopping for supper at Atcham, decided to carry on with his return journey to Hurn. Ten minutes after departing from Atcham, however, the engine began faltering as he flew down the Severn river valley and so he,

> … figured to follow the river until I came to the low-lands and could put it into a sizeable field. I couldn't climb out of it for fear the engine would cut during the climb and at low airspeed I would have no choice but to put down right there. As I passed the town of Iron Bridge, I thought of wires, began lifting to avoid any. Airspeed dropped to 75-80, was climbing slowly. Shortly beyond the town I hit three high tension wires. It knocked part of the prop off and there was a violent vibration. Also smashed the wind shield and bent a wing strut. The stub of a prop was sufficient to stretch my glide to the field I put down in. The field was just off the river and very small---covered by 8 strands of high tension wire. I put into a slip of maximum proportions, power off, set down just under the wires and on the field. As the field was so short there was no chance to dissipate speed---had to jam on brakes immediately. Nose dipped, caught, and nosed over.

2 Lt (pilot) Roger S Manchester (O-1578807), USAAF, had attended college in Cairo before the war, following which he spent the summer of 1939 cycling across Europe, returning to the USA just before the outbreak of war. He completed his schooling and then began work at an auto repair shop in Westport, Connecticut. After enlisting in the Air Force, he finished his training in the USA and was posted to the UK, where he completed a tour with the 598th Squadron, before returning to the USA and settling down with his wife Elizabeth Lewis.

14 August (Monday)
Low-level cross-country exercise. 21 (P)AFU (RAF Wheaton Aston, Staffordshire)
Airspeed Oxford I (N4588) crashed at Norton in Hales (at wartime map reference 703383), near Market Drayton, at 11.40 hrs. According to the pilot's statement, he had ducked instinctively when something smashed into the windscreen, causing him to push forward on the control column. The aircraft then struck some high tension power lines and the collision caused the starboard engine to fail. The pilot attempted a forced landing in a field but the aircraft crashed and overturned, injuring the two occupants. In the subsequent investigation, the pilot's explanation was dismissed as fiction and a charge of deliberate low flying was brought but, as there were no witnesses to the incident, the charge had to be dropped.

F/Sgt (instructor pilot) John Alan Beanland (1548790), RAFVR. He survived the war.

Sgt (pilot u/t) Raymond Stanley Dickinson (R.179872), RCAF, was later commissioned and survived the war.

15 August (Tuesday)
Training flight. 28 EFTS (Penderford, Staffordshire)
De Havilland Tiger Moth II (T7353) crashed into the River Severn at 'High Rock', Bridgnorth. The pilot was flying low along the river valley when he failed to notice some high-tension power cables spanning the river ahead and collided with them, crashing into the river but suffering only slight injuries.

Lt (pilot u/t) Ozsu, Turkish Air Force.

16 August (Wednesday)
Battle formation and interception training. 551st FTS, 495th FTG (Station 342, Atcham, Shropshire)
Republic P-47D Thunderbolt (42-76128, bearing the fuselage code VM-?) crashed at Fenns Bank (at eyewitness map reference 515398), near Whitchurch, at 10.40 hrs. After taking off at 09.20 hrs, 1 Lt Adam J Wisniewski led his flight in a climb to 23,000 feet, at which height he ordered the men into string formation and began 'rat-racing'. During the course of the 'rat race' the flight began an 'Immelmann' manoeuvre, which meant performing a half loop, at the top of which the pilot would roll the aircraft into an upright position. According to the pilot's account he:

> ... pulled up and was nearly on top of the loop when my engine cut out. I immediately switched gas tanks but my engine did not cut back in. I stalled out and snapped and went into an inverted spin. I tried a normal spin recovery and then I tried rolling into a normal spin without result. I used stick and rudder with and against the spin. After trying this and with no power, I opened my canopy and bailed out.

The subsequent investigation concluded that the pilot, who is believed to have landed safely at Wirswall, was a little premature in leaving the aircraft and, had he persisted further, he would probably have experienced little difficulty in regaining control.

2 Lt (pilot u/t) James B Allison Jr (O-708630), USAAF. On completion of his training he flew P-47s with the 83rd Fighter Squadron, 78th Fighter Group, between September 1944 and March 1945.

17 August (Thursday)

Formation and interception training. 551st FTS, 495th FTG (Station 342, Atcham, Shropshire)

Republic P-47D Thunderbolt (42-8469, bearing the fuselage code VM-Q) crash-landed 'near Wellington' (possibly at map reference 606115, just west of Wrockwardine, where a P-47 was wirnessed lying in the field), at 08.45 hrs. A flight of four aircraft took off at 07.30 hrs and had climbed to 10,000 feet, where they were 'bounced' by another flight of four aircraft. After approximately forty-five minutes the pilot of this aircraft (call sign Redmond 44) became separated from his flight and decided to return to the vicinity of the airfield in an attempt to locate them. He descended below cloud to 3,000 feet, where he saw his formation but, just as he was about to join up with them, his engine failed for technical reasons. He immediately requested clearance for an emergency landing but, unable to reach the airfield, he chose a field and 'brought it in wheels up. On landing I undershot by a few feet and hit a hedge of small trees with the tail surfaces. I waited with the ship until the ambulance and MP arrived.'

2 Lt Paeth's Thunderbolt after he belly-landed in a field near Wellington. [USAAF]

2 Lt (pilot u/t) Norman Lee Paeth (O-770371), USAAF. Born in Fremont, Ohio on 19 May 1923, he subsequently joined the 367th Fighter Squadron, 358th Fighter Group and flew operationally until the end of the war.

18 August (Friday)

Transition training flight. 552nd FTS, 495th FTG (Station 342, Atcham)

Lockheed P-38J Lightning (42-67490, bearing the fuselage code DQ-G) crash-landed at Wroxeter (at map reference 576091), at 15.00 hrs. The pilot was an instructor at the unit but was on his first transition flight in a P-38 aircraft, during which he feathered his port engine as he 'wanted to see how it would operate on one engine'. When he went to unfeather the engine, however, it lost all power. The pilot attempted to make a single-engine landing at the airfield but 'the aircraft reactions caused him to overshoot'. Unable to maintain height he was forced to belly-land in a field but, after touching down, the aircraft flipped onto its back and caught fire. The pilot, who suffered third degree burns to his right arm and left thigh (amongst other injuries), was rushed to hospital but succumbed to his injuries on 22 September.

1 Lt (instructor pilot) Luther Joe Abel (O-686799), DFC & 2 OLC, AM & 2 OLC, USAAF, aged 23 (?), was

the son of Luther and Joe Ann Abel of Gladewater, Texas. Before arriving at Atcham he had flown P-47s with the 84th Fighter Squadron, 78th Fighter Group, between January and July 1944 and was credited with two enemy aircraft destroyed and one shared. He is buried in Cambridge (Madingley) Cemetery.

1 Lt Luther Abel pictured in the cockpit of his P-47 Mickey II *while serving with 84th Fighter Squadron. [Peter Randall]*

19 August (Saturday)
Cross-country exercise. 1655 Mosquito Training Unit (RAF Wyton, Cambridgeshire)
De Havilland Mosquito B.XX (KB224) broke up in the air and scattered wreckage over a large area between Leebotwood and Downes' Farm, Longnor, at 12.55 hrs. Having taken off at 10.00 hrs, the crew climbed to 28,000 feet at midday. A short while later the pilot is believed to have been thrown onto the control column by a violent jolt, as he was not wearing his safety belt. The resultant 'bunt' exerted such strain on the wings that they broke off and the aircraft disintegrated over a wide area of land, killing the two crew members.

F/Lt (pilot) John Mansfield Pearce (125871), RAFVR, aged 23, was the son of Charles Clifford and Mary Elisabeth Pearce of Cheltenham. He is commemorated at the Cheltenham Crematorium.

P/O (Nav) Arthur Alan Young (164218), RAFVR, aged 20, was the son of George L and Margaret Hilda Young of West Denton. He is buried in Newburn (Lemington) Cemetery, Northumberland.

24 August (Thursday)
Aerobatics practice. 5 (P)AFU (RAF Condover, Shropshire – satellite to RAF Tern Hill)
Miles Master II (AZ841) crashed at Park Farm (at wartime map reference 472998), near Leebotwood, at 17.15 hrs. After entering a roll at 4,000 feet (lower than he had been instructed), the pilot had nearly completed the manoeuvre when the engine cut, causing the aircraft to lose speed and enter a spin from which it did not recover.

Sgt (pilot u/t) Noël Elie Soubde (36646), FFAF, aged 23, was born in Riscle on 21 December 1920 and had escaped to the UK, via Morocco, in 1943. He is buried in Tournay, south-west France.

26 August (Saturday)
Night navex. 3 (O)AFU (RAF Halfpenny Green, Staffordshire)
Avro Anson I (DJ663) crashed at Lindridge Farm (at map reference 793870), just south of Tuckhill, to the south east of Bridgnorth, at 19.45 hrs. The crew were making a 'back beam approach' through cloud when the aircraft struck trees on the high ground to the south-west of the airfield and crashed. Three crewmen were killed instantly and the remaining two were seriously injured, of whom one, P/O Welham succumbed to his injuries two days later in the station hospital at RAF Bridgnorth. Local farmer, Mr J E Brown, provided an account of the accident which appeared in the Wartime Aircraft Recovery Group newsletters (now held in the county archives):

> The weather during this period was very wet and this particular evening was misty and overcast. I hadn't been asleep long that night when I was awoken by an aircraft circling the area. On waking the following morning a very agitated farmworker knocked on my door to ask whether I knew there was an aircraft down in my field.
>
> We were soon on the scene, although the farmworker was very reluctant to go near the wreckage. At first it appeared that all on board had been killed but a slight movement from the rear told us otherwise and soon we

were dragging one of the injured clear. I remember he had a Canadian flash on his shoulder and this turned out to be Pilot Officer Staples. To our amazement, amid all this destruction, his first comment was 'mind my bloody watch!' Very soon a detachment from the nearby airfield arrived to remove the injured and dead.

F/O Norm Trusty
[Robert Trusty]

F/Sgt (pilot) Michael Francis Joseph Cox (1158185), RAFVR, aged 22, was the son of Mr and Mrs Hubert Cox of Edgbaston, Birmingham. He is buried in Stourbridge Cemetery, Worcestershire.

F/O (Nav) Norman Edward (Norm) Trusty (J.38191), RCAF, aged 29, was the son of Robert and Edith Trusty of Owen Sound, Ontario. He is buried in Chester (Blacon) Cemetery.

P/O (Nav) Alfred John (Jack) Welham (165193), RAFVR, aged 27, was the son of Ruth Welham of Hintlesham and the husband of Gladys Speed. Educated at Felixstowe Grammar School, where he excelled in rugby, Jack had joined the Suffolk Constabulary as a police constable after leaving school and had served for a number of years before volunteering for the RAFVR. Prior to the accident, he had undergone training in London, Ontario, where he came top of his class and was presented with the Leavens Brothers Training Ltd trophy and a Waterman's pen set. He is buried in Hintlesham (St Nicholas) Churchyard, Suffolk.

P/O Jack Welham
[Jack Welham]

Sgt (W/Op) Clarence Douglas Rhys Verrier (1313490), RAFVR, aged 23, was the son of Sidney and Anne Louise Verrier of Aberbeeg and the husband of Elaine Mary Verrier (née Dayton) of Llanhilleth. He is buried in Aberbeeg (Christ Church) Cemetery, Monmouthshire.

P/O (W/AG) Joseph Lorne (Joe) Staples (J.37904), RCAF. Born in Kindersley, Saskatchewan, on 26 July 1920, he had joined up in June 1942 and underwent training in Canada before sailing to the UK in June 1944. Following the accident he spent a considerable time in hospital in Oxford, before being repatriated to Canada in January 1945. On his return, he settled in Kindersley, where he bought a farm and raised a family with his wife, Marion Perrin. He died in December 2000.

28 August (Monday)
P/O A J Welham died in RAF Hospital, Bridgnorth, from injuries received on 26 August.

P/O Joe Staples
[Donald Staples

31 August (Thursday)
Night training flight. 41 OTU (RAF Poulton, Cheshire – satellite airfield to RAF Hawarden, Flintshire)
Hawker Hurricane IIc (LF341) crashed at Booley House Farm (at map reference 580252), near Stanton upon Hine Heath, at 04.00 hrs. Flying on instruments, in conditions of patchy cloud and occasional showers, the pilot is believed to have lost control while flying through a rain shower, and the aircraft dived into the ground.

F/O (pilot u/t) Leslie Clarence Watts (141362), RAFVR, aged 30, was the son of Walter William and Annie Laura Watts and the husband of Ella Watts (née Crabtree) of Stalybridge, Cheshire. He is commemorated at the Manchester Crematorium.

7 September (Thursday)
Test flight in preparation for night flying. 21 (P)AFU (RAF Wheaton Aston, Staffordshire)
Airspeed Oxford I (LX509) crashed at 'Colonel's Covert, Hatton Grange' (at wartime map reference 765036), near Albrighton, at 15.20 hrs. Shortly after the instructor took off for a daytime test flight, with a member of staff from the Nottingham Air Training Corps (ATC) riding as passenger, the aircraft was seen to dive into the ground. The cause could not be established.

F/Lt (instructor pilot) Sydney Donald Harrison (151136), RAFVR, aged 21, was the son of Donald and Minnie Harrison of Hernes Road, Oxford. He is buried in Church Eaton (St Edith's) Churchyard, Staffordshire.

P/O Warren Herbert Cheale (177869), RAFVR, aged 44, was the son of Herbert J and Hilda Cheale of Ore, Sussex and the husband of Rose Cheale of Burton Joyce, Nottinghamshire. At the time of his death he was leading a weeklong annual training camp at RAF Wheaton Aston for a group of Nottingham ATC cadets. He is commemorated at the Nottingham Crematorium.

8 September (Friday)
Dive-bombing, glide-bombing, skip-bombing and strafing exercise. 551st FTS, 495th FTG (Station 342, Atcham, Shropshire)
Republic P-47D Thunderbolt (42-8384, bearing the fuselage code VM-I) crash-landed at Charlton Farm, near Uppington (believed to be at map reference 598119, where a P-47 was witnessed lying in a field), at 12.25 hrs. A flight of four aircraft had taken off at 10.15 hrs and was returning to the airfield, after completing their exercise, when Lt Farley (flying N° 2) called his leader to inform him that he was running low on fuel. The message was, apparently, not heard by the leader, 1 Lt Claude G Godard, who therefore made a normal wide orbit approach to land, during which Lt Farley's engine started to splutter and fail. He immediately broke away and headed straight for the airfield but was unable to reach it and belly-landed in a field. The subsequent investigation concluded that the pilot

> ... did not apply his full knowledge of fuel conservation as instructed, as the other members of his flight had ample fuel remaining after landing. If Lt Farley had broken off and landed independently, which all pilots are instructed to do when they get low on fuel, he would have had ample time to land successfully.

Above & right: 2 Lt Farley's Thunderbolt, pictured (left and below) near Uppington following the accident, had previously been in service with the 328th Fighter Squadron, 352nd Fighter Group and bore the nose art, Hildegarde. *[USAAF]*

2 Lt (pilot u/t) John W Farley (O-774068), USAAF. On completion of his training he flew P-47s with the 387th Fighter Squadron, 365th Fighter Group, from October 1944 until the end of the war.

8 September (Friday)
Cross-country exercise from Base–Northampton–Fishguard–St Tudwalls–Skegness–Newbury–Tetbury–Northampton–Base. 29 OTU (RAF Bruntingthorpe, Leicestershire)
Vickers Wellington III (BK552) crashed at Mile Oak (at map reference 303277), to the south east of Oswestry, at 13.43 hrs. Before taking off on the exercise the trainee crews were cautioned that heavy cumulonimbus was forecast, rising from 3,500 feet to 15,000 feet, with a few isolated tops up to 22,000 feet and icing high up in the cloud. When such weather was encountered, the crews were instructed to climb above or around it and, if this was not possible, to return to base. During the course of the flight, however, the pilot of this aircraft entered cloud and is believed to have lost control after ice built up on the wings. The aircraft was then heard by David Meredith Hamer, who was on duty in the Royal Observer Corps N°. 3 post (Oswestry):

> I had previously reported this aircraft coming in from WNW, estimated height on sound between 3,000-4,000 feet at 13.36 hours. It was making a noise as if it was diving and circling. It made three or four dives but didn't break cloud until the final vertical dive to earth at 13.43 hours. From the position of this post it appeared to make a vertical dive out of the clouds and burst into flames immediately. It was raining very hard at the time and I estimated the cloud base to be 2,000 feet above sea level. The height of my post is 500 feet above sea level. Before hitting the ground I did not notice the aircraft to be on fire. This incident was reported to Wrexham Centre at 13.43 who then advised Rednal aerodrome.

F/O (pilot) Desmond De Villiers Clarke (160076), RAFVR, aged 22, came from South Africa. He is buried in Chester (Blacon) Cemetery.

P/O (Nav) Harold James Holmes (164590), RAFVR, aged 23, was the son of Henry and Agnes Holmes of Bedworth and the husband of Marian Mary Holmes (née Sills) of Exhall, Coventry. He is buried in Bedworth Cemetery, Warwickshire.

Sgt (Second Navigator) Gordon Edward Manning (1520513), RAFVR, aged 20, was the son of William Edward Francis and Katharine Manning of Malahide. He is buried in Malahide (St Andrew) Church of Ireland Churchyard, Dublin.

Sgt (AB) Clifford Taylor (1671845), RAFVR, aged 30, was the son of Harold and Frances Taylor of Low Newton. He is buried in Lindale (St Paul) Churchyard, Lancashire.

F/Sgt (W/Op) Thomas Donovan Potter (432260), RAAF, aged 19, was the son of Fred and Susan Eliza Potter of Thornley, New South Wales. He is buried in Chester (Blacon) Cemetery.

Sgt (AG) Leslie Edward Bowler Walker (1852244), RAFVR, aged 19, was the son of Thomas Bowler Walker and Beatrice Annie Florence Walker of Boar's Hill, Berkshire. He is buried in Abingdon New Cemetery, Berkshire.

Sgt (AG) John Stanley Alexander Nicholson (1597145), RAFVR, aged 20, was the son of John Joseph and Adelaide Martha Nicholson of Holmrook, Cumberland. He is buried in Chester (Blacon) Cemetery.

10 September (Sunday)
Simulated combat training. 551st FTS, 495th FTG (Station 342, Atcham, Shropshire)
Republic P-47D Thunderbolt (42-74684, bearing the fuselage code VM-?) crashed at Betton Abbots Farm, near Cross Houses (at map reference 518080), at 18.45 hrs. Lt Eskew and 2 Lt Willie A Eschenfelder took off together to practise simulated combat (using camera guns), during the course of which they were 'bounced' by another P-47 piloted by Lt Kerfoot. After a series of turns, Lt Kerfoot manoeuvred onto Lt Eskew's tail and followed him into a climb, at approximately 8,000 feet. During the climb Lt Eskew

is believed to have cut his throttle, in an attempt to shake off his 'attacker', but Lt Kerfoot was too close to take evasive action and his port wing sliced Lt Eskew's tail clean off. The two aircraft were sent out of control and crashed. Sadly, Lt Kerfoot went down with his aircraft, while Lt Eskew attempted to bale out, but his parachute failed to open in time (investigation later showed that it had become snagged on the aircraft).

2 Lt (pilot u/t) John Rolfe Kerfoot (O-774185), USAAF, aged 27, was the son of Horace Rolfe Kerfoot and Bertha Kerfoot (née Raine) of Wilder, Canyon County, Idaho. He is buried in Cambridge (Madingley) Cemetery.

Simulated combat training. 551st FTS, 495th FTG (Station 342, Atcham, Shropshire)
Republic P-47D Thunderbolt (42-7986, bearing the fuselage code VM-R) crashed at Cronkhill Farm, Cross Houses, following the incident described above.

2 Lt (pilot u/t) John Charles Eskew Jr (O-774080), USAAF, aged 20, was the son of John Charles and Norma Eskew of Alexandria City, Louisiana. He is buried in Greenwood Memorial Park Cemetery, Pineville, Louisiana.

13 September (Wednesday)
Local flight to observe bomber group forming up. 13th Combat Bombardment Wing, 8th Air Force (Station 119, Horham, Suffolk)
Republic P-47D Thunderbolt (42-8536) crashed at Sibdon Carwood (at map reference 416829), near Craven Arms, at 09.30 hrs. On the morning of 13 September, 390th Bombardment Group (which made up part of the 13th CBW) was due to fly a mission over north-west Europe and Colonel Wittan attended the early morning pre-mission briefing. In what is presumed to have been a spur-of-the-moment decision, Colonel Wittan took off at 07.16 hrs in the Combat Wing's P-47 Thunderbolt, apparently to watch the group forming up. The aircraft was subsequently witnessed 'flying above and somewhat to the east of the 390th as it departed the south coast of England', after which Colonel Wittan is thought to have turned around and headed back inland. Why he ended up so far west is unknown but, upon reaching south Shropshire, he encountered very thick cloud down to 500 feet and visibility of less than 3,000 feet, with even worse localised weather over the higher ground. In the prevailing conditions it is thought that he became lost and, not having R/T on the aircraft, began feeling his way north in an attempt to find a break in the clouds. Realising then that his fuel was nearly exhausted and that dropping down through the cloud to carry out a forced landing was far too dangerous, he decided to take to his parachute. Tragically, because he was over high ground, his parachute failed to open in time and he was killed instantly on striking the ground, while his aircraft crashed, inverted, half a mile to the north.

Col Ed Wittan
[390th Bombardment Group Association]

Colonel (pilot) Edgar (Ed) Milton Wittan (O-21612), SS, DFC & 2 OLC, AM & 2 OLC, USAAF, aged 33, was born in Baltimore on 26 November 1910, the son of David and Anna Wittan. After graduating from Staunton Military Academy in 1928 he studied at the University of Pittsburgh before receiving a commission in the Air Corps Reserve in 1932 and gaining his wings early the following year. The next five years were spent in the reserve but, in 1940, he was promoted to major and flew with the Neutrality Patrol off Florida. Following the attack on Pearl Harbour in December 1941 he joined the Army Air Force tactical unit set up in Newfoundland, where he also gained his senior pilot's wings in 1942 and was promoted to lieutenant-colonel. In February 1943 he was assigned to command and train the 390th Bombardment Group, which he then took overseas and into combat, earning the Group the nickname 'Wittan's Wallopers'. He was assigned to command the 13th Combat Bombardment Wing on 17 April 1944. Col Wittan is buried alongside his brother, Robert (who died at Anzio), in Arlington National Cemetery Virginia.

15 September (Friday)
Formation flying exercise. 61 OTU (RAF Rednal, Shropshire)
Supermarine Spitfire IIA (P7280) crashed at Crickheath Farm (at map reference 301233), between Llynclys and Maesbrook, at 09.50 hrs. Although he had failed to ensure that his pupils were capable of cloud flying, the flight commander authorised a formation exercise, during which the pilot of this aircraft is believed to have lost control in cloud and crashed.

F/Sgt (pilot u/t) Gordon Leonard Smith (1320299), RAFVR, aged 22, was the son of Henry and Phyllis Smith of Walthamstow, Essex. He is buried in Oswestry General Cemetery, Shropshire.

16 September (Saturday)
Height climb to 25,000 feet. 61 OTU (RAF Rednal, Shropshire)
Supermarine Spitfire IIA (P8088, presentation aircraft named *The Borough of Lambeth*) crashed between Prees Green and Fauls (at wartime map reference 576319), at 09.05 hrs. The pilot is believed to have lost consciousness due to failure of his oxygen supply, and the aircraft dived into the ground from a great height.

Sgt (pilot u/t) John Cashel Barry (423588), RAAF, aged 22, was the son of Michael Joseph and Florence Kathleen Barry of Wahroonga, New South Wales. He is buried in Chester (Blacon) Cemetery.

16 September (Saturday)
Local training mission. 552nd FTS, 495th FTG (Station 342, Atcham)
Lockheed P-38J Lightning (42-67701, bearing the fuselage code DQ-Q ?) crash-landed south of Bayston Hill (at map reference 484080), near the Condover turning, at 15.50 hrs. Lt Green took off at 14.05 hrs, with 2 Lt John W Mahoney as his wingman. The two had completed their training exercise and were returning to the airfield when Lt Green's starboard engine failed, due to a lack of fuel. He immediately radioed Lt Mahoney to inform him and an instructor, who was on the same frequency, heard the message and instructed Lt Green to climb to 4,000 feet and use the fuel cross-feed before unfeathering his engine. Lt Green was seen to climb to 2,200 feet and attempt the procedure, but it was subsequently determined that he 'made the mistake of leaving his empty tank 'on' and switching 'off' the tank which had fuel remaining'. This caused both engines to fail and, in the resultant belly-landing, the aircraft hit a sharp rise in the ground and Lt Green struck his head on the instrument panel, when his seat broke loose, suffering fatal injuries.

2 Lt (pilot u/t) Alan Stewart Green (O-708677), USAAF, aged 22, was the son of English-born Emanuel George and Winifred Green of Lakewood, Ohio. He is buried in Cambridge (Madingley) Cemetery.

The wreckage of 2 Lt Green's P-38 after he crash-landed on the lower slopes of Lyth Hill. [USAAF]

16 September (Saturday)
Return flight to base. Empire Central Flying School (RAF Hullavington, Wiltshire)
Martin Baltimore I (AG689) crashed into woodland at Tedsmore Hall (at map reference 371257, where a wooden memorial cross marks the spot), east of West Felton, at 13.50 hrs. Five officers from the Empire Central Flying School (ECFS) had arrived at RAF Rednal the previous day to observe the training programme carried out by 61 OTU and had spent the night at the airfield. The following day the same five officers left to fly back to Hullavington but, soon after taking off, the pilot lost control due to a 'defect in the rudder mechanism' and the aircraft crashed into a hillside, bursting into flames. Two passengers were killed instantly, while the pilot and one passenger were taken to Copthorne Military Hospital and an American passenger to the US 68th General Hospital, Whitchurch, by RAF Rednal's ambulance.

S/Ldr (pilot) Frederick William Westley (43624), AFC, RAF. Born in Greenwich, on 27 March 1909, he had joined the RAF in 1924 and spent the inter-war years flying with a number of operational units including 24 Squadron, HMS *Eagle*, 8 Squadron (flying light bombers during the Arab revolts in Aden) and 17 Squadron (flying as part of the UK's air defence network). In July 1934, he began a number of non-operational postings in the UK but, following the outbreak of war, was chosen for instructor duties. He subsequently spent three years in Canada, during which he was awarded the AFC, in October 1942, for his outstanding abilities as an instructor, before returning to the UK in October 1943. On his arrival in the UK he was posted to ECFS for training and, after completing the course in April 1944, was asked to stay on as a member of staff. Following the crash at Tedsmore, he underwent treatment at RAF Hospital, Cosford until April 1945 and subsequently retired in February 1947 on grounds of medical unfitness. He died in Enfield in March 1999.

W/Cdr (pilot, but travelling as passenger) David Scott Shearman 'Wilkie' Wilkerson (62281), DSO, DFC, RAFVR, aged 27, was the son of John Shearman Wilkerson and Jane Elizabeth Wilkerson of Snaresbrook, Essex. 'Wilkie', as he was known, had been awarded the DFC in March 1942 during his first tour of ops with 35 Squadron, piloting Halifax bombers. Following promotion he was given command of 51 Squadron in November 1943 and, in January 1944, he helped form (and subsequently commanded) 578 Squadron out of a nucleus of 51 Squadron personnel. In May 1944 he was awarded the DSO, the recommendation for which read:

> This officer has completed many sorties on his second tour of operations. He has displayed high powers of leadership, great skill and determination, qualities which have earned him much success. He is a devoted and zealous squadron commander, whose great drive and tactical ability have contributed in a large measure to the high standard of operational efficiency of the squadron.

W/Cdr 'Wilkie' Wilkerson [Hugh Cawdron]

He relinquished his command of the squadron in August 1944 and was posted to ECFS. Following his death he was posthumously awarded the American DFC. He is buried in Selby Cemetery, Yorkshire.

Maj (pilot, but travelling as passenger) James Wilfred Cross (102809V), SAAF, aged 33, was the son of Albert H and Ellen Cross and the husband of Henriette A Cross of Worcester, in the Cape Province of South Africa. Born on 28 July 1911, he appears to have served in the navy between 1929 and 1933 before becoming an architect for the public works department and also serving with the Transvaal Air Training Squadron (TATS) between 1936 and 1939. Commissioned in November 1939, he was posted to 12 (Bomber) Squadron, SAAF, the following month but was soon selected for an instructors' course at the CFS in South Africa. He subsequently remained in South Africa until 1944, serving in a wide variety of instructor roles, before being posted to the UK as Chief Ground Instructor at ECFS in August 1944. He is buried in Chester (Blacon) Cemetery.

S/Ldr Jeffrey [or Jeffery?] (service number unknown), RCAF.

Lt Cdr A Packard (service number unknown), USN.

22 September (Friday)
Lt Luther J Abel died from injuries received in an aircraft crash at Wroxeter on 18 August.

23 September (Saturday)
Non-operational battle formation flight. 551st FTS, 495th FTG (Station 342, Atcham, Shropshire)
Republic P-47C Thunderbolt (41-6233, bearing the fuselage code VM-?) crashed at 'Tibberton Green Farm, Tibberton', near Wellington, at 15.40 hrs. A flight of four aircraft, led by 1 Lt Rupert M Tumlin, was flying in battle formation when they were bounced by two other P-47s at 5,000 feet. Lt Tumlin immediately ordered the formation to break right but it is thought that Lt Heagney, in No. 4 position, either misheard and turned left, or hesitated too long and collided with No. 3, which was turning to the right. No. 3's starboard wing buckled approximately four feet from the wing tip and the aircraft was thrown into a series of uncontrollable rolls before crashing and killing the pilot (whose body was found 100 yards from the wreckage, suggesting that he may have tried to bale out). Lt Heagney's aircraft was, similarly, thrown into an uncontrollable dive and crashed, killing him instantly.

2 Lt Jackie Heagney
[Linda Parker]

2 Lt (pilot u/t) John Dominick Heagney Jr (O-714413), USAAF, aged 25, was the son of John Dominick and Blanche Alma Heagney (née Lester) of St Louis, Missouri. Jackie, as he was known to his family, was educated at Ritenaur High School and Brasley Architectural School in St Louis, before enlisting in the Air Force in November 1942. According to his family, he was a bit of a daredevil, enjoying motorbikes and fast cars, so joining the Air Force was the natural choice for him. He is buried in Arlington National Cemetery, Virginia.

23 September (Saturday)
Non-operational battle formation flight. 551st FTS, 495th FTG (Station 342, Atcham, Shropshire)
Republic P-47D Thunderbolt (42-74640, bearing the fuselage code VM-?) crashed at 'Tibberton Green Farm, Tibberton' (although the map reference 711196, converts to a site just north-west of Edgmond), following the incident described above.

2 Lt (pilot u/t) Donald Eugene Casebier (O-567611), USAAF, aged 23, was the son of Thomas Roscoe Casebier and Stella McDonald and the husband of Ruth Casebier (née Underwood). He is buried in Fort Leavenworth National Cemetery, Kansas.

26 September (Tuesday)
Training flight. 28 EFTS (Penderford, Staffordshire)
De Havilland Tiger Moth II (T6039) crashed at 'Llwyn-y-mapsis field', near Morda crossroads, Oswestry. The aircraft was being flown by two pupil pilots when it crashed while flying over Sgt Woodward's family home in Oswestry. Sgt Wilkinson was killed instantly, while Sgt Woodward was injured and admitted to the Agnes Hunt and Robert Jones Orthopaedic Hospital suffering from shock and slight facial injuries.

Sgt (pilot u/t) Robert Arnold Wilkinson (1165064), RAFVR, aged 26, was the son of Robert Samuel and Caroline Wilkinson of Sutton in Ashfield and the husband of Marjorie Edith Wilkinson (née Morris) of Mansfield. He is buried in Sutton in Ashfield Cemetery, Nottinghamshire.

Sgt (pilot u/t) Willoughby Woodward (1577955), RAFVR, was born in Oswestry in 1923, the family living at Oswyn House where his father ran a dental practice. Nothing further is known of his military service other than that he survived the war.

28 September (Thursday)
Gunnery practice . 5 (P)AFU (RAF Tern Hill, Shropshire)
Miles Master II (DK822) crashed at Heathcote (at wartime map reference 655283), between Stoke on Tern and Wistanswick, at 09.00 hrs. The pilot took off at 08.35 hrs with instructions to carry out gunnery practice with another Miles Master but, as there was a delay in the other Master's taking off, he began orbiting the airfield at 2,000 feet, during which time he allowed the aircraft to stall and crash.

Sgt (pilot u/t) Samuel Alexander Gault (1352418), RAFVR, aged 29, was born in Shettleston, Glasgow, in 1915. He is buried in Chester (Blacon) Cemetery.

28 September (Thursday)
Formation training mission. 552nd FTS, 495th FTG (Station 342, Atcham, Shropshire)
Republic P-47C Thunderbolt (41-6267, bearing the fuselage code DQ-W) crashed near the railway crossing at Brick Kiln Farm, north of Whitchurch, at 14.55 hrs. A flight of four P-47s, led by Lt Richard W Oxley, was climbing in close formation when a Spitfire suddenly appeared and began trying to join the formation. In an attempt to lose the Spitfire the flight leader made a sharp downwards turn to the left but, as the flight pulled out at 1,500 feet, Lt Clark (in number 3 position) lost control and crashed, possibly after being caught in his wingman's slipstream.

The wreckage of 2 Lt Clark's P-47 being hosed down following the crash near Whitchurch. [USAAF]

2 Lt (pilot u/t) Fay H Clark (O-714874), USAAF, aged 20 (?) was the son of Fay Johnfin Clark and Mary Agnes Clark of Shelbyville, Indiana. He is buried in Cambridge (Madingley) Cemetery.

29 September (Friday)
Sector reconnaissance and R/T homing exercise. 60 OTU (RAF High Ercall, Shropshire)
De Havilland Mosquito II (W4086) crashed 'one mile west of Peplow' (putting it in the area between Radmoor and High Hatton) at 15.50 hrs. After being given various vectors as part of his exercise, the pilot was instructed to return to the vicinity of the airfield and reduce height to 1,800 feet (200 feet below the cloud base). This instruction was acknowledged but, thirty seconds later, the aircraft was seen to drop its nose suddenly and dive steeply into the ground, exploding on impact. The subsequent investigation determined that the cause of the crash was a failure of the

F/Lt Alfred Roberts [TNA]

starboard engine after the pilot omitted to switch to his inner fuel tanks when his outer tanks had run dry. While trying to turn the fuel cocks, 'which are in an exceedingly awkward position behind the pilot's back, he stalled the aircraft and had insufficient height to recover from the resulting dive and probable spin'.

F/Lt (pilot u/t) Alfred Thomas Roberts (413666), RAAF, aged 26, was the son of Alfred Albert and Mabel Lydia Roberts of Burwood, New South Wales and the husband of Doreen Chambers of Montreal (whom he had presumably met during pilot training in Canada). Born on 9 March 1918, he had worked as a metallurgical clerk before enlisting in September 1941. He is buried in Chester (Blacon) Cemetery.

4 October (Wednesday)
Solo formation training flight. 5 (P)AFU (RAF Tern Hill, Shropshire)
Miles Master II (AZ731) force-landed at 'Bolas Common Farm' (presumably Common Farm in Bolas Heath), near Tibberton, at 10.35 hrs. After his engine failed and caught fire, the pupil pilot managed to extinguish the flames before belly-landing the aircraft in a field.

Sgt (pilot u/t) Maurice Hubert Paul Remy (1424995), RAFVR. On completion of his training this Belgian citizen was posted to 349 (Belgian) Squadron and flew Spitfires (and Tempests briefly) over the advancing Allied armies in Europe. Sadly, having survived the war, he was fatally injured in a crash on 18 December 1945 when his aircraft's engine failed during take-off. W/O Remy was twenty-four years old and is buried in Hotton War Cemetery, Belgium.

12 October (Thursday)
Night cross-country exercise. 83 OTU (RAF Peplow, Shropshire)
Vickers Wellington X (HE700) crashed at Stoke Grange, to the south-west of Tern Hill airfield, at 05.30 hrs. The trainee crew were being recalled to base because of reports of worsening weather, when the pilot is believed to have lost control in cloud. In the resultant spin, the aircraft began to disintegrate before crashing.

P/O (pilot) James Claude Hubble (186586), RAFVR, aged 21, was the son of James William and Rachel George Hubble of Crawley Green Road, Luton. Born on 15 November 1922, he was educated at Waller Street Boys' School and had worked as an accountant for the Percival Aircraft Company before enlisting. He is buried in Luton Church burial yard.

Sgt (pilot) Patrick Noel Gent (1615002), RAFVR, aged 21, was the son of Arthur John and Mabel Anne Gent of Peterborough, Northamptonshire. He is buried in Chester (Blacon) Cemetery.

F/Sgt (Nav) Thomas Robert Terrence Gooding (1416452), RAFVR, aged 24, was the son of Percy Lewis and Catherine Elizabeth Gooding of Mountain Ash. He is buried in Mountain Ash (Maes yr Arian) Cemetery, Glamorganshire.

Sgt (W/AG) Eric Evans (2204517), RAFVR, aged 19, was the son of Isaac and Edith Evans of Holyhead. He is buried in Holyhead (Maes Hyfryd) Cemetery, Anglesey.

Sgt (AG) John Eaton Maddocks (2226577), RAFVR, aged 36, was the son of Samuel William and Sarah Jane Maddocks of Liverpool and the husband of Elizabeth Maddocks (née Adamson), also of Liverpool. He is buried in Chester (Blacon) Cemetery.

Sgt (AG) Jack Lambe Doveton (2235927), RAFVR, aged 21, was the son of Cecil Lambe Doveton and Violet Maud Doveton of Bishops Waltham, Hampshire. He is buried in Winchester (Magdalen Hill) Cemetery.

12 October (Thursday)
Formation flying practice. 41 OTU (RAF Hawarden, Flintshire)
Hawker Hurricane IIc (LF394) force-landed between Ollerton and Stoke on Tern (at wartime map

reference 643262) at 12.45 hrs. During the course of the flight the engine began to fail due to a broken con rod. The pilot was unable to maintain height and had to make a forced landing in a field.

P/O (pilot u/t) Fredrick Arthur George (175345), RAFVR. He survived the war and attained the rank of flying officer.

15 October (Sunday)
Instrument flying and camera gunnery. 551st FTS, 495th FTG (Station 342, Atcham, Shropshire)
Republic P-47D Thunderbolt (42-74674, bearing the fuselage code VM-S) crashed at Park Farm, Leebotwood, near Church Stretton, at 09.15 hrs. Two pilots took off together at 07.50 hrs and climbed to 8,000 feet, where they levelled off and took it in turns to practise instrument flying while the other observed. Having completed the exercise the two pilots flew around for a few minutes, 'looking the country over', before starting simulated combat with camera guns. Soon afterwards, however, they saw a combat formation nearby and decided to dive and make an 'attack'. In the melee that ensued Lt Kuehl began a climbing right-hand turn in an attempt to shake off two aircraft but, failed to notice that his wingman, Lt Borden, had left the 'dogfight' and was orbiting ahead. The resultant collision slightly damaged Lt Borden's aircraft but he was able to return to Atcham. Lt Kuehl meanwhile found that his port wing was

> … wrecked to within about a foot and a half of the inboard edge of the gun cover. My aileron was almost jammed tight. Using the rudder and applying extreme pressure on the aileron I kept the plane straight and notified the field of the situation. They told me to use my own judgment so I headed the plane west, cut the throttle, rolled the plane over and fell out.

After leaving the aircraft at 10,000 feet, the pilot floated down at Frodesley, where he 'phoned the station and was picked up by the station ambulance.

2 Lt (pilot u/t) Richard I Kuehl (O-716011), USAAF. On completion of his training he flew Mustangs with the 83rd Fighter Squadron, 78th Fighter Group and was credited with two enemy aircraft destroyed and one shared destroyed. On 10 April 1945 he was forced to bale out again after being hit by flak over Helmstadt but managed to return to Allied lines without being captured.

Instrument flying and camera gunnery. 551st FTS, 495th FTG (Station 342, Atcham, Shropshire)
Republic P-47D Thunderbolt (42-8466, bearing the fuselage code VM-T) landed at base after colliding with the above-mentioned aircraft.

2 Lt (pilot u/t) George Borden Jr (O-829808), USAAF.

17 October (Tuesday)
Stalling and spin recovery practice. 5 (P)AFU (RAF Tern Hill, Shropshire)
Miles Master II (W9060) crash-landed at Ashwood Farm, between Ash Magna and Ightfield (at wartime map reference 591396), at 11.30 hrs. The pilot was flying at 2,000 feet when his engine failed. In the ensuing belly-landing he suffered lacerations to his right eye and was taken to Tern Hill sick quarters by RAF Tilstock's ambulance.

F/O (pilot u/t) Han J Doornbos (134306), RAFVR. On completion of his training this Dutch citizen was posted to 322 (Dutch) Squadron on 18 April 1945 and flew Spitfires operationally during the final weeks of the war.

18 October (Wednesday)
Battle formation training mission. 552nd FTS, 495th FTG (Station 342, Atcham, Shropshire)

Republic P-47D Thunderbolt (42-7974, bearing the fuselage code DQ-?) crashed at Muckleton Hall Farm, Muckleton, to the east of Shawbury, at 08.45 hrs. A flight of four P-47s took off at 06.45 hrs and climbed to 7,000 feet in close formation, at which point the leader, 1 Lt George W Franklin, ordered them into battle formation while continuing to climb. At approximately 10,000 feet the flight was 'bounced' in quick succession by a pair of P-38s and the flight leader ordered a 'break to left'. During this break it is believed that Lt Maxwell, flying No. 2, tightened his turn too much and struck the right side of Lt Clary's aircraft, which was flying No. 3. The impact sent 2 Lt Maxwell's aircraft crashing out of control and he was killed instantly. According to Lt Clary's account,

> It [Lt Maxwell's aircraft] evidently hit my left [sic] wing and fuselage as I was thrown violently against the right side of my cockpit, losing consciousness momentarily. When I revived I was in a spin and attempted one recovery with no results. Was low on altitude so bailed out at approximately 4,000 feet.

2 Lt (pilot u/t) William E Maxwell (O-830272), USAAF, aged 20(?), was the son of Bert and Helen A Maxwell of Kenmore, New York State. He is buried in Cambridge (Madingley) Cemetery.

Battle formation training mission. 552nd FTS, 495th FTG (Station 342, Atcham, Shropshire)
Republic P-47D Thunderbolt (42-75071, bearing the fuselage code DQ-K) crashed at Grange Farm, Ellerdine, one mile east of Muckleton, following the collision described above.

1 Lt (pilot u/t) Dallas J Clary (O-816748), USAAF. On completing his training he flew P-47s with the 397th Fighter Squadron, 368th Fighter Group and was credited with one Me109 destroyed on 18 December 1944.

19 October (Thursday)
Night training flight. 61 OTU (RAF Montford Bridge, Shropshire – satellite airfield to RAF Rednal)
Supermarine Spitfire VB (W3621) crashed at Ensdon House Farm, to the south-west of the airfield, at 21.50 hrs. Shortly after taking off on a south-westerly heading, the pilot attempted to change from instruments to visual flying and allowed the aircraft to lose height and strike the ground, injuring himself. According to an account in the Wartime Aircraft Recovery Group magazines held in the county archives;

> The aircraft lost height and flew for about 800 yards at very low level, passing between two trees about 50 feet apart, brushing a hedge top, crossing an area of wooded land, under the branches of an oak tree, through two wooden fences and crossing the A5 trunk road before crashing into a five bar gate at Ensdon House Farm. One heavy stone gate-post was smashed and the other hurled about 20 yards as the wings were broken from the aircraft. The fuselage struck the ground and broke up over a distance of about 150 yards, the largest remaining section being the area from the engine bulkhead to the radio compartment. The machine guns which had broken away from the wings and travelled further than any other wreckage, were later collected by a guard and placed in a tent on the site for security reasons!

F/Lt (pilot u/t) Cecil Henry Arthur Harrison (119555), RAFVR. Born in Woolwich on 31 October 1910, he was commissioned in the RAFVR in January 1942 and had, presumably, served in another branch before being accepted for pilot training. He remained in the RAF after the war and relinquished his commission as a flight lieutenant in October 1955. He died in Bristol in 1988.

23 October (Monday)
'Training on new type'. 5 (P)AFU (RAF Chetwynd, Shropshire – satellite to RAF Tern Hill)
Hawker Hurricane I (P3961) force-landed 'near Chetwynd airfield' (at wartime map reference 740223,

just east of Puleston) at 15.10 hrs. The pilot was approaching the airfield to land when he changed to his reserve tank (which was full). Due to a possible airlock the fuel did not feed through and the engine failed. With his wheels already down, the pilot quickly attempted to retract them for a belly-landing, but there was not enough time and the partly-raised undercarriage caught in the soft ground, flipping the aircraft onto its back.

F/O (pilot u/t) Lawrence Donald Morrow (J.36492), RCAF. Born on 10 January 1917, he had enlisted in Hamilton, Ontario, in November 1940 and, after completing his training, was selected to remain in Canada for instructor duties. Commissioned in July 1943, he finally sailed to the UK in May 1944 and at the time of the accident was undergoing training on single-engine aircraft. He retired from the RCAF in November 1945.

23 October (Monday)
Cross-country exercise. 1656 HCU (RAF Lindholme, Yorkshire)
Handley Page Halifax II (BB284) crashed at Upper Whittingslow Farm, Marshbrook (at map reference 433886), to the south of Church Stretton, at 15.15 hrs. The trainee crew had been in the air for just over three hours when the starboard outer engine caught fire. As he was unable to extinguish it, the pilot ordered his men to bale out. Sadly, there were not enough parachutes on board and both pilots were killed after control of the aircraft was lost while descending through cloud (perhaps due to icing on the wings). In the subsequent inquiry, emphasis was placed on the fact that the pilot had failed to check the correct number of parachutes on board before taking off.

P/O (pilot) Thomas Arthur Ellison (56151), RAF, aged 28, was the son of Thomas and Jemima Elizabeth Ellison and the husband of Cynthia Kathleen Ellison (née Perryman) of East Preston, Sussex. He is buried in Chester (Blacon) Cemetery.

Sgt (pilot) John Francis Charles Wheeler (1586690), RAFVR, aged 22, was the son of Ethel Maude and the late Francis James Wheeler of Bridgwater. He is buried in Bridgwater (Quantock Road) Cemetery, Somerset.

Sgt Brownhill, RAFVR.

Sgt A E Parker, RAFVR.

Sgt (W/AG) Trevor P Roberts, RAFVR. Following the accident he spent three months in RAF Hospital, Cosford, undergoing treatment for 15 multiple fractures he suffered due to his parachute spilling while he tried to avoid trees.

Sgt Robinson, RAFVR.

Sgt Pointer, RAFVR.

25 October (Wednesday)
Training flight. 81 OTU (RAF Sleap, Shropshire)
Airspeed Horsa (LH441) force-landed at Loppington, near Wem, after the pilot cast off from the tug aircraft prematurely, slightly damaging the nose wheel.

The names of the crew are unknown.

2 November (Thursday)
Ferry flight to unknown airfield. Station Flight, Hawkinge (RAF Hawkinge, Kent)
Supermarine Spitfire VB (EP388) crash-landed at North Tasley, on the north-western outskirts of Bridgnorth, at 17.45 hrs. The pilot was flying at 1,000 feet when his engine started cutting out and the aircraft began to lose height. In the ensuing crash-landing the pilot suffered a fractured vertebra and was taken to RAF Hospital, Bridgnorth, before being transferred the following day for specialist treatment at RAF Hospital, Cosford.

F/Lt (pilot) Alan Johnstone (C.5210), RCAF. Born in the USA on 19 October 1911, he had travelled to Canada in September 1940 and volunteered for the RCAF. Before arriving in the UK, in August 1943, he had spent 15 months flying Kittyhawk fighters with 118 and 132 Squadron, RCAF, as part of the air defence of Canada. Following his arrival in the UK, he was posted to 441 Squadron in April 1944 and, over the following months, was credited with one aircraft destroyed, two shared destroyed and one damaged. At the time of the accident, the squadron was operating out of Hawkinge, although it is unclear what duty F/Lt Johnstone was performing when the crash occurred. As a result of the accident he did not return to flying duties and was repatriated to Canada in July 1945.

8 November (Wednesday)
Glider towing practice. 81 OTU (RAF Sleap, Shropshire)
Airspeed Horsa I (LH502 or LJ502) force-landed at 'Fields Farm', to the south-west of the airfield (at wartime map reference 468267), at 20.30 hrs. The pilot was taking off from the airfield when a sharp jerk at 100 feet caused a faulty shackle-pin on the tug's tow rope attachment to break and the pilot landed in a field ahead.

Staff Sgt (1st pilot) W R Fisher (4278476), GPR.
Sgt (2nd pilot) J Topp (2891054), GPR.

8 November (Wednesday)
Cloud flying training. 61 OTU (RAF Montford Bridge, Shropshire – satellite to RAF Rednal)
Supermarine Spitfire VB (AA943) crash-landed at 'Farm Hall, Sandford' (although the wartime map reference 332193 converts to a point near Farm Hall, Kinnerley) at 14.58 hrs. While flying at 5,000 feet the engine failed, due to a 'probable bearing failure', and the pilot was forced to belly-land in a field.

F/O (instructor? pilot) Clifford Denzel Wilson (J.29906), RCAF. Born on 6 September 1920, he had enlisted in Hamilton, Ontario in July 1941 and underwent pilot training in Canada before sailing to the UK in September 1943. Little is known of his movements after his arrival, but he had presumably flown operationally before becoming an instructor at 61 OTU. He survived the war and returned to Canada in September 1945.

F/O Feliks Nowak [TNA]

9 November (Thursday)
Circuits and landings. 60 OTU (RAF High Ercall, Shropshire)
De Havilland Mosquito NF II (DZ244) crashed at Haughmond Farm (at map reference 544153), to the east of Shrewsbury, at 00.53 hrs. After taking off for his sixth circuit of the airfield the pilot is thought to have lost control and crashed when the port engine failed, due to a glycol leak.

F/O (pilot u/t) Feliks Pawel Nowak (P2284), PAF, aged 28, was the husband of Delphine Nowak of Poland. According to the Borders Historical Aviation Archaeology Group, he had fought with the Polish 59th Infantry Regiment during the German invasion of Poland, prior to escaping to France and joining the Polish Forces there. He is believed to have then been taken prisoner of war for a time, before managing to escape to England, via Spain and Portugal, in July 1942. He is buried in Shrewsbury General Cemetery, Shropshire.

9 November (Thursday)
Cross-country exercise. 82 OTU (RAF Ossington, Nottinghamshire)
Vickers Wellington X (LP840) crashed at Woodhouse, just north of Rednal airfield (at map reference

365295), near Oswestry, at 16.45 hrs. The trainee crew had been in the air for five hours and fifteen minutes when they encountered thick cloud, through which the pilot decided to continue, despite having being told to turn back if it was encountered. Soon afterwards it is believed that he lost control, and the aircraft was witnessed by airmen at RAF Rednal diving out of cloud and exploding on impact. The pilot's loss of control was subsequently attributed to either an 'inability to fly on instruments through a very dense and turbulent cloud', or failure of his airspeed indicator due to icing, or build-up of ice on the controls.

F/O (pilot) Raymond Phillip Willison (J.39140), RCAF, aged 22, was the son of Albert and Ruth Hazel Willison of Moose Jaw, Saskatchewan and the husband of Jean Catherine Willison, also of Moose Jaw. Born on 15 March 1922, he had joined the RCAF in June 1940 and underwent training in Canada, after which he served as an instructor from May 1941 until his posting to the UK in April 1944. He is buried in Chester (Blacon) Cemetery.

F/O Raymond Willison [Library and Archives Canada]

F/O (Nav) Thomas McLaren Young (J.42722), RCAF, aged 26, was the son of Thomas B and Maude M Young of West Summerland, British Columbia. Before enlisting he had studied at the University of British Columbia. He is buried in Chester (Blacon) Cemetery.

P/O (AB) Arthur Rosen (J.44604), RCAF, aged 23, was the son of Joseph and Rose Rosen of Toronto. He is buried in Chester (Blacon) Cemetery.

Sgt (W/AG) Joseph Anthony Austin Giroux (R.220910), RCAF, aged 20, was the son of Anthony and Inez Giroux of Demers Centre, Quebec. He is buried in Chester (Blacon) Cemetery.

Sgt (AG rear) Donald Goodwin (R.290583), RCAF, aged 19, was the son of Peter and Alice Goodwin of Arnprior, Ontario. He is buried in Chester (Blacon) Cemetery.

F/O Thomas Young [Library and Archives Canada]

10 November (Friday)
Training flight. 81 OTU (RAF Sleap, Shropshire)
Airspeed Horsa (LH384) crashed on the edge of the airfield at 02.50 hrs. After casting off from his tug aircraft too high, the pilot thought he was going to overshoot the airfield and began a 360 degree turn to lose height. In the process the glider struck a contractor's hut on the edge of the airfield, killing the pilot instantly and injuring his co-pilot.

Staff Sgt (1st pilot) Hadyn Reginald Browne (7620222), GPR, aged 35, was the son of Albert Richmond Browne and Peggy Browne of St Anne's-on-Sea, Lancashire. He is buried in Lytham St Anne's (Park) Cemetery, Lancashire.

Sgt (2nd pilot) C Clegg (893614), GPR.

11 November - Armistice Day (Saturday)
Operational mission to bomb the Buer synthetic oil plant at Gelsenkirchen, Germany. 360th Bombardment Squadron, 303rd Bombardment Group, 8th Air Force (Station 107, Molesworth, Cambridgeshire)
Boeing B-17G Flying Fortress (44-8422, bearing the nose art *Duffy's Tavern*) wreckage scattered over a wide area in the vicinity of Grange Farm, near Much Wenlock, at 08.30 hrs. The crew took off at 07.35 hrs, for their eleventh mission together, and immediately began climbing up through cloud to 12,000 feet, where they broke through into brilliant sunshine. Moments later, it is believed, the pilot 'lost control

after hitting the slipstream of an aircraft ahead, was then confronted with an instrument recovery but failed to pull out soon enough, thus allowing an excess speed to build up'. The 'abnormal stresses' consequently placed on the aircraft caused it to disintegrate, spreading wreckage over a wide area and killing all but two of the crew. Sgt Phillips, who was in the top turret, had heard the metal straining and strapped his parachute on just in time, while Sgt Sorenson gave the following account of his escape in the subsequent investigation:

> ... it felt to me as though the aircraft was doing a slow roll and I was thrown against the floor. It took all the energy I had to pick up my chute and hook it on my harness. I looked up and saw that the waist door came off by itself, and I couldn't crawl at all towards the door. I turned around and saw that the aircraft was broken in two just ahead of the ball turret, I let loose my hold and was thrown clear of the aircraft. I pulled my rip cord but my chute didn't open so I pulled it out with my hands. Just after untangling myself from the chute I touched down. The chute just broke my fall.

In the November 1984 newsletter for the 303rd Bomb Group Association, an account was written of the aftermath by local man, Edward Townsend, who had rushed to the scene with Harry Murdoch:

> When we got out of town, Burt Luscott, another of the Home Guard, was stopping traffic from Much Wenlock since the road ahead was blocked by flaming wreckage. Murdoch and I set off across the marshy fields to search for any survivors. It was misty and we couldn't see too far, but in the second field from the road, we thought we heard a faint 'Help.' We set off in the direction indicated and shortly came upon an airman leaning over some wooden rails in the hedgerow. He [Sorenson] looked in a very bad state and was only half conscious. He apparently had walked or crawled 60 or 70 yards from a large oak tree where we later found the burnt and torn remains of a parachute. He was still holding the metal grip of the parachute ripcord. Two more local men came up and together, we placed the injured airman on an iron hurdle (gate) from the hedge and carried him to the road. Shortly an ambulance arrived and took him off to the hospital.

1 Lt (pilot) Paul Curtis Stephan (O-766108), AM, USAAF, aged 26, was the son of Curtis Edward and Catherine Margaret Stephan (née Coman) of Ellinwood, Kansas. He is buried in Cambridge (Madingley) Cemetery.

2 Lt (co-pilot) John Robert Clingler (O-205889), USAAF, aged 24, was the son of Roscoe and Lula B

The crew of Duffy's Tavern pictured in front of their aircraft in the autumn of 1944. Back row L–R: Sgt Dwight Phillips, 2 Lt Paul Stephan, 2 Lt John Clingler and 2 Lt Harold Lewis. Front row L–R: Sgt Raymond Ladurini, Sgt Edgar Harris, Sgt Thomas Tapley, Sgt Robert Sorenson and Sgt Stanton Keyes. [Robert Sorenson, via the 303rd Bomb Group website, www.303BG.com]

Clingler, and the husband of Helen I Clingler of Lebanon, Indiana. He is buried in Oak Hill Cemetery, Lebanon, Indiana.

Sgt (engineer and upper gunner) Dwight A Phillips (14173925), USAAF. Following lengthy treatment for a compound fracture of the back he was repatriated to the USA, where he worked as a truck driver and settled in Riverdale, Georgia.

2 Lt (Nav) Harold G Lewis (O-926767), AM, USAAF, came from Massachusetts. He is buried in Cambridge (Madingley) Cemetery.

Sgt (togglier) Thomas William (Tom) Tapley (14170363), AM, USAAF, aged 19(?), was the son of Lester Leroy and Anna Lillian Tapley (née Clark) of Shaw Township, Mississippi. He is buried in Cambridge (Madingley) Cemetery.

S/Sgt (radio operator) Raymond R Ladurini (17107147), USAAF, aged 22, was born on 5 July 1922 and enlisted in October 1942. He is buried in Fort Snelling National Cemetery, South Minneapolis.

Sgt (ball turret gunner) Stanton (Stan) W Keyes (39341328), USAAF, aged 19, is buried in Golden Gate National Cemetery, San Francisco. His next of kin are unknown.

Sgt (waist gunner) Robert J Sorenson (36391908), USAAF, eventually recovered from his injuries and returned to his native Michigan, where he married, before moving to Texas.

Sgt (tail gunner) Edgar (Ed) P Harris Jr (140955565), AM, USAAF, was a resident of Hinds County, Mississippi. He is buried in Cambridge (Madingley) Cemetery.

13 November (Monday)

Training flight. 61 OTU (RAF Montford Bridge, Shropshire – satellite to RAF Rednal)

Supermarine Spitfire VB (BL850) crash-landed near Montford Bridge airfield at 15.20 hrs. The pilot was coming in to land when the engine failed. Realising that he was undershooting, he tried to bounce the aircraft on a road to clear a hedge but the wheels collapsed and the aircraft crashed through the hedge, seriously injuring him.

P/O (pilot u/t) Peter Bremner (J.39138), RCAF. Born on 6 March 1919, he had enlisted in Toronto in August 1941 and underwent pilot training in Canada. Remaining in Canada presumably to undertake instructor duties, he sailed to the UK in June 1944 and stayed there until September 1945, when he returned home.

14 November (Tuesday)

Training flight. 81 OTU (RAF Sleap, Shropshire)

Airspeed Horsa (aircraft serial unknown), bearing the fuselage code '20' force-landed 'two miles north of the airfield' (putting it roughly in the area of Horton, between Loppington and Wem). The pilot 'made a false release from tug and force-landed', undamaged, in a field.

The name of the pilot is unknown

20 November (Monday)

Cross-country exercise. 14 OTU (RAF Market Harborough, Leicestershire)

Vickers Wellington X (LN428) crashed near the 'Red House Inn, Brockton', between Lilleshall and Newport, at 11.55 hrs. The trainee crew were flying in adverse weather conditions when a collision occurred with a Seafire (LR872), causing both aircraft to crash out of control.

RAF Peplow's crash crew and medical officer were quickly on the scene and the remains of the crew were taken to the station mortuary.

F/Sgt (pilot) John George Lamb (1324182), RAFVR, aged 23, was the son of George Rene and May Ethel Lamb of Hornchurch, Essex. He is buried in Chester (Blacon) Cemetery.

F/Sgt (Nav) Eric Richard Southern (1581192), RAFVR, aged 23, was the son of Richard and Gladys

Southern of Mansfield, Nottinghamshire. He is buried in Chester (Blacon) Cemetery.

Sgt (AB) Stanley Edward Witz (1524174), RAFVR, aged 30, was the son of Louis Edward and Martha L Witz (née Brown) of Sunderland. He is buried in Chester (Blacon) Cemetery.

Sgt (W/Op) Benjamin Kelly (1594719), RAFVR, aged 19, was the son of James and Margaret Kelly of Gateshead, County Durham. He is buried in Chester (Blacon) Cemetery.

Sgt (AG) Donald William Herbert Hall (1869433), RAFVR, aged 19, was the son of William Charles and May Pretoria Hall of Dagenham, Essex. He is buried in Chester (Blacon) Cemetery.

Sgt (AG) William Bratton Forsyth (1597691), RAFVR, aged 20, was the son of William B and Esther Forsyth of Wallsend. He is buried in Wallsend (Holy Cross) Cemetery, Northumberland.

Flight from RAF Mona, Anglesey, to RNAS Lee-on-Solent, Hampshire. 887 Squadron, Fleet Air Arm Supermarine Seafire III (LR872) crashed at 'Ketley Brook', in what is now part of Telford, after colliding in the incident described above.

Sub Lt (A) John Vincent Brooke, RN, aged 19, was the son of Vincent E and Maud Brooke of Sherwood, Nottingham and the husband of Betty Brooke (née Minister). He is buried in Arnold Cemetery, Nottinghamshire.

Cpl 'Billy' Bean [Lynda Bean]

25 November (Saturday)

'Routine passenger flight' from Stansted to Station 597 (Langford Lodge), in Northern Ireland, via Burtonwood. 40th Depot Repair Squadron, 40th Air Depot Group (Station 169, Stansted, Essex)

Boeing B-17G Flying Fortress (43-38847) crashed into the slopes of Clee Hill (at map reference 598759), near Ludlow, at 15.20 hrs. The pilot had taken off at 14.31 hrs for the first leg of the journey but, having failed to check the weather map beforehand, ran into bad weather en route. He attempted to skirt westwards around it but, having become totally lost, decided to descend below cloud in an endeavour to locate his position. However, finding himself surrounded by high ground, he tried to gain height to fly out of it and the aircraft was last witnessed flying up the hillside and disappearing into thick cloud at 800 feet. Moments later the port wing struck the ledge of a quarry, at 1,300 feet, causing the aircraft to cartwheel and disintegrate. Five of the occupants, including a British MTC driver who was travelling as a passenger, were killed instantly, while the radio operator, Cpl Bean, was seriously injured and died on his way to Ludlow Hospital.

1 Lt (pilot) George C Johnson Jr (O-800548), USAAF, aged 24, came from Westchester County, New York. According to the accident investigation he was a very experienced pilot and had completed thirty operational missions piloting B-17s. He is buried in Lakeview Cemetery, New Canaan, Connecticut.

S/Sgt (engineer) Francis O Hull (36505160), USAAF, aged 26, is believed to be the son of George W and Rity E Hull from Wayne County, Michigan. He is buried in Woodlawn National Cemetery, Elmira, New York.

Cpl (W/Op) John Elliot 'Billy' Bean (34331239), USAAF, aged 23, was born on 25 May 1921 in Yolande, Alabama. He is buried in Elmwood Cemetery, Birmingham, Alabama.

Maj (passenger) Kenneth Theodore Omley (O-415251), USAAF, aged 24, was the son of Norwegian-born Theodore Kristian Omley and Oline Andrea Omley of Hoboken, New Jersey. Born on 29 January 1920, he had studied at Union Hill High School and Rutgers College (the State University of New Jersey), where he graduated with a BSc in Agriculture. He is buried in Hackensack Cemetery, New Jersey.

Lt Col (passenger) Hartford Hardie Vereen (O-901433), USAAF, aged 35, was the son of Jeremiah Cookson Vereen and Agnes Vereen and the husband of Constance Mary Sebold of Miami, Florida. He joined the USAAF in March 1942 while at the University of Michigan Law School and was posted to the UK as a member of the Air Intelligence Service, 8th Air Force. He is buried in Florida.

Capt (passenger) Priscilla Corry Gotto, MTC, aged 27, was the daughter of Charles Corry Gotto and Ethel Millar Pinion of Malone, Belfast. Born in Belfast, in 1916, she was a 'lively, charming and amusing person', according to her sister-in-law. Her job in the MTC involved driving VIPs around Northern Ireland and included many visits to Langford Lodge airfield, where she became friendly with some of the American officers (hence her ability to get a lift to London to spend some of her leave). She is buried in Falls Cemetery, Belfast.

Capt Priscilla Gotto [Gwyneth Gotto]

26 November (Sunday)
'Into wind 500 feet release'. 23 HGCU (RAF Peplow, Shropshire)
Airspeed Horsa II (RN348) force-landed at Howle Manor, between Newport and Hinstock, at 04.10 hrs. The glider pilot landed in a field, ran through a hedge and struck a windmill, having had to release when one of the tug aircraft's engines failed.

F/O (1st pilot) Joseph Neilson Nicol (164984), RAFVR. Born on 9 January 1924, he had joined the RAFVR and was commissioned in April 1944, before being seconded to the Glider Pilot Regiment (as were a great number of RAF pilots, to compensate for the terrible losses suffered in Normandy and at Arnhem). On completing his training he participated in the Rhine crossings on 24 March 1945 and survived the war, eventually retiring from the RAFVR as a flight lieutenant in 1959. He died in Dudley in October 1996.

Sgt (2nd pilot) Neville Howard Thackray (1584212), RAFVR.

6 December (Wednesday)
Circuits and landings. 1665 HCU (RAF Tilstock, Shropshire)
Handley Page Halifax V (LL281) crashed on the edge of the airfield at 11.30 hrs. The trainee crew were taking off from the airfield when the port inner engine failed. Unable to gain height, the aircraft smashed into trees on the edge of the airfield and caught fire, killing two crew members instantly. The remainder of the crew were taken to the station sick quarters for treatment, including the wireless operator who suffered burns to the head. The pilot, who was seriously injured, was later transferred to RAF Hospital, Cosford but succumbed to his injuries at 02.00 hrs the following day.

F/O (pilot) Charles Peter Adams (147612), RAFVR, aged 22, was the son of S/Ldr Godfrey Adams and Mary Beatrice Adams (née Cable) of Radlett. He is buried in Bell Hill burial ground, Hertfordshire.

Sgt (F/Eng) Kenneth John Harmer (1897935), RAFVR, aged 19, was the son of William James and Annie Doreen Harmer of Reading. He is buried in Reading Cemetery.

F/O (AB) Harry Webster (154071), RAFVR, aged 30, was the son of George Henry and Edith Webster of Sheffield and the husband of Edith Webster of Ecclesall, Sheffield. He is buried in Sheffield (Shiregreen) Cemetery.

The names of the surviving crew are unknown.

7 December (Thursday)
F/O C P Adams died in RAF Hospital, Cosford, from injuries received in a crash the day before.

10 December (Sunday)

Transit flight from Broadwell to Belfast, Northern Ireland. 575 Squadron (RAF Broadwell, Oxfordshire) Avro Anson X (NK448) crashed at Banbury Covert, on Brown Clee Hill (at map reference 601844), near Ludlow, at 14.30 hrs. The pilot was flying twelve miles off track and, apparently, trying to map-read when the aircraft crashed into the hillside, which was obscured by bad weather. In a poignant letter, written soon after the accident to the pilot's family, Mr W E Pearce, the local farmer at Burwarton Farm, wrote:

> It was about 2.30 P.M. on Dec. 10, an awful snowy foggy day. The plane went up over my farm flying very low and we made sure he would not get over the hill as we up nearly 2,000 ft so we being in the H.G. [Home Guard] started up after them towards the hill. We heard it crash and when we arrived some 20 minutes afterwards the medical officer was just breathing his last poor chap. Flt Lt Potter and Flt Sgt Staple were both killed. There were 6 people there before me, but the medical officer never spoke. There was no fire at all. They crashed into a coppice on the hill, if they had have been up only 50 yards higher they would have cleared the hill at that point. I helped to carry Lt Potter down on the stretcher. We had to carry the three about 1/2 a mile down to the road to the ambulance [from RAF Bridgnorth].

He finished his letter with a touching postscript; 'it did not hurt the land at all. It matters not about the land neither the plane, but it is this life which we can never replace which matters most, the youth of our land.'

F/Lt Barney Potter [Felicity Potter]

F/Lt (pilot) Geoffrey Barnabas (Barney) Potter (81932), RAFVR, aged 27, was the son of Thomas Harry and Frances Maud Potter of Wembley Park, Middlesex. Born on 19 August 1917, Barney, as he was known to his family, worked in the land registry office between 1934 and 1939 and had joined the RAFVR in 1937. Following the outbreak of war he was called up and subsequently commissioned in July 1940, before being posted to Rhodesia as a pilot instructor. He returned to the UK in 1944 and was posted to 575 Squadron, flying Dakotas on supply running and casualty evacuation flights to and from north-west Europe. He is buried in Bath (Haycombe) Cemetery.

W/O (Nav, W/Op) James Cecil Staples (1681105), RAFVR, aged 22, was the son of James and Cecilia Pirrie Staples of Skellow, Yorkshire. He is buried in Adwick le Street Cemetery, Yorkshire.

F/Lt (RAF doctor, travelling as passenger) Archibald Norman Campbell (156465), MB, BCh, RAFVR, aged 26, was the son of Archibald and Anna B Campbell of Limavady, Northern Ireland and the husband of Margaret C Campbell. He had been commissioned in the medical branch in October 1943. He is buried in Drumachose Parish Churchyard, County Londonderry.

22 December (Friday)

Training flight. 23 HGCU (RAF Peplow, Shropshire)

Airspeed Horsa (unknown serial) force-landed at Great Bolas, to the south-west of the airfield. The tug pilot was 'forced to take evasive action in bad visibility' and the glider was released to land in a field.

The names of the crew are unknown.

28 December (Thursday)

Non-operational bombing exercise. 733rd Bombardment Squadron, 453rd Bombardment Group, 8th Air Force (Station 144, Old Buckenham, Norfolk)

Consolidated B-24J Liberator (42-51361, bearing the fuselage code F8-X) crashed on the banks of the

River Severn, at Shrawardine Farm, Shrawardine, at 14.00 hrs. At the time of the accident the crew had been stood down from operational flying for a long period due to bad weather over north-west Europe and, consequently, were scheduled for a routine training exercise. After taking off, the pilot climbed to 8,000 feet and was heading towards the bombing range when both starboard engines failed simultaneously due to an unknown cause. He immediately feathered both engines and began making for the nearest airfield (Montford Bridge) but, due to a thin layer of haze at 2,000 feet, he is thought to have lost sight of it and overshot his approach. Passing over the airfield, with wheels locked down and only two engines running, the aircraft's low airspeed caused it to stall and then strike the riverbank, disintegrating as it did so. Of the six crew members, three were killed instantly in the crash while the pilot and navigator succumbed to their injuries in Copthorne Military Hospital, Shrewsbury. Incredibly, the bombardier survived the crash and, later in life, wrote an account for his family:

> The last thing I remember until I regained consciousness on a stretcher on the ground was signaling thru the bomb bay that the wheels were down and locked, then jumping over the auxiliary engine to my landing position.

Tail section of Liberator 42-51361 on the banks of the River Severn. [USAAF]

2 Lt (pilot) Elmer Russell Mitchell Jr (O-827906), USAAF, aged 24, was the son of Elmer Russell Mitchell and Georgena Adelle Mitchell (née Noble) of Lena. Born in De Smet, South Dakota, he and his family moved to Lena when he was twelve years old, where he was educated at the local high school. He is buried in Lena Burial Park, Illinois.

2 Lt (co-pilot) James Guy Gilbert Jr (O-833518), USAAF, aged 20, was the son of James Guy and Bonnie Elizabeth Gilbert (née Morgan) of Albermarle County, Virginia. He is buried in Dexter Cemetery, Stoddard County, Missouri.

2 Lt (Nav) Paul W Peterson Jr (O-2064314), USAAF, aged 19, was the son of Paul W and Florence C Peterson of Minneapolis. He is buried in Fort Snelling National Cemetery, Minnesota.

T/Sgt (engineer) Gwilym Richards (33873187), USAAF, aged 26 (?), was the son of the late Thomas Evan Richards and Josephine Blodwyn Young of Harrisburg, Pennsylvania. He is buried in Cambridge (Madingley) Cemetery.

S/Sgt (radio operator) Roger F Batchelder (31366007), USAAF, aged 19, was the son of Harold Worth Batchelder and Reine G Batchelder of Reading, Massachusetts. He is buried in Laurel Hill Cemetery, Reading, Massachusetts.

F/O (bombardier) Walter Ernest Patscheider (T-128618), USAAF. Born in Lynn, Massachusetts, on 1 March 1925, he was the son of Arthur Carl and Nellie Mae Patscheider and had been educated at Cobbet Junior High and Lynn Classical High School. After recovering from his injuries he retrained as a radar

The crew and ground crew in front of their aircraft. Back row, L–R: 2 Lt Elmer Mitchell, 2 Lt James Gilbert, 2 Lt Paul Peterson, Flt Officer Walter Patscheider. Front row, left to right: William Hogan, T/Sgt Gwilym Richards, S/Sgt Roger Batchelder, Robert Self, Russell Nyquist, Tom Selser. [Deborah Harper]

operator and was assigned to the 732nd Bombardment Squadron, completing nine bombing missions over north-west Europe in a B-24 (44-49972). On 31 March 1945, during the crew's tenth mission, the top turret gunner accidentally shot out one of the engines en route to bomb Brunswick and the crew were forced to bale out over Den Helder, in Holland. The remainder of the war was spent in a POW camp before being liberated by the advancing armies and returning to the USA. He died in January 1994.

29 December (Friday)
2 Lt Paul W Peterson, USAAF, died in hospital in Shrewsbury from injuries received in a crash the previous day.

29 December (Friday)
Training flight. 81 OTU (RAF Sleap, Shropshire)
Airspeed Horsa (unknown serial) force-landed at Loppington House, to the north of the airfield. According to the pilot's account in Toby Neal's book, *Shropshire Airfields*, the tow rope came adrift at 500 feet and, with little time to react, he spotted a grass 'runway' between an avenue of trees and aimed for it:

> I came over a road or lane at about 50 feet with full flap and directly I touched down both the wings started to disintegrate, leaving pieces of plywood all over the place … me and my co-pilot and one of the RAF chaps with us walked to the house and this gentleman there said, 'What the hell's happened out there?'. There was an aircraft with no wings and no engines in front of his house. He was really surprised.

Staff Sgt (pilot) Richard Long (service number unknown), GPR.
The name of the co-pilot is unknown.
Eight unknown RAF passengers.

31 December (Sunday)
2 Lt E R Mitchell, USAAF, died in hospital in Shrewsbury from injuries received in a crash on 28 December.

31 December (Sunday)
Instrument flying. 5 (P)AFU (RAF Condover, Shropshire, satellite airfield to RAF Tern Hill)

North American Harvard IIB (KF260) crashed 'one mile west-south-west of Atcham village' (at wartime map reference 534090), at 14.45 hrs. The pupil pilot began a loop at approximately 1,000–1,300 feet but, as the aircraft came out at the bottom, it stalled, flicked over onto its back and crashed out of control.

F/O Bill Leahy [Bill Hall]

F/O (instructor pilot) Thomas William (Bill) Leahy (J.41874), RCAF, aged 26, was born in Brock Township, on 19 April 1918, the son of Leonard William and Florence Alberta Leahy. At the age of twelve he and his family moved to Port Perry, Ontario, where Bill attended Port Perry High School before working in the export department of General Motors in Oshawa. After enlisting in December 1942 he underwent pilot training in Canada before being posted to the UK in April 1944 and selected for instructor duties. He is buried in Chester (Blacon) Cemetery.

Sgt (pilot u/t) Keith Dickinson Howden (4216289), RNZAF, aged 21, was the son of George and Helen Howden (née Dickinson) of Riccarton, Christchurch, New Zealand. He is buried in Chester (Blacon) Cemetery.

The funeral of F/O Bill Leahy at Chester (Blacon) Cemetery on 5 January 1945. [Bill Hall]

1945

8 January (Monday)

Solo training flight. 5 (P)AFU (RAF Condover, Shropshire – satellite airfield to RAF Tern Hill)

Miles Master II (AZ727) belly-landed 'near to the entrance to Atcham airfield' at 11.05 hrs. The pilot was flying at 3,000 feet when the engine caught fire and, despite his managing to extinguish the flames, the revs dropped and he was unable to reach Atcham airfield to make an emergency landing.

F/Lt (pilot u/t) Stanley Mercer Robertson (126652), RAFVR. Born in Partick, Glasgow on 17 June 1917, he is believed to have been undertaking conversion to single-engine types at the time, as he already had a total of 870 flying hours to his name. He survived the war and died in Norwich in June 1991.

12 January (Friday)

Solo training flight. 5 (P)AFU (RAF Tern Hill, Shropshire)

Miles Master II (AZ597) force-landed at Sutton Grange Farm, near the airfield, at 13.25 hrs. Shortly after taking off the engine failed and the pilot was forced to belly-land in a field.

F/O (pilot u/t) David Mervyn Cowan (J.26626), RCAF. Born on 13 October 1921, he enlisted in Windsor, Ontario in April 1942 and after completing his training was posted to 1 Naval Air Gunner School as a staff pilot, in June 1943. He subsequently sailed to the UK in May 1944, but nothing further is known of his military service other than that he was repatriated to Canada in July 1945.

13 January (Saturday)
Night navigation training exercise. 60 OTU (RAF High Ercall)
Avro Anson I (NK890) crashed at Lyneal, three miles east-south-east of Ellesmere, at 00.55 hrs. Although 60 OTU was, primarily, a Mosquito-equipped training unit, a couple of Ansons were kept on strength so that navigation instruction could be given to multiple trainee navigators. It was one such aircraft, with a navigation instructor and four trainee aircrew on board, that crashed and burst into flames after the pilot is thought to have 'lost control at night'.

W/O (pilot instructor) John Alexander Campbell Russell (1368908), RAFVR, aged 25, was the son of John Campbell Russell and Mary Hay Russell of Edinburgh and the husband of Georgina Helen Russell, also of Edinburgh. Prior to joining 60 OTU as a pilot instructor on 8 October 1944, he had completed a tour of ops flying Baltimore bombers in the Mediterranean theatre with 55 Squadron. He is buried in Edinburgh (Rosebank) Cemetery.

F/O (navigator instructor) William Alfred Lovatt (182407), RAFVR, aged 23, was the son of Edwin Oliver and Elizabeth Minnie Lovatt and the husband of Doris May Lovatt (née Bentley) of Coseley. Before being posted to 60 OTU as a navigator instructor on 3 October 1944, he had served on Mosquitos with 140 Wing. He is buried in Coseley (Providence) Baptist chapel yard, Staffordshire.

F/O Donald Tinkess [Royal Bank of Canada Roll of Honour]

F/O (Nav, W/Op u/t) Stanley James Margrie (165657), RAFVR, aged 21, was the son of Arthur James Margrie and Alice Margrie of Hornchurch. He is buried in Hornchurch Cemetery, Essex.

F/O (Nav, W/Op u/t) John Kenneth Langston (165566), RAFVR, aged 22, was the son of John Keeble Langston and Mabel Gertrude Langston of Folkestone. Prior to joining up he had been a student at the University of London. He is buried in Hawkinge Cemetery, Kent.

F/O (Nav, W/Op u/t) Donald Guthrie Tinkess (J.45437), RCAF, aged 24, was the son of Samuel and Edna Tinkess of Ottawa. Prior to joining up he had worked for the Royal Bank of Canada's Hintonburgh branch from December 1937 until his enlistment in May 1941. He is buried in Chester (Blacon) Cemetery.

Sgt (Nav, W/Op u/t) Enoch Gwynfryn Williams (1582620), RAFVR, aged 25, was the son of Thomas and Mary Williams of Borth, Cardiganshire, and the husband of Joyce R Williams (née Leader) of Whitmore Reans. He is buried in Wolverhampton Borough Cemetery.

21 January (Sunday)
Training flight ('pair flying'). 41 OTU (RAF Hawarden, Flintshire, Wales)
Hawker Hurricane IIC (LF372) crashed at Hadley Farm, one mile west of Whitchurch, at 12.30 hrs. The pilot was flying through a snowstorm when he became separated from his flight leader and, consequently, turned onto a reciprocal course to fly out of the blizzard, while requesting a homing from RAF Hawarden. After beginning a gentle turn, at 2,000 feet, the aircraft entered a dive from which the pilot was unable to pull out. He therefore took to his parachute at 1,000 feet, suffering injuries as he did so. On landing, he was taken in by some local inhabitants before an ambulance from RAF Tilstock arrived and took him to RAF Hospital, Cosford, for treatment of a fractured arm, collarbone and back injuries.

F/Lt (pilot u/t) Eric Alan Sawyer (83728), RAFVR, was commissioned in August 1940 and is presumed to have served in another branch of the RAF before beginning pilot training in 1944. He survived the war, relinquished his commission on grounds of medical unfitness in November 1945 and eventually became a farmer.

22 January (Monday)
Night cross-country exercise. 6 (P)AFU (RAF Little Rissington, Gloucestershire)
Airspeed Oxford I (NM606) crash-landed at Brockton, in the Corve Dale, to the south west of Much Wenlock, at 00.15 hrs. After heavy icing began to form on the airframe while the aircraft was being flown through snowstorms, the pilot found that he could no longer maintain height, force-landed in a field and the wheels collapsed.

F/O (instructor pilot) John Thorburn Ballantyne (J.38905), RCAF. Born on 31 October 1923, he enlisted in October 1942 and had been chosen to remain in Canada for instructor duties after completing his training. He eventually sailed to the UK in March 1944, but it is unclear if he flew operationally before being posted to 6 (P)AFU as an instructor. He survived the war and returned to Canada in June 1945.

F/O (pilot u/t) Clifford Collier (162643), RAFVR. He remained in the RAF after the war and eventually relinquished his commission as a flight lieutenant in September 1958.

28 January (Sunday)
Cross-country exercise. 13 OTU (RAF Bicester, Oxfordshire)
De Havilland Mosquito NF.II (HJ645) belly-landed at 'Williams Farm, Hadnall', at 10.40 hrs. After taking off from Bicester the pilot changed from outer to inner fuel tanks. He informed his navigator, so that he could note it in the flight log, but was unaware that the navigator misunderstood his message and had turned the fuel cock back to outer (thinking he was switching to inner). When the aircraft reached Shrewsbury, both engines failed in quick succession due to lack of fuel. By the time the pilot realised the mistake, the aircraft had lost too much height and he was forced to belly-land it in a field, skidding through a hedge before coming to a rest.

F/O (pilot) George Stuart Reid (J.21940), RCAF. Born on 12 July 1920, he had enlisted in August 1941 and, after gaining his wings, was chosen to remain in Canada for instructor duties. He eventually sailed to the UK in October 1944 but nothing further is known of his military service other than that he returned to Canada in May 1945.

The navigator's name is unknown.

1 February (Thursday)
Test flight. 9 MU (RAF Cosford, Shropshire)
Supermarine Spitfire IX (PL136) belly-landed at Donington near Albrighton, at 16.30 hrs. While flying at 2,000 feet the pilot switched to the auxiliary fuel tank when his main fuel tank was running low but, unknown to him, the tank had not been refuelled by the ground crew. The engine therefore failed as the fuel ran out and he was forced to belly-land in a field, sustaining slight injuries.

F/Lt (test pilot) Frank McBean Paul (04159), RAFVR. Commissioned in October 1939, he eventually relinquished his commission as a flight lieutenant in February 1954.

2 February (Friday)
Formation flying exercise. 61 OTU (RAF Rednal, Shropshire)
Supermarine Spitfire VC (AB216, presentation aircraft named *Oyo Province*) crash-landed 'one and a half miles north-north-east of Sleap airfield' (putting it in the area between Commonwood and Horton, near Wem) at 12.45 hrs. The pilot was flying in 'finger four' formation at 2,000 feet when the engine began cutting out due to a glycol leak. In his account of the incident the pilot described how:

> ... as soon as the failure occurred I climbed until my airspeed dropped to 120 mph and reported to my Flight Commander, F/Lt Bignell, who told me to turn starboard and endeavour to reach Sleap aerodrome. This I did, but when at approximately 1,500 feet there was no power coming from my engine at all and to make the

> aerodrome seemed highly improbable so I abandoned the idea and concentrated on the most likely field around which was on my starboard and into which I successfully force-landed. At the time of passing over the field there was no response from my engine at all, and airscrew just turning and the smoke reduced to a negligible amount. I climbed out with my gear and walked away, first turning off the fuel and switches. The aircraft was burning fiercely but was little damaged prior to the fire.

F/Sgt (pilot u/t) Gordon Lindsay Richards (436276), RAAF. Born in Fairfield, New South Wales on 29 February 1924, he had served with the Australian army for six months before transferring to the Air Force in December 1942. Nothing further is known of his military service other than that he survived the war.

2 February (Friday)
Night training flight. 61 OTU (thought to have taken off from RAF Montford Bridge, Shropshire – Satellite to RAF Rednal)
Supermarine Spitfire VC (BM132, presentation aircraft named *Rootes Snipe*) crashed 'on the main Shrewsbury road' at 22.57 hrs. Immediately after taking off the pilot allowed the aircraft to turn to starboard, lose height and fly into the ground due to faulty instrument flying. He was seriously injured.
P/O (pilot u/t) Wiesław Rago (P2767), PAF. Born in Warsaw on 7 February 1915, he arrived in England in May 1943 to join the PAF, having previously served in the Middle East with the Polish Army.

6 February (Tuesday)
Wireless telephony training exercise. 4 Radio School (RAF Madley, Herefordshire)
Percival Proctor III (LZ595) crashed on Mynydd Myfyr near Trefonen, to the west of Oswestry, at 11.10 hrs. The pilot was briefed to carry out the exercise within a ten mile radius of the airfield but, after taking off at 09.30 hrs, he strayed much further afield and eventually became lost. Finding himself unable to use his W/T set to contact Madley (due to high ground between himself and base), the pilot decided to force-land but, as he approached a field, he stalled while trying to avoid a tree. A detailed account published on the Borders Historical Aviation Archaeology website adds that:

> As it approached its chosen field the Proctor pulled up sharply to avoid a big ash tree the pilot hadn't spotted until the last second because of the mist. They got over the tree but had lost too much airspeed. It stalled and dived into the ground into an area of rabbit warrens.
>
> One airman was thrown out by the impact the Pilot, Sgt. C H Gerner, RAAF, was trapped in the wreckage, both had been killed. Locals ran to try and help the crew but soon realized that there was nothing that could be done. The airman who was thrown out was W/OP U/T Sylvain Doucris [sic] a Fleet Air Arm airman. On the tunic of this airman was noted a French flash badge and just sticking out of his chest pocket was a small pair of child's knitted boots, which were respectfully tucked back into the pocket.

F/Sgt (pilot) Christian Henry Gerner (433206), RAAF, aged 20, was the son of Christian Henry and Isabelle Gerner of Singleton, New South Wales. He is buried in Blyth (Cowpen) Cemetery, Northumberland (near his uncle's house).
Matelot (W/Op u/t) Sylvain Isaac Boucris (1087), *Aéronavale* (French Fleet Air Arm), aged 19. Born on 28 February 1925, he had studied at the prestigious Lycée Carnot in Paris before escaping to England in 1942 and volunteering for the Free French forces.

13 February (Tuesday)
Ferry flight. 1 FPP (White Waltham, Berkshire)
Fairey Swordfish III (NS193) force-landed 'near Bridgnorth'. Little is known of the accident other than that the aircraft was slightly damaged in a forced landing.

First Officer (pilot) Victor Richard Baxter-Jones, ATA. Born in Wells, Somerset on 7 June 1918, he lived in Ilford, Essex. He survived the war and gained a civilian pilot's certificate in July 1945.

15 February (Thursday)
'Servicing training.' 21 (P)AFU (RAF Peplow, Shropshire – Satellite to RAF Wheaton Aston, Staffordshire)
Airspeed Oxford I (NM305) crashed at RAF Tern Hill's Stoke Heath site at 12.15 hrs. After the weather deteriorated badly, during the course of the flight, the pilot was diverted to Tern Hill airfield. However, as he approached through thick fog, he was suddenly confronted by a hangar looming ahead and, with the engines throttled back for landing, the aircraft stalled as he tried to avoid the building, and crashed.

F/Lt (pilot u/t) Leslie Albert Hudson (136835), RAFVR, aged 22, was the son of Captain Harry James Hudson and Yvonne Marie Hudson (née Alibert) of Marseilles, France. He is buried in Chester (Blacon) Cemetery.

17 February (Saturday)
Test flight. 9 MU (RAF Cosford, Shropshire)
Supermarine Spitfire VB (BL907, presentation aircraft named *Spirit of Natal*) crashed 'at Donington' (believed to have crashed into a barn at the Blue House, map reference 811051), near Albrighton, at 10.00 hrs. Very little is known of the accident other than that the aircraft crashed during a test flight, as no accident card survives. According to the current owners of Blue House Farm, a Spitfire clipped one of the barn roofs during the war and then smashed into the side of another barn on the opposite side of the courtyard, killing the pilot. As this is the only fatal Spitfire crash known to have occurred so close to Cosford, it is assumed that it must be this aircraft.

F/Lt (test pilot) Roy Harold Phillips (138663), RAFVR, aged 23, was the son of Harold Alexander and Marie Ethel Phillips of Virginia Water, Surrey and the husband of Marjorie Eileen Phillips. He is buried in Donington (St Cuthbert's) Churchyard, Shropshire.

F/Lt Roy Phillips
[Mark Phillips]

21 February (Wednesday)
Dive-bombing exercise. 61 OTU (RAF Rednal, Shropshire)
Supermarine Spitfire VB (BL763) crashed on Baggy Moor, to the east of the airfield. While levelling off for a practice dive-bombing attack on Baggy Moor bombing range, the pilot lost speed and allowed the aircraft to strike the ground, crashing in flames.

Cpl (pilot u/t) Zygmunt Kawczyński (P-703919), PAF, aged 23, was born in the city of Lódź in Poland on 9 February 1922. He had arrived in the UK on 30 May 1942 and volunteered for the PAF soon after. He is buried in Donington (St Cuthbert's) Churchyard, Shropshire.

10 March (Saturday)
Low-level practice attack on the airfield. 61 OTU (RAF Rednal, Shropshire)
North American Mustang III (FZ150) crashed at Station Farm, to the west of the airfield, at 09.30 hrs. A formation of four Mustangs was briefed to carry out a mock attack on the airfield, with special instruction not to descend lower than 200 feet. The pilot of this aircraft, however, was 'overconfident in his flying' and disobeyed the order by approaching 100 feet lower than the rest of the formation. According to a detailed account on the Borders Historical Aviation Archaeology website:

> The left wing tip of the aircraft struck a telegraph pole/breaking part of the wing away. The Mustang then

rolled to an almost inverted attitude before striking the ground and cart wheeling across three fields, the engine coming to rest almost three hundred yards from the first impact point. The body of Sergeant Zgainski was found on a hedge in the same field.

Just after the crash, another of the Mustangs flew slowly and low over the scene before returning to Rednal. The station's fire tender arrived, only to become bogged down in the first field. After being dragged out, it was driven around the edge of the fields to reach the crash site, by which time, the fire was nearly out.

Sgt (pilot u/t) Boleslaw Zgainski, PAF, aged 27, was born in Splawie, near Kościan in Poland on 15 April 1917. He is buried in Arnold Cemetery, Nottingham.

17 March (Saturday)
Training flight. IXth Troop Carrier Command, USAAF (unknown airfield)
Almost certainly a Waco CG-4 Haig glider force-landed 'three miles north west of Tilstock' (putting it in the area between Whitchurch and Alkington). The glider was being towed over Shropshire when it broke loose from its C-47 Dakota tug aircraft and the pilot force-landed in a field.

The name of the pilot is unknown.

18 March (Sunday)
Training flight. 61 OTU (RAF Rednal, Shropshire)
Supermarine Spitfire VC (EE601) belly-landed on Baggy Moor range, near the airfield, at 14.48 hrs. While flying at 1,500 feet the engine failed, due to an internal glycol leak, and the pilot was forced to belly-land in a field.

F/Sgt (pilot u/t) Michael Edward G Dalton (1319396), RAFVR. He survived the war and died in Petersfield, Hampshire in 1995.

26 March (Monday)
Training flight. 61 OTU (RAF Rednal, Shropshire)
North American Mustang III (SR407) force-landed at 'Davis Farm, Haughton, 2 1/2 miles south of Rednal' (although the location is uncertain as Haughton is on the edge of the airfield), at 10.21 hrs. The pilot was returning to the airfield, after his engine had begun cutting intermittently at 2,000 feet, when it failed altogether and he was forced to belly-land in a rough field.

P/O (pilot u/t) Jerzy Tyczyński (P2952), PAF. On completion of his training he was posted to 316 (Polish) Squadron and flew Mustangs operationally during the closing stages of the war.

28 March (Wednesday)
Formation flying exercise. 61 OTU (RAF Rednal, Shropshire)
North American Mustang III (FB190) crash-landed just off the south-east boundary of the airfield at 12.26 hrs. Whilst taking off from the airfield the pilot attempted to lift off with insufficient flying speed, causing the aircraft to swing and crash onto railway lines.

Sgt (pilot u/t) Zbigniew Tadeusz Zablocki (704967), PAF. Born in Poland on 30 October 1924, he had wrecked another of the unit's Mustangs just four days earlier when he swung while overshooting and crashed into a building. Because of these two accidents he was suspended from pilot training.

30 March (Friday)
Solo training flight. 61 OTU (RAF Rednal, Shropshire)
Miles Master II (AZ549) force-landed at Horton Hall, to the west of Wem, at 12.45 hrs. The pilot was flying at 7,000 feet when the engine failed and, despite his efforts to reach RAF Sleap, he was unsuccessful and belly-landed in a field.

P/O (pilot u/t) Tadeusz Linttner (P2943), PAF. On completion of his training he was posted to 302 (Polish) Squadron in August 1945 and flew Spitfires as part of the occupying forces in Germany.

30 March (Friday)
Training flight. 61 OTU (RAF Rednal, Shropshire)
North American Mustang III (SR424) crashed at Wolfshead, to the north west of Nesscliffe, at 14.13 hrs. The pilot had only been in the air for four minutes when he called up over his R/T to say that he had a glycol leak and that a fire had broken out in the cockpit. Unable to bring the flames under control, he took to his parachute, breaking both his legs in the process (either on landing or from striking part of the aircraft) and was taken to hospital in Oswestry, where he succumbed to his injuries three days later.

F/Sgt (pilot u/t) Kenneth Thomas Gill (1333747), RAFVR, aged 22, is believed to be the husband of Barbara F Gill (née Hunt) of Maldon. He is buried in Maldon Cemetery, Essex.

2 April (Monday)
F/Sgt K T Gill died of injuries received in a plane crash three days earlier.

28 April (Saturday)
Practice flight with long-range fuel tanks fitted. 61 OTU (RAF Montford Bridge, Shropshire – Satellite to RAF Rednal)
North American Mustang III (FX977) crashed just south of Montford Bridge airfield at 14.25 hrs. The pilot was making his final turn to line up for a landing when he is believed to have stalled and crashed, possibly due to the extra fitted fuel tanks (which he may not have taken into account for).

P/O (pilot u/t) Jerzy Antoni Fijałkowski (P2402), PAF, aged 27, was born in Ostrów Mazowiecka, to the north-east of Warsaw, on 19 December 1917. Entering the Polish flying school at Deblin in 1937, he had qualified as a pilot by the outbreak of war and managed to escape to England, via France, in the summer of 1940. After undergoing training in the UK in 1941, nothing further is known of his military service and it is unclear why he was undergoing training at Montford Bridge (perhaps converting to single-engine aircraft?). He is buried in Donington (St Cuthbert's) Churchyard, Shropshire.

8 May (Victory in Europe Day)

12 May (Saturday)
Cross-country exercise. 43 OTU (RAF Andover, Hampshire)
De Havilland Tiger Moth II (N6784) crash-landed 'near Condover' (although the wartime map reference 587031 converts to a point near Cressage) at 17.20 hrs. After getting lost during the flight the pilot decided to make a precautionary landing but, as he touched down, he hit a bump and quickly decided to overshoot and make a second attempt. He pulled up sharply to clear a hedge, however, and allowed the aircraft to stall, crashing into the next field and overturning. Fortunately neither occupant was hurt.

F/Lt (pilot) Frederick Henry Wellwood Moncreiff (108236), RAFVR. Born on 13 February 1909, he relinquished his commission on grounds of ill health in December 1945.

Capt (pilot, but travelling as passenger) Charles Elphinstone Wood (40249), Royal Artillery (AOP pilot). Born in Wolstanton, Staffordshire on 27 June 1909, he had received his commission in the army in 1928, but nothing further is known of his military service other than that he was a qualified AOP pilot. He died in Stafford in June 1986.

15 May (Tuesday)
Training flight. 61 OTU (RAF Rednal, Shropshire)

Supermarine Spitfire VB (AB249) belly-landed at Tedsmore, to the south of the airfield, at 13.17 hrs. The pilot was taking off from Rednal when he forgot to alter the propeller from coarse to fine pitch and the aircraft failed to gain height. He was therefore forced to pull it up sharply to avoid a railway embankment, before belly-landing in a field further on. As a result of the accident the pilot, who was slightly injured, had his logbook endorsed for 'gross carelessness'.

Sgt (pilot u/t) Thomas Dinning Spence (5955), RNoAF. He is believed to have left the Air Force after the accident and returned to Norway.

18 May (Friday)
Training flight. 81 OTU (RAF Sleap, Shropshire)
Vickers Wellington X (NC921) crashed near the airfield at 16.37 hrs. After realising that he was approaching the wrong runway, the pilot increased the throttles to go around for another attempt at landing but, as he did so, the port engine failed to respond, causing the aircraft to yaw to port, stall and dive into the ground. Three members of the crew were killed instantly while the rear gunner survived, despite suffering second-degree burns to his hands and face, lacerations to his right leg and shock.

Sgt Robert Taylor [Larry Taylor]

F/O (pilot) Alfred Edward Davis (175038), RAFVR, aged 36, was the son of Alfred William and Mary Davis and the husband of Mabel Joan Davis (née Firrell) of Beckenham, Kent. He is buried in Whitchurch Cemetery, Shropshire.

Sgt (AB) Robert Henry Taylor (1319303), RAFVR, aged 24, was the son of Ernest and Lilian Sarah Ann Taylor (née Long) of Bristol. He is buried in Bristol (Greenbank) Cemetery.

Sgt (W/Op) Joseph Ashbridge Bell (2209924), RAFVR, aged 20, was the son of Joseph Ashbridge Bell and Georgina Bell of Lowca, Cumbria. He is buried in Morseby (St Bridget) Churchyard, Cumberland.

F/O (AG rear) H Rhodes (service number unknown), RAFVR.

30 May (Wednesday)
Practice height climb to 25,000 feet. 61 OTU (RAF Rednal, Shropshire)
North American Mustang III (FX942) crashed in an area concentrated around Mile Bank Farm, one mile north-east of Whitchurch, at 09.57 hrs. The pilot was briefed to take off at 09.30 hrs and climb to 25,000 feet (reporting his progress at 5,000 feet stages) and then 'throw the aircraft about' for approximately fifteen minutes before descending to land. After he had taken off, however, no progress reports were received from the pilot until 09.45 hrs (despite numerous requests), when he finally replied that he was at 25,000 feet and was aware of his location. Ten minutes later the aircraft was seen by an experienced member of the Royal Observer Corps flying northwards at approximately 20,000 feet, when all of a sudden it entered a screaming high-speed vertical dive and began to disintegrate before striking the ground. This loss of control was presumed to have been caused by the pilot's passing out due to a leak in his oxygen supply.

F/O (pilot u/t) James Jamison (166749), RAFVR, aged 27, was the son of Robert and Janetta Jamison of Rasharkin and was a graduate of Queen's University, Belfast. He is buried in Rasharkin (St Andrew) Churchyard, County Antrim.

7 June (Thursday)
Cross-country exercise. 81 OTU (RAF Sleap, Shropshire)

Vickers Wellington X (LP901) crashed at Webscott, near Harmer Hill, at 02.22 hrs. The trainee crew were approaching to land after a three hour cross-country flight, when the pilot saw another aircraft on the runway and began carrying out an overshoot procedure. As the aircraft passed over the boundary at 1,000 feet, however, the pilot displayed an 'error of judgement' by allowing the aircraft to lose height and strike an oak tree, before demolishing a power line post and disintegrating as it struck the ground. Of the five crew, three were killed in the crash, the wireless operator was admitted to RAF Hospital, Cosford, suffering burns to his hands and face, while the rear gunner was only slightly injured. In the subsequent investigation the rear gunner described how, shortly before the crash, he heard the pilot exclaim 'Dammit!' and, moments later, the aircraft crashed and he was thrown from his turret.

Sgt (pilot) James Robert Howard (1624902), RAFVR, aged 30, was the son of John Thomas and Ada Howard and the husband of Kathleen Howard (née Pease) of Askern. He is buried in Askern Cemetery, Yorkshire.

Sgt (Nav) John Robert Pickover (702329), RAFVR, aged 26, was the son of Fred and Blanche Pickover of Earby. He is buried in Earby (Wheatlands) Cemetery, Yorkshire.

Sgt (AB) William Robert Symonds (1629992), RAFVR, aged 20, was the son of Percy and Doris Mary Symonds of Drayton, Norfolk. He is buried in Little Plumstead (SS Gervasius and Protasius) Churchyard, Norfolk.

P/O (W/Op) Alexander Blewes Robertson (188123), RAFVR.

Sgt (AG rear) W Stirling (service number unknown), RAFVR.

3 July (Tuesday)

Aerobatics practice. 5 (P)AFU (RAF Tern Hill, Shropshire)

North American Harvard IIB (KF325) force-landed at New Lodge Farm (at map reference 733128), between Lilleshall and Sheriffhales, at 10.05 hrs. While completing a roll at 5,000 feet the pilot tried to open up the throttles, but the engine failed to respond because of a fractured hydraulic pipe. Moments later the engine burst into flames as the hydraulic fluid ignited and the pilot belly-landed the aircraft in a field, before extinguishing the flames.

Sub Lt Derek Sadd [Ginny Waters]

Sub Lt (A) Derek Ian Sadd (180366), RNVR. Born in Leicestershire on 20 December 1924, he had enlisted in the RAFVR in 1943 and gained his wings in the USA before returning to the UK and transferring to the Royal Navy in May 1945. He left the Navy at the end of the war but, after an unsuccessful foray into business, re-enlisted in February 1953 and subsequently flew helicopters in Aden, Cyprus and the Far East. He finally left the service for the second time in February 1959 and worked for a shipping company in London. He died in Braintree, Essex in October 1995.

11 July (Wednesday)

Cross-country exercise. 10 OTU (RAF Stanton Harcourt, Oxfordshire)

Vickers Wellington X (NC714) crashed at Walton Grange (at map reference 629985), Much Wenlock, at 01.15 hrs. The trainee crew were on a routine exercise when the pilot is believed to have lost control in cloud due to 'faulty instrument flying' and crashed, killing the entire crew. According to the *Shrewsbury Chronicle*, men from the Much Wenlock National Fire Service (NFS) were soon on the scene 'in commendable smartness' and managed to put the fires out by 04.15 hrs with the help of Ironbridge NFS.

W/O (pilot) Richard Muir Morrison (1395952), RAFVR, aged 24, was the son of William and Helen

Morrison and the husband of Ghislaine Doreen Morrison (née Griffiths) of Gloucester. He is buried in Bognor Regis Cemetery, Sussex.

F/Sgt (Nav) Norman Drayton Rendle (1587030), RAFVR, aged 22, was the son of Stanley and Ivy Drayton Rendle of Bristol. He is buried in Chester (Blacon) Cemetery.

Sgt (AB) Norman Hooley (1589206), RAFVR, aged 20, was the son of Herbert and Maud Hooley and the husband of Doris Hooley of Barnton. He is buried in Barnton Cemetery, Cheshire.

Sgt (W/AG) Stanley Williams (1499900), RAFVR, aged 24, was the son of Mr and Mrs M Williams of Tonyrefail. He is buried in Llantrisant (Trane) Cemetery, Glamorganshire.

Sgt (AG) Alfred John Franklin (1851045), RAFVR, aged 22, was the son of Alfred John and Mary Rose Franklin of Cowley, Oxford. He is buried in Chester (Blacon) Cemetery.

31 July (Tuesday)

Cross-country exercise from Base–Prestatyn–a sea position near the Isle of Man–Nuneaton–Stratford–Base. 81 OTU (RAF Tilstock, Shropshire)

Vickers Wellington X (NA962, bearing the fuselage code EZ-H) crashed at Ivy Farm (at map reference 573329), Prees Lower Heath, at 23.13 hrs. The trainee crew were briefed to take off with three other aircraft for a cross-country flight, during the course of which gun firing practice was to be carried out over the Irish Sea (using a drogue target trailed behind the aircraft). On completion of the exercise the crew returned to the vicinity of the airfield at 6,000 feet, where the pilot requested permission to join the circuit. Flying Control replied and instructed him not to descend below 4,000 feet as another Wellington was preparing to land but, shortly afterwards, the aircraft was witnessed to dive steeply out of cloud and crash. The crash was subsequently attributed to the pilot's allowing the aircraft to stall while reducing height through cloud, due to his 'comparative inexperience'.

Sgt Jack Tallentire
[Vic Tyler-Jones]

F/Sgt (pilot) Thomas Alfred Holmes (1802278), RAFVR, aged 29, was the son of Thomas William and Charlotte Holmes and the husband of Lily Ethel Holmes (née Robinson) of Feltham, Middlesex. He is commemorated at Woking (St John's) Crematorium.

Sgt (Nav) John Maurice Tallentire (2213870), RAFVR, aged 29, was the son of John and Mildred Tallentire of Gateshead, County Durham. He is commemorated at Newcastle-upon-Tyne (West Road) Crematorium.

W/O (AB) William James Evans (1313499), RAFVR, aged 29, was the son of William John Draper Evans and Ellen May Evans of Bagshot and the husband of Clarissa Evans, also of Bagshot. He had previously completed a tour of ops with 570 Squadron between August 1944 and spring 1945 (which had involved numerous Special Operations Executive supply drops and towing gliders for the Arnhem landings) so it is unclear exactly why he was back at a training unit. He is buried in Windlesham (Lightwater) burial ground, Surrey.

W/O William Evans
[John Evans]

Sgt (W/Op) Stanley Rickards (1800002), RAFVR, aged 23, is buried in Enfield Highway (St James) Churchyard, Middlesex. His next of kin are unknown.

Sgt (AG) George Edward Anthony Hulbert (1866695), RAFVR, aged 20, was the son of William H and Rose Hulbert of Upper Norwood, Surrey. He is buried in Beckenham Cemetery, Kent.

15 August – Victory over Japan day

25 September (Tuesday)
Dual instruction training flight. 5 (P)AFU (RAF Atcham, Shropshire – Relief Landing Ground to RAF Tern Hill)
North American Harvard IIB (FX386) crashed adjacent to Atcham airfield at 15.50 hrs. The instructor was approaching the airfield, to demonstrate a precautionary landing to his pupil, when he turned into the wind at a very low altitude, struck a forty foot tree and crashed, injuring both himself and his pupil. Despite his failure to see the tree, no disciplinary action was taken against the instructor in view of his 'excellent record' (he had previously completed 2,100 hours of flying without incident).

W/O (instructor pilot) Herbert James Studley (1246514), RAFVR. He died in Dorset in 1994.

F/O (pilot u/t) John Jeffrey Dennis Forrester (1246514), RAFVR. Commissioned in June 1944, he was himself an experienced pilot with 1103 flying hours to his credit, so it is probable that he was retraining on single-engine types at the time of the accident. He resigned his commission as a flight lieutenant in January 1947.

17 December (Monday)
Triangular training flight from Base–Condover–Shawbury–Base. 21 (P)AFU (RAF Wheaton Aston, Staffordshire)
Airspeed Oxford I (LX530) crashed at Wrekin Farm near Little Wenlock (at map reference 633073), at about 18.30 hrs. The aircraft had been in the air for nineteen minutes when it was witnessed descending in a shallow dive to 100 feet, before diving vertically into the ground. It was thought that 'some part of the airframe failed' and caused the accident but, due to the state of the wreckage, it was impossible to draw any firm conclusions.

F/O Billie Cull [Penny Handley]

W/O (instructor pilot) Victor Thomas William Servis (1607118), RAFVR, aged 22, was the son of Marshall Henry and Charlotte Servis and the husband of Dorothy Hilda Rose Servis (née Gams) of Seven Kings, Ilford. He is buried in Woodrange Park Cemetery, East Ham.

F/O (pilot u/t) Billie Richard Gordon Cull (55506), RAFVR, aged 25, was the son of Thomas and Violet Cull. Born on 28 November 1920, he had joined the RAF in the summer of 1939 and served as a ground crew airman for most of the war (including time with 231 Squadron in Northern Ireland in 1941), before being accepted for pilot training. He is buried in Chester (Blacon) Cemetery.

W/O Victor Servis [Paul Sanders)

20 December (Thursday)
Cross-country exercise. 1380 (Transport) Conversion Unit (RAF Tilstock, Shropshire)
Vickers Wellington X (LP912, bearing the fuselage code EZ-A) crashed at Ashfield Farm, Ash Magna, to the north-east of the airfield, at 22.15 hrs. The pilot was carrying out an overshoot of runway 15 when he raised his flaps too soon as he passed the boundary, causing the aircraft to sink back to the ground and crash through some electricity cables, plunging the airfield into darkness. The navigator was killed in the crash while the pilot was conveyed to the Royal Salop Infirmary by one ambulance and the remainder of the crew were sent to RAF Hospital, Cosford, to be treated for multiple injuries.

F/O (pilot) Ieuan Morus Jones (184016), DFC, RAFVR. His DFC had been awarded in December 1944 following a tour of ops flying Wellington bombers in the Mediterranean theatre with 150 Squadron. After recovering from his injuries he continued to serve in the RAF until December 1947, when he relinquished his commission.

F/O Bob Struthers
[Fiona Budd]

F/O (Nav) Robert (Bob) Struthers (163161), RAFVR, aged 22, was the son of Alexander and Mary McKenzie Struthers of Crosshill, Glasgow. He is buried in Glasgow (Eastwood) Cemetery.

F/O (AB) John Stanway Bower (193219), RAFVR. Born on 4 June 1921, he became a solicitor after leaving the military and worked in the West Midlands. He died in October 2000 in Lichfield.

W/O (W/Op) Walker (1068223), RAFVR.

1946

10 January (Thursday)
Solo training flight. 5 (P)AFU (RAF Tern Hill, Shropshire)
North American Harvard IIB (FX258) belly-landed 'near Whitchurch' (at military map reference 555428, near Blakemere) at 10.50 hrs. The pupil pilot had been in the air for fifty-five minutes when his engine failed, after he neglected to switch over to his reserve fuel tanks, forcing him to belly-land in a field.

Sub Lt (A) (pilot u/t) Peter Moulton, RNVR. He had transferred from the RAFVR to the RNVR in August 1945, but appears to have returned to the RAFVR training branch in August 1954. He eventually resigned his commission as a squadron leader in August 1968.

21 February (Thursday)
Air test. Empire Air Navigation School (RAF Shawbury, Shropshire)
Handley Page Halifax III (NA952) crashed 'one mile from the airfield' at 15.23 hrs. After overshooting on a three-engine landing, the pilot was unable to gain sufficient height to go around again and, as he attempted a belly-landing in a field ahead, the aircraft clipped some trees and crashed. The pilot, who was not strapped in, was thrown out of the aircraft and suffered lacerations to the scalp, cheek and left foot, while the flight engineer, who was standing at his side, was also thrown out but, amazingly, only suffered lacerations to his fingers. The remainder of the crew had braced themselves in the centre of the aircraft and, fortunately, all escaped with minor injuries.

F/Lt (staff pilot) Henry Selvin Schwass (428822), DFC, RNZAF. Born in Redwoods Valley, Nelson, New Zealand, he had been awarded his DFC in January 1945 following a tour of ops with 166 Squadron. He returned to New Zealand after leaving the Air Force and died in Glen Eden, Auckland in January 1981.

F/Sgt (F/Eng) Clay, RAFVR.
W/O (W/AG) Hurst, RAFVR.
W/O (W/AG) Thurland, RAFVR.
LAC (Fitter IIA) Scott, RAFVR.

19 March (Tuesday)
Ferry flight from RAF Hamble, Hampshire, to RAF High Ercall. 29 MU (RAF High Ercall, Shropshire)
Supermarine Spitfire XIV (NH695) crashed at Postensplain (at map reference 750791), near Buttonoak, in the Wyre Forest, at 13.40 hrs. The aircraft, which was being piloted by a female ATA pilot, was witnessed performing minor aerobatics in the vicinity of Bewdley at a height of 3,000–4,000 feet. After completing a slow roll it was seen to enter a 45-degree dive, from which the pilot failed to recover, before striking trees on a hilltop, crossing a small valley and crashing on the hillside opposite. The accident was subsequently attributed to the pilot's failing to pull up in time, although mechanical failure could not be ruled out altogether.

First Officer (pilot) Rosamund King Everard-Steenkamp, ATA, aged 32, was the daughter of Charles Joseph and Bertha Everard of Moedig in Transvaal, South Africa and the wife of the late Lt H N F Steenkamp, who had lost his life serving with the SAAF in December 1942. Born in Bonnefoi, in Transvaal, she had learned to fly (along with her brother) in the 1930s and regularly toured Europe in her own aircraft. During the war she had served as an instructor in South Africa as well as being employed on a shuttle service between South Africa and Cairo. In 1944 she volunteered for the ATA and proceeded to the UK, where she flew all types of aircraft and clocked up over 3,500 flying hours. She also held the distinction of being the first female pilot to fly a jet aircraft when she took Vampire TO300 on a test flight on 22 February 1946, commenting afterwards that it was 'wizard to fly and roll.' She is buried in Maidenhead Cemetery.

First Officer Rosamund Everard-Steenkamp [South African Military History Society]

16 June (Sunday)
Ferry flight. Royal Aircraft Establishment (RAF Farnborough, Hampshire)
Avro Anson I (NK728) force-landed 'near Shrewsbury' at 17.00 hrs. After encountering bad weather en route to an unknown airfield, the pilot decided to continue his flight, rather than return to base, until conditions became so bad that he was forced to land in a field.

W/Cdr (pilot) George Bruce Milligan Rhind (18226), RAF. Born in Portsmouth, in 1904, he had joined the RAF in 1924 and on completion of his training was posted to 111 Squadron in February 1925, flying Siskin fighters. He remained with the squadron until 1927, when he attended Cambridge University, before returning to the RAF in 1931 and starting a posting as an engineering officer at the Aircraft Depot in Iraq. Posted to 54 Squadron as a flight commander in January 1934, then to 3 Squadron the following year, he was subsequently posted as Equipment Staff Officer to HQ, Coastal Command, in November 1936. Little is known of his career during the war other than that he was posted to AHQ Iraq and Persia in April 1943 and remained in the RAF until April 1957, retiring as an air commodore. He died in 1962.

The names of the two other occupants are unknown.

27 June (Thursday)
Solo navigation flight. 780 Squadron, HMS *Godwit* (RNAS Peplow, Shropshire)
Fairey Firefly I (MB463) crashed adjacent to Peplow airfield at 10.43 hrs. The pilot was taking off from the airfield when his aircraft was seen suddenly to climb vertically to 100 feet, turn onto its back and dive into the ground just off the edge of the runway. Following a thorough examination of the wreckage, it was discovered that the navigation computer, which was usually strapped to the pilot's leg, was loose in the cockpit. It was concluded that it had fallen to the cockpit floor and then become jammed under the elevator control, causing the aircraft to climb uncontrollably. Had the pilot secured the instrument properly then the accident would have been avoided.

Lt (pilot u/t) Albert Edward Payne, RN, aged 28, was the son of Albert Edward and Ellen Payne of Southall. He is buried in Havelock Cemetery, Middlesex. His brother, Sgt George William Payne, had lost his life serving with the RAF on 12 August 1943.

1 August (Thursday)
Cross-country flight from Shawbury to Debden, Essex. Empire Air Navigation School (RAF Shawbury, Shropshire)
Avro Anson I (NK503) crashed at Abbey Farm in Hawkstone Park, between Prees Green and Marchamley, at 15.23 hrs. After taking off at 15.12 hrs, the experienced pilot began unauthorised low

flying in the vicinity of the airfield, during the course of which he entered a valley at 300 feet, stalled while banking to port and crashed out of control into trees. The accident was witnessed by a large number of golfers on the local course, including an RAF officer who stated that his 'attention was drawn to an aircraft of the Anson type flying about 300 feet above the level of the hill. The plane was normal but travelling too low for that type and too fast, yet it did not appear to be in any difficulty.'

F/Lt (pilot) Patrick John (Pat) Boothman (139973), DFC, RAF, aged 22, was the only son of the famous Schneider Trophy winner, Air Vice-Marshal John Boothman, CB, DFC, AFC, CdeG and his wife Gertrude, and the husband of Pamela Ann Boothman of George, Cape Province, South Africa. His DFC had been awarded in the New Year of 1945, following a tour of ops with 178 Squadron, and he held the distinction of being the only person to be awarded the DFC at the same investiture as his father. He is buried in Chester (Blacon) Cemetery.

F/O (Nav) William Broughton Gingell (56168), DFC, DFM, RAF, aged 27, was the son of William Henry and Christine Frances Gingell of Wadhurst, Sussex. His DFM was gazetted in September 1940 for a particular action on 10 August 1940, when his Blenheim (N3574) of 101 Squadron crashed into the sea off Lowestoft. The citation read:

> In August 1940, Pilot Officer Bicknell was the pilot and Sergeant Gingell the observer, of an aircraft detailed to carry out a night attack on Antwerp Aerodrome. As the aircraft reached the Dutch coast the port engine failed, and Pilot Officer Bicknell therefore decided to abandon his original target and bomb Haamsted aerodrome; this was located by Sergeant Gingell and successfully attacked from 5,000 feet. On the return journey, just before reaching the coast, the aircraft commenced to lose height, and in spite of the efforts of the crew it became necessary to make a forced landing in a rough sea close to a trawler. The pilot and observer forced their way out of the aircraft and made repeated but unsuccessful attempts to extricate the unconscious air gunner before the aircraft sank. Some thirty minutes later, the pilot, who was suffering from head injuries, and the unconscious observer were picked up by the trawler. Pilot Officer Bicknell displayed great determination in pressing home an alternative attack, after one of his engines had failed, and both he and Sergeant Gingell showed great courage in endeavouring to free the unconscious air gunner.

His DFC was gazetted in July 1943 following a tour of ops flying Baltimore bombers in the Mediterranean theatre with 223 Squadron. He is buried in Chester (Blacon) Cemetery.

F/O (Nav, but acting as W/Op on the flight) George Morrell (Bob) Harrison (200737), RAFVR, aged 28, was the son of Arthur and Eva Harrison and the husband of Georgina Kathleen Harrison of Earlsdon, Coventry. He is buried in Coventry (London Road) Cemetery.

F/Sgt (passenger) Charles Henry John Wheeler (1814074), RAFVR, aged 22, was the son of Harry Herbert and Agnes Amelia Wheeler of 176 Dawling Road, Hammersmith, London. He is buried in Chester (Blacon) Cemetery.

11 August (Sunday)
Navigation and 'Gee' training exercise. 540 Squadron (RAF Benson, Oxfordshire)
De Havilland Mosquito P.R.XXXIV (RG241) belly-landed at Bomere Heath (at either military map

F/Lt Pat Boothman (right), pictured at Buckingham Palace when both he and his father, John (left), received the DFC. [Martin Boothman]

reference 482190 or 478220) at 11.53 hrs. After landing at RAF Shawbury, where it is believed that S/Ldr Sutton was picked up, the pilot took off for the next leg of the journey to Blackbushe in Surrey. Moments after leaving the airfield, however, the starboard engine failed at 400 feet, due to a petrol pipeline fault. The pilot was forced to belly-land the aircraft in a field ahead and S/Ldr Sutton was injured in the landing. RAF Shawbury quickly dispatched their ambulance and the injured officer was taken to Oswestry Orthopaedic Hospital, where he was diagnosed as suffering from three fractured thoracic vertebrae, while the two crew members were taken back to Shawbury.

F/Lt (pilot) Ian Robert Campbell (33557), RAF. Born on 5 October 1920, he was educated at Eton and was living at Thistleton Grange, Oakham, in Rutland, when he enlisted. Posted to 203 Squadron on completion of his pilot training, he was shot down in a Blenheim (V5861) on 23 January 1942, during an operation to shadow the Italian battle fleet and spent the remainder of the war as a POW. Following his repatriation to the UK, he remained in the RAF and was awarded the AFC in the New Year's Honours list of 1948 and invested with a CBE in 1968. Promoted to Air Vice-Marshal in 1970, he worked for the Ministry of Defence and Chief of Staff until 1975 and was invested as CB the following year.

F/Lt (Nav) Frederick Edward Thayer (151186), RAF. Born in Romford, Essex in 1921, he had served in the RAFVR during the war. Following the accident he transferred to the Aircraft Control Branch in September 1952 and was invested with the MBE in June 1971, before retiring as a squadron leader three years later.

S/Ldr (pilot, but travelling as passenger) Denys Herschel Sutton (41492), RAF. Born on 3 December 1920, he had joined the RAF before the war and flew operationally with 226, 35, 98 and 53 Squadron on Liberators. According to his son, his tours passed largely without major incident, although he flew as co-pilot to the squadron commander of 53 Squadron on one occasion when they, unfortunately, attacked a neutral Spanish submarine. He remained in the RAF after the war and was mentioned in despatches in January 1945 for what his son believes was his role as a planner. He was subsequently invested with a CBE in the New Year's Honours list of 1971 and promoted to air commodore in July 1971. He died in Bath in January 2004.

1947

17 April (Thursday)
Cross-country flight. HQ, FTS Communication Flight, 25 Group (RAF Tern Hill, Shropshire)
North American Harvard IIB (KF653) belly-landed near Lacon Hall, one and a half miles north-east of Wem, at 12.05 hrs. While flying at low altitude the engine suddenly cut, due to a lack of fuel, and the pilot was forced to belly-land the aircraft in a field. In the subsequent investigation it was revealed that the pilot 'did not have sufficient knowledge of petrol cocks and system' and mishandled the petrol cocks, for which he was reprimanded.

F/O (pilot) Stanley Richards (202571), RAF. He retired from the RAF as a flight lieutenant in June 1961.

16 May (Friday)
Ferry flight from RAF Chivenor to 12 MU, RAF Kirkbride, Cumbria. 691 Squadron (RAF Chivenor, Devon)
Vultee Vengeance TT.IV (HB468) belly-landed 'nine miles south of Shrewsbury' (putting it roughly in the area of Leebotwood). The pilot was travelling northwards over south Shropshire when the engine failed and he was forced to belly-land the aircraft in a field.

F/Lt (pilot) Harris (service number unknown), RAF.

18 December (Thursday)
Staff training flight. Empire Air Navigation School (RAF Shawbury, Shropshire)
Avro Lancaster VII (NX719) overshot the runway onto the Carradine road, on the south side of the airfield, at 14.24 hrs. While practising a three-engine landing the pilot's foot slipped off the rudder bar and became trapped, causing the aircraft to career off the runway towards the airfield boundary. Despite an attempt to stop the aircraft by retracting the wheels, it slid through the boundary hedge and came to rest on top of a civilian car. The three occupants of the car were injured and taken to the Royal Salop Infirmary along with the navigator, who fractured his skull, but all eventually recovered.

F/Lt (pilot) Reginald Garner 'Timber' Woods (123838), RAF. Born on 26 August 1915, he had flown Lancaster bombers operationally during the war. He eventually became a senior air traffic controller and retired as a flight lieutenant in August 1965. He died in Birkenhead in 1969

F/Lt (F/Eng) Tyler, RAF.

F/Lt (Nav) Kenneth Shapley Delbridge (162793), DFC, RAF. Born in Chiswick in 1922, he was educated at Chiswick Central School and enlisted in the RAFVR in 1941. After undergoing training in Canada he completed a tour of ops with 432 (RCAF) Squadron and, in June 1944, was gazetted with the DFC for his 'outstanding navigational ability'.

Sig II (W/Op) Lewsley, RAF.

The three civilian occupants of the car were:

Mrs (driver) H H Crow of Hardwicke Home Farm.

Mrs (passenger) Gertrude Brettell of Smethcote Manor Farm, Hadnall.

Miss (passenger) Isobel Brettell of Smethcote Manor Farm, Hadnall.

1948

S/Ldr Chris Garvey
[Brian Garvey]

14 January (Wednesday)
Ferry flight from RAF Edzell to 27 MU, RAF Shawbury. 44 MU (RAF Edzell, Angus, Scotland)
De Havilland Mosquito NFXXX (NT552) crashed at Castle Farm, Moreton Corbet, at 11.20 hrs. The experienced pilot was making his final landing approach when it is believed that the port engine faltered as he increased the throttle, causing the aircraft to yaw to port and dive steeply into the ground. The pilot, who was cleared of all blame in the subsequent investigation, was seriously injured and, sadly, died within twenty minutes of the station ambulance's arrival on the scene.

S/Ldr (pilot) Richard Francis Christopher (Chris) Garvey (44811), DFC & bar, RAFVR, aged 29, was the son of Mr and Mrs R C Garvey and the husband of Patricia Mary Sutton. Born in County Mayo, Ireland, on 11 July 1918, he had served as the intelligence officer of the Royal Irish Fusiliers during the retreat to Dunkirk before transferring to the RAFVR in 1940. His first DFC had been awarded in February 1944 for his actions with 170 Squadron, the citation for which read:

> Flight Lieutenant Garvey has taken part in a large number of operational sorties and photographic reconnaissances, achieving some excellent results. In June 1943, whilst on a shipping reconnaissance, he sighted and photographed a large convoy of enemy shipping as a result of which five enemy vessels were sunk. Recently this officer completed five special photographic missions very successfully. He has, at all times, displayed enthusiasm, courage and a fine fighting spirit.

His second DFC was awarded just nine months later for his actions with 541 Squadron, the citation for which read:

> This officer has completed numerous reconnaissance sorties, setting an example of great courage and devotion to duty. In October 1944 he was detailed to obtain photographs of a certain objective. After completing his photographic runs, F/Lt Garvey noticed two enemy fighters behind him. Their leader opened fire. F/Lt Garvey spiralled almost to ground level, pulling out of his dive at the last moment. His attacker, who had followed him down, dived into a wood and burst into flames. This incident is characteristic of the skill and determination consistently displayed by this officer.

Following the war he became a ferry pilot and it was while serving with 5 FPP that he was tasked with the fatal ferry flight to RAF Shawbury. He is buried in Shawbury (St Mary's) Churchyard, Shropshire.

8 March (Monday)
Air test. 9 MU (RAF Cosford, Shropshire)
De Havilland Mosquito FBVI (VL731) belly-landed '500 yards beyond the airfield boundary' at 15.30 hrs. The test pilot was making a single-engine landing approach after an engine failed, when he used excessive throttle on his 'good' engine, sending the aircraft temporarily out of control and resulting in his overshooting the runway and belly-landing in a field.

F/Lt (test pilot) Mieczyslaw M Wyszkowski (P1584), PAF. Born in Nowy Sącz, Poland, on 9 December 1918, he had learned to fly gliders in the mid-1930s, while living in Torun, and subsequently joined the Polish Air Force. Following the German invasion in 1939, he fled to Romania where he was interned for a while before escaping to France to continue the fight. After the collapse of France he arrived in the UK and completed two tours of ops with 306 (Polish) Squadron and then 145 Squadron, during which he was credited with one enemy aircraft probably destroyed. He returned to Poland after the war and died in Warsaw in 1976.

24 October (Sunday)
Low-level cross-country flight. 25 Reserve Flying School (Penderford, Staffordshire)
De Havilland Tiger Moth II (R5102) crashed in Longford Hall park (at military map reference 723182), to the west of Newport, at 15.40 hrs. The pupil pilot was in control and flying at a low level on the Whitchurch-Bewdley leg of the flight, when he failed to see a large tree ahead, collided with it and crashed. Amazingly, neither occupant was injured.

F/O (instructor pilot) Hubert Edward Gibson (152535), RAF. Commissioned in the RAFVR in June 1943, he eventually relinquished his commission as a flight lieutenant in October 1957.

PII (pilot u/t) John Darlington (2602779), RAF.

The wreckage of the Tiger Moth (R5102) in Longford Hall park.
[Newport & Market Drayton Advertiser]

6 December (Monday)
Test flight. 9 MU (RAF Cosford, Shropshire)
De Havilland Mosquito PRXXXIV (RG295) force-landed in a field '1/2 mile from the airfield' at 15.04 hrs. The test pilot was taking off from the airfield when the port engine failed and he was forced to land in a field ahead, running through a hedge before hitting some trees and coming to rest.

F/Lt (test pilot) Henry David Costain (143384), RAF. Commissioned in March 1943, he was appointed an MBE in the New Year's Honours list of 1966 and retired as a wing commander in March 1977.

Mr (fitter, travelling as passenger) T Hargreaves, civilian MU employee.

1949

2 March (Wednesday)
Circuits and landings. 6 FTS (RAF Tern Hill, Shropshire)
De Havilland Tiger Moth II (N9331) crashed 'two miles south of Tern Hill' (putting it in the area around Stoke upon Tern) at 10.10 hrs. After forty-five minutes in the air the pilot 'spun off a bad turn', recovered, but had lost so much flying speed that he stalled and crashed through a wire fence and hedge.

Cadet pilot (pilot u/t) Richard Peter John King (4032246), RAF. He retired from the RAF as a squadron leader in December 1967.

1950

F/O Alec Davies [RAeC Aviator's Certificate]

7 February (Tuesday)
Night familiarisation flight. 6 FTS (RAF Tern Hill, Shropshire)
Percival Prentice T.1 (VS370) crashed at Cliff Grange, just north of the airfield, at 18.58 hrs. The instructor and his pupil pilot had been in the air for fifty-two minutes and were in the circuit preparing to land when they collided with a Harvard (FT164) which was also lining up to land. The Provost, which struck the Harvard's windscreen and starboard wing, was sent crashing out of control, while the Harvard pilot was able to maintain control and was diverted to RAF Shawbury.

F/O (instructor pilot) Alec Stanley Davies (1318391), RAF, aged 27,was born in Lancaster on 11 June 1922, but was living in Alexandra Road, Market Drayton, at the time of his death. He is commemorated at the Stafford Crematorium.

Officer Cadet (pilot u/t) Sidney Harry Harrex (4035671), RAF, aged 23, was the son of Sidney George and Lucy Harrex of Southall, Middlesex. He is buried in Moreton Say Churchyard, Shropshire.

Training flight. 6 FTS (RAF Tern Hill, Shropshire)
North American Harvard IIB (FT164) landed at RAF Shawbury following the collision described above.

P/O (instructor pilot) Edward Richardson (1807229), RAF, aged 25. He subsequently transferred to the Photographic Interpretation Branch and retired as a squadron leader in June 1978.

Lt (pilot u/t) A Shaikhli, RIrAF, aged 27.

13 February (Monday)
Night cross-country flight. 6 FTS (RAF Tern Hill, Shropshire)
North American Harvard IIB (FX400) belly-landed 'one mile south-east of the airfield boundary' at 20.03 hrs. The pilot was approaching to land when he was obliged to overshoot and, as he did so, the motor cut due to a lack of fuel, forcing him to belly-land the aircraft in a field.

Lt (pilot u/t) M Kessar, RIrAF.

10 March (Friday)
'School of Air Traffic Control detail'. CNCS (RAF Shawbury, Shropshire)
Avro Anson T.21 (VV988) belly-landed '400 yards west of the airfield' at 11.35 hrs. The pilot was making a single-engine landing approach when the student air traffic controller told him to overshoot, as another aircraft needed to make an emergency landing. Despite an attempt to un-feather his engine, the pilot was unable to maintain height as he passed over the airfield boundary and belly-landed the aircraft in a field ahead.

P/O (pilot) Edwyn John Huband (578599), RAF. Born in Cricklade, Swindon on 24 May 1924, he eventually retired on medical grounds as a squadron leader in June 1980. He died in Wiltshire in April 1997.

15 May (Monday)
General flying training. 6 FTS (RAF Tern Hill, Shropshire)
North American Harvard IIB (KF411) belly-landed 'three miles south-east of Newport' (putting it in the area around Woodcote) at 15.00 hrs. While climbing away from a practice forced landing the engine cut, from an unknown cause, and the pilot was forced to belly-land the aircraft in a field.

Officer Cadet (pilot u/t) Richard John Warr (2426344), RAF. Little is known of his military service other than that he was promoted to flying officer in September 1954. He died in Gloucestershire in 2001.

1951

12 March (Monday)
Circuits and landings. 6 FTS (RAF Tern Hill, Shropshire)
North American Harvard II (FE910) crash-landed 'near the airfield' at 22.05 hrs. The instructor and his pupil had been in the air for an hour and five minutes and were climbing away, after overshooting a practice landing, when the engine began to lose power (possibly as a result of ice forming in the carburettor intake). Unable to maintain height, the instructor took control but failed to retract the undercarriage before making a forced landing and the aircraft flipped onto its back, damaging a chicken coop and some wire fencing. Fortunately, neither officer was injured.

S/Ldr (instructor pilot) Vernon William Hinkley (77463), RAF. Born on 28 May 1917, he had served in the RAF during the war and eventually retired as a wing commander in January 1962. He died in Tenbury in 1996.

F/Lt (pilot u/t) William Maurice Robinson (55684), RAF. He had joined the RAFVR in 1943, but it is likely that he had served in another trade prior to retraining as a pilot. He eventually retired as a flight lieutenant in April 1963.

31 March (Saturday)
Training flight. 6 FTS (RAF Tern Hill, Shropshire)
North American Harvard IIB (KF587) belly-landed 'near Newport'. The pilot belly-landed the aircraft in a field 'owing to shortage of fuel and ice'.

Officer Cadet (pilot u/t) Wright (service number unknown), RAF.

11 April (Wednesday)
Low flying practice. 25 Reserve Flying School (Penderford, Staffordshire)
De Havilland Tiger Moth II (DE568) crashed 'one mile west of Ackleton', between Albrighton and

Bridgnorth, at 15.35 hrs. While flying between 100–200 feet, the pilot inadvertently turned towards higher ground and collided with a line of high-tension power cables running along the crest. The aircraft crashed and he was injured. In the subsequent investigation it was concluded that the cause was 'pilot error' but added that he had been 'badly briefed by instructor and given no minimum height'.

F/O (pilot u/t) James Geoffrey Hamer (205136), RAF. Born in Builth Wells on 15 September 1923, he later relinquished his commission on grounds of medical unfitness in October 1951. He died in Wellington, Shropshire in December 1991.

16 November (Friday)
Low flying & circuits and landings. 6 FTS (RAF Tern Hill, Shropshire)
North American Harvard IIB (KF578) crashed at Field Farm, between Onneley and Woore, at 09.45 hrs. Thirty minutes after taking off the aircraft was seen, by civilian eyewitnesses, to start rotating rapidly around its longitudinal axis, losing height as it did so, before striking the ground and exploding. The subsequent investigation concluded that the pupil pilot's foot became jammed between the aileron controls and that the opposing efforts of the pupil to free his foot and the instructor trying to regain control resulted in the aircraft going completely out of control.

F/Lt (instructor pilot) Douglas Gilbert (166032), RAF, aged 27, was born in Brighton on 6 January 1924. He is commemorated at the Brighton Crematorium, Sussex.

Acting P/O (pilot u/t) Kenneth Robert Smith (583516), RAF, aged 21, was born in Highbury, London, on 25 November 1929. He is buried in Moreton Say Churchyard, Shropshire.

1952

1 August (Friday)
Stalling, spinning and forced landing practice. 6 FTS (RAF Tern Hill, Shropshire)
North American Harvard IIB (KF322) force-landed at Lodgebank, near Hopton, to the south of Hodnet, at 10.05 hrs. On noticing smoke coming from behind the instrument panel the pilot assumed that he had an engine fire and carried out a forced landing, damaging the aircraft as it ran through a hedge and hit a hidden mound. In the subsequent investigation it was concluded that 'a more experienced pilot would have realised that it was safe to fly back to base'.

Acting P/O (pilot u/t) Peter John Miller (3510806), RAF. He relinquished his commission as a flight lieutenant in August 1963.

20 August (Wednesday)
Circuits and landings. 6 FTS (RAF Tern Hill, Shropshire)
North American Harvard IIB (FS742) crashed at Mickley, between Fauls and Bletchley, at 22.10 hrs. On taking off from the airfield the pilot 'failed to maintain adequate control whilst climbing away' and the aircraft entered a descending turn to starboard and crashed. It was considered a contributory factor that the pilot had only just been woken from sleep as he 'did not realise that he was required to fly.'

Acting P/O (pilot u/t) John David Campbell McLean (2523806), RAF, aged 19, was born in Bombay, India on 26 September 1932. He is buried in Bexleyheath Cemetery, London.

12 September (Friday)
'Day flying control training flight'. CNCS (RAF Shawbury, Shropshire)
Avro Anson T.21 (VV987, bearing the code letter N) crashed into Wenlock Woods (at map reference 635084), on the east side of the Wrekin, near Willowmoor Farm, at 08.27 hrs. The pilot took off at 07.55

hrs and had completed one controlled descent through cloud (known as a 'QGH exercise'), after which he flew away from the airfield to repeat the exercise. Soon afterwards, however, he reported a temporary loss of elevator control and, while regaining control, it is believed that he became unsure of his position and flew into the side of the Wrekin, which was totally obscured by mist and cloud. Mr Frank Johnson, of Willowmoor Farm, told the *Wellington Journal* afterwards how,

> [He] was looking through a window directly at the spot where it crashed. There was an explosion and a burst of smoke and flame. With Douglas Jones, who works on the farm, I dashed to the scene and located the wreckage about 150 feet up on the side of the Wrekin. We heard the plane coming over the farm beforehand. There was a mist over the Wrekin at the time practically to the spot where the plane crashed. We were the first on the scene and found the body of the pilot about forty yards away from the wreckage.

F/Sgt (pilot u/t) Alexander Walter Arthur Gee (1066637), RAF, aged 35, was the husband of Margaret L Gee (née Aves) of Henllan, Denbighshire. Born in Moscow on 24 September 1916, he had been commissioned in the RAFVR in November 1941 and attained the rank of flight lieutenant by the war's end. He is buried in Shawbury (St Mary's) Churchyard.

21 October (Tuesday)
Instrument training flight. 1689 Flight (RAF Aston Down, Gloucestershire)
Airspeed Oxford I (PH713) crashed at Loughton, near Burwarton, at 14.32 hrs. The instructor and his pupil took off at 14.05 hrs and were flying at 1,700 feet when one of the starboard propeller blades broke off due to 'metal fatigue' and smashed into the nose of the aircraft. As the seriously damaged aircraft began to lose height the two officers baled out but, sadly, the pupil pilot's parachute failed to deploy before he struck the ground. The instructor injured his leg, striking the tailplane as he left the aircraft, but survived.

F/Lt (instructor pilot) Amos John Rendell (55400), RAF. Born in Beaminster, Dorset on 24 April 1919, he had served in the RAFVR during the war and eventually retired as a flight lieutenant in April 1962. He died in Hampshire in 1982.

F/O (pilot u/t) John Pryse (172118), RAF, aged 29, was born in Aberystwyth, Cardiganshire on 7 May 1923, the son of Iorwerth and Lydia Pryse (née Hughes). He is buried in Kingston-upon-Thames Cemetery, Surrey.

28 October (Tuesday)
Forced landing practice. 6 FTS (RAF Tern Hill, Shropshire)
North American Harvard IIB (FS773) belly-landed at Hawkstone Abbey Farm, between Prees Green and Marchamley, at 09.20 hrs. Having taken off at 08.35 hrs the pilot was climbing away from a practice forced landing when the engine failed, possibly due to icing in the carburettor, and he was forced to belly-land the aircraft ahead.

Acting P/O (pilot u/t) Peter Ettore Giovanni Freddi (4078064), RAF. Born in Lambeth on 19 May 1933, little is known of his military service other than that he served into the 1970s. He died in Barnstable, Devon in October 1993.

1953

29 January (Thursday)
Stalling and aerobatics. 6 FTS (RAF Tern Hill, Shropshire)

North American Harvard IIB (KF472) belly-landed '$2^1/_2$ miles north of the airfield' (putting it roughly in the area of Longford) at 16.05 hrs. The pilot was carrying out a maximum rate climb when the engine began to run rough and then cut completely, due to a 'fractured push rod in the number four cylinder', forcing him to belly-land the aircraft in a field.

Acting P/O (pilot u/t) Bernard Eugene McGourlay (3135421), RAF. Born in Rochdale, Lancashire, in 1929, little is known of his military service other than that he was promoted to flying officer in March 1954.

13 April (Monday)
'Stalling, forced landings etc'. 6 FTS (RAF Tern Hill, Shropshire)
North American Harvard IIB (FX199) belly-landed in a field '$1^1/_2$ miles from Tern Hill' at 11.02 hrs. The pilot was turning onto his final approach when the engine failed, due to a shortage of fuel, and he was forced to belly-land the aircraft into a field. As a result of the accident the pilot was 'suspended from further training'.

Acting P/O (pilot u/t) Pat Frederick Plummer (3512996), RAF. He eventually resigned his commission as a pilot officer in January 1960.

22 June (Monday)
Aerobatics training (stalling, turning and spinning). 6 FTS (RAF Tern Hill, Shropshire)
North American Harvard IIB (FS753) crashed '$3^1/_2$ miles north west of the airfield' (putting it in the area around Bletchley and Moreton Say) at 15.45 hrs. During the course of the aerobatics practice the pupil pilot pulled back sharply on the control column while recovering from a spin, causing his instructor and himself to black out. When the instructor regained consciousness, he attempted to recover from the resulting dive but, by then, the aircraft had lost too much height and crashed into the ground, seriously injuring the two occupants.

F/Lt (instructor pilot) Douglas Edward Read (154156), RAF. He had served in the RAFVR during the war and eventually relinquished his commission in August 1955.

Acting P/O (pilot u/t) Brian Michael McClelland (3513785), RAF. Born in Oldham on 27 July 1931, nothing is known of his military service. He died in Yorkshire in 2001.

22 November (Sunday)
Training flight. RAF Cosford Gliding Club (RAF Cosford, Shropshire)
Slingsby Sedbergh T.21.B glider crashed on the station sports field. The instructor and his pupil had just 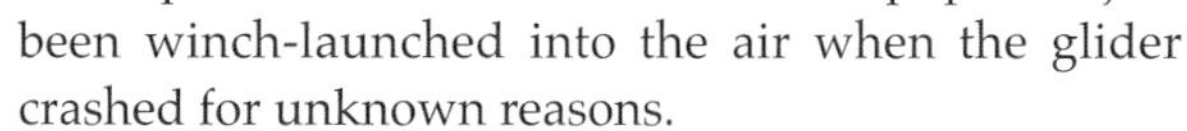
been winch-launched into the air when the glider crashed for unknown reasons.

S/Ldr (glider instructor) Reginald Herbert Havelock (Reg) Pelling (44376), RAF, aged 46, was born in Alverstoke, Hampshire on 1 June 1907. After training as an engineer in the RAF in the early 1930s, he was posted to Hong Kong, where he met and married Agnes F W Black in 1934. During the Second World War he was involved in the British retreat from mainland Greece to Crete and subsequently escaped to

Reg Pelling (in white) pictured in the cockpit of a Sedbergh T.21.B at Cosford. [Richard Pelling]

North Africa in a commandeered Blenheim after the German assault on the island in May 1941. Little else is known of his military service other than that he took an interest in gliding while stationed at RAF Lüneburg in Germany, and eventually qualified as a gliding instructor. In May 1952 he was posted to RAF Cosford to command 'B' Squadron (the engine mechanics' squadron) and subsequently became the station gliding instructor (while also helping to form the West Midland Area Gliding Club). He is buried in Donington (St Cuthbert's) Churchyard, Shropshire.

Cpl (pupil glider pilot) Donald John MacKintosh (4031151), RAF, aged 23, was born in Ross-shire on 23 August 1930. At the time of his death he was stationed at Cosford as a radar fitter and instructor for the boy entrant wing, but was also learning to fly gliders. He is buried in Kiltearn Cemetery, Ross-shire.

1954

4 March (Thursday)
Meteorological flight from Base–Worcester–Base. THUM Flight (RAF Woodvale, Lancashire) Supermarine Spitfire PRXIX (PM577) crashed in the back yard of Lower House Farm (at map reference 431027), Church Pulverbatch, at 10.18 hrs. The 'THUM' (Temperature and Humidity) flight was operated by Short Brothers Ltd and was responsible for taking weather readings every day of the year (except the Christmas holiday) by flying specially fitted Spitfires from Woodvale to Worcester and back, collecting data along the way. On the day of the accident the pilot was on his return leg from Worcester when his engine began 'overspeeding' and he sent out a mayday signal saying, 'I'm in trouble, I'm going to bale out.' However, since he did not do so, it is thought that he decided to force-land instead. The aircraft was subsequently seen passing low over Cothercott Hill and Pulverbatch, with its engine spluttering and trailing smoke, before making an 'almighty roar' and crashing vertically into the

Above and left: The wreckage of Spitfire PM577 pictured at Pulverbatch. [Stuart Leigh-Davies]

Photo-reconnaissance Spitfire PM577 at Woodvale.

F/Lt Tommy Heyes in the cockpit of Spitfire PM577 [Stuart Leigh-Davies]

farmyard. Local belief is that the pilot had remained at the controls to avoid the village school (where children were sitting at their desks) although, according to the accident investigation, it was believed that the pilot 'became overcome by fumes from a fractured cooling pipe'.

F/Lt (pilot) Thomas Victor (Tommy) Heyes (172597), DFC, aged 39, was the husband of Iris Heyes of Acrefair, Denbighshire. He was awarded the DFC in April 1944 after completing 29 operations (of which 11 were to Berlin) flying Lancaster bombers with 100 Squadron. After being demobilised in 1946 he subsequently returned to flying as an instructor at a Reserve Flying School before taking up an appointment as a THUM pilot in approximately 1951. He is buried in Acrefair, near Ruabon, Denbighshire.

26 March (Friday)

Training flight. 6 FTS (RAF Tern Hill, Shropshire)

Percival Provost T.1 (WV490) crashed on the airfield at 14.14 hrs. After completing their respective training flights, two pupil pilots joined the circuit simultaneously in preparation for landing but, as they approached the airfield, the controller saw that they were too close for safety and fired off a warning flare. Both pilots immediately began overshoot procedure but, as the pilot of this aircraft climbed and turned to starboard, he failed to notice that the other aircraft was above and slightly in front of him and the two collided. Acting P/O Walker was killed instantly in the resulting crash, while Acting P/O Quirk was seriously injured and taken to the Royal Salop Infirmary, where he succumbed to his injuries later in the day.

Acting P/O (pilot u/t) John Rooper Walker (4135085), RAF, aged 18, was born in Billingham, County Durham on 17 January 1936. At the time of his death his address was given as 60 Oxcliffe Road, Morecambe. He is buried in an unknown location.

Training flight. 6 FTS (RAF Tern Hill, Shropshire)
Percival Provost T.1 (WV500) crashed on the airfield following the accident described above.

Acting P/O (pilot u/t) Herbert Edgar Quirk (2583670), RAF, aged 23, was the son of Owen Herbert and Rosa Gwendoline Quirk (née Stanbury) of 12 Upper Park Street, Llanelli, Carmarthenshire. He is buried in Llanelli Cemetery.

18 May (Tuesday)
Formation training flight. 6 FTS (RAF Tern Hill, Shropshire)
Percival Provost T.1 (WV488) crash-landed at Colehurst Manor, to the north-east of the airfield, at 14.40 hrs. The pilot of this aircraft was flying in number two position in a line astern formation of three aircraft, which entered the airfield circuit at 1,300 feet in preparation for landing. At the same time, another Provost, piloted by P/O Golder, had joined the circuit at 2,300 feet and was also descending in a right-hand pattern when it collided with this aircraft from above and behind. Amazingly, the pilots of both aircraft were able to maintain control and carry out emergency forced landings in fields nearby. In the subsequent investigation the leader of the formation and P/O Golder were held to blame as 'neither maintained an effective lookout for other aircraft in the circuit', although it was added that there were mitigating circumstances in that two different methods of joining the circuit were in use. The first involved coming in 'at 2,300 feet and letting down to 1,300 feet on the dead side of the runway', while the second was to join 'tangentially at 1,300 feet providing a complete downwind leg was carried out', which is how the two aircraft had joined the circuit.

Acting P/O (pilot u/t) Richard Thompson Green (4130848), RAF, aged 23. He retired from the RAF as a flight lieutenant in June 1970.

Training flight. 6 FTS (RAF Tern Hill, Shropshire)
Percival Provost T.1 (WV567) crash-landed at Sutton Grange, to the north-east of the airfield, following the collision described above.

Acting P/O (pilot u/t) Peter James Golder (2711106), RAF, aged 19. Nothing further is known of his military service.

26 July (Monday)
'Formation fly-past flight'. 6 FTS (RAF Tern Hill, Shropshire)
Percival Provost T.1 (WV483) crashed 'one and a half miles west of the airfield' (putting it roughly in the area of Fauls and Bletchley) at 15.40 hrs. A flight of 12 aircraft was flying in three boxes in line astern formation, when a change of configuration was ordered to form an 'arrowhead', while turning to port at 1,000 feet. On nearing completion of the turn the pilot of this aircraft, who was flying in number 3 position, increased his angle of bank and the tailplane struck the propeller of the aircraft behind him. The collision was so severe that the tail was completely severed and the aircraft immediately fell into an uncontrollable dive and crashed, killing the two occupants. The pilot of the other aircraft managed to land safely at the airfield.

F/Lt (instructor pilot) Harry Bridle (1339250), RAF, aged 32, was born in Swindon, on 13 May 1922. He is buried in Nunhead Cemetery, London.

Acting P/O (pilot u/t, but travelling as passenger) Gordon Syer (4147544), RAF, aged 20, was the son of James and Nora Emma Syer of Stepney, London. Educated at Colfes Grammar School, he had gained a place at the University of London but turned it down in order to join the RAF. He is buried in Stoke upon Tern (St Peter's) Cemetery, Shropshire.

'Formation fly-past flight'. 6 FTS (RAF Tern Hill, Shropshire)
Percival Provost T.1 (WV603) landed at RAF Tern Hill following the collision described above.

F/O (pilot u/t) William Black (2360115), RAF, aged 25. He retired from the RAF as a flight lieutenant in June 1967.

F/Lt David Hytch [Samantha Bossi]

3 August (Tuesday)
Instrument flying in low flying area. 6 FTS (RAF Tern Hill, Shropshire)
Percival Provost T.1 (WV545) crashed at Lees Farm, Adderley, near Market Drayton, at 14.50 hrs. The instructor and his pupil were flying at just 35 feet when the aircraft struck high-tension power cables, which wrapped around the port wheel and caused the aircraft to nosedive into a barn full of straw and catch fire. The subsequent investigation concluded that the instructor should have maintained slightly more height to avoid such obstacles, but also that warning notices should be attached to all low flying area maps, drawing attention to the existence of overhead cables.

F/Lt (instructor pilot) David Idwall Hytch (56206), RAF, aged 33, was the son of the late Frederick Arnold Hytch and Winifred Hitch, and husband of Olive Margaret Hytch (née Long) of Gloucester. He had joined the RAF during the war and, after completing his pilot training, was posted to 49 Squadron in December 1944, piloting Lancaster bombers. On 19 April 1945, he and his crew had to be rescued from the sea after their Lancaster (ME357) crashed in The Wash during air–sea firing practice. Having left the squadron in 1946, he spent a short period in civilian life before deciding to re-join the RAF and eventually becoming an instructor at Tern Hill. He was cremated and his ashes spread in an unknown location (but believed to have been in Shropshire).

Acting P/O (pilot u/t) Leonard Harold Stafford (1921013), RAF, aged 22, was the son of Harold B and Ada Stafford (née Cottingham) of Dartford, Kent. He is buried in an unknown location.

1955

1 March (Tuesday)
Communications flight. CNCS (RAF Shawbury, Shropshire)
Avro Anson T.21 (WB463) belly-landed '2½ miles south-west of the airfield' (putting it in the area around Hadnall) at 09.04 hrs. Moments after taking off, the port engine failed at a height of 150 feet, and the pilot displayed 'good airmanship' in belly-landing the aircraft ahead, skidding through a hedge before dropping three feet onto a small lane.

F/Sgt (pilot) Robert Wall (1435469), RAF, aged 33. He had served as an officer in the RAFVR during the war but nothing further is known of his military service.

The names of the other crew members are unknown.

3 April (Sunday)
Low-level cross-country flight to RAF Llandow, Glamorgan. 663 (AOP) Squadron, Royal Auxiliary Air Force (RAF Hooton Park, Cheshire)
Auster AOP 6 (TW539) crashed '3½ miles east-south-east of Whitchurch' (putting it in the area around Ash Magna and Ightfield). The pilot was flying in dull conditions, at just twenty-five feet, when he saw

Auster TW539 pictured in 1954. [Wikipedia]

high-tension power cables directly ahead. As he attempted to fly under them the aircraft struck the ground and crashed, injuring him and seriously injuring his observer. In the subsequent investigation it was concluded that the pilot was flying too low for the conditions but also added that there was 'a lack of general supervision on Squadron'.

Capt (pilot) John Ulric Steiger (78128), RA (TA). Born on 21 June 1914, he had been commissioned in 4 The Loyal Regiment in November 1938, but little else is known of his military career. He died in Macclesfield in January 1996.

Lance Bombardier (observer) B O'Donnell (22184832), RA (TA).

1956

11 January (Wednesday)
Circuits and landings. 6 FTS (RAF Tern Hill, Shropshire)
Percival Provost T.1 (WV498) crashed near the bridge over the River Tern, between Stoke upon Tern and Hodnet, at 10.10 hrs. The instructor and his pupil had just taken off and were climbing away from the airfield when the instructor decided to demonstrate engine failure after take-off procedure, by gliding the aircraft down to a low level, before climbing away steeply. On completion of the procedure the instructor climbed back up to rejoin the circuit but, as he did so, he flew into the path of another Provost (WV514) which was making a normal circuit. Both aircraft were immediately sent crashing out of control and only Squadron Leader Wilson survived after taking to his parachute with just moments to spare.

S/Ldr (instructor pilot) Fergus Connon Wilson (47900), RAF, aged 36. Born on 2 June 1919, he had been commissioned in the RAFVR in February 1942 and eventually retired as a squadron leader in January 1959. He died in Suffolk in 1999.

Acting P/O (pilot u/t) Andrew Robin Dawson (504467), RAF, aged 23, was born in Johannesburg, South Africa on 29 October 1929, although at the time of his death his family lived in Pretoria. He is buried in Stoke upon Tern (St Peter's) Cemetery, Shropshire.

Training flight. 6 FTS (RAF Tern Hill, Shropshire)
Percival Provost T.1 (WV514) crashed near the bridge over the River Tern, between Stoke upon Tern and Hodnet, following the collision described above.

F/O (instructor pilot) Michael Edward Preskett (4059918), RAF, aged 23, was the son of Albert E and Hilda Annie Preskett (née Hawkins) of Swanley. He is buried in Swanley Junction (St Mary's) Churchyard, Kent.

P/O (pilot u/t) Donald James Grant (4111044), RAF, aged 22, was the son of Laurence J and Dorothy C Grant (née Jones) of Headington. He is buried in Headington Cemetery, Oxford.

1 July (Sunday)
Army co-operation exercise. 1844 Squadron, HMS *Gamecock* (RNAS Bramcote, Warwickshire)
Grumman Avenger AS.5 (XB323) crashed at Crabtree Farm, Prees Higher Heath, at 12 noon. The aircraft

The wreckage of Avenger XB323 at Crabtree Farm, Prees Higher Heath. [The Shrewsbury Advertiser]

was taking part in an army exercise when the engine failed due to a loose nut in the carburettor. The pilot fought to avoid some farm buildings before the aircraft dived into a herd of cows. Sadly, two of the crew were killed instantly, while the third member was rushed to the Royal Salop Infirmary suffering a fractured arm and leg. According to the account of Mr Wallace Jones of Crabtree Farm, which appeared in the *Shrewsbury Advertiser* at the time,

> I was loading milk onto a lorry when I saw the plane skim over the roof of the farmhouse and hit the ground only ten yards from the buildings. The aircraft ploughed along the pasture for 50 yards before overturning and breaking its back. I ran to the plane and then got an axe from the farmhouse and with soldiers who had been taking part in the exercise we managed to get the crew out.

Lt (A) (pilot) Raymond Charles (Ray) Barkway, RNVR, aged 31, was born in Northwood, Middlesex on 24 August 1924 and was the husband of Barbara R Bennet of Bristol. Educated at Harrow School, he was a noted hurdler (having competed in the 1948 Olympics) and held the claim to fame that he started the race for Roger Bannister's first sub four-minute mile on 6 May 1954. He is buried in an unknown location.

Lt (A) Gordon Hedley Capps, RNVR, aged 33, was the son of the late Thomas Ambrose Sumpter Capps and Nellie Capps (née Whittemore) of Kettering and husband of Ethel Capps (née Jackson). Born in Kettering on 10 September 1922, he had been commissioned in the RAFVR in December 1944 and subsequently transferred to the Royal Navy in September 1953. He is buried in an unknown location.

Sub Lt (A) Christopher Cavill Hutchinson, RNVR. He lived in Derby, but nothing further is known of him.

9 July (Monday)
Training flight (?). CNCS (RAF Shawbury, Shropshire)
De Havilland DHC-1 Chipmunk T.10 (WK561) force-landed 'four miles north of Shrewsbury' (putting it roughly in the area between Bomere Heath and Hadnall). The pilot force-landed in a field after the aircraft's engine failed and came to rest after striking a hedge.

The name of the pilot is unknown.

5 October (Friday)
Training flight. 6 FTS (RAF Tern Hill, Shropshire)
Percival Provost (serial number unknown) force-landed 'north of Wellington'. The instructor force-landed the aircraft in a field after allowing it to run out of fuel during a training flight. It then had to

be re-fuelled in situ before being flown out. As a consequence of the accident the instructor was 'sentenced to take rank and precedence as though his appointment to the rank of flight lieutenant bore date of 4 December 1953' (six months later than his original appointment) and was also 'severely reprimanded'.

F/Lt (instructor pilot) Ronald Mosley (1571583), RAF. He eventually relinquished his commission as a flight lieutenant in July 1963.

The name of the pupil pilot is unknown.

1957

11 April (Thursday)
'Final handling test flight'. 6 FTS (RAF Tern Hill, Shropshire)
Percival Provost T.1 (XF902) crash-landed 'one mile north of Tern Hill' (putting it to the south of Longford) at 11.32 hrs. Immediately after taking off, the instructor ordered his pupil to carry out an engine failure after take-off procedure by putting the aircraft into a glide, before being instructed to open up the throttle and climb away. When the pupil hesitated in response to the order, the instructor was forced to open up the throttle himself, but the engine did not respond quickly enough, causing the aircraft to sink down and clip a railway signal. This damaged the elevator, causing the aircraft to climb steeply and, in an attempt to get the aircraft down, the instructor closed the throttle, causing the nose to drop and the aircraft crash-landed, injuring him.

S/Ldr (instructor pilot) George Robert Stewart McKay (120741), DFC, RAF, aged 36. Commissioned in the RAFVR in March 1942, his DFC was awarded during a tour of ops flying ground-attack Spitfires with 145 Squadron in Italy. He retired from the RAF in November 1959 and died in Aylesbury in 1980.

Acting P/O (pilot u/t) Barry Jennett Stott (4181850), RAF, aged 19. He was awarded the Queen's Commendation for Valuable Services in the Air in the New Year's Honours list of 1973 and retired two years later as a flight lieutenant in October 1975.

20 September (Friday)
Dual low-level navigation training. 7 FTS (RAF Valley, Anglesey)
Vampire T.11 (WZ496) crashed at Paddolgreen, two miles north of Wem, at 11.30 hrs. During a routine training flight a defect in the fire warning system occurred and the instructor, F/Lt Rufus Heald, 'carried out the correct fire drill in accordance with current instructions' while looking for somewhere to land. His account of the accident, which he wrote for the author in 2008, describes the event in detail:

> On this occasion, I had been on a dual low-level navigation trip round the Cheshire plain. Having completed the route, I told the student to climb to an appropriate flight level above 10,000 feet, and to head back towards Valley. There was a layer of cloud between 1,500 feet and 4,000 feet but visibility above was excellent. As we passed 11,000 feet I was alerted by a very bright red light in the centre top of the instrument panel. Naturally, my brain went into neutral instantly but when it had recovered, I reached past the student to turn off the low pressure fuel cock, and to flick the radio changeover switch to 2 box , which was always pre-set on 243 mhz. I transmitted a 'Mayday' call and, as the speed fell, pressed the fire extinguisher. In the Vampire, the fire detection switches are not resetting, so I had no way of knowing if the fire was out except by flying a tight turn and looking back to see if I had a trail of smoke. As far as I could see, we didn't! The D + D Cell at Preston Centre gave us a heading and distance to go to Shawbury. I remember thinking that 34 miles was a hell of a long way to try to glide from 11,000 feet into wind! They told me that there was nowhere nearer, although they did

mention a disused airfield at Sleap, but we were still in cloud when we passed it. It became obvious that we were not going to get to Shawbury so I had all the time in the world to brief my student and to remind him about how to 'fly' a parachute. At about 2,000 feet we jettisoned the canopy and at 1,500 feet I ordered him to bail out. I carried on a bit further and at some 500 feet above ground level, I followed him. All the equipment worked perfectly and when I looked down I found myself descending towards some 33,000 volt power lines. I pulled on the rear lift webs to drift back, away from the cables and hit the ground with an almighty wallop, but I missed the power lines and the farm house which had materialised from behind me. There was a nasty crunching noise as I hit the ground so I let myself fall down the pile of brick rubble which I had managed to land on and I slid myself onto a patch of reasonably clean grass. Next problem was to attract attention. There was smoke coming out of the farm house chimney so I got my whistle out of my life jacket and blew loud and long. After a few minutes a lovely lady looked over the wall. She was at least 50 years old and still had her hair in curlers and her bedroom slippers on. 'What's all that noise?' she asked. I apologised for disturbing her, told her that my aircraft had crashed somewhere 'over there' and asked if she was on the telephone. She was, so I asked her to pop back indoors and dial 999 and tell the police that my aircraft had crashed, that I was there and that I needed an ambulance. She was back in a very few minutes with her hair curlers out, but still in her slippers and, being typically British, she had a tray with a pot of tea, a milk jug a bowl of sugar and what looked like the best china. It was strong, but one of the best drinks I have ever had. While I was sipping it, my student walked up - he was totally uninjured – and then two of the farm workers arrived out of breath. They had seen it all happen and had run over to see if they could help. Some 15–20 minutes after the accident, the RAF ambulance arrived, picked me up and took me to Shawbury where we were given lunch and afterwards flown back to Valley in an elderly Avro Anson. That evening, as I lay in the Station Medical Centre, with a compression fracture of the spine and seven broken bones in my left foot, there was a knock on the door and in came my student and his very pregnant wife. Not only that, but they were carrying a case of Guinness! Since his wife was pregnant she couldn't drink, and since he was detailed for night flying later that night, he couldn't drink either, so I had to drink it all! It can be hard work being a flying instructor!

F/Lt (instructor pilot) Michael Arthur Rufus Heald (1813102), RAF, aged 32. Born on 14 July 1925, he grew up in London and was educated at St Peter's Court Prep School and Wellington College, Berkshire. Enlisting in the RAFVR in 1942, he was subsequently selected for pilot training at the end of the war and sent to Rhodesia, following which he was posted to 20 Squadron in Agra, at the time of the Indian independence in 1947. The following year (by which time he had joined 213 Squadron in the Middle East) he flew operationally during the Arab-Israeli War and was involved in combat with Ezra Weisman (who later became the President of the state of Israel). During the engagement his wingman was shot down and his own aircraft badly damaged. After returning to the UK, Rufus spent twelve months studying mathematics to degree level, before returning to the RAF full time and converting to the Meteor jet (and subsequently the Vampire). Following his jet conversion he was posted to 28 Squadron in Hong Kong, where he 'got involved several times with various Chinese aircraft – mostly Mig 15 aircraft'. He returned to the UK in 1955, underwent weapons training and then a long instructor's course at the CFS, before arriving at RAF Valley to instruct naval pilots on Vampires. He was awarded the MBE in June 1978 and retired two years later, but still runs an aviation consultancy business in Devon.

Lt (pilot u/t) John Lawrence Williams, RN, aged 24. Born in St Georges, Shropshire on 20 December 1932, he had gained a private pilot's licence in April 1951 at the Wolverhampton Aero Club, whilst serving as a Royal Navy cadet. His address at the time was given as 33 The Crescent, Compton, Wolverhampton.

1961

16 June (Friday)

Delivery flight from Prestwick, South Ayrshire, to Base. Aeroplane & Armament Experimental Establishment (RAF Boscombe Down, Wiltshire)

Scottish Aviation Pioneer CC.1 (XL664) crash-landed at Catsley Farm, Kinlet, in south-east Shropshire, at 16.25 hrs. The experienced pilot was tasked with picking up the aircraft from the makers in Prestwick and was on the return leg, cruising straight and level at a height of 2,000 feet, when the engine began to run rough. After throttling back slightly the engine appeared to run normally for a few seconds but, on opening up to zero boost, it cut completely and the pilot was forced to land in a small field, wrecking the aircraft as it came to rest in a small copse.

The subsequent investigation found the engine failure was due to the pilot's not switching over to his starboard fuel tanks when the port tank ran dry, adding that he had 'inexperience on this type of aircraft'.

S/Ldr (test pilot) Alastair McNaughton Christie (3114812), RAF, aged 32. Commissioned in 1951, he was awarded the Queen's Commendation for Valuable Service in the Air in June 1963 and the AFC in the New Year's Honours list of 1969. He retired from the RAF as a group captain in October 1983.

The wrecked Pioneer lies in a field at Kinlet after the pilot was forced to crash-land following engine failure. [Bridgnorth Journal]

1963

29 March (Friday)

Low-level map reading to Chetwynd airfield, torque turns and quick stops. CFS (H) (RAF Tern Hill, Shropshire)

Bristol Sycamore HR.14 helicopter (XE309) crashed at Eaton upon Tern. The pilot was instructed to fly to Chetwynd at no lower than 100 feet but, twelve minutes after taking off, his helicopter was witnessed flying at approximately 40 feet on an easterly heading. Moments later, the pilot is believed to have lost control after an attempted recovery from a 'quick stop' in a downwind position, displaying 'inexperience on type' and a disregard of his briefing instructions. Sadly, despite being airlifted to RAF Hospital, Cosford, he died of his injuries shortly after being admitted.

P/O (pilot u/t) Arthur Barry Watson (507247), RAF, aged 28, was the son of Arthur Roland and Irene Watson (née Von Sturmer) of Waverley on the outskirts of Dunedin, New Zealand. Educated at King's High School, Dunedin, he was a member of the school Air Training Corps and was granted a scholarship to take his pilot's licence at the Otago Aero Club. After leaving school he studied science at the University of Otago and then qualified at the College of Optometry (attached to Melbourne University for a time) before returning to Dunedin to practice as an optician. Throughout his studies at the University of Otago he served as a member of the Territorial Air Force (undergoing jet grading in May 1956) and, when he went to Melbourne to study, he was placed on the reserve. He evidently continued to crave flying, however, and, in 1962, gave up practising as an optician and travelled to the UK to join the RAF. Cremated at Wolverhampton Crematorium, his ashes were scattered from a helicopter over Tern Hill airfield by an RAF padre.

30 September (Monday)
Dual airways crossing navigation exercise. 8 FTS (RAF Swinderby, Lincolnshire)
De Havilland Vampire T.11 (WZ578) crashed at Rea Farm, one mile east of Upton Magna, at 16.49 hrs. The instructor and his student took off at 16.10 hrs and were part-way through their exercise when a serious vibration developed in the engine. The instructor therefore took control and began 'flaming out'. On sending out a distress signal he was homed towards RAF Shawbury by Northern Air Traffic Control and began a spiral descent through cloud to make an emergency landing. However, on breaking out of the cloud at 3,500 feet the crew were unable to locate RAF Shawbury and, when they sighted the disused wartime airfield at Atcham, put up a landing pattern there instead. During their approach, however, the instructor noticed numerous obstructions on the runway and realising that a landing would be extremely dangerous he ordered his pupil to eject at 900 feet and followed suit himself moments later. According to a contemporary newspaper report, the aircraft continued in flight for a few moments before striking the ground and sliding along for 100 yards, while one of the pilots landed within ten yards of the River Tern and was helped by farm-workers. Soon afterwards, the local police, an ambulance and two fire engines arrived at the scene, followed by a Whirlwind helicopter from RAF Tern Hill, which landed and conveyed the crew to RAF Shawbury.

Vampire WZ578's wreckage lies in a field near Upton Magna with the Wrekin in the background. [Shropshire Star]

F/Lt (instructor pilot) Peter Rory Callaghan (2758359), RAF. He had joined the RAF in 1955 and eventually retired as a squadron leader in January 1995.

P/O (pilot u/t) Douglas Aylward (4231380), RAF. A resident of Richmond in Yorkshire, he went on to serve with 11 and 92 Squadrons (piloting Lightning jets) and eventually retired as a wing commander in July 1985.

1964

25 March (Wednesday)
'Vortex ring' demonstration. CFS (H) (RAF Tern Hill, Shropshire)
Bristol Sycamore HR.14 (XL820) crashed at Tern Hill railway station at 14.37 hrs. After taking off at 14.25 hrs the instructor climbed to 3,000 feet to demonstrate a 'vortex ring' to his student (a state in which airflow over the blades causes the helicopter, in effect, to stall and become uncontrollable) but, soon after he began a sharp descent, pieces of rotor blade were seen to fly off at approximately 1,000 feet and the helicopter crashed out of control. The subsequent investigation attributed the structural failure to 'the main rotor blades and gearbox becoming detached due to overstressing during the

demonstration' and, as a result, HQ Flying Training Command examined the possibility of deleting the 'vortex ring' demonstration from its syllabus.

F/Lt (instructor pilot) Brian Richard Galletly (3045932), RAF, aged 35, was the son of Ernest George and Lily M Galletly (née Bryant) of Rochester, Kent, and husband of Gillian Galletly (née Stokes). After enlisting in the RAF in October 1946, his first operational posting was in December 1949 when he joined 56 Squadron, piloting Meteor jets out of Thorney Island. He left the squadron in November 1951 and, following a couple of postings, was assigned to 20 Squadron in May 1953, flying the ground attack Sabre jet out of Oldenburg in Germany. Over the following seven years he was posted to various airfields in Germany, Cyprus and the UK, before undergoing helicopter pilot training in Malaya in 1960. He then joined 110 Squadron flying the Sycamore helicopter out of Butterworth and, the following February, was posted to Singapore, before flying during the Indonesian confrontation in Borneo. He returned to the UK in July 1963 and became a helicopter instructor. He is buried in Stoke upon Tern (St Peter's) Cemetery, Shropshire.

F/Lt Brian Galletly [TNA]

F/Lt (pilot u/t) Bruce Sinclair Northway (607312), RAF, aged 32, was born in Victoria, London, on 16 February 1932. After joining the RAF in 1950 he was posted to 54 Squadron in November 1953 and flew Meteor jets out of RAF Chivenor. In March 1955, he underwent training on the all-weather Hunter jet but, four months later, was posted to 96 Squadron at Ahlhorn in Germany and flew night-fighter Meteors. He returned to the UK in August 1958 and spent time as an instructor before beginning his helicopter training. He is buried in an unknown location.

F/Lt Bruce Northway [TNA]

1965

13 October (Wednesday)
Advanced autorotation exercise. CFS (H) (RAF Tern Hill, Shropshire)
Bristol Sycamore HR.14 (XE320) crashed at The Moors, Great Bolas, to the south of Peplow airfield, at 17.42 hrs. The pilot had carried out an advanced autorotation exercise in the morning, under the supervision of an instructor, before being briefed to take off at 17.13 hrs and repeat the exercise solo. The exercise was to be carried out in the vicinity of Peplow, starting at 1,500 feet and recovering by 200 feet, but after beginning the exercise it is believed that the helicopter entered a state known as a 'vortex ring' and crashed. The subsequent investigation commented that an experienced pilot might have been able to react to a 'vortex ring' quickly enough to recover, but this pilot was on appointment from the engineering branch and had not had enough flying experience.

F/Lt (pilot u/t) Ian Rennie Harvey (609097), RAF, aged 27, was the son of Norman C and Isabella D Harvey (née Rennie) of Bristol. He is buried in an unknown location.

1966

2 June (Thursday)
Joint training exercise. CFS (H) (RAF Tern Hill, Shropshire)
Westland Whirlwind HAR.10 (XP342) crashed close to Llyn Rhuddwyn, near Rhydycroesau, four miles

The wreckage of Whirlwind XP342 after it crashed into a wood near Oswestry. Amazingly, both pilots escaped with only minor injuries. [Shropshire Star]

west of Oswestry, at 11.45 hrs. Four helicopters had just dropped off soldiers from 17 Training Regiment, Park Hall Camp, at Llansilin rifle range and were making their way back to the airfield at low level, up a steep, wooded ravine, when the lead helicopter struck some high-tension power cables spanning the valley. The collision was so severe that the tail cone was torn off and the fuselage crashed into a clearing in the wood about 300 yards further on. Amazingly, the two pilots survived. The pilots of two of the remaining helicopters immediately landed nearby and the injured men were taken directly to Gobowen Orthopaedic Hospital, where the student was treated for head injuries while his instructor was treated for shock and cuts.

F/Lt (instructor pilot) John Frederick Dickin (504303), RAF. Born in Derby on 16 January 1929, he had previously flown Belvedere helicopters with 66 Squadron during the Borneo campaign, for which he was mentioned in despatches in June 1965. He retired from the RAF as a flight lieutenant in April 1972 and died in West Sussex in 2002.

P/O (pilot u/t) Richard Kingston (608487), RAF, aged 22. A native of Newport Pagnell, Buckinghamshire, he joined 66 Squadron on completion of his training and flew Belvedere helicopters.

23 June (Thursday)
Training flight. 8 Air Experience Flight (RAF Shawbury, Shropshire)
De Havilland DHC-1 Chipmunk T.10 (WK631) crashed at Tibberton Grange (at map reference 685188), near Newport, at 10.15 hrs. Three aircraft were seen manoeuvring at low altitude 'in a manner of a dogfight', although one seemed to be flying 'more steadily than the other two' and subsequently flew off on its own. The remaining two continued 'dogfighting' but, shortly afterwards, the pilot of WP834 struck the starboard tailplane of this aircraft with his port wing and the two aircraft crashed out of control. RAF Tern Hill was called for assistance and dispatched their medical officer on board a Whirlwind helicopter but, after landing, it was clear that all three occupants had been killed instantly and their bodies were taken to RAF Hospital, Cosford.

P/O (pilot) Geoffrey Wallace Dowd (4232410), RAF, aged 25, was the son of Ronald and Kathleen M Dowd (née Wallace) of the Wirral, Merseyside. He is buried in an unknown location.

P/O (pilot) Robert Anthony Spooner (4232340), RAF, aged 25, was born in Oldham, Lancashire, on 2 December 1940. He is buried in an unknown location.

Training flight. Birmingham University Air Squadron (RAF Shawbury, Shropshire)
De Havilland DHC-1 Chipmunk T.10 WP834 crashed at Tibberton Grange following the collision described above.

Cadet Pilot (pilot u/t) Michael David Fox (2607663), RAF, aged 21, was born in Birmingham, on 22

October 1944, and was a student at Birmingham University. He is buried in Donington (St Cuthbert's) Churchyard, Shropshire.

12 August (Friday)
Flight from Sleap to Abbotsinch, Glasgow, on a 'business trip'. Privately owned aircraft
Bellanca Model 14-19-3 (aircraft registration G-ASRD) crashed at Oakleigh Farm, Welshampton, to the east of Ellesmere, at 17.00 hrs. The aircraft, which was owned by Salopian Industries Ltd, was being piloted by an RAF staff officer (on leave at the time) from the Shawbury detachment of the Birmingham University Air Squadron and had just taken off, when it was seen to crash at high speed out of cloud into a hillock, killing all three on board. The cause of the accident was obscure, as no technical defect could be found, although the pilot had 'a moderately severe cold at the time and had taken medication which could have made him feel drowsy, but insufficient evidence was found to come to any firm conclusions'.

F/Lt (pilot) John Joseph McMahon (588231), RAF, aged 31, was born in Liscannor, County Clare, on 17 June 1935. He was an experienced pilot and was an 'instrument rating examiner' with the Birmingham University Air Squadron at RAF Shawbury. He is buried in Shawbury (St Mary's) Churchyard, Shropshire.

Mr (co-pilot) Stanley W Barnett, aged 35. He was the owner of S Barnett (Builders) Ltd, which was a subsidiary of Salopian Industries Ltd.

Mr (passenger) Robert Burns Malcolm, aged 62. He was a poultry dealer from Auchengate in Scotland and was a customer of Salopian Industries Ltd.

12 September (Monday)
Low-level tactical formation flying. CFS (H) (RAF Tern Hill, Shropshire)
Westland Whirlwind HAR.10 (XP394) crash-landed at Cheswardine at 11.15 hrs. The pilot was flying number 2 in a formation of three helicopters, when he 'pulled in the power after a turn to port in order to keep station with the lead aircraft' and immediately felt the aircraft falter and sink. At the same time his RPM's and compressor fell rapidly, while a smell of hot vaporising fuel entered the cockpit. He immediately 'lowered the collective lever and started to turn into the wind but had to flare the aircraft immediately and landed without being able to switch anything off'. As the helicopter settled down on the ground the pilot heard a loud crack as the rotor blades struck the tail cone and he quickly switched off all power and jumped clear of the helicopter, only returning to operate the fire extinguisher. The wreckage was subsequently airlifted by a salvage team from 60 MU, RAF Leconfield, to RAF Tern Hill, where an examination found that 'computer instability caused throttle trim back' and a sudden loss of power.

P/O (pilot u/t) Christopher John Taylor (4232465), RAF, aged 22. He was designated 'specialist aircrew' in May 1982 and eventually retired as a flight lieutenant in March 1994.

Whirlwind XP394 pictured in a field near Cheswardine following the accident. [Shropshire Star]

1969

The tail unit of the Jet Provost lies on the mist-shrouded hilltop of Brown Clee Hill. [Shropshire Star]

F/Lt John Watson in front of a Jet Provost. [Iain Watson]

24 January (Friday)
Low-level training exercise. CFS (RAF Little Rissington, Gloucestershire)
Hunting Jet Provost T.3 (XM360) crashed at Abdon Burf (at map reference 590870) on Brown Clee Hill, at 12.45 hrs. The aircraft was flying through thick cloud and mist when a sudden increase in engine noise was heard by local residents, suggesting that the instructor had seen high ground ahead but had insufficient time to clear the hilltop.

F/Lt (instructor pilot) John Sims Watson (607747), RAF, aged 31, was born in South Shields on 10 April 1937. He is commemorated at the Cheltenham Crematorium.

P/O (pilot u/t) Ian Scott Primrose (608772), RAF, aged 22, was born in Stirling, Scotland, on 5 October 1947. He is commemorated at the Cheltenham Crematorium.

1970

22 April (Wednesday)
Display team practice flight. CFS (H) (RAF Tern Hill, Shropshire)
Westland Sioux HT.2 (XV310) crashed at Lockleywood, near Hinstock, at 08.48 hrs. Two pilots had completed an early morning practice for the 'Tomahawks' display team at Chetwynd airfield and were returning to base in close formation at 500 feet, when a collision occurred. In an e-mail to the author in 2008 Keith Ifould recalled how:

> Somehow we managed to collide on this routine part of the flight. Our rotors struck each other, which in a helicopter is quite dramatic! To this day I am not sure how it happened but I was held responsible as it was I who struck the lead helicopter in the formation.

In fact, the official accident report stated that he 'failed to appreciate [the] decrease in distance between the main rotors of the two aircraft and eventually got so close that the rotors collided'. It did, however, add that an aggravating factor may have been the distraction caused by 'the procedure adopted to complete the radio frequency change'. As a result of the accident F/O Ifould spent three months in RAF Hospital, Cosford, undergoing treatment for a fractured spine. The pilot of XV316 was less seriously injured but was treated for several broken ribs.

The wreckage of the two Sioux helicopters lying in a field at Hinstock. [Shropshire Star]

F/O (pilot u/t) Keith William Ifould (4232498), RAF, aged 23, was awarded the AFC in the New Year's Honours list of 1983 and appointed CBE in 2000. He retired from the RAF as a group captain in January 2001 and currently works as a director of the RAF Museum.

Display team practice flight. CFS (H) (RAF Tern Hill, Shropshire)
Westland Sioux HT.2 (XV316) crashed at Lockleywood following the collision described above.
F/Lt (pilot u/t) Ronald Henry Cunningham (3509754), RAF, aged 37. He retired from the RAF as a squadron leader in April 1975.

1973

1 November (Thursday)
Final review test. 4 FTS (RAF Valley, Anglesey)
Hawker Hunter T.7 (XL596) crashed at Besford Wood, near Preston Brockhurst, at 14.58 hrs. The instructor and his Jordanian student were carrying out a practice diversion to RAF Shawbury and were approaching at 1,500 feet when instructions were received from the control tower to decrease height. The order was received but the student

Hunter XL596 pictured at RAF Valley three months prior to its loss in Shropshire [Steve Williams]

Left: RAF Shawbury's crash team and ambulance look on at the smouldering wreckage of Hunter XL596. [Shropshire Star]

reacted with too rapid a rate of descent and, when advised of this, he overcorrected and gained too much height. At about 2 3/4 miles distance from the airfield the aircraft was seen to veer rapidly to the right then, 1/2 mile further on, it turned back towards the glide path but dropped below it. The aircraft continued to descend until it disappeared from Shawbury's radar and, moments later, ploughed into trees and crashed. The reason for the crash could not be explained.

S/Ldr (instructor pilot) Ronald Clive Etheridge (2454968), RAF, aged 42, was born in Woolwich, London, on 14 August 1931. He is commemorated at Colwyn Bay Crematorium.

Officer Cadet (pilot u/t) Abdullah Qasim Nasourat, RJAF, aged 20. Burial location unknown.

1975

9 April (Wednesday)

Routine training flight to Wales. 1 Squadron (RAF Wittering, Cambridgeshire)

Hawker Harrier GR.3 (XV776) crashed into Powkesmore Coppice, near Ditton Priors, at 16.25 hrs. Two Harriers were returning to base at 3,000 feet when the main engine bearing in this aircraft failed and the pilot was forced to eject after switching on his emergency frequency. The pilot parachuted to safety at Shipton, while his aircraft continued for approximately three miles before striking the ground and leaving a 1/2 mile long trail of wreckage strewn across two fields and the Ditton Priors–Ashfield road. According to a dramatic article published in the *Shropshire Star*, RAF Shawbury received the pilot's emergency transmission and a big rescue operation was put under way, with two helicopters taking off from RAF Tern Hill to aid in the search. On their arrival in the approximate area, the pilot's ejector seat was located at Willow Hope Farm, Longville in the Dale and, soon afterwards, the pilot was found in a hilly, wooded area during a particularly heavy snowstorm. The first helicopter touched down and picked up the slightly injured pilot but, as it lifted off, it struck some power cables and had to be put down in a field with damaged rotor blades. Fortunately, the second helicopter was able to pick up the Harrier pilot and conveyed him to RAF Shawbury where he was treated for cuts above his eye.

F/Lt (pilot) Jonathan Leslie Buckler (608711), RAF, aged 28. Commissioned in August 1967, he eventually retired as a group captain in July 2001.

Search and rescue flight to locate pilot of crashed Harrier aircraft. CFS (H) (RAF Tern Hill, Shropshire) Westland Whirlwind HAR.10 (XR453) landed 'near Shipton', in the Corve Dale, at approximately 16.45 hrs. As

Harrier XV776 pictured at RAF Gütersloh, in Germany, five months prior to its loss. [Günter Grondstein]

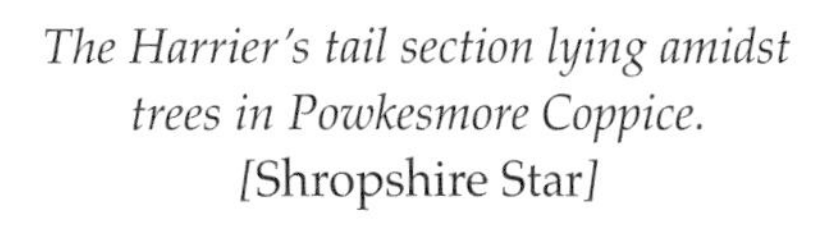

The Harrier's tail section lying amidst trees in Powkesmore Coppice. [Shropshire Star]

a result of the damage to the three rotor blades, the helicopter had to be repaired in situ before it could be flown out again.

F/Lt (pilot) Alexander Campbell Sneddon (4231960), RAF. Commissioned in November 1963, he was appointed an MBE in June 1979 and left the RAF as a squadron leader in March 1988.

F/Sgt (?) Nigel Garden, RAF.

W/Cdr (Doctor) Edward Gilbert, RAF.

Whirlwind XR453 being repaired on site, near Shipton, after suffering a 'wire strike'. [TNA]

1976

8 October (Friday)
Circuit training. 4 FTS (RAF Valley, Anglesey)
Folland Gnat T.1 (XR996) crashed at Besford, near Preston Brockhurst, to the north of Shawbury airfield. Little is known of the accident other than that the instructor and his student were carrying out circuit flying at RAF Shawbury when the aircraft crashed into a stubble field half a mile north of the airfield. According to a contemporary report in the *Shropshire Star* newspaper, among the first people at the scene were Chris Morgan and Rod Oakley, who were working on alterations at nearby Besford Grange. Mr Morgan said that 'We saw the cloud of black smoke and immediately went over the fields to it,' while Mr Oakley added that 'there was nothing left of the plane that was recognizable. It would have been impossible for the pilots to have got out.'

F/Lt (instructor pilot) John Leszek Grzybowski (8024979), RAF, aged 27, was the son of S/Ldr Leszek Kazimierz Grzybowski, AFC, and Joan M Fleming, and the husband of Patricia L Grzybowski (née Harrison) of Faringdon, Oxfordshire. He is commemorated at Shrewsbury Crematorium.

F/O (pilot u/t) Ashley William Smart (5202359), RAF, aged 21, was the son of William L and Nellie Smart (née Amies) of Solihull, although at the time of his death his address was given as Moulsford, Oxfordshire. He is commemorated at Shrewsbury Crematorium.

The wreckage of Gnat XR996 lies strewn across fields near Shawbury airfield. [Shropshire Star]

Non-Flying Fatalities

A record of the men and women who have died in Shropshire, due to non-aviation related causes, while on active duty.

04.10.17 – Gnr WH Herford (AFC), Shawbury
17.10.17 – Miss LM Birch (civilian), Shawbury
10.02.18 – Cpl A Morgan (AFC), Shawbury
05.04.18 – AM2 FW Mason (RAF), 1 Sch of Balloon Inst
10.11.18 – 2 Lt GP Cilliers (RAF), Tern Hill
13.11.18 – Pte OG Kious (USAAS), Shawbury
11.01.19 – Sgt F Richards (RAF), recently discharged
12.04.19 – AM1 E Dyke (RAF), unit unknown
09.08.19 – AC1 CA Jones (RAF), RAF Depot, Harlescott
11.08.19 – Pte F Ogden (RAF), Tern Hill
10.03.20 – Pte TJ Jones (RAF), recently discharged
09.04.20 – AM2 E Lloyd (RAF), unit unknown
25.12.20 – LAC DJ Jeffreys (RAF), Aeroplane Supply Depot
01.07.38 – Cpl JW Holliday (RAF), Shawbury
14.01.39 – Sgt T Greaves (RAF), Buntingsdale Hall
08.03.39 – AC J West (RAF), Cosford
17.11.39 – FW Boon (civilian), Shawbury
11.02.40 – AC2 IE Thomas (RAF), Locking
18.02.40 – AC1 CVM Winn (RAF), Cosford
28.02.40 – AC2 WT Meacham (RAF), Cosford
28.02.40 – Sister AS Ketley (PMRAFNS), Cosford
23.05.40 – Cpl F McCormach (RAF), Cosford
30.05.40 – AC2 GM Mountain (RAF), Hednesford
06.06.40 – AC2 AG Carpenter (RAF), Hednesford
29.06.40 – AC1 JJJ Walker (RAF), Hednesford
11.07.40 – AC2 CJ Chappell (RAF), Tern Hill
10.08.40 – AC2 E Jones (RAF), Kirton in Lindsey
12.08.40 – LAC AEK Briggs (RAF), Shawbury
31.08.40 – AC1 NH Hateley (RAF), Shawbury
01.09.40 – AC1 E Williamson (RAF), Shawbury
06.09.40 – AC2 A Reynard (RAF), Hednesford
10.09.40 – Sapper GB Waugh (Royal Engineers), Tern Hill
24.09.40 – F/Sgt GFJ James (RAF), Cosford
30.10.40 – AC2 J Santer (RAF), Bridgnorth
16.11.40 – AC2 H Smith (RAF), Cosford/Castle Bromwich
24.11.40 – P/O RE Dease (RAF), Air Ministry Unit, London
20.11.40 – HJ Ardley (civilian), Tern Hill
25.12.40 – AC2 RW Baker (RAF), Bridgnorth
24.01.41 – LAC E Orlowski (PAF), Shawbury
25.01.41 – AC2 GW Robinson (RAF), Bridgnorth
30.01.41 – W/O J Campbell (RAF), Castle Bromwich
11.02.41 – Cpl SE Lyons (RAF), Wythall
02.03.41 – AC2 DR Hilton (RAF), Bridgnorth
12.03.41 – AC2 M Blue (RAF), Bridgnorth
13.03.41 – LAC KR Taylor (RAF), Tern Hill
15.04.41 – AC2 AF Prior (RAF), Pembrey
16.05.41 – AC2 J Morrison (RAF), Bridgnorth
20.05.41 – W/O J Burke (RAF), Bridgnorth
02.06.41 – AC2 EJ Griffiths (RAF), Shawbury
24.06.41 – LAC RJ McLintock (RAF), Monkmoor
06.08.41 – AC2 JF Mahoney (RAF), Hednesford
11.08.41 – AC2 CF Gale (RAF), Bridgnorth
17.08.41 – AC2 GS Freeman (RAF), Bridgnorth
18.08.41 – AC2 I Trim (RAF), Cosford
01.09.41 – P/O GB Rushton (RAF), High Ercall
10.09.41 – AC2 PA Pacitto (RAF), Perton
13.09.41 – AC2 H Fairhurst (RAF), Hednesford
24.09.41 – LAC J McKeever (RAF), Tern Hill
29.09.41 – LAC CHJ Clements (RAF), Leeming
17.11.41 – ACW2 KM Threshie (WAAF), Bridgnorth
18.11.41 – W/O T Webb (RAF), Stafford
24.11.41 – Cpl JH Jones (RAF), Tern Hill
07.12.41 – LAC RJ Ogborn (RAF), Cosford
16.12.41 – Cpl JE Jones (RAF), Cosford
25.12.41 – AC1 WA Elliott (RAF), Penrhos
02.02.42 – Sgt WE Elliott (RAF), Bridgnorth
08.02.42 – F/Sgt W Ware (RAF), Cosford
08.02.42 – AC2 AJ Joyner (RAF), Stafford
09.02.42 – AC2 J Sneddon (RAF), Kirkham
15.02.42 – AC2 AR Davies (RAF), West Bromwich
03.03.42 – AC2 RH Lucas (RAF), Cosford
08.03.42 – AC2 CP Thompson (RAF), Shawbury
21.03.42 – LAC JJ Ayres (RAF), Stafford
03.04.42 – LAC J Kyle (RAF), Atcham
10.04.42 – Cpl J McElin (RAF), Atcham (?)
13.04.42 – ACW2 PD Shevlin (WAAF), Buntingsdale Hall
17.05.42 – Cpl FA Cunliffe (WAAF), Buntingsdale Hall
21.05.42 – AC2 FG Byrne (RAF), Cosford
22.06.42 – AC1 G Bate (RAF), Bobbington
19.07.42 – ACW2 MG Todd (WAAF), Bridgnorth
10.08.42 – LAC ME Nicholls (RAF), Monkmoor
20.08.42 – ACW1 WV Sweet (WAAF), Cosford
23.08.42 – ACW1 DW Oliver (WAAF), High Ercall
25.08.42 – LAC MJ O'Brien (RAF), Rednal/Montford Bridge
27.08.42 – LAC E Evans (RAF), High Ercall
03.09.42 – AC1 F Hulme (RAF), Shawbury
03.09.42 – AC2 HJ Foster (RAF), Monkmoor
07.09.42 – Cpl JW Witney (RAF), Atcham
16.09.42 – F/Sgt GO Clement (RAF), Ludlow
24.09.42 – F/Lt W BBH Griffith (RAF), Condover
04.10.42 – Cpl D O'Shea (RAF), Cosford
08.10.42 – AC1 GC Milne (RAF), Tern Hill
12.10.42 – LAC WE Deas (WAAF), Stafford
14.10.42 – AC2 WA Barton (RAF), Whitchurch Heath
19.10.42 – Sgt RE Nicholson (RAF), Cosford
09.11.42 – LAC KCritchlow (RAF), Bobbington
11.11.42 – P/O HCN Adams (RAF), Wheaton Aston
15.11.42 – AC1 MW Armitage (RAF), Hixon
17.11.42 – Sgt H Roscoe (RAF), Hixon
29.11.42 – Sgt WJ Clinton (RAF), Cosford
01.12.42 – AC1 CE Hole (RAF), Perton
14.01.43 – AS Pitt (civilian), Whitchurch Heath
25.01.43 – LAC WMM Farmer (WAAF), Tern Hill
31.01.43 – Cpl R Roberts (RAF), Towyn

31.01.43 – G/Capt FG Sherriff, OBE, MC, MiD (RAF), Cosford
02.02.43 – AC2 RF Bonnick (RAF), Shawbury
11.02.43 – AM2 CEF Handy (RN), Hednesford
12.02.43 – 3rd Officer JJ Wallis (ATA), ATA
17.02.43 – ACW1 EN Snape (WAAF), Cosford
20.02.43 – LAC JW Lines (RAF), Alness
24.02.43 – W/O C Stovell (RAAF), Valley
28.03.43 – F/Sgt R Platt (RAF), Cosford
08.04.43 – F/O JHW Harrison-Broadley (RAF), Atcham
12.04.43 – Cpl SJ Tipler (RAF), unit unknown
02.05.43 – LAC TJ Williams (RAF), Whitchurch Heath
05.05.43 – Air Fitter WJ Abbott (RN), Hednesford
09.05.43 – Sgt HE Boyd (RAF), Portreath
21.05.43 – AC2 J Hook (RAF), Cosford
25.05.43 – AC2 A Hughes (RAF), Bridgnorth
31.05.43 – LACW BI Howl (WAAF), Bridgnorth
02.06.43 – LAC AW Clear (RAF), Rednal
30.07.43 – F/Lt HR Hunt (RAF), Biggin Hill (?)
08.08.43 – Cpl L Thorpe (WAAF), Sutton Coldfield
17.08.43 – P/O BW Norman (RAF), Sleap
20.08.43 – P/O DR Ford (RAF), Sleap
25.08.43 – LAC WBHM Turner (WAAF), Rednal
ACW1 B Robertson (WAAF), Rednal
26.08.43 – F/Sgt CW Early (RNZAF), Rednal
18.09.43 – LAC J Campbell (RAF), Tern Hill
24.09.43 – Sgt AJ Sedgwick (RAF), Cosford
01.10.43 – ACW2 JM Lord (WAAF), Peplow
07.10.43 – Cpl AT Darke (RAF), Bridgnorth
04.11.43 – AC2 PJ McIlroy (RAF), Tilstock
20.11.43 – Cpl SR Smyth (RAF), Tilstock
28.11.43 – LAC WN Rosser (WAAF), Rednal
12.12.43 – P/O FC McCrae (RAAF), Lichfield
04.01.44 – Sgt LD Higgins (RAF), Tern Hill
20.01.44 – W/O H Cross (RAF), 93 Group
20.01.44 – Sjt RG Bates (GPR), Sleap or Tilstock
31.01.44 – Cpl HA Maxwell (RAF), Wellesbourne Mountford
08.02.44 – LAC E Waite (RAF), Bridgnorth
09.02.44 – W/O FJ Harper (RAF), Cosford
13.02.44 – Cpl WG Daltry (RAF), Cosford
15.02.44 – Cpl JT Payne (RAF), Peplow
11.03.44 – LAC AHW Brockman (RAF), Cosford
20.03.44 – LAC ER Maggs (RAF), Filton
27.03.44 – AC2 KW Pilbrow (RAF), Bridgnorth
20.04.44 – Cpl JV Benkel (USAAF), Atcham
17.05.44 – LAC WH Siggins (RAF), Cosford
25.05.44 – ACW2 BM Taylor (WAAF), Hednesford
25.07.44 – Cpl R Motley (RAF), unit unknown
27.07.44 – Airman E Knutel (*Luftwaffe*), POW
06.08.44 – F/O RSM Lees (RAF), Air Ministry
08.08.44 – Sgt D Gaymer (RAF), South Cerney
18.09.44 – LAC OW Phillips (RAF), Tilstock
19.09.44 – AC1 C Archer (RAF), Tilstock
01.10.44 – ACW1 ED Hobbs (WAAF), Aston Down
02.10.44 – AC2 TJ Lucyna (PAF), Croughton
27.10.44 – AC2 R Garrat (RAF), Bridgnorth
05.11.44 – Cpl LCL Cawthorn (RAF), Spilsby
13.11.44 – AM2 RS Liversage (RN), Tern Hill
15.11.44 – S/Ldr NB Silk (RAF), Hartlebury
01.12.44 – F/O FW Evans (RAF), Bridgnorth
24.12.44 – LAC AG Jelfs (RAF Regt), Gatwick
04.01.45 – LAC R Willoughby (RAF), Tilstock
06.01.45 – Cadet Sgt RB Biddulph, ATC
25.01.45 – AC1 E Aston (RAF), Shawbury
29.01.45 – Naval Airman 2 EH Simpson (RN), Hinstock
04.02.45 – AC1 GH Parton (RAF), Bridgnorth
15.02.45 – Cpl R Salter (RAF), West Kirby
17.03.45 – Cpl HK Ellis (RAF), unit unknown
23.03.45 – LAC DP Holloway (RAF), recently discharged
24.03.45 – AM1 GC McCallum (RN), Tern Hill
02.04.45 – AC1 J Wightman (RAF), Aston Down
07.04.45 – LAC WM Nicholson (WAAF), Aston Down
13.05.45 – AC2 DA Lee (RAF), Hartlebury
18.07.45 – LAC E Williams (RAF), Monkmoor
30.07.45 – Air Artificier 3 WV Snowdon (RN), Hinstock
03.08.45 – LAC RF Hall (RAF), Tern Hill
11.08.45 – AM1 JD Harding (RN), Hinstock
11.08.45 – LAC JH Hall (RAF), Stafford
08.09.45 – W/O S Theaker (RAF), Full Sutton
14.09.45 – F/Lt HR Evans (RAF), Innsworth
08.10.45 – ACW1 H Bacchus (WAAF), Wheaton Aston
16.10.45 – 3rd Officer MJ Pearson (WRNS), Hinstock
21.12.45 – LAC WBA Fisher (WAAF), Cosford
22.01.48 – AC2 JE Gaines (RAF), Bridgnorth
26.06.48 – AC1 SH Bond (RAF), Tern Hill
23.08.48 – MP Roberts (civilian), Cosford
07.11.48 – LAC RR Stephen (RAF), Lichfield
18.11.48 – AC1 HN Nicholls (RAF), Bridgnorth
17.12.48 – AC2 AK Palmer (RAF), Cosford
17.12.48 – AC2 W Anderson (RAF), Bridgnorth
18.12.48 – F/Lt EG Taylor (RAF), Shawbury
02.01.49 – AC2 CG Porter (RAF), Bridgnorth
12.02.49 – Sgt EP Davies (RAF), Stoke Heath
24.10.49 – F/Lt WF Jones (RAF), Shawbury
06.12.49 – F/Sgt RW Wright (RAF), Bridgnorth
17.12.49 – F/Lt PJ Carney (RAF), Tern Hill
29.09.50 – AC2 KA Thomas (RAF), Bridgnorth
09.12.50 – Sgt EC Baldwin (RAF), Stoke Heath
08.03.51 – Officer Cadet RS Cross (RAF), Tern Hill
18.04.51 – F/Lt M Bennetts, MC (RAF), Bridgnorth
28.05.51 – AC1 NE Hodgkinson (RAF), Tern Hill
01.09.51 – Sgt E Cullen (RAF), Cosford
14.02.52 – F/O IB Bond (RAF), Shawbury
18.04.52 – Jnr Tech H Hutchinson (RAF), Stoke Heath
28.05.52 – Boy Ent PM Watkins (RAF), Cosford
01.11.52 – LAC IG Holden (RAF), Tilstock
24.12.52 – LAC WGH Humphreys (RAF), Stoke Heath
30.04.53 – AC2 AWS Seymour (RAF), Bridgnorth
15.10.53 – LAC S Plant (RAF), Stoke Heath
11.03.54 – AC2 PC Barnes (RAF), Bridgnorth
28.05.54 – SAC JG Sankey (RAF), Cosford
19.06.54 – F/Lt K Polton (RAF), Shawbury
31.07.54 – Boy Entrant D Heyworth (RAF), Cosford
04.10.54 – S/Ldr R Alexander, AFC (RAF), Stoke Heath
23.01.55 – Jnr Tech AP Jones (RAF), Bridgnorth
15.08.55 – SAC FT Morris (RAF), Stoke Heath
31.10.55 – LAC GA Fox (RAF), Stoke Heath
09.01.56 – Jnr Tech GA Murphy (RAF), Stoke Heath
13.02.56 – LAC P Drury (RAF), Stoke Heath
26.02.56 – AC2 DK Steven (RAF), Stoke Heath
19.11.56 – Master Pilot FV Ryans (RAF), Shawbury
23.07.57 – WH Massey (civilian), Buntingsdale Hall
30.07.57 – P/O ED Gollan (RAF), Shawbury
07.11.57 – A/Cpl RD Smith (RAF), Stoke Heath
25.04.58 – Cpl JR Connell (RAF), Bridgnorth
03.06.58 – AC2 TB McNeill (RAF), Bridgnorth
13.02.59 – Boy Ent MR Kennedy (RAF), Cosford
03.04.59 – Cpl PAM Ogilvie (RAF), Bridgnorth
05.04.59 – Master Pilot RE Phillips (RAF), Shawbury
02.05.59 – Chief Tech CC Brotheridge (RAF), Cosford

28.06.59 – Master Gunner JF Dowsing (RAF), Shawbury
14.09.59 – Sgt ME Townley (WRAF), Malvern
15.12.59 – AC2 RM Craig (RAF), Bridgnorth
29.07.60 – SAC PJ Rodway (RAF), Shawbury
23.03.61 – Boy Ent KJ Munro (RAF), Cosford
26.08.61 – SAC PI Woodhouse (RAF), Shawbury
27.08.61 – ACW1 BM Hutchison (WRAF), Shawbury
15.10.61 – Chief Tech AC Challoner (RAF), Tern Hill
28.09.61 – Sgt HA Erwin (RAF), Innsworth
24.10.61 – Boy Ent M Shaw (RAF), Cosford
03.12.61 – Jnr Tech DF Hughes (RAF), Shawbury
17.05.62 – W/O G Jinks (RAF), Cosford
27.10.62 – F/Sgt J Paterson (RAF), Cosford
26.02.64 – F/Lt PJ Burridge (RAF), Cosford
19.03.65 – S/Ldr R Williams (RAF), Stafford
23.12.65 – F/Lt A Jones (RAF), Shawbury
11.09.66 – W/O KW Hazel (RAF), Cosford
15.10.66 – SAC PJ McMeeken (RAF), Cosford
09.03.67 – F/Sgt DR Barker (RAF), Swanton Morley
10.03.67 – SAC T Timney (RAF), Cosford
20.08.67 – S/Ldr WC Rees, MBE (RAF), Shawbury
08.11.67 – SAC ME Judge (RAF), Cosford
01.05.68 – W/O J Duffield (RAF), Innsworth
06.08.68 – G/Capt WG Thomson, MRCS, LRCP (RAF), Cosford
20.01.69 – W/O PC McCann, BEM (RAF), Cosford
26.11.69 – Sgt GJF Birch (RAF), Cosford
30.01.71 – ACW RJS Smith (RAF), Cosford
13.02.71 – A/Sgt T Moran (RAF), Cosford
14.06.71 – A/Cpl PD Lewis (RAF), Cosford
14.04.72 – F/Lt T Currie AFC (RAF), Shawbury
18.06.72 – Sgt H Dudey (RAF), Cosford
12.07.72 – W/O AE Stinson (RAF), Cosford
12.01.74 – F/Lt RL Shenton (RAF), Cosford
08.05.74 – F/Lt K MacDonald (RAF), Tern Hill
30.08.74 – Cpl JF Chalker (RAF), Tern Hill
17.03.75 – Cpl CA Synnott (RAF), Tern Hill
22.12.78 – Sgt D Nesbitt (RAF), Cosford
15.05.79 – F/Lt BH Sparks, MBE (RAF), Shawbury
30.04.80 – SAC RCE North (RAF), Shawbury
20.11.81 – Sgt ME Bundy (RAF), Shawbury
10.10.83 – Cpl C Vast (RAF), Cosford
11.10.84 – App Tech DN McCaffer (RAF), Cosford
30.05.86 – SAC MA Cronshaw (RAF), Shawbury
SAC DP Pendred (RAF), Shawbury
16.08.86 – F/Lt GL McCracken (RAF), Shawbury
15.03.88 – Able Seaman GM Davies (RN), Cosford
24.03.92 – App Tech A Downey (RAF), Cosford
30.04.97 – AC LA Smith (RAF), Cosford
03.05.98 – F/Sgt PP Fallon (RAF), Cosford
18.11.99 – SAC MT Wilkes (RAF), Cosford

Sources

Archive Documentation:

Aviation Archaeology Investigation and Research (AAIR), Falcon Field, Mesa, Arizona, USA
Report of air accident files (USAAF).
Photos from crash reports.

Library and Archives Canada
Personnel and casualty files
WW1 attestation papers

The National Archives at Kew, London:
Air Force award citation (AIR 2)
Air Force Lists
AVIA files
Navy Lists
Operations Record Books (AIR 27, 28 & 29)
POW Questionnaires (WO344)
Personnel Files in AIR 4 Series
RAF intelligence documents on downed German aircraft and crews (AIR 40)

National Archives of Australia
A705 casualty files
A9301 RAAF Personnel files, 1921–48
B2455 AIF Personnel Dossiers,1914–20

Polish Institute and Sikorski Museum London
Personnel files

RAF Museum Department of Research and Information Services (DORIS), Hendon, London:
Aircraft accident cards
Aircraft movement cards
1939–45 RAF casualty list
ATA personnel files
Aircrew logbooks
First World War casualty cards

Shropshire Archives, Shrewsbury:
Shropshire ARP HQ War Diary (1818/106)
WARG documents

South African Department of Defence Documentation Centre
Personnel files

Newspapers:

The Border Counties Advertiser
The Bridgnorth Journal
The Newport and Market Drayton Advertiser
The Shrewsbury Advertiser
The Shrewsbury Chronicle
The Shropshire Star
The Wellington Journal

Index to Crash Sites

Ackleton, 277
Acton Burnell, 64, 86, 128, 220, 228
Acton Lea (near Shawbury), 46, 87
Adderley, 152, 158, 230, 284
Admaston, 81
Albrighton (near Cosford), 71, 239, 261, 263, 277
Alcaston, 174
Alkington, 101, 213, 264
Allscott, 73, 115
All Stretton, 128
Alveley, 85, 148, 153, 204
Ashford Carbonell, 226
Ash Magna, 96, 167, 209, 247, 269, 284
Asterley, 232
Aston, 188, 189, 195
Aston on Clun, 166
Atcham airfield, 89, 95, 112, 157, 170, 183, 205, 221, 224, 259, 269
Atcham village, 144, 259
Baggy Moor, 229, 263, 264
Bagley/Bagley Marsh, 117, 133, 229
Baschurch, 38, 40, 53, 61, 114, 174, 217, 218
Battlefield, 67, 173, 191
Bayston Hill, 60, 77, 242
Beckbury, 148
Bedstone, 183
Bettisfield, 37
Betton Strange, 77, 240
Billingsley, 51, 163
Bing's Heath, 167
Bishop's Castle, 62, 160
Bletchley, 35, 62, 66, 73, 91, 173, 278, 280, 283
Bobbington, 128, 178
Bolas Heath (see Great Bolas)
Bomere Heath, 82, 120, 148, 151, 203, 204, 272, 286
Brandwood, 60
Bratton, 91, 98, 144, 218
Bridgnorth, 43, 44, 51, 52, 54, 56, 64, 85, 103, 106, 122, 140, 141, 148, 150, 153, 156, 163, 165, 192, 204, 234, 235, 237, 249, 262, 277
Bridleway Gate, 110, 171
Brockton (Corve Dale), 261
Brockton (near Lilleshall), 253
Brockton (near Shifnal), 200
Broseley, 127, 174, 211
Brown Clee Hill (see Clee Hill)
Buntingsdale, 65
Burlton, 60
Burwarton, 101, 124, 145, 279
Buttonoak, 99, 270
Callaughton, 58, 127
Calverhall, 63
Cardington, 187
Cherrington, 80, 196, 231
Cheswardine, 43, 63, 73, 75, 100, 293
Chetwynd airfield, 92, 122, 135, 137, 202, 248
Chetwynd Aston, 103
Chetwynd Heath, 105
Child's Ercall village, 30, 37, 76, 82, 86, 122, 208, 214
Child's Ercall airfield (see Peplow airfield)
Chirbury, 110
Church Stretton, 40, 41, 106, 131, 151, 187, 205, 247, 249
Claverley, 54, 106
Clee Hill, 50, 61, 68, 101, 106, 124,125, 131, 145, 150, 180, 254, 256, 294
Clee St Margaret, 106
Cleobury Mortimer, 155
Clun, 215
Clungunford, 164
Cockshutt, 71
Colehurst, 21, 159, 283
Commonwood, 261
Condover, 60, 191, 198, 199, 208, 242, 265
Condover airfield, 152, 155, 190
Corve Dale, 32, 46, 179, 261, 296
Cosford, 50, 71, 75, 82, 86, 88, 192, 275, 280
Cotonwood, 213
Coxbank, 158, 230
Crackley Bank, 180
Craven Arms, 46, 174, 193, 194, 241
Cressage, 55, 56, 105, 134, 186, 191, 207, 265
Cross Houses, 144, 240, 241
Cruckton, 102, 233
Crudgington, 185
Dawley, 223
Derrington, 58
Ditton Priors, 32, 296
Donington (Albrighton), 261, 263
Dorrington, 186, 210
Dudleston Heath (Old Dudleston), 67, 109, 111, 113
Eaton (near Bishop's Castle), 62
Eaton Constantine, 55, 103, 137
Eaton on Tern, 201, 289
Edgmond, 35, 83, 103, 244
Elbridge, 114, 115
Ellerdine, 128, 248
Ellerton, 36, 72, 169
Ellesmere, 34, 47, 51, 55, 56, 67, 71, 100, 109, 111, 113, 117, 118, 121, 123, 150, 152, 156, 197, 260, 293
Ensdon, 122, 248
Eyton on Severn, 207
Eyton upon the Weald Moors, 134
Fauls, 49, 62, 71, 105, 242, 278, 283
Fenns Bank, 235
Ford, 200, 213, 233
Forton Heath, 34
Gobowen, 64, 107
Grafton, 95
Great Bolas, 37, 246, 256, 291
Great Chatwell, 169
Grinshill, 108, 138
Hadley, 35, 141
Hadnall, 54, 108, 261, 284, 286
Hampton Loade, 150
Hanwood, 102, 152, 233
Hardwick, 108
Harley, 191, 220

Harmer Hill, 131, 218, 267
Harnage, 186, 220
Haughmond Hill, 138, 215, 250
Haughton, 113, 119, 139, 264
Haughton (Haughmond Hill), 138
Hawkstone, 271, 279
Helshaw Grange (near Tern Hill), 70, 79, 199, 225
High Ercall, 39, 85, 94, 110, 130, 148
High Ercall airfield, 101, 124, 159, 185, 200, 210, 220
High Hatton, 47, 52, 245
Highley, 74, 103
Hinstock, 30, 36, 48, 65, 72, 73, 84, 89, 123, 169, 179, 255, 294
Hinton, 40
Hodnet, 20, 33, 51, 60, 63, 88, 92, 102, 113, 116, 142, 190, 219, 278, 285
Hopton, 63, 113, 142, 278
Hordley / Hordley Grange, 34, 51, 55, 67, 100, 208
Horton, 253, 261, 264
Howle (near Newport), 79, 255
Hughley, 64
Hungryhatton, 123, 180
Ightfield, 107, 198, 247, 284
Ironbridge, 43, 219
Isombridge, 115, 168, 206, 209
Kemberton, 200
Kenley, 64, 86
Kenstone, 51
Kenwick, 71
Ketley, 254
Kingsnordley, 141
Kinlet, 103, 289
Kinnerley, 109, 250
Kynnersley, 49
Lawley (near Wellington), 225, 226
Leaton, 203, 204
Leebotwood, 205, 237, 247, 273
Lee Brockhurst, 43, 78, 102
Leegomery, 142
Leighton, 105, 225
Lilleshall, 75, 79, 83, 160, 253, 267
Linley, 160
Little Stretton, 147
Little Wenlock, 269
Llynclys, 96, 242
Lockleywood, 294, 295
Longden Common, 191
Longdon on Tern, 85, 115, 168, 190, 206
Longford / Longford Grange, 37, 63, 177, 178, 280, 287
Long Mynd (The), 106, 117, 128, 151
Longnor, 210, 237
Longville in the Dale, 296
Loppington, 147, 249, 253, 258
Loughton, 279
Lower Ledwyche, 145
Ludlow, 50, 56, 61, 84, 145, 207, 226, 254, 256
Lyneal, 260
Madeley, 140
Maesbrook, 207, 208, 242
Maesbury, 159
Marchamley, 271, 279
Market Drayton, 27, 35, 37, 39, 42, 43, 63, 66, 87, 91, 152, 154, 158, 162, 173, 179, 184, 185, 197, 212, 223, 230, 235, 284
Melverley, 109
Middleton, 154
Montford Bridge, 32, 34, 200, 234
Montford Bridge airfield, 95, 99, 135, 143, 168, 198, 253, 265
Morda, 114, 244
More, 62
Moreton Corbet, 51, 70, 72, 156, 274
Moreton Say, 173, 223, 280
Morville, 56
Much Wenlock, 42, 58, 127, 167, 168, 203, 251, 261, 267
Muckleton, 113, 128, 248
Myddle, 131, 147, 199, 218
Nesscliffe, 68, 176, 265
Newport, 35, 36, 62, 79, 103, 105, 117, 169, 216, 253, 255, 275, 277, 292
Norton, 95
Norton in Hales, 235
Oakengates, 121
Ollerton, 20, 65, 76, 230, 246
Oswestry, 39, 44, 64, 65, 88, 96, 104, 107, 111, 114, 115, 154, 159, 175, 182, 183, 206, 207, 240, 244, 251, 262, 292
Paddolgreen, 287
Pant, 104
Park Hall, 175
Pell Wall, 110
Peplow, 47, 52, 60, 88, 214, 230, 231, 245
Peplow airfield, 41, 76, 83, 271
Picklescott, 117, 222
Pitchford, 228
Pontesbury, 40, 99, 232
Poynton Green, 94
Prees / Prees Green / Prees Lower Heath / Prees Higher Heath, 88, 153, 178, 242, 268, 271, 279, 285
Preston Brockhurst, 78, 143, 182, 295, 297
Preston Gubbals, 151
Preston Montford, 233
Preston on the Weald Moors, 91
Priorslee, 118, 129, 180
Puleston / Puleston Common, 97, 249
Pulverbatch, 224, 281
Quatford, 64
Quatt, 52, 141
Quina Brook, 153
Rednal airfield, 120, 166, 184, 201, 250, 263, 264
Rhydycroesau, 183, 291
Roden, 130, 148
Rodington, 115, 148
Rowton (near High Ercall), 123
Ruyton-XI-Towns, 48, 109, 134
Ryton, 186
Sambrook, 84, 146
Sandford, 250
Selattyn, 64, 88, 183, 206
Shawbury airfield, 19, 20, 21, 24, 25, 26, 27, 28, 41, 45, 46, 54, 68, 72, 77, 82, 83, 85, 120, 138, 172, 187, 226, 227, 270, 274, 277
Shawbury village, 47, 61, 113, 137, 167, 216, 248
Sheinwood, 43
Sheriffhales, 84, 89, 121, 169, 180, 267
Shifnal, 52, 82, 84, 90, 200
Shipton, 296
Shirlett, 167, 168
Shrawardine, 257
Shrewsbury, 22, 30, 33, 43, 55, 59, 60, 67, 149, 150, 173, 191, 250, 262, 271, 273
Sibdon Carwood, 241
Sleap, 60, 147
Sleap airfield, 161, 164, 198, 250, 251, 261, 266
Snailbeach, 193
Spoonhill, 127
Spoonley, 27, 184
Stanton Long, 32
Stanton upon Hine Heath, 50, 238
Stapleton, 155
Stiperstones, 192
Stirchley, 80, 172
Stoke Grange, 70, 110, 246
Stoke upon Tern, 70, 71, 180, 245,

246, 276, 285
Stoney Stretton, 111
Sugdon, 115
Sutton Grange, 185, 259, 283
Sutton upon Tern, 66, 80
Swancote, 106
Tedsmore, 243, 266
Telford, 129, 140, 141, 172,223, 254
Tern Hill airfield, 19, 20, 21, 22, 23, 24, 26, 28, 29, 31, 45, 48, 49, 52, 61, 65, 69, 73, 74, 76, 78, 79, 90, 162, 195, 255, 263, 276, 277, 280, 282, 290
Tetchill, 100, 117, 156, 197
Tibberton, 35, 52, 56, 80, 196, 231, 244, 246, 292
Tilstock airfield, 125, 135, 143, 182, 198, 211, 213
Titterstone Clee Hill (see Clee Hill)
Tong, 75, 192
Trefonen, 262
Tuckhill, 141, 237
Uffington, 48, 59, 232
Uppington, 149, 195, 220, 239
Upton Cressett, 192
Upton Magna, 290
Walcot, 115, 209
Walford, 114, 217
Wappenshall, 49
Webscott, 131, 267
Wellington, 35, 46, 49, 73, 76, 81, 85, 91, 134, 188, 218, 225, 226, 236, 244, 286
Welshampton, 293
Welsh Frankton, 197
Welshpool, 172
Wem, 43, 60, 147, 178, 182, 199, 249, 253, 261, 264, 273, 287
Westbury, 111
West Felton, 48, 111, 115, 243
Whitchurch, 96, 97, 101, 107, 130,167, 213, 235, 245, 260, 264, 266, 270, 284
Whitchurch Heath (see Tilstock)
Whittingslow, 147, 249
Whittington, 65, 114, 182
Whixall, 88, 213
Wistanswick, 48, 230, 245
Withington, 73, 107
Wollerton, 49, 71, 92, 105, 108, 116, 219
Woodcote, 277
Woodseaves, 179, 189, 212
Woofferton, 207
Woore, 42, 92, 154, 162, 278
Wooton, 52
Wrekin (The), 41, 81, 99, 103, 188, 189, 195, 269, 278
Wrockwardine, 236
Wroxeter, 95, 134, 170, 207, 236
Wykey, 109
Wyre Forest, 99, 270
Yeaton Peverey, 114
Yockleton, 111, 213

Index to Airfields

Andover, 42, 56, 265
Annan, 204
Aston Down, 64, 151, 279
Atcham, 89, 94, 95, 99, 102, 105, 112, 118, 127, 130, 135, 136, 137, 141, 142, 144, 148, 149, 156, 157, 162, 163, 167, 168, 170, 174, 182, 190, 191, 194, 195, 200, 205, 207, 209, 210, 215, 216, 217, 218, 220, 221, 222, 223, 224, 225, 226, 228, 229, 232, 233, 234, 235, 236, 237, 239, 240, 241, 242, 244, 245, 247, 248, 269, 290
Benson, 40, 272
Bicester, 32, 54, 261
Bobbington (see Halfpenny Green)
Boscombe Down, 289
Bottesford, 158
Bovingdon, 193
Bramcote, 180, 182, 285
Bratton, 91, 98, 144, 219, 230
Breighton, 138
Bridleway Gate, 110, 112, 113, 171
Brize Norton, 47
Broadwell, 256
Brockworth, 99
Bruntingthorpe, 240
Burtonwood, 52, 234, 254
Calveley, 197
Cardiff, 62
Chalgrove, 203
Chetwynd, 72, 92, 97, 105, 136, 188, 189, 202, 248, 289, 294
Child's Ercall (see Peplow)
Chipping Warden, 165, 166
Chivenor, 273
Colerne, 191
Condover, 128, 134, 137, 151, 152, 155, 173, 186, 187, 190, 191, 198, 199, 207, 208, 210, 237, 258, 259
Cosford, 71, 75, 85, 86, 87, 88, 89, 90, 101, 111, 123, 126, 129, 131, 132, 143, 144, 148, 158, 161, 164, 169, 170, 178, 181, 187, 191, 199, 209, 212, 218, 227, 249, 255, 260, 261, 263, 267, 269, 275, 280, 289, 292, 294
Cottesmore, 96
Cranage, 56, 67
Debden, 32, 271
Defford, 207
Derby, 107
Dunsfold, 150
Dyce, 147
Edzell, 274
Farnborough, 88, 271
Filton, 37, 40, 53, 95
Finningley, 33
Grantham, 46
Halfpenny Green, 104, 106, 107, 116, 127, 140, 145, 150, 160, 170, 178, 237
Hamble, 270
Hatfield, 156
Hawarden, 55, 64, 68, 97, 98, 99, 100, 107, 109, 122, 130, 150, 223, 230, 238, 246, 260
Hawkinge, 66, 249
High Ercall, 73, 77, 81, 85, 94,101, 103, 110, 113, 115, 123, 124, 140, 149, 155, 156, 157, 159, 167, 168, 171, 179, 183, 185, 200, 210, 220,

245, 250, 260, 270
Hinstock, 188, 199, 219
Hooton Park, 62, 284
Horham, 241
Hucknall, 74, 80, 89
Hullavington, 84, 243
Hurn, 234
Ingham, 179
Kemble, 42, 43, 65, 66
Kidlington, 56
Kirkbride, 103, 273
Langford Lodge, 254
Lee on Solent, 205, 254
Lichfield, Staffordshire, 103
Lindholme, 249
Linton on Ouse, 66
Litchfield, Hampshire, 100
Little Rissington, 50, 154, 261, 294
Llandow, 284
Madley, 183, 262
Market Harborough, 253
Middle Wallop, 64, 140
Molesworth, 251
Mona, 254
Monkmoor, 30, 70
Montford Bridge, 95, 122, 135, 143, 149, 150, 151, 152, 168, 175, 198, 233, 248, 250, 253, 257, 262, 265
Moreton-in-Marsh, 108, 183
Moreton Valance, 125
Netheravon, 226
Northolt, 44, 74
North Coates, 52
Old Buckenham, 256
Ossington, 250
Penrhos, 35, 39, 117
Peplow, 41, 76, 82, 83, 86, 90, 169, 179, 180, 196, 197, 201, 208, 212, 214, 231, 246, 253, 255, 256, 263, 271
Pershore, 147
Perth, 41
Peterborough, 172
Poulton, 223, 238
Rednal, 109, 111, 113, 114, 115, 116, 117, 118, 119, 120, 121, 122, 123, 131, 133, 139, 147, 150, 152, 154, 159, 160, 166, 175, 176, 182, 183, 184, 189, 195, 201, 206, 207, 208, 213, 218, 240, 242, 243, 251, 261, 263, 264, 265, 266
Ringway, 52, 62, 74
Sealand, 32, 33, 37, 42, 46, 51, 53, 64, 95, 120
Shawbury, 19, 20, 21, 22, 24, 25, 26, 27, 28, 33, 34, 35, 36, 38, 39, 41, 43, 44, 45, 46, 47, 50, 51, 52, 53, 54, 55, 56, 57, 61, 62, 65, 68, 69, 70, 72, 77, 81, 82, 83, 87, 98, 106, 108, 110, 111, 113, 114, 120, 128, 131, 138, 143, 148, 156, 160, 172, 174, 176, 186, 187, 198, 216, 226, 227, 228, 270, 271, 273, 274, 276, 277, 278, 284, 286, 288, 290, 292, 293, 295, 296, 297
Shobdon, 145, 164, 174
Silloth, 103
Sleap, 147, 151, 161, 162, 164, 191, 192, 193, 198, 199, 203, 213, 218, 227, 249, 250, 251, 253, 258, 261, 264, 266, 288, 293
South Cerney, 43, 46
Stanton Harcourt, 267
Staverton, 125
St Athan, 41, 56
Stoke Orchard, 148
Stretton, 205
Swinderby, 290
Sywell, 63, 86
Tern Hill, 19, 20, 21, 22, 23, 24, 26, 27, 28, 29, 30, 31, 32, 33, 35, 36, 37, 39, 40, 41, 42, 43, 44, 45, 47, 48, 49, 51, 52, 55, 59, 60, 61, 62, 63, 64, 65, 66, 67, 68, 69, 70, 71, 72, 73, 74, 75, 76, 77, 78, 29, 80, 82, 83, 84, 85, 86, 88, 89, 90, 91, 92, 94, 100, 101, 103, 105, 110, 111, 115, 116, 122, 123, 134, 136, 140, 142, 146, 152, 159, 162, 167, 169, 172, 173, 177, 178, 185, 189, 190, 199, 202, 204, 206, 212, 213, 219, 225, 227, 231, 245, 246, 247, 259, 267, 270, 273, 276, 277, 278, 279, 280, 282, 283, 284, 285, 286, 287, 289, 290, 291, 292, 293, 294, 295, 296
Thame, 192
Thorney Island, 50
Tilstock, 153, 158, 167, 171, 209, 211, 213, 234, 247, 255, 260, 268, 269
Topcliffe, 178
Upper Heyford, 120, 128, 131, 153
Upwood, 61, 86, 95, 102
Valley, 94, 185, 287, 295, 297
Warton, 193
Wellesbourne Mountford, 128, 129
West Freugh, 88
Wheaton Aston, 180, 230, 235, 239, 269
Whitchurch (near Bristol), 95, 99
Whitchurch Heath (see Tilstock)
White Waltham, 48, 51, 52, 53, 74, 124, 262
Wittering, 47, 296
Woodvale, 281, 282
Worthy Down, 200
Wrexham, 96
Wyton, 237
Yeovil, 44